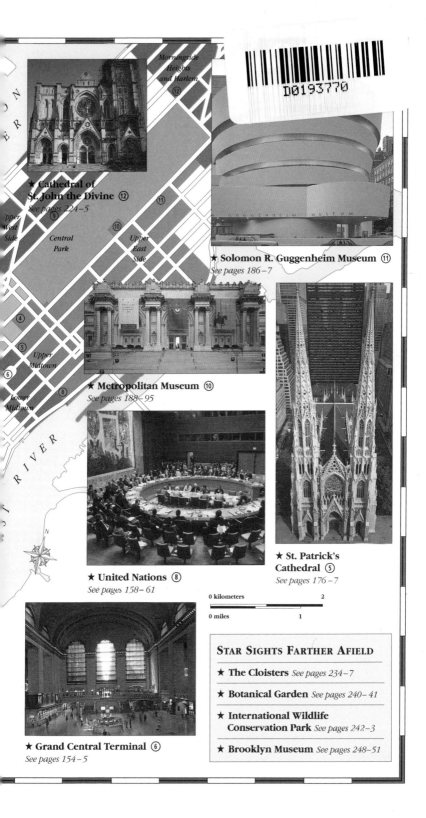

★ Cathedral of
St. John the Divine ⑫
See pages 224–5

Morningside
Heights
and Harlem ⑫

D0193770

Upper
West
Side

Central
Park

Upper
East
Side

★ Solomon R. Guggenheim Museum ⑪
See pages 186–7

Upper
Midtown

Lower
Midtown

RIVER

★ Metropolitan Museum ⑩
See pages 188–95

EAST RIVER

★ United Nations ⑧
See pages 158–61

★ St. Patrick's
Cathedral ⑤
See pages 176–7

0 kilometers   2

0 miles   1

★ Grand Central Terminal ⑥
See pages 154–5

STAR SIGHTS FARTHER AFIELD

★ **The Cloisters** *See pages 234–7*

★ **Botanical Garden** *See pages 240–41*

★ **International Wildlife
Conservation Park** *See pages 242–3*

★ **Brooklyn Museum** *See pages 248–51*

NEW YORK

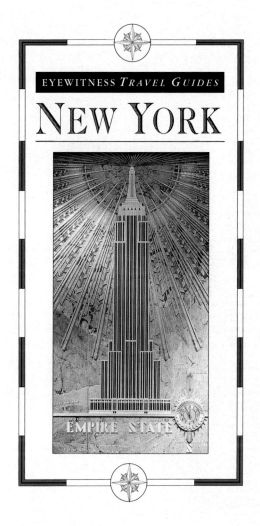

EMPIRE STATE

EYEWITNESS *TRAVEL GUIDES*

NEW YORK

Main contributor:
ELEANOR BERMAN

DORLING KINDERSLEY
LONDON • NEW YORK • STUTTGART

A DORLING KINDERSLEY BOOK

PROJECT EDITOR Fay Franklin
ART EDITOR Tony Foo
EDITORS Donna Dailey, Ellen Dupont
DESIGNERS Steve Bere, Louise Parsons, Mark Stevens
EDITORIAL ASSISTANT Fiona Morgan

MANAGING EDITOR Douglas Amrine
MANAGING ART EDITORS Stephen Knowlden, Geoff Manders
SENIOR EDITOR Georgina Matthews
SERIES DESIGN CONSULTANT Peter Luff
EDITORIAL DIRECTOR David Lamb
ART DIRECTOR Anne-Marie Bulat

PRODUCTION CONTROLLER Hilary Stephens
PICTURE RESEARCH Susan Mennell, Sarah Moule
DTP DESIGNER Andy Wilkinson

CONTRIBUTORS
Lester Brooks, Patricia Brooks, Susan Farewell

MAPS
Andrew Heritage, James Mills-Hicks, Chez Picthall,
John Plumer (Dorling Kindersley Cartography)

PHOTOGRAPHERS
Max Alexander, Dave King, Michael Moran

ILLUSTRATORS
Richard Draper, Robbie Polley, Hamish Simpson

SUPERVISING EDITOR IN NEW YORK
Mary Ann Lynch

•

This book was produced with the assistance of
Websters International Publishers.

Film outputting bureau PLS (London)
Reproduced by Colourscan (Singapore)
Printed and bound by Graphicom (Italy)

First American Edition, 1993
2 4 6 8 10 9 7 5 3 1
Published in the United States by
Dorling Kindersley, Inc., 232 Madison Avenue
New York, New York 10016

Copyright 1993 © Dorling Kindersley Limited, London

Library of Congress Cataloging-in-Publication Data
Berman, Eleanor. 1934–
    New York / Eleanor Berman. – – 1st American ed.
    p.   cm. – – (Eyewitness travel guides)
    Includes index.
    ISBN 1-56458-184-5
    1. New York (N.Y.) – – Guidebooks.   I. Title.   II. Series.
F128.18.B42 1993   92-53471
917.47'10443– –dc20   CIP

Every effort has been made to ensure that the information in this
book is as up-to-date as possible at the time of going to press. However,
details such as telephone numbers, opening hours, prices, gallery hanging
arrangements and travel information are liable to change. The
publishers cannot accept responsibility for any consequences
arising from the use of this book.

We would be delighted to receive any corrections and suggestions
for incorporation in the next edition.
Please write to the Managing Editor, Eyewitness Travel Guides,
Dorling Kindersley, 9 Henrietta Street, London WC2E 8PS, UK.

THROUGHOUT THIS BOOK, FLOORS ARE REFERRED TO IN ACCORDANCE WITH
AMERICAN USAGE, I.E. THE "FIRST FLOOR" IS AT GROUND LEVEL.

CONTENTS

Baseball star
Babe Ruth
(1895–1948)

INTRODUCING
NEW YORK

South Manhattan skyline

Vesuvio Bakery, SoHo

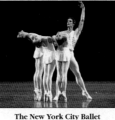

The New York City Ballet

Tug boat at the North Wind
Undersea Institute Museum

TRAVELERS'
NEEDS

Bagel from a New York deli

SURVIVAL GUIDE

Trump Tower, Upper Midtown

Solomon R. Guggenheim Museum, Upper East Side

How to Use this Guide

THIS EYEWITNESS TRAVEL GUIDE helps you get the most from your stay in New York with the minimum of practical difficulty. The opening section, *Introducing New York*, locates the city geographically, sets modern New York in its historical context and describes the highlights of the year. *New York at a Glance* is an overview of the city's attractions. Section two, *New York Area by Area*, guides you through the city's sightseeing areas. It describes all the main sights with maps, photographs and detailed illustrations. In addition, five planned walks take you step-by-step through special areas.

Well-researched tips on where to stay, eat, shop, and on sports and entertainment are in section three, *Travelers' Needs. Children's New York* lists highlights for young visitors, and section four, *Survival Guide*, shows you how to do everything from mailing a letter to using the subway.

NEW YORK AREA BY AREA

Manhattan has been divided into 15 sightseeing areas, each described separately. Each area opens with a portrait, summing up the area's character and history and listing all the sights to be covered. Sights are numbered and clearly located on an *Area Map*. After this comes a large-scale *Street-by-Street Map* focusing on the most interesting part of the area. Finding your way around each area is made simple by the numbering system. This refers to the order in which sights are described on the pages that follow.

Sights at a Glance lists the sights in the area by category, including: Historic Streets and Buildings, Modern Architecture, Museums and Galleries, Churches, Monuments, and Parks and Squares.

The area covered in greater detail on the *Street-by-Street Map* is shaded red.

Numbered circles pinpoint all the listed sights on the area map. Trump Tower, for example, is ❷

1 The Area Map

For easy reference, the sights in each area are numbered and located on an Area Map. *To help the visitor, the map also shows subway stations, heliports and ferry embarkation points.*

Photographs of facades and distinctive details of buildings help you locate the sights.

Color-coding on each page makes the area easy to find in the book.

Travel tips help you reach the area quickly by public transportation.

2 The Street-by-Street Map

This gives a bird's-eye view of the heart of each sightseeing area. The most important buildings are illustrated, to help you spot them easily as you walk around.

A locator map shows you where you are in relation to surrounding areas. The area of the *Street-by-Street Map* is shown in red.

Trump Tower ❷ is also shown on this map.

A suggested route for a walk takes you past some of the area's most interesting sights.

Red stars indicate the sights that no visitor should miss.

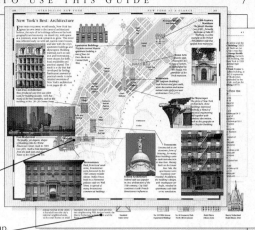

NEW YORK AT A GLANCE
Each map in this section concentrates on a specific theme: *Museums, Architecture, Multicultural New York,* and *Celebrated New Yorkers.* The top sights are shown on the map; other sights are described on the two pages following and cross-referenced to their full entries in the *Area by Area* section.

Each sightseeing area is color-coded.

The theme is explored in greater detail on the pages following the map.

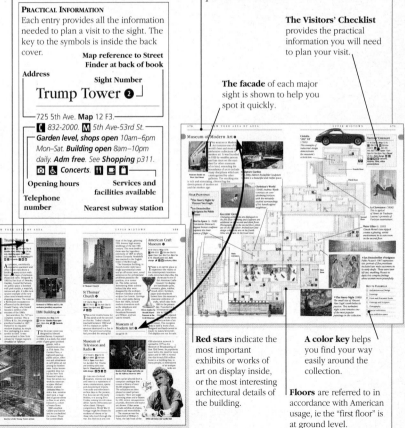

3 Detailed information on each sight
All important sights in each area are described in depth here. They are listed in order, following the numbering on the opening Area Map. *Practical information is also provided.*

PRACTICAL INFORMATION
Each entry provides all the information needed to plan a visit to the sight. The key to the symbols is inside the back cover.

Map reference to Street Finder at back of book

Address

Sight Number

Trump Tower ❷

725 5th Ave. **Map** 12 F3.
◖ 832-2000. Ⓜ 5th Ave-53rd St.
Garden level, shops open 10am–6pm
Mon–Sat. ***Building open*** 8am–10pm
daily. **Adm** free. See **Shopping** p311.
◙ ◬ **Concerts.** 🏠 ▮ ◙

Opening hours

Services and facilities available

Telephone number

Nearest subway station

4 New York's major sights
These are given two or more full pages in the sightseeing area in which they are found. Important buildings are dissected to reveal their interiors; museums have color-coded floor plans to help you find particular exhibits.

The Visitors' Checklist provides the practical information you will need to plan your visit.

The facade of each major sight is shown to help you spot it quickly.

Red stars indicate the most important exhibits or works of art on display inside, or the most interesting architectural details of the building.

A color key helps you find your way easily around the collection.

Floors are referred to in accordance with American usage, ie the "first floor" is at ground level.

INTRODUCING
NEW YORK

Putting New York on the Map

NEW YORK is a city of over seven million people, covering 301 sq miles (780 sq km). The city gives its name to the state of New York, the capital of which is Albany, 156 miles (251 km) to the north. New York is also a good base from which to visit the historic towns of Boston and Philadelphia, as well as the spectacular Niagara Falls.

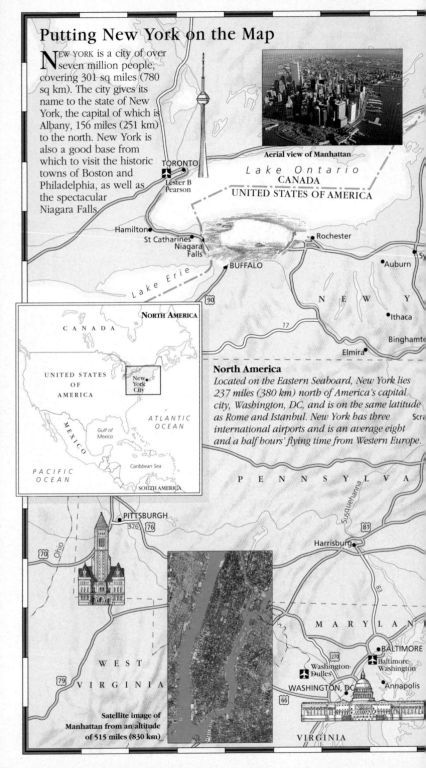

Aerial view of Manhattan

Lake Ontario

CANADA
UNITED STATES OF AMERICA

TORONTO

Lester B Pearson

Hamilton

St Catharines
Niagara Falls

BUFFALO

Lake Erie

Rochester

Auburn

Sy

N   E   W   Y

Ithaca

Binghamte

Elmira

90

17

North America

Located on the Eastern Seaboard, New York lies 237 miles (380 km) north of America's capital city, Washington, DC, and is on the same latitude as Rome and Istanbul. New York has three international airports and is an average eight and a half hours' flying time from Western Europe.

Scra

NORTH AMERICA

C A N A D A

UNITED STATES
OF
AMERICA

New
York
City

ATLANTIC
OCEAN

M
E
X
I
C
O

Gulf of
Mexico

Caribbean Sea

PACIFIC
OCEAN

SOUTH AMERICA

PITTSBURGH

376   76

Ohio

70

P E N N S Y L V A

Susquehanna

81

Harrisburg

83

M A R Y L A N

BALTIMORE

Baltimore-
Washington

Washington-
Dulles

WASHINGTON, DC

66

Annapolis

WEST

79

V I R G I N I A

**Satellite image of
Manhattan from an altitude
of 515 miles (830 km)**

VIRGINIA

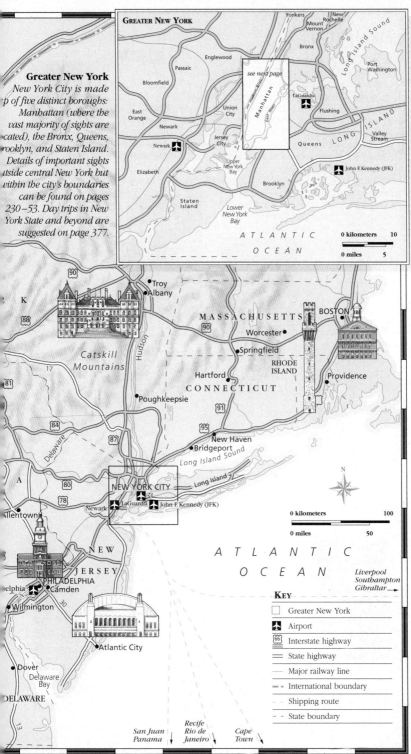

GREATER NEW YORK

Greater New York
*New York City is made
up of five distinct boroughs:
Manhattan (where the
vast majority of sights are
located), the Bronx, Queens,
Brooklyn, and Staten Island.
Details of important sights
outside central New York but
within the city's boundaries
can be found on pages
230–53. Day trips in New
York State and beyond are
suggested on page 377.*

see next page

Hudson River

East River

Yonkers   New Rochelle
Mount Vernon
Bronx
Port Washington
Englewood
Passaic
Manhattan   LaGuardia
Bloomfield
Flushing
East Orange
Union City
Valley Stream
Newark
Jersey City   Queens
Newark
Upper New York Bay
John F Kennedy (JFK)
Elizabeth
Brooklyn
Staten Island   Lower New York Bay

ATLANTIC OCEAN

0 kilometers   10
0 miles   5

Troy
Albany

90

K

88

MASSACHUSETTS   BOSTON
90
Worcester
Springfield
Catskill Mountains
Hudson
RHODE ISLAND
17
Hartford
81   CONNECTICUT   Providence
Poughkeepsie
91
84   87
95
New Haven
A   80   Bridgeport
Long Island Sound
78   NEW YORK CITY
Long Island
llentown   Newark   LaGuardia   John F Kennedy (JFK)
N
NEW   0 kilometers   100
0 miles   50
JERSEY
PHILADELPHIA
elphia   Camden   ATLANTIC
Wilmington   OCEAN   Liverpool
30   Southampton
Gibraltar
Atlantic City

Dover
Delaware Bay
DELAWARE
13

San Juan   Recife   Cape
Panama   Rio de   Town
Janeiro

KEY

	Greater New York
Airport
Interstate highway
State highway
Major railway line
International boundary
Shipping route
State boundary

Manhattan

MOST OF THE SIGHTS described in this book lie within 15 areas of Manhattan. Each of these has its own section in the book. If you are short of time, you could restrict your sightseeing to one or two areas. Many of New York's oldest and newest buildings rub shoulders in Lower Manhattan. It is from here, too, that you can take the Staten Island ferry for breathtaking views of the famous skyline and the Statue of Liberty. The Theater District and Midtown offer Fifth Avenue's glittering shops as well as museums, entertainment and such landmark skyscrapers as the glorious Chrysler Building. Museum Mile on the Upper East Side is a cultural paradise, and, since it runs alongside Central Park, you can rest en route and watch New Yorkers at play.

PAGES 138–47
*Street Finder maps
8, 11–12*

PAGES 128–37
*Street Finder maps
7–8*

PAGES 106–13
*Street Finder maps
3–4*

PAGES 100–105
*Street Finder map
4*

PAGES 64–79
*Street Finder maps
1–2*

PAGES 80–91
*Street Finder maps
1–2*

PAGES 92–9
*Street Finder maps
4, 5*

Chelsea and
the Garment
District

Gramer
and th
Flatiro
Distric

Greenwich
Village

East
Village

SoHo
and
TriBeCa

Lower
East Side

Lower
Manhattan

Seaport
and the
Civic
Center

N

HUDSON RIVER

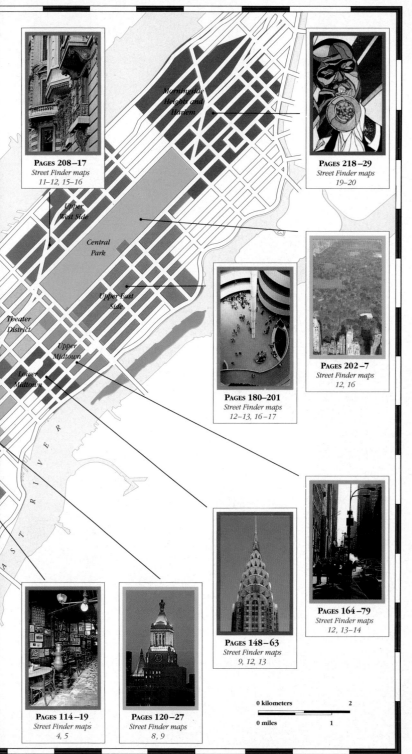

Morningside
Heights and
Harlem

PAGES 208–17
*Street Finder maps
11–12, 15–16*

PAGES 218–29
*Street Finder maps
19–20*

Upper
West Side

Central
Park

Upper East
Side

PAGES 202–7
*Street Finder maps
12, 16*

Theater
District

Upper
Midtown

Lower
Midtown

PAGES 180–201
*Street Finder maps
12–13, 16–17*

EAST RIVER

PAGES 148–63
*Street Finder maps
9, 12, 13*

PAGES 164–79
*Street Finder maps
12, 13–14*

PAGES 114–19
*Street Finder maps
4, 5*

PAGES 120–27
*Street Finder maps
8, 9*

0 kilometers   2

0 miles   1

THE HISTORY OF NEW YORK

ROM ITS FIRST sighting almost 500 years ago by Giovanni da Verrazano, New York's harbor was the prize that all of Europe wanted to capture. The Dutch first sent fur traders to the area in 1621, but they lost the colony they called New Amsterdam to the English in 1664. The settlement was re-christened New York and the name stayed, even after the English lost the colony in 1783, at the end of the Revolutionary War.

A shell-work cloak worn by an Indian chief

THE GROWING CITY

In the 19th century, New York grew rapidly and became a major port. Ease of shipping spawned manufacturing, commerce was king and great fortunes were made. In 1898, Manhattan was joined with the four outer boroughs to form the world's second-largest city. From 1800 to 1900, the population grew from 79,000 to 3 million people. New York City became the country's cultural and entertainment mecca as well as its business center.

THE MELTING POT

The city continued to grow as thousands of immigrants came seeking a better life. Overpopulation meant that many at first lived in slums. Today, the mix of cultures has enriched the city and become its defining quality. Its nine million inhabitants speak 80 languages.

Manhattan's skyline took shape as the city grew skyward to make space for its ever-increasing population. Throughout its history, the city has experienced alternating periods of economic decline and growth, but in both good times and bad, it remains one of the world's most vital cities.

The following pages illustrate significant periods in New York's history.

A deed signed by New Amsterdam's last Dutch governor, Peter Stuyvesant, in 1664

The southern half of Manhattan and part of Brooklyn in 1767

Early New York

Indian husk mask

MANHATTAN WAS a forested land populated by Algonquian-speaking Indians when the Dutch West India Company established a fur trading post called New Amsterdam in 1625. The first settlers built houses helter-skelter, so even today the streets of Lower Manhattan still twist. Broadway, then called by the Dutch name *Breede Wegh*, began as an Indian trail known as the Week-quaesgeek Trail. Harlem has also kept its Dutch name. The town was unruly until Peter Stuyvesant arrived to bring order. But the colony did not produce the expected revenues, and in 1664 the Dutch let it fall to the English, who renamed it New York.

GROWTH OF THE METROPOLIS
☐ *1664*   ☐ *Today*

Seal of New Netherland
The beaver pelt and wampum (Indian shell beads) on the seal were the currency of the colony of New Netherland.

FIRST VIEW OF MANHATTAN (1626)
The southern tip of Manhattan resembled a Dutch town, down to the windmill. Although shown here, the fort had not yet been built.

Dutch ships

The First New Yorkers
Algonquian-speaking Indians were the first inhabitants of Manhattan.

Iroquois Pot
Iroquois Indians were frequent visitors to early Manhattan.

Indian Village
Some Algonquians lived in longhouses on Manhattan before the Dutch arrived.

Indian canoe

TIMELINE

1524 Giovanni da Verrazano sails into New York harbor

1626 Peter Minuit buys Manhattan from the Indians

1625 Dutch establish first permanent trading post

1653 Wall is built for protection from attack; adjacent street is called Wall Street

1600	1620	1640

1609 Henry Hudson sails up the Hudson River in search of the Northwest Passage

1625 First black slaves brought from Africa

1643–45 Indian skirmishes end with temporary peace treaty

1647 Peter Stuyvesant becomes colonial governor

1654 First Jewish settlers arrive

Dutch Delftware
Colonists brought this popular tin-glazed earthenware pottery from Holland.

***Tiger* timbers**

Manhattan Skyline
The Strand, now Whitehall Street, was the site of the city's first brick house.

WHERE TO SEE DUTCH NEW YORK
Dug up by workmen in 1916, these remnants of a Dutch ship, the *Tiger*, which burned in 1613, are the earliest artifacts of the period and are now in the Museum of the City of New York (*see p197*). Rooms in this museum, as well as in the Morris-Jumel Mansion (*see p233*) and the Van Cortlandt House Museum (*see p238*), display Dutch pottery, tiles and furniture.

Purchase of Manhattan
Peter Minuit bought the island from the Indians in 1626 for $24 worth of trinkets.

Dutch windmill

Fort Amsterdam

Peter Stuyvesant
The last Dutch governor was a tyrant who imposed strict laws – such as an edict closing all the city's taverns at 9 o'clock.

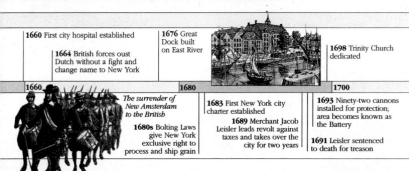

1660 First city hospital established

1664 British forces oust Dutch without a fight and change name to New York

1676 Great Dock built on East River

1698 Trinity Church dedicated

1660 ———————————— 1680 ———————————— 1700

The surrender of New Amsterdam to the British

1680s Bolting Laws give New York exclusive right to process and ship grain

1683 First New York city charter established

1689 Merchant Jacob Leisler leads revolt against taxes and takes over the city for two years

1693 Ninety-two cannons installed for protection; area becomes known as the Battery

1691 Leisler sentenced to death for treason

Colonial New York

Colonial gentleman

U NDER BRITISH RULE, New York prospered and the population grew rapidly. The bolting of flour (grinding grain) was the main commercial enterprise. Shipbuilding also flourished. As the city prospered, an elite emerged that could afford a more refined way of life, and fine furniture and household silver were made for use in their homes during the Colonial period. During more than a century of governing New York, Britain proved more interested in profit than in the welfare of the colony. The Crown imposed hated taxes, and the spirit of rebellion grew, although especially in New York, loyalties were divided. On the the eve of Revolution, New York was the second-largest city in the 13 colonies, with 20,000 citizens.

GROWTH OF THE METROPOLIS

☐ *1760*   ☐ *Today*

Colonial currency

Bedroom

Dining room

Colonial Street
Pigs and dogs roamed free on the streets of Colonial New York.

Kas
This Dutch-style pine wardrobe was made in New York's Hudson River valley around 1720.

Shipping
Trade with the West Indies and Britain helped New York prosper. In some years, 200 or more vessels visited the port.

TIMELINE

1702 Lord Cornbury appointed Colonial governor; he often wore women's clothes

1711 Slave market set up at the foot of Wall Street

1720 First shipyard opens

1700

1710

1720

1730

1710 Iroquois chief Hendrick visits England

1725 *New York Gazette,* city's first newspaper, is established

1732 First city theater opens

Captain Kidd

The English pirate William Kidd was a respected citizen, loaning a block and tackle to help build Trinity Church (see p68).

VAN CORTLANDT HOUSE

Frederick Van Cortlandt built this Georgian-style house in 1748 on a wheat plantation in what is now the Bronx. Today a museum (see p238), it shows how a well-to-do Dutch-English family once lived.

West parlor

WHERE TO SEE COLONIAL NEW YORK

Colonial buildings are open to the public at Historic Richmond Town on Staten Island *(see p252)*. Fine examples of Colonial silver and furniture are on display at the Museum of the City of New York *(see p197)*.

Richmond Town General Store

Colonial Kitchen

Plain white cheese, called "white meat," was often served in place of meat. Waffles, introduced by the Dutch, were popular. Fresh fruit was rare, but preserved fruits were eaten.

Pewter baby bottle   **Cheese mold**   **Waffle iron**

Decorative Carvings
A face carved in stone peers over each of the front windows.

Sucket fork, for eating preserved fruits

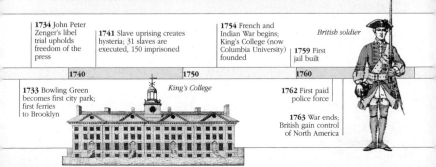

1734 John Peter Zenger's libel trial upholds freedom of the press

1741 Slave uprising creates hysteria; 31 slaves are executed, 150 imprisoned

1754 French and Indian War begins; King's College (now Columbia University) founded

British soldier

1759 First jail built

1740   1750   1760

1733 Bowling Green becomes first city park; first ferries to Brooklyn

King's College

1762 First paid police force

1763 War ends; British gain control of North America

Revolutionary New York

George Washington, Revolutionary general

DUG UP INTO TRENCHES for defense, heavily shelled by British troops and scarred by recurring fires, New York suffered during the American Revolution. But despite the hardships, many continued to enjoy cricket games, horse races, balls and boxing matches. After the British took the city in 1776, it became their headquarters. The Continental army did not return to Manhattan until November 25, 1783, two years after the fighting ended.

GROWTH OF THE METROPOLIS

▨ 1776   ☐ Today

Soldier's Haversack
American soldiers in the War of Independence carried their supplies in haversacks.

Battle Dress
The Continental (Patriot) army wore blue uniforms, while the British wore red. **American soldier**

TOPPLING THE KING
New Yorkers tore down the statue of King George III in Bowling Green and melted it down to make ammunition.

British soldier

Battle of Harlem Heights
Washington won this battle on September 16 , 1776. But he did not have enough troops to hold New York so retreated, leaving it to the British.

Patriot

Death of a Patriot
While working behind British lines in 1776, Nathan Hale was captured and hanged by the British without trial for spying.

TIMELINE

1765 British pass Stamp Act; New Yorkers protest; Sons of Liberty formed

1767 New duties imposed with Townshend Act; after protests, the act is repealed

1770 Sons of Liberty fight British in the "Battle of Golden Hill"

1774 Rebels dump tea in New York harbor to protest taxes

1760   1770   1780

St. Paul's Chapel

1766 St. Paul's Chapel completed; Stamp Act repealed; Statue of George III erected on Bowling Green

General William Howe, commander in chief of the British troops

1776 War begins; 500 ships under General Howe assemble in New York harbor

Fire Fighters

Fires had long threatened the city, but during the war a series of fires nearly destroyed it. In the wake of the patriot retreat, on September 21, 1776, a devastating fire razed Trinity Church and 1,000 houses.

Leather fire bucket

Flags of the Revolution

Washington's army flew the Continental colors, with a stripe for each of the 13 colonies and a Union Jack in the corner. The Stars and Stripes became the official flag in 1777.

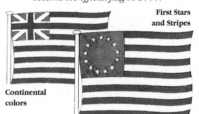

First Stars and Stripes

Continental colors

Statue of George III

General Washington Returns

Washington received a hero's welcome when he reentered New York on November 25, 1783, after the British withdrawal.

Cheering patriots

WHERE TO SEE THE REVOLUTIONARY CITY

In 1776, George Washington used the Morris-Jumel Mansion in upper Manhattan as a headquarters (*see p233*). He also slept at the Van Cortlandt House (*see p19 and p238*). After the war he bade farewell to his officers at Fraunces Tavern (*see p76*).

Morris-Jumel mansion

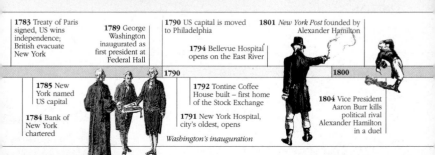

1783 Treaty of Paris signed, US wins independence; British evacuate New York

1785 New York named US capital

1784 Bank of New York chartered

1789 George Washington inaugurated as first president at Federal Hall

1790 US capital is moved to Philadelphia

1794 Bellevue Hospital opens on the East River

1792 Tontine Coffee House built – first home of the Stock Exchange

1791 New York Hospital, city's oldest, opens

Washington's inauguration

1790

1800

1801 *New York Post* founded by Alexander Hamilton

1804 Vice President Aaron Burr kills political rival Alexander Hamilton in a duel

New York in the 19th Century

Governor De Witt Clinton

FIRMLY ESTABLISHED as the nation's largest city and preeminent seaport, New York grew increasingly wealthy. Manufacturing increased due to the ease of shipping; tycoons like John Jacob Astor made millions. The rich moved uptown; public transportation followed. With rapid growth came fires, epidemics and financial panics. Immigrants from Ireland, Germany, and other nations arrived. Some found prosperity; others crowded into slums in Lower Manhattan.

GROWTH OF THE METROPOLIS

☐ 1840   ☐ Today

Sheet Music
The Stephen Foster ballad Jeanie With the Light Brown Hair *was popular at this time.*

Croton Distributing Reservoir was built in 1842. Until then, New Yorkers had no fresh drinking water – they relied on deliveries of bottled water.

Omnibus
The horse-drawn omnibus was introduced for public transportation in 1832 and remained on New York streets until World War I.

Keeping Fit
Gymnasiums such as Dr. Rich's Institute for Physical Education were established in New York in the 1830s and 1840s.

TIMELINE

1805 First free state schools established in New York

1811 Randel Plan divides Manhattan into grid pattern above 14th Street

1812–14 War of 1812; British blockade New York harbor

The Constitution, *most famous ship in War of 1812*

1835 Much of old New York razed in city's worst fire

| 1810 | 1820 | 1830 |

1807 Robert Fulton launches first steamboat, on the Hudson River

1822 Yellow fever epidemic; people evacuate to Greenwich Village

1823 New York surpasses Boston and Philadelphia to become nation's largest city

1827 New York abolishes slavery

1837 New Yorker Samuel Morse sends first telegraph message

The Brownstone

Many brownstone row houses were built in the first half of the century. The raised stoop allowed separate entry to the parlor and ground-floor servants' quarters.

Crystal Palace was an iron and glass exhibition hall erected for the 1853 World's Fair.

NEW YORK IN 1855

Looking south from 42nd Street, Crystal Palace and the Croton Distributing Reservoir stood where the public library and Bryant Park are today.

THE PORT OF NEW YORK

New York's importance as a port city grew by leaps and bounds in the early 19th century. Robert Fulton launched his first steamboat, the *Clermont*, in 1807. Steamboats made travel much quicker – it now took 72 hours to reach Albany, which was both the state capital and the gateway to the West. Trade with the West by steamboat and canal boat, and with the rest of the world by clipper ship, made the fortunes of many New Yorkers.

The steamboat *Clermont*

Crystal Palace in Flames
On October 5, 1858, New York's Crystal Palace exhibition hall burned to the ground, just as its predecessor in London did.

Grand Canal Celebration

Ships in New York harbor lined up to celebrate the 1825 Erie Canal opening. In connecting the Great Lakes with Albany, the state capital, on the Hudson River, the canal opened a water link between the Midwest and the Port of New York. New York realized huge profits.

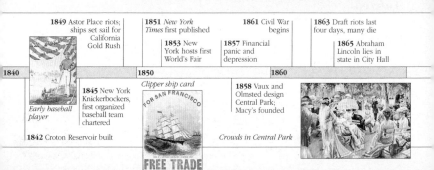

1849 Astor Place riots; ships set sail for California Gold Rush

1851 *New York Times* first published

1853 New York hosts first World's Fair

1861 Civil War begins

1857 Financial panic and depression

1863 Draft riots last four days, many die

1865 Abraham Lincoln lies in state in City Hall

1840

1850

1860

Early baseball player

1845 New York Knickerbockers, first organized baseball team chartered

Clipper ship card

FOR SAN FRANCISCO

FREE TRADE

1858 Vaux and Olmsted design Central Park; Macy's founded

Crowds in Central Park

1842 Croton Reservoir built

The Age of Extravagance

Industrialist Andrew Carnegie

A S NEW YORK'S merchant princes grew ever wealthier, the city entered into a gilded era during which many of its most opulent buildings went up. Millions were lavished on the arts with the founding of the Metropolitan Museum, Public Library and Carnegie Hall. Luxury hotels like the Plaza and the original Waldorf-Astoria were built, and elegant department stores arose to serve the wealthy. Such flamboyant figures as William "Boss" Tweed, political strongman and king of corruption, and circus man Phineas T. Barnum were also larger than life.

GROWTH OF THE METROPOLIS

☐ *1890*   ☐ *Today*

Overlooking the Park
The Dakota (1880) was the first grand luxury apartment house on the Upper West Side (see p216).

Palatial Living
Mansions lined Fifth Avenue. When it was built in 1882, W.K. Vanderbilt's Italianate palace at 660 Fifth Avenue, was one of the farthest north.

Fashion City
Lord & Taylor built a new store on Broadway's Ladies' Mile; 6th Avenue between 14th and 23rd streets was known as Fashion Row.

BATHING SUITS.

A GREAT SPECIALTY AT
LORD & TAYLOR'S, Broadway and 20th Street, N.Y.
CHEAPEST AND BEST QUALITY OF BATHING SUITS IN THE CITY.

THE ELEVATED RAILROAD
By the mid 1870s, elevated railroads or "Els" ran along 2nd, 3rd, 6th and 9th avenues. They made travel faster, but left noise, grime and pollution in their wake.

TIMELINE

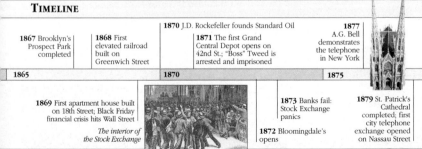

1867 Brooklyn's Prospect Park completed

1868 First elevated railroad built on Greenwich Street

1870 J.D. Rockefeller founds Standard Oil

1871 The first Grand Central Depot opens on 42nd St.; "Boss" Tweed is arrested and imprisoned

1877 A.G. Bell demonstrates the telephone in New York

1865

1870

1875

1869 First apartment house built on 18th Street; Black Friday financial crisis hits Wall Street

The interior of the Stock Exchange

1872 Bloomingdale's opens

1873 Banks fail: Stock Exchange panics

1879 St. Patrick's Cathedral completed; first city telephone exchange opened on Nassau Street

Mark Twain's Birthday
Mark Twain, whose 1873 novel The Gilded Age *portrayed the decadent lifestyle of New Yorkers, celebrated his birthday at Delmonico's.*

WHERE TO SEE THE AGE OF EXTRAVAGANCE

The Gold Room in the Henry Villard Houses *(see p174)* is a good place to experience the city's past. Formerly the Music Room, it is now a venue for afternoon tea. The Museum of the City of New York also has two period rooms (p197).

The Tweed Ring
William "Boss" Tweed led Tammany Hall, which dominated city government. He stole millions in city funds.

Nast's cartoon of "Boss" Tweed

Tammany Tiger
The Museum of the City of New York has "Boss" Tweed's cane, which sports a gold Tammany Tiger mascot on its handle.

Elevated train

Bowery

Streetcar

Rural Fifth Avenue
This painting by Ralph Blakelock shows a shanty-town at 86th Street. Today it is one of New York's most expensive addresses.

1880 Canned fruits and meats first appear in stores; Metropolitan Museum of Art opens; streets lit by electricity

1883 Metropolitan Opera opens on Broadway; Brooklyn Bridge completed

1886 Statue of Liberty unveiled

1891 Carnegie Hall opens

1880

1885

1890

1888 Great Blizzard dumps 22 in (56 cm) of snow

1890 First moving picture shows appear in New York

Grand display of fireworks over Brooklyn Bridge, 1883

1892 Cathedral of St. John the Divine begun; Ellis Island opens

New York at the Turn of the Century

Horse-drawn carriage

By 1900, NEW YORK was a hub of American industry: 70% of the country's corporations were based there, and the port handled two-thirds of all imported goods. The rich got richer, but in the crowded slums, disease spread. Even so, immigrants kept their rich traditions alive, and political and social reform emerged. In 1900, the International Ladies' Garment Workers' Union was founded to battle for the rights of the women and children who toiled in dangerous factories for low wages. The Triangle Shirtwaist Factory fire in 1911 also sped reform.

GROWTH OF THE METROPOLIS

☐ *1914*   ☐ *Today*

Gateway to America
Almost five times as crowded as the rest of New York, the Lower East Side was the most densely populated place in the world.

Crowded Conditions
Tenements were unhealthy and overcrowded. They often lacked windows, air shafts or proper sanitary facilities.

WHERE TO SEE TURN-OF-THE-CENTURY NEW YORK
The Lower East Side Tenement Museum *(see p97)* has exhibits on tenement life.

Hip bath

Tailor's scissors

Inside a Sweatshop
Workers toiled long hours for low wages in the overcrowded sweatshops of the garment district. This view of Moe Levy's shop was taken in 1912.

Streetcars on Broadway

TIMELINE

1895 Olympia Theater is first to open in the Broadway area

1896 First bagel served in a Clinton Street bakery

1897 Waldorf-Astoria Hotel opens: the largest hotel in the world

1898 Five boroughs merge to form world's second-largest city

1895

1900 Mayor Robert Van Wyck breaks ground for city's first subway with silver shovel

1900

1901 Macy's opens Broadway department store

1903 Lyceum Theater opens – oldest Broadway house still in use

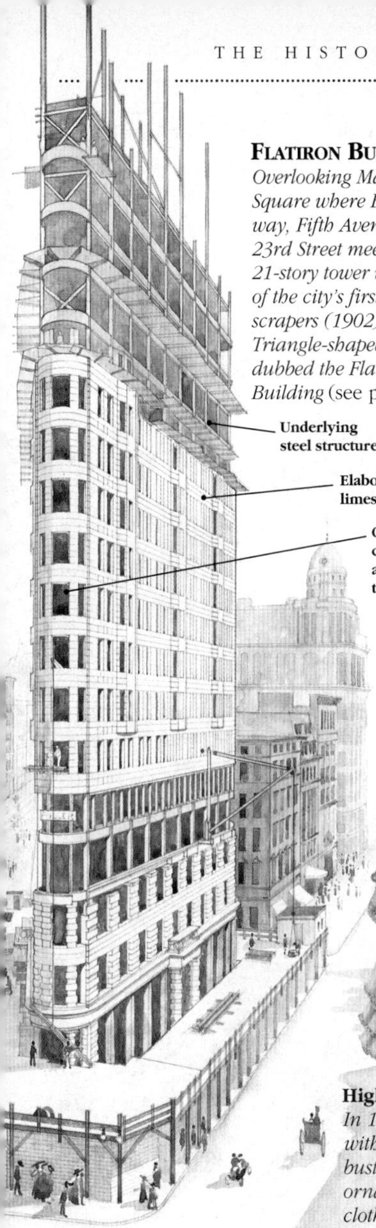

FLATIRON BUILDING

Overlooking Madison Square where Broadway, Fifth Avenue and 23rd Street meet, the 21-story tower was one of the city's first skyscrapers (1902). Triangle-shaped, it was dubbed the Flatiron Building (see p125).

Underlying steel structure

Elaborate limestone facade

Only 6 ft (185 cm) wide at apex of triangle

Supper in the Saddle
Decadent parties were all the rage. C.K.G. Billings's horseback dinner at Sherry's restaurant in 1903 was the talk of all New York.

Plaza Promenade
The section of Fifth Avenue in front of the Plaza Hotel was considered the most elegant in the city.

Ventilated hairpiece

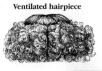

High Fashion
In 1900 styles were stiff, with wire hoops and bustles worn beneath ornate dresses. Later, clothes became softer and more practical.

Long bustle

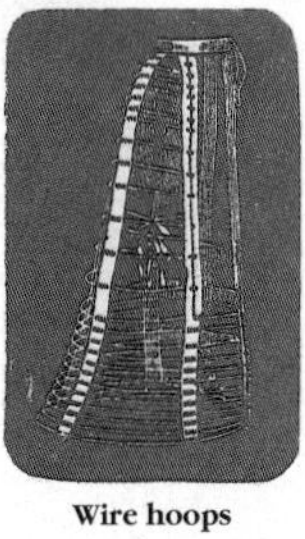

Wire hoops

1906 Architect Stanford White shot at Madison Square Garden, which he had built in 1890

1909 Wilbur Wright flies first plane over New York

1910 Pennsylvania Station opens

1913 Woolworth Building is world's tallest; new Grand Central Terminal opens; Harlem's Apollo Theater opens

1905

1910

1915

1905 First crossing of the Staten Island Ferry

1907 First metered taxicabs; first Ziegfield Follies

1911 Triangle Shirtwaist Factory fire kills 146 sweatshop workers; New York Public Library completed

Woolworth Building

New York Between the Wars

Entrance card to the Cotton Club

T HE 1920s WERE a time of high living for many New Yorkers. Mayor Jimmy Walker set the pace, whether squiring chorus girls, drinking in speakeasies or watching the Yankees. But the good times ended with the 1929 stock market crash. By 1932, Walker had resigned, charged with corruption, and one-quarter of New Yorkers were unemployed. With Mayor Fiorello La Guardia's 1933 election, New York began to recover and thrive.

GROWTH OF THE METROPOLIS
☐ *1933*   ☐ *Today*

Exotic Costumes
Chorus girls were a major Cotton Club attraction.

THE COTTON CLUB
This Harlem nightclub was host to the best jazz in town, as first Duke Ellington and then Cab Calloway led the band. People flocked from all over the city to hear them.

Defying Prohibition
Although alcohol was outlawed, speakeasies – semi-secret illegal drinking dens – still sold it.

Home-Run Hitter
In 1927, baseball star Babe Ruth hit a record 60 home runs for the Yankees. Yankee Stadium (see p239) became known as "the house that Ruth built."

Sawed-off shotgun concealed in violin case

Gangsters
Dutch Schultz was the kingpin of an illegal booze racket.

TIMELINE

1918 End of World War I		*Opening of the Holland Tunnel*	**1931** Empire State Building becomes world's tallest
1919 18th Amendment bans alcohol, launches Prohibition Era	**1926** Jimmy Walker becomes mayor		
1920 US women get the vote			

1920		**1925**		**1930**

1924 Novelist James Baldwin is born in Harlem

1925 *The New Yorker* magazine is launched

1927 Lindbergh flies across the Atlantic; first talking movie, *The Jazz Singer,* opens; Holland Tunnel opens

1929 Stock market crash; Great Depression begins

1930 Chrysler Building completed

Big Band Leaders
Banned from many downtown clubs, black artists like Cab Calloway starred at the Cotton Club.

Broadway Melodies
The 1920s were the heyday of the Broadway musical, with a record number of plays opening.

THE GREAT DEPRESSION

The Roaring Twenties ended with the stock market crash of October 29, 1929, which set off the Depression. New York was hard hit: squatters' shacks sprang up in Central Park and thousands were out of work. But art flourished as artists went to work for the Works Projects Administration (WPA), creating outstanding murals and artworks throughout the city.

Waiting to receive benefits in 1931

Breakfast menu

Lindbergh's plane, *Spirit of St. Louis*

Lindbergh's Flight
New Yorkers celebrated Lindbergh's nonstop solo flight across the Atlantic in 1927 in a variety of ways, including a breakfast in his honor.

Rockefeller Center
Millionaire John D. Rockefeller drives the final rivet to celebrate the opening of Rockefeller Center on May 1, 1939.

Mass Event
Forty-five million people visited the 1939 World's Fair in New York.

NEW YORK WORLD'S FAIR
1939

1933 Prohibition ends; Fiorello LaGuardia begins three terms as mayor

1940 Queens-Midtown Tunnel opens

1942 Times Square blacked out during World War II; Idlewild International Airport (now JFK) opens

1935

1940

1945

1936 Parks Department headed by Robert Moses; new parks created

1939 Rockefeller Center is completed

1941 US enters World War II

1944 Black leader Adam Clayton Powell elected to Congress

Postwar New York

SINCE WORLD WAR II, New York has seen both the best of times and the worst. Although established as the financial capital of the world, the city itself almost went bankrupt in the 1970s. Wall Street hit its peak in the 1980s, then experienced its worst crash since 1929. Recently the city has had to cope with racial tensions and an increase in homelessness and crime. Yet New York always bounces back. The city is the cultural and financial hub of the United States, and while new buildings continue to spring up, many of the city's older buildings, such as Grand Central Station, are being restored.

BILTMORE THEATER

1967 Hippie musical *Hair* opens on Off-Broadway, then transfers to the Biltmore Theater – total run: 1,836 performances

1963 Pennsylvania Station razed

1966 Newspaper and transit strikes

1953 Merce Cunningham founds dance company

1959 Guggenheim Museum opens

1965 New York blacked out in power failure for 13 hours

1945 End of World War II

1946 UN headquarters established in New York

1954 Ellis Island closes

1945	1950	1955	1960	1965

MAYORS:	O'DWYER	IMPELLITERI	WAGNER		LINDSAY

1945	1950	1955	1960	1965

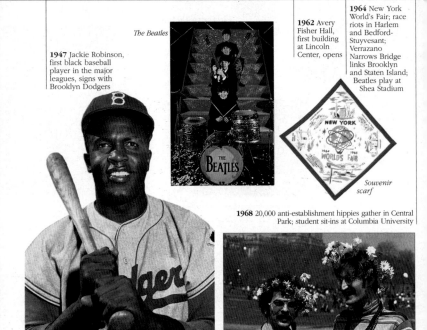

The Beatles

1962 Avery Fisher Hall, first building at Lincoln Center, opens

1964 New York World's Fair; race riots in Harlem and Bedford-Stuyvesant; Verrazano Narrows Bridge links Brooklyn and Staten Island; Beatles play at Shea Stadium

1947 Jackie Robinson, first black baseball player in the major leagues, signs with Brooklyn Dodgers

NEW YORK WORLD'S FAIR

Souvenir scarf

1968 20,000 anti-establishment hippies gather in Central Park; student sit-ins at Columbia University

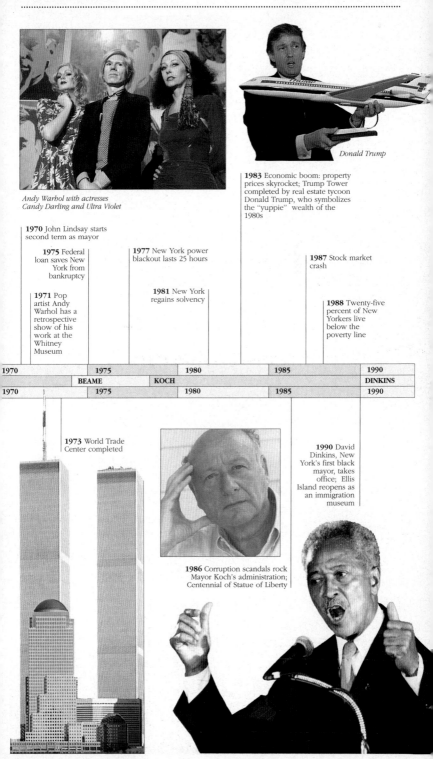

Donald Trump

Andy Warhol with actresses
Candy Darling and Ultra Violet

1983 Economic boom: property prices skyrocket; Trump Tower completed by real estate tycoon Donald Trump, who symbolizes the "yuppie" wealth of the 1980s

1970 John Lindsay starts second term as mayor

1975 Federal loan saves New York from bankruptcy

1977 New York power blackout lasts 25 hours

1987 Stock market crash

1971 Pop artist Andy Warhol has a retrospective show of his work at the Whitney Museum

1981 New York regains solvency

1988 Twenty-five percent of New Yorkers live below the poverty line

1970	1975	1980	1985	1990
BEAME	KOCH			DINKINS
1970	1975	1980	1985	1990

1973 World Trade Center completed

1990 David Dinkins, New York's first black mayor, takes office; Ellis Island reopens as an immigration museum

1986 Corruption scandals rock Mayor Koch's administration; Centennial of Statue of Liberty

NEW YORK AT A GLANCE

THERE ARE ALMOST 300 places of interest described in the *Area by Area* section of this book. They range from the bustling New York Stock Exchange *(see pp70–71)* to Central Park's peaceful Strawberry Fields *(see p206)* and from synagogues to skyscrapers. The following 16 pages are a time-saving guide to New York's most interesting sights. Museums and architecture each have a section, and there are guides to the people and cultures that have given the city its unique character. Each sight is cross-referenced to its own full entry. Below are the top ten tourist attractions to start you off.

NEW YORK'S TOP TEN

TOURIST ATTRACTIONS

Ellis Island
See pp78–9.

Empire State Building
See pp134–5.

South Street Seaport
See p84.

Rockefeller Center
See p142.

Museum of Modern Art
See pp170–73.

Central Park
See pp202–7.

Statue of Liberty
See pp74–5.

Metropolitan Museum of Art
See pp188–95.

Brooklyn Bridge
See pp86–9.

Chinatown
See p96.

Park Avenue's relentless flow of traffic

New York's Best: Museums

NEW YORK'S MUSEUMS range from the vast scope of the Metropolitan Museum to the personal treasures of financier J. Pierpont Morgan's own collection. Several museums celebrate New York's heritage, giving visitors an insight into the people and events that made the city what it is today. This map features some highlights, with a detailed overview on pages 36 and 37.

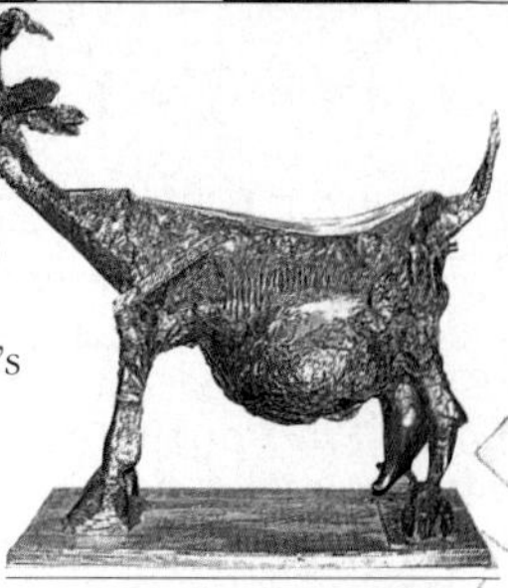

Museum of Modern Art
The world's most comprehensive collection of modern art includes such gems as Picasso's Goat (1950).

Intrepid **Sea-Air-Space Museum**
Situated on a large aircraft carrier on the Hudson River, this naval museum also traces the progress of flight and undersea exploration.

Pierpont Morgan Library
One of the world's finest collections of manuscripts, prints and books includes this rare French Bible from 1230.

Old Merchant's House
This perfectly preserved 1820s house belonged to a wealthy trader.

Ellis Island
This museum vividly re-creates the experiences of many millions of immigrant families.

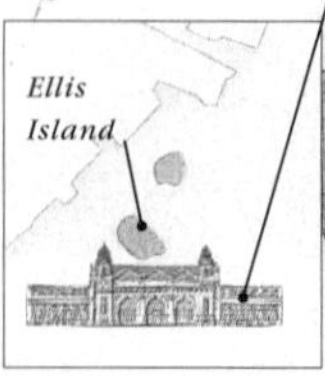

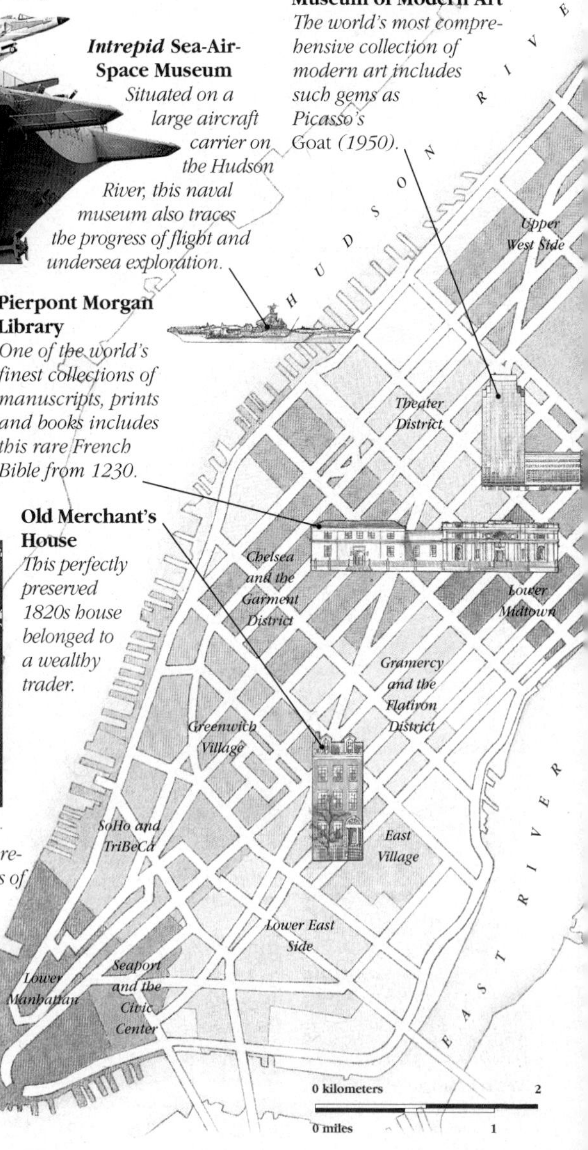

Upper West Side

Theater District

Chelsea and the Garment District

Lower Midtown

Gramercy and the Flatiron District

Greenwich Village

SoHo and TriBeCa

East Village

Lower East Side

Lower Manhattan

Seaport and the Civic Center

Ellis Island

| 0 kilometers | | 2 |
| 0 miles | 1 | |

American Museum of Natural History
Dinosaurs, meteorites and much more have fascinated generations of visitors here.

Morningside Heights and Harlem

Central Park

Upper East Side

Upper Town

Museum of the City of New York
Costumes, works of art and household objects (such as this 1725 silver dish) create an intricate and detailed picture of New York's past.

Cooper-Hewitt Museum
A wealth of decorative arts is displayed in the handsome Upper East Side mansion of the late Andrew Carnegie.

Solomon R. Guggenheim Museum
Ellsworth Kelly's Blue, Green, Yellow, Orange, Red *(1966) is part of the collection housed in Frank Lloyd Wright's only New York building.*

Metropolitan Museum of Art
Of the millions of works in its collection, this 12th-dynasty Egyptian faïence hippo is the museum's own mascot.

Frick Collection
The collection of 19th-century railroad magnate Henry Clay Frick is displayed in his former home. Masterpieces include St. Francis in the Desert *(about 1480) by Giovanni Bellini.*

Whitney Museum of American Art
This exceptional collection includes many views of New York. One of the best is Brooklyn Bridge: Variation on an Old Theme *(1939), by Joseph Stella.*

Exploring New York's Museums

Richmond Town tobacco tin

YOU COULD DEVOTE an entire month to visiting New York's museums and still not do them justice. There are more than 60 in Manhattan alone, and half that number in the other boroughs. The wealth of art and the huge variety of offerings – from old masters to old fire engines, dinosaurs to dolls, Tibetan tapestries to African masks – is equal to that of any city in the world. Note that some museums may be closed on Monday as well as on another day. Many stay open late one or two evenings a week, and some have one evening when admission is free. Not every museum charges for admission, but donations are always welcome.

PAINTING AND SCULPTURE

NEW YORK is best known for its art museums. The **Metropolitan Museum of Art** houses an extensive collection of American art as well as world-famous masterpieces. The **Cloisters**, a branch of the "Met" in Upper Manhattan, is a treasury of medieval art and architecture. The **Frick Collection** has a superb display of Old Masters. In contrast, the **Museum of Modern Art (MoMA)** has some of the world's most famous Impressionist and modern paintings. **The Whitney Museum of American Art** and the **Solomon R. Guggenheim Museum** also specialize in modern art, the Whitney's biennial show being the foremost display of contemporary work by living artists. The cutting edge of today's art is to be seen at the **New Museum of Contemporary Art**, and the work of untrained artists can be seen at the **Museum of American Folk Art**. The **National Academy of Design** displays a collection of 19th- and 20th-century art, donated by its members. In Harlem, the **Studio Museum** shows the work of black artists.

CRAFTS AND DESIGN

IF YOU ARE interested in textiles, porcelain and glass, embroideries and laces, wallpaper and prints, visit the **Cooper-Hewitt Museum**, the decorative arts outpost of Washington's Smithsonian Institution. The design collections at **MoMA** are as well known as the paintings, tracing the history of design from clocks to couches. The **American Craft Museum** offers the finest work of today's skilled artisans in mediums from furniture to art glass, while the **Museum of American Folk Art** presents folk forms, from quilts to canes. Silver collections are notable at the **Museum of the City of New York**. The fine displays of native art at the **Museum of the American Indian** include jewelry, rugs and pottery.

PRINTS AND PHOTOGRAPHY

THE SMALL but excellent **International Center of Photography** is the only museum in New York totally devoted to this medium. Collections can also be seen at the **Metropolitan Museum of Art** and **MoMA**, with many examples of early photography at the **Museum of the City of New York** and **Ellis Island**.

Prints and drawings by such great book illustrators as Kate Greenaway and John Tenniel are featured at the **Pierpont Morgan Library**. The **Cooper-Hewitt Museum** has examples of the use of prints in the decorative arts.

FURNITURE AND COSTUMES

THE ANNUAL exhibition of the Costume Institute at the **Metropolitan Museum of Art** is always worth a visit. Also impressive is the American Wing, with its 24 rooms of original furnishings tracing life from 1640 to the 20th century. Period rooms depicting New York in various settings, beginning with the 17th century Dutch, are on display at the **Museum of the City of New York**. There are also some house museums that give a realistic picture of furnishings and life in old New York. The **Old Merchant's House**, a preserved residence from the 1820s, was occupied by the same family for 98 years. **Gracie Mansion**, the residence of the mayor, was the 1799 country house of a wealthy shipping merchant and is open periodically for public tours. The **Theodore Roosevelt Birthplace** is the brownstone where the 26th president of the United States grew up, and the **Abigail Adams Smith Museum** was part of an 18th-century estate.

Corn husk doll, American Museum of Natural History

The Peaceable Kingdom (c.1840–1845) by **Edward Hicks, at the Brooklyn Museum**

HISTORY

Palm pistol at the Police Academy Museum

AMERICAN HISTORY unfolds at **Federal Hall**, the first US capital – George Washington took his oath as America's first president on the balcony in April 1789 – and now a museum of constitutional history. For the history of colonial New York, visit the **Fraunces Tavern Museum**. The restored **Ellis Island** and **Lower East Side Tenement Museum** re-create the hardships faced by immigrants. The **New York City Fire Museum** and the **Police Academy Museum** chronicle heroism and tragedy, while the **South Street Seaport Museum** re-creates early maritime history, complete with the original tall ships.

TECHNOLOGY AND NATURAL HISTORY

Forest-dwelling bonga, American Museum of Natural History

SCIENCE MUSEUMS hold exhibitions from nature to space-age technology. The **American Museum of Natural History** has vast collections covering flora, fauna and cultures from around the world. Here, too, the Hayden Planetarium offers unique laser-light shows. The **Intrepid** Sea-Air-Space **Museum** is a repository of technology that chronicles military progress. It is based on the decks of an aircraft carrier.

If you missed a classic Lucille Ball sitcom or footage of the first man on the moon, the place to visit is the **Museum of Television and Radio**, which holds these and many other classics of TV and radio.

ART FROM OTHER CULTURES

ARTWORK of other nations is the focus of several special collections. Oriental art is the specialty of the **Asia Society** and the **Japan Society**. The **Jewish Museum** features major collections of Judaica and has changing exhibitions of Jewish life. **El Museo del Barrio** is dedicated to the arts of Puerto Rico, including many pre-Columbian artifacts. For an impressive review of African-American art and history, visit the **Schomburg Center for Research in Black Culture**. Finally, the **Metropolitan Museum of Art** excels in its multicultural displays of art, ranging from ancient Egypt to contemporary Africa.

Egyptian mummy, Brooklyn Museum

LIBRARIES

NEW YORK'S notable libraries, such as the **Pierpoint Morgan Library**, offer some superb art collections as well as a chance to view pages from rare books. The **New York Public Library** shows a collection that includes manuscripts of many famous works.

BEYOND MANHATTAN

OTHER MUSEUMS worth a visit include **The Brooklyn Museum,** with its one and a half million paintings. The **American Museum of the Moving Image** in Queens has a unique collection of motion-picture history. The **Jacques Marchais Center of Tibetan Art** is a rare find on Staten Island. Also on Staten Island is **Historic Richmond Town**, a well-restored village dating from the 1600s.

New York's Best: Architecture

EVEN WHEN FOLLOWING world trends, New York has given its own twist to the turns of architectural fashion, the style of its buildings influenced by both geography and economy. An island city, with space at a premium, must look upward to grow. This trend was reflected early on with tall, narrow town houses

and later with the city's apartment buildings and skyscrapers. Building materials such as cast-iron and brownstone were chosen for their local availability and practical appeal. The result is a city that has developed by finding flamboyant answers to practical needs. A more detailed overview of New York's architecture is on pages 40 to 41.

Apartment Buildings
The twin-towered Majestic apartment building is one of four Art Deco blocks on Central Park West.

Cast-Iron Architecture
Mass-produced cast-iron was often used for building facades. SoHo has many of the best examples, such as this building at 28–30 Greene Street.

Post-Modernism
The quirky, yet elegant, shapes of buildings like the World Financial Center, built in 1985 (see p69), mark a bold departure from the sleek steel-and-glass boxes of the 1950s and 1960s.

Brownstones
Built from local sandstone, brownstones were favored by the 19th-century middle classes. India House, built in a Florentine palazzo style on Wall Street, is typical of many brownstone commercial buildings.

Theater District · Chelsea and the Garment District · Greenwich Village · Gramercy and the Flatiron District · SoHo and TriBeCa · East Village · Lower East Side · Lower Manhattan

Morningside Heights and Harlem

Upper West Side

Central Park

Upper East Side

Upper Midtown

Lower Midtown

EAST RIVER

0 kilometers

0 miles 1

19th-Century Mansions

The Jewish Museum (see p184), formerly the home of Felix M. Warburg, is a fine example of the French Renaissance style that typified these mansions.

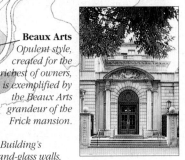

Beaux Arts

Opulent style, created for the richest of owners, is exemplified by the Beaux Arts grandeur of the Frick mansion.

Modernism

The Seagram Building's sleek bronze-and-glass walls, scant decoration and monumental scale typify postwar architecture. (See p173.)

The Skyscraper

The glory of New York architecture, these buildings expressed a perfect blend of practical engineering skill together with fabulous decoration, such as this gargoyle on the Chrysler Building.

Federal Architecture

Federal style was popular in civic architecture of the 19th century; City Hall combines it with French Renaissance influences.

Tenements

Constructed as an economic form of housing, for many these buildings were a stark introduction to new lives. Mainly built on the Lower East Side, the apartments were hopelessly overcrowded. In addition, the buildings' design, with inadequate air shafts, resulted in apartments with little or no ventilation.

Exploring New York's Architecture

A Federal-style front door

IN ITS FIRST 200 YEARS, New York, like all of America, looked to Europe for architectural inspiration. None of the buildings from the Dutch colonial period survive in Manhattan today; most were lost in the great fire of 1776 or torn down to make way for new developments in the early 1800s. Throughout the 18th and 19th centuries, the city's major architectural trends followed those of Europe. With the advent of cast-iron architecture in the 1850s, the Art Deco period and the ever-higher rise of the skyscraper, New York's architecture came into its own.

FEDERAL ARCHITECTURE

THIS AMERICAN adaptation of the Neoclassical Adam style flowered in the early decades of the new nation, featuring square buildings two or three stories tall, with low hipped roofs, balustrades and decorative elements – all carefully balanced. **City Hall** (1811, John McComb, Jr. and Joseph François Mangin) is a blend of Federal and French Renaissance influences. The restored warehouses of **Schermerhorn Row** (c1812) in the Seaport district are also in Federal style.

BROWNSTONES

PLENTIFUL AND CHEAP, the brown sandstone found in the nearby Connecticut River Valley and along the banks of the Hackensack River in New

A typical brownstone with stoop leading up to the main entrance

Jersey was the most common building material in the 1800s. It is found all over the city's residential neighborhoods, used for small homes or small

apartments – some of the best examples of brownstone can be found in **Chelsea**. Because street space was limited, these buildings were very narrow in width, but also very deep. A typical brownstone has a flight of steps, called a stoop, leading up to the living floors. Separate stairs lead down to the basement, which was originally the servants' quarters.

TENEMENTS

TENEMENTS WERE built to house the huge influx of immigrants who arrived from the 1840s up to World War I. The six-story blocks, 100 ft (30 m) long and 25 ft (8 m) wide, offered very little light and air except from tiny sidewall air shafts and windows at each end, leaving the middle rooms in darkness. The tiny apartments were called railroad flats after their similarity to railway cars. Later designs had air shafts between buildings, but these helped the spread of fire. The **Lower East Side Tenement Museum** has scale models of the old tenements.

CAST-IRON ARCHITECTURE

AN AMERICAN architectural innovation of the 19th century, cast iron was cheaper than stone or brick and allowed ornate features to be prefabricated in foundries from molds and used as building facades. Today, New York has the world's largest concentration of full and partial cast-iron facades. The best, built in the 1870s, are in the **SoHo Cast-Iron Historic District**.

The original cast-iron facade of 72–76 Greene Street, SoHo

BEAUX ARTS

THIS FRENCH school of architecture dominated public buildings and wealthy residential properties during New York's gilded age. This era (from 1880 to about 1920) produced many of the city's most prominent architects, including Richard Morris Hunt (**Carnegie Hall**, 1891; **Metropolitan Museum**, 1895), who in 1845 was the first American architect to study in Paris; Cass Gilbert (**Custom House**, 1907; **New York Life Insurance**

ARCHITECTURAL DISGUISES

Some of the most fanciful forms on the New York skyline were devised by clever architects to disguise the city's essential but utilitarian – and rather unattractive – rooftop water tanks. Look skyward to discover the ornate cupolas, spires and domes that transform the most mundane of features into veritable castles in the air. Examples that are easy to spot are atop two neighboring Fifth Avenue hotels: the Sherry Netherland at 60th Street and the Pierre at 61st Street.

Standard water tower

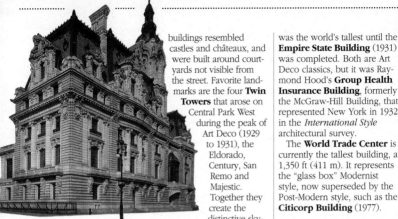

buildings resembled castles and châteaux, and were built around courtyards not visible from the street. Favorite landmarks are the four **Twin Towers** that arose on Central Park West during the peak of Art Deco (1929 to 1931), the Eldorado, Century, San Remo and Majestic. Together they create the distinctive skyline seen from the park.

Beaux Arts mansion built for Cornelius Vanderbilt II (1843–99); it has since been demolished

Building, 1928; the **US Courthouse**, 1936; the teams of Warren & Wetmore (**Grand Central Terminal**, 1913; **Helmsley Building**, 1929); Carrère & Hastings (**New York Public Library**, 1911; **Frick mansion**, 1914); and McKim, Mead & White, the city's most famous firm of architects (**Villard Houses**, 1884; **United States General Post Office**, 1913; **Municipal Building**, 1914).

APARTMENT BUILDINGS

AS THE CITY'S population grew and space became ever more precious, family homes in Manhattan became much too expensive for most New Yorkers, and even the wealthy joined the trend toward communal living. In 1884 Henry Hardenbergh's Dakota *(see p216)*, one of the first luxury apartment buildings, started a spate of turn-of-the-century construction on the Upper West Side. Many of the

SKYSCRAPERS

ALTHOUGH CHICAGO gave birth to the skyscraper, New York has seen some of the greatest innovations in this style. In 1902 Daniel Burnham, a Chicago architect, built the **Flatiron Building**, so tall at 300 ft (91 m) that sceptics said it would collapse. By 1913, the **Woolworth Building** had risen to 792 ft (241 m). Soon, zoning laws were passed requiring "setbacks" – upper stories were stepped back to allow light to reach street level. This suited the Art Deco style. The **Chrysler Building** (1930)

Art Deco arched pattern on the spire of the Chrysler Building

was the world's tallest until the **Empire State Building** (1931) was completed. Both are Art Deco classics, but it was Raymond Hood's **Group Health Insurance Building**, formerly the McGraw-Hill Building, that represented New York in 1932 in the *International Style* architectural survey.

The **World Trade Center** is currently the tallest building, at 1,350 ft (411 m). It represents the "glass box" Modernist style, now superseded by the Post-Modern style, such as the **Citicorp Building** (1977).

245 Fifth Avenue (Apartment Bulding)

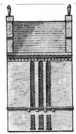

60 Gramercy Park North (Brownstone)

Hotel Pierre (Beaux Arts)

Sherry Netherland Hotel (Beaux Arts)

Multicultural New York

WHEREVER YOU GO in New York, even in pockets of the hectic high-rise city center, you will find evidence of the richly ethnic flavor of the city. A bus ride can take you from Madras to Moscow, Hong Kong to Haiti. Immigrants are still coming to New York, though numbers are fewer than in the peak years from 1880 to 1910, when 17 million people arrived. In the 1980s, a million newcomers, largely from Caribbean countries and Asia, arrived and found their own special corner of the city. Throughout the year you will encounter crowds celebrating one of many festivals. To find out more about national celebrations and parades, see pages 50 to 53.

Hell's Kitchen
The Irish community first settled here; now they color Fifth Avenue green for St. Patrick's Day on March 17 every year.

Little Ukraine
Services are held at Taras Sevchenko Place as part of the May 17 festivities to mark the Ukrainians' conversion to Christianity.

Little Korea
Not far from Herald Square, a small enclave of Koreans has made a niche.

Theatre District

Chelsea and the Garment District

Gramercy and the Flatiron District

Greenwich Village

Little Italy
For ten days in September, the Italian community gathers around the Mulberry Street area, and the streets are taken over by the celebrations of the Festa di San Gennaro.

SoHo and TriBeCa

East Village

Chinatown
Every year, around the end of January, Mott Street is packed with revelers as Chinatown celebrates its New Year.

Seaport and the Civic Center

Lower Manhattan

Lower East Side

| 0 kilometers | | 2 |
| 0 miles | 1 | |

The Lower East Side
The synagogues around Rivington Street reflect the religious traditions of this old Jewish area.

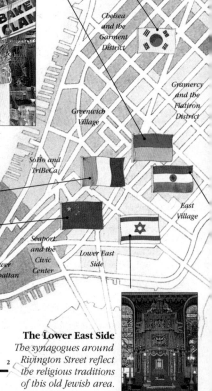

Morningside Heights and Harlem

Upper West Side

Central Park

Upper East Side

Upper Midtown

Lower Midtown

Harlem
The Sunday morning gospel service at the Abyssinian Baptist Church is one of Harlem's finest.

El Barrio
The vibrant Hispanic community of Harlem's El Barrio district is centered around the street market, La Marquetta.

Yorkville
A few cafés and bierkellers remain to keep the flavor of this former uptown German district. The Steuben Day Parade is held here each September.

Upper East Side
The magnificent St. Nicholas Russian Orthodox Cathedral on East 97th Street is a reminder of the dispersed White Russian community. Mass is held in Russian each Sunday.

Little India
The restaurants of East 6th Street offer Eastern atmosphere at affordable prices.

Exploring New York's Many Cultures

Stained glass at the Cotton Club

EVEN "NATIVE" NEW YORKERS have ancestral roots in other countries. Throughout the 17th century, the Dutch and English settled here, establishing trade colonies in the New World. Soon America became a symbol of hope for the downtrodden elsewhere in Europe. Many flocked across the ocean, some penniless and with little knowledge of the language. The potato famine of the 1840s led to the first wave of Irish immigrants, followed by German and other European workers displaced by political unrest and the Industrial Revolution. Immigrants continue to enrich New York in countless ways, and today an estimated 80 languages are spoken.

Turkish immigrants arriving at former Idlewild Airport in 1963

THE JEWS

THERE HAS BEEN a Jewish community in New York since 1654. The first synagogue, Shearith Israel, was established by refugees from a Dutch colony in Brazil and is still active today. These first settlers, Sephardic Jews of Spanish descent, included such prominent families as the Baruchs. They were followed by the German Jews, who set up successful retailing enterprises, like the Straus brothers at Macy's. Russian persecution led to the mass immigration that began in the late 1800s. By the start of World War I, there were 600,000 Jews living on the Lower East Side. Today, this area is more Hispanic than Jewish, but it holds reminders of its role as a place of refuge and new beginnings.

THE GERMANS

THE GERMANS began to settle in New York in the 18th century. From Peter Zenger onward *(see p19)*, the city's German community has championed the freedom to express ideas and opinions. It has also produced giants of industry, such as John Jacob Astor, the city's first millionaire.

THE ITALIANS

ITALIANS FIRST came to New York in the 1830s and 1840s. Many came from northern Italy to escape the failing revolution at home. In the 1870s, poverty in southern Italy drove many more Italians across the ocean. In time, they became a potent political force in the city, exemplified by Fiorello La Guardia, one of New York's finest mayors.

THE CHINESE

THE CHINESE were late arrivals to New York. In 1880, the population of the Mott Street district was a mere

Eastern States Buddhist Temple, in central Chinatown *(see pp96–7)*

700. By the 1940s, they were the city's fastest-growing and most upwardly mobile ethnic group, extending the old boundaries of Chinatown and establishing new neighborhoods in parts of Brooklyn and Queens. Once a closed community, Chinatown now bustles with tourists exploring the streets and markets, and sampling the restaurant food.

THE HISPANIC AMERICANS

Hispanic religious carving at El Museo del Barrio *(see p229)*

PUERTO RICANS were in New York as early as 1838, but it was not until after World War II that they arrived in large numbers in search of work. Most live in El Barrio, formerly known as Spanish Harlem. Professionals who fled Fidel Castro's Cuba have moved out of the city itself but are still very influential in Hispanic commerce and culture. Washington Heights is home to the Dominican and Colombian communities.

THE IRISH

THE IRISH, who first arrived in New York in the 1840s, had to overcome harsh odds. Wretched with starvation, and with barely a penny to their names, they labored hard to escape the slums of Five Points and Hell's Kitchen, helping to build the modern city in the process. Many joined the police and fire-fighting forces, rising to high rank through dedication to duty. Others set up successful businesses, such as the Irish bars that act as a focus for the now-scattered New York Irish community.

THE AFRICAN AMERICANS

Arguably the best-known black inner-city community in the Western world, Harlem is noted for the Harlem Renaissance of writing *(see pp28-9)* as much as it is for great entertainment, gospel music and soul food. The move of black African Americans from the south to the north began with emancipation in the 1860s and increased markedly in the 1920s, when Harlem's black population rose from 83,000 to 204,000. Today Harlem is undergoing revitalization in many areas. The African American population has also dispersed throughout the city.

THE MELTING POT

Other New York cultures are not distinctly defined but are still easily found. Ukrainians gather in the East Village, around St. George's Ukrainian Catholic Church on East 7th Street. Little India can be spotted by the restaurants along East 6th Street. Koreans own many of the small grocery stores in Manhattan, but most tend to live in the Flushing area of Queens. The religious diversity of New York can be seen in the Islamic Center on Riverside Drive, the

A woman celebrating at the Greek Independence Day parade

Russian Orthodox Cathedral on East 97th Street *(see p197)*; and the new Islamic Cultural Center on 96th Street – Manhattan's first major mosque.

THE OUTER BOROUGHS

Brooklyn is by far the most international borough. Caribbean newcomers from Jamaica and Haiti are one of the fastest-growing immigrant groups. West Indians tend to cluster along Eastern Parkway between Grand Army Plaza and Utica Avenue, the route of the lavish, exotically-costumed West Indian Day Parade in September. Recently arrived Russian Jewish immigrants have turned Brighton Beach into "Little Odessa by the Sea," and the Scandinavians and Lebanese have settled in Bay Ridge and the Finns in Sunset Park. Borough Park and Williamsburg are home to Orthodox Jews, and Midwood has an Israeli – Middle East accent. Italians live in the Bensonhurst area. Greenpoint is little Poland, and Atlantic Avenue is home to the largest Arab community in America.

The Irish were among the earliest groups to cross the Harlem River into the Bronx. Japanese executives favor the more exclusive Riverdale area. One of the most distinctive ethnic areas is Astoria, Queens, which has the largest Greek population outside the motherland. Jackson Heights is home to a large Latin American quarter, including 300,000 Colombians. Indians also favor this area and neighboring Flushing. But it is the Asians who have transformed Flushing, so much so that the local train is known as "The Orient Express."

The New York police, a haven for Irish Americans

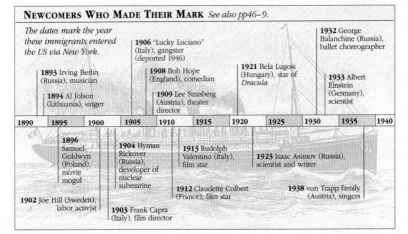

NEWCOMERS WHO MADE THEIR MARK See also pp46–9.

The dates mark the year these immigrants entered the US via New York.

1893 Irving Berlin (Russia), musician

1894 Al Jolson (Lithuania), singer

1906 "Lucky Luciano" (Italy), gangster (deported 1946)

1908 Bob Hope (England), comedian

1909 Lee Strasberg (Austria), theater director

1921 Bela Lugosi (Hungary), star of *Dracula*

1932 George Balanchine (Russia), ballet choreographer

1933 Albert Einstein (Germany), scientist

1890	1895	1900	1905	1910	1915	1920	1925	1930	1935	1940

1896 Samuel Goldwyn (Poland), movie mogul

1902 Joe Hill (Sweden), labor activist

1903 Frank Capra (Italy), film director

1904 Hyman Rickover (Russia), developer of nuclear submarine

1912 Claudette Colbert (France), film star

1913 Rudolph Valentino (Italy), film star

1923 Isaac Asimov (Russia), scientist and writer

1938 von Trapp family (Austria), singers

Celebrated Visitors and Residents

Nᴇᴀʀʟʏ ᴀʟʟ New Yorkers have immigrant roots if you go back far enough. Indeed, many of the city's most prominent residents have migrated here, coming to New York to find creative freedom and sometimes fleeing from constraints or repression in their native countries. As a result, some of the most brilliant contributions to New York's colorful history and culture have been made by first-generation immigrants and visitors.

George Balanchine *(1904–83)*
The ballet choreographer migrated from Russia in 1933 and formed the New York City Ballet.

Dylan Thomas
(1914–53)
The Welsh poet drank himself to a tragically early death; he frequented the White Horse Tavern in Greenwich Village.

Marcel Duchamp
(1887–1968)
In 1917 the French Dadaist climbed Washington Square arch to protest against US partici-pation in World War I.

Guiseppe Garibaldi *(1807–82)*
A statue in Greenwich Village honors the Italian freedom fighter who spent four years in exile on Staten Island before returning to unify Italy.

Irving Berlin *(1888–1989)*
Born Israel Baline in Siberia, he grew up on the Lower East Side and composed the hit tune "White Christmas."

Theater District

Chelsea and the Garment District

Lower Midtow

Gramercy and the Flatiron District

East Village

Greenwich Village

SoHo & TriBeCa

Lower East Side

Seaport and the Civic Center

Lower Manhattan

Isaac Bashevis Singer (1904–91) The Polish Jewish novelist lived on West 86th Street for many years.

Morningside Heights and Harlem

John Audubon (1785–1851) America's most famous ornithologist grew up in France. His New York estate was in Washington Heights.

Marcus Garvey (1887–1940) During the 1920s Jamaican-born Garvey lived in Harlem, where he was an influential black leader.

Upper West Side

Central Park

John Lennon (1940–80) The Liverpool-born musician and his wife, Yoko Ono, made their home on the Upper West Side.

Upper East Side

Harry Houdini (1874–1926) The escape artist from Budapest had a vision of his death at age 52 and left his West 113th Street house weeping.

Upper Midtown

Andrew Carnegie (1835–1918) The Scottish-born industrialist and philanthropist's home is now the Cooper-Hewitt Museum (see p184).

Sarah Bernhardt (1844–1923) The French actress attended services at the Little Church Around the Corner (see p127) during her time in New York.

0 kilometers 2

0 miles 1

Jacob Riis (1849–1914) A Danish immigrant, he slept in Bowery doorways before writing How the Other Half Lives, which helped alleviate New York's squalor.

Remarkable New Yorkers

N EW YORK HAS NOURISHED some of the best creative talents of this century. Pop art began here, and Manhattan is still the world center for modern art. The alternative writers of the 1950s and '60s – known as the Beat Generation – took inspiration from the city's jazz clubs. And since it is the financial capital, many leading world financiers have made New York their home.

WRITERS

Novelist James Baldwin

M UCH GREAT AMERICAN literature was created in New York. *Charlotte Temple, A Tale of Truth,* first published in 1791 by Susanna Rowson (c1762–1824), was a tale of seduction in the city and a best-seller for 50 years.

America's first professional author was Charles Brockden Brown (1771–1810), who came to New York in 1791. The novels of Edgar Allan Poe (1809–49), the pioneer of the modern detective story, expanded the thriller genre. Henry James (1843–1916) published *The Bostonians* (1886) and became the master of the psychological novel, and his friend Edith Wharton (1861–1937) became known for her satirical novels about American society.

American literature finally received international recognition with Washington Irving's (1783–1859) satire, *A History of New York* (1809). It earned him $2,000. Irving coined the names "Gotham" for New York and "Knickerbockers" for New Yorkers. He and James Fenimore Cooper (1789–1851), whose books gave birth to the "Western" novel, formed the Knicker-

bocker group of US writers. Greenwich Village has always attracted writers, including Herman Melville (1819–91) whose masterpiece, *Moby Dick* (1851), was very poorly received at first. Jack Kerouac (1922–69), Allen Ginsberg and William Burroughs all went to Columbia University and drank at the San Remo Café in Greenwich Village. Dylan Thomas (1914–53) lived at the Chelsea Hotel *(see p137).* Novelist Nathanael West (1902– 40) worked in the Gramercy Park Hotel, and Dashiell Hammett (1894–1961) wrote *The Maltese Falcon* while living there. James Baldwin (1924– 87), born in Harlem, wrote *Another Country* (1963) on his return to New York from Europe.

ARTISTS

T HE NEW YORK School of Abstract Expressionists founded the first influential American art movement. It was launched by Hans Hofmann (1880–1966) with Franz Kline and Willem de Kooning, whose first job in America was as a house-painter. Adolph Gottlieb, Mark Rothko (1903–70) and Jackson Pollock (1912–56) went on to popularize this style. Pollock, Kline and de Kooning all had their studios on the Lower East Side.

Pop art began in New York in the 1960s with Roy Lichtenstein and

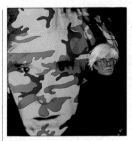

Pop artist Andy Warhol

Andy Warhol (1926–87), who made some of his cult films at 33 Union Square. Keith Haring (1958–90) was a very prolific graffiti artist whose work as a pop artist is now receiving recognition.

Robert Mapplethorpe (1946–89) acquired notoriety for his homoerotic photos of men. Jeff Koons has now superseded him as the *bête noire* of the art establishment.

The illusionistic murals by Richard Haas enliven many walls throughout the city.

ACTORS

I N 1849 the British actor Charles Macready started a riot by saying Americans were vulgar. A mob stormed the Astor Place Opera House, where Macready was playing Macbeth, police opened fire, and 22 rioters were killed. In 1927 Mae West (1893–1980) spent 10 days in a workhouse on Roosevelt Island and was fined $500 for giving a lewd performance in her Broadway show *Sex*. Marc Blitzstein's radical pro-labor opera *The Cradle Will Rock* produced by Orson Welles (1915–85) and John Houseman (1902–88), was immediately banned and the show had

Vaudeville actress Mae West   to move to

another theater. The actors managed to get around the ban by buying tickets and singing their roles from the audience.

The musical has been New York's special contribution to the theater. Florenz Ziegfeld's (1869–1932) *Follies* ran from 1907 to 1931. The opening of *Oklahoma!* on Broadway in 1943 began the age of musicals by Richard Rodgers (1902–79) and Oscar Hammerstein, Jr. (1895–1960).

Off Broadway, the Provincetown Players at 33 MacDougal Street were the first to produce Eugene O'Neill's (1888–1953) *Beyond the Horizon* (1920). His successor as the major innovative force in US theater was Edward Albee, author of *Who's Afraid of Virginia Woolf?* (1962).

MUSICIANS AND DANCERS

LEONARD BERNSTEIN (1918–90) followed a long line of great conductors at the New York Philharmonic, including Bruno Walter (1876–1962), Arturo Toscanini (1867–1957) and Leopold Stokowski (1882–1977). Maria Callas (1923–77) was born in New York but moved to Europe.

Carnegie Hall (*see p146*) has featured Enrico Caruso (1873–1921), Bob Dylan and the Beatles. A record concert attendance was set in 1991 when Paul Simon drew a million people for his free concert in Central Park.

The legendary swinging jazz clubs of the 1930s and 1940s are now gone from 52nd Street. Plaques on "Jazz Walk" outside the CBS building honor such

Josephine Baker

famous performers as Charlie Parker (1920–55) and Josephine Baker (1906–75).

Between 1940 and 1965, New York became a world dance capital with the founding of George Balanchine's (1904–83) New York City Ballet and the American Ballet Theater. In 1958, choreographer Alvin Ailey (1931–89) started the American Dance Theater, a showcase for modern dance works by a multiracial troupe.

INDUSTRIALISTS AND ENTREPRENEURS

Tycoon Cornelius Vanderbilt

THE RAGS-TO-RICHES story is an American dream. Andrew Carnegie (1835–1919), "the steel baron with a heart of gold," started with nothing and died having given away $350 million. His beneficiaries included public libraries and universities throughout America. Many other foundations are legacies of wealthy philanthropists. Some, like Cornelius Vanderbilt (1794–1877) tried to shake off their rough beginnings by patronizing the arts.

In business, New York's "robber barons" did what they liked with apparent impunity. Financiers Jay Gould (1836–92) and James Fisk (1834–72) beat Vanderbilt in the war for the Erie Railroad by manipulating stock. In September 1869 they caused Wall Street's first "Black Friday" when they tried to corner the gold market, but fled when their fraud was discovered. Gould died a happy billionaire and Fisk was killed in a fight over a woman.

Modern entrepreneurs have included Donald Trump (*see p31*), owner of Trump Tower, and Harry and Leona Helmsley. Despite Leona's imprisonment for tax evasion, their property empire remains intact and includes such New York sites as the Helmsley Building (*see p156*).

ARCHITECTS

CASS GILBERT (1858–1934), who built such Neo-Gothic skyscrapers as the Woolworth Building of 1913 (*see p91*) was one of the men who literally shaped the city. His caricature can be seen in the lobby, clutching a model of his masterpiece. Stanford White (1853–1906) was as well known for his scandalous private life as for his fine Beaux Arts buildings, such as the Players Club (*p124*). For most of his life, Frank Lloyd Wright (1867–1959) spurned city architecture. When he was persuaded to leave his mark on the city, it was in the form of the Guggenheim Museum (*pp186–7*). German-born Ludwig Mies van der Rohe (1886–1969), who built the Seagram Building, did not believe in "inventing a new architecture every Monday morning," although some might argue that this is just what New York has always done best.

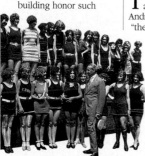
Musical producer Florenz Ziegfeld

NEW YORK THROUGH THE YEAR

SPRINGTIME IN NEW YORK sees Park Avenue filled with blooms, while Fifth Avenue goes green for St. Patrick's Day, the first of the year's many big parades. Summer in the city is hot and humid, but it is worth forsaking an air-conditioned interior to step outside, where parks and squares are the setting for free open-air music and theater. The first Monday in September marks Labor Day and the advent of comfortable temperatures and the orange-red colors of autumn. Then, as Christmas nears, the shops and streets begin to sparkle with dazzling window displays.

Dates of the events on the following pages may vary. For details consult the listings magazines *(see p353)*. The New York Convention and Visitors Bureau *(see p352)* also issues a useful quarterly free calendar of events.

SPRING

EVERY SEASON in New York brings its own tempo and temptations. In spring, the city shakes off the winter with tulips and cherry blossoms in the parks and spring fashions in the stores. Everyone window shops and gallery hops. The hugely popular St. Patrick's Day Parade draws the crowds, and thousands don their finery for the Easter Parade down Fifth Avenue.

Inventive Easter bonnets in New York's Easter Parade

MARCH

St. Patrick's Day Parade
(Mar 17), Fifth Ave, from 44th to 86th St. Green clothes, green flowers – even green beer.
Greek Independence Day Parade *(Mar 25)*, Fifth Ave, from 49th to 59th St. Greek dancing and food.
New York City Opera Spring Season *(Mar–mid-Apr)*, Lincoln Center *(p338)*.
Ringling Bros and Barnum & Bailey Circus *(late Mar–end May)*, Madison Square Garden *(p133)*.

EASTER

Easter Flower Show *(week before Easter)*, Macy's department store *(pp132–3)*.
Easter Parade *(Easter Sun)*, Fifth Ave, from 44th to 59th St. Paraders in costumes and outrageous millinery gather around St. Patrick's Cathedral.

APRIL

Cherry Blossom Festival *(late Apr–May)*, Brooklyn Botanic Garden. Famous for Japanese cherry trees and beautifully laid out ornamental gardens.
Gramercy Park Flower Show *(last weekend)* *(p126)*.
Baseball *(Apr–May)*, Major league season starts for Yankees and Mets *(p344)*.
New York City Ballet Spring Season *(Apr–Jun)*, New York State Theater and Metropolitan Opera House in Lincoln Center *(p212)*.

MAY

Brooklyn Bridge Day *(second Sun)*. Celebrations on the bridge *(pp86–9)*.
Martin Luther King, Jr. Day Parade *(third Sun)*, Fifth Ave, from 44th to 86th St. Parade to honor the memory of

Parading in national costume on Greek Independence Day

the assassinated black civil rights leader.
Ninth Avenue Street Festival *(mid-May)*, from W 37th to W 57th St. A feast of ethnic foods, music and dance.
Washington Square Outdoor Art Exhibit *(last weekend in May and first weekend in Jun)*. Paintings, sculpture, crafts and food.

Yellow tulips and cabs shine on Park Avenue

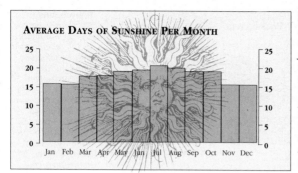

AVERAGE DAYS OF SUNSHINE PER MONTH

Jan Feb Mar Apr May Jun Jul Aug Sep Oct Nov Dec

Days of Sunshine
New York enjoys long hours of summer sun from June to August, with July the month of greatest sunshine. The winter days are much shorter, but many are clear and bright. Autumn has more sunshine than spring, although both are sunny.

SUMMER

NEW YORKERS escape the hot city streets when possible, for picnics, boat rides and the beaches. Macy's fireworks light up the Fourth of July skies, and more sparks fly when the New York Yankees and Mets baseball teams are in town. Summer also brings street fairs, outdoor concerts, and free Shakespeare and opera in Central Park.

Policeman dancing in the Puerto Rican Day Parade

JUNE

Puerto Rican Day Parade *(first Sun)*, Fifth Ave, from 44th to 86th St. Floats and marching bands.
Museum Mile Festival *(second Tue)*, Fifth Ave, from 82nd to 105th St. Free entry to museums.
L'eggs Mini-Marathon *(late Jun)*, from Central Park West and W 66th St to Central Park West at W 67th St. Women's road-running race.
Metropolitan Opera Parks Concerts. Free evening concerts in parks throughout the city *(pp338–9)*.
Goldman Memorial Band Concerts *(Jun–Aug)*, Lincoln Center *(p212)*. Traditional band concerts.

Shakespeare in the Park *(Jun–Sep)*. Broadway stars take on the bard at Delacorte Theater, Central Park *(p335)*.
Lesbian and Gay Pride Day Parade *(late Jun)*, from Columbus Circle along Fifth Ave to Washington Sq *(p113)*.
JVC Jazz Festival *(late Jun–early Jul)*. Top jazz musicians perform in various halls in the city *(p341)*.

JULY

Macy's Firework Display *(Jul 4)*, East River. High point of the city's Independence Day celebrations.
American Crafts Festival *(early July)*, Lincoln Center *(p212)*. High-quality crafts.
Chinatown Cultural Festival *(mid-Jul–mid-Sep)*, Chinatown *(pp96–7)*.
Mostly Mozart Festival, *(mid-Jul–end Aug)*, Avery Fisher Hall, Lincoln Center *(pp338-9)*.
NY Philharmonic Parks Concerts *(late Jul–early*

Festivities at a summer street fair in Greenwich Village

Aug). Free concerts in parks throughout the city *(p339)*.
Summer Festival *(Jul–Aug)*, Snug Harbor Cultural Center, Staten Island. Music and art.

AUGUST

Harlem Week *(mid-Aug)*. Films, art, music, dance, fashion, sports and tours.
Out-of-Doors Festival *(mid-Aug–early Sep)*, Lincoln Center. Free dance and theater performances *(p334)*.
US Open Tennis Championships *(late Aug–early Sep)*, Flushing Meadows *(p345)*.

Independence Day (July 4) fireworks display on the East River

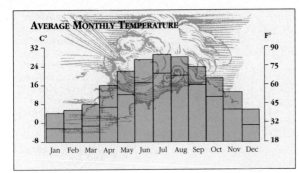

AVERAGE MONTHLY TEMPERATURE

Jan Feb Mar Apr May Jun Jul Aug Sep Oct Nov Dec

Temperature
The chart shows the average minimum and maximum temperatures for each month in New York. With top temperatures averaging 84° F (29° C), the city can become hot and humid. In contrast, the months of winter, although rarely below freezing, can seem bitterly cold.

AUTUMN

LABOR DAY marks the end of the summer. The Giants and the Jets kick off the football season, the Broadway season begins and the Festa di San Gennaro in Little Italy is the high point in a succession of colorful neighborhood fairs. Macy's Thanksgiving Day Parade is the nation's symbol that the festive season has arrived.

SEPTEMBER

Richmond County Fair
(Labor Day weekend), in the grounds of Historic Richmond Town *(p252)*. New York's only authentic county fair.
West Indian Carnival
(Labor Day weekend), Brooklyn. Parade, floats, music, dancing and food.
One World Festival *(second week)*, E 35th St, between First and Second avenues.

Exotic Caribbean carnival costume in the streets of Brooklyn

International antiques, arts and crafts, and food.
New York is Book Country *(mid-Sep)*, Fifth Ave, from 48th to 59th sts. Book fair.
Festa di San Gennaro *(third week)*, Little Italy *(p96)*. Ten days of festivities and processions.
New York Film Festival *(mid-Sep – early Oct)*, Lincoln Center *(p212)*. American films and international art films.
Von Steuben Day Parade *(third week)*, Upper Fifth Ave. German-American celebrations.
American Football *(season begins)*, Giants Stadium, home to the Giants and the Jets *(p344)*.

OCTOBER

Columbus Day Parade *(Oct 12)*, Fifth Ave, from 44th to 86th sts. Parades and music to celebrate Columbus's first sighting of America.
Pulaski Day Parade *(Sun closest to Oct 5)*, Fifth Ave, from 26th to 52nd sts. Celebrations for Polish-American hero Casimir Pulaski.
Halloween Parade *(Oct 31)*, Greenwich Village. Brilliant event with fantastic costumes.
Big Apple Circus *(Oct – Jan)*, Damrosch Park, Lincoln Center. Special themes are presented each year *(p347)*.
Basketball *(season begins)*, Madison Square Garden. Local team is the Knicks *(p344)*.
New York City Marathon *(last Sun Oct or first Sun Nov)*. From Staten Island through all the city boroughs.

Huge Superman balloon floating above Macy's Thanksgiving Day Parade

NOVEMBER

Macy's Thanksgiving Day Parade *(fourth Thu)*, from Central Park West and W 79th St to Broadway and W 34th St. A joy for children, with floats, huge balloons and Santa.
Christmas Star Show *(Nov – Jan)*, Hayden Planetarium *(p216)*. Re-creation of Bethlehem's sky on the night that Christ was born.
Magnificent Christmas Spectacular *(Nov – Jan)*, Radio City Music Hall. Variety show, with the Rockettes.

Revelers in Greenwich Village's Halloween Parade

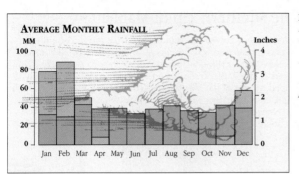

AVERAGE MONTHLY RAINFALL

MM — Jan Feb Mar Apr May Jun Jul Aug Sep Oct Nov Dec — Inches

Rainfall

March and August are the months of heaviest rainfall in New York. Rainfall in spring is unpredictable, so be prepared. Sudden heavy snowfalls in winter can cause chaos in the city.

 Rainfall

Snowfall

WINTER

Nᴇᴡ ʏᴏʀᴋ is magical at Christmas – even the stone lions at the Public Library don wreaths for the occasion, and shops become works of art. From Times Square to Chinatown, New Year celebrations punctuate the season, and Central Park becomes a winter sports arena.

Statue of Alice in Wonderland in Central Park

DECEMBER

Tree-Lighting Ceremony *(early Dec)*, Rockefeller Center *(p142)*. Lighting of the giant Christmas tree in front of the RCA Building.
Messiah Sing-In *(mid-Dec)*, Lincoln Center *(p212)*. The audience rehearses and performs under the guidance of various conductors.
Hanukkah Menorah *(mid–late Dec)*, Grand Army Plaza, Brooklyn. Lighting of the huge menorah (candelabra) every night during the eight-day Festival of Lights.
New Year's Eve. Fireworks display in Central Park *(pp204–5)*; festivities in Times Square *(p145)*; 5-mile (8-km) run in Central Park; poetry reading in St. Mark's Church.

JANUARY

National Boat Show *(mid-Jan)*, Jacob K. Javits Convention Center *(p136)*.
Chinese New Year *(late Jan)*, Chinatown *(pp96–7)*. Dragons, fireworks and food.
Winter Antiques Show *(late Jan)*, Seventh Regiment Armory *(p185)*. The city's most prestigious antiques fair.

FEBRUARY

Black History Month. African-American events take place throughout the city.
Empire State Building Run-Up *(early Feb)*. Runners race to the 102nd floor *(pp134–5)*.
Lincoln and Washington Birthday Sales *(Feb 12–22)* Big department stores sales throughout the city.
Westminster Kennel Club Dog Show *(mid-Feb)*, Madison Square Garden *(p133)*. Major dog show.

Chinese New Year celebrations in Chinatown

PUBLIC HOLIDAYS

New Year's Day (Jan 1)
Martin Luther King Day (3rd Mon, Jan)
President's Day (mid-Feb)
Memorial Day (end May)
Independence Day (Jul 4)
Labor Day (1st Mon, Sep)
Columbus Day (2nd Mon, Oct)
Election Day (1st Tue, Nov)
Veterans Day (Nov 11)
Thanksgiving Day (4th Thu, Nov)
Christmas Day (Dec 25)

The giant Christmas tree and decorations at Rockefeller Center

The Southern Tip of Manhattan

THIS VIEW OF Lower Manhattan, seen from the Hudson River, encompasses some of the most striking modern additions to the New York skyline, including the instantly recognizable twin towers of the World Trade Center, and the newer, distinctively topped quartet of the World Financial Center. You will also catch glimpses of an earlier Manhattan: Castle Clinton set against the green space of Battery Park and, behind it, the noble Custom House building.

LOCATOR MAP

☐ *The Southern Tip*

World Trade Center
Twin 110-story steel-and-glass towers (see p72) dominate the skyline. Below is a plaza bigger than St. Mark's Square in Venice.

World Financial Center
At the heart of this complex is the Winter Garden – a place to shop, dine, be entertained or just enjoy the Hudson River views (see p69).

The Upper Room
This walkaround sculpture by Ned Smyth is one of many works of art in Battery Park City (see p72).

An Earlier View
This 1898 photograph shows a skyline now changed beyond recognition.

Detail from the *Upper Room*

Downtown Athletic Club
The Heisman Trophy for football is kept in this fine Art Deco building.

US Custom House
This magnificent 1907 Beaux Arts building now houses the Museum of the American Indian (see p73).

East Coast War Memorial
In Battery Park, a huge bronze eagle by Albino Manca honors the dead of World War II.

26 Broadway
The tower of the former Standard Oil Building resembles an oil lamp. The interior is still decorated with company symbols.

Bank of New York

17 State Street

26 Broadway

1 Liberty Plaza

Liberty View

Castle Clinton

US Custom House

Shrine of Mother Seton
The first US-born saint lived here (see p76).

American Merchant Mariners' Memorial (1991)
This sculpture by Marisol is on Pier A, the last of Manhattan's old piers. The pier also has a clock tower that chimes the hours on ships' bells.

Lower Manhattan from the East River

AT FIRST SIGHT, this stretch of East River shoreline, running up from the tip of Manhattan Island, is a seamless array of 20th-century office buildings. But from sea level, streets and slips are still visible, offering glimpses of old New York and the Financial District to the west. On the skyline itself, a few of the district's early skyscrapers still proudly display their ornate crowns above their more anonymous modern counterparts.

LOCATOR MAP

☐ *East River View*

India House
The handsome brownstone at One Hanover Square is one of the finest of its kind.

Vietnam Veterans Plaza
An engraved green-glass memorial dominates the former Coenties Slip, a wharf filled in to make a park in the late 19th century (see p76).

Hanover Square
A statue of one of the Dutch mayors, Abraham De Peyster, sits near the house where he was born in 1657.

One New York Plaza

55 Water Street

Barclay Bank Building

Battery Maritime Building
This historic ferry terminal serves only Governor's Island (see p77).

Downtown Heliport
Air-Sea Rescue and sightseeing flights operate from here.

Delmonico's
High society dined here a century ago.

New York Stock Exchange
Although hidden from view by more modern edifices, this is still the hub of the hectic Financial District (see pp70–71).

40 Wall Street
In the 1940s, the pyramid-topped tower of the former Bank of Manhattan was hit by a light aircraft.

70 Pine Street
Replicas of this elegant Gothic-style tower can be seen near the Pine and Cedar Street entrances.

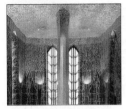

Bank of New York
This serene 1928 interior is part of the bank set up in 1784 by Alexander Hamilton (see p21).

Morgan Bank
Columns from lobby to rooftop are the theme of this striking modern building.

1 Financial Square

New York Stock Exchange

Chase Manhattan Bank Tower

120 Wall Street

100 Old Slip
Now in the shadow of One Financial Square, the small palazzo-style First Precinct Police Department was the city's most modern police station when it was built in 1911.

Citibank Building

Carved medallion, 100 Old Slip

***Queen Elizabeth* Monument**
The ocean liner that sank in 1972 is remembered here.

South Street Seaport

AS THE FINANCIAL DISTRICT ends, the skyline, as seen from the East River or Brooklyn, changes dramatically. The corporate headquarters are replaced by the piers, low-rise streets and warehouses of the old seaport area, now restored as the South Street Seaport *(see pp82–3)*. The Civic Center lies not far inland, and a few of its monumental buildings can be seen. The Brooklyn Bridge marks the end of this stretch of skyline. Between here and midtown, apartment blocks make up the majority of riverside features.

LOCATOR MAP

South Street Area

Stonework on the Woolworth Building

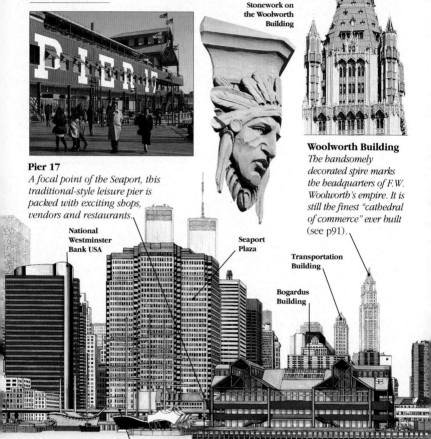

Pier 17
A focal point of the Seaport, this traditional-style leisure pier is packed with exciting shops, vendors and restaurants.

National Westminster Bank USA

Seaport Plaza

Transportation Building

Bogardus Building

Woolworth Building
The handsomely decorated spire marks the headquarters of F.W. Woolworth's empire. It is still the finest "cathedral of commerce" ever built (see p91).

Maritime Crafts Center
At Pier 15, craftspeople demonstrate traditional seafaring skills such as woodcarving and model-making.

Sweets
This seafood restaurant was in this Schermerhorn Row site from 1847 to 1993.

Fulton Fish Market
The largest wholesale fish market in the US takes place at the Seaport before dawn.

Police Plaza
Five in One *(1971–4), in Police Plaza, is a sculpture by Bernard Rosenthal. It represents the five boroughs of New York.*

United States Courthouse
The Civic Center is marked on the skyline by the golden pyramid of architect Cass Gilbert's courthouse (see p85).

Surrogate's Court and Hall of Records
Archives dating back to 1664 are stored and displayed here (see p85).

Municipal Building
Among the offices of this vast building is the Marriage Chapel, where weddings "at City Hall" actually take place. The copper statue on the skyline is Civic Fame *by Adolph Weinman* (see p85).

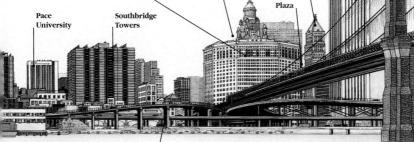

Pace University

Southbridge Towers

Police Plaza

New York Telephone Company

Con Edison Mural
In 1975, artist Richard Haas re-created the Brooklyn Bridge on the side wall of a former electrical substation.

Brooklyn Bridge
Views of, and from, the bridge have made it one of New York's best-loved landmarks (see pp86–9).

Midtown Manhattan

T HE SKYLINE OF midtown Manhattan is graced with some of the city's most spectacular towers and spires – from the familiar beauty of the Empire State Building's Art Deco pinnacle to the dramatic wedge shape of Citicorp's modern headquarters. As the shoreline progresses uptown, so the architecture becomes more varied; the United Nations complex dominates a long stretch, and then Beekman Place begins a strand of exclusive residential enclaves that offer the rich and famous some seclusion in this busy part of the city.

LOCATOR MAP

Midtown

Chrysler Building
Glinting in the sun by day or lit up by night, this stainless-steel spire is, for many, the ultimate New York skyscraper (see p153).

Empire State Building
At 1472 ft (449 m), this was the tallest building in the world for many years (see p134–5).

Grand Central Terminal
Now dwarfed by its neighbors, this landmark building is full of period details, such as this fine clock (see pp154–5).

The Highpoint

MetLife Building

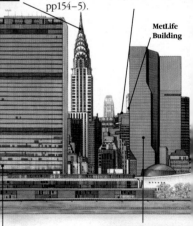

Tudor City
Built in the 1920s, this complex is mock Tudor on a grand scale, with over 3,000 apartments (see p156).

United Nations
Works of art from member countries include this Barbara Hepworth sculpture, a gift from Britain (see pp160–63).

1 and 2 UN Plaza
Angular glass towers house offices and the UN Plaza Hotel (see pp156 and 280).

General Electric Building
Built of red brick in 1931, this Art Deco building has a tall spiked crown. The present tenant is RCA Victor (see p172).

Waldorf–Astoria
Twin copper-capped towers rise high above one of the city's finest hotels. The interior is also splendid (see p173).

Citicorp Center
St. Peter's Church nestles in one corner of the Citicorp Center with its raked tower (see p173).

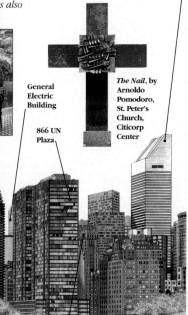

Rockefeller Center
The outdoor skating rink and walkways of this complex of office buildings are a great place to people watch (see p142).

General Electric Building

The Nail, by Arnoldo Pomodoro, St. Peter's Church, Citicorp Center

866 UN Plaza

100 UN Plaza

St. Mary's Garden
The garden at Holy Family Church is a peaceful haven.

Japan Society
Japanese culture, from avant-garde plays to ancient art, can be seen here (see p156–7).

Beekman Tower
Now an all-suite hotel, this Art Deco tower was built in 1928 as a hotel for women who were members of US college sororities.

New York
Area by Area

LOWER MANHATTAN

THE OLD AND THE NEW converge at the lower tip of Manhattan, where Colonial churches and early American monuments stand in the shadow of skyscrapers. New York was born here, and this was the site of the nation's first capitol. Commerce has flourished since 1626, when Dutchman Peter Minuit made one of

Minuit memorial on Bowling Green

history's most famous property deals, purchasing the island of Man-a-hatt-ta from the Algonquian Indians for beads and goods valued at $24 *(see p17)*. The stakes have become higher, but finance remains at the heart of this part of the city: it is home to Wall Street, the Federal Reserve Bank, the World Trade Center and the Stock Exchange.

Trinity Church at the foot of Wall Street

SIGHTS AT A GLANCE

Historic Streets and Buildings
Federal Reserve Bank **1**
Federal Hall **2**
New York Stock Exchange pp70–71 **3**
Downtown Athletic Club **8**
Cunard Building **9**
Fraunces Tavern Museum **13**
Battery Maritime Building **16**

Museums and Galleries
US Custom House **11**
Ellis Island pp78–9 **18**

Castle Clinton National Monument **20**

Monuments and Statues
Statue of Liberty pp74–5 **17**

Churches
Trinity Church **4**
Shrine of Elizabeth Ann Seton **12**

Modern Architecture
World Financial Center **5**
World Trade Center **6**
Battery Park City **7**

Parks and Squares
Bowling Green **10**
Vietnam Veterans' Plaza **14**
Battery Park **19**

Boat Trips
Staten Island Ferry **15**

Bronze statue of a bull, symbol of Wall Street, near the Custom House

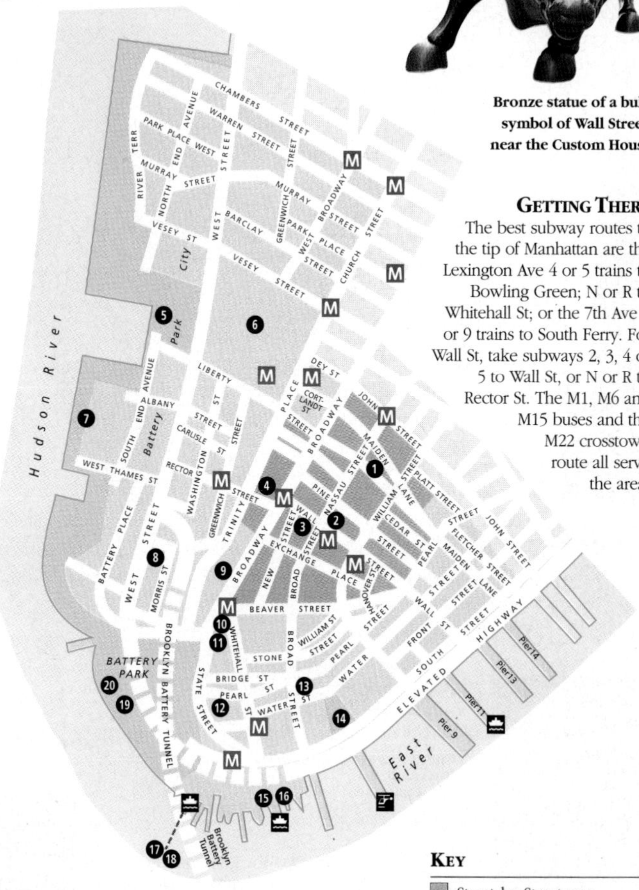

GETTING THERE
The best subway routes to the tip of Manhattan are the Lexington Ave 4 or 5 trains to Bowling Green; N or R to Whitehall St; or the 7th Ave 1 or 9 trains to South Ferry. For Wall St, take subways 2, 3, 4 or 5 to Wall St, or N or R to Rector St. The M1, M6 and M15 buses and the M22 crosstown route all serve the area.

SEE ALSO

0 meters   500

0 yards   500

KEY

▨ Street-by-Street map

Ⓜ Subway station

⬛ Ferry boarding point

⬛ Heliport

Street by Street: Wall Street

No intersection has been of greater importance to the city, past or present, than the corners of Wall and Broad streets. Three important sites are located here. Federal Hall National Monument marks the place where, in 1789, George Washington was sworn in as president. Trinity Church is one of the nation's oldest Anglican parishes. The New York Stock Exchange, founded in 1817, is to this day a financial nerve center whose ups and downs cause tremors around the globe. The surrounding buildings are the very heart of New York's famous financial district.

The Marine Midland Bank rises straight up 55 stories. This dark, glass tower occupies only 40% of its site. The other 60% is a plaza in which a large red sculpture by Isamu Noguchi, *Cube*, balances on one of its points.

Trinity Building, an early 20th-century Gothic skyscraper, was designed to complement nearby Trinity Church.

The Equitable Building (1915) deprived its neighbors of light, prompting a change in the law: skyscrapers had to be set back from the street.

★ Trinity Church
Built in 1846 in a Gothic style, this is the third church on this site. Once the tallest structure in the city, the bell tower is now dwarfed by the skyscrapers that surround it. Many famous early New Yorkers are buried in the churchyard ❹

Wall Street subway (lines 4, 5)

The Irving Trust Company, built in 1932, has an outer wall patterned to look like fabric. In the lobby is an Art Deco mosaic in shades of flame and gold.

26 Broadway was built as the home of the Standard Oil Trust. An oil lamp rests on top of it.

New York Stock Exchange ★
The hub of the world's financial markets is housed in a 17-story building constructed in 1903. Its visitors' center explains the history and workings of the Stock Exchange ❸

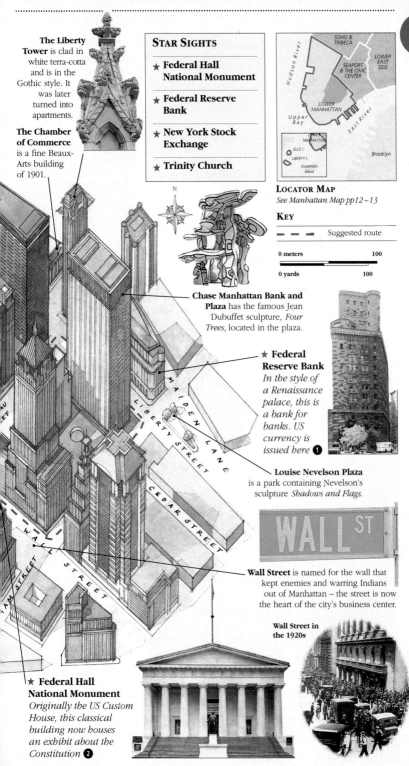

The Liberty Tower is clad in white terra-cotta and is in the Gothic style. It was later turned into apartments.

The Chamber of Commerce is a fine Beaux-Arts building of 1901.

STAR SIGHTS

★ **Federal Hall National Monument**

★ **Federal Reserve Bank**

★ **New York Stock Exchange**

★ **Trinity Church**

LOCATOR MAP
See Manhattan Map pp12–13

KEY

— — — Suggested route

0 meters 100

0 yards 100

Chase Manhattan Bank and Plaza has the famous Jean Dubuffet sculpture, *Four Trees*, located in the plaza.

★ **Federal Reserve Bank**
In the style of a Renaissance palace, this is a bank for banks. US currency is issued here ❶

Louise Nevelson Plaza is a park containing Nevelson's sculpture *Shadows and Flags.*

Wall Street is named for the wall that kept enemies and warring Indians out of Manhattan – the street is now the heart of the city's business center.

Wall Street in the 1920s

★ **Federal Hall National Monument**
Originally the US Custom House, this classical building now houses an exhibit about the Constitution ❷

Federal Reserve Bank ❶

33 Liberty St. **Map** 1 C2. 720-6130. **M** Wall St. **Open** 9:30am–2:30pm Mon–Fri. **Closed** public hols.

Entrance to Federal Reserve Bank

THIS IS A GOVERNMENT bank for banks – it is one of the 12 Federal Reserve banks, and therefore issues US currency. You can identify bank notes originating from this branch by the letter B in the Federal Reserve seal on each note.

Below ground is a five-story vault that serves as the largest storehouse for gold owned by the nations of the world. Each nation's gold is stored in its own compartment within the subterranean vault, guarded by 90-ton doors. Payments between nations used to be made by physical transfers of gold, but this is no longer so.

Designed by York & Sawyer, the building was completed in 1924. It occupies a full block and is liberally adorned with fine wrought-iron grillwork. It was inspired by the palaces of the Italian Renaissance.

Federal Hall ❷

26 Wall St. **Map** 1 C3. 264-8700. **M** Wall St. **Open** 9am–5pm Mon–Fri. **Closed** public holidays.

A BRONZE STATUE of George Washington on the steps of Federal Hall marks the site where the nation's first president took his oath of office in 1789. Thousands of New Yorkers jammed Wall and Broad streets for the occasion. They roared their approval when the Chancellor of the State of New York shouted, "Long live George Washington, President of the United States."

The present imposing structure was built between 1834 and 1842 as the United States Custom House and is one of the finest Classical designs in the city. Display rooms off the Rotunda include the Bill of Rights Room and an interactive computer exhibit about the Constitution.

New York Stock Exchange ❸

See pp70–71.

Trinity Churchyard

Trinity Church ❹

Broadway at Wall St. **Map** 1 C3. 602-0872. **M** Wall St, Rector St. **Open** 7am–6pm Mon–Fri, 8am–4pm Sat, 7am–4pm Sun. 11:15am Sun. except during services. 2pm daily. **Concerts.**

THIS SQUARE-TOWERED Episcopal church at the head of Wall Street is the third one on this site in one of America's oldest Anglican parishes, founded in 1697. Designed in 1846 by Richard Upjohn, it was one of the grandest churches of its day, marking the beginning of the best period of Gothic Revival architecture in America. Richard Morris Hunt's design for the sculpted brass doors was inspired by Ghiberti's *Doors of Paradise* in Florence.

Restoration has uncovered the original rosy sandstone, long buried beneath layers of city grime. The 280-ft (26-m) steeple, the tallest structure in New York until the 1860s, still commands respect despite its towering neighbors.

Many prominent early New Yorkers were members of Trinity parish. Statesman Alexander Hamilton; steamboat inventor Robert Fulton; and William Bradford, founder of New York's first newspaper in 1725, are among those buried in the venerable graveyard beside the church.

Marble-columned rotunda within Federal Hall

World Financial Center ❺

West St. **Map** 1 A2. 945-0505. 1, 2, 3, 9, A, C, E to Chambers St, 1, 9, N, R to Cortlandt St. M1, M6, M9, M10, M22.

A MODEL OF URBAN design by Cesar Pelli & Associates, this development is a vital part of the revival of Lower Manhattan. Four office towers soar skyward, each topped with a different geometric shape. Some of the world's most important financial companies are headquartered here, and overpasses link the Center with its World Trade counterpart. But this is far more than an office complex.

At the heart of the Center is the dazzling Winter Garden, a vast glass-and-steel public space, flanked by 45 restaurants and shops, opening onto a lively piazza and marina on the Hudson River. The sweeping marble staircase leading down to the Winter Garden often doubles as seating for free arts and events, varying from the classic to the contemporary in music, dance and theater.

Main floor of the Winter Garden

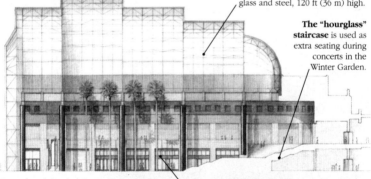

The atrium is a sparkling vault of glass and steel, 120 ft (36 m) high.

The "hourglass" staircase is used as extra seating during concerts in the Winter Garden.

An esplanade borders the Hudson.

Cafés and shops line the atrium.

Sixteen 45-ft (14-m) palm trees from the Mojave Desert make this a 1990s version of the "palm court" of yesteryear.

Inaugurated in 1988 and still expanding, this is a place designed for people and for pleasure, and it has been hailed as the Rockefeller Center of the 21st century by even the most stringent of architectural critics.

World Financial Center viewed from the Hudson River

New York Stock Exchange ❸

IN 1790, TRADING in stocks and shares took place haphazardly on or around Wall Street, but in 1792, 24 brokers who traded under a buttonwood tree at 68 Wall Street signed an agreement to deal only with one another, and the basis of the New York Stock Exchange was formed. Membership is strictly limited. In 1817, a "seat" cost $25; today it can cost up to a million dollars, and a rigorous test of suitability is required. Visitors can watch the bustle of the trading posts from a gallery overlooking the trading floor. The NYSE has weathered slumps ("bear markets") and booms ("bull markets"), and has seen advances in technology, from tickertape to microchip, turn a local marketplace into a global one.

Computerized stock tickers flash a steady stream of prices as fast as the human eye is able to read them.

Ticker-tape Machine
Introduced in the 1870s, these machines printed out up-to-the-minute details of purchase prices on ribbons of paper tape.

Public entrance, Broad Street

WHAT A TRADING POST DOES

The 17 trading posts each consist of 22 groups or "sections" of traders and technology, each trading the stock of up to 10 listed companies.

Post display units show stock prices.

Free-arm CRTs display prices and trades for the specialist.

The pages help on the busy exchange floor, bringing orders from the booths to the brokers and specialists.

The supervisor's job is to monitor the smooth and legal running of the post.

A specialist trades in just one stock at a time, quoting bids to other brokers.

Independent floor brokers handle orders for busy brokerage firms.

Commission brokers work for brokerage firms, and rush between booth and trading post, buying and selling securities (stocks and bonds) for the public.

Clerks process the orders that come into the trading post via SuperDOT computer, and log the results of trading into the Exchange's Market Data System.

The 48-Hour Day
During the 1929 Crash, stock exchange clerks worked nonstop for 48 hours. Their mood stayed cheerful despite the panic outside.

Public viewing gallery

Trading post

Trading Floor
Amid the frenzy of the trading floor, 200 million shares are traded each day for more than 2,000 companies. The advanced electronics that support the Designated Order Turnaround (SuperDOT) computer are carried above the chaos in a web of gold piping.

Great Crash of 1929
On Tuesday, October 29, over 16 million shares changed hands as the stock market crashed. Investors thronged Wall Street in bewilderment but, contrary to popular myth, traders did not leap from windows in panic.

Members' entrance, Wall Street

TIMELINE

1792 Buttonwood Agreement signed on May 17	**1867** Ticker-tape machines introduced		**1903** Present Stock Exchange building opens	**1987** "Black Monday" crash, October 19. Dow Jones Index drops 508 points	
	1844 Invention of the telegraph allows trading nationwide			**1976** DOT system replaces ticker tape	

1750	**1800**	**1850**	**1900**	**1950**

1817 New York Stock & Exchange Board created	**1863** Name changed to New York Stock Exchange		**1929** Wall St. Crash, October 29	
Crowds gather outside during the 1929 Crash		**1869** "Black Friday" gold crash, September 24		**1981** Trading posts upgraded with electronic units
		1865 New Exchange Building opens at Wall and Broad Sreets		

World Trade Center ⑥

Map 1 B2. **M** *Chambers St, Rector St.* **Observation Deck** *Two World Trade Center.* **(** *435-7377.* **Open** *winter: 9:30am–9:30pm daily; summer: 9:30am–11:30pm daily (last adm: 9:30pm).* **Adm charge.** 📷 🚻 *but not to outside viewing platform.* 🍴 🎁 **Commodities Exchange** *9th Floor, Four World Trade Center.* **(** *938-2018.* **Open** *9:30am–3pm Mon–Fri.* 🚫 🚻 ♿

T HE 110-STORY twin towers of the World Trade Center dominate the skyline of lower Manhattan. The enormous weight of each building is supported by an inner wire mesh cage, instead of a steel frame, depriving workers inside of large windows. Spectacular views can be seen only from the top. Critics describe the buildings as giant, upended boxes. Built from 1966 to 1977, the complex consists of five office buildings and a hotel, connected by a vast underground concourse lined with shops and restaurants.

The World Trade Center is home to 450 businesses and 50,000 workers. Large numbers of visitors come to see the unparalleled views from the observation deck or the rooftop promenade at Two World Trade Center. The express elevator takes just 58 seconds to reach the 107th floor. At One World Trade Center, make this speedy ascent to the 107th floor for drinks or dining at the Windows on the World restaurant *(see p295).*

When you look across from one

tower to the next, think of Philippe Petit who, on August 7, 1974, stepped out onto a tightrope between towers One and Two, and entertained amazed office workers for almost an hour with his high-rise balancing act.

If you've more of a head for high finance than for heights, a visitors' gallery on the ninth floor of Four World Trade Center overlooks the trading floor of the bustling Commodities Exchange.

The tightrope act in progress

Philippe Petit about to step out between the two towers in 1974

Battery Park City ⑦

Map 1 A3. **M** *1,9 to Cortland St.* 📷 🚻 🍴 🎁

Battery Park City esplanade

G OVERNOR MARIO CUOMO set the tone for this project in 1983 when he urged the developers, "Give it a social purpose – give it a soul." The city's newest neighborhood is an ambitious development on 92 reclaimed acres (37 ha)

along the Hudson River. The offices, buildings, restaurants, apartments, sculptures and gardens emphasize quality and are based very much on a human scale.

In due course, Battery Park City will house over 25,000 people. The most visible part is the World Financial Center, four towers centered around the Winter Garden, with its huge atrium lined with palm trees. The total cost has been estimated at $4 billion.

The esplanade along the river offers unobstructed views of the Statue of Liberty.

Downtown Athletic Club ⑧

19 West St. **Map** 1 B4. **(** *425-7000.* **M** *4, 5 to Bowling Green. Tourists, public welcome.*

O NE OF DOWNTOWN'S most striking buildings, this Art Deco creation from 1926 features a front arcade of

arches with a Moorish flavor and a facade of patterned salt-glazed tiles in a range of colors from burnt orange to brown. The tiles have kept their fresh look, thanks to a natural glaze that has resisted the city soot. The rooms of the cub, open to members and their guests, have the calm, sleek atmosphere of an old-fashioned ocean liner.

Downtown Athletic Club facade

Ornate ceiling of the Cunard Building's Great Hall

Cunard Building ⑨

25 Broadway. **Map** 1 C3.
⟨ 363-9490 **M** Bowling Green.
Open post office hours, see **Practical Information** p361.

STEP PAST the Renaissance facade, through the brass doors and beyond the fine wrought–iron gates of what is now the US Post Office to see the elaborate, domed Great Hall of this fine building of 1921. It was here that tickets were booked on classic liners such as the *Lusitania*, the *Titanic*, the *Queen Mary* and the original *Queen Elizabeth*, when the Cunard Line was the largest passenger ship company in the world.

The hall has magnificent murals and frescoes, including maps of the world by Barry Faulkner and a remarkable, ornately decorated ceiling. Paintings by Ezra Winter on the supporting vaulting show the ships of Christopher Columbus, John Cabot, Sir Francis Drake and the Viking explorer Leif Eriksson.

Bowling Green ⑩

Map 1 C4. **M** Bowling Green.

THIS TRIANGULAR plot north of Battery Park was the city's earliest park, used first as a cattle market and later as a bowling ground. A statue of King George III stood here until the signing of Declaration of Independence,

when, as a symbol of British rule, the statue was hacked to pieces and smelted for ammunition *(see pp20–21)*. The wife of the governor of Connecticut is said to have melted down enough pieces to mold 42,000 bullets.

The fence, erected in 1771, is still standing, but minus the royal crowns that once adorned it. They met the same fate as the statue. The Green was once surrounded by elegant homes. Beyond it is the start of Broadway, which runs the length of Manhattan and, under its formal name of Route 9, all the way north to the State capital in Albany.

Top of a column at the US Custom House

US Custom House ⑪

1 Bowling Green St. **Map** 1 C4.
⟨ 283-2420 for latest information on opening date & hours.
M Bowling Green.

ONE OF NEW YORK'S finest Beaux Arts designs, this 1907 granite palace by Cass Gilbert is a fitting monument to the city's role as a great seaport, incorporating the talents of the best sculptors and artists of the time. Forty-four stately Ionic columns stand guard, adorned with an ornate frieze. Four heroic sculptures by Daniel Chester French depict four continents as seated women: Asia (contemplative), America (facing optimistically forward), Europe (surrounded by symbols of past glories) and Africa (still sleeping).

Inside, murals by Reginald Marsh decorate the fine marble rotunda, showing the progress of ships into the harbor. Look to your right, opposite the entrance, to see a portrait of movie star Greta Garbo giving a press conference on board ship. In 1973 the US Customs Service moved out, leaving the building empty but for a small bankruptcy court.

The Custom House will take on a new function in 1994, when the George Gustav Heye Center of the National Museum of the American Indian is scheduled to open on three floors of the building *(see p232)*. The museum's superb collection of about a million artifacts, along with an archive of many thousands of photographs, spans the breadth of the native cultures of North, Central and South America. An intermediary exhibition, featuring a representative sample from the vast range of material held, was selected by Native American representatives.

Fountain at Bowling Green

Statue of Liberty ⓱

A GIFT FROM THE FRENCH to the American people, the statue was the brainchild of sculptor Frédéric-Auguste Bartholdi and has become a symbol of freedom throughout the world. In Emma Lazarus's poem, which is engraved on the base, Lady Liberty says: "Give me your tired, your poor,/ Your huddled masses yearning to breathe free." The statue loomed over Paris before its home on Bedloe's Island (now called Liberty Island) was ready. Unveiled by President Grover Cleveland on October 28, 1886, the statue was restored in time for its 100th anniversary in 1986.

★ **Golden Torch**
In 1986, a new torch replaced the corroded original. The replica's flame is coated in 24-carat gold leaf.

The crown is the highest level open to visitors.

The frame was designed by Gustave Eiffel, who later built the Eiffel Tower. The copper shell hangs on iron bars from a central iron pylon.

A central pylon anchors the 225-ton statue to its base.

From Her Toes to Her Torch
Three hundred molded copper sheets riveted together make up Lady Liberty.

354 steps lead from the entrance to the crown.

Observation deck and museum

THE STATUE
With a height of 305 ft (93 m) from ground to torch, the Statue of Liberty dominates New York harbor.

The pedestal is set within the walls of an army fort. It was the largest concrete mass ever poured.

★ **Statue of Liberty Museum**
Posters featuring the statue are among the items on display.

The original torch now stands in the main lobby.

★ **Views of Lower Manhattan**
Lady Liberty has some of the best views of the city; see them from the observation deck, the crown or the ferry.

Portrait of Liberty
Bartholdi's mother was the model for Liberty. The seven rays of her crown represent the seven seas and seven continents.

Making the Hand
To mold the copper shell, the hand was made first in wood, then plaster.

A Model Figure
A series of graduated scale models enabled Bartholdi to build the largest metal statue ever constructed.

FRÉDÉRIC-AUGUSTE BARTHOLDI

The French sculptor who designed the Statue of Liberty intended it as a monument to the freedom he found lacking in his own country. He said "I will try to glorify the Republic and Liberty over there, in the hope that someday I will find it again here." Bartholdi devoted 21 years of his life to making the statue a reality, even traveling to America in 1871 to talk President Ulysses S. Grant and others into funding it and installing it in New York's harbor.

STAR FEATURES

★ **Golden Torch**

★ **Statue of Liberty Museum**

★ **Views of Lower Manhattan**

Restoration Celebration
On July 3, 1986, after a $69.8 million clean-up, the statue was unveiled. The $2 million fireworks display was the largest ever seen in America.

Shrine of Elizabeth Ann Seton ⑫

7–8 State St. **Map** 1 C4. 269-6865. Whitehall, South Ferry. **Open** 6:30am–5:30pm Mon–Fri, 7:30am–3pm Sat, Sun. frequent.

Elizabeth Ann Seton

Eₗᵢᵤₐᵦₑₜₕ ₐₙₙ Seton (1774–1821), the first native-born American to be canonized by the Catholic Church, lived here from 1801 to 1803. Mother Seton founded the American Sisters of Charity, the first order of nuns in the United States.

After the Civil War, the Mission of Our Lady of the Rosary turned the building into a shelter for homeless Irish immigrant women – 170,000 passed through on their way to a new life in America. The adjoining church was built in 1883. The Mission established and maintains the shrine to Mother Seton.

The house itself was built in 1793, and in 1806 a Federal wing was added, with a curved, columned porch. The Georgian-style and Federal facades have been carefully restored according to an 1859 print. They are all that survives of the early mansions of Lower Manhattan.

Fraunces Tavern Museum ⑬

54 Pearl St. **Map** 1 C4. 425-1778. South Ferry, Bowling Green. **Open** 10am–4:45pm Mon–Fri, noon–4pm Sat. **Closed** public hols, day after Thanksgiving. **Lectures, films.**

Nₑw york's only full remaining square block of 18th-century commercial buildings contains an exact replica of the Fraunces Tavern, originally built in 1719, where George Washington said farewell to his officers in 1783. The tavern had been an early casualty of the Revolution: the British ship *Asia* shot a cannonball through its roof in August 1775. The building was purchased in 1904 by the Sons of the Revolution in the State of New York. Its restoration in 1907 was one of the nation's first efforts to preserve its heritage.

The restaurant on the ground floor has wood-burning fireplaces and great charm. Upstairs is a museum, with changing exhibits of paintings, prints and decorative arts that interpret the history and culture of early America.

Vietnam Veterans Plaza ⑭

Between Water St and South St. **Map** 2 D4. Whitehall, South Ferry.

Tₕᵢₛ ᵢₛ ₐ ᵣₐₜₕₑᵣ sterile multilevel brick plaza with a shopping mall below. However, in its center is a huge wall of translucent green glass, engraved with excerpts from speeches, news stories and moving letters to families from servicemen and women who died in the war.

Staten Island Ferry – one of the city's best bargains

Staten Island Ferry ⑮

Whitehall St. **Map** 2 D5. 806-6901. South Ferry. **Open** 24 hrs daily. **Adm charge.** See **Practical Information** p353.

Tₕₑ ᵣᵢᵣₛₜ business venture of a promising Staten Island boy named Cornelius Vanderbilt, the ferry has operated since 1810, carrying island commuters to and from the city and offering visitors

The 18th-century Fraunces Tavern Museum and restaurant

an unforgettable close-up of the harbor, the Statue of Liberty, Ellis Island and Lower Manhattan's incredible skyline. The fare is still the city's best bargain, although it doubled in 1991 – to 50 cents.

Battery Maritime Building ⑯

11 South St. **Map** 2 D4. Ⓜ *South Ferry.* **Not open** to the public.

FROM 1909 TO 1938, the municipal terminal for ferries to Brooklyn operated here on the site of a small wharf known as Schreijers Hoek, from which Dutch Colonial ships once set sail for the mother country. At the height of the ferry era, 17 lines made regular runs from these bustling piers, which are used now only by the Coast Guard service for Governors Island.

The building was designed in 1907. Arriving boats face 300-ft (91-m) arched openings guarded by tall, ornately scrolled columns and adorned with latticework, molding and rosettes typical of the Beaux Arts period. This is actually a false front of sheet metal and steel, painted green to resemble copper.

Ironwork railing on the Battery Maritime Building

Statue of Liberty ⑰

See pp74–5.

Ellis Island ⑱

See pp78–9.

Castle Clinton National Monument with Liberty Island beyond

Battery Park ⑲

Map 1 B4. Ⓜ *South Ferry, Bowling Green.*

Beaux Arts subway entrance at the corner of Battery Park

NAMED FOR the line of cannon that once protected the harbor, the park is a wedge of green between the water and the crush of buildings, and is one of the best places in the city for gazing out to sea. Over the years, landfill has extended the greenery far beyond its original State Street boundary.

The park is rimmed with statues and monuments, including the Netherlands Memorial Monument as well as memorials to New York's first Jewish immigrants, early Walloon (Celtic) settlers; the city's first wireless telegraph operators; the Salvation Army and the Coast Guard. Others honored are Giovanni da Verrazano, the first explorer to see these shores, and also the poet Emma Lazarus.

Castle Clinton National Monument ⑳

Battery Park. **Map** 1 B4. Ⓒ *344-7220.* Ⓜ *Bowling Green, South Ferry.* **Open** 8:30am–5pm daily. **Closed** Dec 25. Ⓞ Ⓔ Ⓕ **Concerts.** Ⓗ

CASTLE CLINTON WAS built in 1807 as a defense post for the artillery. Originally, it stood about 300 ft (91 m) offshore, connected to Battery Park by a causeway; but landfill gradually linked it to the mainland. None of its 28 guns were ever used in battle.

The fort was enclosed in 1824 and became a fashionable theater known as Castle Garden. Phineas T. Barnum introduced "Swedish nightingale" Jenny Lind here in 1850. It later preceded Ellis Island as the city's immigration center in 1855, processing 7.5 million newcomers. In 1896, the building was remodeled by McKim, Mead & White to become the New York Aquarium, a popular attraction that later moved to Coney Island in 1941 *(see p253).*

Now it is a monument and the main visitors' center for the National Park Service sites in Manhattan, with exhibits featuring panoramas of New York history. The complex is also the departure point for the Statue of Liberty–Ellis Island ferry *(see p353).*

Ellis Island ⑱

Main building

Half of America's population can trace its roots to Ellis Island, which served as the country's immigration depot from 1892 until 1954. Nearly 17 million people passed through its gates and dispersed across the country in the greatest wave of migration the world has ever known. Today the site is a national museum. Exhibits such as *Through America's Gate* retrace the steps through the entry inspections. *Peopling of America* is an electronic map showing the many nationalities that comprise the population. Much of this story is told with photos and the voices of actual immigrants. No other place or museum explains so well the "melting pot" that formed the unique character of New York and the nation.

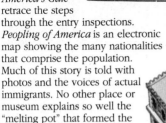

Rail Ticket
A special fare for emigrants led many on to California.

The railroad office sold tickets onward to the final destination.

★ **Dormitory**
There were separate sleeping quarters for male and female detainees.

THE RESTORATION
Ellis Island lay in ruins until 1990. A $156 million renewal project replaced the copper roof domes, cleaned the mosaic tiles and restored the interior using any surviving original fixtures.

The ferry office sold tickets to New Jersey.

★ **Baggage Room**
The immigrants' meager possessions were checked here on arrival.

Great Hall ★
Immigrant families were made to wait for "processing" in the Registry Room. The old metal railings were replaced with wooden benches in 1911.

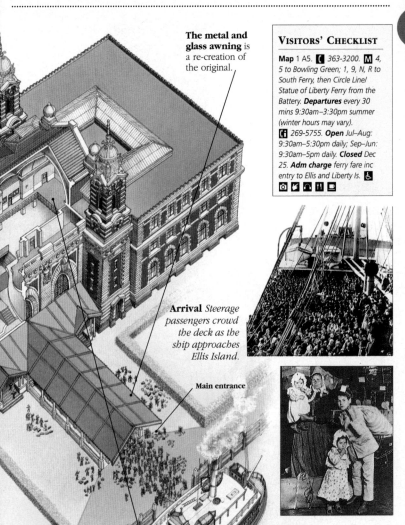

The metal and glass awning is a re-creation of the original.

Arrival *Steerage passengers crowd the deck as the ship approaches Ellis Island.*

Main entrance

VISITORS' CHECKLIST

Map 1 A5. (363-3200. M 4, 5 to Bowling Green; 1, 9, N, R to South Ferry, then Circle Line/ Statue of Liberty Ferry from the Battery. **Departures** every 30 mins 9:30am–3:30pm summer (winter hours may vary). 269-5755. **Open** Jul–Aug: 9:30am–5:30pm daily; Sep–Jun: 9:30am–5pm daily. **Closed** Dec 25. **Adm charge** ferry fare inc entry to Ellis and Liberty Is.

Immigrant Family
An Italian mother and her children arrive in 1905.

STAR FEATURES

★ **Great Hall**

★ **Dormitory**

★ **Baggage Room**

Medical Examining Rooms
Immigrants with contagious diseases could be refused entry and sent back home.

SEAPORT AND THE CIVIC CENTER

M ANHATTAN'S BUSY Civic Center is the hub of the city, state and federal governments' court systems and the city's police department. In the 1880s it was the heart of the newspaper publishing business as well. The area is still a handsome enclave of imposing architecture with fine landmarks from every period in the city's history, from the 20th-century Woolworth Building to 19th-century City Hall and 18th-century St. Paul's

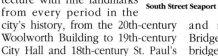

Ship's figurehead, South Street Seaport

Chapel, New York's oldest building in continuous use. Nearby is South Street Seaport. Called the "street of sails" in the 19th century because of the many ships that were moored there, the seaport underwent a decline when sailing ships became unprofitable. The area has now been restored and is home to a museum and many shops and restaurants. The Brooklyn Bridge, once the largest suspension bridge in the world, lies to the north.

SIGHTS AT A GLANCE

Historic Streets and Buildings
South Street Seaport ❶
Schermerhorn Row ❷
Brooklyn Bridge pp86–9 ❸
Criminal Courts Building ❹
New York County Courthouse ❺
United States Courthouse ❻
Municipal Building ❼
Surrogate's Court, Hall of Records ❽
Old New York County Courthouse ❾
City Hall ❿
Woolworth Building ⓬
AT&T Building ⓮

Churches
St. Paul's Chapel ⓭

Parks and Squares
City Hall Park and Park Row ⓫

GETTING THERE
Many subway lines serve the area: the 7th Ave/Broadway 2 and 3 trains to Park Pl; the Lexington Ave 4, 5 and 6 to Brooklyn Bridge; the 8th Ave A, C and E to Chambers St and the N and R to City Hall. By bus take the M1, M6, M9, M10, M15, M101/102 or the M22 crosstown.

SEE ALSO
• *Street Finder,* map 2
• *Restaurants* pp290–92
• *Lower Manhattan Walk* p257

KEY
▨ Street-by-Street map
Ⓜ Subway station
⛴ Riverboat boarding point

0 meters — 500
0 yards — 500

South Street Seaport

Street by Street: South Street Seaport

PART COMMERCIAL, part historical, the development of South Street Seaport has turned the former heart of the 19th-century port of New York, which had long been neglected, into a lively part of the city. Shops and cafés abound; tall ships are once again moored here. The South Street Seaport museum tells the story of New York's maritime past through craft demonstrations, ship tours and river cruises. Workers from Wall Street come here to eat and drink.

★ **South Street Seaport**
Once full of sailors and sailing ships, the seaport is now a lively complex of shops, restaurants and museums ❶

The Titanic Memorial is a lighthouse built in 1913 in memory of those who died on the *Titanic*. It now stands on Fulton Street.

To Fulton St. subway (4 blocks)

Cannon's Walk is a 19th- and 20th-century block of buildings, with an outdoor café, shops and a very lively marketplace.

Schermerhorn Row
Built as warehouses (1811–13), the buildings now house several eateries, including the North Star Pub (see p308) and Sloppy Louie's ❷

The Boat-Building Shop lets you watch as skilled craftspeople build and restore small wooden vessels.

At the Maritime Crafts Center woodcarvers and painters can be seen at work on models, ship carvings and figureheads.

Ship in a bottle

The Pilothouse was originally from a steam tugboat built in 1923 by New York Central. The Seaport's admission and information center is to be found here.

STAR SIGHTS

★ **Brooklyn Bridge**

★ **South Street Seaport**

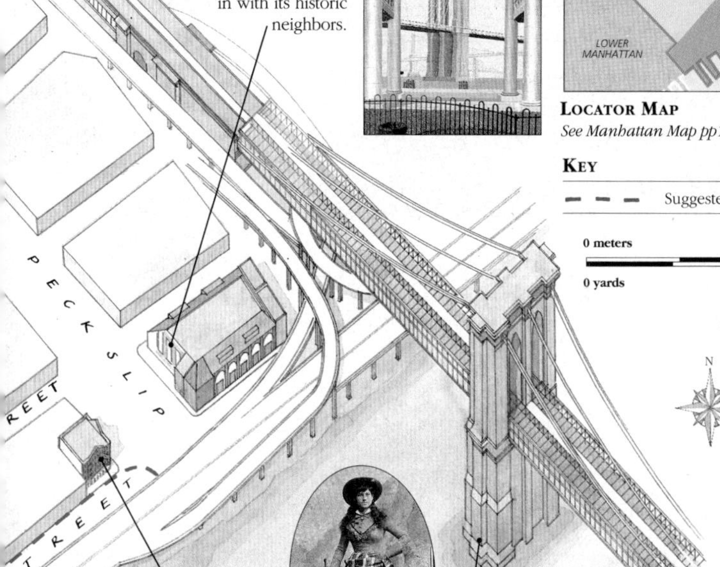

The Consolidated Edison electrical substation, built in 1975, has an illusionistic mural of the Brooklyn Bridge by Richard Haas on one side to help it blend in with its historic neighbors.

LOCATOR MAP
See Manhattan Map pp12–13

KEY

‒ ‒ ‒ Suggested route

0 meters	100
0 yards	100

N

Meyer's Hotel, built in 1873, became a hotel in 1881. Now a bar, it retains a feel of days gone by when marks-woman Annie Oakley stayed here.

★ Brooklyn Bridge
An engineering wonder when it was built in 1883, the bridge is still remarkable. From the pedestrian walkway there are fine views of the city and the bridge itself ❸

The Fulton Fish Market has been here for over 150 years. Once sold fresh from the boat, the fish now come in by road. The market is only open in the early morning hours *(see p347)*.

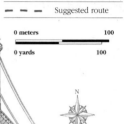

Pier 17 offers three floors of shops, restaurants and food stands, with fine views from the top floor of the Brooklyn Bridge and historic ships.

The paddlewheeler *Andrew Fletcher* is used for river cruises. You can also sail on the schooner *Pioneer* or the traditional steamboat *DeWitt Clinton (see p355)*.

East River harbor at South Street Seaport

South Street Seaport ❶

Fulton St. **Map** 2 E2. 📞 732-7678.
Ⓜ *Fulton St.* **Open** 10am–9pm daily.
📷 ♿ 🎫 *Concerts.* 🍴 🎭
South Street Seaport Museum
📞 669-9400. 📠 669-9424. **Open**
10am–5pm daily (last adm: 4:30pm).
Closed Jan 1, Thanksgiving, Dec 25.
Adm charge. 📷 ♿ 🎫 *Lectures,*
exhibits, films. 🍴 🎭

THE HEART of New York's
19th-century seaport has
been given an imaginative
new lease of life. Glitzy stores
and restaurants sit harmoni-
ously beside seafaring craft,
historic buildings and museum
exhibits, with spectacular
views of Brooklyn Bridge
and the East River from the
cobbled streets.

The historic ships docked
alongside the piers range
from the little tugboat
W.O. Decker to the grand
four-masted bark *Peking*, the
second-largest sailing ship in
existence. A 19th-century
paddlewheeler offers
atmospheric harbor cruises,
and there are mini–sailing
voyages on the schooner
Pioneer (see p353).

The Fulton Fish Market has
been here since 1821. Though

Fulton Fish Market at dawn

fish are no longer delivered
from boats in the harbor but
arrive in refrigerated trucks,
many still find the busy
morning action an enjoyable
sight; however, you'll need to
be there before dawn.

**Historic seaport restaurant in
Schermerhorn Row**

Schermerhorn Row ❷

Fulton and South Sts. **Map** 2 D3.
Ⓜ *Fulton St.*

THIS IS THE architectural
showpiece of the seaport.
Built in 1811 by shipowner
and chandler Peter Schermerhorn on a piece of land
reclaimed from the river, the
buildings were originally
warehouses and counting-
houses. The opening of the
Brooklyn Ferry terminus in
1814 and of Fulton Market in
1822 made the block very
desirable property. One of its
oldest restaurants – Sloppy
Louie's – makes use of the
nearby fish market and is justly
famous for its bouillabaisse.

The Row has been restored
as part of the South Street
Seaport development, and it
now houses a visitors' center,
shops and restaurants.

Brooklyn Bridge ❸

See pp86–9.

Criminal Courts Building ❹

100 Centre St. **Map** 4 F5.
Ⓜ *Canal St.* **Open** 9am–5pm
Mon–Fri. **Closed** public hols.

THIS 1939 BUILDING is Art
Moderne in style, with
towers reminiscent of a
Babylonian temple. The
three-story-high entrance is
set back in a court, behind
two huge, square free-
standing granite columns –
an intimidating sight for the
accused. The building also
houses the Manhattan
Detention Center for Men,
which was formerly across
the street in a building known
as "The Tombs" because of its
Egyptian-style architecture.
The nickname has stuck,
although the original is long
gone. An aerial walkway, or
"bridge of sighs," links the
courts with the correctional
facility across Centre Street.

The building also houses
the night courts, where cases
are heard from 5pm to 1am
on weekdays.

**Entrance to the Criminal
Courts Building**

New York County Courthouse ❺

60 Centre St. **Map** 2 D1.
Ⓜ *Brooklyn Br-City Hall.* **Open** 9am–
5pm Mon–Fri. **Closed** public hols.

BUILT TO REPLACE the Tweed
Courthouse *(see p90)*, this
new county courthouse was
completed in 1926.

The fluted Corinthian portico at the top of a wide staircase is the main feature of the hexagonal building. The austere exterior is offset by a circular-columned interior rotunda featuring Tiffany lighting fixtures and a series of rich marble and ceiling murals by Attilio Pusterla on themes of law and justice. Six wings radiate from the rotunda, each housing a single court and its facilities.

The courtroom drama *Twelve Angry Men,* starring Henry Fonda, was filmed here.

New York County Courthouse

United States Courthouse ❻

40 Centre St. **Map** 2 D1. Ⓜ
Brooklyn Br–City Hall. **Open**
9am–5pm Mon–Fri. **Closed** *public hols.*

T HIS COURTHOUSE is the last work by noted architect Cass Gilbert, designer of the Woolworth Building. Begun in 1933, the year before his death, it was finished by his son. The 31-story structure is

United States Courthouse

a pyramid-topped tower set on a classical temple base. The bronzework on the doors is handsome, but the interior lacks the colorful decoration Gilbert had outlined in his sketchbooks. Aerial walkways link the building with its Police Plaza Annex.

Municipal Building ❼

1 Centre St. **Map** 1 C1. Ⓜ
Brooklyn Br–City Hall. Ⓞ &

T HE MUNICIPAL Building, constructed in 1914, dominates the Civic Center and straddles Chambers Street. It was McKim, Mead & White's first skyscraper and houses government offices and a marriage chapel. The exterior, in harmony with City Hall, has no excess detail to detract from the earlier building. The most notable feature is the top, a fantasy of towers capped by Adolph Wienman's statue *Civic Fame.*

A railway passage (no longer in use) through the base, and the plaza joining the building to the IRT subway station entrance were built as concessions to modern transportation needs. The building has had a far-reaching influence on architectural style; the main building at Moscow University is said to have been modeled on its design.

Surrogate's Court, Hall of Records ❽

31 Chambers St. **Map** 1 C1. Ⓜ *City Hall.* **Open** *10am–3pm Mon–Fri.*
Closed *public hols.* Ⓞ & ▮

A BEAUX ARTS triumph, the original Hall of Records was begun in 1899 and completed in 1911. The elaborate columned facade is of white Maine granite, with a high mansard roof. The figures by Henry K. Bush-Brown in the roof area represent life's stages from childhood to old age; the statues by Philip Martiny over the colonnade are of notable New Yorkers

Municipal Building

such as Peter Stuyvesant. Martiny also made the representations of New York in its infancy and New York in revolutionary times at the Chambers Street entrance.

The Paris Opéra was the inspiration for the twin marble stairways and painted ceiling of the dazzling central hall. The ceiling mosaic by William de Leftwich Dodge features the signs of the zodiac as well as symbols of record keeping.

The Hall of Records holds public records dating back to 1664. A permanent exhibition, *Windows on the Archives,* features historical papers, drawings, letters and photographs illustrating what life was like in New York from 1626 to the present.

Surrogate's Court

Brooklyn Bridge ❸

Cℴℳℙℒℰℸℰᴅ ⁱℕ 1883, the Brooklyn Bridge was the largest suspension bridge and the first to be constructed of steel. Engineer John A. Roebling conceived of a bridge spanning the East River while ice-bound on a ferry to Brooklyn. The bridge took 16 years to build, required 600 workers and claimed over 20 lives, including Roebling's. Most died of caisson disease (now known as the bends) after coming up from the underwater excavation chambers. When finished, the bridge linked Manhattan and Brooklyn, then two separate cities.

Souvenir medal cast for the opening of the bridge

BROOKLYN BRIDGE
From making the wire to sinking the supports, the bridge was built using new techniques.

Anchorage
The ends of the bridge's four steel cables are fastened to a series of anchor bars that are held in place by anchor plates. These are held down by giant granite vaults up to three stories high. Their vast interiors were once used for storage.

Granite vault

Cable to tower

Anchor bar

Anchor plate

Vault

Caisson
The towers rose up above caissons, each the size of four tennis courts, which provided a dry area for underwater excavation. As work went on, they sank deeper beneath the river.

Shaft

Anchor Plates
Each of the four cast-iron anchor plates holds one cable. The masonry was built up around them after they were placed in position.

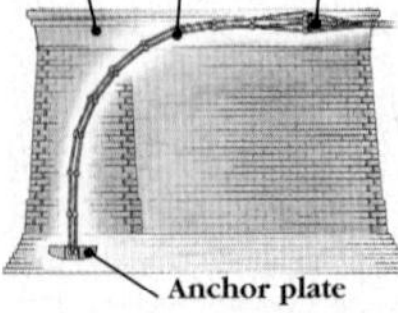

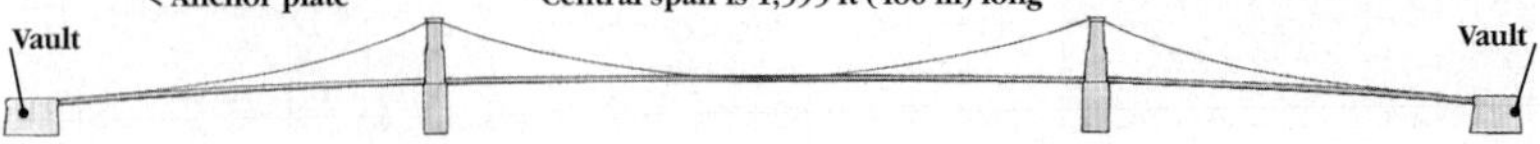

Anchor plates

Central span is 1,595 ft (486 m) long

Vault

Roadway from anchorage to anchorage is 3,579 ft (1,091 m)

First Crossing
Master mechanic E.F. Farrington in 1876 was the first to cross the river on the bridge-in-progress, using a steam-driven traveler rope. His journey took 22 minutes.

VISITORS' CHECKLIST
Map 2 D2. M 4, 5, 6 to Brooklyn Bridge-City Hall (Manhattan side); A, C to High St, Brooklyn Bridge (Brooklyn side). M9, M22, M101, M102.

Steel Cable Wire
Each cable contains 3,515 miles (5,657 km) of wire, galvanized with zinc for protection from the wind, rain and snow.

Brooklyn Tower (1875)
Two Gothic double arches, each 277 ft (84 m) high, one in Brooklyn, the other in Manhattan, were meant to be the portals of the cities.

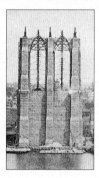

JOHN A. ROEBLING
The German-born Roebling designed the bridge. In 1869, just before construction started, his foot was crushed between an incoming ferry and the ferry slip. He died three weeks later. His son, Washington Roebling, finished the bridge, but in 1872 he was taken from a caisson suffering from the bends and became partly paralyzed. His wife, under his tutelage, then took over.

Inside the Caisson
Immigrant workers broke up rocks in the riverbed.

MAKING THE CABLES

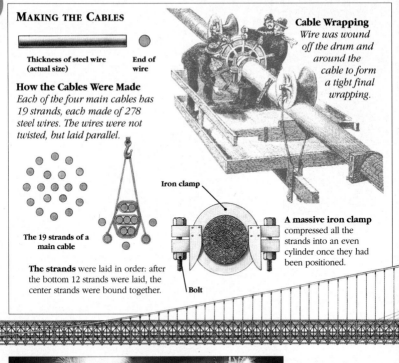

Thickness of steel wire (actual size)   **End of wire**

How the Cables Were Made
Each of the four main cables has 19 strands, each made of 278 steel wires. The wires were not twisted, but laid parallel.

The 19 strands of a main cable

The strands were laid in order: after the bottom 12 strands were laid, the center strands were bound together.

Cable Wrapping
Wire was wound off the drum and around the cable to form a tight final wrapping.

Iron clamp

A massive iron clamp compressed all the strands into an even cylinder once they had been positioned.

Bolt

Fireworks over the Brooklyn Bridge
Each year, the Fourth of July is celebrated with a fireworks display.

Bustling Bridge
This 1883 view from the Manhattan side shows the original two outer lanes for horse-drawn carriages, two middle lanes for cable cars and the elevated center walkway.

Panic of May 30, 1883
After a woman tripped on the bridge, panic broke out. Of the estimated 20,000 people on the bridge, 12 were crushed to death.

Holding the Cables
Saddle plates anchor the cables at the top of each of the two towers.

Cable

Nearing Completion (1883)
Vertical suspender wires lashed to diagonal stays hold the floor beams in place.

Suspender wires

Diagonal stays

Floor Beams
The steel floor beams weigh 4 tons each.

Odlum's Jump
Robert Odlum was the first to jump off the bridge, on a bet, in May 1885. He later died from internal bleeding.

Elevated Walkway
Poet Walt Whitman said that the view from the walkway – 18 ft (5.5 m) above the road – was "the best, most effective medicine my soul has yet partaken."

Old New York County Courthouse ❾

52 Chambers St. **Map** 1 C1.
Ⓜ *Chambers St-City Hall.* **Open**
9am–5pm Mon–Fri. 🅾 ♿

T HIS BUILDING is best known
for the scandal it caused.
It is nicknamed the "Tweed
Courthouse" after the political
boss who spent 20 times the
budget for the building and
pocketed $9 million of the
total $14 million cost. "Boss"
Tweed even bought a marble
quarry and sold materials to
the city at huge profit. Public
outrage eventually led to his
downfall in 1871 – ironically,
he was tried in his own
courthouse and died in a New
York jail *(see p25).*

However, Tweed left
behind a handsome Italianate
building. Now used to house
city offices, it has survived
many threats of demolition.
Work has begun on a $6.3
million renovation.

**City Hall's imposing early 19th-
century facade**

City Hall ❿

City Hall Park. **Map** 1 C1. 🄲 *788-
3071.* Ⓜ *Brooklyn Br-City Hall.*
Open *10am–4pm Mon–Fri.* **Closed**
public hols. 🅾 ♿ 🎟 *788-6865.*
Concerts.

C ITY HALL, the seat of New
York city government
since 1812, is one of the
finest examples of early
19th-century American architecture. A stately Georgian
building (with a bit of French

P.T. Barnum's museum blazes as crowds watch from City Hall Park

Renaissance influence), it was
designed by John McComb,
Jr., the first prominent
American-born architect, and
French emigré Joseph Mangin.

Marble cladding was not
used for the building's rear,
since it was not expected that
the city would ever develop
farther to the north. In
1954, restoration remedied
this and the interior was
refurbished.

Mangin is usually given
credit for the exterior,
McComb for the beautiful
interior with its fine domed
rotunda encircled by 10
columns. Beneath it, an
elegant marble stairway leads
to the splendid second-floor
City Council chambers and
the Governor's Room, which
houses a portrait gallery of
early New York leaders. This
magnificent entrance has
welcomed rulers and heroes
for nearly 200 years. In
1865 Abraham Lincoln's
body lay in state in
this hall.

Stand on the steps
and look to your
right to see
a statue of
Nathan Hale,
a US soldier
hanged by the British
as a spy in September
1776 during the
Revolutionary War. His
last words – "My only
regret is that I have not
more lives than one to
offer in the service of my
country" – won him a
permanent place in the
history books and hearts
of America.

City Hall Park and Park Row ⓫

Map 1 C2. Ⓜ *Brooklyn Br-City Hall.*

T HIS WAS New York's village
green 250 years ago,
complete with stocks and
whipping post. It was the
scene of pre-Revolution
protests against English rule,
and there is a memorial to the
"Liberty Poles" (symbols of
revolt) on City Hall's west
lawn. The Declaration of
Independence was read to
George Washington and his
troops here on July 9, 1776.

Later, Phineas T. Barnum's
American Museum at the
park's southern tip drew
crowds from 1842 until it
burned down in 1865. The
Park Row building was
the site of the Park
Theater. From 1798 to
1848, the best actors
of the day, such
as Edmund Kean
and Fanny
Kemble, per-
formed there.
Park Row runs
along the east
side of City
Hall Park.
Once called
"Newspaper
Row," it was
lined with the
lofty offices of
the *Sun, World,
Tribune* and other
papers. Printing

**Statue of Benjamin
Franklin in Printing
House Square**

House Square has a statue of Benjamin Franklin with his *Pennsylvania Gazette*.

Time was not kind to the newspaper business. In 1893 New York had 19 daily papers; in 1993 there were four.

Woolworth Building ⑫

233 Broadway. **Map** 1 C2. Ⓜ *City Hall.* **Open** *office hours.*

The Georgian interior of St Paul's Chapel

Bas-relief caricature of architect Gilbert in the Woolworth lobby

IN 1879, SALESCLERK Frank W. Woolworth opened a new kind of store, where shoppers could see and touch the goods for sale and everything cost five cents. The chain of stores that followed made him a fortune, and changed the face of retailing forever.

The Gothic headquarters of his retail empire, completed in 1913, was New York's tallest building until 1930. It set the standard for the great skyscrapers, and no office building is finer.

Architect Cass Gilbert's soaring two-tiered design, adorned with gargoyles of bats and other wildlife, is topped with a pyramid roof, flying buttresses, pinnacles and four small towers. The marble interior is rich with filigree, sculptured reliefs and painted decoration, and has a high glass-tile mosaic ceiling that almost seems to glow. The lobby is one of the city's treasures. Gilbert showed his sense of humor here, in bas-relief caricatures of the store's founder F.W. Woolworth counting out his fortune in nickels and dimes; of the real estate broker closing a deal; and of Cass Gilbert himself cradling a large model of the building. Paid for with $13.5 million in cash, the building has never had a mortgage, and the Woolworth company is still here.

St. Paul's Chapel ⑬

Broadway. **Map** 1 C2. 📞 *602-0872.* Ⓜ *Fulton St.* **Open** *9am–3pm Mon–Fri, 7am–3pm Sun.* **Closed** *most public hols.* ⛪ *8am Sun.* 📷 ✏ *by appt.* **Concerts.**

IN THE LONG SHADOW of the World Trade Center stands Manhattan's only remaining church built before the Revolutionary War. It is a Georgian gem. The colorful interior, lit by Waterford chandeliers, is the setting for free concerts. The pew where newly inaugurated George Washington prayed has been preserved. In the churchyard, the Actor's Monument commemorates George Frederick Cooke, who played many great roles at the Park Theater and finally drank himself to death at the Shakespeare Tavern on Fulton Street.

AT&T Building ⑭

195 Broadway. **Map** 1 C2. Ⓜ *Broadway-Nassau.* **Open** *office hours.*

COLUMNS, columns everywhere mark this former headquarters designed by Welles Bosworth from 1915 to 1922. The facade is said to have more columns than any other building in the world, and the interior of the building is a forest of marble pillars. The whole edifice looks like a gigantic square-topped layer cake.

A sea sprite above the door of the AT&T (American Telephone and Telegraph) Building

LOWER EAST SIDE

NOWHERE DOES the strong ethnic flavor of New York come through more clearly than in Lower Manhattan, where many immigrants first settled. Here Italians, Chinese and Jews established distinct neighborhoods, preserving their languages, customs, foods and religions in the midst of a strange land. New immigrants from many

**19th-century tin,
Lower East Side
Tenement Museum**

nations now occupy some of these neighborhoods of low-rise buildings, but the old flavor remains. The area brims with restaurants, some of the city's greatest bagains and a spirit found nowhere else. The composer Irving Berlin grew up here. Looking back on those days he said: "Everybody ought to have a Lower East Side in their life."

SIGHTS AT A GLANCE

**Historic Streets and
Buildings**
Home Savings of America ❶
Police Headquarters
Building ❷
Little Italy ❸
Chinatown ❹
Orchard Street ❽
Delancey Street ❿

Puck Building ⓬
Engine Company No. 31 ⓮

Parks and Squares
Columbus Park ❺

Museums and Galleries
Lower East Side Tenement
Museum ❼

Churches and Synagogues
Eldridge Street Synagogue ❻
Bialystoker Synagogue ❾
Old St. Patrick's Cathedral ⓭

Landmark Stores
Schapiro's Winery ⓫

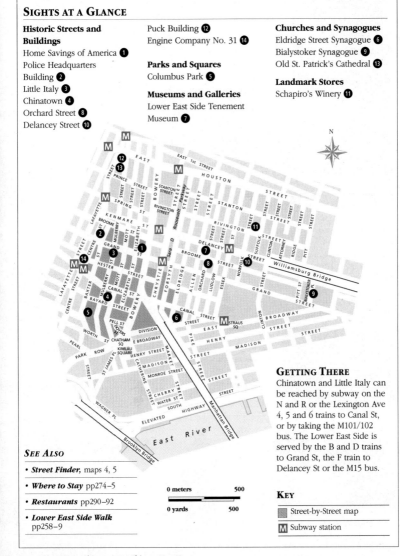

SEE ALSO

- **Street Finder,** maps 4, 5
- **Where to Stay** pp274–5
- **Restaurants** pp290–92
- **Lower East Side Walk**
  pp258–9

| 0 meters | 500 |
| 0 yards | 500 |

GETTING THERE

Chinatown and Little Italy can be reached by subway on the N and R or the Lexington Ave 4, 5 and 6 trains to Canal St, or by taking the M101/102 bus. The Lower East Side is served by the B and D trains to Grand St, the F train to Delancey St or the M15 bus.

KEY

▨ Street-by-Street map

Ⓜ Subway station

Dragon puppet in Chinatown at Chinese New Year

Street by Street: Little Italy and Chinatown

NEW YORK'S LARGEST and most colorful ethnic neighborhood is Chinatown, which is growing so rapidly that it is overrunning nearby Little Italy as well as the Lower East Side. Streets here teem with grocery stores, gift shops and hundreds of Chinese restaurants; even the plainest offer good food. What is left of Little Italy can be found at Mulberry and Grand streets, where old-world flavor abounds.

★ **Little Italy**
The scents of Italy still waft from the restaurants and bakeries of this area, once home to thousands of immigrants. ❸

The Market on Canal Street has a wide range of bargains in new and used clothes and other goods.

Ⓜ **Canal Street subway (lines N, R, 4, 5, 6)**

The Eastern States Buddhist Temple at 64b Mott Street contains over 100 golden Buddhas.

★ **Chinatown**
Home to a thriving – and still expanding – community of Chinese immigrants, this area is famous for its restaurants and hectic street life. The area truly comes alive around the Chinese New Year in January or February ❹

The Wall of Democracy on Bayard Street is covered with newspapers and posters describing the situation in China.

Columbus Park ❺
This park was once the site of 19th century New York's worst slum.

Confucius Plaza is marked by sculptor Liu Shih's monument to the Oriental philosopher.

Chatham Square has a memorial to Chinese-American war dead.

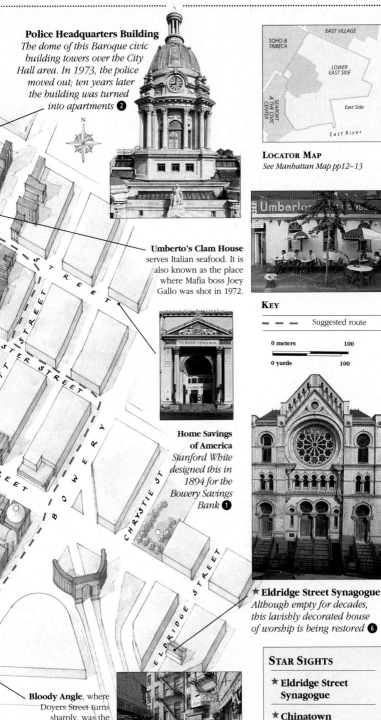

Police Headquarters Building
The dome of this Baroque civic building towers over the City Hall area. In 1973, the police moved out; ten years later the building was turned into apartments ❷

Umberto's Clam House
serves Italian seafood. It is also known as the place where Mafia boss Joey Gallo was shot in 1972.

Home Savings of America
Stanford White designed this in 1894 for the Bowery Savings Bank ❶

Bloody Angle, where Doyers Street turns sharply, was the gruesome site of many gangland ambushes during the 1920s.

LOCATOR MAP
See Manhattan Map pp12–13

KEY

– – –   Suggested route

0 meters	100
0 yards	100

★ **Eldridge Street Synagogue**
Although empty for decades, this lavishly decorated house of worship is being restored ❻

STAR SIGHTS

★ **Eldridge Street Synagogue**

★ **Chinatown**

★ **Little Italy**

Home Savings of America ❶

130 Bowery. **Map** 4 F4. **M** Grand St,
Bowery. **Open** banking hours.

IMPOSING INSIDE and
out, this Classical
Revival building
was built for the
Bowery Savings
Bank in 1894.
Architect Stanford
White designed the **Detail from Home**
ornamented lime- **Savings of America**
stone facade to wrap
around the rival Butchers' and
Drovers' Bank, which refused
to sell the corner plot. The
interior is decorated with
marble pillars and a ceiling
scattered with gilded rosettes.
By the middle of the 20th
century, the bank was a
contrast to the Bowery with
its vagrants and flophouses.

Police Headquarters Building ❷

240 Centre St. **Map** 4 F4. **M** Canal
St. **Not open** to the public.

COMPLETED IN 1909, this was
a fitting home for the
city's new professional police
force. Corinthian columns line
the main portico and the end
pavilions, and the dome dominates the skyline. However,
lack of space meant the headquarters had to conform to an
awkward, wedge-shaped site
in the midst of Little Italy.
For nearly three-quarters of
a century, this was where
"New York's finest" came to

work. During Prohibition,
Grand Street from here to the
Bowery was known as
"Bootleggers' Row," and
alcohol was easily
obtained except
when a police raid
was due. The liquor
merchants paid
handsomely for a
tip-off from inside
police headquarters.
The police moved
to new headquarters
in 1973, and in 1985
the building was
converted into a luxury
cooperative apartment project.

Little Italy ❸

Streets around Mulberry St.
Map 4 F4. **M** Canal St.

THE SOUTHERN
Italians who came
to New York in the
late 19th century
found themselves
living in the squalor
of "dumbbell" apart-
ments. These were
built so close together
that sunlight never
reached the lower
windows or back-
yards. With over 40,000
people living in 17 small,
unsanitary blocks, diseases
such as tuberculosis were rife.
Despite the privations of life
on the Lower East Side, the
community that grew up
around Mulberry Street was
lively with the colors, flavors
and atmosphere of its
homeland. These have
lingered on, although the
Italian population has

dwindled to a mere 5,000 and
the boundaries of Chinatown
have encroached on the
traditional "Little Italy."
The most exciting time to
visit is during the Feast of San
Gennaro, which is held
around September 19 (see
p52). For nine days each year,
Mulberry Street is renamed
Via San Gennaro. On the
saint's day, his shrine and
relics are paraded through the
streets. Throughout the feast
the milling crowds enjoy
music, dancing, fairground
sideshows and stalls selling
every conceivable kind of
Italian food and drink, as well
as other ethnic cuisines.
Little Italy's restaurants offer
simple, rustic food served in
friendly surroundings at
reasonable prices.

Italian café in Little Italy

Chinatown ❹

Streets around Mott St. **Map** 4 F5.
M Canal St. **Eastern States Buddhist
Temple open** 9am–7pm daily.

THE CHINATOWN of the early
20th century was primarily
a male community, made up
of immigrants who had first
gone to California. Wages
were sent home to their
families in China who were
prevented from joining them
by US immigration laws. The
men relaxed by gambling at
mahjong. The community
remained isolated from the
rest of the city, financed and
controlled by its own secret
organizations, the Tongs.
Some of the Tongs were
simply family associations
who provided loans. Others,
such as the On Leong and the
Hip Sing, who were at war
with one another, were
criminal fraternities. Tiny,
crooked Doyers Street was
called "Bloody Angle"; enemies
were lured there and set

Stonework figures adorning the Police Headquarters Building

A Chinese grocer tending his shop on Canal Street

upon by gang members waiting around the bend.

A truce between the Tongs in 1933 brought peace to Chinatown. By 1940 it was home to many middle-class families. Immigrants and businesses from Hong Kong also brought postwar prosperity to the community. Today over 80,000 Chinese-Americans live here.

Many people visit the neighborhood simply to feast on Chinese cuisine, but there is more to do here than eat. There are also galleries, antiques and curio shops, and Oriental festivals *(see p53)*. To glimpse another side of Chinatown, step into the incense-scented dimness of the Eastern States Buddhist Temple at 64b Mott Street, where offerings are piled up and over 100 golden Buddhas gleam in the candlelight.

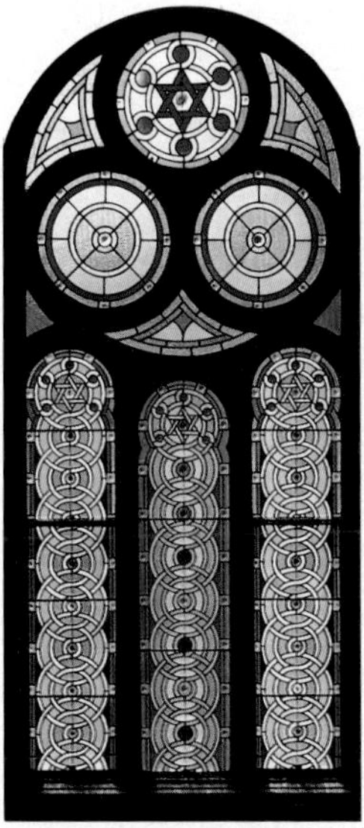

Stained glass from the Synagogue

Columbus Park ❺

Map 4 F5. [M] *Canal St.*

THE TRANQUILLITY of Columbus Park today could not be further removed from the scene near this site in the early 1800s. The area, known as Mulberry Bend, was a red-light district, part of the infamous Five Points slum. Gangs with names like the Dead Rabbits and the Plug Uglies roamed the streets. A murder a day was commonplace; even the police were afraid to pass through. Partly as a result of the writings of reformer Jacob Riis *(see p47)*, the slum was finally taken down in 1892. Now the park is the only open space in all of Chinatown.

Eldridge Street Synagogue ❻

12 Eldridge St. **Map** 5 A5. ☎ *219-0888.* [M] *East Broadway.* ***Open*** *10am–4pm Sun, by appt during week.* ✡ *Fri at sundown, Sat 9am onward.* 🚫📷 ♿ 🛍

WHEN THIS HOUSE of worship was built by the Orthodox Ashkenazi from Eastern Europe in 1887, it was the most flamboyant temple in the neighborhood. But many immigrant Jews saw the Lower East Side as just the beginning of a new life and later moved up and out. Massive synagogues were no longer needed.

In the 1930s, the huge sanctuary, rich with stained glass, brass chandeliers, marbelized wood paneling and fine carving, was closed. Three decades later a group of citizens raised funds for preservation, and restoration is now in progress. A brief audiovisual presentation recounts the history of the synagogue and its renovation.

Even after years of neglect, the facade, with touches of Romanesque, Gothic and Moorish designs, is impressive. Inside, the Italian hand-carved ark and sculpted wooden balcony show why this building was the pride of the area.

Lower East Side Tenement Museum ❼

97 Orchard St. **Map** 5 A4. ☎ *431-0233.* [M] *Delancey, Grand St.* ***Open*** *11am–4pm Tue–Fri, 10am–4pm Sun.* ***Closed*** *Jan 1, Thanksgiving, Dec. 25* ***Donation.*** 🚫📷 ♿ 🎞 ***Lectures, films, videos.***

Street vendor's pushcart (1890s) from the museum

THE INTERIOR of this building is being restored to how it was at the turn of the century. There were no regulations on tenement living conditions until 1879. Many rooms had no windows. Indoor sinks, hallway toilets, even air shafts between buildings were rare. The re-created rooms give a sense of the cramped and deplorable conditions in which so many lived. The museum program includes changing exhibits about the early immigrants, slide shows and excellent walking tours of the neighborhood.

Orchard Street ❽

Map 5 A3. Ⓜ *Delancey, Grand St.*
See **Shopping** p312.

JEWISH IMMIGRANTS founded
the New York garment
industry on Orchard Street,
named after the orchards that
once stood here on James De
Lancey's colonial estate. For
many years the street was
filled with pushcarts loaded
with goods for sale, many of
which were made at home in
the teeming tenements of the
neighborhood.

The pushcarts are long
gone and not all the shop-
keepers are Jewish, but the
flavor remains and the stores
still close on Saturday, the
Jewish Sabbath. On Sunday
there is an outdoor market,
and shoppers fill the street
from Houston to Canal, looking for clothing bargains at
any of the 300 shops.

Zodiac mural from the synagogue

Bialystoker Synagogue ❾

7–11 Willett St. **Map** 5 C4.
Ⓒ 475-0165. Ⓜ *Essex St.*
✪ *frequent services.* ⓞ

THIS 1826 Federal-style
building was originally the
Willett Street Methodist
Church. It was bought in 1905
by Jewish immigrants from
the Bialystok province in
Poland, (now Russia) who
converted it into a synagogue.
For this reason, it faces west
instead of the traditional east.
It has a beautiful interior, with
lovely stained-glass windows,

Canal Street Market vegetable stall

a three-story carved wooden
ark and murals representing
the signs of the zodiac and
views of the Holy Land.

Delancey Street ❿

Map 5 C4. Ⓜ *Essex St.* See
Shopping p312.

ONCE A MAJESTIC boulevard,
Delancey Street today is
little more than an obligatory
entrance to the Williamsburg
Bridge. The street was named
for James De Lancey, whose
farm was situated here during
colonial days. De Lancey remained loyal to George III
during the Revolution and fled
to England after the war,
before his land was seized.

Most of the stores on this
once-grand shopping street
are now run-down, but you
can still buy an authentic
English bowler hat (not to
mention an authentic
American Stetson cowboy hat,
or almost any other kind of
hat) at the Buranelli Hat
Company at 101 Delancey.

Schapiro's Winery ⓫

126 Rivington St. **Map** 5 B3.
Ⓒ 674-4404. Ⓜ *Essex St.* **Open**
10am–5pm Mon–Fri, 11am–4pm
Sun. **Closed** Jewish hols. **Adm
charge.** ⓞ ♿ ⓩ *compulsory, every
hour, make reservations.*

SCHAPIRO'S was founded in
1899 so that Jewish
immigrants to New York
could have their traditional
kosher wines for the Sabbath

and holidays. It has survived
Prohibition, the Depression
and the dwindling numbers
of local Jewish residents. The
owner swears it will still be in
business when his grand-
children have grandchildren.

Today, Schapiro's produces
32 different types of wine.
Though the grapes are now
crushed in upstate New York,
fermenting and bottling are
still done on the premises.
The operation can be seen on
"quickie" tours; afterward,
you can taste the sweet, thick
wine that gave rise to
Schapiro's motto: "You can
almost cut it with a knife!"

Farther east along Rivington
Street at No. 150, Streit's
Matzoh is another long-
established neighborhood
landmark, where visitors can

Schapiro's kosher wine

watch the freshly baked unleavened bread rolling off conveyor belts behind the sales counter.

Puck Building

295–309 Lafayette St. **Map** 4 F3.
Ⓜ *Lafayette. **Not open** to the public.*

Puck statue on building's north-east corner

THIS BLOCK-SQUARE architectural curiosity was built in 1885 by Albert and Herman Wagner. It is an adaptation of the German *Rundbogenstil*, a mid-19th-century style characterized by horizontal bands of arched windows and the skillful use of molded red brick.

The building is part of the city's publishing history. Situated on the edge of Manhattan's old printing district, from 1887 to 1916 it housed the satirical *Puck*, a magazine similar to the British *Punch*. At the turn of the century it was the largest building in the world devoted to lithography and publishing.

Today it is used as the site of some of New York's most stylish parties and artiest fashion-photography shoots. The only connection remaining to the mythical Puck is the gold-leaf statue on the third-floor corner of Mulberry and Houston, and the smaller version over the entrance on Lafayette Street.

Walk half a block and you will see a display of *Puck* covers in Bars and Backbars at 49 East Houston.

Old St. Patrick's Cathedral ⓭

263 Mulberry St. **Map** 4 F3.
📞 226-8075. Ⓜ *Prince St.*
Open *for mass only.*
✝ *9:30am, 11am (Spanish), 12:30pm Sun.*

THE FIRST St. Patrick's was begun in 1809, making it one of the oldest churches in the city. When fire destroyed the original in the 1860s, it was rebuilt much as it is today, with a somewhat austere exterior. When the archdiocese moved the cathedral uptown *(see pp176–7)*, this became the local parish church, and it has flourished with a constantly changing ethnic congregation.

Below the church are vaults containing the remains of, among others, one of New York's most famous families of restaurateurs, the Delmonicos. Pierre Toussaint was also buried here. In 1990 his remains were moved from the old graveyard beside the church to a more prestigious burial place in a crypt in the uptown St. Patrick's. Born as a slave in Haiti in 1766, Toussaint was brought to New York, where he became

Old St. Patrick's Cathedral

a prosperous wig-maker as a free man. He later devoted himself to the poor, tending cholera victims and using his money to build an orphanage. The Vatican is now considering him for sainthood.

Engine Company No. 31 ⓮

87 Lafayette St. **Map** 4 F3.
📞 966-4510. Ⓜ *Canal St.* **Open**
10am–6pm daily. **Closed** *public hols.* 📷

IN THE 19TH CENTURY, fire stations were considered important enough to merit memorable architecture, and the Le Brun firm was the acknowledged master of the art. This 1895 station is one of their best. The building resembles a Loire château, with its steep roof, dormers and towers, seeming almost fairy tale-like in this location.

The present day tenant is the Downtown Community Television Center, which offers courses, workshops and exhibitions of local filmmakers' and artists' work.

Facade of Engine Company 31, in the style of a French château

SoHo and TriBeCa

ART AND architecture are the twin lures that have transformed these formerly industrial districts. SoHo (south of Houston) was threatened with demolition in the 1960s until preservationists drew attention to the rare cast-iron architecture lining the streets. The district was saved, and artists began to move into

Shopfront of a SoHo bakery

the loft spaces. Galleries, cafés and shops followed. Brunch and gallery hopping in SoHo is now a favorite weekend outing. As rents rose, many artists were priced out of SoHo and moved to TriBeCa (triangle below Canal). Now, trendy TriBeCa not only attracts galleries but also has many of the city's newest restaurants.

SIGHTS AT A GLANCE

Historic Streets and Buildings
Haughwout Building ❶
St. Nicholas Hotel ❷
Greene Street ❸
Singer Building ❹

Harrison Street ❽
White Street ❾

Museums and Galleries
Guggenheim Museum SoHo ❺

New Museum of Contemporary Art ❻
New York City Fire Museum ❼

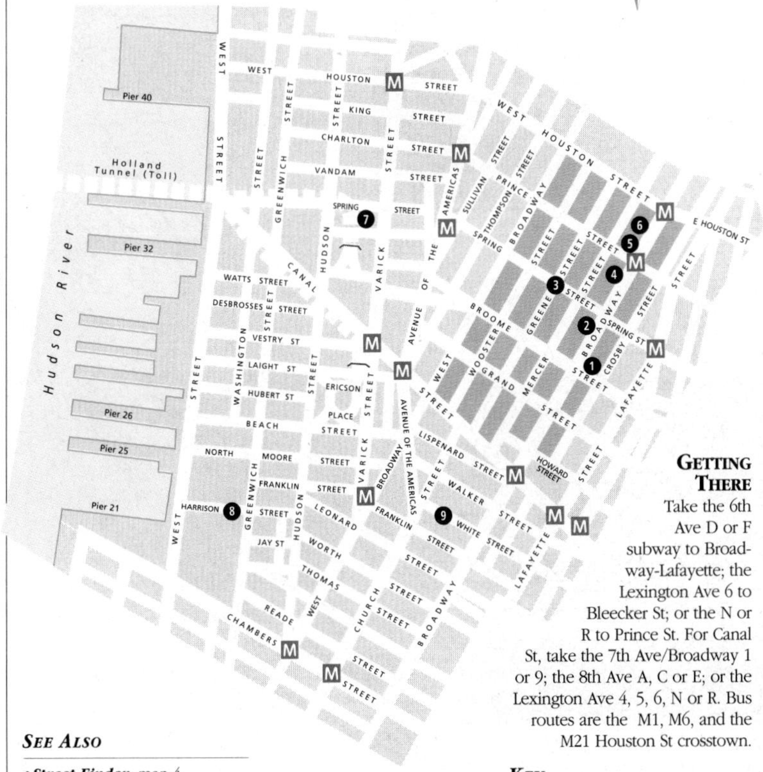

GETTING THERE
Take the 6th Ave D or F subway to Broadway-Lafayette; the Lexington Ave 6 to Bleecker St; or the N or R to Prince St. For Canal St, take the 7th Ave/Broadway 1 or 9; the 8th Ave A, C or E; or the Lexington Ave 4, 5, 6, N or R. Bus routes are the M1, M6, and the M21 Houston St crosstown.

SEE ALSO

- *Street Finder,* map 4
- *SoHo Walk* pp260
- *Restaurants* pp290–92

0 meters   500

0 yards   500

KEY

☐ Street-by-Street map

Ⓜ Subway station

Cast-iron facades on Greene Street

Street by Street: SoHo Cast-Iron Historic District

THE LARGEST concentration of cast-iron architecture in the world *(see pp40–41)* survives in the area between West Houston and Canal streets. The heart of the district is Greene Street, where 50 buildings erected between 1869 and 1895 are found on five cobblestoned blocks. The intricately designed facades were mass-produced in a foundry but are now rare works of industrial art, well suited to the character of the district.

West Broadway, as it passes through SoHo, combines striking architecture with a string of prestigious art galleries, including Charles Cowles, Hirsch & Adler, Sonnabend, Leo Castelli and Mary Boone. *(See p324.)*

Zona at 97 Greene Street stocks original and imaginative items for the home.

Creature from the Enchanted Forest

Enchanted Forest casts a magic spell, just as its name suggests, selling children's toys and books in a fairy-tale forest setting. *(See p314.)*

72–76 Greene Street, the "King of Greene Street," is a splendid Corinthian-columned building. It was the creation of Isaac F. Duckworth, one of the masters of cast-iron design.

Performing Garage is a tiny experimental theater that pioneers the work of avant-garde artists.

★ **Greene Street**
Of all Greene Street's fine cast-iron architecture, one of the best is 28–30, the "Queen," which was built by Duckworth in 1872, and has a tall mansard roof ❸

Canal Street-Broadway subway (2 blocks)

10–14 Greene Street dates from 1869. Note the glass circles in the risers of the iron stoop, which allowed daylight to reach the basement.

15–17 Greene Street is a late addition from 1895, in a simple Corinthian style.

Pace Gallery is one of a group
of influential galleries housed in a
Tuscan-style cast-iron building by
Henry Fernbach. *(See p324.)*

Guggenheim Museum SoHo
*Museum Mile's modern giant
has branched out into
the heart of SoHo,
to rapturous
acclaim* **5**

★ **Singer Building**
*This terra-cotta beauty
was built in 1904 for
the famous sewing
machine company* **4**

LOCATOR MAP
See Manhattan Map pp12–13

KEY

– – –   Suggested route

**New Museum of
Contemporary Art**
*This museum is dedicated
to showing innovative
work by living artists* **6**

**Prince Street
subway station
(lines N, R)**

Dean & DeLuca is one
of the best gourmet
food stores in
New York. Its
range includes
a global
choice of
coffee beans.
(See p326.)

Richard Haas, the prolific
muralist, has transformed a
blank wall into a convincing
cast-iron frontage.

101 Spring Street, with its
simple, geometric facade and
large windows, is a fine
example of the style that led to
the skyscraper.

St. Nicholas Hotel
*During the Civil War, this
former luxury hotel was
used as a headquarters for
the Union Army* **2**

0 meters   100

0 yards   100

STAR SIGHTS

★ **Greene Street**

★ **Singer Building**

Haughwout Building
*In 1857 this was a smart store,
featuring the first Otis safety
elevator* **1**

Haughwout Building ❶

88–92 Broadway. **Map** 4 E4.
M Canal St.

Haughwout Building facade

THIS CAST-IRON building was erected in 1857 for the E.V. Haughwout china and glassware company, which once supplied the White House. Beneath the grime, the design is superb: rows of windows are framed by arches set on columns flanked by taller columns. Mass-produced sections repeat the pattern over and over. The building was the first to use a steam-driven Otis safety elevator, an innovation that made the skyscraper a possibility.

St. Nicholas Hotel ❷

521–523 Broadway. **Map** 4 E4.
M Prince St.

ENGLISH PARLIAMENTARIAN W.E. Baxter, visiting New York in 1854, reported of the recently opened St. Nicholas Hotel: "Every carpet is of velvet pile; chair covers and curtains are made of silk or satin damask…and the embroidery on the mosquito nettings itself

St. Nicholas Hotel in its heyday

might be exhibited to royalty." It is small wonder, then, that it cost over $1 million to build – and with profits of over $50,000 for that year it must have seemed money well spent. Its glory was short-lived, however. In the Civil War it served as a Union Army headquarters. After-ward, the better hotels followed the entertainment district uptown, and by the mid-1870s the St. Nicholas had closed. There is little left on the ground floor to attest to its former opulence, but look up to the remains of its once-stunning marble facade.

Greene Street ❸

Map 4 E4. **M** Canal St.

Haas mural on Greene Street

THIS IS THE HEART of SoHo's Cast-Iron District. Along five cobblestoned blocks are 50 cast-iron buildings dating from 1869 to 1895. The block between Broome and Spring streets has 13 full cast-iron facades and from 8–34 is the longest row of cast-iron buildings anywhere. Those at 72–76 are known as the "King of Greene Street," but 28–30, the "Queen," is considered to be the finest. Although some buildings are of special note, the architecture is best appreciated as a streetscape, with row upon row of columned facades. Walk into any of the galleries housed within to see the spacious interior lofts. At the corner of Greene and Prince streets, the illusionistic muralist Richard Haas has been hard at work, disguising a plain brick side wall as a cast-iron frontage. Look for the detail of the little gray cat, which sits primly in an "open window."

Singer Building ❹

561–563 Broadway. **Map** 4 E3.
M Prince St.

THE "LITTLE" Singer Building built by Ernest Flagg in 1904 is the second and smaller Flagg structure by this name, and many critics think it superior to the 41-story tower on lower Broadway that was torn down in 1967. The charmingly ornate building is adorned with wrought-iron balconies and graceful arches painted in striking dark green. The 12-story facade of terra-cotta, glass and steel was advanced for its day, a forerunner of the metal and glass walls to come in the 1940s and 1950s. The building was an office and warehouse for the Singer sewing machine company, and the original Singer name can be seen cast in iron above the entrance to the store on Prince Street.

Early electric-powered Singer sewing machine

Guggenheim Museum SoHo ❺

575 Broadway. **Map** 4 E3. **☎** 423-3600. **Ⓜ** *Prince St.* **Open** *11am–6pm Sun, Mon, Wed, 11am–10pm Thu–Sat.*

Tʜɪs ᴅʀᴀᴍᴀᴛɪᴄ gallery opened in 1992 to critical acclaim. Designed by architect Arata Isozake, it features displays that complement those at the main Guggenheim Museum *(see p186)*.

New Museum of Contemporary Art ❻

583 Broadway. **Map** 4 E3. **☎** 219-1222. **Ⓜ** *Prince St.* **Open** *noon–6pm Wed–Thu, Sun, noon–8pm Fri, Sat.* **Adm charge.** 🚫 ♿ *limited.* 🎤 *Lectures, readings, events.* 📷

Mᴀʀᴄɪᴀ ᴛᴜᴄᴋᴇʀ created quite a stir in the art world when, in 1977, she left her post as the Whitney Museum's Curator of Painting

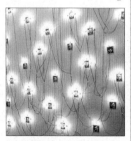

Les Enfants de Dijon **by Christian Boltanski, at the New Museum**

and Sculpture to found this museum showing work by living artists. Jeff Koons and the late John Cage are among those whose work has at some time been featured in thematic shows of paintings, sculpture and performance arts. There is no permanent collection; the point is to exhibit the kind of work Tucker felt was missing from more traditional museums. The provocative shows attract attention for artists who might otherwise be overlooked by the art establishment.

New York City Fire Museum ❼

278 Spring St. **Map** 4 D4. **☎** 691-1303. **Ⓜ** *Houston St, Spring St.* **Open** *10am–4pm Tue–Sat.* 📷 ♿

Hᴏᴜsᴇᴅ ɪɴ ᴀ Beaux Arts–style 1904 firehouse, the city's splendid collection of fire-

1901 La France horse-drawn steam pumper in the City Fire Museum

fighting equipment and memorabilia from the 18th century to 1917 includes scale models, hydrants and bells. Upstairs, a row of gleaming fire engines is lined up for an 1890 parade. Special exhibitions are sometimes held.

Federal houses in Harrison Street

Harrison Street ❽

Map 4 D5. **Ⓜ** *Chambers St.*

Sᴜʀʀᴏᴜɴᴅᴇᴅ ʙʏ high-rise blocks, this rare row of eight restored Federal town houses, with their pitched roofs and dormer windows, almost seems like a stage set. The houses were built in the late 1700s and early 1800s. Two were designed by John McComb, Jr., New York's first major native-born architect, and were transplanted here from Washington Street for preservation. The houses had been used as warehouses and were about to be razed when, in 1969, the Landmarks Preservation Commission

intervened and helped secure funding to restore them. They are now privately owned.

On the other side of the high-rise complex is Washington Market Park, site of the city's former wholesale produce center. The market moved to the Bronx in the early 1970s.

White Street ❾

Map 4 E5. **Ⓜ** *Franklin St.*

Wʜɪʟᴇ ɴᴏᴛ as fine as some SoHo blocks, this sampling of TriBeCa cast-iron architecture shows a wide range of styles. Two White Street has Federal features and a rare gambrel roof, in contrast with the mansard roof of No. 17 (the Alternative Museum). Numbers 8 to 10 White, designed by Henry Fernbach in 1869, have Tuscan columns and arches, with Neo-Renaissance shorter upper stories to give an illusion of height. 38 White is the home of neon artist Rudi Stern's gallery, Let There Be Neon.

Let There Be Neon gallery

GREENWICH VILLAGE

NEW YORKERS call it simply "the Village," and it did indeed begin as a country village, an escape for city dwellers during the yellow fever epidemic of 1822. The crazy-quilt pattern of streets, reflecting early farm boundaries or streams, could not be made to conform to the city's grid plan, and Greenwich Village has remained an enclave apart, a bohemian haven that has been home to many celebrated artists and writers. A popular gay district is here, but on the whole the area has become mainstream and very high-priced. Near Washington Square, it is dominated by New York University students. Nonconformists tend to live in the cheaper East Village.

Jazz club flag on West 3rd Street

SIGHTS AT A GLANCE

Historic Streets and Buildings
St. Luke's Place ❶
75½ Bedford Street ❷
Isaacs-Hendricks House ❸
Grove Court ❹
Jefferson Market Courthouse ❻
Patchin Place ❼
Salmagundi Club ❾
Washington Mews ⓬
New York University ⓭

Museums and Galleries
Forbes Magazine Building ❽

Churches
First Presbyterian Church ❿
Church of the Ascension ⓫
Judson Memorial Church ⓮

Parks and Squares
Sheridan Square ❺
Washington Square ⓯

GETTING THERE
By subway, take lines A, B, C, D, E, F or Q to West 4th St-Washington Sq, the 7th Ave 1 and 9 to Christopher St-Sheridan Sq or the R to 8th St. By bus take the M1, M5, M6 or the M8 crosstown.

0 meters 500
0 yards 500

KEY
▨ Street-by-Street map
Ⓜ Subway station

Billboards on the corner of Christopher Street and Seventh Avenue South

Street by Street: Greenwich Village

A STROLL THROUGH HISTORIC Greenwich Village is a feast of unexpected small pleasures – charming row houses, hidden alleys and leafy courtyards. The often quirky architecture suits the bohemian air of the Village. Many famous people, particularly artists and writers, such as playwright Eugene O'Neill and actor Dustin Hoffman, have made their homes in the houses and apartments that line these old-fashioned narrow streets. By night, the Village really comes alive. Late-night coffeehouses and cafés, experimental theaters and music clubs, including some of the best jazz venues, beckon you at every turn.

The Lucille Lortel Theater is at 121 Christopher Street; it opened in 1955 with *The Threepenny Opera.*

Christopher Street, a part of New York's gay community, is lined with all kinds of shops, bookstores and bars.

Twin Peaks at 102 Bedford Street began life in 1830 as an ordinary house. It was rebuilt in 1926 by architect Clifford Daily to house artists, writers and actors. Daily believed that the quirky house would help their creativity flourish.

Grove Court *Six houses dating from 1853 to 1854 are set at the back of a leafy courtyard* ❹

Chumley's at 86 Bedford Street *(see p309)*, once a speakeasy, now a restaurant, still seems secret. There is no sign outside, just a small menu.

75½ Bedford Street *Built in 1873 in an alley, this is the city's narrowest house* ❷

★ **St. Luke's Place** *This beautiful row of Italianate houses was built in the 1850s* ❶

To Houston Street subway (2 blocks)

The Cherry Lane Theater was founded in 1924. Originally a brewery, it was one of the first of the Off-Broadway theatres.

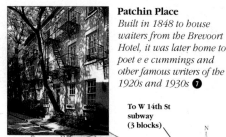

Patchin Place
Built in 1848 to house waiters from the Brevoort Hotel, it was later home to poet e e cummings and other famous writers of the 1920s and 1930s

To W 14th St subway (3 blocks)

LOCATOR MAP
See Manhattan Map pp12–13

STAR SIGHTS

★ **St. Luke's Place**

★ **Jefferson Market Courthouse**

Balducci's *(see p327)* sells some of the best food in town – fine cheeses and many Italian specialties and produce. Balducci's is still run by three generations of one food-loving family.

Gay Street and its fine Federal houses feature in Ruth McKenney's novel of Village life, *My Sister Eileen.*

To West 4th Street subway (2 blocks)

KEY

— — — Suggested route

0 meters   100

0 yards   100

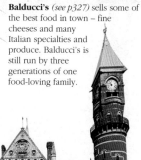

The Northern Dispensary has offered free medical care to the poor since 1827. Edgar Allan Poe was treated here for a cold.

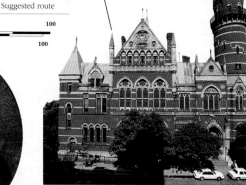

★ **Jefferson Market Courthouse**
Now a public library, it was built as a courthouse in 1877 and voted the fifth most beautiful building in America. Empty for over 20 years, it was restored and turned into a library in 1967

Row houses on St. Luke's Place

St. Luke's Place ❶

Map 3 C3. **M** *Houston St.*

FIFTEEN ATTRACTIVE row houses, dating from the 1850s, line the north side of this street. The park opposite is named after a previous resident of St. Luke's Place, Mayor Jimmy Walker, the popular dandy who ran the city from 1926 until he was forced to resign after a financial scandal in 1932. In front of No. 6 are the lamps that always identify a mayor's home in New York. In recent years, the most recognizable house on the block has been No. 10, shown on television as the home of the Huxtable family in *The Cosby Show* (although the series sets it in Brooklyn). This is also the block where *Wait Until Dark* was filmed, starring Audrey Hepburn as a blind woman living at No. 4. Theodore Dreiser was one of several writers, including the poet Marianne Moore, who lived here. He wrote *An American Tragedy* while living at No. 16. One block north, the corner of Hudson and Morton Streets marked the edge of the Hudson River three centuries ago.

Mayor's lamp at No. 6

75½ Bedford Street ❷

Map 3 C2. **M** *Houston St.* **Not open** to the public.

NEW YORK'S narrowest home, just 9½ ft (2.9 m) wide, was built in 1893 in a former passageway. The poet Edna St. Vincent Millay lived here briefly, followed by the actor John Barrymore, and later Cary Grant. Sadly, the three-story building is now empty and partially boarded up, and there is no plaque.

Just around the corner, at 38 Commerce Street, Miss Millay founded the Cherry Lane Theater in 1924 as a site for avant-garde drama. It still premieres new works. Its biggest hit was the 1960s musical *Godspell*.

Cottage on Bedford Street

Isaacs-Hendricks House ❸

77 Bedford St. **Map** 3 C2. **M** *Houston St.* **Not open** to the public.

THIS IS THE OLDEST surviving home in the Village, built in 1799. The old clapboard walls are visible on the sides

Isaacs-Hendricks House

and rear; the brickwork and third floor came later. The first owner, John Isaacs, bought the land for $295 in 1794. Next came Harmon Hendricks, a copper dealer and associate of revolutionary Paul Revere. Robert Fulton, who used copper for the boilers in his steamboat, was a customer.

Grove Court ❹

Map 3 C2. **M** *Christopher St/ Sheridan Sq.*

AN ENTERPRISING grocer named Samuel Cocks was responsible for this group of six town houses, fitting snugly into an area formed by the bend in the street. (The bends in this part of the Village originally marked divisions between colonial properties.) Cocks reckoned that having residents in the empty passage between Nos. 10 and 12 Grove Street would help his business at No. 18.

But residential courts, now prized as exclusive private addresses, were not considered respectable in 1854, and the lowbrow residents attracted to the area soon earned it the nickname "Mixed Ale Alley." O Henry later used this block as the setting for his 1902 work *The Last Leaf.*

The mid-19th-century town houses at Grove Court

Sheridan Square ❺

Map 3 C2. Ⓜ *Christopher St-Sheridan Sq.*

THIS IS THE HEART of the Village, where seven streets come together in such a maze that early guidebooks called it "the mousetrap." It was named after the Civil War General Philip Sheridan who became commander in chief of the US Army in 1883. His statue stands in nearby Christopher Park.

The Draft Riots of 1863 took place in the square, when mobs revolting against army service tried to lynch freed slaves. More than a century later, another famous disturbance rocked the

Sheridan Square scene

square. The Stonewall Inn on Christopher Street was a gay bar that had stayed in business (it was then illegal for gays to gather in bars) by paying off the police. However, on June 28, 1969, the patrons rebelled, and the pitched close combat that resulted found police officers barricaded inside the bar for hours while crowds taunted them from outside. It was a landmark moral victory for the budding Gay Rights movement. The inn still stands but is no longer a bar. The Village remains a focus for the city's gay community. The spirited gay Halloween Parade *(see p52)* through the Village, noted for its outrageous costumes, brings thousands out.

Pointed tower of "Old Jeff"

Jefferson Market Courthouse ❻

425 6th Ave. **Map** 4 D1. Ⓒ *243-4334.* Ⓜ *W 4th St-Washington Sq.* **Open** *10am–6pm Mon, 1–6pm Tue, Thu, 1–8pm Wed, 10am–5pm Sat* **Closed** *Fri, Sun, public hols.* ♿

PERHAPS THE MOST treasured Village landmark, "Old Jeff" was saved from the wrecking ball and converted into a branch of the New York Public Library through a spirited campaign that began at a local Christmas party in the late 1950s.

The site became a market in 1833, named after former president Thomas Jefferson. Its fire lookout tower had a giant bell that alerted the neighborhood's volunteer fire fighters. In 1865, the founding of the municipal fire department made the bell obsolete, and the Third Judicial District, or Jefferson Market, Courthouse was built. With its Venetian Gothic-style spires and turrets, it was named one of the 10 most beautiful buildings in the country when it opened in 1877. The old

Statue of General Sheridan in Christopher Park

GENERAL PHILIP HENRY
SHERIDAN

fire bell was installed in the tower. Here, in 1906 Harry Thaw was tried for Stanford White's murder *(see p124).*

By 1945, the market had moved, court sessions were discontinued, the four-sided clock had stopped and the building was endangered. In the 1950s, preservationists campaigned first to restore the clock and then the whole building. Architect Giorgio Cavaglieri has preserved many original details, including the stained glass and a spiral staircase that now leads to a dungeonlike reference room.

Facade and an ailanthus tree at Patchin Place

Patchin Place ❼

W 10th St. **Map** 4 D1. Ⓜ *W 4th St-Washington Sq.*

ONE OF MANY delightful unexpected pockets in the Village is this tiny block of small residences, lined with ailanthus trees planted in order to "absorb the bad air." The houses were built in the mid-19th century to house Basque waiters from the Fifth Avenue Brevoort Hotel.

Later the houses became fashionable addresses, with many writers living here. The poet e e cummings lived at No. 4 from 1923 until his death in 1962. English poet laureate John Masefield also lived on the block. So did playwright Eugene O'Neill and John Reed, whose eyewitness account of the Russian Revolution, *Ten Days That Shook The World* was filmed by Warren Beatty as *Reds.*

Toy battleship from the Forbes Magazine Collection

Forbes Building and Galleries ⑧

62 5th Ave. **Map** 4 E1. 📞 206-5548. Ⓜ 14th St-Union Sq. **Galleries open** 10am–4pm Tue, Wed, Fri, Sat (times may vary). 🚫 Thu.

Sᴏᴍᴇ ᴀʀᴄʜɪᴛᴇᴄᴛᴜʀᴀʟ critics have called this 1925 limestone cube by Carrère & Hastings pompous. It was originally the headquarters of the Macmillan Publishing Company. When Macmillan moved uptown, the late Malcolm Forbes moved in with his financial magazine, *Forbes*. The Forbes Magazine Galleries show Forbes's diverse tastes, with Fabergé eggs made for the last Russian czar; over 500 antique toy boats; 12,000 toy soldiers; and a signed copy of Abraham Lincoln's Gettysburg Address, among other presidential memorabilia. There are also exhibitions of paintings, ranging from French to American Military works.

Salmagundi Club ⑨

47 5th Ave. **Map** 4 E1. 📞 255-7740. Ⓜ 14th St-Union Sq. **Open** 1–5pm daily. 🚫

Aᴍᴇʀɪᴄᴀ's ᴏʟᴅᴇsᴛ club for artists is housed in the last remaining mansion on lower Fifth Avenue. Built in 1853 for Irad Hawley, it is now the home of the American Artists' Professional League, the American Watercolor Society and the Greenwich Village Society for Historic Preservation. *The Salmagundi Papers,* the satiric periodical by Washington Irving, gave the club its name. Founded in 1871, the club moved here in 1917. Periodic art exhibits open the late 19th-century interior to the public.

Exterior of the Salmagundi Club

First Presbyterian Church ⑩

5th Ave at 12th St. **Map** 4 D1. 📞 675-6150 Ⓜ 7th Ave-Union Sq. **Open** 9am–5pm Mon–Fri. 🕇 12:15pm Wed, Fri;11am Sun.

Dᴇsɪɢɴᴇᴅ ʙʏ Joseph C. Wells in 1846, this Gothic church was modeled on the Church of Saint Saviour in Bath, England. The church is noteworthy for its brownstone tower. The carved wooden plaques on the altar list every pastor since 1716. The south transept by McKim, Mead & White was added in 1893. The fence of iron and wood was built in 1844 and then restored in 1981.

Church of the Ascension ⑪

36–38 5th Ave. **Map** 4 E1. 📞 254-8620. Ⓜ 14th St-Union Sq. **Open** noon–2pm, 5–7pm daily. 🕇 6pm daily, 9am, 11am, 6pm Sun. 📷 (not during services).

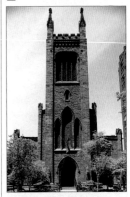

Church of the Ascension

Tʜɪs ᴇɴɢʟɪsʜ Gothic Revival church was designed in 1840–41 by Richard Upjohn, architect of Trinity Church. The interior was redone in 1888 by Stanford White, with an altar relief by Augustus Saint-Gaudens. Above the altar hangs *The Ascension*, a mural by John La Farge, who also designed some of the stained glass. The belfry tower is lit at night to show off the colors.

In 1844 President John Tyler married Julia Gardiner here; she lived in nearby Colonnade Row (see p118).

Washington Mews ⑫

Washington Sq N at E 8th St. **Map** 4 E2. Ⓜ W 4th St.

Bᴜɪʟᴛ ᴀs sᴛᴀʙʟᴇs, this hidden enclave was turned into carriage houses around 1900. The south side was added in 1939. Gertrude Vanderbilt Whitney, founder of the Whitney Museum, lived and worked there.

On the corner of University Place is NYU's French House, remodeled in a French style, where movies, lectures and classes in French are held.

New York University ⑬

Washington Sq. **Map** 4 E2.
Ⓜ W 4th St. **Open** 8am–9pm Mon–Sat.

Ⓞ RIGINALLY CALLED the University of the City of New York, NYU was founded in 1831 as an alternative to Episcopalian Columbia University. It is now the largest private university in America and extends for blocks around Washington Square.

Construction of the school's first building on Waverly Place sparked the Stonecutters' Guild Riot of 1833, when contractors protested about the use of inmates from a state prison to cut stone. The National Guard had to restore order. The original building no longer exists, but a memorial with a piece of the original tower can be seen on a pedestal set into the pavement on Washington Square South. Samuel Morse's telegraph, John W. Draper's first-ever photographic

Bust of Sylvette by Picasso, between Bleecker and West Houston streets

portrait and Samuel Colt's six-shooter were invented here.

The Brown Building, on Washington Place near Greene Street, was the site of the Triangle Shirtwaist Company. In 1911, 146 factory workers died in a fire here, leading to new fire safety and labor laws.

A 36-ft (11-m) enlargement of Picasso's *Bust of Sylvette* is in University Village.

Judson Memorial Church ⑭

55 Washington Sq S. **Map** 4 D2.
Ⓒ 477-0351. Ⓜ W 4th St.
Open 9am–noon, 1–5pm Mon–Fri.
✝ Sun 11am.

Ⓑ UILT IN 1892, this McKim, Mead & White church is an impressive Romanesque building with stained glass by John La Farge. Designed by Stanford White, it is named after the first American missionary sent to foreign soil, Adoniram Judson, who served in Burma in 1811. A copy of his Burmese translation of the Bible was put in the cornerstone when the building was dedicated.

It is the unique spirit of this church, not the architecture, that makes it stand out. Judson Memorial has played an active role in local and world concerns and has been the site of activism on issues ranging from AIDS to the arms race. It is also home to avant-garde art exhibitions and off-Off Broadway plays.

Arch on the north side of Washington Square

Washington Square ⑮

Map 4 D2. Ⓜ W 4th St.

Ⓝ OW ONE OF the city's most vibrant open spaces, Washington Square was once marshland through which the quiet Minetta Brook flowed. By the late 1700s, the area had been turned into a public cemetery – when excavation began for the park, some 10,000 skeletal remains were exhumed. The square was used as a dueling ground for

a time, then as a site for public hangings until 1819. The "hanging elm" in the northwest corner remains. In 1826 the marsh was filled in and the brook diverted underground, where it still flows; a small sign on a fountain at the entrance to Two Fifth Avenue marks its course.

The magnificent marble arch by Stanford White, completed in 1895, replaced an earlier wooden version that had spanned lower Fifth Avenue to mark the centenary of George Washington's inauguration. A stairway is hidden in the right side of the arch. In 1916, a group of artists led by Marcel Duchamp and John Sloan broke in, climbed atop the arch, and declared the "free and independent republic of Washington Square, the state of New Bohemia."

Across the street is "the Row." Now part of NYU, this block was once home to New York's most prominent families. The Delano family, writers Edith Wharton, Henry James, and John dos Passos, and artist Edward Hopper all lived here. Number 8 was once the mayor's official home.

Today students, families and free spirits mingle and enjoy the park side by side. A few drug dealers frequent the park, but it is safe by day.

Window on the corner of West 4th Street and Washington Square

EAST VILLAGE

PETER STUYVESANT had a country estate in the East Village, and in the 19th century, the Astors and Vanderbilts lived here. But around 1900, high society moved uptown and immigrants moved in. The Irish, Germans, Jews, Poles, Ukrainians and Puerto Ricans all left their mark in the area's churches, landmarks and the city's most varied

Mosaic, facade of St George's Ukrainian Catholic Church

and least expensive ethnic restaurants. In the 1950s low rents attracted the "beat generation." Later, Hippies were followed by punks. The area's experimental music clubs and theaters still feature the latest styles. Astor Place buzzes with students. To the east are Avenues A, B, C and D, an area known as "Alphabet City," which is slowly being redeveloped.

SIGHTS AT A GLANCE

Historic Streets and Buildings
Cooper Union ❶
Colonnade Row ❸
Bayard-Condict Building ❽

Museums and Galleries
Old Merchant's House ❹

Churches
St. Mark's-in-the-Bowery Church ❺
Grace Church ❻

Parks and Squares
Tompkins Square ❼

Famous Theaters
Public Theater ❷

SEE ALSO

• *Street Finder*, map 4, 5

• *Where to Stay* pp274–5

• *Restaurants* pp290–92

GETTING THERE
By subway, the Lexington Ave 6 train stop at Astor Pl is the most convenient; the area is also served by the M15 and M101/102 buses and the M8 crosstown bus.

| 0 meters | 500 |
| 0 yards | 500 |

KEY

▨ Street-by-Street map

Ⓜ Subway station

Gothic bas-relief on the facade of Grace Church

The interior of McSorley's Old Ale House

Street by Street: East Village

AT THE SPOT WHERE Tenth and Stuyvesant streets now intersect, Peter Stuyvesant's country house once stood. His grandson, also named Peter, inherited most of the property and had it divided into streets in 1787. Among the prize sites of the St. Mark's Historic District are the St. Mark's-in-the-Bowery Church, the Stuyvesant-Fish house and the 1795 home of Nicholas Stuyvesant, both on Stuyvesant Street. Many other homes in the district were built between 1871 and 1890 and still have their original stoops, lintels and other architectural details.

Astor Place subway (line 6)

Astor Place saw rioting in 1849. English actor William Macready, playing *Hamlet* at the Astor Place Opera House, criticized American actor Edwin Forrest. Forrest's fans revolted and there were 34 deaths.

Alamo is the title of the 15-ft (4.5-m) steel cube in Astor Place designed by Bernard Rosenthal. It revolves when pushed.

ASTOR PLACE

8 TH ST

LAFAYETTE STREET

FOUR

STABLE COURT

BOWERY

Colonnade Row
Now in shabby disrepair, these buildings were once expensive town houses. The houses, of which only four are left, are unified by one facade in the European style. The marble was quarried by Sing Sing prisoners ❸

Public Theater
In 1965 the late Joseph Papp convinced the city to buy the Astor Library (1849) as a home for the theater. Now restored, it sees the opening of many famous plays ❷

STAR SIGHTS

★ **Cooper Union**

★ **Old Merchant's House**

★ **Old Merchant's House**
This museum contains the house's original Federal, American Empire and Victorian furniture ❹

★ Cooper Union
Founded by self-made man Peter Cooper in 1859, it still provides a free education to its students ❶

The Stuyvesant-Fish House (1803–4) was constructed out of brick. It is a classic example of a Federal-style house.

LOCATOR MAP
See Manhattan Map pp12–13

St. Mark's-in-the-Bowery-Church
The church was built in 1799 and the steeple added in 1828 ❺

Renwick Triangle is a group of 16 houses built in 1861 in the Italianate style.

Stuyvesant Polyclinic was founded in 1857 as the German Dispensary and it is still a health clinic. The facade is decorated with the busts of many famous physicians and scientists.

St. Mark's Place was once the main street of hippie life. It is still the hub of the East Village youth scene. Funky shops now occupy many of the basements.

Little India, the row of Indian eateries on the south side of East Sixth Street, offers a taste of India at budget prices.

Little Ukraine is home to 30,000 Ukrainians. The focus of the community is St. George's Ukrainian Catholic Church.

KEY

– – – Suggested route

0 meters   100

0 yards   100

McSorley's Old Ale House still brews its own ale and serves it in surroundings seemingly unchanged since it opened in 1854. *(See p309.)*

Great Hall at Cooper Union, where Abraham Lincoln spoke

Cooper Union ❶

41 Cooper Sq. **Map** 4 F2.
🅲 353-4100. Ⓜ *Astor Pl.*
Open by appointment only, and for lectures and concerts in Great Hall.
Closed Jun–Aug, public hols. 🚫 ⚿

PETER COOPER, the wealthy industrialist who built the first US steam locomotive, made the first steel rails and was a partner in the first transatlantic cable venture, had no formal schooling. To make education easier for others, Cooper founded New York's first free, nonsectarian co-educational college. Still free, the school inspires intense competition for places. The six-story building was the first with a steel frame, made of Cooper's own rails. The building was renovated in 1973–74. The Great Hall was inaugurated in 1859 by Mark Twain, and Lincoln delivered his "Right Makes Might" speech there in 1860. Cooper Union continues to sponsor a provocative Public Forum.

Public Theater ❷

425 Lafayette St. **Map** 4 F2. 🅲 598-7150 (box office). Ⓜ *Astor Pl.*
See also **Entertainment** p333.

THE LARGE redbrick and brownstone building that is the home of the New York Shakespeare Festival began its life in 1849 as the Astor Library, the city's first free library, now part of the New York Public Library. It is a prime American example of German Romanesque Revival style. When the building was threatened with demolition in 1965, Joseph Papp, founder of the Shakespeare Festival, persuaded New York City to buy it as a home for the company. Renovation began in 1967, and much of the handsome interior was preserved during conversion into six theaters. Although much of the work shown is experimental, the Public Theater was the original home of hit musicals *Hair* and *A Chorus Line*. The latter moved uptown to become the longest-running Broadway production.

Colonnade Row ❸

428–434 Lafayette St. **Map** 4 F2.
Ⓜ *Astor Pl.* **Not open** to the public.

THE CORINTHIAN columns across these four buildings are all that remain of a once-magnificent row of nine Greek Revival town houses. They were completed in 1833 by developer Seth Geer and were known as "Geer's Folly" by skeptics who thought no one would live so far east. They were proved wrong when the houses were taken by such eminent citizens as John Jacob Astor and Cornelius Vanderbilt. Washington Irving, author of *Rip Van Winkle* and other classic American tales, lived here for a time, as did two English novelists, William Makepeace Thackeray and Charles Dickens. Five of the houses were lost when the John Wanamaker Department Store razed them early this century to make room for a garage. Neglect has been cruel to the remaining buildings.

Old Merchant's House ❹

29 E 4th St. **Map** 4 F2.
🅲 777-1089. Ⓜ *Astor Pl.*
Open 1–4pm Sun–Thurs. **Adm charge.** 🚫 📷 **Lectures** 🎟

The original 19th-century iron stove in the kitchen of the Old Merchant's House

THIS REMARKABLE Greek Revival brick town house, improbably tucked away on an East Village block, is a time capsule of a vanished way of life. It still has both its original fixtures and its kitchen, and is filled with the actual furniture, ornaments and utensils of the family that lived here for almost 100 years. Built in 1832, it was bought in 1835 by Seabury Tredwell, a wealthy merchant, and stayed in the family until Gertrude Tredwell, the last member, died in 1933. She had maintained her father's home just as he would have liked it, and a relative convinced the city to buy it and preserve it as a museum. The first-floor parlors are very grand, a sign of how well New York's merchant class lived in the 1800s.

The Public Theater on Lafayette Street

St. Mark's-in-the-Bowery Church **5**

131 E 10th St. **Map** 4 F1. **C** 674-6377. **M** Astor Pl. **Open** 9am–4pm Mon–Fri. **Closed** public hols. **⚡**

ONE OF New York's oldest churches, this building, dating from 1799, replaced a 1660 church on the *bouwerie* (farm) of Governor Peter Stuyvesant. He is buried here with seven generations of his descendants and many other prominent early New Yorkers. Poet W.H. Auden, who was a member of the parish, is also commemorated here.

In 1878, a grisly kidnapping took place in the churchyard, when the remains of department store magnate A.T. Stewart were removed and held for $20,000 ransom.

The church rectory at 232 East 11th Street is a little-known work, from 1900, by Ernest Flagg. He achieved renown for his Singer Building *(see p104).*

Grace Church **6**

802 Broadway. **Map** 4 F1. **C** 254-2000. **M** Astor Pl. **Open** 10am–5:30pm Mon–Fri, noon–4pm Sat. **Closed** public hols. **✝** 6pm Wed, 9am, 11am Sun. **⚡** **♿** Concerts.

JAMES RENWICK, JR., the architect of St. Patrick's Cathedral, was only 23 when he designed this church, yet many consider it his finest achievement. Its delicate early Gothic lines have a grace befitting the church's name. The interior is just as beautiful, with Pre-Raphaelite stained glass and a handsome mosaic floor.

The church's peace and serenity were briefly shattered in 1863, when Phineas T. Barnum

staged the wedding of midget General Tom Thumb here; the crowds turned the event into complete chaos.

The marble spire replaced a wooden steeple in 1888 amid fears that it might prove too heavy for the church – and it has since developed a distinct lean. The church is visible from afar, because it is on a bend on Broadway. Henry Brevoort forced the city to bend Broadway to divert it around his apple orchard.

Grace Church altar and window

Tompkins Square **7**

Map 5 B1. **M** 2nd Ave, 1st Ave.

THIS ENGLISH-STYLE park has the makings of a peaceful spot, but its past has more often been dominated by strife. It was the site of America's first organized labor demonstration in 1874, the main gathering place during the neighborhood's hippie era of the 1960s and, in 1991, an arena for violent riots when the police tried to evict homeless people who had taken over the grounds. The square also contains a poignant monument to the neighborhood's greatest tragedy. A small statue of a boy

Tom Thumb and his bride at Grace Church

and a girl looking at a steamboat commemorates the deaths of over 1,000 local residents in the *General Slocum* steamer disaster. On June 15, 1904, the boat caught fire during a pleasure cruise on the East River. The boat was crowded with women and children from this then-German neighborhood. Many local men lost their entire families and moved away, leaving the area and its memories behind.

Bayard-Condict Building **8**

65 Bleecker St. **Map** 4 F3. **M** Bleecker St.

THE GRACEFUL columns, elegant filigreed terra-cotta facade and magnificent cornice on this 1898 building mark the only New York work by Louis Sullivan, the great Chicago architect who taught Frank Lloyd Wright. He died in poverty and obscurity in Chicago in 1924.

Sullivan is said to have objected vigorously to the sentimental angels supporting the Bayard-Condict Building's cornice, but he eventually gave in to the wishes of Silas Alden Condict, the owner.

Because this building is squeezed into a commercial block, it is better appreciated from a distance. Cross the street and walk a little way down Crosby Street for the best view.

The Bayard-Condict Building

GRAMERCY AND THE FLATIRON DISTRICT

FOUR SQUARES were laid out in this area by real estate developers in the 19th century to emulate the quiet, private residential areas in many European cities. Gramercy Park, still mainly residential, was one of them. The townhouses around the square

Toy in the Police Academy Museum

were designed by some of the city's best architects and occupied by some of its most prominent citizens. Today, not far away, boutiques and trendy cafés are moving to the once-dowdy stretch of lower Fifth Avenue just south of the famous Flatiron Building.

SIGHTS AT A GLANCE

Historic Streets and Buildings
New York Life Insurance Company **2**
Appellate Division of the Supreme Court of the State of New York **3**
Metropolitan Life Insurance Company **4**
Flatiron Building **5**
Ladies' Mile **6**
National Arts Club **8**
The Players **9**
Block Beautiful **11**
Con Edison Headquarters **14**

Museums and Galleries
Theodore Roosevelt Birthplace **7**
Police Academy Museum **12**

Churches
The Little Church Around the Corner **16**

Parks and Squares
Madison Square **1**
Gramercy Park **10**
Stuyvesant Square **13**
Union Square **15**

SEE ALSO

• **Street Finder,** maps 8, 9
• **Where to Stay** pp274–5
• **Restaurants** pp290–92

GETTING THERE
The closest subway station is at 23rd St, where the Lexington Ave No. 6 train stops. Buses to the area include the M101/102 on 3rd Ave, and the M1, M2 or M3 on 5th and Madison avenues. The crosstown bus is the M26.

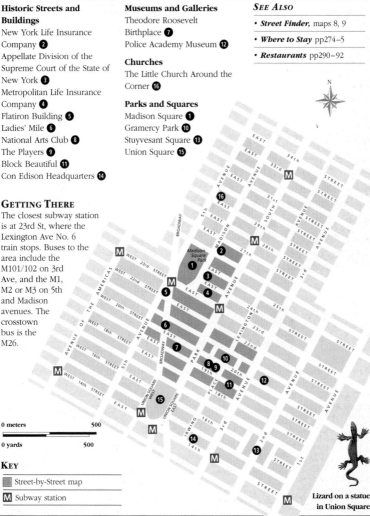

0 meters 500
0 yards 500

KEY

Street-by-Street map

M Subway station

Lizard on a statue in Union Square

Con Edison Headquarters by night

Street by Street: Gramercy Park

GRAMERCY PARK AND nearby Madison Square tell a tale of two cities. Madison Square is ringed by offices and traffic and is used mainly by those who work nearby, but the fine surrounding commercial architecture and statues make it well worth visiting. It was once the home of Stanford White's famous pleasure palace, the old Madison Square Garden, a place where revelers always thronged. Gramercy Park, however, retains the air of dignified tranquility it has become known for. Here, the residences and clubs remain, set around New York's last private park, for which only those who live on the square have a key.

★ **Madison Square**
The Knickerbocker Club played baseball here in the 1840s and was the first to codify the game's rules.
Today office workers enjoy the park's many statues of 19th-century figures, among them Admiral David Farragut ❶

Statue of Diana atop the old Madison Square Garden

23rd Street subway (lines N, R)

M

M

★ **Flatiron Building**
The triangle made by Fifth Avenue, Broadway and 23rd Street is the site of one of New York's most famous early skyscrapers. When it was built in 1903, it was the world's tallest building ❺

A sidewalk clock found in front of 200 Fifth Avenue marks the very end of the once-fashionable shopping area, known as Ladies' Mile.

Ladies' Mile
Broadway from Union to Madison squares was once New York's finest shopping area. A few buildings remain ❻

Theodore Roosevelt Birthplace
The house is a replica of the one in which the 26th American president was born ❼

BROADWAY (LADIES' MILE)

E 21 ST STRE

E 19TH ST

E 17TH ST

National Arts Club
This is a private club for the arts, on the south side of the park ❽

KEY

– – – Suggested route

0 meters	100
0 yards	100

Appellate Court
This small marble palace is said to be the world's busiest court-house ❸

LOCATOR MAP
See Manhattan Map pp12–13

New York Life Insurance Company
This spectacular building by Cass Gilbert bears his trade-mark pyramid-shaped top ❷

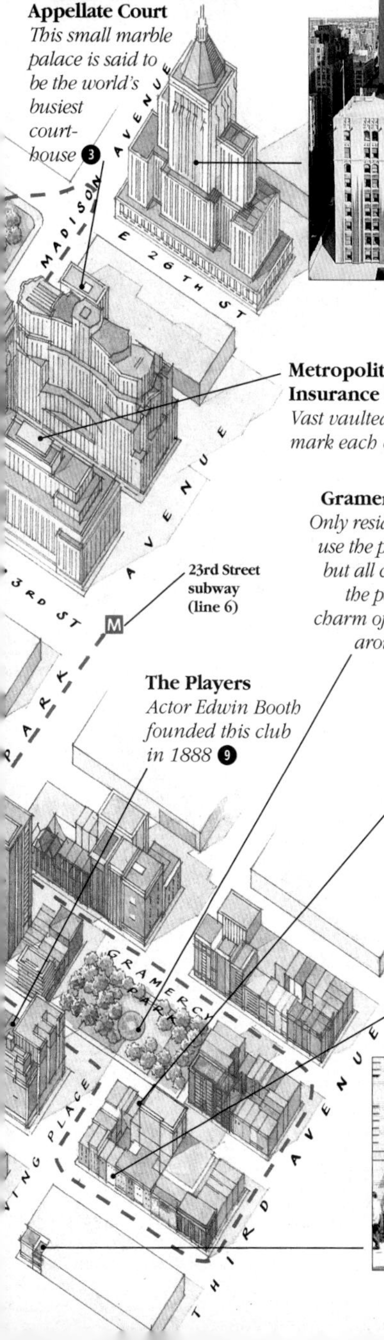

STAR SIGHTS
- ★ **Flatiron Building**
- ★ **Madison Square**

Metropolitan Life Insurance Company
Vast vaulted entrances mark each corner ❹

Gramercy Park
Only residents can use the park itself, but all can enjoy the peace and charm of the area around it ❿

23rd Street subway (line 6)

The Players
Actor Edwin Booth founded this club in 1888 ❾

The Brotherhood Synagogue was a Friends Meeting House from 1859 to 1975, when it became a synagogue.

The Block Beautiful
This is a tree-lined stretch of East 19th Street. No particular house is outstanding, but the street as a whole is lovely ⓫

Pete's Tavern has been here since 1903. Short story writer O Henry, a well-known chronicler of the city, wrote "The Gift of the Magi" in the second booth.

Madison Square ❶

Map 8 F4. Ⓜ *23rd St.*

Farragut's statue, Madison Square

PLANNED AS the center of a fashionable residential district, this square became a popular entertainment center after the Civil War. It was bordered by the elegant Fifth Avenue Hotel, the Madison Square Theater and Stanford White's Madison Square Garden. The torch-bearing arm of the Statue of Liberty was exhibited here in 1884.

Quiet once again, it is a lunchtime spot for neighbor-hood office workers, and a place to stroll and admire the sculptures. The 1880 statue of Admiral David Farragut is by Augustus Saint-Gaudens, with a pedestal by Stanford White. Farragut was the hero of a Civil War sea battle; figures representing Courage and Loyalty arising from the waves are carved on the base. The statue of Roscoe Conkling commemorates a US senator who died of exposure during the great blizzard of 1888. The Eternal Light flagpole, by Carrère & Hastings, honors the soldiers who fell in France during World War I.

New York Life Insurance Company ❷

45–55 Madison Ave. **Map** 9 A3. Ⓜ *28th St.* **Open** *office hours.*

THIS IMPOSING building was designed in 1928 by Cass Gilbert of Woolworth Building fame. The interior is a master-piece, adorned with enormous hanging lamps, bronze doors and paneling, and a grand staircase leading, of all places, to the subway station.

Other famous buildings have stood on this site. Barnum's Hippodrome was here in 1874, then the first Madison Square Garden opened in 1879. A wide range of entertainments were put on, including the prizefights of heavyweight boxing hero Jack Dempsey in the 1880s. The next Madison Square Garden – Stanford White's legendary pleasure palace – opened on the same site in 1890. Lavish musical shows and social events were attended by New York's elite, who paid over $500 for a box at the prestigious annual horse show.

The building had street-level arcades and a tower modeled on the Giralda in Seville. A gold statue of the goddess Diana stood atop the tower. Her nudity was shocking, but far more scandalous was the decadent life and death of White himself. In 1906, while watch-ing a revue in the roof garden, he was shot dead by millionaire Harry K. Thaw, the husband of White's former mistress, showgirl Evelyn Nesbit. The headline in the journal *Vanity Fair* summed up popular feeling: "Stanford White, Voluptuary and Pervert, Dies the Death of a Dog." The ensuing trial's revelations about decadent Broadway high society leave modern soap operas far behind.

New York Life Insurance Company's golden pyramid roof

Appellate Division of the Supreme Court of the State of New York ❸

E. 25th St. at Madison Ave. **Map** 9 A4. 【 *340 0400.* Ⓜ *23rd St.* **Open** *9am–5pm Mon–Fri (court in session from 2pm Tue, Wed, Thu, from 10am Fri).* **Closed** *public hols.* 🚫

APPEALS RELATING TO civil and criminal cases for New York and the Bronx are heard here, in what is widely considered to be the busiest court of its kind in the world. James Brown Lord designed the small yet noble Palladian Revival building in 1900.

Statues of *Justice* and *Study* above the Appellate Court

It is decorated with more than a dozen handsome sculptures, including Daniel Chester French's *Justice* flanked by *Power* and *Study*. During the week, the public is invited to step inside to admire the fine interior, designed by the Herter brothers, including the courtroom when it is not in session. Among the elegant details worth looking for are the fine stained-glass windows and dome, the murals and the striking cabinetwork.

Displays in the lobby often feature some of the more famous cases that have been heard in this court. Among the celebrity names that have been involved in appeals settled here are Babe Ruth, Charlie Chaplin, Fred Astaire, Harry Houdini, Theodore Dreiser and Edgar Allan Poe.

Clock tower of the Metropolitan Life Insurance Company

Metropolitan Life Insurance Company ❹

1 Madison Ave. **Map** 9 A4. 578-2211. 23rd St. **Open** office hours.

I N 1909, THE ADDITION of a 700-ft (210-m) tower to this 1893 building ousted the Flatiron as the tallest in the world. The huge four-sided clock has minute hands said to weigh 1000 lb (454 kg) each. The building is lit up at night, and is a familiar part of the evening sky-line. It served as the company symbol "the light that never fails."

A series of historical murals by N.C. Wyeth, the famed illustrator of such classics as *Robin Hood, Treasure Island* and *Robinson Crusoe* (and the father of painter Andrew Wyeth), once graced the walls of the cafeteria. They are now on display in the lobby.

Flatiron Building ❺

175 5th Ave. **Map** 8 F4. 23rd St. **Open** office hours.

O RIGINALLY NAMED the Fuller Building after the construction company that owned it, this building by Chicago architect David Burnham was the tallest in the world when it was completed in 1902. One of the first buildings to use a steel frame, it heralded the era of the skyscrapers.

It soon became known as the Flatiron for its unusual triangular shape, but some called it "Burnham's folly," predicting that the winds created by the building's shape would knock it down. It has withstood the test of time, but the winds along 23rd Street did have one notable effect. In the building's early days, they drew crowds of males hoping to get a peek at women's ankles as their long skirts got blown about. Police officers had to keep people moving along, and their call, "23-skidoo" became slang for "scram."

The stretch of Fifth Avenue to the south of the building was, un-til recently, rather run down but is fast coming to life with smart shops such as Emporio Armani and Paul Smith, giving the area new cachet and a new name, "the Flatiron District."

Flatiron Building during its construction

Ladies' Mile ❻

Broadway (Union Sq. to Madison Sq.). **Map** 4 E1 to 8 F4. 14th St, 23rd St.

Arnold Constable store

I N THE 19TH CENTURY, the "carriage trade" came here in shiny traps from their town houses nearby, to shop at stores such as Arnold Constable (Nos. 881–887) and Lord & Taylor (No. 901). The ground-floor exteriors have changed beyond recognition; look up to see the remains of once-grand facades.

President Teddy Roosevelt

Theodore Roosevelt Birthplace ❼

28 E. 20th St. **Map** 9 A5. 260-1616 14th St.-Union Sq. **Open** 9am–5pm Wed–Sun (last adm: 4:30pm). **Closed** public hols. **Adm** charge. Lectures, concerts, films, videos.

T HE RECONSTRUCTED boyhood home of the colorful 26th president displays everything from the toys with which the young Teddy played to cam-paign buttons and emblems of the trademark "Rough Rider" hat that Roosevelt wore in the Spanish-American War. One exhibit features his explor-ations and interests; the other covers his political career.

Bas-relief faces of great writers at the National Arts Club

National Arts Club ❽

15 Gramercy Pk S. **Map** 9 A5. **C** 475-3424. **M** *14th St-Union Sq, 6 to 23rd St.* **Open** *for exhibitions.*

DESIGNED BY Calvert Vaux in 1881–84, this large brownstone was the residence of New York governor Samuel Tilden, who condemned "Boss" Tweed *(see p25)* and established a free public library. The National Arts Club bought the home in 1906 and kept the original high ceilings and stained glass. Members have included most of the leading American artists of the late 19th and early 20th century. Early members were asked to donate a painting or sculpture in lieu of a subscription for life membership, and these gifts form the permanent collection. The club is open to the public several times a year for exhibitions.

The Players ❾

16 Gramercy Pk S. **Map** 9 A5. **C** 228-7610. **M** *14th St-Union Sq, 6 to 23rd St.* **Not open** *exc for pre-booked group tours.* ▨

THIS TWO-STORY brownstone was the home of actor Edwin Booth, brother of President Lincoln's assassin, John Wilkes Booth. Edwin Booth hired architect Stanford White to remodel the building as a club in 1888. Although the club was intended primarily for actors, members have included White himself, author Mark Twain, publisher Thomas Nast and Winston Churchill, whose mother, Jennie Jerome, was born nearby. A statue of Booth playing Hamlet is across the street in Gramercy Park.

Decorative grille at The Players club

Gramercy Park ❿

Map 9 A4. **M** *14th St-Union Sq, 6 to 23rd St.*

GRAMERCY PARK is one of four squares (with Union, Stuyvesant and Madison) laid out in the 1830s and 1840s to attract society residences. It is the city's only private park, and residents in the surrounding buildings have keys to the park gate as the original owners once did. Look through the railings at the southeast corner to see Greg Wyatt's fountain, with giraffes leaping around a smiling sun.

The buildings around the square were designed by some of the city's most famous architects, including Stanford White, whose house was located on the site of today's Gramercy Park Hotel. Particularly fine are 3 and 4, with graceful cast-iron gates and porches. The lanterns in front of 4 serve as symbols marking the house of a former mayor of the city, James Harper. Number 34 (1883) has been the home of the sculptor Daniel Chester French, the actor James Cagney and circus impresario John Ringling (who had a massive pipe organ installed in his apartment).

Block Beautiful ⓫

E. 19th St. **Map** 9 A5. **M** *3rd Ave, 14th St-Union Sq, 6 to 23rd St.*

House facade on the Block Beautiful on East 19th Street

THIS IS A SERENE, tree-lined block of 1920s residences, beautifully restored. None of them is exceptional on its own, but together they create a wonderfully harmonious whole. Number 132 had two famous theatrical tenants: Theda Bara, silent movie star and Hollywood's first sex symbol, and the fine Shakespearean actress Mrs. Patrick Campbell, who originated the role of Eliza Doolittle in George Bernard Shaw's *Pygmalion* in 1914. The hitching posts outside 141 and the ceramic relief of giraffes outside 147-149 are two of the many details to look for as you walk along the block.

Fountain with sun and giraffes by Greg Wyatt in Gramercy Park

Police Academy Museum **⑫**

235 E 20th St. **Map** 9 B4.
🅒 477-9753. **Ⓜ** 14th St-Union Sq.
Open 9am–2pm Mon–Fri.**Closed** Sat,
Sun, **public** hols, & for meetings – call
for appt. 📷

A COLORFUL SALUTE to "New
York's finest," the museum
possesses one of the largest
collections of police force
memorabilia anywhere. On
display are daily registers
describing liquor raids during
the Prohibition era,
sensational ax murders, bank
robberies and kidnappings.
There is a whole arsenal of
weapons – nightsticks, billy
clubs and an enormous gun
collection. Also on display are
antique uniforms and caps,
and every badge issued by
the Police Department since
1845. On a more somber
contemporary note, an
educational exhibit details the
tragic consequences of drug
addiction and youth gangs.

**Gangster Al Capone's gun at the
Police Academy Museum**

Stuyvesant Square **⑬**

Map 9 B5. **Ⓜ** 14th St-Union Sq.

T HIS OASIS, in the form of a
pair of parks divided by
Second Avenue, was part of
Peter Stuyvesant's original
farm in the 1600s. It was still
in the Stuyvesant family when
the park was designed in
1836; Peter G. Stuyvesant sold
the land to the city for the
nominal sum of $5 (much to
the delight of those living
nearby, who saw real estate
values jump). A statue of
Stuyvesant by Gertrude
Vanderbilt Whitney stands in
the park. The park separated
the Stuyvesant area from the
poorer Gas House district.

The towers of Con Edison (right), Metropolitan Life and the Empire State

Con Edison Headquarters **⑭**

4 Irving Pl. **Map** 9 A5. **Ⓜ** 3rd Ave,
14th St-Union Sq. **Museum** 🅒 460-
6244. **Open** 10am– 4pm Tue–Sat.
Guided tours by reservation. **Closed**
public hols.

T HE CLOCK TOWER of this
1911 building is a local
landmark. The Con Edison
Energy Museum
next door at 145
East 14th Street traces progress from Thomas Edison to
solar power. There is a working model of Edison's 1882
generator and a cutaway view
of underground New York.

Union Square **⑮**

Map 9 A5. **Ⓜ** 14th St-Union Sq.
Farmers' Market Wed, Sat.

Greenmarket day at Union Square

O PENED IN 1839, this park
joined Bloomingdale
Road (now Broadway) with
the Bowery Road (Fourth
Avenue or Park), and hence
its name. Later, the center of

the square was lifted up for a
subway to run beneath it.
The park became popular
with soapbox orators. During
the Depression in 1930, more
than 35,000 unemployed
people rallied here, before
marching on to City Hall to
demand jobs. The square
hosts a popular greenmarket
on Wednesdays and Satur-
days, when farmers bring
their produce to sell.

The Little Church Around the Corner **⑯**

1 E 29th St. **Map** 8 F3.
🅒 684-6770. **Ⓜ** 28th St. **Open**
7:30am–6pm daily. 🕇 11am Sun.
📷 ♿ 🎼 Sun after 11am service.
Lectures, concerts, recitals.

B UILT FROM 1849 to 1856, the
Episcopal Church of the
Transfiguration is a tranquil
retreat. It has been known by
its nickname since 1870 when
Joseph Jefferson tried to
arrange the funeral of fellow
actor George Holland. The
pastor at a nearby church
refused to bury a person of so
lowly a profession. Instead, he
suggested "the little church
around the corner." The name
stuck and the church has had
special ties with the theater
ever since. Sarah Bernhardt
attended services here.
The south transept window,
by John La Farge, shows
Edwin Booth playing Hamlet.
Jefferson's cry of "God bless
the little church around the
corner" is commemorated in a
window in the south aisle.

CHELSEA AND
THE GARMENT DISTRICT

THIS WAS FARMLAND in 1750, but by the 1830s it was a city suburb, and in the 1870s, with the coming of the elevated railroads *(see pp24–5)*, it had become quite commercial. Music halls and theaters lined 23rd Street. Fashion Row grew in the shadow of the El, with department stores serving middle-class New York. But, as fashion moved uptown, Chelsea drifted downhill. It became a warehouse district, until the Els were removed and New Yorkers rediscovered the charming 19th-century town houses. While Chelsea's fortunes were waning, Herald Square to the north was thriving, changing from bawdy to busy as Macy's arrived and New York's retailing and garment districts grew up around it.

Statue of garment worker, at 555 7th Avenue

Inside Chelsea's Empire Diner

SIGHTS AT A GLANCE

Historic Streets and Buildings
Empire State Building
pp134–5 2
General Post Office 7
General Theological
Seminary 10

Chelsea Historic District 11
Hugh O'Neill Dry Goods
Store 13

Churches
Marble Collegiate Reformed
Church 1
St. John the Baptist Church 5

Monuments
Worth Monument 14

Modern Architecture
Madison Square Garden 6
Jacob K. Javits Convention
Center 8

Parks and Squares
Herald Square 3

**Landmark Hotels and
Restaurants**
Empire Diner 9
Chelsea Hotel 12

Landmark Stores
Macy's 4

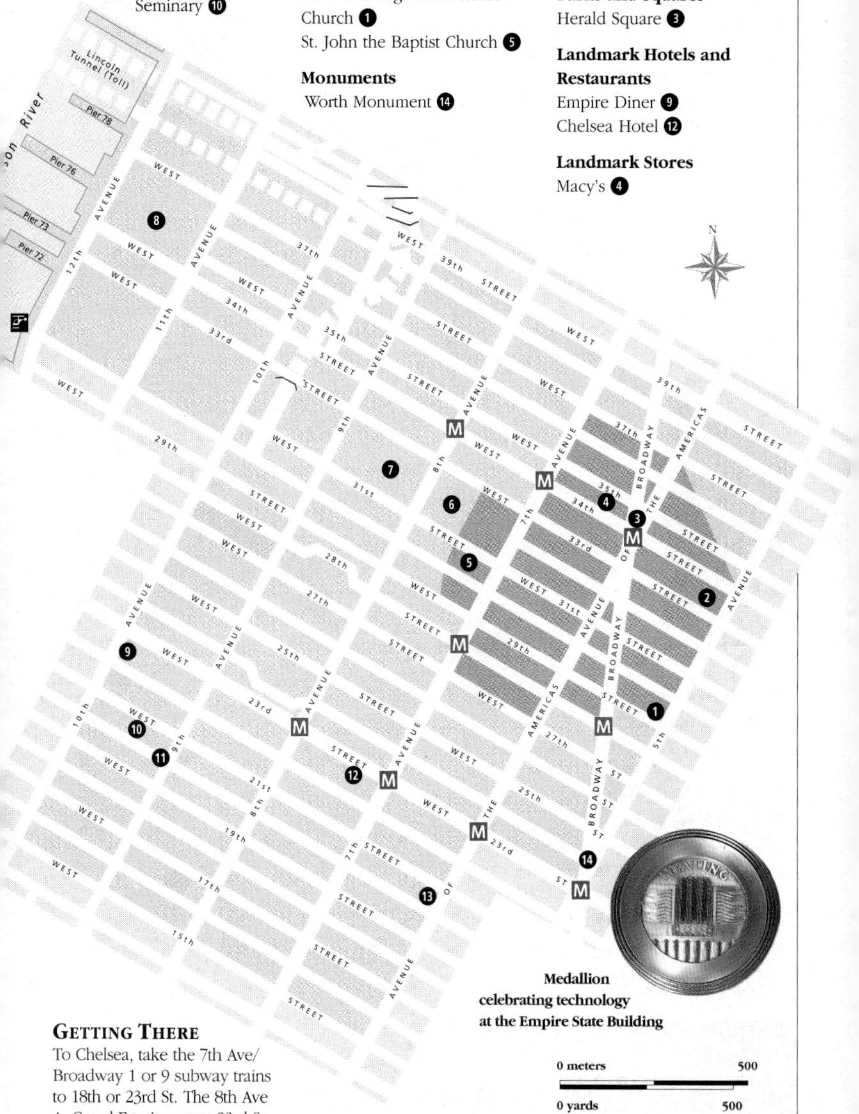

Medallion
celebrating technology
at the Empire State Building

GETTING THERE
To Chelsea, take the 7th Ave/
Broadway 1 or 9 subway trains
to 18th or 23rd St. The 8th Ave
A, C and E trains go to 23rd St.
Buses include the M10 and
M11, M14 or the M26
crosstown. To reach the area
around Macy's, take the 1 or 9
or the 2 or 3 express trains to
34th St/Penn Station. The 8th
Ave trains also stop at 34th St.

SEE ALSO
• *Street Finder*, maps 7–8
• *Where to Stay* pp274–5
• *Restaurants* pp290–92

0 meters   500
0 yards   500

KEY

Street-by-Street map

M Subway station

Heliport

Street by Street: Herald Square

HERALD SQUARE is named for the New York *Herald*, which had its office there from 1894 to 1921. Today full of shoppers, the area was once one of the raunchiest parts of New York. During the 1880s and '90s, it was known as the Tenderloin District and was filled with dance halls and bordellos. When Macy's opened in 1901, the focus moved from flesh to fashion. New York's Garment District now fills the streets near Macy's on and around Seventh Avenue, also known as Fashion Avenue. To the east on Fifth Avenue is the Empire State Building, with the city's best eagle's-eye views from the observation deck.

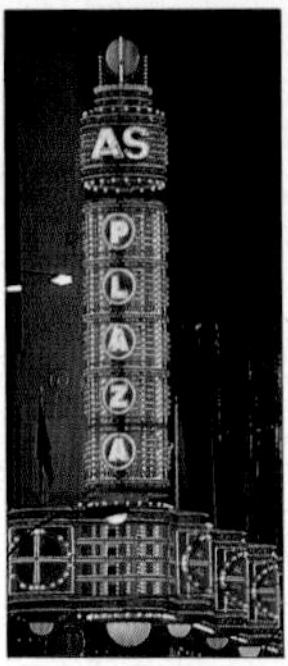

A&S Greeley Square Plaza is a branch of Brooklyn's Abraham & Straus. Once the site of Macy's arch-rival, Gimbel's, it was remodeled in 1988 for A&S.

Fashion Avenue is another name for the stretch of Seventh Avenue around 34th Street. This area is the heart of New York's garment industry. The streets are full of men pushing trolleys of clothes and furs.

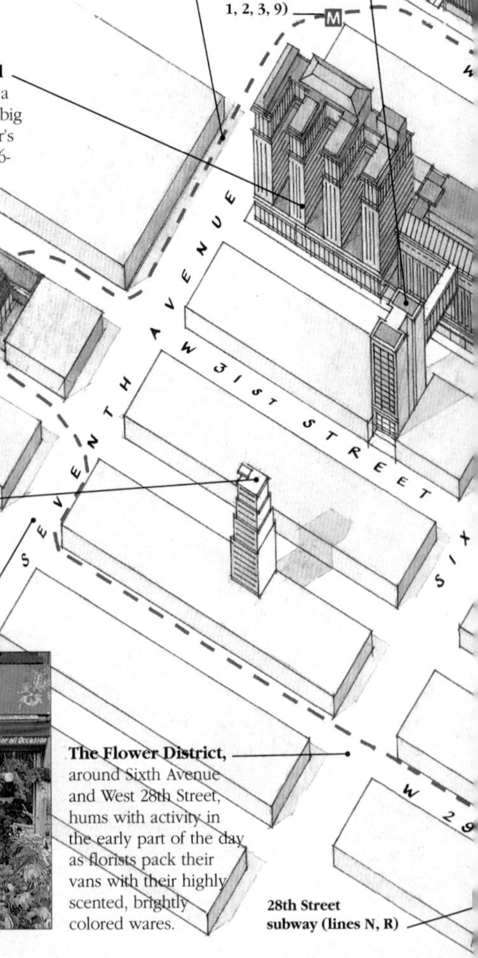

34th Steet-Penn Station subway (lines 1, 2, 3, 9)

The Ramada Hotel Pennsylvania was a center for the 1930s big bands – Glenn Miller's song "Pennsylvania 6-5000" made its telephone number famous.

St. John the Baptist Church
A beautiful set of carved Stations of the Cross is hung on the walls of the white marble interior of this church ❺

The SJM Building is at 130 West 30th Street. Mesopotamian-style friezes adorn the outside of the building.

The Fur District is at the southern end of the Garment District. Furriers ply their trade between West 27th and 30th streets.

The Flower District, around Sixth Avenue and West 28th Street, hums with activity in the early part of the day as florists pack their vans with their highly scented, brightly colored wares.

28th Street subway (lines N, R)

★ Macy's
The biggest department store in the world has something for everyone ④

The Greenwich Savings Bank (now the CrossLand Savings Bank) is a Greek temple to banking with huge columns on three sides.

34th Street subway (lines B, D, F, N, Q, R)

Herald Square
The New York Herald Building's clock now is situated where Broadway meets Sixth Avenue ③

LOCATOR MAP
See Manhattan Map pp12–13

KEY

- - - Suggested route

| 0 meters | 100 |
| 0 yards | 100 |

Greeley Square is more of a traffic island than a square, but it does have a fine statue of Horace Greeley, founder of the New York *Tribune*.

★ Empire State Building
The observation deck of this quintessential skyscraper is a great place to view the city ②

N

Little Korea is an area of Korean businesses. In addition to shops, there are restaurants nearby on West 31st and 32nd streets.

W 33RD STREET

The Life Building at 19 West 31st Street housed *Life* magazine when it was a satirical weekly. Carrère & Hastings designed the building in 1894. It is now a hotel (see p276).

Marble Collegiate Church
This 1854 church was built in the Gothic Revival style. It became famous when Norman Vincent Peale was pastor here ①

STAR SIGHTS

★ **Macy's**

★ **Empire State Building**

Marble Collegiate's Tiffany stained-glass windows

Marble Collegiate Reformed Church ❶

1 W. 29th St. **Map** 8 F3. 🄲 686-
2770. Ⓜ 28th St. **Open**
10am–noon, 2–4pm Mon–Fri,
9am–3pm Sat. 🔔 Sep–Jun: 11:15am
Sun; Jun–Sep: 10:30am Sun.
🚫 during services. ♿

THIS CHURCH is best known
for its former pastor
Norman Vincent Peale, who
wrote *The Power of Positive*

Thinking. Another positive
thinker, ex-president Richard
M. Nixon, attended services
here when he was a lawyer in
his pre–White House days.
 The church was built in
1854 using the marble blocks
that give it its name. At that
time, Fifth Avenue was a
dusty country road, and the
cast-iron fence around the
church kept livestock out.
 The original white and gold
interior walls were replaced
with a stenciled gold *fleur-de-
lis* design on a soft rust background. Two stained-glass
Tiffany windows, depicting Old
Testament scenes, were placed
in the south wall in 1893.

Empire State Building ❷

See pp134–5.

Herald Square ❸

6th Ave. **Map** 8 E2. Ⓜ 34th St-Penn
Station. See **Shopping** p313.

NAMED AFTER the New York
Herald, which occupied a
fine Stanford White building
here until 1921, the square

was the hub of the rowdy
Tenderloin district at the turn
of the century. The ornamental
clock is now all that is left of
the Herald Building.
 Herald Square is also the site
of the now-defunct Gimbel
Brothers Department Store,
once arch rival to Macy's. (The
rivalry was affectionately
portrayed in the New York
Christmas movie *A Miracle on
34th Street*). In 1988 the store
was converted into a vertical
mall with a glittery neon front.

A&S Plaza in Herald Square area

Macy's ❹

151 W. 34th St. **Map** 8 E2. 🄲 695-
4400 Ⓜ 34th St-Penn Station.
Open 9:45am–8:30pm Mon, Thu, Fri;
9:45am–6:45pm Tue, Wed;
10am–6:45pm Sat; 10am–6pm Sun.
See **Shopping** p311.

THE "WORLD'S LARGEST STORE"
covers a square block and
the merchandise inside covers
just about any item you could
imagine in every price range.
 Macy's was founded by a
former whaler named Rowland
Hussey Macy, who opened a
small store on West 14th Street
in 1857. The store's red star
logo came from Macy's tattoo,
a souvenir of his sailing days.
 By the time Macy died in
1877, his little store had grown
to a row of 11 buildings. It was
to expand further under two
brothers, Isidor and Nathan
Straus, who had operated
Macy's china and glassware
department. By 1902 Macy's
had outgrown its 14th Street
premises, and the firm
acquired its present site. The
eastern facade has a new

Macy's 34th Street facade

The nave of St. John the Baptist Church

entrance but still bears the bay windows and Corinthian pillars of the 1902 design. The 34th Street facade still has its original caryatids guarding the entrance, along with the clock, canopy and lettering.

The sea featured again in Macy's history in 1912 – a plaque by the main entrance commemorates the death of Isidor and his wife in the sinking of the *Titanic*.

Macy's sponsors New York's Thanksgiving Day parade and Fourth of July fireworks. The store's spring flower show draws thousands of visitors. But the recession has taken its toll even on this New York institution, and the 1990s have not been easy.

St. John the Baptist Church ❺

210 W. 31st St. **Map** 8 E3. 564-9070. 34th St-Penn Station. **Open** 6am–6pm daily. through-out the day. ⬛ ♿ ⬛

FOUNDED IN 1840 to serve a congregation of newly arrived immigrants, today this small Roman Catholic church is almost lost in the heart of the Fur District. The exterior has a single spire. Although the brownstone facade on 30th Street is dark with city soot, many treasures lie within this dull exterior. The entrance is through the modern Friary on 31st Street.

The sanctuary by Napoleon Le Brun is a marvel of Gothic arches in glowing white marble surmounted by gilded capitals. Painted reliefs of religious scenes line the walls; sunlight streams through the stained-glass windows. Also off the Friary is the Prayer Garden, a small, green and peaceful oasis with religious statuary, a fountain and stone benches.

Madison Square Garden ❻

4 Pennsylvania Plaza. **Map** 8 D2. 465-6741. 34th St-Penn Station. **Open** Mon–Sun, times vary according to shows. **Adm charge**. See **Entertainment** p344.

THERE'S ONLY ONE good thing to be said for the razing of the extraordinarily lovely McKim, Mead & White Pennsylvania Station building in favor of this undistinguished 1968 complex: it so enraged city preservationists that they formed an alliance to ensure that such a thing would never be allowed to happen again.

Madison Square Garden itself, which sits atop underground Pennsylvania Station, is a cylinder of precast concrete, functional enough as a 20,000-seat, centrally located home for the famous New York Knickerbockers (the Knicks) basketball and New York Rangers hockey teams. It also has a packed calendar of other events: rock concerts, championship tennis and boxing, outrageously staged wrestling, the Ringling Bros. and Barnum & Bailey Circus, an antiques show, a dog show and more. There is also a 5,600-seat theater.

In spite of some recent renovation work, Madison Square Garden lacks the panache of its earlier location, which combined a truly stunning Stanford White building with equally extravagant entertainment *(see p124)*.

The massive interior of Madison Square Garden

General Post Office ❼

421 8th Ave. **Map** 8 D2. 967-8585. 34th St-Penn Station. **Open** 24 hrs a day, every day, (incl public hols). See **Practical Information** p361.

DESIGNED BY McKim, Mead & White in 1913, in a style to complement their 1910 Pennsylvania Station across the street, the Post Office is a perfect example of a public building of the Beaux Arts period. The imposing, two-block-long structure has a broad staircase leading to a facade adorned with 20 Corinthian columns and a pavilion at each end. The 280-ft (85-m) inscription across it is loosely based on a description by Herodotus of the Persian Empire's postal service: "Neither snow nor rain nor heat nor gloom of night stays these couriers from the swift completion of their appointed rounds."

The Corinthian colonnade of the General Post Office

Empire State Building ❷

102nd-floor observatory

Empire State Building

Aᴌᴛʜᴏᴜɢʜ ɪᴛ ʟᴏsᴛ its title as the world's tallest building to the World Trade Center in the 1970s, the Empire State is still New York's most famous skyscraper, a symbol of the city all over the world. Construction began only weeks before the Wall Street Crash of 1929, and by the time it opened in 1931, space was so difficult to rent that it was nicknamed "the Empty State Building." Only the immediate popularity of the observatories saved the building from bankruptcy – to date, they have attracted more than 79 million visitors.

The Empire State was planned to be 86 stories high, but then a 150 ft (46 m) mooring mast for zeppelins was added. Now the mast transmits TV and radio to the city and four states.

Colored floodlighting of the top 30 floors marks special and seasonal events.

Symbols of the modern age are depicted on these bronze Art Deco medallions placed over the doorways.

Cᴏɴsᴛʀᴜᴄᴛɪᴏɴ
The building was designed for ease and speed of construction. Everything possible was prefabricated and slotted into place at a rate of about four stories per week.

High-speed elevators travel at up to 1,200 ft (366 m) a minute.

The framework is made from 60,000 tons of steel and was built in 23 weeks.

Aluminum panels were used instead of stone around the 6,500 windows. The steel trim masks rough edges on the facing.

Ten million bricks were used to line the whole building.

Eleven minutes is all it takes fit runners to race up the 1,860 steps from the lobby to the 102nd floor, in the annual Empire State Run-Up.

Sandwich space between the floors houses the wiring, pipes and cables.

Over 200 steel and concrete piles support the 365,000-ton building.

Sᴛᴀʀ Fᴇᴀᴛᴜʀᴇs

★ **Fifth Avenue Entrance Lobby**

★ **Views from 86th- and 102nd-floor Observatories**

★ Views from the Observatories

The 86th floor has outdoor observation decks for bird's-eye views of Manhattan. From the 102nd floor, 1,250 ft (381 m) high, you can see more than 80 miles (125 km) on a clear day, but check the visibility rating in the lobby first.

Sky Boy

Photographer Lewis Hine documented the workers' bravery during the 1930s construction. Here, a worker climbs up a cable. The wide Hudson River appears small in the background.

Empire State 1454 ft (443 m)

Eiffel Tower 1045 ft (319 m)

Great Pyramid 350 ft (107 m)

Big Ben 220 ft (67 m)

Pecking Order

New Yorkers are justly proud of their city's symbol, which towers above the icons of other countries.

Lightning Strikes

The Empire State is a natural lightning conductor, struck up to 500 times a year. The outside deck is closed during storms, the inside viewing area open.

★ Fifth Avenue Entrance Lobby

A relief image of the skyscraper is superimposed on a map of New York State in the marble-lined lobby.

ENCOUNTERS IN THE SKY

The Empire State Building has been seen in many films. However, the finale from the 1933 classic *King Kong* is easily its most famous guest appearance, as the giant ape straddles the spire to do battle with army aircraft. In 1945 a real bomber flew too low over Manhattan in fog and struck the building just above the 78th floor. The luckiest escape was that of a young elevator operator whose cabin plunged 79 floors to the basement. The emergency brakes saved her life.

Jacob K. Javits Convention Center ❽

655 W. 34th St. **Map** 7 B2. 📞 *216-2000.* Ⓜ *34th St-Penn Station.* **Opening times** *vary with shows.* **Closed** *on non-show days.* **Adm charge.** 🚫 ♿ 📷 🍴

The Convention Center – modern New York architecture at its best

S TRIKINGLY MODERNISTIC in appearance, this glass building facing the Hudson was designed by I.M. Pei to give New York the space for large-scale expositions. It has served its purpose well since it opened in 1986, hosting political conventions and such events as the annual automobile show that draws more than a million people. The 15-story building is constructed of 16,000 panes of glass, the two main halls can accommodate thousands of delegates and the lobby is high enough to hold the Statue of Liberty. In 1989 the final completion of the Galleria River Pavilion added another 40,000 sq ft (3,750 sq m) of dramatic open space and two new outdoor terraces that overlook the river.

The building is often used for fashion shoots and has been a setting for movies. By day the walls are opaque, but at night light glows brilliantly through the glass.

Empire Diner ❾

210 10th Ave. **Map** 7 C4. 📞 *243-2736.* Ⓜ *23rd St.* **Open** *24hrs daily.* See **Restaurants and Bars** *p306.*

T HIS ART DECO beauty is a faithful refurbishing of a classic 1929 American diner, complete with stainless steel bar and elegant black and chrome trim. Bette Davis reputedly declared it her favorite diner.

Its cuisine and clientele, however, are pure 1990s New York. At dawn on a Sunday morning it is bustling with the young and beautiful, who spill out of fashionable clubs and gravitate here to gossip over breakfast.

A 15th-century Gutenberg Bible from the Seminary's collection

General Theological Seminary ❿

20th–21st Sts. **Map** 7 C4. 📞 *243-5150.* Ⓜ *23rd St. or 34th St.-Penn Station.* **Open** *noon–3pm Mon–Fri, 11am–4pm Sat, 2–4pm Sun.* 🚫 ♿

F OUNDED IN 1817, this block-square campus accepts 150 students at a time to train for the priesthood. Clement Clarke Moore, a professor of Biblical Learning, donated the site, officially known as Chelsea Square. The earliest remaining building dates from 1836; the most modern, St. Mark's Library, was built in 1960 and holds the largest collection of Latin Bibles in the world.

The campus can be entered from Ninth Avenue only. Inside, the garden is laid out in two quadrangles like an English cathedral close: it is especially lovely in spring.

The Empire Diner before hungry club-goers arrive for breakfast

Chelsea Historic District ⓫

From 9th to 10th Aves. and from W. 20th to 21st Sts. **Map** 8 D5. **M** *18th St.*

ALTHOUGH HE is more well-known as the author of "A Visit from St. Nicholas" than as an urban planner, Clement Clarke Moore owned an estate here and divided it into lots in the 1830s creating handsome rows of town houses. Restoration has since rescued many of the original buildings.

Of these, the finest are seven houses known as Cushman Row, running from 406–418 West 20th Street, which were built from 1839–1840 for Don Alonzo Cushman. He was a merchant who also founded the Greenwich Savings Bank. He joined Moore and James N. Wells in the development of Chelsea. Rich in detail and intricate ironwork, Cushman Row is ranked with Washington Square North as supreme examples of Greek Revival architecture. Look for cast-iron wreaths around attic windows and the pineapples on the newel posts of two of the houses – old symbols of hospitality.

Farther along West 20th Street, from 446–450, there are fine examples of the Italianate style for which Chelsea is also renowned.

A house on Cushman Row

The detailed brickwork arches of windows and fanlights subtly implied the wealth of the owner, being able to afford this expensive effect.

Hugh O'Neill Dry Goods Store

Chelsea Hotel ⓬

222 W. 23rd St. **Map** 8 D4. **C** 243-3700. **M** *23rd St, 34 St.-Penn Station.*

FEW HOTELS ANYWHERE can match the Chelsea for artistic and literary heritage – and notoriety. Many of its former guests have been commemorated in the brass plaques on the hotel's facade.

A guest's-eye view of the Chelsea Hotel's cast-iron stairwell

They include Tennessee Williams, Mark Twain, Jack Kerouac and Brendan Behan. Dylan Thomas spent his last years here. In 1966, the hotel was the setting for the Andy Warhol movie *Chelsea Girls*, reviving its cult status, and in 1978 punk band member Sid Vicious killed his girlfriend in the hotel. For many, all this adds to the Chelsea's seedy mystique, and it still draws musicians, artists and writers who hope their names will one day be remembered.

Hugh O'Neill Dry Goods Store ⓭

655–671 6th Avenue. **Map** 8 E4. **M** *23rd St.*

THOUGH THE STORE is long gone, the 1876 cast-iron columned and pilastered facade clearly shows the scale and grandeur of the emporiums that once lined Sixth Avenue from 18th to 23rd streets, the area known as Fashion Row. O'Neill, whose sign can still be seen on the facade, was a showman and super-salesman whose trademark was a shiny fleet of delivery wagons. His customers came in droves via the conveniently close Sixth Avenue El. They were not the "carriage trade" enjoyed by Ladies' Mile *(see p125)*, but their numbers allowed the Row to flourish until the turn of the century, when the retailing district continued its move uptown. The grand buildings remain, and many are now under renovation. All it takes is a look upward to imagine what they were like in their heyday.

Worth Monument ⓮

5th Ave. **Map** 8 F4. **M** *34th St, 34th St-Penn Station.*

HIDDEN AWAY BEHIND a water meter on a triangle amid city traffic is an obelisk erected in 1857 to mark the grave of the one public figure to be buried under the streets of Manhattan. That honor belongs to General William J. Worth, a hero of the Mexican wars of the mid-1800s. A cast-iron fence of swords embedded in the ground surrounds the monument.

The Worth Monument

THEATER DISTRICT

IT WAS THE move of the Metropolitan Opera House to Broadway at 40th Street in 1883 that first drew lavish theaters and restaurants to this area. In the 1920s, movie palaces added the glamor of neon to Broadway, the signs getting bigger and brighter until the street became known as the "Great White Way."

Lee Lawrie design in Rockefeller Center

After World War II, the pull of the movies waned and glitter was replaced by grime. Now a redevelopment program has brought the public and the bright lights back. Pockets of calm also exist away from the bustle. Explore the Public Library or relax in Bryant Park. For the best of both worlds, though, visit Rockefeller Center.

Main Reading Room of the New York Public Library

SIGHTS AT A GLANCE

Historic Streets and Buildings

New York Yacht Club **5**
American Standard Building **7**
New York Public Library **8**
Times Square **9**
Group Health Insurance Building **11**
Paramount Building **12**
Shubert Alley **13**
Alwyn Court Apartments **18**

Museums

Intrepid Sea-Air-Space Museum **19**

Modern Architecture

Rockefeller Center **1**
MONY Tower **14**

Parks and Squares

Bryant Park **6**

Famous Theaters

Lyceum Theater **3**
New Amsterdam Theater **10**
City Center of Music and Drama **15**
Carnegie Hall **16**

Landmark Hotels and Restaurants

Algonquin Hotel **4**
Russian Tea Room **17**

Landmark Stores

Diamond Row **2**

GETTING THERE

Convenient subway routes are the 7th Ave/Broadway 1, 2, 3 and 9 trains to 50th or 42nd St, and N or R trains to 57th or 49th St. Other nearby lines include the 8th Ave A, C or E trains and 6th Ave, D, F or M trains. Bus routes through the area are the M5, M6, M7, M10, M34, M42, M50, M57 and the M58 Street crosstown.

KEY

▨ Street-by-Street map
Ⓜ Subway station
◧ Riverboat boarding point

SEE ALSO

- **Street Finder,** maps 8, 11–12
- **Where to Stay** pp274–75
- **Restaurants** pp290–92

0 meters   500

0 yards   500

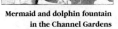

Mermaid and dolphin fountain in the Channel Gardens

Street by Street: Rockefeller Center

THE FIRST COMPLEX in the world to integrate offices with shops, entertainment, dining and gardens, Rockefeller Center is one of the most visited sights in New York. Night and day, throughout the year, the Center is alive with people. There are workers from some of the world's major companies, shoppers browsing in the stores and tourists admiring the wealth of American art and architecture. In winter skaters glide beneath the famous Christmas tree. You can rent skates and try it. The colorful flower displays change with the seasons.

The Winter Garden has housed hit revues and musicals since 1911.

Rockefeller Center expanded to the west in the 1960s, with a series of four towers providing a bland backdrop to the older buildings.

Equitable Center has the Roy Lichtenstein *Mural with Blue Brushstroke (1984–5)* in its lobby.

50th St subway (lines 1, 9)

Cort Theater has a facade based on the Petit Trianon at Versailles, and a bust of Marie Antoinette overlooking the ticket lobby. Both *The Diary of Anne Frank* and *Sarafina!* were premiered here.

George M. Cohan's statue, in front of the TKTS booth in Duffy Square, honors the man who wrote "Give My Regards to Broadway."

The Miller Building was "The Show Folks' Shoe Shop" before World War II. Four statues of American actresses by A. Stirling Cooper are all that remain to show for its former role.

Lyceum Theater
This is the oldest New York theater still in use, although it is "dark" more often than not these days. It was built in 1903 for producer Daniel Froman, who had an apartment in the building complete with a trap door looking down over the stage ❸

Detail from the facade of the Lyceum

Sun Triangle in the Lower Plaza mixes science and symbolism to show the relationship of the sun with the planets, using a reflecting pool and shining steel globes.

Radio City Music Hall
has a year-round schedule
of top entertainment, but
the high point is the
Christmas Spectacular
featuring the Rockettes
chorus line. *(See p333.)*

**47-50th St
subway (lines B,
D, F, Q)**

See Manhattan Map pp12–13

LOCATOR MAP
See Manhattan Map pp12–13

KEY

－－－　Suggested route

0 meters　　　　100

0 yards　　　　100

STAR SIGHTS

★ **Rockefeller Center**

★ **Diamond Row**

★ **Rockefeller Center**
*The towering General
Electric Building is the
"flagship" of the Center. It
is brilliantly lit at night* ❶

News, by Isamu
Noguchi, is a ten-ton
stainless steel panel at the
main entrance to the
Associated Press Building.

The ice rink at
Rockefeller Plaza
becomes a café
area in summer.

Atlas, by Lee
Lawrie, stands
in the main
entrance to
the International
Building. Cast in
bronze and weighing
4,000 lb (1,800 kg) it is
one of 12 works by
Lawrie in the Center.

**The Rainbow
Room**, atop the GE
Building, is the place
for a luxury night out,
dining and dancing in
a 1930s-style setting.
(See p341.)

**Channel
Gardens**
separates the
British Empire
Building and La
Maison Française.
It is a pleasant
place to sit and
relax amid the
floral displays
and fountains.

★ **Diamond Row**
*This block of West
47th Street is the hub
of New York's gem trade.
Almost every window
gleams with jewels* ❷

The Rockefeller Center, looking toward the General Electric Building

within the complex. It hosts dazzling shows and the annual Christmas show featuring the Rockettes, a perennial favorite.

Diamond Row ❷

47th St. **Map** 12 F5. **M** *47th–50th Sts. See* **Shopping** *p320.*

N EARLY EVERY SHOP window on 47th Street glitters with gold and diamonds. The buildings are filled with booths and workshops where jewelers vie for customers while, upstairs, millions of dollars change hands. The diamond district was born in the 1930s, when the Jewish diamond cutters of Antwerp and Amsterdam fled to America to escape Nazism. Hasidic Jews with black hats, beards and long sidelocks are still an integral part of the scene. Although mainly a wholesale district, individual customers are welcome. Bring cash, compare prices, haggle, and stay away if you know nothing about the value of diamonds. In the midst of all this, look for the sign saying "Wise men fish here" – here is the Gotham Book Mart, a tiny, much-loved treasure house of literary gems *(see p319).*

Diamond Row's main commodity

Rockefeller Center ❶

Map 12 F5. **M** *47th–50th Sts.*

W HEN THE New York City Landmarks Preservation Commission unanimously voted to declare Rockefeller Center a landmark in 1985, they rightly called it "the heart of New York . . . a great unifying presence in the chaotic core of midtown Manhattan."

It is the largest privately owned complex of its kind and the inspiration for dozens of cities that try to emulate its almost perfect urban mix. The Art Deco design was by a team of top architects headed by Raymond Hood. Works by 30 artists can be found in foyers, on facades, and in the gardens.

The site, once a botanic garden owned by Columbia University, was leased in 1928 by John D. Rockefeller, Jr., as an ideal central home for a new opera house. When

the 1929 Depression scuttled the plans, Rockefeller, stuck with a long-term lease, decided to go ahead with his own development. The 14 buildings that were erected between 1931 and 1940 provided jobs for 225,000 people during the worst of the Depression. More development between 1957 and 1973 brought the Center to a total of 19 buildings in all.

In December 1932, Radio City Music Hall opened

Wisdom by Lee Lawrie, on the GE Building

Lyceum Theater ❸

149 W 45th St. **Map** 12 E5. **C** *Telecharge 239-6200.* **M** *42nd St–5th Ave. See* **Entertainment** *p330.*

T HE OLDEST New York theater still active is a Baroque-style bandbox as frilly as a wedding cake. This 1903 triumph was the first theater by Herts and Tallant, later renowned for their extravagant style. The Lyceum made history with a record run of 1,600 performances of the comedy *Born Yesterday.* It was the first theater to be designated a historic landmark but, though it is safe from change, it is often dark now that the Theater District has shifted westward.

The Rose Room in the Algonquin Hotel

Algonquin Hotel ❹

59 W 44th St. **Map** 12 F5. ☎ *840-6800.* [M] *42nd St-5th Ave. See* ***Where to Stay*** *p278.*

THE EXTERIOR is a bit fussy – iron bay windows in vertical rows, red brick, too much detail – but it is the ambience, not the 1902 architecture, that makes the Algonquin special. In the 1920s, the Rose Room was home to America's best-known luncheon club, the Round Table, with literary lights such as Alexander Woollcott, Franklin P. Adams, Dorothy Parker, Robert Benchley and Harold Ross. All were associated with the *New Yorker* (Ross was the founding editor), whose 25 West 43rd Street headquarters had a back door opening into the hotel.

A recent renovation has preserved the old-fashioned, civilized feel of the Rose Room, as well as the cozy, paneled lobby where publishing types and theater-goers still like to gather for drinks, settling into comfortable armchairs and ringing a small brass bell to summon the waiters.

Statue of poet William Cullen Bryant in Bryant Park

New York Yacht Club ❺

37 W 44th St. **Map** 12 F5. [M] *42nd St-5th Ave.* ***Not open*** *to the public (access to members only).*

A WHIMSICAL 1899 creation, this private club has the carved sterns of 18th-century sailing ships in the three bay windows. The prows of the ships are borne up by sculpted dolphins and waves spilling over the windowsills and splashing down to the pavement.

This is the birthplace of the America's Cup yacht race, which was based in the US from 1857 to 1983. That was the year the much coveted prize was taken from the table where it had stood for more than a century, when the *Australia II* sailed to a historic victory.

The America's Cup, the coveted yachting prize

Bryant Park ❻

Map 8 F1. [M] *42nd St-5th Ave.*

IN 1853, WITH the New York Public Library site still occupied by Croton Reservoir, Bryant Park (then Reservoir Park) housed a dazzling Crystal Palace, built for the World's Fair of that year *(see p22).*

In the 1960s the park was a hangout for drug dealers and other undesirables. In 1989 the city closed and renovated it, reclaiming it for workers and visitors to relax in. Food is available at lunch-time, and a Music & Dance Tickets Booth *(see p329)* offers half-price seats for same-day performances.

Over three million library books lie in storage stacks beneath the park.

American Standard Building ❼

40 W 40th St. **Map** 8 F1. [M] *42nd St-Grand Central.* ***Not open*** *to the public.*

THIS WAS the first major New York work by Raymond Hood, who went on to design the News Building *(see p153)* and Rockefeller Center. The structure, from 1924, is reminiscent of the Gothic building Hood was best known for at that time, Chicago's Tribune Tower. Here, the design is sleeker, giving the building the illusion of being taller than its actual 21 stories. The black brick facade is set off by gold terra-cotta trim, evoking images of flaming coals: a comparison that would have suited its original owners well, since they made heating equipment. Stand across the street in Bryant Park to appreciate the striking golden tower top.

In 1989, the building was sold to a Japanese company. Their intention was to turn it into a hotel, but this did not happen and the building remains empty.

The American Standard Building seen from Bryant Park

The New York Public Library ❽

5th Ave and 42nd St. **Map** 8 F1.
📞 869-8089. Ⓜ 42nd St-Grand
Central. **Open** Tue–Sat; hours vary.
Closed public hols. 🅿 ♿ ✓
Lectures, workshops, readings. 📷

**The doorway leading to the Main
Reading Room**

I N 1897 THE COVETED JOB of
designing New York's main
public library was awarded to
architects Carrère & Hastings.
Their plan was influenced by
the library's first director. He
envisaged a light, quiet, airy
place for study, where millions
of books could be stored and
yet be available to readers as
promptly as possible. In the
hands of Carrère & Hastings,
his vision came true, in what
is considered the epitome of
New York's Beaux Arts period.

Built on the site of the
former Croton Reservoir *(see
p22)*, it opened in 1911 to
immediate
acclaim,
despite
having
cost the
city $9
million.

**One of the library's two stone lions, named
Patience and Fortitude by Mayor LaGuardia**

**Barrel vaults of carved
white marble over the
stairs in the Astor Hall**

The vast, paneled Main
Reading Room stretches
two full blocks and is
suffused with daylight
from the two interior
courtyards. Below it
are 88 miles (140 km)
of shelves, holding over
two million volumes.
A staff of over 100 and
a computerized dumb-
waiter can supply any
book within 10 minutes.

The Periodicals Room
holds 10,000 current
periodicals from 128
countries. On its walls
are murals by Richard
Haas, honoring New York's
great publishing houses. The
original library combined the
collections of John
Jacob Astor and James
Lenox. Its collections
today range from
Thomas Jefferson's
handwritten copy of
the Declaration of
Independence to
T.S. Eliot's typed
copy of "The
Waste Land." More
than 1,000 queries

**The Main Reading Room, with its
original bronze reading lamps**

are answered daily, using the
vast database of the CATNYP
computer catalog.

This library is the hub of a
network of 82 branches, with
nearly seven million users.
Some branches are very well
known, such as the New York
Public Library for the Performing Arts at the Lincoln Center
(see p210) and the Schomburg
Center in Harlem *(see p227)*.

Times Square, ablaze with neon

Times Square ❾

Map 8 E1. **M** *42nd St-Times Sq.*

KNOWN AS Longacre Square in the late 19th century, this was the home of horse traders, blacksmiths and stables, marking the edge of "Thieves' Lair," a haven for pickpockets. Oscar Hammerstein built the Victoria and Republic theaters in 1899; and the Republic later became Minsky's, featuring the stylishly scandalous Gypsy Rose Lee. Broadway blossomed, and Times Square became the heart of the Theater District.

The Depression ruined many theaters, and Broadway's "guys and dolls" were replaced by much sleazier types. The 1980s saw a huge civic plan to transform the square into a safe and vibrant place for theatergoers and tourists.

Times Square was named in 1904, after the 25-story *New York Times* tower. The *Times* moved in on New Year's Eve with a fireworks display, and the celebration has continued every year, with a countdown to midnight, when a lighted ball is lowered to mark the new year. Thousands jam the square to watch and millions more follow the events on television across the country.

In 1928, the *Times* posted election returns on the world's first moving sign, a band of 14,800 lights running around the building. The newspaper has moved on, but the ever-busy newswire remains.

New Amsterdam Theater ❿

214 W 42nd St. **Map** 8 E1.
M *42nd St-Times Sq.* **Not open** to the public.

W.C. Fields (far left) and Eddie Cantor (holding top hat, right) in the 1918 *Ziegfeld Follies* at the New Amsterdam Theater

THIS WAS the most opulent theater in the United States when it opened in 1903, and the first to have an Art Nouveau interior. It was owned for a time by Florenz Ziegfeld, who produced his famous *Follies* revue here between 1914 and 1918 – with Broadway's first $5 ticket price. He remodeled the roof garden into another theater, the Aerial Gardens. This is one of a row of fine early theaters on 42nd Street that fell on hard times and became second-rate movie houses. It is now dark, and almost derelict.

The Art Deco top of the Paramount Building

Group Health Insurance Building ⓫

330 W 42nd St. **Map** 8 D1. **M** *42nd St.* **Open** office hours.

THIS 1931 design by Raymond Hood was the only New York building selected for the influential International Style survey of 1932 *(see p41).* Its unusual design gives it a stepped profile seen from east and west, but a slab effect viewed from north or south. The exterior's horizontal bands of blue-green terra-cotta have earned it the nickname "jolly green giant." Step inside to see the classic Art Deco lobby of opaque glass and stainless steel.

One block west is Theater Row, a pleasant group of Off-Broadway theaters and cafés.

Paramount Building ⓬

1501 Broadway. **Map** 8 E1.
M *34th St.*

THE FABULOUS ground-floor movie theater where bobby-soxers stood in line in the 1940s to hear Frank Sinatra perform is gone, but there's still a theatrical feel to the massive building designed by Rapp & Rapp in 1927. On each side are symmetrical setbacks, 14 in all, rising like building blocks to an Art Deco crown – a tower, clock and globe. In the heyday of the "Great White Way," the tower was lit, with an observation deck at the top.

Shubert Alley ⓭

Between W 44th and W 45th St.
Map 12 E5. Ⓜ *42nd St-Times Sq.*

T HE PLAYHOUSES on the
streets west of Broadway
are rich in theater lore – and
in notable architecture. Two
classic theaters built in 1913
are the Booth (22 West 45th
Street), named after actor
Edwin Booth, and the Shubert
(221 West 44th), after theater
baron Sam S. Shubert. They
form the west wall of Shubert
Alley, where aspiring actors
lined up, hoping for a casting
in a Shubert play.

A *Chorus Line* ran at the
Shubert until 1990, for a
record 6,137 performances;
Katharine Hepburn starred
earlier in *The Philadelphia
Story.* Across from the 44th
Street end of the alley is the
St. James, where Rodgers and
Hammerstein made their
debut with *Oklahoma!* in
1941, followed by *The King
and I.* Nearby is Sardi's, the
restaurant where actors
waited for opening night
reviews. Irving Berlin staged
The Music Box Revue opposite
the other end of the alley in
1921. His Music Box Theater
has since housed many
famous shows.

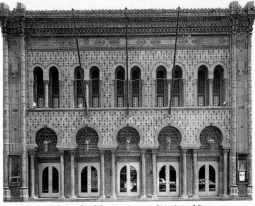

The tiled Moorish facade of the City Center of Music and Drama

MONY Tower ⓮

1740 Broadway. **Map** 12 E4.
Ⓜ *57th St.* **Not open** to the public.

B UILT IN 1950, the head office
of the Mutual of New York
insurance company (now
MONY Financial Services) has
a weather vane that tells you
everything except the wind
direction. The mast turns green
for fair, orange for cloudy,
flashing orange for rain and
white for snow. Lights moving
up the mast mean warmer
weather; lights going down
mean get out your overcoat!

City Center of Music and Drama ⓯

131 W 55th St. **Map** 12 E3.
🎫 581-7907. Ⓜ *57th St.* 🚫 ♿
▯ See **Entertainment** *p332.*

T HIS HIGHLY ornate Moorish
structure with its dome of
Spanish tiles was designed in
1924 as a Masonic Shriners'
Temple. It was saved from
the developers by Mayor La
Guardia, becoming home to
the New York City Opera and
Ballet in 1943. When the
troupes moved to Lincoln
Center, City Center lived on
as a major venue for dance.
Recent renovation work has
preserved the delightful
excesses of the architecture.

Carnegie Hall ⓰

154 W 57th Street. **Map** 12 E3.
🎫 903-9600. Ⓜ *57th St, 59th St.*
Museum open 11am–4:30pm daily
& during concerts. 🚫 ♿ 🎁 🍴 ▯
See **Entertainment** *p337–9.*

F INANCED BY millionaire
philanthropist Andrew
Carnegie, New York's first
great concert hall opened in
1891 in what was then a
suburb of the city. The
terra-cotta and brick Italian
Renaissance–style building is
said to have among the best
acoustics in the world. On
opening night, when
Tchaikovsky was a guest
conductor, all of New York's
finest families were in

Auditorium of the Shubert Theater, built by Henry Herts in 1913

attendance; they waited on line for up to an hour before they could alight from their horse-drawn carriages.

For many years Carnegie Hall was home to the New York Philharmonic, under such conductors as Arturo Toscanini, Leopold Stokowski, Bruno Walter and Leonard Bernstein. Playing Carnegie Hall quickly became an international symbol of success for both classical and popular musicians.

A campaign led by violinist Isaac Stern in the late 1950s saved the building from redevelopment as offices, and in 1964 the hall was made a national landmark. Interior renovation in 1986 brought the bronze balconies and the ornamental plaster back to their original splendor. The corridors are lined with memorabilia of artists who have performed here. In 1991, a museum opened adjacent to the first-tier level, telling the story of the illustrious first 100 years of "The House that Music Built."

Millionaire Andrew Carnegie

Today, top orchestras and performers from around the world still fill Carnegie Hall with their great music. A tour of the hall is also available.

Russian Tea Room ⓱

150 W 57th St. **Map** 12 E3. **⒞** 265-0947. **Ⓜ** 57th St. **Open** 11:30am–midnight Mon–Fri, 11am–midnight Sat & Sun. See **Restaurants and Bars** p303.

THIS IS A New York classic for Russian caviar, blinis and stargazing at the many show-business luminaries who dine here, especially at lunch. The lavish paintings, gleaming brass and red walls make it look like Christmas all year. The Tea Room has recently revived its upstairs

Interior of the Russian Tea Room on West 57th Street

cabaret, a popular spot in the 1930s and 1940s, which features popular singers in an intimate setting.

Alwyn Court Apartments ⓲

180 W 58th St. **Map** 12 E3. **Ⓜ** 57th St. **Not open** to the public.

YOU CAN'T miss it – not with the fanciful crowns, dragons and other French Renaissance-style terra-cotta carvings covering the exterior of this 1909 Harde and Short apartment building. The ground floor has been altered and lost its cornice in the process, but the rest of the building is intact, an intricate stone tapestry, and one of a kind in the city.

The facade follows the style of François I, whose reign saw the building of some of the finest Loire châteaux, and whose symbol, a crowned salamander, can be seen above the entrance at 58th Street.

Residents and their guests are fortunate to be able to

Salamander on Alwyn Court

enjoy the interior courtyard, which features a dazzling display of the illusionistic skills of artist Richard Haas, in which plain walls are transformed into "carved" stonework.

Flight deck of the *Intrepid*

Intrepid Sea-Air-Space Museum ⓳

Pier 86, W 46th St. **Map** 11 A5. **⒞** 245-2533. **⒡** 245-0072. **Ⓜ** 50th St. **Open** Jun–Aug: 10am–5pm daily; Sep–May: 10am–5pm Wed–Sun (last adm: 4pm). **Adm charge**. **⒧**

ON THE *Intrepid*, a World War II US aircraft carrier, the control room and flight decks are open for exploration. Exhibits range from real fighter planes from the 1940s to space-age wonders like the A12, fastest spy plane in the world. The *Growler*, a guided-missile submarine, and the destroyer *Edson* are also here.

Pioneers Hall traces the development of flying and the workings of today's super-carriers; Technologies Hall looks at ocean exploration and the rockets of the future.

LOWER MIDTOWN

FROM BEAUX ARTS to Art Deco, this section of midtown boasts some fine architecture. Quiet, residential Murray Hill was named for a country estate that once occupied the site. By the turn of the century, it was home to many of New York's first families, including the financier J.P. Morgan, whose library,

Brass door, Fred F. French Building

now a museum, reveals the grandeur of the age. The commercial pace quickens at 42nd Street, near Grand Central Terminal, where tall office buildings line the streets. However, few of the newer buildings have equaled the Beaux Arts Terminal itself or such Art Deco beauties as the Chrysler Building.

SIGHTS AT A GLANCE

Historic Streets and Buildings
Grand Central Terminal pp154–5 ❷
Home Savings of America ❸
Chanin Building ❹
Chrysler Building ❺
News Building ❻
Tudor City ❼
Helmsley Building ❽
Fred F. French Building ⓬
Sniffen Court ⓯

Museums and Galleries
Pierpont Morgan Library pp162–3 ⓮
Japan Society ⓫

Modern Architecture
MetLife Building ❶
Nos. 1 and 2 United Nations Plaza ❾
United Nations pp158–61 ❿

Churches
Church of the Incarnation ⓭

GETTING THERE
By subway, take the Lexington Avenue 4, 5 or 6 trains to 42nd Street–Grand Central. Buses M15, M101/102, M1, M2, M3 and M4 run along the area's avenues, while the M34 and M42 are the crosstown buses.

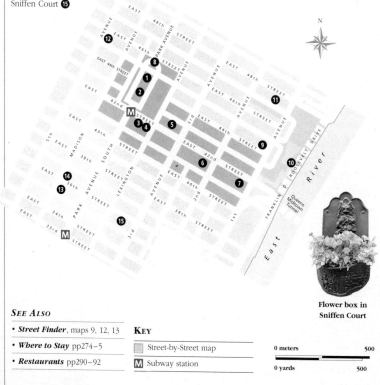

Flower box in Sniffen Court

SEE ALSO

- *Street Finder*, maps 9, 12, 13
- *Where to Stay* pp274–5
- *Restaurants* pp290–92

KEY

	Street-by-Street map
M	Subway station

0 meters 500
0 yards 500

The stainless-steel–coated spire of the Chrysler Building

Street by Street: Lower Midtown

A WALK IN THE neighborhood allows you to see an eclectic mix of New York's architectural styles. Step back to appreciate the contours of the tallest skyscrapers, and step inside to experience the many fine interiors, from modern atriums such as those in the Philip Morris Building and Ford Foundation buildings to the ornate details of the Home Savings Bank and the soaring spaces of Grand Central Terminal.

MetLife Building
This skyscraper, built by Pan Am in 1963, towers above Park Avenue. ❶

★ **Grand Central Terminal**
The vast, vaulted interior is a splendid reminder of the heyday of train travel ❷

The Philip Morris Building is the headquarters of a tobacco company. It houses a branch of the Whitney Museum, which specializes in modern American art.

Grand Central-42nd St. subway (lines S, 4, 5, 6, 7)

STAR SIGHTS

★ **Grand Central Terminal**

★ **Chrysler Building**

★ **Home Savings of America**

★ **Daily News Building**

Chanin Building
Built for self-made real estate mogul Irwin Chanin in 1922, this building has a fine Art Deco lobby ❹

The Mobil Building has a self-cleaning stainless steel facade that is embossed in geometric patterns to prevent it from warping. It was built in 1955.

Brass door, Home Savings Bank

★ **Home Savings of America**
Formerly the headquarters of the Bowery Savings Bank, this is one of the finest bank buildings in New York. Architects York & Sawyer designed it to resemble a Romanesque palace ❸

Helmsley Building
Its ornate entrance symbolized the wealth of the New York Central Railroad, the first occupants. It straddles Park Avenue near Grand Central **8**

Mailbox in the Chrysler Building

LOCATOR MAP
See Manhattan Map pp12–13

KEY

- - - -	Suggested route

0 meters 100

0 yards 100

★ **Chrysler Building**
Ornamented with automotive motifs, this Art Deco delight was built in 1930 for the Chrysler car company **5**

Worker resting during construction of the Chrysler Building

The Ford Foundation Building
is the headquarters of Ford's philanthropic arm. It has a lovely interior garden surrounded by a cube-shaped building made of pinkish gray granite, glass and steel.

Ralph J. Bunche Park

E 43RD STREET

E 42ND STREET

THIRD AVENUE

SECOND AVENUE

FIRST AVENUE

Daily News ★ **Building**
The Art Deco home of the newspaper has a revolving globe in the lobby **6**

Tudor City
This 1928 private residential complex has 3,000 apartments. Built in the Tudor style, it features fine stonework details **7**

MetLife Building ❶

200 Park Ave. **Map** 13 A5.
Ⓜ *42nd St-Grand Central.*
Open *office hours.* 🚻 🔏

Lobby of the MetLife Building

ONCE, THE SCULPTURES atop the Grand Central Terminal stood out against the sky. Then this colossus, formerly called the Pan Am Building and designed by Walter Gropius, Emery Roth and Sons and Pietro Belluschi, rose up in 1963 to block the Park Avenue view. It dwarfed the terminal and aroused universal dislike. At the time it was the largest commercial building in the world, and the dismay over its scale helped thwart a later plan to build a tower over the terminal itself.

It is ironic that the New York skies were blocked by Pan Am, a company that had opened up the skies as a means of travel for millions of people. When the company began in 1927, Charles Lindbergh, fresh from his solo trans-atlantic flight, was one of their pilots and an adviser on new routes. By 1936, Pan Am managed to introduce the first trans-Pacific passenger route, and in 1947 they introduced the first round-the-world route.

The building's famous roof-top heliport was abandoned in 1977 after a freak accident showered debris on to the surrounding streets. Now Pan Am itself has gone, too, and in 1981 the entire building was sold to the Metropolitan Life organization.

Grand Central Terminal ❷

See pp154–5.

Home Savings of America ❸

110 E 42nd St. **Map** 9 A1.
Ⓜ *42nd St-Grand Central.* **Open** *banking hours.*

MANY CONSIDER this 1923 building the best work of the best bank architects of the 1920s. York & Sawyer chose the style of a Romanesque basilica for the uptown offices of the venerable Bowery Savings Bank (now Home Savings of America). An arched entry leads into the vast banking room, with a high beamed ceiling, marble mosaic floors and marble columns that support the stone arches that soar overhead.

Facade of Home Savings of America building

Between the columns are unpolished mosaic panels of marble from France and Italy. The rich detailing includes symbolic animal motifs, such as a squirrel representing thrift and a lion for power.

Chanin Building ❹

122 E 42nd St. **Map** 9 A1.
Ⓜ *42nd St-Grand Central.*
Open *office hours.*

Stonework detail on the Chanin Building

ONCE THE headquarters of Irwin S. Chanin, one of New York's leading real estate developers, the 56-story tower was the first skyscraper in the Grand Central area, a harbinger of things to come. It was designed by Sloan & Robertson in 1929 and is one of the best examples of the Art Deco period. A wide bronze band, patterned with birds and fish, runs the full length of the facade; the terra-cotta base is decorated with a luxuriant tangle of stylized leaves and flowers. Inside, Radio City's sculptor René Chambellan worked on the reliefs and the bronze grills, elevator doors, mailboxes, clocks and pattern of waves in the floor. The vestibule reliefs chart the career of Chanin, who was a self-made man.

Carved detail in the banking hall of Home Savings of America

Chrysler Building 5

405 Lexington Ave. **Map** 9 A1.
682-3070. **M** *42nd St-Grand Central.* **Open** *office hours.*

Stainless steel gargoyle on the Chrysler Building

W ALTER P. CHRYSLER began his career in a Union Pacific Railroad machine shop, but his passion for the motor car helped him rise swiftly to the top of the new industry, to found, in 1925, the corporation bearing his name. His wish for a headquarters in New York that symbolized his company led to a building that will always be linked with the golden age of motoring. Following Chrysler's wishes, the stainless-steel Art Deco spire resembles a car radiator grill; the building's series of stepped setbacks are emblazoned with winged radiator caps, wheels and stylized automobiles; and there are gargoyles modeled on hood ornaments from the 1929 Chrysler Plymouth.

Though it lost the title of tallest building in the world to the Empire State Building only a few months after its completion in 1930, William Van Alen's 77-story Chrysler Building and its shining crown are still among the city's best-known and most-loved landmarks.

The crowning spire was kept a secret until the last moment, when, having been built in the fire shaft, it was raised into position through the roof, ensuring that the building would be higher than the Bank of Manhattan, then just completed downtown by Van Alen's great rival, H. Craig Severance.

Van Alen was poorly rewarded for his labors. Chrysler accused him of accepting bribes from contractors and refused to pay him. Van Alen's career never recovered from the slur.

The stunning lobby, once used as a showroom for Chrysler cars, was perfectly restored in 1978. It is lavishly decorated with patterned marbles and granite from around the world and has chromed steel trim. A vast painted ceiling by Edward

Elevator door at the Chrysler Building

Trumball shows transportation scenes of the late 1920s.

Although the Chrysler Corporation never occupied the building as their headquarters, their name remains, as firm a fixture as the gargoyles.

Entrance to the News Building

News Building 6

220 E 42nd St. **Map** 9 B1.
M *42nd St-Grand Central.*
Open *8am–6pm Mon–Fri.*

T HE *DAILY NEWS* WAS founded in 1919, and by 1925 it was a million-seller. It was known, rather scathingly, as "the servant girl's bible," for its concentration on scandals, celebrities and murders, its readable style and its heavy use of illustration. Over the years it has stuck to what it does best, and for years the formula paid off handsomely. It revealed stories such as the romance of Edward VIII and Mrs. Simpson, and has become renowned for its punchy headlines that sum up the mood of the moment. Though in recent years it has lost money, its circulation figures are still among the highest in the United States.

Its headquarters, designed by Raymond Hood in 1930, has rows of brown and black brick alternating with windows to create a vertical striped effect. Hood's lobby is familiar to many as that of the *Daily Planet* in the 1980s *Superman* movies. It includes the world's largest interior globe, an illuminated, rotating geography lesson with details constantly updated. Bronze lines on the floor indicate the direction of world cities and the position of the planets. At night, the intricate Deco detail over the front entrance of the building is lit from within by neon.

Grand Central Terminal ❷

IN 1871 CORNELIUS VANDERBILT opened a railway station on 42nd Street. Although often revamped, it was never large enough and was finally demolished. The present station opened in 1913. This Beaux Arts gem has been a gateway to and symbol of the city ever since. Its glory is the soaring main concourse and the way it separates auto, pedestrian and train traffic. The building has a steel frame covered with granites and marbles. Reed & Stem was in charge of the logistical planning; Warren & Wetmore for the overall design. It is now being restored by the architects Beyer Blinder Belle.

42nd Street colonnaded facade

Statuary on the 42nd Street Facade
Jules-Alexis Coutans sculptures of Mercury, Hercules and Minerva crown the main entrance.

Park Avenue ramp

Main concourse level

Subway

Cornelius Vanderbilt
The railway magnate was known as the "Commodore."

Commuters use the terminal. Half a million people pass through it each day. An escalator leads up into the MetLife Building, and other nearby buildings can be reached through tunnels.

STAR SIGHTS
★ **Grand Staircase**
★ **Main Concourse**
★ **Central Information**

Grand Central Oyster Bar
This popular restaurant, with its yellow Guastavino tiles, attracts over three million seafood lovers a year. But beware – the acoustics carry whispers from one corner to another (see p294).

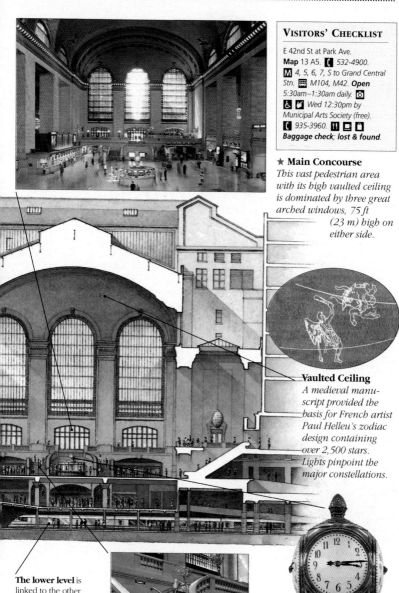

VISITORS' CHECKLIST

E 42nd St at Park Ave.
Map 13 A5. 532-4900.
4, 5, 6, 7, S to Grand Central
Stn. M104, M42. **Open**
5:30am–1:30am daily.
Wed 12:30pm by
Municipal Arts Society (free).
935-3960.
Baggage check; lost & found.

★ **Main Concourse**
This vast pedestrian area with its high vaulted ceiling is dominated by three great arched windows, 75 ft (23 m) high on either side.

Vaulted Ceiling
A medieval manuscript provided the basis for French artist Paul Helleu's zodiac design containing over 2,500 stars. Lights pinpoint the major constellations.

The lower level is linked to the other levels by stairways and by a clever system of ramps.

Grand Staircase ★
The double flight of marble steps, styled after the grand staircase in the Paris Opéra, is a vivid reminder of the glamorous days of early rail travel.

★ **Central Information**
This four-faced clock tops the travel information booth on the main concourse.

Tudor City 🄻

E. 42nd St. **Map** 9 B1.
Ⓜ *42nd St.-Grand Central.*

THIS EARLY URBAN renewal
effort, developed between
1925 and 1928 by the Fred
F. French Company, was
designed as a middle-class
city within the city. Rents
were modest, thanks to the
"large-scale production." There
are 12 buildings containing
3,000 apartments, a hotel,
shops, restaurants, a post office
and two small private parks, all
built in the Tudor Gothic style.
   Now a tranquil corner of
the modern city, in the mid-
19th century the area was the
haunt of criminals and was
known as Corcoran's Roost,
after Paddy Corcoran, the
leader of the notorious "Rag
Gang." The East River shore
was lined with glue factories,
slaughterhouses, breweries
and a gasworks. Some were
still there when Tudor City
was planned, so its buildings
have few outward-facing
windows from which residents
might enjoy what is
now a great view
of the river.

Upper stories of Tudor City

Helmsley Building 🄼

230 Park Ave. **Map** 13 A5.
Ⓜ *42nd St-Grand Central.* **Open**
office hours.

ONE OF THE GREAT New
York views looks south
down Park Avenue to the
Helmsley Building straddling
the busy traffic flow beneath.
There is just one flaw – the
monolithic MetLife Building
(which was built by Pan Am
as its corporate headquarters

Performance at the Japan Society

in 1963) that towers behind it,
replacing the building's
former backdrop, the sky.
   Built by Warren & Whetmore
in 1929, the Helmsley Building
was originally the headquarters
of the New York Central Railroad Company. Its current
owner is aging property
magnate Harry
Helmsley, a
billionaire who
began his career
as a New York
office boy for
$12 per week.
Helmsley is
perhaps best
known for his
wife, Leona,
who was a
prominent
feature in all the advertisements for their hotel chain –
until her imprisonment in
1989 for tax evasion on a
grand scale. Many observers
believe that the extravagant
glitter of the building's
face-lift is due to
Leona's over-
blown taste
in decor.

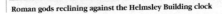

Roman gods reclining against the Helmsley Building clock

---

1 & 2 United Nations Plaza 🄽

Map 13 B5. Ⓜ *42nd St.-
Grand Central.*

THESE TWO
GREAT columns
of lovely blue-
green mirrored
glass are set at an
angle to each other;
the play of light and reflections
on their gleaming sides and
sloping setbacks make them
seem an ever-changing,
giant work of modern art.
The marble and mirrored
interiors are also stunning.
They house streamlined
modern offices and, in
No. 1, the United
Nations Plaza Hotel
(see p280). Here,
the guest list
frequently
includes many UN delegates
from all over the world as
well as a number of visiting
heads of state. Even the
stresses of international
diplomacy must ease when
one is floating lazily in the
glassed-in swimming pool,
enjoying the bird's-eye views
of the city and the United
Nations itself.

United Nations 🄾

See pp158–61.

Japan Society 🄿

333 E 47th St. **Map** 13 B5.
Ⓒ *832-1155.* Ⓜ *42nd St.-Grand
Central.* **Gallery open** *11am–5pm
Tue–Sun.* 🚫 ♿ 📷

THE HEADQUARTERS of the
Japan Society, which was
founded in 1907 to foster
understanding and cultural
exchange between Japan
and the United States,
was underwritten
by John D.
Rockefeller
III at a cost

of some $4.3 million. The striking black building with its delicate sun grilles was designed by Tokyo architects Junzo Yoshimura and George Shimamoto in 1971. It includes an auditorium, a language center, a research library, a museum gallery and serene, traditional Oriental gardens.

Changing exhibits open to the public include a variety of Japanese arts, from swords to kimonos to scrolls. The society offers programs of Japanese performing arts, lectures, language classes and many business workshops for American and Japanese executives and managers.

Fred F. French Building ⓬

521 5th Ave. **Map** 12 F5.
Ⓜ *42nd St.-Grand Central.* **Open** *office hours.*

Built IN 1927 to house the best-known real estate firm of the day, this is a fabulously opulent creation. It was designed by French's chief architect, H. Douglas Ives, in collaboration with Sloan & Robertson, whose other work included the Chanin Building *(see p152)*. They handsomely blended Near Eastern, ancient Egyptian and Greek styles with early Art Deco forms.

Multicolored faïence ornaments decorate the upper facade, and the water tower is hidden in a false top level of the building. Its disguise is an elaborate one, with reliefs showing a rising sun flanked by griffins and bees and symbols of virtues such as integrity and industry. Winged Assyrian beasts ride on a bronze frieze over the entrance. These exotic themes continue into the vaulted lobby, with its elaborate polychrome ceiling decoration and 25 gilt-bronze doors.

This was the first building project to employ members of the Native Canadian Caughnawaga tribe as construction workers. They did not fear heights and soon became highly sought-after scaffolders for many of the city's most famous skyscrapers.

Tiffany stained-glass window in the Church of the Incarnation

Lobby of the Fred F. French Building

Church of the Incarnation ⓭

205 Madison Ave. **Map** 9 A2.
☎ *689-6350.* Ⓜ *42nd St.-Grand Central.* **Open** *11:30am–1pm Mon–Wed, Fri.* 🕆 *11am Sun.* 📷
🚻 *By appointment.* 🎫

This EPISCOPAL church and its parish house date from 1864, when Madison Avenue was home to the elite. Its patterned sandstone and brownstone exterior is representative of the period.

The interior includes an oak communion rail by Daniel Chester French; a chancel mural, *Adoration of the Magi*, by John La Farge; and stained-glass windows by La Farge, Louis Comfort Tiffany, William Morris and Edward Burne-Jones.

Pierpont Morgan Library ⓮

See pp162–3.

Sniffen Court ⓯

150–158 E 36th St. **Map** 9 A2.
Ⓜ *33rd St.*

Here IS a delightful, intimate courtyard of ten brick Romanesque revival carriage houses, built by John Sniffen in the 1850s.

They are perfectly and improbably preserved off a busy block in modern New York. The house at the south end was used as a studio by the American sculptor Malvina Hoffman, whose plaques of Greek horsemen decorate the exterior wall.

Malvina Hoffman's studio

United Nations ⑩

Founded in 1945 near the end of World War II with 51 members, the United Nations now numbers some 180 nations. Its aims are to preserve world peace, promote self-determination and to aid economic and social well-being around the globe. New York was chosen as the UN headquarters when John D. Rockefeller, Jr. donated $8.5 million for the purchase of the East River site. The chief architect was American Wallace Harrison, who worked with an international Board of Design Consultants. The 18-acre (7-ha) site is not on US territory. It is an international zone and has its own stamps and post office. Daily guided tours show visitors the various council chambers and General Assembly hall.

Flag of the United Nations

United Nations headquarters

Secretariat building

The Conference Building houses meeting rooms for the Security Council, the Trusteeship Council and the Economic and Social Council.

Trusteeship Council

★ **Security Council**
Delegates and their assistants confer around the horseshoe-shaped table while verbatim reporters and other UN staff members sit at the long table in the center.

Economic and Social Council

STAR FEATURES

★ **General Assembly**

★ **Security Council**

★ **Peace Bell**

★ **Reclining Figure**

★ **Peace Bell**
Cast from the coins of 60 nations, this gift from Japan hangs on a cypress pagoda shaped like a Shinto shrine.

Rose Garden
Twenty-five varieties of roses adorn the manicured gardens on the East River.

★ Reclining Figure *(1982)*
This bronze statue was a gift from the Henry Moore Foundation.

General ★ Assembly
This is the only UN organ in which all member states are represented. One regular, three-month session is held each year.

Colors of the World
Flags of member nations fly in front of the UN complex.

Non-Violence *(1988)*
Luxembourg donated this peace sculpture by Swedish artist Karl Fredrik Reuterswärd.

The statue of peace was a gift from Yugoslavia.

Visitors' entrance

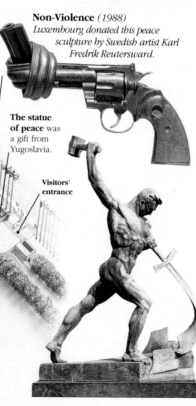

Let Us Beat Swords Into Plowshares
This bronze statue (1958) by Soviet sculptor Evgeny Vuchetich symbolizes the main goal of the United Nations.

The Work of the United Nations

THE GOALS of the United Nations are pursued by three UN councils and a General Assembly comprising all member nations. The Secretariat carries out the administrative work of the organization. Guided tours allow visitors to see the Security Council Chamber and General Assembly Hall.

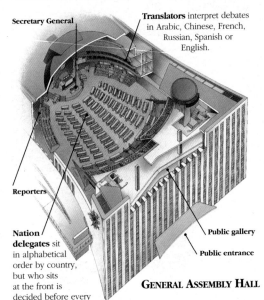

Secretary General

Translators interpret debates in Arabic, Chinese, French, Russian, Spanish or English.

Reporters

Nation delegates sit in alphabetical order by country, but who sits at the front is decided before every session by drawing lots.

Public gallery

Public entrance

GENERAL ASSEMBLY HALL

GENERAL ASSEMBLY

THE GENERAL ASSEMBLY is the governing body of the UN and has regular sessions each year from mid-September to mid-December. Special sessions are also held when the Security Council or a majority of members request one. All member states are represented with an equal vote, regardless of size. The General Assembly may discuss any international problem raised by the members or by other UN bodies. Although it cannot enact laws, recommendations strongly influence world opinion; these require a two-thirds majority vote.

Lots are drawn before each session to determine the seating in the chamber for the delegations. All 2,070 seats in the chamber are equipped with earphones that offer simultaneous translations in

several languages. The General Assembly also appoints the Secretary General (on the recommendation of the Security Council), approves the UN budgets and elects the non-permanent members of

Foucault's Pendulum (Holland); its slowly rotating swing is proof of the earth's rotation on its axis

the Councils. Together with the Security Council, it also appoints the judges of the International Court of Justice, based in the Netherlands.

SECURITY COUNCIL

THE MOST POWERFUL part of the UN is the Security Council. It strives to achieve

Mural symbolizing peace and freedom by Per Krohg (Norway)

international peace and security and intervenes in crises such as the fighting in Kuwait and the former Yugoslavia. It is the only body whose decisions member states are obliged to obey as well as the only one in continuous session.

Five of its members – China, France, the Russian Federation, the United Kingdom and the United States – are permanent. The other nations are elected by the General Assembly to serve two-year terms.

When international conflicts arise, the Council first tries to seek agreement by mediation. If fighting breaks out, it may issue cease-fire orders and impose military or economic sanctions. It could also decide to send UN peace-keeping missions into troubled areas to separate opposing factions until issues can be resolved through diplomatic channels.

Military intervention is the Council's last resort. UN forces may be deployed, and peace-keeping forces are resident in such places as Cyprus and the Middle East.

TRUSTEESHIP COUNCIL

THE SMALLEST OF the councils, this is the only UN body whose workload is decreasing. The council was established in 1945 with the goal of fostering peaceful independence for non–self-governing territories or colonies. Since then, more than 80 colonies have gained self-rule, and the number of people living in dependent territories has been reduced from 750 million to about 3 million. The council currently consists of the five permanent members of the Security Council.

Zanetti mural (Dominican Republic) in the Conference Building depicting the struggle for peace

plays a key role as a spokesperson in the organization's peace-keeping efforts. The Secretary General is appointed by the General Assembly for a five-year term.

military support from members. As a result, it has had successes and failures in its efforts to keep the peace. In 1948, the UN declared South Korea the legitimate government of Korea; two years later, it played a leading role in defending South Korea against the invading North Korean armies. In 1949, the UN helped negotiate a cease-fire between Indonesia and the Netherlands and set up a conference that led to the Dutch granting independence to Indonesia. In 1974, the People's Republic of China – long refused membership in favor of Taiwan – gained UN membership, restoring it to the international community.

Trusteeship Council Chambers

ECONOMIC AND SOCIAL COUNCIL

THE 54 MEMBERS OF this Council work to improve the standard of living and social welfare around the world, goals that consume 80% of the UN's resources. It makes recommendations to the General Assembly, to each member nation and to the UN's specialized agencies. The Council is assisted by commissions dealing with regional economic problems, human rights abuses, population, narcotics and women's rights. It also works with the International Labor Organization, the World Health Organization, UNICEF and other global welfare organizations.

SECRETARIAT

AN INTERNATIONAL STAFF of 16,000 works for the Secretariat to carry out the day-to-day work of the United Nations, providing services to all UN councils, commissions and agencies. The Secretariat is headed by the Secretary General, who

IMPORTANT EVENTS IN UN HISTORY

Soviet premier Krushchev speaking to the General Assembly in 1960

WITH NO PERMANENT police force to deal with disputes, the UN depends on voluntary compliance and

The most persistent problems have been in the Middle East. When Israel was invaded by five Arab nations after it was declared a state in 1948, the UN negotiated a cease-fire; UN forces have been present in the area since 1974, but the Palestinians' status is unresolved.

The UN was instrumental in negotiating the independence of Cyprus from Britain in 1957, and in 1964 it created a UN military force in Cyprus to keep peace between the Greeks and Turks.

WORKS OF ART AT THE UN

The UN Building has acquired numerous works of art and reproductions by major artists; many have been gifts from member nations. Most of them have either a peace or international friendship theme. The legend on Norman Rockwell's *The Golden Rule* reads "Do unto others as you would have them do unto you." Marc Chagall designed a large stained-glass window as a memorial to former Secretary General Dag Hammarskjöld, who was accidentally killed while on a peace mission in 1961. A Henry Moore sculpture graces the grounds. There are many other sculptures and paintings by the artists of many nations.

The Golden Rule (1985), a large mosaic by Norman Rockwell

Pierpont Morgan Library 🄮

T HE PIERPONT MORGAN LIBRARY came into being
as the private collection of banker J. Pierpont
Morgan. In 1902, architects McKim, Mead & White
designed a magnificent palazzo-style building to
house it. Morgan's son, J. Pierpont Morgan, Jr.,
established the library as a public institution in
1924. Today it has one of the world's finest
collections of rare manuscripts, books and prints,
displayed in a complex that includes the original
library and J.P. Morgan, Jr.'s home.

Exterior of the original library building

★ **Garden Court**
*This three-story skylit garden
area links the library with
the Morgan house.*

**Morgan
House**

Key to Floor Plan

☐ Exhibition space

☐ Non-exhibition space

**The Pied Piper of
Hamelin** *(1887)*
*Kate Greenaway's vision
of Robert Browning's
poem is one of her
finest works.*

**Forecourt
Gallery**

The Nursery Alice
*Lewis Carroll's characters
are immortalized in John
Tenniel's classic illus-
trations (c. 1865).*

Exhibition Room

Star Exhibits

★ **Livre de la Chasse**

★ **Adam and Eve by
Albrecht Dürer**

★ **Garden Court**

★ **Manuscript of
Mozart's Horn Con-
certo in E-flat Major**

Puss-in-Boots *(1695)*
*This is an original page
from the* Tales of Mother
Goose *by Charles Perrault.*

VISITORS' CHECKLIST

29 E. 36th St. **Map** 9 A2.
📞 685-0008. Ⓜ 6 to 33rd St.
🚌 M1, M2, M3, M4.
Open 10:30am–5pm Tue–Sat;
1pm–5pm Sun (last adm: 4:50pm).
Closed Jan 1, Jul 4, Thanksgiving,
Dec 25. **Adm charge.** 🚫 ♿ 🎧
Concerts, lectures, film/video
presentations. 🎞

LIBRARY GUIDE
Mr. Morgan's Study and the original library contain some of his favorite paintings, objets d'art and rare acquisitions. Medieval manuscripts and early books are in the Exhibition Room. The children's books are in the Forecourt Gallery.

★ Mozart's Horn Concerto in E-flat Major
The six surviving leaves of this score are written in different colored inks.

West Room
(Mr. Morgan's study)

Rotunda

Main entrance

East Room
The walls are lined from floor to ceiling with triple tiers of bookcases. Murals show historical figures and their muses, and signs of the zodiac.

★ Adam and Eve (1504)
One of Albrecht Dürer's most celebrated works, this drawing reflects his quest for the perfect representation of the human figure.

★ Livre de la Chasse
This copy of Gaston Phébus's illustrated book on hunting was made in about 1410.

J. PIERPONT MORGAN
J.P. Morgan (1837–1913) was not only a leading financier but also one of the great collectors of his time. Rare books and original manuscripts were his passion, and inclusion in his collection was an honor. In 1909, when Morgan requested the donation of the manuscript of *Pudd'nhead Wilson*, Mark Twain responded, "One of my high ambitions is gratified."

UPPER MIDTOWN

U PMARKET NEW YORK in all its diversity is here, in this area of churches, synagogues, clubs, museums, luxury hotels, famous stores, trend-setting skyscrapers and pockets of luxury living. For almost 30 years from 1833, it was home to society names

1946 Cisitalia in the MoMA

such as Astor and Vanderbilt. In the 1950s, architectural history was made when the Lever and Seagram buildings were erected. These first great modern towers marked midtown Park Avenue's change from a residential street to a prestigious office address.

SIGHTS AT A GLANCE

Historic Streets and Buildings
Villard Houses **9**
General Electric Building **11**
Sutton Place and Beekman Place **17**
Roosevelt Island **18**
Fuller Building **20**

Modern Architecture
Trump Tower **2**
IBM Building **3**
Lever House **13**
Seagram Building **14**
Citicorp Center **15**

Museums and Galleries
Museum of Modern Art (MoMA) pp170–73 **5**
American Craft Museum **6**

Museum of Television and Radio **7**

Churches and Synagogues
St. Thomas' Church **4**
St. Patrick's Cathedral pp176–7 **8**
St. Bartholomew's Church **10**
Central Synagogue **16**

Landmark Hotels
Waldorf–Astoria **12**
Plaza Hotel **21**

Landmark Stores
Fifth Avenue **1**
Bloomingdale's **19**

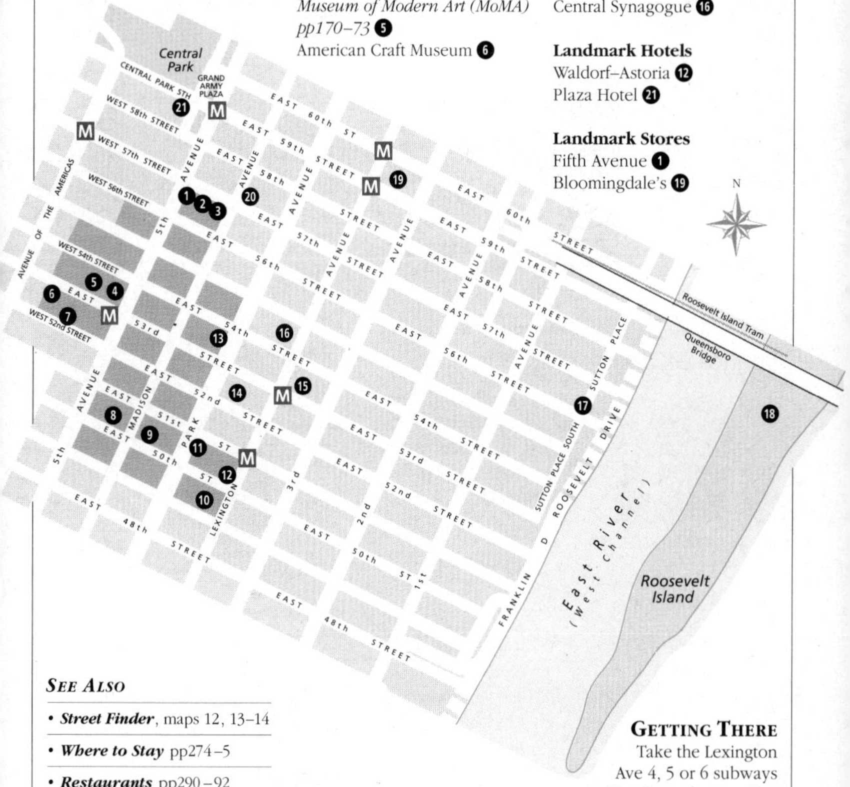

SEE ALSO

• *Street Finder*, maps 12, 13–14

• *Where to Stay* pp274–5

• *Restaurants* pp290–92

0 meters	500
0 yards	500

KEY

▨ Street-by-Street map

Ⓜ Subway station

GETTING THERE
Take the Lexington Ave 4, 5 or 6 subways to 51st St, or the E or F to 5th Ave. Bus routes are the M15, M101/102 and M1, M2, M3 and M4. Crosstown buses are the M50, M57 and M58.

View down Fifth Avenue

Street by Street: Upper Midtown

THE LUXURY STORES that are synonymous with Fifth Avenue first blossomed as society moved on uptown. In 1917, Cartier's acquired the mansion of banker Morton F. Plant in exchange for a string of pearls, setting the style for other retailers to follow. But this stretch of midtown is not simply for shoppers. There are three distinctive museums and an equally diverse assembly of architectural styles to enjoy, too.

Fifth Avenue
Today's carriage rides offer a taste of past elegance ❶

The University Club was built in 1899 as an elite club for gentlemen.

American Craft Museum
This is a showcase for crafts – from ceramics to furniture ❻

St. Thomas' Church
Much of the interior carving was designed by sculptor Lee Lawrie ❹

★ **Museum of Modern Art**
This is one of the finest collections of modern art in the world ❺

Museum of Television and Radio
Exhibitions, seasons of special screenings, live events and a vast library of historic broadcasts are offered at this media museum ❼

Fifth Avenue subway (lines E, F)

Saks Fifth Avenue has offered goods in impeccable taste to generations of New Yorkers. *(See p311.)*

★ **St. Patrick's Cathedral**
This, the largest Catholic cathedral in the United States, is a magnificent Gothic Revival building ❽

Olympic Tower
combines offices, apartments and a skylit atrium within its sleek walls.

Villard Houses
Five handsome brownstone houses now form part of the New York Palace Hotel ❾

STAR SIGHTS

★ Museum of Modern Art

★ St. Patrick's Cathedral

Trump Tower
Donald Trump's tower houses many expensive shops ❷

Paley Park is a tiny green oasis, known as a "vest-pocket" park.

LOCATOR MAP
See Manhattan Map pp12–13

KEY
--- Suggested route

0 meters 100
0 yards 100

IBM Building
A restful atrium is to be found at the base of this polished black granite building ❸

Sony Building has a very distinctive "chippendale" top.

Lever House
This building is one of the most prominent "glass-box" buildings in New York ⓭

N

Tiffany & Company is renowned for its discreet luxury. The store contains many precious jewels. *(See p321.)*

Park Avenue Plaza is a bulky glass prism containing an airy atrium.

Racquet Club, a Renaissance palazzo–style building, provides squash and tennis courts for its members.

General Electric Building
The spiky pinnacle of this building, built in 1931, is meant to symbolize electrical waves ⓫

St. Bartholomew's Church
A Byzantine dome sets this place apart from other midtown churches ❿

51st Street subway (line 6)

Waldorf-Astoria
Old-world elegance has attracted many famous guests to this hotel, including the late Duke and Duchess of Windsor ⓬

Window display at Bergdorf Goodman *(see p311)*

Fifth Avenue **1**

Map 4 F1–16 E1. **M** *5th Ave-53rd St.*

In 1883, when William Henry Vanderbilt built his mansion at Fifth Avenue and 51st Street, he started a trend that resulted in palatial residences stretching as far as Central Park, built for top families such as the Astors, Belmonts and Goulds. Only a few remain to attest to the grandeur of the era.

One of these is the Cartier store at 651 Fifth Avenue, originally the home of Morton F. Plant, millionaire and commodore of the New York Yacht Club. As retailers swept north up the avenue – a trend that began in 1906 – society gradually moved to better locations uptown. In 1917, Plant moved to a new mansion at 86th Street, and legend has it that he traded his old home to Pierre Cartier for a perfectly matched string of pearls.

Fifth Avenue has been synonymous with luxury goods ever since. From Cartier at 52nd Street to Tiffany and Bergdorf Goodman at 57th, you will find a range of famous brands symbolizing wealth and social standing today, just as Vanderbilt and Astor did more than a century ago.

Trump Tower **2**

725 5th Ave. **Map** 12 F3.
C 832-2000. **M** *5th Ave-53rd St.*
Garden level, shops open 10am–6pm
Mon–Sat. **Building open** 8am–10pm
daily. See **Shopping** *p311.*
◯ ⬤ *Concerts.* **⬛ ⬛ ⬛**

A glittering, exorbitantly expensive apartment and office tower rises above a lavish six-story atrium with layer upon layer of exclusive shops and cafés. Designed in 1983 by Der Scutt of Swanke, Hayden, Connell & Partners, the public space is lavished with pink marble, a waterfall, mirrors and glitz. It is the most opulent example of the new urban trend toward vertical shopping centers. The tower is a flamboyant monument to affluence by the developer Donald Trump, a symbol of the excesses of the 1980s.

Next door, 727 Fifth is a complete contrast: Tiffany & Co., the prestigious jewelers founded in 1837. Famed for its exquisite window displays, the store uses understated but elegant blue packaging as a status symbol in itself. Tiffany's was immortalized in New York culture by Truman Capote's *Breakfast at Tiffany's*.

Entrance to Tiffany and Co., the exclusive jewelry emporium

IBM Building **3**

590 Madison Ave. **Map** 12 F3.
M *5th Ave.* **Garden Plaza open**
8am–10pm daily. **⬛ ⬤** *Concerts.*
⬛ ⬛

This 43-story tower was designed by Edward Larrabee Barnes. Completed in 1983, it is a sleek, five sided prism of gray-green polished granite, with a cantilevered corner at 57th Street. The Garden Plaza, a light and spacious public atrium, offers rest and refreshment at café tables set out among the bamboo trees. It also houses a garden shop run by the New York Botanical Garden. Near the atrium is a work by American sculptor Michael Heizer, entitled *Levitated Mass*. Inside a low, stainless steel tank, a huge slab of granite seems to float on air while beneath it, a sheet of water flows.

IBM's excellent Gallery of Science and Art is scheduled for closure. Phone for current details.

Interior of the Trump Tower atrium

St. Thomas' Church

St. Thomas' Church ❹

1 W 53rd St. **Map** 12 F4.
📞 757-7013. Ⓜ 5th Ave-53rd St.
Open 7am–6pm daily. 🚇 frequent.
Ⓟ ♿ 🎥

THIS IS THE FOURTH home for this parish and the second on this site. Today's church was built between 1909 and 1914 to replace an earlier structure destroyed in a fire in 1905. The previous building had provided the setting for most of the large, glittering Fifth Avenue high society weddings of the late 19th century. The most lavish of these was the legendary ceremony of 1895 in which heiress Consuela Vanderbilt was married to the English duke of Marlborough.

The limestone building, in French–Gothic style, has a single asymmetrical tower and an off-center nave, novel solutions to the architectural problems posed by the position, on a corner lot. The richly carved, shimmering white screens behind the altar were designed by the architect Bertram Goodhue and the sculptor Lee Lawrie. Carvings in the choir stalls, dating from the 1920s, include modern inventions such as the telephone and radio, as well as Presidents Roosevelt and Wilson, and Lee Lawrie himself.

Museum of Modern Art ❺

See pp170–73.

American Craft Museum ❻

40 W 53rd St. **Map** 12 F4.
📞 956-3535. Ⓜ 5th Ave-53rd St.
Open 10am–5pm Wed–Sun, 10am–8pm Tue. **Closed** public hols. **Adm charge**. Ⓟ ♿ 🎥 Lectures, films.

THERE IS NO BETTER place to experience the vitality of the contemporary American crafts movement than this, the showcase home of the American Crafts Council. On display are handmade quilts, ceramics, glass, textiles, wood, silver, furniture, paper and metalwork drawn from the museum's extensive collection of crafts, which date from 1900 to the present day. Founded as a brownstone on this site in 1956, the museum reopened in 1987 in the three-story atrium of an office tower. The reception desk is itself a work of art, designed and hand-carved in maple by James Schneider. The displays are not for sale.

Silver chalice by Ronald Hayes Pearson at the Craft Museum

Museum of Television and Radio ❼

25 W 52nd St. **Map** 12 F4.
📞 621-6600. Ⓜ 5th Ave-53rd St. **Open** noon–6pm Tue–Sun (8pm Thu). Theaters and screening rooms close 9pm Fri. **Closed** public hols. **Adm charge**. Ⓟ ♿ 🎥 📷 📱

IN THIS one-of-a-kind repository museum, visitors can watch and listen to news and a collection of entertainment and sports documentaries from radio and television's earliest days to the present. Pop fans can see the early Beatles or a young Elvis Presley making his television debut. Sports enthusiasts can relive classic Olympic competitions. World War II footage might be chosen by students of history or by those who lived through the war. Six choices at any one

Beatles Paul, Ringo and John on the "Ed Sullivan Show" in 1964

time can be selected from a computer catalogue that covers a library of over 50,000 programs. The selections are then played on small private areas. There are larger screening areas and a theater for 200, where retrospectives of artists, directors and topics are shown. There are also photo exhibits, posters and memorabilia.

The museum was the brainchild of William S. Paley, who was a former head of the CBS television network. It opened in 1975 as the Museum of Broadcasting on East 53rd Street. It proved to be so popular that in 1991 it moved into this hi-tech $50 million home in a building that to many people is reminiscent of an antique radio set.

I love Lucy

1960s television star Lucille Ball

Museum of Modern Art ❺

Museum facade on West 53rd Street

The MUSEUM of Modern Art contains one of the world's best and most comprehensive collections of modern art. It was founded in 1929 by wealthy patrons and has since set the standard for other museums of its kind, extending the boundaries of art to include many disciplines which are unrecognized by other galleries. The resulting mix is rich and stimulating, chronicling the development of modern art and the modern age.

Sculpture Garden
The Abby Aldrich Rockefeller Sculpture Garden is a beautiful and restful space.

Christina's World
(1948) Andrew Wyeth contrasts an overwhelming horizon with the minutely-studied surroundings of his handicapped neighbor.

STAR PAINTINGS

★ **The Starry Night by Vincent Van Gogh**

★ **Les Demoiselles d'Avignon by Pablo Picasso**

Bird in Space *(c. 1928)*
Constantin Brancusi's elegant bronze sculpture captures the sheer essence of flight.

GALLERY GUIDE
Changing exhibitions are displayed on the first floor. Painting and sculpture are exhibited on the second and third floors. Photography is on the second floor, prints are on the third floor. Architecture and design collections are on the fourth. Films are shown on the lower level.

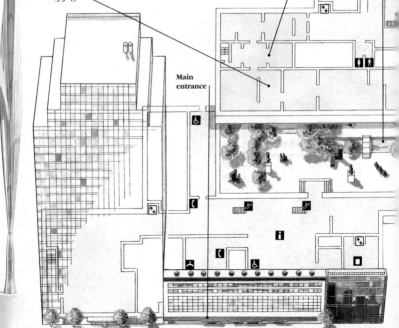

Main entrance

Cisitalia "202" GT *(1946)*
This example of industrial design demonstrates the museum's eclecticism.

Fourth floor

Third floor

La Clownesse *(1896)*
*This is typical
of Henri de Toulouse-
Lautrec's portraits of
Parisian entertainers.*

Second floor

Water Lilies *(c. 1920)*
*Claude Monet's late triptych
creates a glowing, serene
environment in its own room
on the second floor.*

★ **Les Demoiselles d'Avignon**
*Pablo Picasso's 1907 expression-
istic portrait of five prostitutes
included two male customers in
its early drafts. These were later
left out, enabling Picasso to
depict his complex feelings
about women more powerfully.*

First floor

KEY TO FLOORPLAN

☐ Architecture and Design
☐ Drawings
☐ Prints and Illustrated Books
☐ Paintings and Sculpture
☐ Photography
☐ Special exhibitions
☐ Non-exhibition space

★ **The Starry Night** *(1889)*
*The small size of Vincent
Van Gogh's work belies its
passion. This turbulent
night scene remains one
of the most popular
paintings in the collection.*

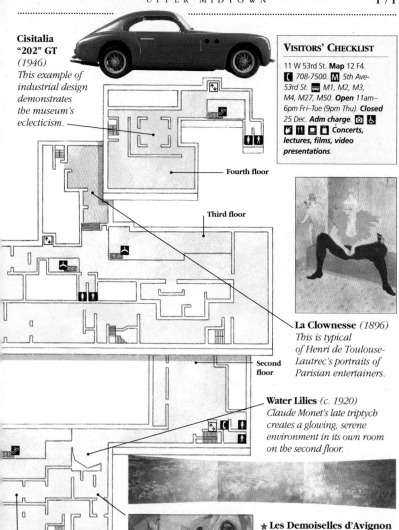

Exploring the Collection

T HE MUSEUM OF MODERN ART houses approximately 100,000 works of art – ranging from a collection of Post-Impressionist classics to an unrivaled collection of modern American art, from fine examples of design to early masterpieces of photography and film.

1880s To 1940s
PAINTING AND SCULPTURE

The Persistence of Memory **by the Surrealist Salvador Dalí (1931)**

P AUL CEZANNE'S monumental *The Bather* and Vincent van Gogh's passionate and transcendent *The Starry Night* are two of the seminal works in the museum's collection of late 19th-century painting. Both Fauvism and Expressionism are well represented with works by Matisse, Derain, Kirchner and others, while Pablo Picasso's *Les Demoiselles d'Avignon* marks a transition to a new style of painting.

The museum also has an unparalleled collection of Cubist paintings, providing an overview of a movement that radically challenged our perception of the world. Among the vast display are Picasso's *Girl with a Mandolin*, Georges Braque's *Man with a Guitar* and *Soda*, and *Guitar and Flowers* by Juan Gris. Works by the Futurists, who brought color and movement to Cubism to depict the dynamic modern world, include Gino Severini's *Dynamic Hieroglyphic of the Bal Tabarin* and *Dynamism of a Soccer Player* by Umberto Boccioni, plus works by Balla, Carrà and Villon.

The geometric abstract art of the Constructivists is included in a strong display of Malevich, Lissitzky and Rod-chenko: De Stijl's influence is seen in paintings by Piet Mondrian, including *Broadway Boogie Woogie*. An entire room is devoted to work by Matisse, such as *Dance I* and *The Red Studio*. Dalí, Miró and Ernst feature among the collection of bizarre, strangely beautiful Surrealist works.

POSTWAR PAINTING AND SCULPTURE

A N EXTENSIVE display of postwar art begins on the third floor, with a series of works by Bacon, Dubuffet and others. The collection of Abstract Expressionist art includes Jackson Pollock's *Autumn Rhythms* and *One [Number 31, 1950]*, Willem de Kooning's *Woman, I*, Arshile Gorky's *Agony* and *Red, Brown, and Black* by

Dog **(1952), an oil painting by British artist Francis Bacon**

Mark Rothko. The following galleries exhibit works such as Jasper Johns' *Flag* and Robert Rauschenberg's *First Landing Jump*, composed from urban refuse, and *Bed*, composed of bed linen. The Pop Art on show includes Roy Lichtenstein's *Girl with Ball* and *Drowning Girl*, Andy Warhol's famous *Gold Marilyn Monroe* and Claes Oldenburg's *Giant Soft Fan*. Works after about 1965 are displayed on a rotating basis and can include pieces by Judd, Flavin, Serra and Beuys among many others.

DRAWINGS AND OTHER WORKS ON PAPER

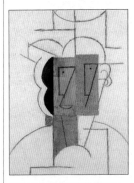

Man with a Hat **by Pablo Picasso (1912), in collage and charcoal**

T HE MUSEUM of Modern Art has one of the most comprehensive collections of modern drawings anywhere in the world. This collection has a range of works in traditional mediums – pencil, ink and charcoal – and also in watercolor, gouache and collage. Some are early studies for famous paintings; Picasso's *Head of the Medical Student* is a study for *Les Demoiselles d'Avignon*. Special strengths are the works representing the School of Paris, Dada and Surrealism. The rotating exhibition in the department's second-floor galleries may include the works of Matisse, Ernst, Klee, Pollock, Dubuffet and Rauschenberg. At various times some of this collection is shown outside the drawings department to complement the museum's other exhibitions.

PRINTS AND ILLUSTRATED BOOKS

The Game of Solitaire by Jacques Villon (1903 but dated 1904)

W IDE-RANGING examples of historical and contemporary printmaking include works in such traditional techniques as lithography, etching, screenprinting and woodcuts, as well as in more experimental techniques. There are fine examples of portraiture, notably a *Self-portrait with Grimace* by Marc Chagall. The collection is strong in the works of Redon, Munch, Klee, Matisse, Picasso, Dubuffet, Villon and Johns. Prints by these and other artists are always displayed in the constantly rotating exhibition in the department's second-floor galleries.

At the entrance to the Print galleries is a reading room containing catalogs and books about prints. The first gallery has a changing survey of printed art from the 1880s up to the 1950s. The next displays art from the 1960s onward, introducing recent and contemporary work.

PHOTOGRAPHY

T HE PHOTOGRAPHY collection begins with the invention of the medium around 1840. It includes pictures by fine artists, journalists, scientists and entrepreneurs, as well as amateur photographers. The first of the department's third-floor galleries is devoted to temporary exhibitions. The other galleries offer an ever-changing chronological series of the collection's highlights. Included in these are photographs by Atget, Stieglitz, Lange, Arbus, Steichen,

FILM DEPARTMENT

With a collection of some 10,000 films and four million stills, the museum offers a wide range of programs, including retrospectives of individual directors and actors, films in specific genres and experimental work, as well as a broad range of other exhibitions. Film conservation is a key part of the department's work. Today's top directors are now donating copies of their films to help fund this expensive but vital work.

Film still of Charlie Chaplin and Jackie Coogan in *The Kid* (1921)

Cartier-Bresson and Kertesz, plus a range of contemporary photographers, most notably Friedlander, Sherman and Nixon. There is an extensive variety of subject matter – covering delicate landscapes, scenes of urban desolation, abstract imagery and stylish portraiture, including some

Sunday on the Banks of the Marne, photographed by Henri Cartier-Bresson in 1939

beautiful silver-gelatin print nudes by the French Surrealist Man Ray. Together, they form a complete history of photographic art and represent one of the finest collections in existence.

ARCHITECTURE AND DESIGN

T HE MUSEUM of Modern Art was the first art museum to include utilitarian objects in its collection. These range from household appliances, stereo equipment, furniture, lighting, textiles and glassware to industrial ball bearings and silicon chips. Architecture is represented in the displays of scale models, drawings and photographs. Graphic design is shown in typography and posters. Architectural models and drawings are displayed in the first gallery, and selections from the design collection follow. Pinin Farina's Cisitalia car and the Bell helicopter are on permanent display in the fourth-floor galleries.

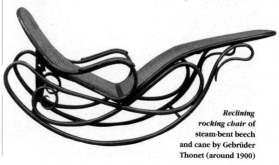

Reclining rocking chair of steam-bent beech and cane by Gebrüder Thonet (around 1900)

St. Patrick's Cathedral 8

See pp176–7.

Villard Houses 9

457 Madison Ave (New York Palace Hotel). **Map** 13 A4. 🄲 *935-3960.* Ⓜ *51st St.* **Urban Center open** *11am–5pm Mon–Wed, Fri, Sat.* 📷 🏢

Henry Villard was a Bavarian immigrant who became publisher of the *New York Evening Post* and founder of the Northern Pacific Railroad. In 1881, he bought the land opposite St. Patrick's Cathedral and hired McKim, Mead & White to design town houses, one for himself, the rest for sale. The inspired result has six four-story houses built around a central court opening to the street and the church. The south wing was Villard's, but financial difficulties forced him to sell before it was finished.

Ownership passed to the Roman Catholic Archdiocese, but the houses were then threatened when the church outgrew its space in the 1970s. The problem was resolved when the Helmsley chain purchased air rights for the 51-story Helmsley (now New York) Palace Hotel. The south wing became the formal entrance to the hotel and the grand public rooms of the Villard suite were incorporated as a tearoom and lounge, restored to their former glory. The Urban Center occupies the entire north wing and its large bookshop is the best place in New York to find architectural books on the city.

St. Bartholomew's Church

St. Bartholomew's Church 10

109 E 50th St. **Map** 13 A4. 🄲 *751-1616.* Ⓜ *51st St.* **Open** *8am–6pm daily.* **Closed** *public hols exc Dec 25 & Easter.* ✝ *9am, 11am Sun.* 📷 ♿ **Lectures, concerts.** 🎵 *on Sundays.*

Known fondly to New Yorkers as "St. Bart's," this Byzantine structure with its ornate detail, pinkish brick, open terrace and a poly-chromed gold dome brought color and variety to Park Avenue in 1919.

Architect Bertram Goodhue incorporated into the design the Romanesque entrance portico created by Stanford White for the original 1903 St. Bartholomew's on Madison Avenue, and marble columns from the earlier church were used in the chapel.

St Bartholomew's musical programs are well known, their Jazz Nativity being a special favorite. They are now concentrating on classical, choral and organ music.

General Electric Building 11

570 Lexington Ave. **Map** 13 A4. Ⓜ *Lexington Ave.* **Not open** *to the public.*

In 1931 architects Cross & Cross were commissioned to design a skyscraper that would be in keeping with its neighbor, St. Bartholomew's Church. Not an easy task, but the result won unanimous acclaim. The colors were chosen to blend and contrast, and the design of the tower complemented the church's polychrome dome.

The General Electric Building on Lexington Avenue

View the pair from the corner of Park and 50th to see how well it works. However, the General Electric is no mere backdrop but a work of art in its own right and a favorite part of the city skyline. It is an Art Deco gem from its chrome and marble lobby to its spiky "radio waves" crown.

Walk one block north on Lexington Avenue to find a place much cherished by movie fans. It is right at this spot that Marilyn Monroe, in a billowing white frock, stood so memorably in the breeze from the Lexington Avenue subway grating in the movie *The Seven-Year Itch.*

Villard Houses, now the entrance to the New York Palace Hotel

Waldorf–Astoria @

301 Park Ave. **Map** 13 A5.
📞 355-3000. Ⓜ *Lexington Ave, 53rd St. See* **Where to Stay** *p281.*

THIS ART DECO classic, which covers an entire city block, was designed by Schultze & Weaver in 1931. The earlier Waldorf–Astoria Hotel at 34th Street was demolished to make way for the Empire State Building.

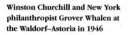

Winston Churchill and New York philanthropist Grover Whalen at the Waldorf–Astoria in 1946

Still deservedly one of New York's most prestigious hotels, the Waldorf–Astoria serves, too, as a reminder of a more glamorous era in the city's history. The 625-ft (190-m) twin towers, where the Duke and Duchess of Windsor lived, have hosted numerous celebrities, including every US president since 1931. The giant lobby clock, executed for the Chicago World's Fair of 1893, is from the original hotel, and the piano in the Peacock Alley cocktail lounge belonged to Cole Porter when he was a resident of the hotel's exclusive Towers.

Lever House ⓭

390 Park Ave. **Map** 13 A4.
📞 888-1260. Ⓜ *5th Ave–53rd St.* **Lobby open** *10am–5pm Mon–Fri, 1–5pm Sun.* **Closed** *public hols & Sun during summer.* 📷

IMAGINE A PARK AVENUE lined with sturdy, residential buildings – and then imagine the sensation when they were suddenly reflected here in the first of the city's glass-walled skyscrapers, one of the most influential buildings of the modern era. The design, by

The pool at the Four Seasons in the Seagram Building

Skidmore, Owings & Merrill, is simply two rectangular slabs of stainless steel and glass, one laid horizontally, the other stacked to stand tall above it, to allow light in from every side. The crisp and bright design was always intended to symbolize many of the Lever Brothers' products – they make soaps and other cleaning products. Revolutionary though it was in 1952, Lever House is now dwarfed by the many imitators that have grown up around it, but its importance as an architectural pacesetter remains undiminished.

Lever House on Park Avenue

Seagram Building ⓮

375 Park Ave. **Map** 13 A4. 📞 572-7000. Ⓜ *5th Ave–53rd St.* 🕐 *3pm Tue.* 🍽

SAMUEL BRONFMAN, the late head of Seagram distillers, was prepared to put up an ordinary commercial building until his architect daughter, Phyllis Lambert, intervened and persuaded him to go to the best – Mies van der Rohe.

The result, which is widely considered the best of the many Modernist buildings of the 1950s, consists of two rectangles of bronze and glass that let the light pour in.

Within is the exclusive Four Seasons Restaurant *(see p293)*, a landmark in its own right. Designer Philip Johnson has created two linked rooms, with the centerpiece of one a pool, and the other a bar that is topped by a quivering Richard Lippold sculpture.

Office workers at lunch in the spacious Citicorp atrium

Citicorp Center ⓯

153 E 53rd St. **Map** 13 A4. Ⓜ *53rd St-Lexington Ave.* **Open** *7am–11pm daily.* 🍽 ⛪ **St. Peter's Lutheran Church** 📞 935-2200. **Open** *9am–9pm daily* ✝ *8:45am, 11am Sun.* **Jazz vespers** *5pm Sun.* **Concerts** *daily except Mon.* **Theater at St. Peter's Church** 📞 935-2200.

AN ALUMINUM-CLAD spire built on ten-story stilts with a sliced-off roof, Citicorp Center is one of a kind and caused a sensation when it was completed in 1978. The unusual base design had to incorporate St. Peter's Lutheran Church. The church is separate both in space and design, a granite sculpture below a corner of the tower. Step inside to see the handsome modern interior and the Erol Beker Chapel by sculptor Louise Nevelson. The church is well known for its organ concerts and jazz vespers, and has a small theater. Citicorp's slanting top never functioned as a solar collector as intended, but it makes the building's outline an unmistakable landmark on the skyline.

Saint Patrick's Cathedral ❽

Fifth Avenue facade

THE ROMAN CATHOLIC Church originally intended this site for use as a cemetery, but in 1850 Archbishop John Hughes decided to build a cathedral instead. Many thought that it was foolish to build so far beyond the (then) city limits, but Hughes went ahead anyway. Architect James Renwick built New York's finest Gothic Revival building, the largest Catholic cathedral in the United States. The cathedral, which seats 2,500 people, was completed in 1878, though the spires were added from 1885 to 1888.

Lady Chapel ★
This chapel honors the Blessed Virgin. The stained-glass windows portray the mysteries of the rosary.

Pièta
American sculptor William O. Partridge created this statue of the Pièta in 1906; it stands at the side of the Lady Chapel.

★ Baldachin
The great baldachin rising over the high altar is made entirely of bronze. Statues of the saints and prophets adorn the four piers supporting the canopy.

STAR FEATURES

★ Baldachin

★ Great Bronze Doors

★ Lady Chapel

★ Great Organ and Rose Window

Cathedral Facade
The exterior wall is built of white marble. The spires rise 330 ft (101 m) above the pavement.

Stations of the Cross
Carved of Caen stone in Holland, these reliefs won first prize in the field of religious art at the Chicago World's Fair in 1893.

VISITORS' CHECKLIST

Fifth Ave and 50th St. **Map** 12 F4. 753-2261. 6 to 51st St.; E, F to Fifth Ave. M1, M2, M3, M4. **Open** 6am–9pm daily (last adm: 8:30pm). frequent Mon–Sat; 7, 8, 9, 10:15am & 12 noon, 1, 4 & 5:30pm Sun. **Concerts & lectures.**

Shrine of St. Elizabeth Ann Seton
The bronze statue and screen depict the life of the first native American to be canonized a saint, who founded the Sisters of Charity (see p76).

Great Organ ★ and Rose Window
Measuring 26 ft (8 m) in diameter, the rose window shines above the great organ, which has more than 7,000 pipes.

Main entrance

Great Bronze Doors ★
The massive doors weigh 20,000 lb (9,000 kg) and are adorned with statues that depict the saints of New York.

Central Synagogue ⑯

652 Lexington Ave. **Map** 13 A4.
📞 838–5122. Ⓜ 51st St, Lexington
Ave. **Open by appt only.** ✪
5:30pm Fri (except 8:15pm first Fri
each month), 10:30am Sat. ⌀

THIS IS NEW YORK'S
oldest building in
continuous use as a
synagogue. It was
designed in 1870 by
Silesian-born Henry
Fernbach, America's
first prominent Jewish
architect. He also
designed some of
SoHo's finest cast-iron
buildings. The Central
Synagogue is considered
the city's best example
of Moorish-Islamic
Revival architecture
The congregation was
originally founded in
1846 as Ahawath
Chesed (Love of
Mercy), by 18 newly-
arrived immigrants,
most of them from
Bohemia, in much
humbler surroundings
on Ludlow Street on
the Lower East Side.

The stenciled interior is a
colorful mix of red, blue,
ochre and gilt and was
inspired by Victorian
prints of a Moorish
Palace in Spain
called the
Alhambra.

**Banded
"horseshoe"
arches** are an
Hispano-
Mooresque
design.

The ark holds
the sacred scrolls
of the Jewish Holy
Book, The Torah.

The twin towers represent
the two columns which stood
outside Solomon's Temple. The
domed minarets, which rise 122 ft
(37 m) are onion-shaped and
made of green copper.

The facade
is an understated
Moorish design in
local brownstone.

Sutton Place and Beekman Place ⑰

Map 13 C3, 13 C5. Ⓜ 59th St.

SUTTON PLACE IS A posh and
pleasant neighborhood,
delightfully devoid of busy
traffic, made up of elegant
low-rise apartment houses
and town houses designed by
noted architects. The arrival of
New York society in the 1920s
transformed an area that had
once been the province of
factories and tenements.
Three Sutton Square is the
residence of the secretary-
general of the United Nations.

Look beyond Sutton Square
and 59th Street for a glimpse
of Riverview Terrace, a
private street of five ivy-
covered brownstones fronting
on the river. The tiny parks at
the end of 55th Street and
jutting out at 57th Street offer
views of the river and the
Queensboro Bridge.

Smaller than Sutton Place,
and even more tranquil, is
Beekman Place, a virtually
private two-block enclave
of 1920s town houses and
some small-scale apartments.
Famous residents here have
included Gloria Vanderbilt,
Rex Harrison, Irving Berlin
and members of the large
Rockefeller family.

Between Beekman and
Sutton places is River House,
a twin-towered apartment
building built in 1931. Its
squash and tennis courts, large
private yacht moorings, pool
and lavish ballroom gave it an
immediate cachet that has
stood the test of time, even

**Park at Sutton Place, looking toward Queensboro Bridge and
Roosevelt Island**

though the moorings had to make way for FDR Drive.

At Turtle Bay Gardens, two rows of brownstone houses dating from the 1860s hide a charming Italianate garden. Among the residents enticed by this privacy have been the film stars Tyrone Power and Katharine Hepburn, and modern composer Stephen Sondheim.

Roosevelt Island ⓲

Map 14 D2. Ⓜ *59th St. Tram departs from 2nd Ave-60th St.*

Since 1976 a Swiss cable car has offered a quick ride across the East River to Roosevelt Island, with eagle's-eye views of the city and the Queensboro Bridge.

Near the tram station are the remains of the Blackwell farmhouse, which stood from 1796 to 1804 and gave the island its name until the 1920s, when real estate development began. From the 1920s to the 1970s, the island housed a succession of hospitals, an almshouse, a jail, a workhouse and an insane asylum, and became known as Welfare Island.

In 1927, Mae West was held in the penitentiary here for eight days after a "lewd performance." She requested, and got, her silk lingerie to wear under her prison uniform. The ruins of 19th-century hospitals still remain, as does an 1872 lighthouse built by an asylum inmate.

The island's present buildings are not noteworthy, but the cable car affords fine city views.

The clock statues above the Fuller Building entrance

Bloomingdale's store sign

Bloomingdale's ⓳

1000 3rd Ave. **Map** 13 A3.
Ⓒ *355-5900.* Ⓜ *59th St.* **Open**
10am–7pm Mon–Wed, Fri; 10am–9pm Thu; 10am–6pm Sat; 11am–6pm Sun. See **Shopping** *p311.*

For a while in the booming 1980s, "Bloomies" was synonymous with the good life. Founded by Joseph and Lyman Bloomingdale in 1872, this famous department store had a bargain-basement image until the 3rd Avenue El was taken down in the 1960s. Then came the store's transformation to the epitome of trendy, sophisticated shopping. But the late 1980s brought new ownership and eventual bankruptcy. While not as flashy as in the past, Bloomingdale's is operating normally and remains one of the city's best-stocked stores.

Fuller Building ⓴

45 E 57th St. **Map** 13 A3. Ⓒ *André Emmerich Gallery 752-0124.* **Open** *10am–5:30pm Tue–Sat. Pace Gallery 421-3292.* **Open** *9:30am–5:30pm Tue–Fri, 10am–6pm Sat.* Ⓜ *59th St.*

This slim-towered black, gray and white 1929 beauty by Walker & Gillette is a prime example of geometric Art Deco design. The striking statues on either side of the clock above the entry are by Elie Nadelman. Step inside to see the intricate mosaic tile floors; one panel shows the Fuller Company's

former home in the Flatiron Building. The Fuller Building is a hive of exclusive art galleries, including the prestigious André Emmerich and Pace galleries.

French Renaissance–style facade of the Plaza Hotel

Plaza Hotel ㉑

768 5th Ave. **Map** 12 F3.
Ⓒ *759-3000.* Ⓜ *59th St. See* **Where to Stay** *p281.*

The city's grande dame of hotels was designed by Henry J. Hardenbergh, known for the Dakota *(see p216)* and the original Waldorf–Astoria. Completed in 1907 at the exorbitant cost of $12.5 million, the plaza was proclaimed "the best hotel in the world," with 800 rooms, 500 baths, a two-story ballroom, five marble staircases, and 14- to 17-room apartments for such families as the Vanderbilts and the Goulds *(see p49)*.

The 18-story cast-iron structure resembles a French Renaissance château on a larger scale. Much of the interior decoration came from Europe. The Palm Court still has mirrored walls and Italian carvings of the four seasons as supporting columns.

Owner Donald Trump has restored the hotel's original glitter (too much of it for some) with elaborate new Bavarian glass chandeliers, lush carpet and miles of gold leaf. Public areas have been refurbished without losing their original ambience.

UPPER EAST SIDE

AT THE TURN of the century, New York society moved to the Upper East Side – and stayed. Many of the Beaux Arts mansions are now museums and embassies, but the well-to-do still occupy grand apartment buildings on Fifth and Park avenues. Chic shops and galleries line Madison. Farther east, the area includes German Yorkville in the East 80s, Hungarian Yorkville to the south and little Bohemia, with its Czech population, below 78th Street. Many Germans, Czechs and Hungarians have left the area, but their churches, restaurants, and ethnic shops still remain.

African urn, Metropolitan Museum of Art

Looking down into the lobby of the Guggenheim Museum

SIGHTS AT A GLANCE

Historic Streets and Buildings
Seventh Regiment Armory [10]
Henderson Place [14]
Gracie Mansion [16]

Museums and Galleries
International Center of Photography [1]
Jewish Museum [2]
Cooper-Hewitt Museum [3]
National Academy of Design [4]
Solomon R. Guggenheim Museum pp186–87 [5]
Metropolitan Museum of Art pp188–95 [6]
Whitney Museum of American Art pp198–99 [7]
Frick Collection pp200–1 [8]
Asia Society [9]
Society of Illustrators [12]
Abigail Adams Smith Museum [13]
Museum of the City of New York [19]

Churches and Synagogues
Temple Emanu-El [11]
Church of the Holy Trinity [17]
St. Nicholas Russian Orthodox Cathedral [18]

Parks and Squares
Carl Schurz Park [15]

GETTING THERE

The Lexington Ave 4 and 5 express trains stop at 59th and 86th streets. The local (No. 6) also stops at 68th, 77th and 96th streets. Buses include: M1, M2, M3 and M4 on Fifth/Madison Aves, M101/102 on Lexington/Third and M15 on First/Second. The crosstown buses are the M66, M72, M79, M86 and M96.

SEE ALSO

- ***Street Finder***, maps 12–13, 16–17
- ***East Side Walk*** pp262–63
- ***Where to Stay*** pp274–75
- ***Restaurants*** pp290–92

KEY

- Street-by-Street map
- [M] Subway station
- Ferry terminal
- Heliport

0 meters 500
0 yards 500

Statue of Diana, National Academy of Design

Street by Street: Museum Mile

Many of New York's museums are clustered on the Upper East Side, in homes ranging from the former Frick and Carnegie mansions to the modernistic Guggenheim, designed by Frank Lloyd Wright. The displays are as varied as the architecture, running the gamut from old masters to photographs to decorative arts. Presiding over the scene is the vast Metropolitan Museum of Art, America's answer to the Louvre. Many of the museums stay open late on Tuesday evenings, and some offer free admission.

Jewish Museum
The most extensive collection of Judaica in the world is housed here. It includes coins, archaeological objects and ceremonial and religious artifacts ❷

Cooper-Hewitt Museum★
The decorative arts, including ceramics, glass, furniture and textiles, are well represented here ❸

The Church of the Heavenly Rest was built in 1929 in the Gothic style. The madonna in the pulpit is by sculptor Malvina Hoffman.

National Academy of Design
The Academy, founded in 1825, moved here in 1940. Its fine collection includes paintings and sculptures by its members ❹

★ **Solomon R. Guggenheim Museum**
Floodlit at dusk, architect Frank Lloyd Wright's building looks purple. It is in the form of a spiral. Take the elevator to the top and walk down to see one of the world's best collections of modern art ❺

Graham House is an apartment building with a splendid Beaux Arts entrance. It was built in 1892.

Star Sights

★ **Solomon R. Guggenheim Museum**

★ **Cooper-Hewitt Museum**

International Center of Photography
This museum houses one of the world's finest photography collections ❶

The facade of the Squadron A Armory is all that remains of the original building. It is now the west wall of the play-ground of Hunter High School. The school was built to complement the style of the armory.

Public basketball court

To 96th Street subway (2 blocks)

The Smithers Alcoholism Center occupies a mansion that was once the home of theatrical producer Billy Rose.

The Synod of Bishops of the Russian Orthodox Church Outside of Russia is housed in a lovely 1931 mansion.

Night Presence IV (1972), a modern work in rusting steel, was created by Louise Nevelson. Some New Yorkers feel it is out of place among its staid, old-fashioned neighbors on Park Avenue.

At **120 and 122 East 92nd Street** are two of the few wooden houses left in Manhattan. Built in 1859 and 1871, respectively, they have a charming Italianate air.

The Marx Brothers spent their boyhoods in a three-bedroom apartment in a modest row house at 179 East 93rd Street.

International Center of Photography

International Center of Photography ❶

1130 5th Ave. **Map** 16 F2.
█ *860-1777.* Ⓜ *86th St, 96th St.*
Open *11am–8pm Tue, 11am–6pm*
Wed–Sun. **Closed** *public hols.* **Adm**
charge. Ⓧ 🅿 🅳

T HIS MUSEUM, often referred
to as the ICP, was
founded by Cornell
Capa in 1974 to
conserve the work
of such outstanding
photojournalists as his
brother Robert, who was
killed on assignment in 1954.
The ICP's collection of 12,500
original prints includes much
work by some of the world's
greatest photographers, such
as Ansel Adams and Henri
Cartier-Bresson. There are
also excellent wide-ranging
exhibitions, and a program of
films, lectures and classes.

One of upper Fifth Avenue's
last grand residences, this brick
six-story Neo-Georgian house
was built in 1915 for Willard
Straight, a diplomat, financier
and founder of the magazines
The New Republic and *Asia.*

Jewish Museum ❷

1109 5th Ave. **Map** 16 F2.
█ *423-3200.* Ⓜ *86th St, 96th St.*
Open *11am–5.45pm Mon, Wed, Thu,*
Sun, 11am–8pm Tue. **Closed** *Fri, Sat,*
major public & Jewish hols. **Adm**
charge. Ⓧ 🅱 🅿 🖵 🅳

T HE EXQUISITE château-like
residence of Felix M.
Warburg, financier and leader
of the Jewish community, was
designed by C.P.H. Gilbert in
1908. It now houses one of
the world's largest collections

of Jewish fine and ceremonial
art, and historical Judaica.
Renovation has almost doubled
the display space. The stonework in the new extension is
by the stonemasons of St.
John the Divine *(see pp224–5)*.

Objects have been brought
here from all over the world,
some at great risk of persecution to the donors. Covering
4,000 years, artifacts include
Torah crowns, candelabras,
kiddush cups, plates, scrolls
and silver ceremonial objects.

There is a Torah ark from
the Benguiat Collection, the
exquisite faience entrance
wall of a 16th-century Persian
synagogue and the powerful
Holocaust by sculptor George
Segal. Changing exhibitions
reflect Jewish life
and experience
around the
world.

19th-century
ewer and basin from Istanbul
at the Jewish Museum

Cooper-Hewitt Museum ❸

2 E 91st St. **Map** 16 F2. █ *860-6868.*
Ⓜ *86th St.* **Open** *10am–9pm Tue,*
10am–5pm Wed–Sat, noon–5pm Sun.
Closed *public hols.* **Adm charge.** 🅱
🅿 🅳

O NE OF THE largest design
collections in the world,
this museum occupies the
former home of industrialist
Andrew Carnegie. It was
amassed by the Hewitt sisters,
Amy, Eleanor and Sarah. The
museum opened in 1897 at
Cooper Union *(see p118)*; the
Smithsonian Institution acquired the collections in 1967,
and the Carnegie Corporation
offered the mansion.

Carnegie's house is an
appropriate setting for the
museum. He asked for "the
most modest, plainest and
most roomy house in New
York," but the house set some
new trends with its central

Cooper-Hewitt Museum entrance

heating, passenger elevator
and air-conditioning. Visitors
can enjoy the wooden staircase, rich paneling and
carving and sunny solarium.

National Academy of Design ❹

1083 5th Ave. **Map** 16 F3.
█ *369-4880.* Ⓜ *86th St.* **Open**
noon–5pm Wed–Sun, noon–8pm Fri.
Adm charge *except 5–8pm Fri.* 🅿
🅱 🅳

M ORE THAN 6,000 paintings,
drawings and sculptures,
including works by Thomas
Eakins, Winslow Homer,
Raphael Soyer and Frank
Lloyd Wright, comprise the
collection of the National
Academy of Design, founded
in 1825 by a group of artists.
The group's mission was
(and is) to train artists and
exhibit their work. In 1940,
Archer Huntington, an art
patron and philanthropist,
donated his house, an
attractive building with
patterned marble floors and
decorative plaster ceilings.
The grand entrance foyer has
a statue of Diana by sculptor
Anna Hyatt Huntington.

Statue of Diana in the National
Academy of Design entrance foyer

Solomon R. Guggenheim Museum ❺

See pp186–7.

Metropolitan Museum of Art ❻

See pp188–95.

Whitney Museum of American Art ❼

See pp198–9.

Frick Collection ❽

See pp200–1.

Asia Society ❾

725 Park Ave. **Map** 13 A1.
[288-6400. M 68th St.
Open 11am–6pm Tue–Sat (8pm Fri),
noon–5pm Sun. **Closed**
Mon, public hols. **Adm**
charge except 6–8pm
Fri. ∅ & ▢ ▯

Founded by
John D.
Rockefeller III
in 1956 to
increase American
understanding of
Asian culture,
the society is a
forum for 30
countries from
Japan to Iran,
Central Asia to
Australia.
Built in
1981, the **South Asian**
eight-story **sculpture at the**
building is **Asia Society**
made of red
granite. It was designed by
Edward Larrabee Barnes. There
are several galleries, one
permanently devoted to
Rockefeller's own collection of
Asian sculptures, ceramics,
bronzes and wood sculptures,
amassed by him and his wife
on frequent trips to the East.
Changing exhibits show a
wide variety of Asian arts,
and the society has a full
program of films, dance,
concerts and lectures. There
is a well-stocked shop with
books on Asia.

Entrance Hall of the Seventh Regiment Armory

Seventh Regiment Armory ❿

643 Park Ave. **Map** 13 A2.
[439 0300. M 68th St.
Open Mon–Fri by appt only.
Closed public hols. ∅ & ▢

From the war of 1812
through two world wars,
the Seventh Regiment has
played a vital role. They were
an elite corps of "gentlemen
soldiers" from prominent
families, and their armory is
unlike any other in the US.
Within the stern fortresslike
exterior are extraordinary
rooms filled with
lavish furnishings of
the Victorian era,
objets d'art and
regimental
memorabilia.
The design by
Charles W.
Clinton, a veteran
of the regiment,
had offices facing
Park Avenue, with
a vast drill hall
stretching behind
to Lexington
Avenue. The
reception rooms
include the
Veterans' Room
and the Library
by Louis Comfort
Tiffany. The
drill hall is now
the site of the
Winter Antiques
Show (see p53)
and a favorite
place to hold
the city's many
charity balls.

Temple Emanu-El ⓫

1 E 65th St. **Map** 12 F2.
[744-1400. M 68th St, 60th St.
Open 10am–4:45pm Sun–Fri,
noon–4:45pm Sat (last adm on Fri
3:30pm) **Closed** Jewish hols. ✡
5:30pm Sun–Thu, 5:15pm Fri,
10:30am Sat. ▢ & ▢ ▯

This impressive limestone
edifice of 1929 is one of
the largest synagogues in the
world, seating 2,500 in the
main sanctuary alone. It is
home to the oldest Reform
congregation in New York.
Among the many fine details
are the bronze grille doors of
the Ark, and stained glass
showing the Shield of David
and the Lion of Judah. The
dominant feature of the Fifth
Avenue exterior is the great
recessed arch enclosing a
magnificent wheel window.
The Beth-El Chapel is a
twin-domed structure with
a Byzantine influence.
The synagogue stands on
the site of the palatial home
of the legendary society
hostess Mrs. William Astor.
She left her midtown mansion
when her nephew, who was
feuding with her, built the
Waldorf Hotel next door. The
formidable Mrs. Astor moved
to the Upper East Side,
taking society with
her, while her son
built the Astoria Hotel
on the site of her
previous home.

The Ark at Temple Emanu-El

The Solomon R. Guggenheim Museum ❺

HOME TO ONE of the world's finest collections of modern and contemporary art, the Guggenheim building itself is perhaps the museum's greatest masterpiece. It was designed by architect Frank Lloyd Wright and has been likened to a giant white shell. As you walk along the spiral ramp that curves down and inward from the dome, and visit the new Small Rotunda and tower galleries, you will see special exhibitions featuring major works by many important 19th- and 20th-century artists. A new downtown site opened in 1992, the Guggenheim Museum SoHo (see p105).

Fifth Avenue facade

Paris Through the Window
The vibrant colors of Marc Chagall's 1913 masterpiece illumine the canvas, conjuring up images of a magical and mysterious city where nothing is quite what it appears to be.

Small Rotunda

THE SOLOMON

Sculpture terrace

Main entrance

i

Woman Ironing (1904)
A work from Pablo Picasso's Blue Period, this painting is his quintessential image of hard work and fatigue.

Yellow Cow (1911)
Franz Marc's work was influenced by a German back-to-nature movement.

Nude (1917)
This sleeping figure is typical of Amedeo Modigliani's stylized work.

MUSEUM GUIDE

The Great Rotunda features special exhibitions. The Small Rotunda shows some of the museum's celebrated Impressionist and Post-Impressionist holdings. The new Tower galleries feature exhibitions of work from the permanent collection as well as contemporary pieces. A fifth-floor sculpture terrace overlooks Central Park. Not all of the collection is on display at any one time.

Tower

Great Rotunda

Before the Mirror *(1876)*
In trying to capture the flavor of 19th-century society, Edouard Manet often used the image of the courtesan.

VISITORS' CHECKLIST

1071 5th Ave at 88th St.
Map 16 F3. 423-3500.
4, 5, 6 to 86th St. M1, M2, M3, M4. **Open** 10am–8pm Fri–Wed. **Closed** Dec 25, Jan 1. **Adm charge.** Concerts, lectures, performing art series.

Woman Holding a Vase
Fernand Léger incorporated elements of Cubism into this work from 1927.

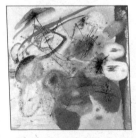

Black Lines *(1913) This is one of Vasily Kandinsky's earliest examples of his work in "non-objective" art.*

Woman with Yellow Hair
(1931) The gentle, voluptuous figure of Picasso's mistress often appears in his work.

FRANK LLOYD WRIGHT

During his lifetime, Wright was considered the great innovator of American architecture. Characteristic of his work are Prairie-style homes and office buildings of concrete slabs, glass bricks and tubing. Wright received the Guggenheim commission in 1942; it was completed after his death in 1959, his only New York building.

Interior of the Guggenheim's Great Rotunda

Metropolitan Museum of Art ❻

Founded in 1870 by a group of artists and philanthropists who dreamed of an American arts institution to rival those of Europe, this collection is thought to be the most comprehensive in the Western world. Works date from prehistoric times to the present. It moved to its current site in 1880 and houses collections from all continents, including ancient Egyptian art and American sculpture and decorative art since colonial times.

The entrance of the Metropolitan Museum of Art

Robert Lehman Collection

★ **Gertrude Stein** *(1905–6)*

This portrait of the American writer Gertrude Stein is by Pablo Picasso. The masklike face is evidence of his debt to African and Roman art.

Pendant Mask
The kingdom of Benin (now part of Nigeria) was renowned for its art. This mask was made in the 16th century.

Seated Man with Harp
This statuette was made in the Cyclades c.3,000 BC.

Lower Floor

GALLERY GUIDE
Most of the collections are housed on the two main floors. Works from 19 curatorial areas are in the permanent galleries, with designated galleries for temporary exhibitions. Central on the first and second floors are European painting, sculpture and decorative art. Other collections can be found radiating out from the center on both levels.

The Marriage Feast at Cana
This rare 16th-century panel painting by Juan de Flandes is part of the Linsky Collection.

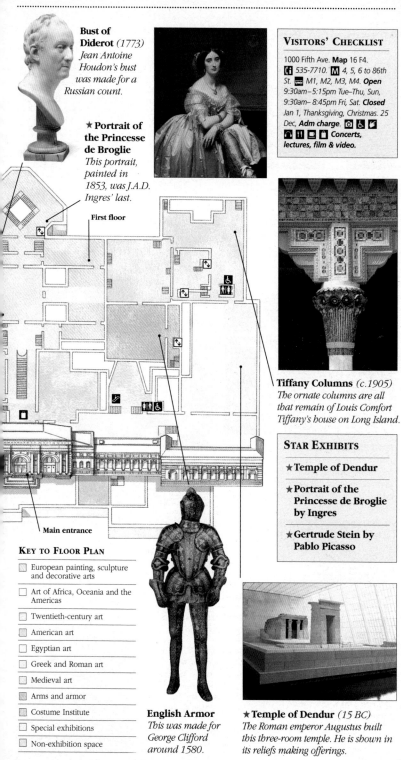

Bust of Diderot (1773)
Jean Antoine Houdon's bust was made for a Russian count.

★ Portrait of the Princesse de Broglie
This portrait, painted in 1853, was J.A.D. Ingres' last.

First floor

Tiffany Columns (c.1905)
The ornate columns are all that remain of Louis Comfort Tiffany's house on Long Island.

STAR EXHIBITS

★ **Temple of Dendur**

★ **Portrait of the Princesse de Broglie by Ingres**

★ **Gertrude Stein by Pablo Picasso**

Main entrance

KEY TO FLOOR PLAN

- European painting, sculpture and decorative arts
- Art of Africa, Oceania and the Americas
- Twentieth-century art
- American art
- Egyptian art
- Greek and Roman art
- Medieval art
- Arms and armor
- Costume Institute
- Special exhibitions
- Non-exhibition space

English Armor
This was made for George Clifford around 1580.

★ Temple of Dendur (15 BC)
The Roman emperor Augustus built this three-room temple. He is shown in its reliefs making offerings.

Metropolitan Museum of Art: Upper Levels

Marrakech
This 1964 work is one of Frank Stella's "Moroccan" paintings. Within a square format, fluorescent strips form the painting's main focus.

Sculpture Garden
These modern sculptures, on top of the 20th-century wing, are changed annually.

Card Players (1890)
Paul Cézanne departed here from his traditional landscapes, still lifes and portraits to paint this scene of peasants intently playing cards.

Islamic art

Second floor

First floor

★ **Cypresses** (1889)
Vincent Van Gogh painted this the year before he died. The heavy brushstrokes and the swirling style mark his later work.

Eagle-headed Winged Being Pollinating the Sacred Tree (about 900 BC)
This relief comes from an Assyrian palace.

STAR EXHIBITS

★ **Self-portrait of 1660 by Rembrandt**

★ **George Washington Crossing the Delaware by Leutze**

★ **Cypresses by Vincent Van Gogh**

★ **Diptych by Jan van Eyck**

★ **Diptych**
(1425–30)
Flemish painter
Jan van Eyck was
one of the earliest
masters of oil
painting. These
scenes of the
Crucifixion and
Last Judgment
show him to be
a forerunner of
realism, too.

★ **Washington Crossing the Delaware**
In 1851 Emanuel Gottlieb Leutze painted
this romanticized – and inaccurate –
view of the famous crossing.

KEY TO FLOOR PLAN

☐ European painting, sculpture
and decorative arts

☐ Ancient Near Eastern and
Islamic art

☐ Twentieth-century art

☐ American art

☐ Asian art

☐ Greek and Roman art

☐ Musical instruments

☐ Drawings, prints and
photographs

☐ Special exhibitions

▨ Non-exhibition space

The Death of Socrates (1787)
*Jacques Louis David shows
Socrates about to take poison
rather than renounce his beliefs.*

Astor Court

★ **Self-portrait** (1660)
Rembrandt painted almost
100 self-portraits. This one
shows him at the age of 54.

THE ASTOR COURT

In 1979, 27 crafts-
people from China,
responsible for the
care of Souzhou's
historic gardens,
came to New York
to replicate a Ming-
style scholar's garden in the Metropolitan Museum.
They used centuries-old techniques and handmade
tools that had been passed down for generations. It was
the first cultural exchange between the United States
and the People's Republic of China. The result
is a quiet garden for meditation, a Western parallel
to Souzhou's Garden of the Master of the Fishing Nets.

Exploring the Metropolitan

T HE TREASURES OF "THE MET" include a vast collection of American art and more than 3,000 European paintings, including masterpieces by Rembrandt and Vermeer. There are also many Islamic exhibits, plus the greatest collection of Egyptian art outside Cairo.

AFRICA, OCEANIA AND THE AMERICAS

A painted gold funerary mask (10th–14th century) from the necropolis of Batán Grande, Peru

N ELSON ROCKEFELLER built the Michael C. Rockefeller Wing in 1982 in memory of his son, who lost his life on an art-finding expedition in New Guinea. The wing showcases a superb collection of over 2,000 objects from Africa, the islands of the Pacific and the Americas.

Among the African works, the ivory and bronze sculptures from the royal kingdom of Benin (Nigeria) are outstanding, as is the wooden sculpture by the Dogon, Bamana and Senufo peoples of Mali. From the Pacific come carvings by the Asmat people of New Guinea and decorations and masks from the Melanesian and Polynesian islands. From Mexico and Central and South America come pre-Columbian gold, ceramics and stonework. The wing also contains fine Native American artifacts by the Inuit and other groups.

AMERICAN ART

G ILBERT STUART'S first portrait of George Washington, George Caleb Bingham's *Fur Traders Descending the Missouri*, John Singer Sargent's notorious portrait of *Madame X* and the monumental *George Washington Crossing the*

Delaware by Emanuel Leutze are among the icons of the American Wing. It holds one of the world's finest collections of American painting, including several works by Edward Hopper, and sculpture and decorative arts from colonial times to this century. Period rooms, with original woodwork and furnishings, range from the saloon hall in which George Washington celebrated his last birthday to the elegant prairie-style living room from the Little house in Minnesota, designed by Frank Lloyd Wright in 1912.

Engelhard Court is an indoor sculpture garden with large-scale architectural elements, including the lovely stained-glass and mosaic loggia from Louis Comfort Tiffany's Long Island estate and the facade of an 1824 United States Branch Bank that stood on Wall Street.

The Lighthouse at Two Lights (1929) by Edward Hopper

ANCIENT NEAR EASTERN AND ISLAMIC ART

M ASSIVE STONE SCULPTURES of human-headed winged lions, once guardians of the 9th-century BC Assyrian

Mysterious in identity and origin, a rare 5,000-year-old copper head from the Near East

palace of Assurnasirpal II, sit at the entrance to the Ancient Near Eastern galleries. Inside is a collection spanning 7,000 years, rich in Iranian bronzes, Anatolian ivories, Sumerian sculptures, and Achaemenian and Sassanian works in silver and gold. An adjacent gallery area displays the diversity of Islamic art from the 7th to the 19th century; glass and metalwork from Egypt, Syria and Mesopotamia; royal miniatures from the courts of Persia and Mughal India; rugs of the 16th and 17th centuries; and an 18th-century room from Syria.

ARMS AND ARMOR

M OUNTED KNIGHTS in full armor charge at each other across the equestrian court here. These galleries are a favorite with children and anyone moved by medieval romance or thrilled by power.

There are suits of armor, rapiers and sabers with hilts of precious stones and gold, firearms inlaid with ivory and mother-of-pearl, plus colorful heraldic banners and shields.

The pistol of Holy Roman Emperor Charles V (16th century)

Highlights include the armor of gentleman-pirate George Clifford, a favorite of Queen Elizabeth I. The rainbow-colored armor of a 14th-century Japanese shogun and a collection of Wild West revolvers that once belonged to gunmaker Samuel Colt are also exhibited here.

ORIENTAL AND ASIAN ART

The Old Plum, a Japanese paper screen from the early Edo period (about 1650)

MANY OUTSTANDING galleries contain masterpieces of Chinese, Japanese, Korean, Indian and Southeast Asian art, dating from the second millennium BC to the 20th century. A full-scale Ming-style Chinese scholar's garden was built by craftspeople from Souzhou as part of the first cultural exchange between the United States and the People's Republic of China. The museum also has one of the finest collections of Sung and Yuan paintings in the world, Chinese Buddhist monumental sculptures, fine Chinese ceramics and jade and an important display of the arts of ancient China.

The full range of Japanese arts is represented in a breathtaking suite of ten galleries featuring chronological and thematic displays of Japanese lacquer, ceramics, painting, sculpture, textiles and screens. Indian, Southeast Asian and Korean galleries display superb sculptures and other arts from these regions.

COSTUME INSTITUTE

THERE IS ALWAYS a portion of the 45,000-piece collection of costumes, dating from the 17th century to the present, on display in these new state-of-the-art galleries. Here, the Institute maintains a definitive compendium of fashionable dress, from the elaborately embroidered dresses of the late 1600s to the shocking-pink evening dresses of Elsa Schiaparelli, complete with hats, scarves, gloves, handbags and other accessories. There are also the designs of Worth, Quant and Balenciaga, as well as gowns from the Napoleonic and Victorian eras, the costumes of the Ballets Russes and even David Bowie's sequined jockstrap.

The regional portion of the collection is rich with folk costumes from Europe, Asia, Africa and the Americas.

The Institute is so sophisticated in its understanding of conservation techniques that it has been called upon to advise NASA on the cleaning of astronauts' spacesuits.

A 17th-century European silk-and-satin doublet

DRAWINGS, PRINTS AND PHOTOGRAPHS

A NEW GALLERY regularly displays selections from the museum's incredible holdings of drawings, prints, etchings and photographs.

Michelangelo's studies of a Libyan Sibyl for the ceiling of the Sistine Chapel (1508)

The drawings collection is especially rich in Italian and French art from the 15th to the 19th century. These are exhibited on a rotating basis because of the light-sensitive nature of works on paper.

Highlights among the 4,000 drawings include works by Michelangelo, Leonardo da Vinci, Raphael, Ingres, Goya, Rubens, Rembrandt, Tiepolo and Seurat.

The encyclopedic print collection of 12,000 individual images (and almost the same number of illustrated books) includes major works by virtually every master printmaker, from an early German woodcut called *Virgin and Child* to some of Dürer's most accomplished works and Goya's *The Giant.* Influential gallery-owner Alfred Stieglitz's donation of his own extensive collection of photographs brought here such gems as Edward Steichen's *The Flatiron.* It formed the core of a photography collection that is now also particularly strong in Modernist works dating from between the world wars.

Ephemera such as posters and advertisements form another part of this collection.

EGYPTIAN ART

ONE OF THE MUSEUM's finest and best-loved areas is the ancient Egyptian wing, which displays every one of its thousands of holdings – from the prehistoric period to the 8th century AD. Objects range from the fragmented jasper lips of a 15th-century BC queen to the massive Temple of Dendur. Other amazing archaeological finds, most of them from museum-sponsored expeditions undertaken early in the 20th century, include sculptures of the notorious Queen Hatshepsut, who seized the Theban throne in the 16th century BC; 100 carved reliefs of Amenhotpe IV's reign; and tomb figures like the blue faïence hippo that has become the museum's mascot.

Young Woman with a Water Jug (1660) by Jan Vermeer

Botticelli's *Last Communion of Saint Jerome* and Bronzino's *Portrait of a Young Man*. The Dutch and Flemish canvases are among the finest in the world, with Brueghel's *The Harvesters*, several works by Rubens and Van Dyck, over a dozen Rembrandts and more Vermeers than any other museum. The collection also has masterpieces by Spanish artists El Greco, Velázquez and Goya, and by French artists Poussin and Watteau.

Some of the finest Impressionist and Post impressionist canvases reside here: 30 Monets, including *Terrace at Sainte-Adresse;* 17 Cézannes; and Van Gogh's *Cypresses.*

In the Kravis wing and adjacent galleries are works from the 60,000-object collection of European sculpture and decorative arts, such as Tullio Lombardo's marble statue of Adam; a bronze statuette of a rearing horse, after a model by Leonardo; and dozens of pieces by Degas and Rodin. Period settings include the patio from a 16th-century

Spanish castle and a series of ornate 18th-century French domestic interiors known as the Wrightsman Rooms. The Petrie European Sculpture Court features French and Italian sculpture in a beautiful garden setting reminiscent of Versailles in France.

GREEK AND ROMAN ART

A ROMAN SARCOPHAGUS from Tarsus, donated in 1870, was the very first work of art in the Met's collections. It can still be seen in the museum's Greek and Roman galleries, along with the breathtaking wall panels from a villa that was buried under the lava of Vesuvius in AD 79, Etruscan mirrors, Roman portrait busts, exquisite objects in glass and silver and hundreds of Greek vases. A monumental 7th-century BC statue of a youth shows the movement toward naturalism in sculpture, and the Hellenistic *Old Market Woman* demonstrates how the Greeks had mastered realism by the 2nd century BC.

An amphora by Exekias, showing a wedding (6th century BC)

Queen Tiye, wife of Amenhotpe III (1417–1379 BC)

EUROPEAN PAINTING, SCULPTURE AND DECORATIVE ARTS

THE HEART of the museum is its awe-inspiring collection of 3,000 European paintings. The Italian works include

EGYPTIAN TOMB MODELS
In 1920, a Met researcher's light illuminated a room, hitherto undiscovered for 2,000 years, in the tomb of the nobleman Mekutra. Within were 23 tiny, perfect replicas of his daily life, to ensure his comfort in the next world – his house and garden, fleet of ships and herd of cattle. Mekutra himself is there, too, on his boat, inhaling a lotus's scent and enjoying the music of his singer and harpist.

LEHMAN COLLECTION

WHAT HAD BEEN one of the finest private art collections in the world, that of investment banker Robert Lehman, came to the museum in 1971. The Lehman Wing is a dramatic glass pyramid housing an extraordinarily varied collection rich in Old Masters and 19th-century French paintings drawings;

A panel from the stained-glass *Death of the Virgin* window, from the 12th-century cathedral of Saint Pierre in Troyes, France

bronzes; Renaissance majolica Venetian glass, furniture and enamels. Among the canvases are works by north–European masters; Dutch and Spanish paintings, French masterworks, Post impressionists and Fauves.

MEDIEVAL ART

THE METROPOLITAN'S medieval collection includes works dating from the 4th to the 16th century, roughly from the fall of Rome to the beginning of the Renaissance. It is split between the main museum and its uptown branch, the Cloisters *(see pp234–7)*. In the main building are a chalice once thought to be the Holy Grail, six silver Byzantine plates showing scenes from the life of David, a 1301 pulpit by Giovanni Pisano in the shape of an eagle, several monumental sculptures of the Virgin and Child, plus a huge choir screen from Spain. Other exhibits include Migration jewelry, liturgical vessels, stained glass, ivories and 14th- and 15-century tapestries.

MUSICAL INSTRUMENTS

THE WORLD'S OLDEST piano, Andrés Segovia's guitars and a sitar shaped like a peacock are some of the features of a broad and sometimes quirky collection of musical instruments that spans six continents and dates from prehistory to the present. The instruments illustrate the history of music and performance, and most of them are conserved to remain in playable condition. Worth particular mention are instruments from the European courts of the Middle Ages and the Renaissance; rare violins, spinets and harpsichords; instruments inlaid with precious materials; a fully equipped traditional violin-maker's work-shop; as well as African drums; Asian *pi-pas;* or lutes; and Native American pipes. Visitors can use audio equipment to hear many of the instruments playing the music of their day.

Stradivari violin from Cremona, Italy (1691)

TWENTIETH-CENTURY ART

SINCE ITS FOUNDATION in 1870, the museum has been acquiring contemporary art, but it was not until 1987 that a permanent home for 20th-century art was built – the Lila Acheson Wallace Wing. Other museums in New York have larger collections of modern art, but this display space is considered among the finest. European and American works from 1900 onward are featured on three levels, starting with Europeans such as Picasso, Kandinsky and Bonnard. The collection's greatest strength lies in its collection of modern American art, with works by New York school "The Eight," including John Sloan; such Modernists as Charles Demuth and Georgia O'Keeffe; American Regionalist Grant Wood; Abstract Expressionists Willem de Kooning; and such Color Field painters as Clyfford Still.

Grant Wood's view of *The Midnight Ride of Paul Revere* (1931)

Special areas of the wing house Art Nouveau and Art Deco furniture and metalwork; a large collection of works on paper by Paul Klee; and the Sculpture Gallery, with its large-scale sculptures and canvases.

Gems of the collection include Picasso's portrait of Gertrude Stein, Matisse's *Nasturtiums and "Dance,"* Demuth's *I Saw the Figure 5 in Gold*, Jackson Pollock's *Autumn Rhythm* and Andy Warhol's last self-portrait.

Each year the Cantor Roof Garden at the top of the wing features a new installation of contemporary sculpture, especially dramatic against the backdrop of the New York skyline and Central Park.

Book cover (1916) by illustrator N.C. Wyeth

Society of Illustrators ⓬

128 E 63rd St. **Map** 13 A2.
📞 838-2560. Ⓜ Lexington Ave.
Open 10am–5pm Tue–Fri, noon–
4pm Sat. 📷 ♿ restricted. ✂ 🛗

ESTABLISHED IN 1901, this
society was formed to
promote the illustrator's art.
Its notable roster included
Charles Dana Gibson, N.C.
Wyeth and Howard Pyle. It
was at first concerned with
education and public service,
and held occasional exhibits.
In 1981, the Museum of
American Illustration opened
in two galleries. Changing
thematic exhibitions show the
history of book and magazine
illustration, with an annual
exhibition of the year's finest
American illustrations.

Abigail Adams Smith Museum ⓭

421 E 61st St. **Map** 13 C3.
📞 838-6878. Ⓜ Lexington Ave,
59th St. **Open** noon–4pm Mon–Fri,
1–5pm Sun (Jun & Jul, also
5:30–8pm Tue). **Closed** Aug, public
hol. **Adm charge.** 🚫 ✂ 🛗

BUILT IN 1799, this federal-
style stone stable once
belonged to Abigail Adams
Smith, President John Adams's
daughter. The house burned

down in 1826; the
stable was reno-
vated as an inn,
then as a home.
    It was acquired
by the Colonial
Dames of America
in 1924 and turned
into a charming
re-creation of a
Federal home.
Costumed guides
show visitors
through the rooms,
pointing out the
treasures, including
Chinese porcelain,
Aubusson carpets,
Sheraton chests
and a Duncan
Phyfe sofa. In one
bedroom, a gown
belonging to
Abigail Adams
Smith is stored in an
antique wardrobe; the same
room holds a baby's cradle
and children's toys. An 18th-
century-style garden has been
planted around the house.

Henderson Place ⓮

Map 18 D3. Ⓜ 86th St.

**Queen Anne row houses
at Henderson Place**

NOW SURROUNDED by mod-
ern apartment blocks, this
enclave of 24 red-brick Queen
Anne row houses was built in
1882. The row houses were
commissioned by John C.
Henderson, a hat-maker, as a
self-contained community.
The elegant Lamb & Rich
design has gray slate roof
gables, pediments, parapets,
chimneys and dormer
windows forming patterns,
and a turret marking the
corner of each block.

Carl Schurz Park promenade

Carl Schurz Park ⓯

Map 18 D3. Ⓜ 86th St.

LAID OUT IN 1891, this park
along the East River has a
wide promenade over the
East River Drive. It offers fine
vistas of the river and the
turbulent waters of Hell Gate,
where the river meets Long
Island Sound. It is named
after Carl Schurz, a native
who became Secretary of the
Interior (1869–75). The first
part of the promenade is the
John Finlay Walk, named for
an editor of the *New York
Times* known for his hiking
prowess. One of the city's
most pleasant green escapes,
the park's grassy areas are
filled with basking New
Yorkers on sunny days.

Gracie Mansion ⓰

East End Ave at 88th St. **Map** 18 D3.
📞 570-4751. Ⓜ 86th St. **Open**
Mar–mid-Nov 10am–2pm Wed for
guided tours by reservation only. **Adm
charge.** 🚫 ✂ 🛗

THIS GRACIOUS, balconied
wooden 1799 country
home is the official mayor's
residence. Built by wealthy
merchant Archibald Gracie, it
is one of the best Federal
houses left in New York.
    The house was acquired by
the city in 1887 and was the
first home of the Museum of
the City of New York. Mayor
Fiorello La Guardia moved in
in 1942 after nine years in

Front view of Gracie Mansion

office, preferring it to a 75-room palace on Riverside Drive – he said that even the modest Gracie Mansion was much too fancy for him. La Guardia, "the Little Flower" (from Fiorello), fought corruption in the city and reformed New York.

Church of the Holy Trinity ⓱

316 E 88th St. **Map** 17 B3.
[289-4100. Ⓜ 86th St. **Open** 9am–5pm Mon–Fri, 7:30am–2pm Sun. ✝ winter: 8:15am, 9:15am, 11am, 7pm Sun; summer: 8:15am, 10am.

Arched doorway of the Church of the Holy Trinity

DELIGHTFULLY PLACED in a serene garden setting, this church was constructed in 1889 of glowing golden brick and terra-cotta in French Renaissance style. It boasts one of New York's best bell towers, which sports a handsome wrought-iron clock with brass hands. The arched doorway is richly decorated with carved images of the saints and prophets.

The complex was donated by Serena Rhinelander in memory of her father and grandfather. The land was part of the Rhinelander farm, which the family had owned for 100 years.

Farther down at 350 E. 88th Street is the Rhinelander Children's Center, also a gift, and the headquarters of the Children's Aid Society.

St. Nicholas Russian Orthodox Cathedral ⓲

15 E 97th St. **Map** 16 F1.
[289-1915. Ⓜ 96 St. **Open** by appt. ✝ 6pm Sat, 10:00am Sun (Russian). ◉

THIS REALLY IS "MOSCOW on the Hudson." Built in Muscovite Baroque style in 1902, it has five onion domes crowned with crosses, and blue and yellow tiles on a red brick and white stone facade. Among the early worshipers were White Russians who had fled the first uprisings at home, mostly intellectuals and aristocrats who soon became a part of New York society. Later, there were more waves of refugees, dissidents and defectors.

The cathedral now serves a scattered community, and the congregation is small. Mass is celebrated in Russian with great pomp and dignity. The cathedral is filled with the scent of incense. The high central sanctuary has marble columns with blue and white trim above. Ornate wooden screens trimmed with gold enclose the altar. It is unique, an unexpected find on a side street in this staid part of Manhattan.

Facade and domes of St. Nicholas Russian Cathedral

Facade of the Museum of the City of New York

Museum of the City of New York ⓳

5th Ave at 103rd St. **Map** 21 C5.
[534-1672. Ⓜ 103rd St. **Open** 10am–5pm Wed–Sat, 1–5pm Sun. **Closed** public hols. **Donations welcome.** ◉ ♿ ▢ ▯

FOUNDED IN 1923 and at first housed in Gracie Mansion, this museum is dedicated to New York's development from its earliest beginnings, shown in costumes, paintings, furnishings, toys and a range of fascinating memorabilia.

Housed in this handsome Georgian Colonial building since 1932, it is noted for its period rooms from actual homes, including John D. Rockefeller's bedroom and dressing room, and for its wonderful collection of toys, dolls and dollhouses dating from 1769. Start with *The Big Apple* video, then visit the exhibition, "Broadway! 125 Years of Musical Theater". The second floor has a magnificent collection of silver objects dating from 1678 to 1984. The Alexander Hamilton Gallery contains furniture and paintings that once belonged to the first Secretary of the Treasury.

The impressive collection housed in the basement includes antique fire equipment, paintings, maps and prints all relating to city history.

Whitney Museum of American Art ●

THE WHITNEY MUSEUM is the foremost showcase for American art of this century. It was founded in 1930 by sculptor Gertrude Vanderbilt Whitney after the Metropolitan Museum of Art turned down her collection of works by living artists including George Bellows and Edward Hopper. In 1966 the museum moved to the present inverted pyramid building designed by Marcel Breuer. The Whitney Biennial show is the most significant survey of new trends in American art.

The cantilevered facade of the Whitney Museum

Green Coca-Cola Bottles
Andy Warhol's 1962 work is a commentary on mass production and monopoly.

The White Calico Flower
Georgia O'Keeffe's enlarged flower paintings have an abstract quality, as in this 1931 example.

Little Big Painting
The 1965 work by Roy Lichtenstein is a comic critique of Abstract Expressionist painting.

Early Sunday Morning (1930)
Edward Hopper's paintings often convey the emptiness of American city life.

MUSEUM GUIDE
There are no permanent displays here; the only item always on exhibit is Alexander Calder's sculpture Circus, *situated on the first floor. Changing exhibitions occupy the second, third and fourth floors.*

Dempsey and Firpo
In 1924, George Bellows depicted one of the most famous prizefights of the century.

Three Flags *(1958)*
Jasper Johns's use of familiar objects in an abstract form was influential in the development of Pop art.

Owh! In San Paõ *(1951)*
In this painting by Stuart Davis, abstract forms are combined with lettering to create a unique and distinctive American style.

Circus *(1926–31)*
Alexander Calder's fanciful creation is always on display.

Tango *(1919)*
This is considered Polish-born Elie Nadelman's greatest wood sculpture.

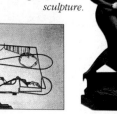

Hudson River Landscape *(1951)*
This steel sculpture is one of David Smith's most influential works.

Frick Collection ⑧

THE PRICELESS ART collection of steel magnate Henry Clay Frick (1849–1919) is exhibited in a residential setting amid the furnishings of his opulent mansion, providing a rare glimpse of how the extremely wealthy lived in New York's gilded age. Frick intended the collection to be a memorial to himself and bequeathed the entire house to the nation on his death. The collection includes old master paintings, French furniture, Limoges enamels and Oriental rugs.

Fifth Avenue facade of the Frick Collection

The Harbor of Dieppe (1826)
J.M.W. Turner was criticized by some sceptical contemporaries for depicting this northern European port suffused with light.

Colonnade
Garden Court

The White Horse (1819)
John Constable based this painting on a familiar scene from his Suffolk home.

Library

West Gallery

Limoges Enamel
The collection of enamels includes The Seven Sorrows of the Virgin *(1500–50).*

STAR PAINTINGS

★ **Sir Thomas More by Hans Holbein**

★ **Mall in St. James's Park by Thomas Gainsborough**

★ **Officer and the Laughing Girl by Jan Vermeer**

★ **Lady Meux by James A.M. Whistler**

★ **Sir Thomas More** (1527)
Holbein's portrait of Henry VIII's Lord Chancellor was painted eight years before More's execution for treason.

Living Hall

GALLERY GUIDE

Of special interest are the skylit West Gallery, offering oils by Vermeer, Hals and Rembrandt; the East Gallery, featuring Whistler; the Library and Dining Room, devoted to English works; and the Living Hall with works by Titian, Bellini and Holbein.

★ Lady Meux *(1881)*
Before marrying a brewery baron, the coquettish young Lady Meux was an actress. This was Whistler's second of three portraits of her.

East Gallery

VISITORS' CHECKLIST

1 E 70th St. **Map** 12 F1. 288-0700. 6 to 68th St. M1, M2, M3, M4. **Open** 10am–6pm Tue–Sat, 1–6pm Sun. **Closed** most public hols. **Adm charge** (children under 10 not admitted). Concerts, lectures, film & video presentations.

★ Officer and the Laughing Girl *(1655–60)*
Jan Vermeer is unique among 17th-century Dutch painters for his bold use of light and shadow.

KEY TO FLOOR PLAN

☐ Exhibition space

☐ Non-exhibition space

Stairs to lower gallery

Main entrance

Fowling and Horticulture *(1750–52)*
François Boucher painted a series of panels for Madame de Pompadour. This one reflects her interest in exotic birds and botany.

Dining Room

Fragonard Room

The Pursuit
This is part of The Progress of Love *(1771–3 and 1790–91), by Jean-Honoré Fragonard. The series of paintings depicts the events of an idealized courtship.*

★ Mall in St. James's Park *(1783)*
The three central figures in Thomas Gainsborough's London landscape may be the daughters of George III.

CENTRAL PARK

THE CITY'S "BACKYARD" was created by Frederick Law Olmsted and Calvert Vaux in 1858 on an unpromising site of quarries, pig farms, swampland and shacks. Ten million cartloads of stone and earth turned it into the lush 843-acre (340-ha) park of today. There are scenic hills, lakes and lush meadows, dotted throughout with outcrops of Manhattan bedrock and planted with more than 500,000 trees and shrubs. Over the years the park has blossomed, with playgrounds and skating rinks, plus ball fields and spaces for everything from chess and croquet to concerts and events for the thousands. Cars are banned on weekends, giving bicyclists and joggers the right-of-way.

Statues, Delacorte Theater *(see p206)*

SIGHTS AT A GLANCE

Historic Buildings
The Dairy **1**
Belvedere Castle **3**

Monuments and Statues
Strawberry Fields **2**
Bethesda Fountain and Terrace **5**
Bow Bridge **4**

Lakes and Gardens
Conservatory Water **6**
Central Park Wildlife
Conservation Center **7**
Conservatory Garden **8**

SEE ALSO

GETTING THERE
Subway lines B and C run the length of the park on the Upper West Side, with stops at 59th, 72nd, 81st, 86th, 96th and 103rd Sts. The 59th St/Columbus Circle stop is served by the 1 and 9 Broadway/7th Ave lines, and the N and R Broadway local trains stop at 57th St and 5th Ave at the southern end of the park. Bus routes M1, M2, M3 and M4 run along the eastern edge of the park.

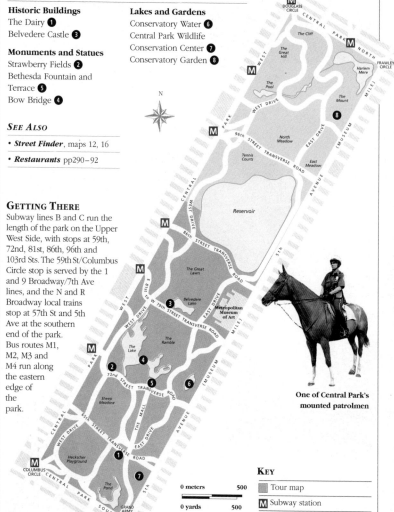

One of Central Park's mounted patrolmen

KEY

	Tour map
M	Subway station

0 meters 500
0 yards 500

Bird's-eye view of the park

A Tour of Central Park

On a short visit, a walking tour from 59th to 79th streets takes in some of Central Park's loveliest features, from the dense wooded Ramble to the open formal spaces of Bethesda Terrace. Along the way, you will see artificial lakes and some of the 30 graceful bridges and arches, no two alike, that link some 58 miles (93 km) of footpaths, bridle paths and roads in the park. In summer the park is often several degrees cooler than the city streets around it, and thus is a favorite retreat.

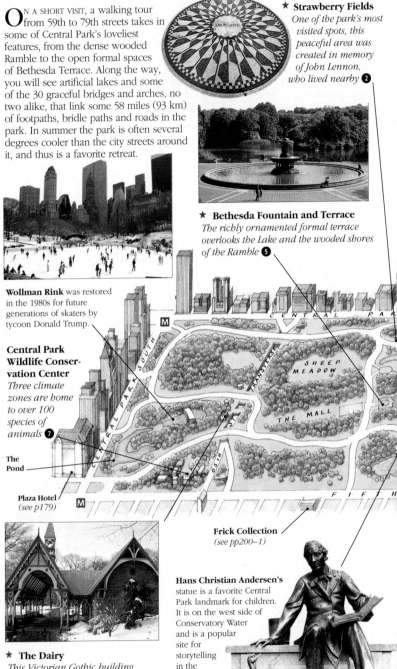

★ **Strawberry Fields**
One of the park's most visited spots, this peaceful area was created in memory of John Lennon, who lived nearby ❷

★ **Bethesda Fountain and Terrace**
The richly ornamented formal terrace overlooks the Lake and the wooded shores of the Ramble ❺

Wollman Rink was restored in the 1980s for future generations of skaters by tycoon Donald Trump.

Central Park Wildlife Conservation Center
Three climate zones are home to over 100 species of animals ❼

The Pond

Plaza Hotel
(see p179)

Frick Collection
(see pp200–1)

Hans Christian Andersen's statue is a favorite Central Park landmark for children. It is on the west side of Conservatory Water and is a popular site for storytelling in the summer.

★ **The Dairy**
This Victorian Gothic building houses the Visitor Center. Make it your first stop and pick up a calendar of park events ❶

Bow Bridge
This cast-iron bridge links the Ramble with Cherry Hill by a graceful arch, 60 ft (18 m) above the Lake **4**

LOCATOR MAP
See Manhattan Map pp12–13

Alice in Wonderland is immortalized in bronze at the northern end of Conservatory Water, along with her friends the Cheshire Cat, the Mad Hatter and the Dormouse. Children love to slide down her toadstool seat.

STAR SIGHTS

- ★ **The Dairy**
- ★ **Strawberry Fields**
- ★ **Belvedere Castle**
- ★ **Bethesda Fountain**
- ★ **Conservatory Water**

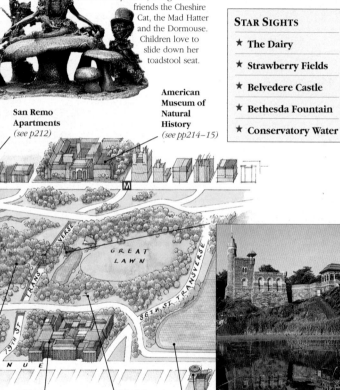

Dakota Building *(see p216)*

San Remo Apartments *(see p212)*

American Museum of Natural History *(see pp214–15)*

WEST

GREAT LAWN

TRANSVERSE

79TH ST TRANSVERSE

86TH ST TRANSVERSE

AVENUE

Metropolitan Museum *(see pp190–95)*

Obelisk

Reservoir

Guggenheim Museum *(see pp186–87)*

The Ramble is a wooded area of 37 acres (15 ha), criss-crossed by paths and streams. It is a paradise for bird-watchers – over 250 species have been spotted in the park, which is on the Atlantic migration flyway.

★ **Belvedere Castle**
From the terraces there are unequaled views of the city and surrounding park. Within the stone walls is the Central Park Learning Center **3**

★ **Conservatory Water**
From March to November, this is the scene of model boat races each Saturday. Many of the tiny crafts are stored in the boathouse that adjoins the Lake **6**

The Carousel, part of the park's Children's Department

The Dairy ❶

Map 12 F2. 397-3156.
360-1333. Fifth Ave. **Open** Mar–Nov: 11am–5pm Tue–Sun (1–5pm Fri); Nov–Mar: 11am–4pm Tue–Sun (1–4pm Fri). **Slide show.**

NOW USED AS the park information center, this charming building of natural stone was planned as part of the "Children's Department" of the park, which included a playground, the Carousel, a Children's Cottage and stable. In 1873, there were cows grazing on the meadows in front of the Dairy, a ewe and her lambs feeding nearby, and chickens, guinea fowl and peacocks roaming the lawn. City children could get fresh milk and other refreshments here. Over the years,

the Dairy deteriorated, being used as a shed until restoration in 1979, done according to original photographs and drawings. The Dairy is the place to begin exploring the park; maps and details of events can be obtained here. The less energetic can rent chess and checkers sets for use on the inlaid boards of the *kinderberg*, the little "children's hill" nearby.

Strawberry Fields ❷

Map 12 E1. 72nd St.

THE RESTORATION of this teardrop-shaped section of the park was Yoko Ono's tribute in memory of her slain husband, John Lennon. They lived in the Dakota apartments overlooking this spot *(see p216)*. Gifts for the garden came from all over the world. A mosaic set in the pathway, inscribed with the word *Imagine* (named for Lennon's famous song), was a gift from the city of Naples in Italy.

This broad expanse of the park's landscape was designed by Vaux and Olmsted. Now it is an international peace garden, with 161 species of plants (one from every country of the world), including jetbead, roses, witch hazel, birches – and strawberries.

Belvedere Castle ❸

Map 16 E4. 772-0288. 81st St. **Open** Mar–Nov: 11am–5pm Tue–Sun (1–5pm Fri); Nov–Mar: 11am–4pm Tue–Sun (1–4pm Fri). to main floor only.

THIS STONE CASTLE atop Vista Rock, complete with tower and turrets, offers one of the best views of the park and the city from its rooftop lookout. Inside is the Central Park Learning Center, with a delightful Discovery Chamber telling young visitors about the park's wildlife.

The view to the north from the castle allows you to look down into

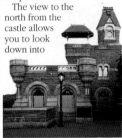

Belvedere Castle with its lookout over the park

the Delacorte Theater, home to the free productions of Shakespeare in the Park every summer, featuring bigname stars *(see p335)*. The theater was the gift of George T. Delacorte. Publisher and founder of Dell paperbacks, Delacorte was a delightful philanthropist who was responsible for many of the park's pleasures.

Bow Bridge ❹

Map 16 E5. 72nd St.

THIS IS ONE of the park's seven original cast-iron bridges and is considered one of the finest. It was designed by Vaux as a bow tying together the two large sections of the lake. In the 19th century, when the Lake was used for ice skating, a red ball was hoisted from a bell tower on Vista Rock to signal that the ice was safe. The bridge offers expansive views of the park and the buildings bordering it on both the east and west sides.

A tranquil scene in Central Park, overlooked by exclusive apartments

An 1864 print of Bethesda Fountain and Terrace

Bethesda Fountain and Terrace ❺

Map 12 E1. Ⓜ *72nd St.*

Sᴵᴛᴜᴀᴛᴇᴅ ʙᴇᴛᴡᴇᴇɴ the Lake and the Mall, this is the architectural heart of the park, a formal element in the naturalistic landscape. The fountain was dedicated in 1873. The statue, *Angel of the Waters*, marked the opening of the Croton Aqueduct system in 1842, bringing the city its first supply of pure water; its name refers to a biblical account of a healing angel at the pool of Bethesda in Jerusalem. The Spanish-style detailing, such as the sculptured double staircase, tiles and friezes, is by Jacob Wrey Mould.

The terrace is one of the best spots to relax and take in some people-watching.

Conservatory Water ❻

Map 16 F5. Ⓜ *77th St.*

Bᴇᴛᴛᴇʀ ᴋɴᴏᴡɴ as the Model Boat Pond, this stretch of water is home to model yacht races every weekend.

At the north end of the lake, a sculpture of Alice in Wonderland is a delight for children. It was commissioned by George T. Delacorte in honor of his wife. He himself is immortalized in caricature as the Mad Hatter. On the west bank, free story hours are held at a statue of Hans Christian Andersen, portrayed reading from his own story, "The Ugly Duckling", while its hero

waddles at his feet. Like that of Alice, this statue is climbed on by small children, who especially like to snuggle in the author's lap.

Conservatory Water's literary links continue into adolescence: it is here that J.D. Salinger's Holden Caulfield comes to tell the ducks his troubles in *The Catcher in the Rye*.

Central Park Wildlife Conservation Center ❼

Map 12 F2. Ⓒ *861-6030.* Ⓜ *Fifth Ave.* **Open** *Apr–Oct: 10:30am–5pm Mon–Fri, 10am–5:30pm Sat & Sun; Nov–Mar: 10am–4:30pm daily.* **Adm charge.** 📷 ♿ 🖥 🚻

Rᴇᴏᴘᴇɴᴇᴅ ɪɴ 1988 after four years of reconstruction, this imaginative zoo won plaudits for its creative and humane use of small space. More than 100 species of animals are represented in three climate zones, the Tropics, the Polar Circle and the California coast. An equatorial rain forest is home to monkeys and free-flying birds, while penguins and polar bears populate an Arctic landscape that allows views both above and under water.

Polar bear in the Wildlife Conservation Center

Near the entrance to the Children's Zoo is the much-loved Delacorte Clock, another example of the whimsical generosity of George T. Delacorte. Every half hour, bronze musical animals (such as a goat playing pan pipes) circle the clock playing nursery rhymes. Toward Willowdell Arch is another children's favorite – the memorial to Balto, lead dog of a team of huskies that made a heroic journey across Alaska to deliver serum for a diphtheria epidemic.

Statue of Balto, the heroic husky sled dog

Conservatory Garden ❽

Map 21 B5. Ⓜ *Central Pk N, 103rd St.* Ⓒ *860-1330.*

Tʜᴇ ᴠᴀɴᴅᴇʀʙɪʟᴛ ɢᴀᴛᴇ on Fifth Avenue is the entry to three formal gardens filled with thousands of flowering trees and shrubs. The Central Garden has a large lawn with yew hedges and ends in a semicircle of hedges and shrubs crowned by a wisteria pergola. On either side are blooming Siberian crabapple trees. The South Garden spills over with perennials. The bronze statue in the reflecting pool is of Mary and Dickon, from Frances Hodgson Burnett's *The Secret Garden*. Beyond is a slope featuring thousands of native wildflowers, spreading into the park beyond. The North Garden, centered around the bronze *Fountain of the Three Dancing Maidens*, puts on a brief but brilliant display of annuals each summer.

UPPER WEST SIDE

THIS AREA became residential only in the 1870s, when the Ninth Avenue El *(see pp24-5)* made commuting to midtown possible for the first time. When the Dakota, New York's first luxury apartment house, was built between 1880 and 1884, the city finally began to grade and level the

Indian mask, Museum of Natural History

streets. Buildings soon sprang up along Broadway and Central Park West, and today the area is bustling and diverse. The cross streets, dating mainly from the 1890s, boast many fine brownstone row houses. Many cultural institutions are here, including Lincoln Center and the American Museum of Natural History.

SIGHTS AT A GLANCE

Historic Streets and Buildings
Twin Towers of Central Park West ❶
The Dakota ❾
Pomander Walk ❸
Riverside Drive and Park ❹
The Dorilton ⓱

Museums and Galleries
Museum of American Folk Art ❼
New-York Historical Society ❿
American Museum of Natural History pp214–15 ⓫
Hayden Planetarium ⓬
Children's Museum of Manhattan ⓯

Famous Theaters
Lincoln Center for the Performing Arts ❷
New York State Theater ❸
Metropolitan Opera House ❹
Lincoln Center Theater ❺
Avery Fisher Hall ❻

Landmark Hotels and Restaurants
Hotel des Artistes ❽
Ansonia Hotel ⓰

GETTING THERE
By subway, take the 7th Ave/Broadway 1, 2 and 3 trains or the 8th Ave A, C and E trains. Buses include the M10 (Central Park West), M7, M11, M104 and M5 or the M66, M72, M79, M86 and M96 crosstown buses.

SEE ALSO

• *Street Finder*, maps 11, 15
• *Where to Stay* pp274-75
• *Restaurants* pp290-92

N

0 meters 500
0 yards 500

The facade of 14 Riverside Drive

Stone figure on the facade of the Hotel des Artistes

KEY

▦ Street-by-Street map

Ⓜ Subway station

Street by Street: Lincoln Center

LINCOLN CENTER was conceived when both the Metropolitan Opera House and the New York Philharmonic required homes, and a large tract on Manhattan's west side was in dire need of revitalization. The notion of a single complex where different performing arts could exist side by side seems natural today, but in the 1950s it was considered both daring and risky. Today Lincoln Center has proved itself by drawing audiences of five million each year. Proximity to its halls prompts both performers and arts lovers to live nearby.

★ **Lincoln Center for the Performing Arts**
Dance, music and theater come together in this fine contemporary complex. It is also a great place to sit around the reflecting fountain and people-watch ❷

Lincoln Center Theater
The Vivian Beaumont and the Mitzi E. Newhouse theaters are both housed in this building ❺

Composer Leonard Bernstein's famous musical *West Side Story*, which was based on the Romeo and Juliet theme, was set in the impoverished streets around what is now Lincoln Center. Bernstein was later instrumental in setting up the large music complex.

The Guggenheim Bandshell in Damrosch Park is the site of free concerts.

The New York State Theater
This is the home of the New York City Ballet, as well as an opera company. The theater seats 2,737 people ❸

Metropolitan Opera House
Lincoln Center's focus is the Opera House. The café at the top of the lobby offers wonderful plaza views ❹

The College Board Building is an Art Deco delight that now houses condominiums and the administrative offices of the College Board, developers of the college entrance exam.

Museum of American Folk Art
Quilting and naïve painting are some of the arts displayed here **7**

Early American quilt

James Dean once lived in a one-room apartment on the top floor at 19 West 68th Street.

★ **Hotel des Artistes**
Artists Isadora Duncan, Noël Coward and Norman Rockwell once lived here. It also houses a much-praised restaurant (see p296) **8**

LOCATOR MAP
see Manhattan Map pp12–13

KEY

– – – Suggested route

0 meters   100
0 yards   100

To 72nd Street subway (4 blocks)

The American Broadcasting Company is housed in this castle-like building, formerly an armory.

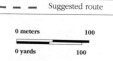

55 Central Park West is the Art Deco apartment building that featured in the film *Ghostbusters*.

The Society for Ethical Culture was one of the city's first Art Nouveau buildings. It also houses a school.

To 59th Street subway (2 blocks)

Central Park West is home to many celebrities, who like the privacy of its exclusive apartments.

STAR SIGHTS

★ **Lincoln Center**

★ **Hotel des Artistes**

Century Apartments
The Century's twin towers are visible from the park, making it a New York landmark **1**

The San Remo, a twin-towered apartment house designed by Emery Roth

Twin Towers of Central Park West ❶

Map 12 D1, 12 D2, 16 D3, 16 D5.
Ⓜ *59th St-Columbus Circle, 72nd St.
Not open to public.*

Aᴍᴏɴɢ ᴛʜᴇ ᴍᴏsᴛ familiar
landmarks on the New
York skyline are the four
twin-towered apartment
houses on Central Park West.
Built from 1929 and 1931, just
before the Great Depression
halted all luxury construction,
they are now among the most
highly sought-after residences
in New York.

Admired today for their
grace and architectural detail,
they were designed in response
to a city planning law allow-
ing taller apartments if set
backs and towers were used.

Emery Roth designed
the San Remo (145
CPW), whose tenants
have included Dustin
Hoffman, Paul Simon
and Diane Keaton.
Madonna was turned
down by the residents'
committee and lives
close by at One West
64th Street, next door to
the New York Society
for Ethical Culture. The

towers on the Eldorado (300
CPW), also designed by Roth,
are crowned by futuristic pinnacles. Celebrities here have
included Groucho Marx, Marilyn
Monroe and Richard Dreyfuss.
The Majestic (115 CPW) and
the Century (25 CPW) are both
sleek classics by Art Deco
designer Irwin S. Chanin.

Lincoln Center for the Performing Arts ❷

Map 11 C2. 【 875-5400. Ⓜ 65th
St. ♿ ⌚ 875-5350. 🚻 🅿 *See
Entertainment pp338–9.*

Iɴ ᴍᴀʏ 1959, President Dwight
D. Eisenhower traveled to
New York to turn a shovelful
of earth, Leonard Bernstein
lifted his baton, the New York
Philharmonic and the Juilliard
Chorus broke into the
Hallelujah Chorus – and New
York's most important cultural
center was born.

It was soon to cover 15
acres (6 ha) on the site of the
slums that had been the
setting for Bernstein's classic
musical *West Side Story.*

The plaza fountain is by
Philip Johnson, and the
sculpture in the reflecting
pool, *Reclining Figure*, is by
Henry Moore.

Guided tours are the best
way to see the complex.

New York State Theater ❸

Lincoln Center. **Map** 11 D2. 【 870-
5570. Ⓜ *66th St.* ♿ ⌚ 🚻 🅿
See Entertainment pp334–5.

Tʜᴇ ʜᴏᴍᴇ ʙᴀsᴇ for the
highly acclaimed New
York City Ballet and the New
York City Opera, a troupe
devoted to presenting opera
at popular prices, is a Philip
Johnson design. It was
inaugurated in 1964.

Gargantuan white marble
sculptures by Elie Nadelman
dominate the vast four-story
foyer. The theater seats 2,800
people. Because of its rhine-
stone lights and chandeliers
both inside and out, some
have described the theater as
"a little jewel box."

Metropolitan Opera House ❹

Lincoln Center. **Map** 11 D2. 【 362-
6000. Ⓜ *66th St.* ♿ ⌚ 🚻 🅿
See Entertainment pp338–9.

Hᴏᴍᴇ ᴛᴏ ᴛʜᴇ Metropolitan
Opera Company and the
American Ballet Theater, "the
Met" is certainly the
most spectacular of
Lincoln Center's build-
ings and the focal
point of the plaza. Five
great arched windows
offer views of the
opulent foyer and two
radiant murals by Marc
Chagall. (You can't see
them in the mornings
when they are pro-
tected from the sun.)

Central plaza at Lincoln Center

Inside there are curved white marble stairs, miles of plush red carpeting and exquisite starburst crystal chandeliers

Free open-air concerts are held at the Guggenheim Bandshell

that are raised to the ceiling just before each performance. All the greats have sung here, including Maria Callas, Jessye Norman and Luciano Pavarotti. First nights are glittering, star-studded occasions.

The Guggenheim Bandshell, in Damrosch Park next to the Met, is a popular concert site featuring music from opera to jazz. The high point of the season is the Lincoln Center Out-of-Doors Festival that takes place in August.

Lincoln Center Theater **5**

Lincoln Center. **Map** 11 C2.
(362-7600 (Beaumont and Newhouse), 870-1630 (Library).
M 66th St. & / 📶 🔲 See
Entertainment pp338–9.

TWO THEATERS MAKE up this innovative complex, presenting eclectic and often experimental drama.

The theaters are the 1000-seat Vivian Beaumont and the smaller, more intimate 280-seat Mitzi E. Newhouse.

Works by some of New York's best modern playwrights have been featured at the Beaumont. The theater's inaugural performance in 1962 was Arthur Miller's *After the Fall*.

The size of the Newhouse suits workshop-style plays, but it can still make the news with theatrical gems such as Robin Williams and Steve Martin in a production of

Samuel Beckett's *Waiting for Godot*. Between the Metropolitan Opera and the Beaumont is the New York Public Library for the Performing Arts. Exhibits include cylinders of early Met performances and original scores and playbills.

Avery Fisher Hall **6**

Lincoln Center. **Map** 11 C2. (875-5030. M 66th St. & / 📶 🔲
See **Entertainment** p338–9.

HOME TO THE New York Philharmonic, America's oldest orchestra, as well as Lincoln Center's own Great Performers; Mostly Mozart Festival; and Jazz at Lincoln Center, Avery Fisher Hall opened in 1962 as Philharmonic Hall. While critics initially complained about the awful acoustics, several structural modifications, including one in 1992, have rendered the Hall an acoustic gem, comparing favorably with the great concert halls of the world.

For a small fee, the public can attend rehearsals on Thursday mornings.

Museum of American Folk Art **7**

Lincoln Sq. **Map** 12 D2.
(977-7170. M 66th St.
Open 11:30am–7:30pm Tue–Sun.
🚫 & / 🔲

CONCERTGOERS ATTENDING Lincoln Center events are among the many to discover and delight in this attractive, small modern gallery, which opened here in 1989 to show American folk art. The exhibits include quilts, carvings and paintings from the museum's permanent collection as well as changing displays. There are also special

programs for children and crafts demonstrations.

A huge weathervane in the shape of an American Indian and named for the legendary chief Tammany, presides over the central atrium. The museum plans a move to larger premises on West 53rd Street, but this location will remain as a branch.

Copper weathervane from the Museum of American Folk Art

Hotel des Artistes **8**

1 W 67th St. **Map** 12 D2.
(362- 6700. M 72nd St. See
Restaurants p296.

BUILT IN 1918 by George Mort Pollard, these two-story apartments were intended as working artists' studios but have attracted a variety of interesting tenants, including Alexander Woollcott, Norman Rockwell, Isadora Duncan, Rudolph Valentino and Noël Coward. The Café des Artistes is well known for its misty, romantic Howard Chandler Christy murals and its fine cuisine.

Decorative figure on the Hotel des Artistes

American Museum of Natural History ⓫

THIS IS THE largest natural history museum in the world. Since the original building by Calvert Vaux and J. Wrey Mould opened in 1877, the complex has grown to cover three city blocks. It holds over 36 million artifacts. The exhibits detail the evolution of life on Earth; many are amazingly lifelike. The most popular areas are the dinosaurs, meteors and the Hall of Minerals and Gems, which contains jewels valued at nearly $50 million. The Hayden Planetarium *(see p216)* adjoins the museum.

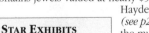

The entrance on 77th Street

STAR EXHIBITS

★ **Barosaurus**

★ **Blue Whale**

★ **Haida Canoe**

★ **Star of India**

★ **Star of India**
This 563-carat gem is the world's largest blue star sapphire. Found in Sri Lanka, it was given to the museum by J.P. Morgan in 1901.

GALLERY GUIDE

Enter at Central Park West on to the second floor to view the magnificent barosaurus exhibit, as well as exhibits on African, Asian, Central and South American peoples and animals. First-floor exhibits include ocean life, meteors, minerals and gems. North American Indians, birds and reptiles occupy the third floor. Dinosaurs, fossil fishes and early mammals are on the fourth floor.

★ **Blue Whale**
The blue whale is the largest of all animals, living or extinct. Its weight can exceed 150 tons. This replica is of a female captured off the southern US coast in 1925.

★ **Haida Canoe**
This 64-ft (19.5-m) seafaring war canoe of the Haida Indians was carved from the trunk of a single cedar. It stands in the 77th Street foyer.

Entrance on W. 77th St.

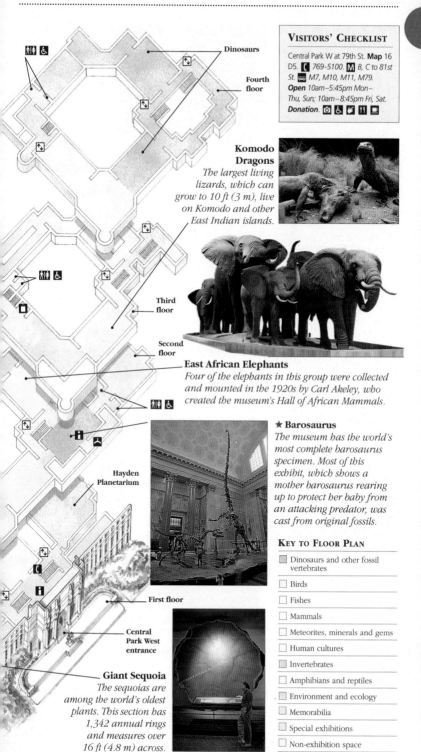

Dinosaurs

Fourth floor

VISITORS' CHECKLIST

Central Park W at 79th St. **Map** 16
D5. ☎ 769-5100. Ⓜ *B, C to 81st
St.* 🚌 *M7, M10, M11, M79.*
Open *10am–5:45pm Mon–
Thu, Sun; 10am–8:45pm Fri, Sat.*
Donation. 🅿 ♿ ✍ 🍴 🛍

Komodo Dragons
The largest living lizards, which can grow to 10 ft (3 m), live on Komodo and other East Indian islands.

Third floor

Second floor

East African Elephants
Four of the elephants in this group were collected and mounted in the 1920s by Carl Akeley, who created the museum's Hall of African Mammals.

★ Barosaurus
The museum has the world's most complete barosaurus specimen. Most of this exhibit, which shows a mother barosaurus rearing up to protect her baby from an attacking predator, was cast from original fossils.

Hayden Planetarium

KEY TO FLOOR PLAN

▨ Dinosaurs and other fossil vertebrates
☐ Birds
☐ Fishes
☐ Mammals
☐ Meteorites, minerals and gems
☐ Human cultures
▨ Invertebrates
☐ Amphibians and reptiles
▨ Environment and ecology
☐ Memorabilia
☐ Special exhibitions
☐ Non-exhibition space

First floor

Central Park West entrance

Giant Sequoia
The sequoias are among the world's oldest plants. This section has 1,342 annual rings and measures over 16 ft (4.8 m) across.

The Dakota 9

1 W 72nd St. **Map** 12 D1. Ⓜ *72nd St.* **Not open** *to the public.*

THE NAME AND STYLE reflect the fact that this apartment building was truly "way out West" when Henry J. Hardenberg, the architect responsible for the Plaza Hotel, designed it in 1880–84. It was New York's first luxury apartment house and was originally surrounded by squatters' shacks and wandering farm animals. Commissioned by Edward S. Clark, heir to the Singer sewing machine fortune, it is one of the city's most prestigious addresses.

The Dakota's 65 luxurious apartments have had many famous owners, including Judy Garland, Lauren Bacall, Leonard Bernstein and Boris Karloff, whose ghost is said to haunt the place. It was the setting for the film *Rosemary's Baby,* and the site of the tragic murder of former Beatle John Lennon. His widow, Yoko Ono, still lives here.

Carved Indian head over the entrance to the Dakota

New-York Historical Society 10

170 Central Park West. **Map** 16 D5. Ⓒ *873-3400.* Ⓜ *81st St.* **Library open** *10am–5pm Wed–Fri.* **Closed** *public hols. (Galleries closed till 1994.)* **Adm charge** *for galleries.* 🚫 ♿ ▣

AUDUBON'S ORIGINAL *Birds of America* prints and over 150 Tiffany lamps are among the treasures of New York's

The Laserium at the Hayden Planetarium

oldest museum. Founded in 1804, the Society has a wide collection of paintings and decorative arts dating back to the 17th century. The portrait collection includes Gilbert Stuart's *George Washington.* There is fine furniture from the Federal period, plus an exceptional silver display.

The Society is currently facing financial problems and its future is uncertain. The galleries are scheduled to reopen in late 1994, but check for the exact date.

American Museum of Natural History 11

See pp214–15.

Hayden Planetarium 12

Central Park West at 81st St. **Map** 16 D4. Ⓒ *769-5920, 769-5100 for times of shows.* Ⓜ *81st St.* **Open** *12:30–4:45pm Mon–Fri, 10am–5:45pm Sat, noon–5:45pm Sun (call for summer hours).* **Closed** *public hols.* **Adm charge.** ▣ ♿ *limited.* ▣

ADJOINING THE American Museum of Natural History is this planetarium, which was named after investment banker Charles Hayden, who donated the original astronomical equipment. In the Sky Theater the Zeiss VI projector re-creates the heavens on a vast dome. There are also 3-D laser light shows to rock music. Exhibits include a black light gallery with luminescent murals depicting a lunar landscape, and, in the Guggenheim Space Theater, a scale model of the solar system, over 40 ft (12 m) in diameter. It shows

the relative size and speed of planets and satellites. Another exhibit focuses on the sun, explaining such things as why the sky is blue. Special children's shows are hosted by and feature the *Sesame Street* Muppets or *Star Wars* robots.

Pomander Walk 13

261–7 W 94th St. **Map** 15 C2. Ⓜ *72nd St.*

LOOK THROUGH the gate for a delightful surprise – a double row of tiny town houses built in 1921 to look like the London mews setting of a popular play of the time.

Appropriately, it was much favored as a home by movie actors, including Rosalind Russell, Humphrey Bogart and the Gish sisters.

Facade of Pomander Walk town house

Riverside Drive and Park 14

Map 15 B4. Ⓜ *103rd St.*

RIVERSIDE DRIVE is one of the city's most attractive streets – broad, with shaded, and lovely views of the Hudson River. It is lined with the opulent original town houses as well as newer apartment buildings. At 40–46, 74–77, 81–89 and 105–107 Riverside Drive are houses designed at the end of the 19th century by local architect Clarence F. True.

Their curved gables, bays and arched windows seem to suit the curves of the road and the flow of the river.

The bizarrely named Cliff Dwellers' Apartments at 243 is a 1914 building with a frieze showing early Arizona cliff dwellers, complete with masks, buffalo skulls, mountain lions and rattlesnakes.

Riverside Park was designed by Frederick Law Olmsted in 1880. He also laid out Central Park (see pp202–5).

Soldiers' and Sailors' monument in Riverside Park

Children's Museum of Manhattan ⓯

212 W 83rd St. **Map** 15 C4. 📞 721-1234. Ⓜ 86th St. **Open** Sep–May: 1:30pm–5:30pm Mon, Wed, Thu; 10am–5pm Fri–Sun; Jun–Aug: 10am–5pm Wed–Mon. **Closed** Jan 1, Dec 25. **Adm charge**. ◻ ♿ ◻

THIS PARTICULARLY imaginative participatory museum was founded in 1973 on the premise that children learn best through play. In the "Brainatarium" the magic of the human mind is revealed in a four-minute multimedia show projected onto the domed ceiling. Using hi-tech, hands-on equipment, children can explore the five senses – not just their own, but also those of birds, insects and animals.

Children's Museum entrance

The Time Warner Center for Media transforms children into budding camera operators, newscasters, animators and technicians in a state-of-the-art TV studio. On weekends and holidays there are guest performers from puppeteers to storytellers in the 150-seat theater. There is also a gallery for free play and an art studio.

Ansonia Hotel ⓰

2109 Broadway. **Map** 11 C1. Ⓜ 72nd St. **Lobby open** to the public.

THIS BEAUX ARTS gem was built in 1899 by William Earl Dodge Stokes, heir to the Phelps Dodge Company fortune, who brought architect Paul E.M. Duboy from France to execute a sumptuous apartment-hotel to rival the Dakota.

The most prominent features are the round corner tower and the two-story mansard roof adorned with single and double dormers. Originally the building had a roof garden (complete with Dodge's menagerie: ducks,

Distinctive rounded turret of the Ansonia Hotel

chickens and a tame bear) and two swimming pools.

The hotel's thick, sound-muffling walls soon made it a favorite with the musical stars of yesteryear. Florenz Ziegfeld, Arturo Toscanini, Enrico Caruso, Leopold Stravinsky and Lily Pons were all once regular guests there.

The Dorilton ⓱

171 W 71st St. **Map** 15 C5. Ⓜ 72nd St. **Not open** to the public.

OPULENT DETAIL and an impressive high mansard roof adorn this apartment house. On the West 71st Street side of the building is a nine-story-high gateway. To the modern eye, the Dorilton is gloriously elaborate, but when it was first built in 1902 it provoked this reaction, reported by the *Architectural Record*: "The sight of it makes

Balcony on the Dorilton, supported by groaning figures

strong men swear and weak women shrink affrighted."

What would the critics have made of the Alexandria Condominium, at 135 West 70th Street, just a block away? Built in 1927 as the Pythian Temple, its current name stems from the lavish Egyptian-style motifs that adorned this former Masonic lodge. Many were stripped away when the building was converted to a condominium, but you can still see what the polychrome designs were like. There are lotus leaves, hieroglyphics, ornately carved columns, mythical beasts, and, in majestic splendor on the roof, two seated pharaohs.

MORNINGSIDE HEIGHTS AND HARLEM

ORNINGSIDE HEIGHTS, near the Hudson River, is home to Columbia University and two of the city's finest churches. Farther east is Hamilton Heights, situated on the border of Harlem, America's most famous black community. One way to see its highlights, which are spread over a large area, is

St. Francis of Assisi, Museo del Barrio

with one of the various tours offered, including a Sunday morning tour *(see p351)*. Many tours start in Hamilton Heights, move east to the St. Nicholas Historic District, stop to enjoy the gospel choir at the Abyssinian Baptist Church, and end with a southern-style brunch at Sylvia's, Harlem's best-known restaurant.

Louis Armstrong in a stained-glass window at the new Cotton Club

SIGHTS AT A GLANCE

Historic Streets and Buildings
Columbia University ❶
St. Paul's Chapel ❷
Low Library ❸
Grant's Tomb ❻
City College of the City University of New York ❼
Hamilton Grange National Memorial ❽
Hamilton Heights Historic District ❾
St. Nicholas Historic District ⓫
Mount Morris Historical District ⓲

Museums and Galleries
Aunt Len's Doll and Toy Museum ⓾
Schomburg Center for Research into Black Culture ⓭
Studio Museum in Harlem ⓱
Museo del Barrio ⓴

Famous Theaters
Harlem YMCA ⓮
Apollo Theater ⓰

Churches
Cathedral of St. John the Divine pp224–25 ❹
Riverside Church ❺
Abyssinian Baptist Church ⓬

Parks and Squares
Marcus Garvey Park ⓳

Landmark Restaurants
Sylvia's ⓯

GETTING THERE

By subway, take the 7th Ave/Broadway local 1 and 9 trains to 116th St./Columbia University. The M4, M5, M11 and M104 buses serve the area. For Harlem, take the A, B, C or D lines to 125th St, or the M1, M2, M7 or M101/102 buses.

Carved stone column, **Cathedral of St. John the Divine**

SEE ALSO

- **Street Finder**, maps 19–20
- **Where to Stay** pp174–75
- **Restaurants** pp290–92

| 0 meters | 500 |
| 0 yards | 500 |

KEY

Street-by-Street map

M Subway station

Street by Street: Columbia University

AGREAT UNIVERSITY is as much spirit as buildings. After admiring the architecture, linger awhile on Columbia's central quadrangle in front of the Low Library, where you will see the jeans-clad future leaders of America meeting and mingling between classes. Across from the campus on both Broadway and Amsterdam Avenue are the coffee-houses and cafés where students engage in lengthy philosophical arguments, debate the topics of the day or simply unwind.

Alma Mater was sculpted by Daniel Chester French in 1903 and survived a bomb blast in the 1968 student demonstrations.

ALMA MATER

116th St./Columbia University subway (lines 1, 9) Ⓜ

The School of Journalism is one of Columbia's many McKim, Mead & White buildings. Founded in 1912 by publisher Joseph Pulitzer, it is the home of the Pulitzer Prize awarded for the best in letters and music.

Butler Library is Columbia's main library.

Low Library
With its imposing facade and high dome, the library dominates the main quadrangle. McKim, Mead & White designed it in 1895–97 ❸

★ Central Quadrangle
Columbia's first buildings were designed by McKim, Mead & White and built around a central quadrangle. This view looks across the quad toward Butler Library ❶

St. Paul's Chapel
Designed by the architects Howells & Stokes in 1907, this church is known for its fine woodwork and magnificent vaulted interior. It is full of light and has fine acoustics ❷

The Sherman Fairchild Center was built in 1977 to house the university's life sciences departments.

LOCATOR MAP
See Manhattan Map pp12–13

KEY

– – – Suggested route

| 0 meters | 100 |
| 0 yards | 100 |

Student demonstrations put Columbia University in the news in 1968. The demonstrations were sparked by the university's plan to build a gymnasium in nearby Morningside Park. The protests forced the university to build elsewhere.

The Eglise de Notre Dame was built for a French-speaking congregation. Behind the altar is a replica of the grotto at Lourdes, France, the gift of a woman who believed her son was healed there.

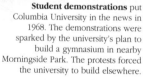

★**Cathedral of St. John the Divine**
If this Neo-Gothic cathedral is ever finished, it will be the largest in the world. Although one third of the structure has not yet been built, it can hold 10,000 parishioners ❹

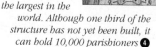

Carved stonework decorates the facade of the Cathedral.

Alma Mater statue at Low Library, Columbia University

Columbia University ❶

Main entrance at W 116th St. **Map** 20 E3. ☎ 854-1754. Ⓜ *116th St-Columbia Univ.* 🎥

THIS IS THE third location to date of one of America's oldest and finest universities. Founded in 1754 as King's College, it was first situated close to where the World Trade Center now stands.

In 1814, when a move uptown was proposed, the university approached the authorities for funding but was instead given a plot of land valued at $75,000, on which to build a new home. The university never built on the land itself, but leased it out and spent the years from 1857 to 1897 in buildings nearby. It finally sold the plot in 1985 to the leaseholders, Rockefeller Center Inc., for the sum of $400 million.

The present campus was begun in 1897 on the site of the Bloomingdale Insane Asylum. Architect Charles

McKim placed the university on a terrace, serenely above street level. Its spacious lawns and plazas still create a sense of contrast in the busy city.

At last count there were over 19,000 students at this campus, 10,400 men and 8,900 women. Columbia, an Ivy League School, is noted for its law, medicine and journalism schools. Its highly distinguished faculty and alumni, past and present, include 53 Nobel laureates. Famous alumni include Isaac Asimov, J.D. Salinger, James Cagney and Joan Rivers.

St. Paul's Chapel ❷

Columbia University. **Map** 20 E3. ☎ 854-6625. Ⓜ *116th St-Columbia Univ.* **Open** *noon–4pm Mon–Fri (term time), noon–2pm (breaks).* **Free organ concerts** *noon Thu.* ✝ *Sun.* ◎ ♿

Interior brick vaulting of St. Paul's Chapel dome

COLUMBIA'S MOST outstanding building, built in 1904, is a mix of Italian Renaissance, Byzantine and Gothic. The interior Guastavino vaulting is of intricate patterns of aged red brick; the whole chapel is bathed in light from above.

The free organ concerts are an exceptionally fine way to appreciate the beauty and acoustics of this church. The Aeolian-Skinner pipe organ is renowned for its fine tone.

Facade of St. Paul's Chapel

Low Library ❸

Columbia University. **Map** 20 E3. Ⓜ *116th St-Columbia Univ.*

A CLASSICAL, columned building atop three flights of stone stairs, the library was donated by Seth Low, a former mayor and college president. The statue in front of it, *Alma Mater* by Daniel Chester French, became familiar as the backdrop to the many 1968 anti–Vietnam War student demonstrations. The building is now used as offices, and its rotunda for a variety of academic and ceremonial purposes. The books have now been moved to Butler Library, across the quadrangle. The university's library collections total some six million volumes.

Cathedral of St. John the Divine ❹

See p224–5.

Riverside Church ❺

490 Riverside Dr at 122nd St. **Map** 20 D2. ☎ 222-5900. Ⓜ *116th St-Columbia Univ.* **Open** *9am–4pm daily.* ✝ *10:45am Sun.* ◎ *with prior permission.* ♿ 🎥 **Carillon bell concerts** *noon, 3pm Sun.* **Theatre** ☎ 864-2929.

A 21-STORY STEEL frame with a Gothic exterior, the church design was inspired by the cathedral at Chartres. It was lavishly funded by John D. Rockefeller, Jr., in 1930. The Laura Spelman Rockefeller Memorial Carillon (in honor of Rockefeller's mother) is the largest in the world, with 74

Columbia University's main courtyard and the Low Library

bells. The 20-ton Bourdon, or hour bell, is the largest and heaviest tuned carillon bell ever cast. The organ, with its 22,000 pipes, is among the largest in the world.

At the rear of the second gallery is a figure by Jacob Epstein, *Christ in Majesty,* cast in plaster and covered in gold leaf. Another Epstein statue, *Madonna and Child,* stands in the court next to the cloister. The panels of the chancel screen honor eight men and women whose lives have exemplified the teachings of Christ. They range from Socrates and Michelangelo to Florence Nightingale and Booker T. Washington.

For quiet reflection, enter the small, secluded Christ Chapel, patterned after an 11th-century Romanesque church in France. For views, take the elevator to the 20th floor and then walk the 140 steps to the top of the 392-ft (120-m) bell tower for a fine panorama of Upper Manhattan from the windy observation deck. (This is definitely not recommended when the bells are tolling.)

Mosaic mural in Grant's Tomb showing Grant (right) and Robert E. Lee

Grant's Tomb ❻

W 122nd St and Riverside Dr. **Map** 20 D2. 𝄡 666-1640. Ⓜ 116th St–Columbia Univ. **Open** 9am–5pm Wed–Sun. **Closed** Jan 1, Jul 4, Thanksgiving, Dec. 25 📷 ✔

THIS GRANDIOSE monument honors America's 18th president, Ulysses S. Grant, the commanding general of the Union forces in the Civil War.

The mausoleum contains the coffins of General Grant and his wife, in accordance with the president's last wish that they be buried together. After Grant's death in 1885, more than 90,000 Americans contributed $600,000 to build the sepulcher, which was inspired by Mausoleus's tomb at Halicarnassus, one of the Seven Wonders of the Ancient World. The tomb was dedicated on what

General Grant on a Civil War campaign

would have been Grant's 75th birthday, April 27, 1897. The parade of 50,000 people, along with a flotilla of 10 American and 5 European warships, took more than seven hours to pass in review.

The interior was inspired by Napoleon's tomb at Les Invalides in Paris. Each sarcophagus weighs 8.5 tons. Two exhibit rooms feature displays on Grant's personal life and his presidential and military career. Surrounding the north and east sides of the building are 17 sinuously curved mosaic benches that seem totally out of keeping with the formal architecture of the tomb. They were designed in the early 1970s by the Chilean-born Brooklyn artist Pedro Silva and built by 1,200 local volunteers under his super-vision. The colorful benches were inspired by the Spanish architect Antonio Gaudi's work in Barcelona. The mosaics depict subjects ranging from the Inuits to New York taxis to Donald Duck.

A short walk north of Grant's Tomb is another, humbler, monument. An unadorned urn on a pedestal marks the resting place of a young child who fell from the riverbank and drowned in the 18th century. His grieving father placed a marker that reads simply: "Erected to the memory of an amiable child, St. Clair Pollock, died 15 July 1797 in his fifth year of his age."

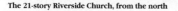

The 21-story Riverside Church, from the north

Cathedral of St. John the Divine ❹

Cram's Gothic West Front

STARTED IN 1892 and still only two-thirds finished, this will be the largest cathedral in the world. The interior is over 600 ft (180 m) long and 146 ft (45 m) wide. It was originally designed in Romanesque style by Heins and LaFarge; Ralph Adams Cram took over the project in 1911, devising a Gothic nave and west front. Medieval construction methods, such as stone supporting buttresses, continue to be used to complete the cathedral, which is also a venue for theater, music and avant-garde art.

Choir
Each of the choir's columns is 55 ft (17 m) tall and made of polished gray granite.

Nave
Rising to a height of over 100 ft (30 m), the piers of the nave are topped by graceful stone arches.

Rose Window★
Completed in 1933, the stylized motif of the Great Rose is symbolic of the many facets of the Christian Church.

★ **West Front Entrance**
The portals of the cathedral's west front are adorned with many fine stone carvings. Some are re-creations of medieval religious sculptures. Others, such as this apocalyptic vision of New York's skyline by local stonemason Joe Kinkannon, highlight the cathedral's involvement in political and social issues of the day.

STAR FEATURES

★ Rose Window

★ West Front Entrance

★ Bay Altars

★ Stoneworks

★ **Stoneworks**
The cathedral's statues are the creations of the Stoneworks program. The project was started in 1978, and employs English master stonemasons to teach local workers skills that have all but died out in the United States.

Baptistry
The Gothic Baptistry has Italian, French and Spanish influences.

THE FINISHED DESIGN

Crossing tower

South transept

West towers

It will cost approximately $400 million to complete the cathedral. The south transept, crossing tower and west towers have yet to be finished. When the money is raised, the proposed design will take at least another 50 years to complete.

Pulpit

St. Ambrose Chapel
Named after a 4th-century Italian bishop, the chapel is decorated with Renaissance-style ironwork.

★ **Bay Altars**
The bay altar windows are devoted to human endeavor. The sports window shows feats of skill and strength.

Bishop's Chair
This is a copy from the Henry VII chapel in Westminster Abbey.

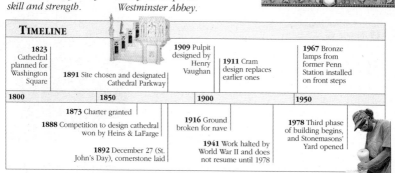

TIMELINE

1823 Cathedral planned for Washington Square	**1891** Site chosen and designated Cathedral Parkway	**1909** Pulpit designed by Henry Vaughan / **1911** Cram design replaces earlier ones	**1967** Bronze lamps from former Penn Station installed on front steps
1800	**1850**	**1900**	**1950**
1873 Charter granted / **1888** Competition to design cathedral won by Heins & LaFarge / **1892** December 27 (St. John's Day), cornerstone laid		**1916** Ground broken for nave / **1941** Work halted by World War II and does not resume until 1978	**1978** Third phase of building begins, and Stonemasons' Yard opened

City College of the City University of New York ❼

Main entrance at W. 138th St. and Convent Ave. **Map** 19 A2. 🅲 650-7000. Ⓜ 137th St-City College.

SET HIGH on a hill adjoining Hamilton Heights, the original Gothic quadrangle of this college, built between 1903 and 1907, is extremely impressive. The material used for the buildings is Manhattan schist, a stone that had been excavated in building the IRT subway. Later, contemporary buildings were added to the school, which enrolls nearly 15,000 students.

Once free to all residents of New York, City College still offers an education at the city's lowest tuition rates. Three-quarters of the students are from minority groups, and a large number of them are the first in their families to attend college.

Shepard Archway at City College of the City University of New York

Hamilton Grange National Memorial ❽

287 Convent Ave. **Map** 19 A1. 🅲 264-4428. Ⓜ 137th St-City College. **Not open** to the public.

BADLY SQUEEZED between a church and apartments is one of the city's most historic buildings, the 1802 columned wooden country home of Alexander Hamilton. He was one of the architects of the federal government system, the first secretary of the treasury and founder of the National Bank. It is his face

Statue of Alexander Hamilton at Hamilton Grange

that appears on the $10 bill. Hamilton lived here for the last two years of his life. He was killed in a duel with political rival Aaron Burr in 1804. Hamilton fired into the air.

The house was acquired by St. Luke's Episcopal Church in 1889 and moved two blocks to this "temporary" site, where it is closed, pending further relocation and renovation.

Hamilton Heights Historic District ❾

W 141st–W 145th St. and Convent Ave. **Map** 19 A1. Ⓜ 137th St-City College.

ORIGINALLY THIS was a setting for the country estates of the wealthy. Also known as Harlem Heights, it was developed during the 1880s following the extension of the El line (*see p24*) into the neighborhood. The privacy of the enclave, on a high hill above Harlem, made it a highly desirable location.

The section known as Sugar Hill was favored by Harlem's elite – Chief Justice Thurgood Marshall, jazz musicians Count Basie, Duke Ellington and Cab Calloway,

and boxer Sugar Ray Robinson, five times world middleweight champion, have all lived there.

The handsome three- and four-story stone row houses were built between 1886 and 1906 mixing Flemish, Romanesque and Tudor influences. In fine condition, many are used as residences by the faculty of City College.

Row houses in Hamilton Heights

Aunt Len's Doll and Toy Museum ❿

6 Hamilton Terr. **Map** 19 A1. 🅲 281-4143. Ⓜ 145th St (B, C, D). **Open** by appointment only. 🚫

THIS COLLECTION, belonging to retired schoolteacher Mrs. Lennon Holder Hoyte, includes over 5,000 dolls and toys, installed in one of Hamilton Terrace's row houses. The hours are at her convenience, so a call is essential before visiting.

Two items from Aunt Len's Doll and Toy Museum

Adam Clayton Powell, Jr. (in dark suit) during a civil rights campaign

St. Nicholas Historic District ⓫

202–250 W 138th & W 139th St.
Map 19 B2. **M** *135th St (B, C).*

KNOWN AS the King Model Houses, these row houses, built in 1891, were designed as a varied yet harmonious group by three different architects. The northern group is Neo–Italian Renaissance; the southern group is Georgian.

Successful blacks were attracted here in the 1920s and 1930s, giving it the nickname "Strivers' Row." Musicians W.C. Handy and Eubie Blake lived here.

Houses in St. Nicholas district

Abyssinian Baptist Church ⓬

132 W. 138th St. **Map** 19 C2.
C 862-7474. **M** *135th St (2, 3).*
🕇 *9am, 11am Sun. Groups of 10 or more need reservations.*

NEW YORK'S OLDEST black church, founded in 1808, became famous through its charismatic pastor Adam Clayton Powell, Jr. (1908–72), a congressman and civil rights leader. Under his leadership it became the most powerful black church in America. A room in the church houses memorabilia from his life.

The church welcomes visitors to its Sunday services in its 1923 Gothic building.

Schomburg Center for Research into Black Culture ⓭

515 Lenox Ave. **Map** 19 C2.
C 491-2200. **M** *135th St. (2, 3).*
Open *noon–8pm Mon–Wed, 10am–6pm Fri–Sat (exhibition hours vary).* **Closed** *Thur, public hols.* 📷 *with prior permission.*
♿ 🖋 🛒 📷

HOUSED IN a sleek contemporary complex opened in 1991, this is the largest research center of black and African culture in the United States. The huge collection was assembled by the late Arthur Schomburg, a black man of Puerto Rican descent, who was told by a

Kurt Weill, Elmer Rice and Langston Hughes at the Schomburg Center

teacher that there was no such thing as "black history."

The Carnegie Corporation bought the collection in 1926 and gave it to the New York Public Library; Schomburg was made curator. The library was the unofficial meeting place for writers involved in what later became known as the black literary renaissance of the 1920s, including Langston Hughes, W.E.B. Du Bois, Zora Neale Hurston and many other great writers of the day. It also hosted many literary gatherings and poetry readings.

The Schomburg Library has excellent facilities for conserving and making available the archive's treasures, which include rare books, art and recordings. The library was designed to double as a cultural center and includes a theater and two art galleries which feature changing shows.

Harlem YMCA ⓮

180 W 135th St. **Map** 19 C3.
C 281-4100. **M** *135th St (2, 3).*

Sociologist W.E.B. Du Bois

PAUL ROBESON and many others made their first stage appearances here in the early 1920s. The Krigqa Players, organized by W.E.B. Du Bois in the basement in 1928, was founded to counter the derogatory images of blacks often presented in Broadway reviews of the time. The "Y" also provided temporary lodgings for some notable new arrivals in Harlem, including writer Ralph Ellison.

Gospel singers performing at Sylvia's during Sunday brunch

Sylvia's ⓕ

328 Lenox Ave. **Map** 21 B1.
📞 996-0660. Ⓜ *125th St (2,3). See*
Restaurants *p294.*

Harlem's best-known soul
food restaurant serves up
southern-fried or smothered
chicken, spicy ribs, black-eyed
peas, collard greens, candied
yams, sweet potato pie and
other southern delicacies

(see p287). Sunday brunch is
served to the accompaniment
of gospel singers.
　Take some time to explore
the market at the corner of
125th Street and Lenox
Avenue (opposite Sylvia's),
extending for a block or more
in either direction. This isn't a
food market: it sells African
clothing, jewelry and art of
varying quality.

Apollo Theater ⓖ

253 W 125th St. **Map** 21 A1.
📞 864-0372. Ⓜ *125th St (A, B, C,
D). Open at showtimes. See*
Entertainment *p341.*

The apollo opened in 1914
as a whites-only opera
house. Its great fame came
when Frank Schiffman, a
white entrepreneur, took over
in 1934. He then opened the
theater to all races and turned

it into Harlem's best-known
showcase, with
legendary black
artists such as
Bessie Smith,
Billie Holiday,
Duke Ellington,
and Dinah
Washington
performing.
　Amateur
nights on
Wednesdays,
with winners

Apollo Theater

determined by audience
applause, were famous, and
there was a long waiting list
for performers. These amateur

nights launched the careers of
Sarah Vaughan, Pearl Bailey,
James Brown and Gladys
Knight, among others, and
they still attract hopefuls.
　The Apollo was *the* place
during the swing band era;
following World War II, a
new generation of musicians,
such as Charlie "Bird" Parker,
Dizzy Gillespie, Thelonius
Monk and Aretha Franklin,
continued the tradition.
　Rescued from decline and
refurbished in the 1980s, the
Apollo still features top black
entertainers performing the
blues, jazz, gospel and dance.

Studio Museum in Harlem ⓗ

144 W 125th St. **Map** 21 B2.
📞 864-4500. Ⓜ *125th St (2, 3).*
***Open** 10am–5pm Wed–Fri, 1–6pm
Sat, Sun.* **Closed** *Jan 1, Thanksgiving,
Dec 25.* **Adm charge.** 🚫 ♿ 🎥
***Lectures, children's programs,
films.*** 📷

The museum was founded in
1967 in a loft on upper
Fifth Avenue with the mission
of becoming the premier
center for the collection and
exhibition of the art and
artifacts of African-Americans.
　The present premises, a
five-story building on
Harlem's main commercial
street, were donated to the
museum by the New York
Bank for Savings in 1979.
The new museum opened
in 1982. There are galleries
on two levels for changing
exhibitions featuring artists
and cultural themes, and
three galleries are devoted to
the permanent collection of
works by major black artists.
　The photographic archives
comprise one of the most

Exhibition space at the Studio Museum in Harlem

complete records in existence of Harlem in its heyday. A side door opens on to a small sculpture garden.

In addition to its excellent exhibitions, the Studio Museum also maintains a national artist-in-residence program, and offers regular lectures, seminars, children's programs and film festivals. An excellent small shop sells a range of books and African crafts.

Mount Morris Historical District ⑱

W 119th–W 124th Sts. **Map** 21 B2. Ⓜ *125th St (2, 3).*

Y OU CAN PLAINLY see that the late 19th-century Victorian-style town houses near Marcus Garvey Park were once grand. This was a favorite neighborhood of German Jews moving up in the world from the Lower East Side. Time has not been kind, and this district shows how the area has deteriorated.

A few impressive churches, such as St. Martin's Episcopal Church, remain. There are also some interesting juxtapositions of faiths to be seen: the columned Mount Olivet Baptist Church, at 201 Lenox Avenue, was once Temple Israel, one of the most imposing synagogues in the

St. Martin's Episcopal Church on Lenox Avenue

city; and at the Ethiopian Hebrew Congregation, 1 West 123rd Street, housed in a former mansion, the choir sings in Hebrew on Saturdays.

Marcus Garvey Park ⑲

120th–124th Sts. **Map** 21 B2. Ⓜ *125th St (2,3).*

The flamboyant black nationalist leader Marcus Garvey

T HIS HILLY, ROCKY, two-block square of green is the site of New York's last fire watchtower, an open cast-iron structure built in 1856, with spiral stairs leading to the observation deck. The bell below the deck used to sound the alarm. Best to view it from a distance, however – this neighborhood is not recommended for carefree wandering. Previously known as Mount Morris Park, it was renamed in 1973 in honor of Marcus Garvey. He came to Harlem from Jamaica in 1916 and founded the Universal Negro Improvement Agency, which promoted self-help, racial pride and a back-to-Africa movement.

Museo del Barrio ⑳

1230 5th Ave. **Map** 21 C5. Ⓜ *103rd St (6).* **Open** *11am–5pm Wed–Sun. (Galleries closed for renovation till early 1994.* ☎ *831-7272 for opening date.)* **Donation expected.** Ø 🚻 ☑

F OUNDED IN 1969, this is North America's only museum devoted to Latin American art, specializing in the culture of Puerto Rico. Exhibitions feature contemporary painting and sculpture, folk art and historical artifacts. The stars of the permanent collection are about 240 wooden Santos, carvings of the saints by folk artisans. Exhibits change often, but some of the Santos are always to be found on display. The pre-Columbian collection contains rare artifacts from the Caribbean. Situated at the far end of Museum Mile, this unusual museum attempts to bridge the gap between the lofty Upper East Side and the cultural heritage of El Barrio (Spanish Harlem).

Folk art at the Museo del Barrio: one of the *Three Wise Men* (left) and the *Omnipotent Hand*

FARTHER AFIELD

THOUGH OFFICIALLY part of New York City, the boroughs outside Manhattan are quite different in feel and spirit. They are residential and don't have the famous skyscrapers that are associated with New York. The difference is evident even in the way residents describe a trip to Manhattan as "going into the city." Yet the outlying areas boast many attractions, including the city's biggest zoo, botanical gardens, museums, beaches and sports arenas. For a guided walk around Brooklyn see pages 264–65.

SIGHTS AT A GLANCE

Historic Streets and Buildings
Morris-Jumel Mansion ❷
George Washington Bridge ❸
Wave Hill ❺
Yankee Stadium ❿
Grand Army Plaza ⓱
Park Slope Historic District ⓲
Historic Richmond Town ㉓
Alice Austen House ㉖

Museums and Galleries
Audubon Terrace ❶
The Cloisters pp234–37 ❹
Van Cortlandt House Museum ❻

New York Hall of Science ⓭
American Museum of the Moving Image and Kaufman Astoria Studio ⓮
Brooklyn Children's Museum ⓯
The Brooklyn Museum pp248–51 ⓴
Jacques Marchais Center of Tibetan Art ㉔
Snug Harbor Cultural Center ㉕

Parks and Gardens
New York Botanical Garden pp240–41 ❽
International Wildlife Conservation Park pp242–43 ❾

Flushing Meadow-Corona Park ⓬
Prospect Park ⓳
Brooklyn Botanic Garden ㉑

Famous Theaters
Brooklyn Academy of Music ⓰

Cemeteries
Woodlawn Cemetery ❼

Beaches
City Island ⓫
Coney Island ㉒
Jamaica Bay Wildlife Refuge Center ㉗
Jones Beach State Park ㉘

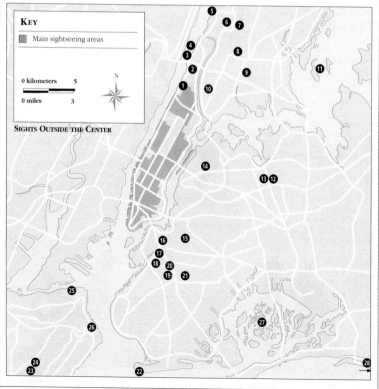

KEY
▢ Main sightseeing areas

0 kilometers 5
0 miles 3

N

SIGHTS OUTSIDE THE CENTER

Jamaica Bay

Upper Manhattan

IT WAS IN UPPER Manhattan that the 18th-century Dutch settlers established their farms. Now a suburban area with little of the bustle of downtown Manhattan, it is a good place to escape the inner city for some relaxed museum and landmark sightseeing. The Cloisters *(see pp234–37)* displays a magnificent collection of medieval art, housed within original European buildings of the period. A piece of New York history is found at the Morris-Jumel Mansion in north Harlem. From his headquarters here, George Washington mounted the defense of Manhattan in 1776.

Facade of the American Academy of Arts and Letters

Audubon Terrace **1**

M *157th St.* **American Numismatic Society** C *234-3130.* **Open** *9am–4:30pm Tue–Sat, 1–4pm Sun.*
🚫 🏛
American Academy of Arts and Letters C *368-5900.* **Open** *during exhibitions.* 🚫
Hispanic Society of America
C *926-2234.* **Open** *10am–4:30pm Tue–Sat, 1–4pm Sun.* **Closed** *public hols.* **Donation expected.** 📷 🏛

THIS 1908 complex of Classical Revival buildings by Charles Pratt Huntington is named after naturalist John James Audubon, whose estate once included this land. Audubon is buried in nearby Trinity Cemetery. His gravestone, a Celtic cross, bears the symbolic images of this adventurous artist's career: the birds he painted, his palette and brushes, and his rifles.

The complex was funded by the architect's cousin, civic benefactor Archer Milton Huntington. His dream was that it should be a center of culture and study. A central plaza contains statues by his wife, the sculptress Anna Hyatt Huntington.

Audubon Terrace contains several theme museums that are worth seeking out. The American Numismatic Society is the leading American museum devoted to coinage and medals, and has one of the world's best collections, with half a million photos and illustrations of coins. A permanent exhibition called "The World of Coins" traces the historical and political role of money, and there is a vast library.

The American Academy of Arts and Letters was set up to honor American writers, artists, and composers, and 75 honorary members from overseas. On the roll are writers John Steinbeck and Mark Twain, painters Andrew Wyeth and Edward Hopper, and the composer Aaron Copland. Exhibitions feature members' work. The library (for scholars, by appointment) has old manuscripts and first editions.

Bronze door at the academy

The Hispanic Society of America is a public museum and library based upon the personal collection of Archer M. Huntington. The Spanish Renaissance-style main gallery holds works by Goya, El Greco and Velázquez. The National Museum of the American Indian, once here, is soon to reopen at the Custom House *(see p73).*

Statue of El Cid by Anna Hyatt Huntington at Audubon Terrace

Morris-Jumel Mansion ❷

Corner W 160th St and Edgecombe Ave. **C** *923-8008.* **M** *163rd St.* **Open** *10am–4pm Tue–Sun.* **Closed** *public hols.* **Adm charge.** **📷** **📹** *by appt.*

THIS IS ONE of New York's few pre-Revolutionary buildings. Now a museum, it was built in 1765 for Roger Morris. His former military colleague George Washington used the house as temporary headquarters while defending Manhattan in 1776.

The house was bought and updated in 1810 by Stephen Jumel, a merchant of French-Caribbean descent, and his wife Eliza. The pair furnished the house with souvenirs of their many visits to France. Her boudoir contains her bed and "dolphin" chair, reputedly bought from Napoleon. Eliza's social climbing and love affairs scandalized New York society. It was rumored that she let her husband bleed to death in 1832 so she could inherit his fortune. She later married Aaron Burr, aged 77, and divorced him three years later on the day he died.

The exterior of this wood-sided Georgian house with its classical portico and octagonal wing – the earliest in the colonies – has been restored. The museum exhibits include many original Jumel pieces.

The 3,500-ft (1,065-m) span of the George Washington Bridge

George Washington Bridge ❸

M *175th St.*

FRENCH ARCHITECT Le Corbusier called this "the only seat of grace in the disordered city." While not as famous a landmark as its Brooklyn equivalent, this bridge by engineer Othmar Ammann and his architect Cass Gilbert has its own character and history. Plans for a bridge linking Manhattan to New Jersey had been in the pipeline for more than 60 years before the Port of New York Authority raised the $59 million needed to fund the project. It was

The lighthouse under Washington Bridge

Ammann who suggested a road bridge rather than the more expensive rail link. Work began in 1927 and the bridge was finally opened in 1931: first across were two young roller skaters from the Bronx. Today the bridge is a vital link for commuter traffic and is in constant use.

Cass Gilbert had plans to clad the two towers with masonry but funds did not permit it, leaving an elegant skeletal structure 600 ft (183 m) in height and 3,500 ft (1,065 m) long.

Ammann had also allowed for a second deck in his original plan, and this lower deck was added in 1962, increasing the bridge's capacity enormously. Now the eastbound toll collection shows a traffic level of over 50 million cars per year.

Below the eastern tower is a lighthouse that was saved from possible demolition in 1951 by sheer force of public pressure. The reason for this unlikely protest has become part of the city's mythology. Many thousands of young New Yorkers and children all around the world have loved the bedtime story *The Little Red Lighthouse and the Great Gray Bridge,* and wrote letters to save the lighthouse. Author Hildegarde Hoyt Swift wove the tale around her two favorite New York landmarks.

The Cloisters ❹

See pp234–37.

Morris-Jumel Mansion, built in 1765, with its original colossal portico

The Cloisters ❹

The Cloisters seen from Fort Tryon Park

THIS WORLD-FAMOUS museum of medieval art resides in a building constructed from 1934 to 1938, incorporating medieval cloisters, chapels and halls. Sculptor George Barnard founded the museum in 1914, having amassed many medieval architectural pieces and sculptures. John D. Rockefeller, Jr., funded the Metropolitan Museum of Art's 1925 purchase of the collection and donated the site at Fort Tryon Park.

Tomb Effigy of Jean d'Alluye
This tomb immortalizes the 13th-century Crusader.

Pontaut Chapter House

★ **Unicorn Tapestries**
The set of beautifully preserved tapestries, woven in Brussels around 1500, depicts the quest and capture of the mythical unicorn.

STAR EXHIBITS

★ **Unicorn Tapestries**

★ **Belles Heures de Jean, Duc de Berry**

★ **Annunciation Altarpiece by Robert Campin**

Boppard Stained-Glass Lancets (1440–47)
Below the lancet of Saint Catherine, angels display the arms of the coopers' guild, of which Catherine was patron.

Bonnefont Cloister

Trie Cloister

★ **Annunciation Altarpiece** (about 1425)
The Campin Room is the location of this Robert Campin of Tournai small triptych, a magnificent example of early Flemish painting.

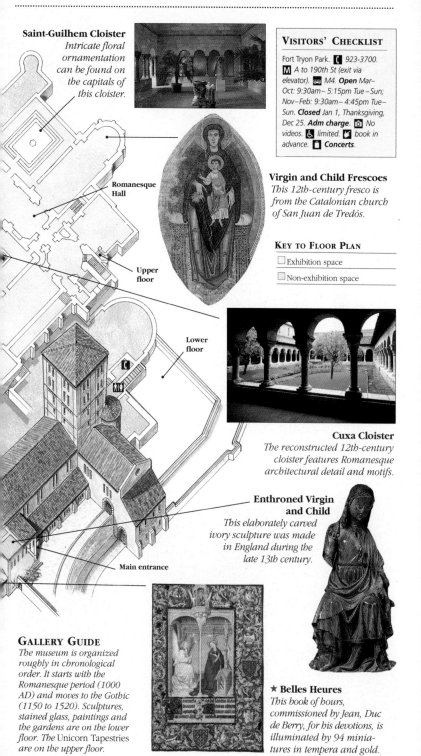

Saint-Guilhem Cloister
Intricate floral ornamentation can be found on the capitals of this cloister.

VISITORS' CHECKLIST

Fort Tryon Park. 923-3700. A to 190th St (exit via elevator). M4. **Open** Mar–Oct: 9:30am–5:15pm Tue–Sun; Nov–Feb: 9:30am–4:45pm Tue–Sun. **Closed** Jan 1, Thanksgiving, Dec 25. **Adm charge.** No videos. limited. book in advance. **Concerts.**

Romanesque Hall

Virgin and Child Frescoes
This 12th-century fresco is from the Catalonian church of San Juan de Tredós.

KEY TO FLOOR PLAN

☐ Exhibition space
☐ Non-exhibition space

Upper floor

Lower floor

Cuxa Cloister
The reconstructed 12th-century cloister features Romanesque architectural detail and motifs.

Enthroned Virgin and Child
This elaborately carved ivory sculpture was made in England during the late 13th century.

Main entrance

GALLERY GUIDE

The museum is organized roughly in chronological order. It starts with the Romanesque period (1000 AD) and moves to the Gothic (1150 to 1520). Sculptures, stained glass, paintings and the gardens are on the lower floor. The Unicorn Tapestries are on the upper floor.

★ Belles Heures
This book of hours, commissioned by Jean, Duc de Berry, for his devotions, is illuminated by 94 miniatures in tempera and gold.

Exploring The Cloisters

K NOWN PARTICULARLY for its Romanesque and Gothic architectural sculpture, The Cloisters collection also includes illuminated manuscripts, stained glass, metalwork, enamels, ivories and paintings. Among its tapestries is the renowned *Unicorn* series. The Cloisters' splendid medieval complex is unrivaled in North America.

ROMANESQUE ART

A lifesized 12th-century Spanish crucifix portraying Christ as the King of Heaven

F ANCIFUL BEASTS and people, acanthus blossoms and scrollwork, top the columns around The Cloisters. Many are in the Romanesque style that flourished in the 11th and 12th centuries. The museum has numerous masterpieces of Romanesque art and architecture, showing the style's powerful rounded arches and intricate details. Highly embellished capitals and warm, pink marble typify the 12th-century Cuxa Cloister from the Pyrenees in France. A griffin, a dragon, a centaur and a basilisk are among the creatures parading over the Narbonne Arch nearby. In the Romanesque Hall, a golden-crowned Christ is depicted as triumphant over death.

In a more solemn style, the apse from the church of Saint-Martín in Fuentidueña, Spain, is a massive rounded vault constructed from 3,000 blocks of limestone. It is decorated with a 12th-century fresco of the Virgin and Child.

More than 800 years ago, Benedictine and Cistercian monks sat on the cold stone benches in the Pontaut Chapter House. By the 19th century it had become so neglected that it was used as a stable. Its ribbed vaulting is a foretaste of the Gothic style to come.

A 16th-century Flemish boxwood rosary bead from the Treasury

GOTHIC ART

W HERE ROMANESQUE art was solid, the Gothic style that followed (from 1150 to around 1520) was open, with pointed arches, glowing stained-glass windows and three-dimensional sculpture. Gothic depictions of the Virgin and Child display exquisite craftsmanship.

The Gothic Chapel's brilliantly colored windows show scenes and figures from biblical stories. Lifesized tomb sculptures include the effigy of the Crusader knight Jean d'Alluye. During the 1790s,

Vaulted ceiling of the Pontaut Chapter House

the statue's original home, La Clarté-Dieu Abbey in France, was vandalized, and the statue was used to bridge a stream.

In the Boppard Room, the lives of the saints are told in marvellous late Gothic stained glass from Germany.

Robert Campin's Flemish masterwork, the *Annunciation* altarpiece, is the focus of the Campin Room. It is an intimate room with furnishings that might have belonged to a wealthy 15th-century family.

THE TAPESTRIES

T HE CLOISTERS' tapestries are full of rich imagery and symbolism, and are among the museum's most highly prized treasures. The four *Nine Heroes Tapestries* bear the coat of arms of Jean, Duc de Berry, who was a brother of the King of France and one of the greatest art patrons of the Middle Ages. These tapestries are one of only two sets that survived from the late 14th century; the other set belonged to Jean's brother, Louis, Duc d'Anjou.

Nine great heroes of the past – three pagan, three Hebrew, three Christian – are shown with members of the medieval court, from cardinals, knights and damsels to musicians.

In an adjacent room is the magnificent *Hunt of the Unicorn*, a series of seven tapestries woven in Brussels around 1500. It depicts the symbolic hunt of the mythical unicorn and capture by a maiden.

Although they were misused in the 19th century to protect fruit trees from frost damage,

the tapestries are remarkably well preserved. They are also astonishing in detail, with

Julius Caesar, entertained by court musicians, in a *Nine Heroes* tapestry

literally hundreds of minutely observed plants and animals. Their story can be read as a tale of courtly love, but the series is also an allegory for the Crucifixion and the Resurrection of Christ.

MEDIEVAL GARDENS

More than 250 varieties of plants grown in the Middle Ages can be found in The Cloisters' gardens. The Bonnefont Cloister has herbal, medicinal and cooking plants. The Trie Cloister features plants shown in the *Unicorn Tapestries* and reveals the use of flowers in medieval symbolism: roses (for the Virgin Mary), pansies (the Holy Trinity) and daisies (the eye of Christ).

Bonnefont Cloister

THE TREASURY

I N MEDIEVAL TIMES, precious objects were stored in sanctuaries for safekeeping. At the Cloisters, they are to be found in the Treasury.

The collection includes several Gothic illuminated "books of hours." These were used for the private devotions of the nobility, such as the Limbourg brothers' *Belles Heures*, made for Jean, Duc de Berry, in 1410, and the tiny, palm-sized version by Gothic master Jean Pucelle for the Queen of France, around 1325.

Other religious artifacts range from a 13th-century English ivory Virgin to the 14th-century silver gilt and enamel reliquary shrine thought to have belonged to Queen Elizabeth of Hungary, along with censers, chalices, candlesticks and crucifixes.

Curiosities here include the "Monkey Cup," an enameled beaker probably made for the 15th-century Burgundian court, showing mischievous monkeys robbing a sleeping peddler; an intricately carved rosary bead the size of a walnut; a 13th-century boat-shaped, jeweled saltcellar; and one of the oldest full sets of playing cards in existence.

Hunting images and symbols depicted on a 15th-century deck of playing cards

The west parlor of the Van Cortlandt House Museum

The Bronx

ONCE A prosperous suburb with a famous Grand Concourse lined with apartment buildings for the wealthy, the Bronx has now become an unfortunate symbol of urban decay. Still, diverse ethnic communities, unique resources and charming areas, such as Riverdale at the northern end, remain. Two major, outstanding attractions are the zoo and the New York Botanical Garden. New Yorkers still flock to see baseball at the Yankee Stadium, now more than 50 years old (see p239).

Wave Hill ❺

W 249th St. and Independence Ave, Riverdale. █ (718) 549-3200. Ⓜ 231st St. then bus Bx7, 10, 24. **Open** 9am–5:30pm Tue–Sun (9am–4:30pm mid-Oct to mid-May). **Adm charge** Sat, Sun; free Tue–Fri.

WHEN CITY concrete begins to overwhelm, come to this 28-acre (11-ha) oasis of calm and beauty, with its fine views over to the New Jersey Palisades across the Hudson River. The former estate of financier and conservationist George W. Perkins, Wave Hill has had a long series of distinguished tenants, including Theodore Roosevelt, Mark Twain and

Arturo Toscanini. Perkins also owned neighboring estates, underneath which he built a subterranean recreation center complete with bowling alley, and a tunnel leading into the main building.

The house and the grounds are open to the public. The house is frequently used for concerts. They often take place in the grand Armor Hall, designed in 1928 for Bashford Dean, who was then the curator of the collection of arms and armor at the Metropolitan Museum of Art.

The gardens were originally designed by Viennese landscape gardener, Albert Millard. There are also greenhouses, lawns, an herb garden and woodlands. Exhibitions range from sculpture to horticulture.

The adjoining Riverdale Park has attractive woodland and paths along the river.

The interior of the grand Armor Hall at Wave Hill

Van Cortlandt House Museum ❻

Van Cortlandt Park. █ (718) 543-3344. Ⓜ 242nd St, Van Cortlandt Park. **Open** 10am–3pm Tue–Fri, 11am–4pm Sat, Sun (last adm: 30 mins before closing). **Closed** most public hols. **Adm charge**.
▣ ▨ █ See **The History of New York** pp18–19.

The facade of Van Cortlandt House

A RESTORED 1748 Georgian Colonial country manor built of rough stone, this was originally the family home of Frederick Van Cortlandt, a New Yorker who inherited great wealth and was related to many of the influential and rich families of his day.

The dining room was used as one of General George Washington's headquarters; the ground behind the house was once the scene of skirmishing during the Revolutionary War.

The interior has American period furnishings as well as a superb collection of delftware and a complete 17thcentury Dutch bedroom.

On the exterior, look for the carved faces in the keystones over the windows.

Woodlawn Cemetery ➐

Jerome and Bainbridge aves.
📞 *(718) 920-0500.* Ⓜ *Woodlawn.*
Open *9am–4:30pm daily.* **Office closed** *public hols.* 🚫 ♿ ⛨

FOR A GLIMPSE into another kind of social history, visit Woodlawn Cemetery, the burial place of many a wealthy and distinguished New Yorker.

Entrance to the Woolworth mausoleum

Memorials and tomb-stones are set in beautiful grounds. F.W. Woolworth and many members of his family are interred in a mausoleum only a little less ornate than the building that carries the family name. The pink marble vault of meat magnate Herman Armour is oddly reminiscent of a ham.

Other New York notables buried here include Mayor Fiorello La Guardia, Roland Macy, the founder of the great department store, author Herman Melville and jazz supremo Duke Ellington.

New York Botanical Garden ➑

See pp240–41.

International Wildlife Conservation Park ➒

See pp242–43.

Yankee Stadium ➓

E 161st St at River Ave, Highbridge.
📞 *(718) 293-6000.* Ⓜ *161st St.*
See **Entertainment** *pp344–45.*

THIS IS THE HOME of the New York Yankees baseball team. Among Yankee heroes are two of the greatest play-ers of all time: Babe Ruth and Joe DiMaggio (who was also famous for marrying, in 1954,

the legendary actress Marilyn Monroe).

The stadium was completed in 1923 by Jacob Ruppert, the owner of the Yankees. It became known as "the house that Ruth built"

Joe DiMaggio in action at Yankee Stadium in 1941

after the famous left-hander Babe Ruth. The Stadium had a face-lift in the mid-1970s, and now seats up to 54,000 people who come for sports, concerts and other events. If you go to a game, take the children along, too.

City Island ⑪

610 City Island Ave. Ⓜ *6 to Pelham Parkway, then Bx12 to City Island.*
North Wind Undersea Institute Museum 📞 *(718) 885-0701.*

SITUATED JUST off the northeast shore of the Bronx, City Island is a small nautical outpost with a very New England feel – it seems a world apart from New York City, and offers a refreshing change of pace. Its scenic marinas are filled with sailing boats, and its seafood restaurants would satisfy any

Diving helmet at the North Wind Undersea Institute Museum

sailor's appetite. Several America's Cup winners have been built in its boatyards.

The main entrance of the North Wind Undersea Institute Museum is constructed from the gaping 9-ft (2.75-m) jaw of a whale. It houses displays on the history of whaling and the only seals in the world that work for the police force. They are trained to retrieve sunken weapons and drugs and to undo the seat belts in sub-merged cars or planes and then to bring humans to the surface. The seals can sometimes be seen practicing in their tanks. City Island is now connected to the rest of the Bronx by bridge. Just to the north on the mainland is Orchard Beach, a popular crescent of white sand edged with 1930s bathing huts.

The best time to visit the beach is during the week, when it is less crowded.

An old tugboat at the North Wind Undersea Institute Museum

New York Botanical Garden ❽

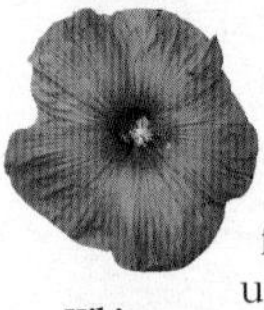

Hibiscus

ONE OF THE oldest and largest botanical gardens in America, founded in 1891, this pastoral oasis covers 250 acres (101 ha), including formal plantings and a large tract of unspoiled woodland along a winding river, the last remnant of New York's primeval forest. The showpiece is the Enid A. Haupt Conservatory, which was added in 1902 and inspired by London's Crystal Palace and the Palm House at Kew Gardens. The garden is not simply a horticulturalist's paradise, however; it is also a center for environmental and ecological research.

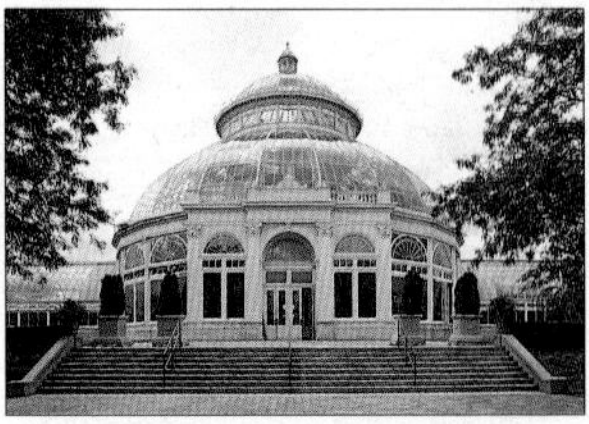

Entrance to Enid A. Haupt Conservatory

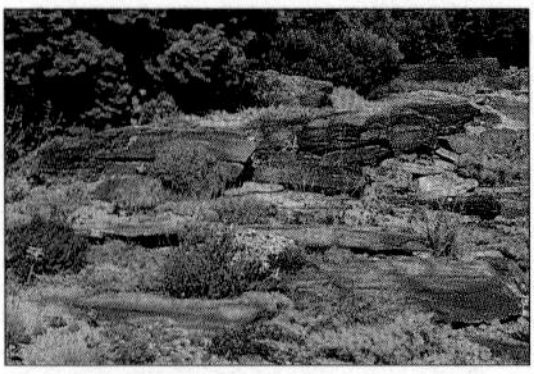

Rock Garden
Giant boulders, ledges, streams and a waterfall create an alpine habitat for plants from the world's rocky and mountainous regions (4)

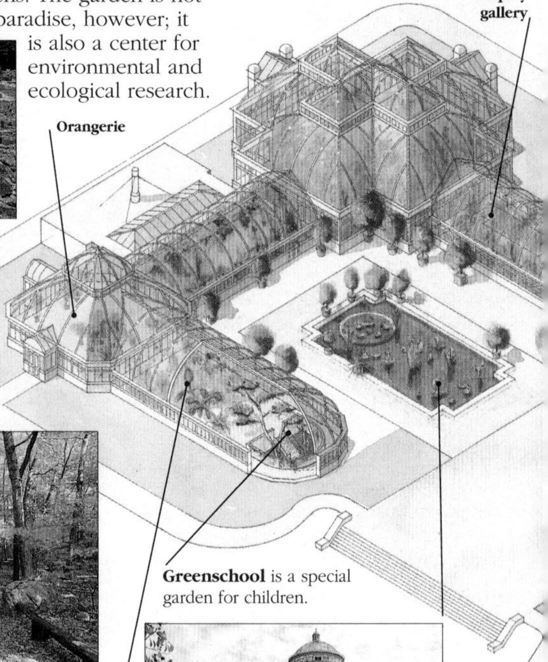
Display gallery
Orangerie
Greenschool is a special garden for children.
Economic plants provide food, medicine and raw materials for industry.

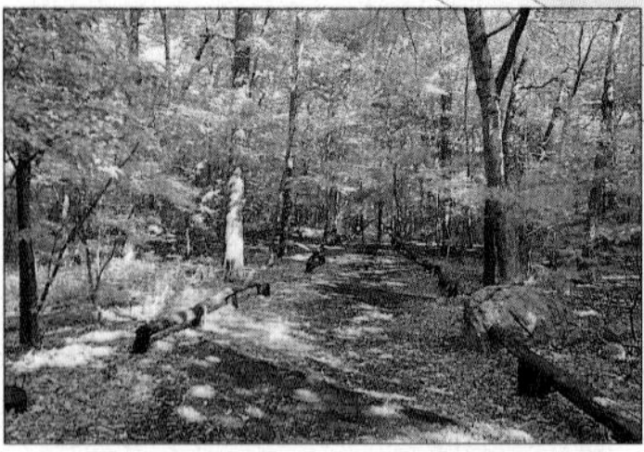

Botanical Garden Forest
New York City's sole surviving natural forest area includes red oak, white ash, tulip trees and hemlock (5)

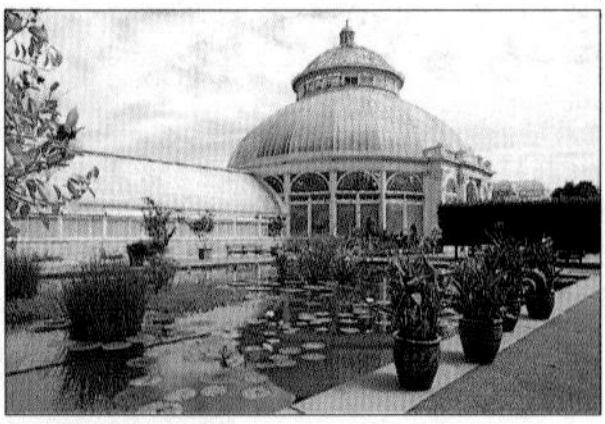

Tropical Pool
Exquisite aquatic plants from all over the world are displayed here.

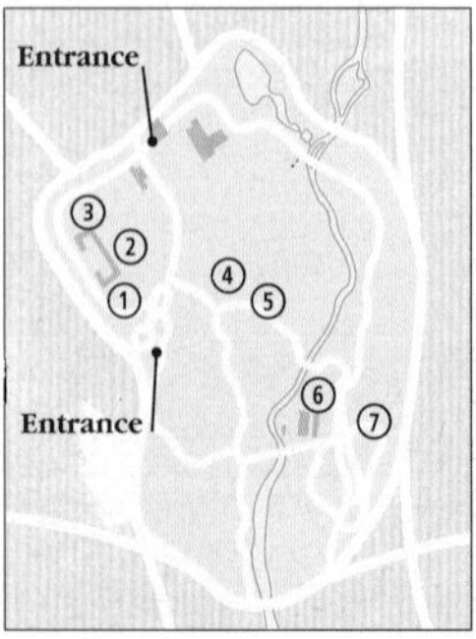
Entrance
3
2
1
4
5
6
7
Entrance

LOCATOR MAP

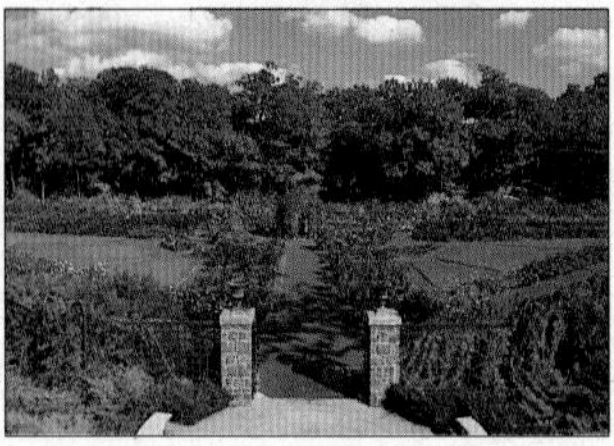

Rose Garden
Over 2,700 roses have been planted in the Peggy Rockefeller Rose Garden, laid out in 1988 according to the original 1915 design (7)

Palm Court
Specimens of one-quarter of the world's palm species are displayed here in a carefully controlled tropical environment.

The Enid A. Haupt Conservatory consists of 11 areas, each with its own botanical or geographical theme. Temperature, light and humidity are all carefully controlled to simulate specific natural environments ①

Demonstration Gardens
Colorful displays are designed to inspire visitors with ideas for their own gardens ③

Jane Watson Irwin Perennial Garden
Flowering perennials are arranged in dramatic patterns according to height, shade, color and blooming time ②

Temperate pool

Tropical flora

Special collections

Old World Desert
displays plants native to arid regions of the Old World.

Fern Forest
Grown in naturalistic habitats, the vast collection of ferns can be viewed from an overhead skywalk.

Main entrance

New World Desert
displays plants from the arid regions of the Americas.

Snuff Mill Terrace Café
Light refreshments are served to garden visitors on the terrace of the Lorillard Snuff Mill near the Bronx River ⑥

International Wildlife Conservation Park ❾

FOUNDED IN 1899, the International Wildlife Conservation Park (formerly the Bronx Zoo) is the largest urban zoo in the US, home to some 4,300 animals representing 764 species, living in realistic representations of their natural habitats. The Park is a leader in the perpetuation of endangered species, such as the hairy rhinoceros and the snow leopard. Its 265 acres (107 ha) of woods, streams and parklands include a children's zoo and a shuttle train that transports visitors around the sprawling park – visitors are also free to walk around. For the best overview of the different areas of the park take the Skyfari cable car.

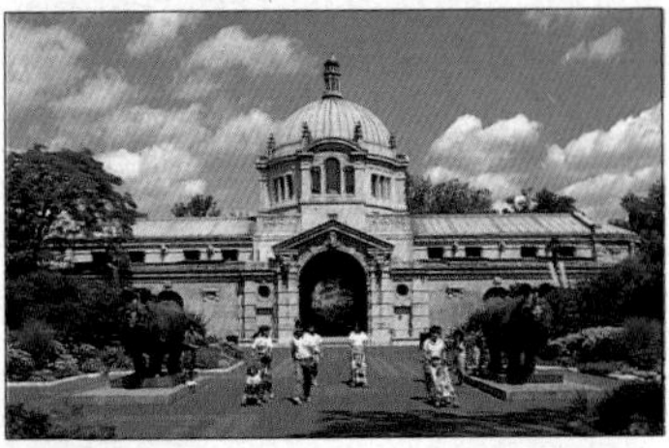

Zoo Center entrance

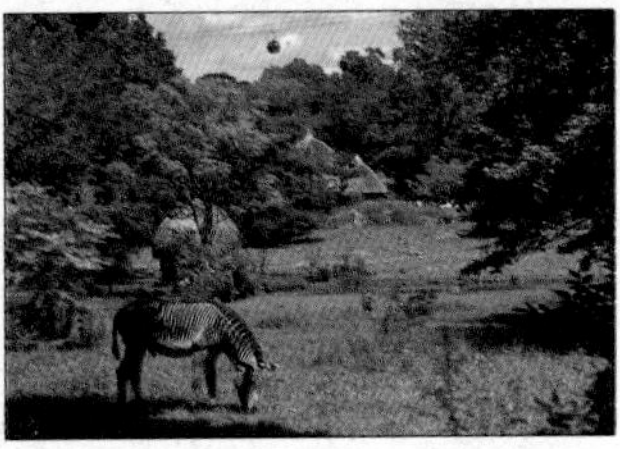

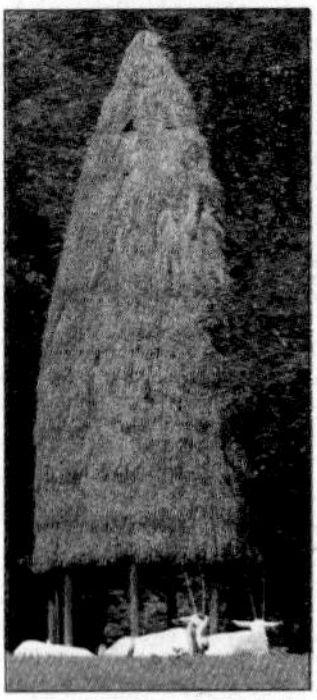

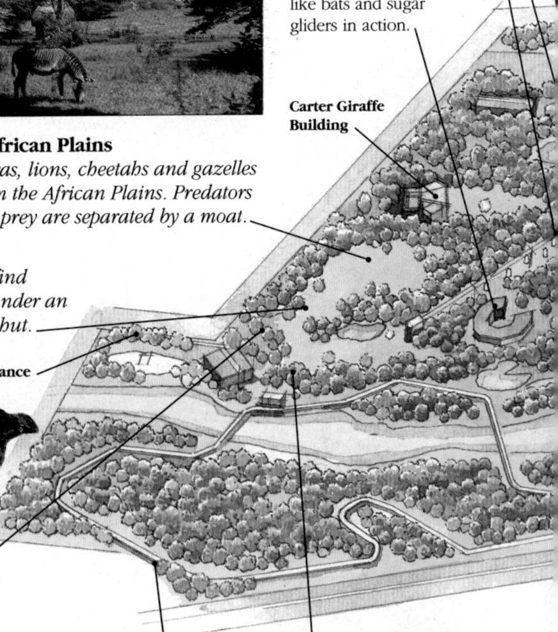

Wildfowl Marsh

World of Darkness
reverses the day/night cycle so visitors can see nocturnal animals like bats and sugar gliders in action.

Mouse-House

Skyfari cable car

Carter Giraffe Building

★ African Plains
Zebras, lions, cheetahs and gazelles roam the African Plains. Predators and prey are separated by a moat.

Africa
Oryxes find shelter under an African hut.

Asia entrance

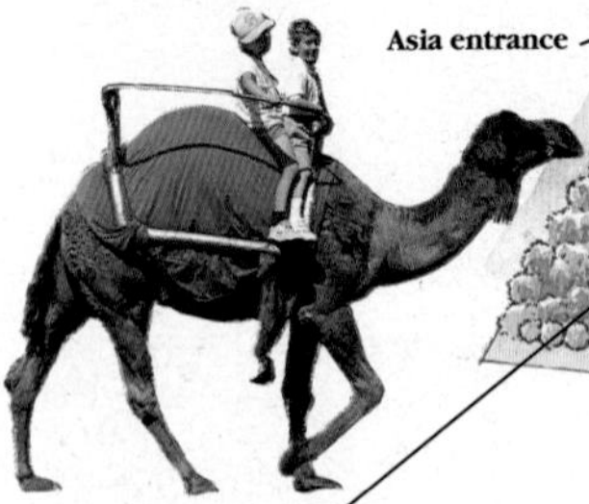

Camel Rides
Children enjoy the zoo's experiences such as camel rides and other attractions.

Bengali Express monorail

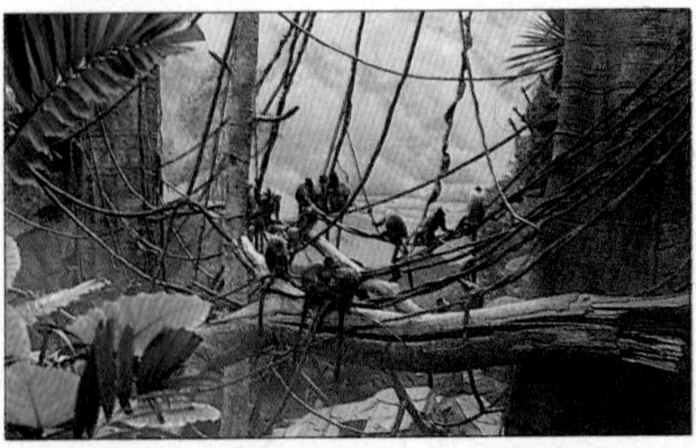

★ JungleWorld
A glass-enclosed tropical rain forest harbors mammals, birds and reptiles from South Asia. The animals are kept apart from visitors by ravines, streams and cliffs.

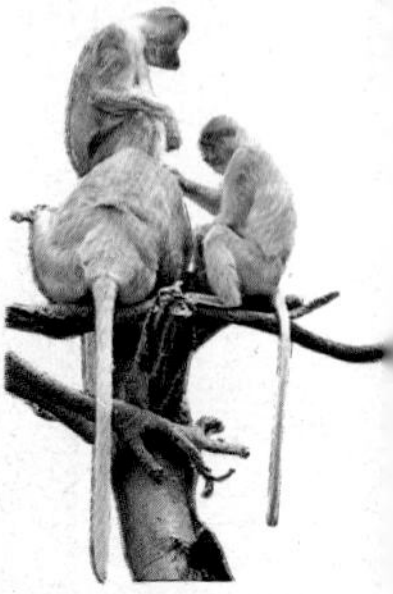

Monkeys in JungleWorld

Baboon Reserve
Visitors walk along a dry riverbed to see wildlife in an Ethiopian mountain habitat.

Children's Zoo
Kids can crawl through a prairie dog tunnel, climb on a spiderweb, try on a turtle shell, and pet and feed the animals.

Great Ape House

World of Reptiles

The Zoo Center houses elephants, rhinos and tapirs.

Southern Boulevard entrance

Aquatic Bird House

Dejur Aviary

Rainey Gate entrance

Monkey House

★ World of Birds
Exotic birds soar free in the lush surroundings of a rain forest. Simulated tropical thunder-storms occur each day at 2pm, and an artificial waterfall rushes down a 50-ft (15-m) fiberglass cliff.

Great hornbill

Bronxdale entrance

Himalayan Highlands
Endangered species, such as snow leopards and red pandas, are kept here.

★ Wild Asia
The Bengali Express monorail journeys through forests and meadows of an Asian habitat, where elephants, rhinoceroses and Siberian tigers roam free.

Queens

A BIG, SPRAWLING borough, Queens has a wide variety of attractions and residential and commercial areas, including a business district known as Long Island City. Development of the borough accelerated after 1909, when the construction of Queensboro Bridge made commuting easier. The city's main airports are here. There are various ethnic enclaves too, including the Greek neighborhood of Astoria, and some Asian communities in Flushing, a district popular with varied ethnic groups.

A 1900 Mutoscope at the Museum of the Moving Image

Flushing Meadow–Corona Park ⑫

M *Willets Point-Shea Stadium. See* **Entertainment** *pp344–45.*

T HE SITE of New York's two World's Fairs now offers expansive waterside picnic grounds and a multitude of attractions. These include the 50,000-seat Shea Stadium, the home of the New York Mets baseball team and a popular site for rock concerts. Flushing Meadow is also home to the US Tennis Center, where the prestigious United States Open is played. The courts are open for would-be Agassis, Grafs and Everts for the remainder of the year. In the 1920s this area was known as the Corona Dump, a nightmarish place of salt marshes and great piles of smoldering trash. In *The Great Gatsby*, author F. Scott Fitzgerald dubbed it the "valley of ashes." It reeked of rotting garbage and glowed red at night. New York's Parks' Commissioner Robert Moses was the driving force behind its transformation. A whole mountain of rubbish was removed and the river was totally re-channeled. The marsh was drained and sewage works were built, helping to restore the area. This site was to serve as the site for the 1939 World's Fair, at which a world on the brink of war saluted the elusive notion of world peace.

The Unisphere, symbol of the 1964 fair, still dominates the remains of the fairground. This giant hollow ball of green steel, built by the US Steel Corporation, is 12 stories high and weighs a massive 350 tons.

The 1964 World's Fair Unisphere at Flushing Meadow-Corona Park

New York Hall of Science ⑬

46th Ave and 111th St Flushing Meadows, Corona Park. **C** *(718) 699-0005.* **M** *111th St.* **Open** *10am–5pm Wed–Sun.* **Closed** *public hols.* **Adm charge.** 📷 ♿ 📱

T HE SCIENCE PAVILION built for the 1964 World's Fair was designed with stained glass set in concrete panels. It is now a hands-on museum for science and technology, with exhibits on color, light and physics. Children love to watch the giant video screens that can magnify the microbes in a drop of water, and the interactive video and laser optical exhibits.

The concrete curtain wall of the New York Hall of Science

American Museum of the Moving Image and Kaufman Astoria Studio ⑭

35th Ave at 36th St, Astoria. **Museum** **C** *(718) 784-0077.* **Studio** **C** *(718) 392-5600.* **M** *36th St.* **Museum open** *noon–4pm Tue–Fri, noon–6pm Sat & Sun.* **Adm charge.** **Studio not open** *to public.* 📷 ♿ 📱

I N NEW YORK'S filmmaking heyday, Rudolph Valentino, W.C. Fields, the Marx Brothers and Gloria Swanson all made films here in the city's largest studio, opened by Paramount Pictures in 1920. When the movies went west, the army took over, making training films here from 1941 to 1971.

The complex stood empty until the 1970s when Astoria Motion Picture and Television Foundation was founded to preserve it. *The Wiz*, Sidney

Poster at the Museum of the Moving Image

Lumet's $24 million musical starring Michael Jackson and Diana Ross, was made here, helping to pay for restoration. Today, the studios house the largest moviemaking facilities on the East Coast and are again in full use. *The Cotton Club* and Woody Allen's *Radio Days* were filmed here.

In 1981 one of the studio buildings was transformed into the American Museum of the Moving Image, with interactive displays on production and theaters for the screening of movies and television.

There is a lot of kitsch and memorabilia on display, from Annie Hall's outfits to the Star Trek costumes. The main gallery on the second floor draws from the permanent collection, containing over 60,000 movie artifacts. These include exhibits such as a mirror in which you can see your own head reflected above the body of Sylvester Stallone in *Rocky*, Marilyn Monroe in *The Seven Year Itch* or Eddie Murphy in *Beverly Hills Cop*.

"Behind the Screen" looks at every aspect of filmmaking, including editing, sound and costumes. Visitors can walk through the original set for Paul Newman's 1988 version of *The Glass Menagerie*. The main floor theater presents film and video programs, from early silent movies to the most avant-garde.

Head for 31st Street for Astoria's big Greek enclave. Here and along Ditmars Boulevard and Broadway are legions of *zacharoplasteia* (pastry shops), *tavernas* (restaurants), nightclubs, 11 Greek Orthodox churches and a Greek cinema. Greek religious processions are very moving, if you're lucky enough to see one.

Brooklyn

The bandstand at Prospect Park *(see p246)*

IF BROOKLYN were a separate city, it would be the USA's fourth largest. It has a character all of its own. Many entertainment greats – Mel Brooks, Phil Silvers, Woody Allen and Neil Simon among them – celebrate their birthplace with great affection and humor. Brooklyn is the ultimate melting pot, with West Indians, Hasidic Jews, Russians, Italians and Arabs, to mention only a few groups, living side by side. Among the diverse neighborhoods are the historic residential districts of Park Slope and Brooklyn Heights.

Brooklyn Children's Museum ⑮

145 Brooklyn Ave. 🄲 *(718) 735-4432.* Ⓜ *Kingston.* **Open** *2–5pm Wed–Fri, noon–5pm Sat, Sun. Jul; Aug; noon–5pm Mon, noon–5pm Wed–Sun.* **Closed** *Jan 1, Thanksgiving, Dec 25.* **Donation expected.** 🄾 ♿

THE BROOKLYN Children's Museum was the first to be designed especially for children and was founded in 1899. Since then, it has been a model, inspiration and consultant to the development of more than 250 museums for children across the country and all over the world. Housed in a high-tech, specially designed underground building dating from 1976, it is one of the most imaginative children's museums anywhere.

The layout of the building is a maze of complex interconnected passageways running off the main "people tube" – a huge drainage pipe that connects the four levels. This is not a passive place where children are meant to stand around and stare – the emphasis is on involvement and hands-on exhibits. Everywhere you look there are curiosities to be discovered, experienced, made or played with. There is even a walk-on piano like the one in the film *Big* – children of every age find it quite irresistible.

Special exhibitions and events are designed to help children learn about the planet, resolve their fears or problems, understand other cultures and discover the past. The squeals of laughter and delight that are always heard are a sign of this well-designed and clever museum's success in teaching children and the young at heart.

A mask from the Children's Museum

The facade of the Brooklyn Academy of Music

Brooklyn Academy of Music ⑯

30 Lafayette Ave. **(** (718) 636-4100. **M** Atlantic Ave. **Adm charge.** **⊘** **&** **❚** See Entertainment pp338–9.

Home to the Brooklyn Philharmonic, the Academy (well-known as BAM) is Brooklyn's leading cultural venue and the oldest, founded in 1858. It offers outstanding performances, often tending toward the innovative and avant-garde.

The classic 1908 building was designed by Herts & Tallant, and inaugurated with a production of Verdi's opera *Faust* featuring the legendary Neapolitan tenor Enrico Caruso. The list of the greats who have performed here is endless and includes actress Sarah Bernhardt, ballerina Anna Pavlova, musicians Pablo Casals and Sergei Rachmaninoff, poets Edna St. Vincent Millay and Carl Sandburg, and statesman Winston Churchill. Many international touring groups have made appearances here, including Britain's Royal Shakespeare Company.

The BAM Next Wave Festival has presented a number of well-known contemporary artists, including musicians Philip Glass and David Byrne, performance artist Laurie Anderson, and choreographers Pina Bausch and Mark Morris. The Brooklyn Academy of Music also runs the Majestic Theater nearby, once a movie theater and now used for dance, drama and music events.

Grand Army Plaza ⑰

Plaza St at Flatbush Ave. **(** (718) 788-0055. **M** Grand Army Plaza. **Arch open** for occasional exhibitions.

The Soldiers' and Sailors' Arch at Grand Army Plaza

Frederick Law Olmsted and Calvert Vaux laid out this grand oval in 1870 as a gateway to Prospect Park. The Soldiers' and Sailors' Arch and its sculptures were added in 1892 as a tribute to the Union Army. The bust of John F. Kennedy here is the only official New York monument to him.

In June, the plaza is the center of the Welcome Back to Brooklyn Festival for the famous – and not-so-famous – people born in Brooklyn.

Park Slope Historic District ⑱

Streets from Prospect Park W below Flatbush Ave, to 8th/7th/5th avenues. **M** Grand Army Plaza.

Relief work on the Montauk Club

This wonderful enclave of beautiful Victorian town houses was developed on the edge of Prospect Park in the 1880s. It served the upper-middle-class professionals who were able to commute into Manhattan after the Brooklyn Bridge was opened in 1883. The shady streets are lined with two- to five-story houses in every architectural style popular in the late 19th century, some with the towers, turrets and curlicues so representative of the era. Particularly fine examples are in Romanesque Revival style, with rounded entry arches.

The Montauk Club at 25 Eighth Avenue combines the style of Venice's Ca' d'Oro palazzo with the friezes and gargoyles of the Montauk Indians, after whom this popular 19th-century gathering place was named.

Prospect Park ⑲

((718) 788-0055. **(** (718) 788-8549. **M** Grand Army Plaza. **☎** (718) 287-3400.

Designers Olmsted and Vaux considered this park, opened in 1867, better than their earlier Central Park. The Long Meadow, a sweep of broad lawns and grand vistas, is the longest unbroken swath of green space in New York.

Olmsted's belief was that "a feeling of relief is experienced by entering them [the parks] on escaping from the cramped, confining and controlling circumstances of the streets of the town." That

The facade of the Brooklyn Public Library on Grand Army Plaza

vision is still as true today as it was a century ago.

Among the many notable features are Stanford White's colonnaded Croquet Shelter, and the pools and weeping willows of the Vale of Cashmere. The Music Grove bandstand shows Japanese influences and hosts both jazz and classical music concerts throughout the summer.

A favorite feature of the park is the Camperdown Elm, an ancient and twisted tree planted in 1872. The Friends of Prospect Park raise money to keep it and all the park trees healthy. This old elm has inspired many poems and paintings. Prospect Park has a wide variety of landscapes, from classical gardens dotted with statues to rocky glens with running brooks. A guided tour with a ranger is the best way to see the park.

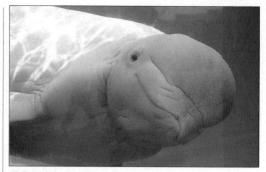
A beluga whale at the New York Aquarium

Carousel horse in Prospect Park

The Brooklyn Museum ❷⓪

See pp248–51.

Brooklyn Botanic Garden ❷①

1000 Washington Ave. 🅲 (718) 622-4433. Ⓜ Prospect Pk, Eastern Pkwy. **Grounds open** Apr–Sep: 8am–6pm Tue–Fri (10am Sat & Sun); Oct–Mar: 8am–4:30pm (10am Sat & Sun). **Closed** Jan 1, Thanksgiving, Dec 25. **Adm charge** for Japanese Garden, Sat & Sun. 🄿 🅯 🄿 🅗 🄿

Tʜᴏᴜɢʜ ɪᴛ is not vast in size, you will find that this 50-acre (20-ha) garden holds many delights. The area was designed by the Olmsted Brothers in 1910 and features a traditional Elizabethan-style

"knot" herb garden and one of North America's largest collections of roses.

The central showpiece is a Japanese hill-and-pond garden, complete with both a teahouse and Shinto shrine. In late April and early May the park promenade is aglow with delicate Japanese cherry blossoms, which have prompted an annual festival featuring typical Japanese culture, food and music.

April is also the time for tourists to appreciate Magnolia Plaza, where some 80 trees display their beautiful, creamy blossoms against a backdrop of daffodils on Boulder Hill.

The Fragrance Garden is planted in raised beds, where the heavily scented, textured and flavored plants are all labeled in Braille, giving blind visitors an opportunity to identify them as well.

The new conservatory now houses one of America's largest bonsai collections and some rare rain forest trees, which are providing scientists with medicinal extracts to produce life-saving drugs.

Brooklyn Botanic Garden lily pond

Coney Island ❷②

Boardwalk and W 8th St, Coney Island. Ⓜ Stillwell Ave, Coney Island. **New York Aquarium** 🅲 (718) 265-3400.

Iɴ ᴛʜᴇ ᴍɪᴅ-19ᴛʜ century, Brooklyn poet Walt Whitman composed many of his works on Coney Island, accompanied by the roar of the surf. At that time it was untamed Atlantic coastline, the tip of the nose on the great "whale" to which the poet compared Long Island.

By the 1920s, Coney Island was starting to bill itself as the "World's Largest Playground." It had grown from three huge fairgrounds built between 1887 and 1904 (Luna Park, Dreamland and Steeplechase Park), providing a popular combination of hair-raising rides and nearby beaches. The subway arrived in 1920, and the addition of the boardwalk in 1921 ensured Coney Island's popularity throughout the Depression. Here was an escape from the city that cost little more than a few nickels.

A main attraction is the New York Aquarium, moved here from Battery Park in 1955 and worth a day's visit. Today, Coney Island remains an exciting experience for all ages: the boardwalk yields ocean views, the wooden Cyclone roller coaster evokes screams and tourists can still enjoy Nathan's Famous hot dogs.

The Brooklyn Museum ⑱

WHEN IT OPENED in 1897, the Brooklyn Museum building, designed to be the largest cultural edifice in the world, was the greatest achievement of New York architects McKim, Mead & White. Though only one-fifth completed, the museum is today one of the most impressive cultural institutions in the United States, with a permanent encyclopedic collection of some 1.5 million objects, which are housed in a grand structure of 450,000 sq ft (41,805 sq m).

North facade, designed by Stanford White

Chinese Jar
Cobalt blue fishes and water plants adorn this 14th-century Yuan dynasty blue-and-white ceramic jar.

KEY TO FLOOR PLAN

- [ ] African, Oceanic and New World art
- [ ] Asian art
- [ ] Prints, drawings and photographs
- [ ] Classical and Egyptian art
- [ ] Decorative arts
- [ ] Painting and sculpture
- [ ] Williamsburg murals
- [ ] Special exhibitions
- [ ] Non-exhibition space

★ **Paracas Textile**
Over 2,000 years old, a woven mantle from Peru still glows with color.

Mother and Child
Figurines like this are carved by the Luluwa tribe of Zaire as amulets for pregnant or nursing women.

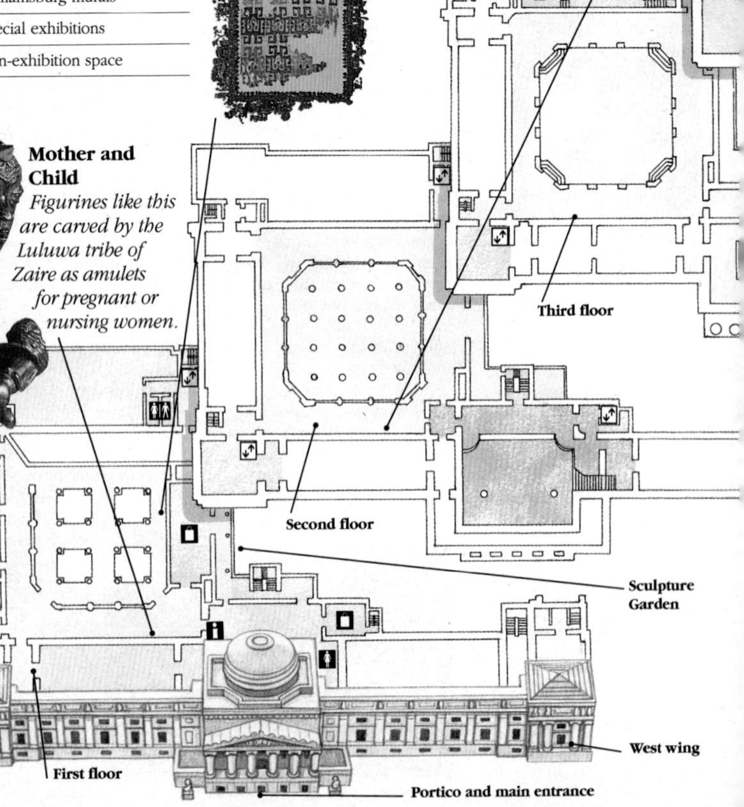

Third floor

Second floor

Sculpture Garden

First floor

West wing

Portico and main entrance

★ Storm in the Rocky Mountains (1866)

A trip to the American West inspired this painting by Albert Bierstadt.

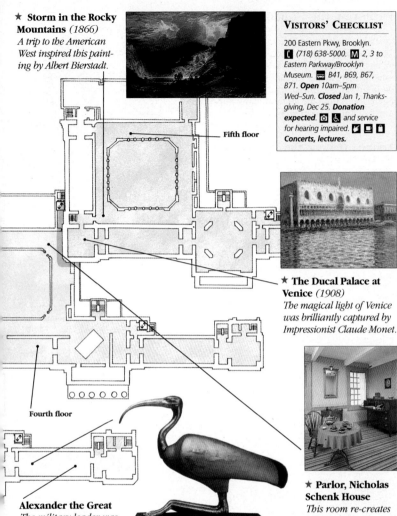

Fifth floor

★ The Ducal Palace at Venice (1908)

The magical light of Venice was brilliantly captured by Impressionist Claude Monet.

Fourth floor

★ Parlor, Nicholas Schenk House

This room re-creates middle-class life in 1820's Brooklyn.

Alexander the Great

The military leader was portrayed in alabaster in the 1st century BC.

Ibis Coffin (332–330 BC)
The sacred bird of ancient Egypt merited a splendid coffin of gold leaf and silver.

STAR EXHIBITS

★ **Paracas Textile**

★ **The Ducal Palace at Venice by Claude Monet**

★ **Storm in the Rocky Mountains – Mount Rosalie by Albert Bierstadt**

★ **Parlor, Nicholas Schenk House**

GALLERY GUIDE

The collection is on five floors, with African, Oceanic and New World art on the first; prints, drawings and Asian art on the second; Egyptian, Classical and ancient Middle Eastern art on the third; decorative art on the fourth; and American, European and contemporary art on the fifth. There is special exhibition space on the first and fourth floors.

Exploring the Collection

T HE BROOKLYN MUSEUM houses one of the finest art collections in the United States. Its strengths include an outstanding collection of Native American art from the Southwest; 28 American period rooms; exquisite examples of ancient Egyptian and Islamic art; and many important American and European paintings.

Seated Buddha torso in limestone, from India (late 3rd century AD)

AFRICAN, OCEANIC AND NEW WORLD ART

T HE BROOKLYN Museum set a precedent in the United States in 1923 by exhibiting African objects as works of art rather than artifacts. Since then, the African art collection has grown steadily in both importance and size.

Exhibits include a rare intricately carved ivory gong from the Benin kingdom of 16th-century Nigeria, one of only five in existence.

The museum also has a notable collection of Native American work, including totem poles, textiles and pottery. A 19th-century deer-skin shirt, once worn by a chief of the Blackfoot tribe, depicts his brave and daring exploits in battle.

Ancient American artistic traditions are represented by Peruvian textiles, Central American gold and Mexican sculpture. A beautifully preserved tunic from Peru, dating from AD 600, is so tightly woven that its vibrant symbolic designs appear to have been painted onto the cloth rather than woven in the traditional manner.

The Oceanic collection includes sculpture from the Solomon Islands, Papua New Guinea and New Zealand.

ASIAN ART

C HANGING EXHIBITIONS from the museum's permanent collection of Chinese, Japanese, Korean, Indian, Southeast Asian and Islamic art are always on display. Japanese and Chinese paintings, Indian miniatures and Islamic calligraphy complement the Asian sculpture, textiles and ceramics. The collections of Japanese folk art, Chinese cloisonné (enamel work) and Oriental carpets are of particular note. Good examples of Buddhist art range from a variety of Chinese, Indian and Southeast Asian Buddhas to a mandala-patterned temple banner from 14th-century Tibet, painted in rich, luminous watercolors.

Blackfoot tribe deerskin shirt, decorated with porcupine quills and glass beads (19th century)

DECORATIVE ARTS

T HE FOCUS of the decorative arts department is a very stylish assembly of 28 superb American period rooms.

The earliest is from a 17th-century Brooklyn Dutch house. It served as a parlor, dining room and sleeping area, with the enclosed "bed boxes" built against the wall opposite the fireplace. The Moorish Smoking Room, from John D. Rockefeller's brown-stone house, is an opulent example of elegant New York living during the 1880s. In complete contrast, the most recent room is a 1928–30 Art Deco study from a Park Avenue apartment, including a walk-in bar that was hidden behind paneling during the Prohibition era (see pp28-29).

Normandie **chrome pitcher, by Peter Müller-Munk (1935)**

Also on exhibit is a wide selection from the museum's vast collection of furniture, ceramics, glass, pewter, silver and metalware, including a 1930s pitcher whose shape was inspired by the stacks of the ocean liner *Normandie*.

EGYPTIAN, CLASSICAL AND ANCIENT MIDDLE EASTERN ART

RECOGNIZED AS among the world's finest, the Egyptian collection holds many masterpieces. It begins with an early female figure dating from 3500 BC, and encompasses sculptures, statues, tomb paintings and reliefs as well as funerary paraphernalia. Of the latter, the most unusual is the coffin of an ibis, probably recovered from the vast animal cemetery of Tuna el-Gebel in Middle Egypt. The ibis was a sacred bird representing the god Thoth, and this coffin is made of solid silver and wood overlaid with gold leaf, with rock crystal for the bird's eyes. These galleries have been renovated into a state-of-the-art, high-tech installation.

Among the artifacts from the Greek and Roman civilizations are statuary, pottery, bronzes, jewelry and mosaics.

Among the Ancient Near and Middle Eastern exhibits are an extensive collection of pottery and 12 alabaster reliefs from the Assyrian palace of King Ashur-nasir-pal II. These date from around 883-859 BC and depict the king fighting, overseeing his crops and purifying the "sacred tree," a major icon in Assyrian religion.

PAINTING AND SCULPTURE

THIS SECTION contains works from the 14th century to the present, including a well-known and outstanding 19th-century French art collection with works by Degas, Rodin, Monet, Cézanne, Matisse and Pissarro. It also boasts one of the largest holdings of Spanish

Pierre de Wiessant (about 1886) by Auguste Rodin, from his *Burghers of Calais* group

Colonial paintings and one of the best collections of North American paintings to be found in the United States.

The museum's 20th-century American collection includes, appropriately, *Brooklyn Bridge* by Georgia O'Keeffe.

The Sculpture Garden has a collection of architectural ornamentation taken from demolished New York buildings, including statues that were rescued from the original Penn Station.

PRINTS, DRAWINGS AND PHOTOGRAPHS

THE PRINTS section displays examples by many masters, ranging from a rare woodcut print by Dürer entitled *The Great Triumphal Chariot* and works by Piranesi to an excellent Impressionist and Post-Impressionist collection. This includes works by Toulouse-Lautrec and Mary Cassatt, the only American woman associated with the Impressionist movement. There are lithographs by James McNeill Whistler, Winslow Homer engravings, and a superb selection of

Rotherbide, an etching by James McNeill Whistler (1860)

drawings by Fragonard, Paul Klee, Van Gogh, Picasso and Gorky, among others, many of them in black and white.

The photography collection consists mainly of works by major 20th-century American photographers, including a 1924 portrait of Mary Pickford by Edward Steichen and work by Margaret Bourke-White and Bernice Abbott. Contemporary examples include photographs by Robert Mapplethorpe.

Sandstone reliefs from Thebes in Egypt (around 760–656 BC), depicting the great god Amun-Re and his consort Mut

Staten Island

APART FROM the famous ferry ride, Staten Island and its attractions are not well known to New Yorkers in general. Residents feel so ignored, they've talked about seceding from the city. Visitors who venture beyond the ferry terminal, however, will be pleasantly surprised to find hills, lakes and greenery, with expanses of open space, amazing harbor views and well-preserved early New York buildings. One of the biggest surprises here is a cache of Tibetan art hidden away in a replica of a Buddhist temple.

Historic Richmond Town ㉓

441 Clarke Ave. **(** (718) 351-1611. **[bus]** S74 from ferry. **Open** Jan–Mar: 1–5pm Wed–Fri; Apr–Jun & Sep–Dec: 1–5pm Wed–Sun; Jul–Aug: 10am–5pm Wed–Fri, 1–5pm Sat & Sun. **Adm charge.** [symbols]

THERE ARE now 29 buildings, 14 of which are open to the public, in New York's only restored village and outdoor museum. The village was first named Coccles-town, after the local shellfish, but was soon corrupted to "Cuckoldstown," much to the annoyance of the

Cologne at the General Store residents. By the end of the Revolutionary War the new name of Richmondtown had been adopted. It was the county seat until Staten Island was made part of the city in 1898, and has been preserved as an example of an early New York settlement.

The Voorlezer House, built in the Dutch era before 1696, is the oldest elementary school to be found in the country. The Stephens General Store, which opened in 1837, doubled as the local post office. It has been well restored, right down to the contents of the shelves. The complex, set on 103 acres (42 ha), includes wagon sheds, a courthouse built in 1837, houses, several shops and a tavern. There are also seasonal workshops where traditional rural crafts are demonstrated to visitors. St. Andrew's Church (1708) and its old graveyard are just across the Mill Pond stream, and the Historical Society Museum is in the County Clerk's and Surrogate's Office. The toy room is a delight.

Jacques Marchais Center of Tibetan Art ㉔

338 Lighthouse Ave. **(** (718) 987-3500. **[bus]** S74 from ferry. **Open** Apr–Nov: 1–5pm Wed–Sun; (4:45pm: last adm) Dec–Mar: by appt. **Closed** public hols. **Adm charge.** [symbols]

A HILLTOP provides a very tranquil setting for one of the largest collections of pri-vately owned Tibetan art out-side Tibet. The main building is a replica of a mountain temple with an authentic altar

Sacred sculpture at the Jacques Marchais Center of Tibetan Art

The Voorlezer House at Richmond Town

in three tiers, crowded with gold, silver and bronze figures.

Another building is used as a library. The garden has some stone sculptures, including life-size Buddhas. The museum was built in 1947 by Mrs. Harry Klauber, a dealer in Asian art trading under the name of Jacques Marchais. The Dalai Lama paid his first visit here in 1991.

A gazebo at the Snug Harbor Cultural Center

Snug Harbor Cultural Center ㉕

1000 Richmond Terrace. **(** (718) 448-2500. **[bus]** S40 from ferry to Snug Harbor Gate. **Grounds open** 8am–midnight daily. **Closed** Jan 1, Thanksgiving, Dec 25 [symbols] limited. [symbols]

FOUNDED IN 1801 as a haven for aged sailors and now an arts center, Snug Harbor is a complex of 28 historical buildings in various stages of restoration. The best are five stately Greek Revival gems, dating from 1831 to 1880. The oldest of these, the Main Hall, is now the Newhouse Center for Contemporary Art, but the ships at sea that decorate the stained-glass windows are a reminder of its origins.

Other buildings house the award-winning Staten Island Children's Museum and the Veterans Memorial Hall, a restored chapel now used for indoor performances.

An annual sculpture festival and summer shows are held on the lawns. The grounds include the Staten Island Botanical Garden, with its noted orchid collection and a beautiful rose garden.

Snug Harbor is the legacy of a Scottish sailor, Robert Richard Randall, who became rich during the Revolutionary War, some say by piracy, and bequeathed his wealth to care for less fortunate seamen. His estate's trustees bought the property so that the sailors could enjoy its harbor views.

Clear Comfort, Alice Austen's lifetime residence

Alice Austen House ㉖

2 Hylan Blvd. **℄** *(718) 816-4506.* **S 51 from ferry to Hylan Blvd. Open** *noon–5pm Thu–Sun.* **Closed** *public hols.* **Donation expected.** 🗾 **ঙ** *limited.* 🗾 🖼

CLEAR COMFORT is a delightfully named small cottage built around 1710, in a setting with splendid harbor views. This was the home of the

photographer Alice Austen. Born in 1866, she lived in this house for most of her life. She documented life on the island, in Manhattan, and also on trips to other parts of the country and on her travels to Europe. She lost all her money in the stock market crash of 1929 and her poverty forced her into a public poorhouse at the age of 84. One year later, her photographic talent was finally recognized by *Life* magazine, which published an article about her, earning her enough money to enter a nursing home. She left 3,500 negatives dating from 1880 to 1930. Today the Friends of Alice Austen House mounts exhibitions of her best work.

Even Farther Afield

The village of Broad Channel at Jamaica Bay

Jamaica Bay Wildlife Refuge Center ㉗

Cross Bay Blvd at Broad Channel. **℄** *(718) 318-4340.* **Ⓜ** *Broad Channel.* **Open** *8:30am–5pm daily.*

THE MARSHES and uplands of the Refuge cover an area almost the size of Manhattan. Over 300 species of birds live here either seasonally or all year round. Situated on the main Atlantic migratory path, the Refuge is at its best in spring and autumn, when the skies are filled with skeins of geese and ducks. The park rangers conduct hikes and nature walks for weekend visitors – be sure to wear

suitable shoes and clothes, and take along a zoom lens camera or binoculars to get the best from your visit. The only village at Jamaica Bay is named Broad Channel, a small collection of houses on pilings along the Cross Bay Boulevard. The Refuge and a 10-mile (16-km) stretch of beach and boardwalk at nearby Rockaway, are accessible by subway straight from the heart of Manhattan.

Jones Beach State Park ㉘

℄ *(516) 785-1600.* **🚆** *Long Island Railroad from Penn Station to Jones Beach.* **Operates** *May 22–Sep 12.* **℄** *(718) 454-5477.* **Jones Beach Theater** **℄** *(516) 221-1000.* **Beaches open** *May 22–Sep 12.*

JONES BEACH was the creation of New York's Parks' Commissioner Robert Moses *(see p244),* who transformed this narrow spit of land into Long Island's most accessible

and popular beach in 1929. There are sand dunes, surf on the Atlantic side and sheltered water in the bay. There is also miniature golf, swimming pools, restaurants and the Jones Beach Theater, which hosts a variety of open-air concerts in the summer.

Robert Moses State Park is on the next island to the east, Fire Island, which is over 30 miles (48 km) long, yet less than 900 yds (800 m) across. Areas of the island are totally unspoiled and unpopulated, with long stretches of white sands, making it a great place for walking and bicycling in peaceful surroundings.

Fire Island's communities are small and very varied – some are favored by singles looking for the company of the opposite sex, others are sedate and family-orientated, others are favorites with New York's large gay community.

Sunbathers basking at Jones Beach

FIVE GUIDED WALKS

ALKING IN NEW YORK is an excellent way to discover the human scale of the city. The following ten pages explore the unique character and charm of New York through five thematic walks. These range from an exploration of Greenwich Village and SoHo's literary and artistic connections *(see pp260–1)* to a trip across the Brooklyn Bridge for spectacular views and a glimpse of 19th-century New York *(see pp264–5)*.

In addition, each of the 15 areas of Manhattan described in the *Area by Area* section of this book has a short walk on its *Street-by-Street* map, taking you past many of the interesting sights in that area. Various organizations and enthusiasts run walking tours of the city. These range from serious appraisals of architectural history to a guide to the ghosts of Broadway. Details of tour organizers are listed on page 353, or you can consult the listings in *New York* magazine. As in any major city, take extra care of your personal belongings while walking *(see p356–7)*. Plan your route ahead; walk only during daylight hours; and, whenever possible, go in a group.

Sculpture outside US Custom House, Lower Manhattan

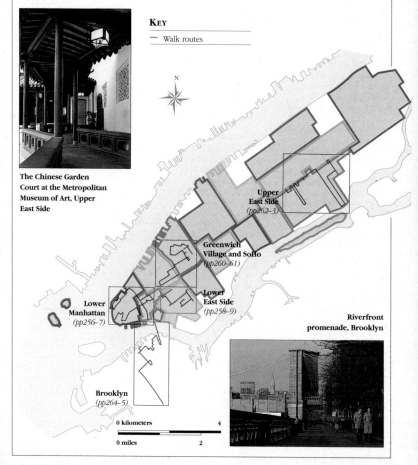

KEY

---- Walk routes

N

The Chinese Garden Court at the Metropolitan Museum of Art, Upper East Side

Upper East Side *(pp262–3)*

Greenwich Village and SoHo *(pp260–61)*

Lower Manhattan *(pp256–7)*

Lower East Side *(pp258–9)*

Riverfront promenade, Brooklyn

Brooklyn *(pp264–5)*

0 kilometers   4

0 miles   2

Relaxing in Grove Street, Greenwich Village

A Two-Hour Walk in Lower Manhattan

THIS WALK takes in the tip of Manhattan from its colonial sites to the World Financial Center, passing through the streets of the financial district. There are detours to the historic South Street Seaport as well as to New York's newest neighborhood, Battery Park City. For more details on Lower Manhattan sights, see pages 64–79; for South Street Seaport sights, see pages 80–91.

Battery Park and Federal New York

Start at Battery Park [1], the tip of the island, named for the line of cannons that once protected the harbor. Visit Castle Clinton, an 1807 fort, to see dioramas of a changing New York. The shoreline is much farther out than it used to be; much of the edge of Manhattan is built on landfill, including most of this park.

Walk a little farther inland past the many statues and monuments and the handsome Beaux Arts US Custom House [2]. The building is the new home of the Museum of the American Indian. Ironically, it was near to this spot, in 1626, that Peter Minuit acquired Manhattan Island from the local Indians, in exchange for $24 worth of beads and other trinkets.

Cross the street to Bowling Green, the city's first park, dating from 1633; turn right on Whitehall, then left to Pearl Street (which, as the old shoreline, was once scattered with pearly shells). You'll soon come to the Fraunces Tavern [3], a restoration of the 1719 building where George Washington bade farewell to his troops after the Revolutionary War. It is now a restaurant with a small museum upstairs. Also in this block are the last few small-scale Federal-style buildings to be found in the financial district.

Minuit memorial, Bowling Green

The Canyon of Wall Street

Walk up Broad Street, an avenue once split by a canal leading to the river. This was eventually filled in, resulting in one of the wider streets downtown. At Wall Street, look left between the high-rises to Trinity Church, a square-towered structure built in 1846. Try to imagine a New York in which this 280-ft (85-m) steeple was the tallest point in New York (until 1860). Among the many prominent early New Yorkers buried in the graveyard is Alexander Hamilton, whose ghost is said to haunt the nearby grave of Matthew Davis, Aaron Burr's second in the duel that took Hamilton's life.

At the junction of Broad and Wall Street stands the New York Stock Exchange [4]. On weekdays, visitors can look down at the trading floor from a balcony. Nearby at 26 Wall Street is Federal Hall [5] where, in 1789, crowds of cheering New Yorkers saw George Washington take his oath of office as president.

The Immigrants' Memorial at Castle Clinton

From Nassau Street to City Hall

Turn uptown at Nassau Street, a continuation of Broad Street, to see some of modern New York at Chase Plaza [6], the first open plaza in the financial district. At the north end of the plaza on Liberty Street is the massive, ornate Federal Reserve Bank [7], built in 1924 and famed for its five stories of bullion vaults. At the far end of the block is the Legion Memorial Square, which was renamed Louise Nevelson

The tower of City Hall [9]

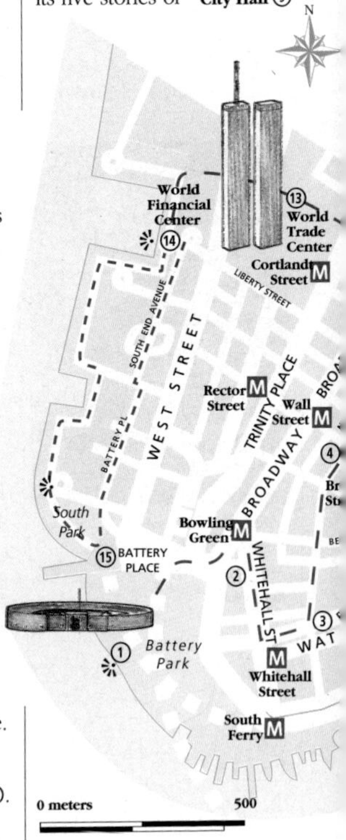
N
World Financial Center
14
13
World Trade Center
Cortlandt Street
LIBERTY STREET
SOUTH END AVENUE
WEST STREET
TRINITY PLACE
Rector Street
Wall Street
BROADWAY
BATTERY PL
4
South Park
Bowling Green
15 BATTERY PLACE
2
WHITEHALL ST
3
Battery Park
1
Whitehall Street
South Ferry
0 meters 500
0 yards 500

KEY

— Walk route

- Detour route

Good viewing point

[M] Subway station

Tips for Walkers

Starting point: *Battery Park.*
Length: *2½ miles (4 km).*
Getting there: *Take subway train 4 or 5 to Bowling Green; or the 1 or 9 to South Ferry. The Fifth Avenue bus M1 and Seventh Avenue-Broadway bus M6 are the closest bus routes.*
Stopping-off points: *Both the Seaport and the World Financial Center offer a good choice. At the Seaport, the best views are from Pier 17. At WFC, choose a café in the Winter Garden, a gourmet feast at the Hudson River Club or a snack to munch along the promenade.*

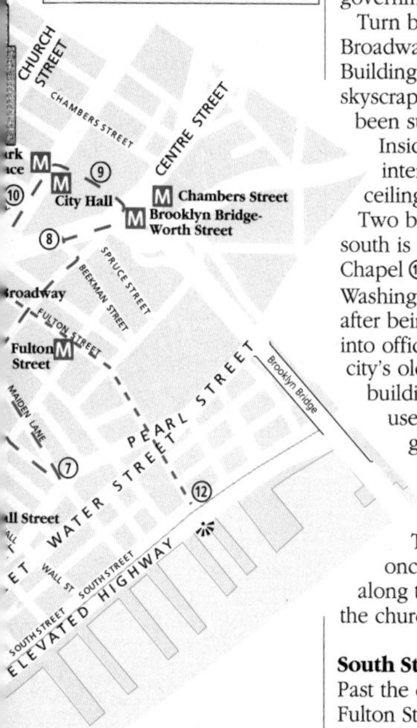

Plaza after the artist, who has seven sculptures on display here. Note the small 1815 building at 90 Maiden Lane opposite the south side of the plaza, a surprising survivor in the high-rise financial district. The fine cast-iron front was added in 1872. Continue north to Park Row ⑧ and the graceful Georgian City Hall ⑨, the seat of New York city government since 1812.

Turn back to 233 Broadway, the Woolworth Building ⑩, a 1913 skyscraper that has never been surpassed in design. Inside is a marvellous interior and mosaic ceiling.

Two blocks farther south is St. Paul's Chapel ⑪, where Washington prayed after being sworn into office. As the city's oldest public building in constant use, this Georgian gem was built in what was then a wheat field. The Hudson once flowed along the edge of the churchyard.

The ***Peking***, **a four-masted bark, in South Street Seaport ⑫**

St. Paul's Chapel ⑪

George Washington, Federal Hall ⑤

South Street Seaport

Past the church, a left turn at Fulton Street and a short walk brings you on to South Street Seaport ⑫ for a waterfront lunch and a tour of one of the tall ships. The red brick Georgian-Federal buildings on Schermerhorn Row have been beautifully restored and now look brand-new, but this is an authentic block of early 1800s warehouses and countinghouses. Sloppy Louie's, on South Street, is a good seafood restaurant. For a water view, stop off at the informal cafés on Pier 17.

From South Street to Battery Park City

Return along Fulton Street past Broadway and then cut through the sculpture-filled courtyard behind the twin towers of the World Trade Center ⑬ and detour for the views from the 107th-floor observation deck. Across the street is the new World Financial Center ⑭, a vital part of the revival of lower New York. (Either use the overpass from the north tower of the World Trade Center or cross over at Vesey Street.) The dazzling Winter Garden is a vast glass and steel atrium filled with tall palms, opening on to a landscaped promenade and a big marina on the Hudson River. The outdoor promenade continues along the river past the striking new Battery Park City ⑮.

Winter Garden at the World Financial Center ⑭

A 90-Minute Walk in the Lower East Side

THIS WALK PASSES through some of the old immigrant neighborhoods that have given New York its unique texture, and gives you the chance to experience a taste of the character, cultures, and cuisine of some of New York's most vibrant communities. Sunday is the best day for local outdoor activity. For more details on sights in the Lower East Side see pages 92–9.

The Lower East Side

Begin at the Lower East Side Tenement Museum ① at 97 Orchard Street between Delancey and Broome. This original tenement building is being restored to show how immigrants lived at the turn of the century. It features a gallery of exhibits on the immigrant experience, giving insights for the remainder of your walk.

Orchard Street itself ② was the center of the Jewish Lower East Side. The pushcarts that once lined the block are gone, but the shops selling fashionable merchandise at discount prices still remain. The stores close on Saturday, the Jewish Sabbath, and so Sunday is the traditional shopping day.

An 1885 iron from the Lower East Side Tenement Museum ①

Much of the Jewish population has moved, but reminders are many. Turn left at Grand Street and right at Essex to 35 Essex, the Essex Street Pickle Company ③, the shop in the film *Crossing Delancey*. Barrels of pickles are outside and people line up to buy. Just a few steps down Hester Street brings you to Kadouri Import (dried fruits, nuts and lots of spices) and Gertel's, an old Jewish bakery. Go back up Essex, cross Delancey and at Rivington, turn right for tours and tastings at Schapiro's Winery ④ at 126 Rivington. At 150 is Streit's Matzoh, the largest manufacturer of unleavened bread in New York.

A cultural mixture

Go back along Rivington. Note the Spanish *bodegas* and the Korean and Chinese grocers serving the new restaurants in this once-Jewish area. This is a gritty street and requires caution, but it shows a true picture of new immigrant life. Across the street at the corner of Forsyth, a synagogue has been converted to a Spanish church ⑤. Detour right to 172 Forsyth ⑥. This looks like a junkyard, but it is in fact a series of strange sculptures by the Rivington School, an avant-garde art group. Turn right on Rivington at Eldridge, a typical tenement street. The junction of Grand and Eldridge is the hub of the textile area, good for discount towels and linens. Beyond Canal Street is the Eldridge Street Synagogue ⑦, the first Eastern European synagogue in New York, now being restored.

Clothes vendors at Orchard Street market ②

TIPS FOR WALKERS

Starting point: *Orchard Street.*
Length: *2 miles (3.2 km).*
Getting there: *Take the subway train F to Delancey; B, D or Q to Grand Street; J or M to Essex Street. The M15 bus stops at the corner of Delancey and Allen Streets. Returning from Chinatown-Little Italy, Canal Street station is served by the 4, 5, 6, N and R trains.*
Stopping-off points: *Your walk will certainly whet your appetite, and you can break or end the tour with a pick of cuisine. Little Italy's cafés are perfect for coffee and luscious cakes. For more substantial fare, 20 Mott Street is recommended for Chinese food, or for Italian, Grotta Azzurra at 387 Broome Street. For a sampling of Jewish dairy delicacies such as blintzes, try Ratner's Dairy Restaurant at 138 Delancey Street.*

KEY

- Walk route
- Detour route
- Good viewing point
- [M] Subway station

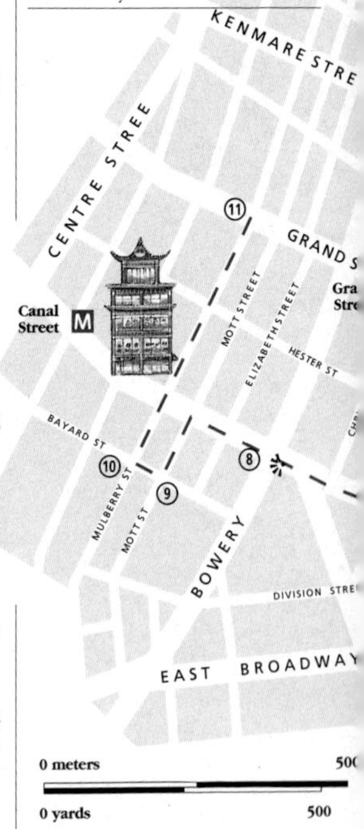

The Essex Street Pickle Company ③

Chinatown
Return to Canal Street and turn left. At the entry to the Manhattan Bridge, you'll see the World Trade Center towering in the distance, framed in stark contrast by the nearby tenements. Cross the Bowery; you'll see many jewelry shops, the remnants of the original Diamond District ⑧. As you continue, they give way to stalls selling an exotic array of vegetables, and butcher shops with

haute cuisine, all offering a chance to taste unusual fare. For spiritual sustenance. visit the Eastern States Buddhist Temple ⑨.

At Bayard Street, turn left to see all the Chinese political posters and messages on the Wall of Democracy, then turn back and to the right, to Mulberry Street. The curve next to Columbus Park was Mulberry Bend ⑩, once notorious for gang murders and mayhem.

An Italian deli in Little Italy ⑪

Little Italy
Turn and walk the other way on Mulberry Street and you are suddenly in Little Italy ⑪. Small in area though it is, and encroached on by Chinatown, this is still a wonderful neighborhood full of old-world restaurants and stores selling homemade pasta, sausages, breads and pastries. The Italian population has dwindled over the years, as the younger generation has moved out. But a staunch community still remains, as does the area's Italian atmosphere.

Pretzel seller on Orchard Street ②

Kam Man Food Products at 200 Canal Street

rows of roast ducks in the windows. At 200 Canal Street is Kam Man Food Products, one of the largest Chinese markets in the area and fascinating to explore.

Turn left from Canal to Mott Street and you'll know you are right in the heart of Chinatown by all the Chinese neon signs. Even the banks and phone booths are shaped like pagodas. There are hundreds of restaurants here, from holes-in-the-wall to

The big event of the year is the Feast of San Gennaro, named for the patron saint of Naples. For eleven nights every September, Mulberry Street is jammed with thousands of locals and visitors enjoying the parades and the Italian food, with rows of stalls selling sizzling sausages.

Little Italy's foothold is Mott to Mulberry on Hester and then from Hester to Grand on Mulberry. If you turn right on to Grand Street you'll soon find yourself passing rows of Chinese grocers again.

A 90-Minute Walk in Greenwich Village and SoHo

A STROLL THROUGH the patchwork quilt of streets in Greenwich Village takes you to where New York's best-known writers and artists have lived, worked and played, and ends with a tour of SoHo's galleries and museums, where today's artists show their work. For more details on sights in Greenwich Village, see pages 106–13, and for SoHo sights, see pages 100–5.

Author Mark Twain, who lived on 10th Street

West 10th Street

The junction of 8th Street and 6th Avenue ① has many book, music and clothing stores nearby. Walk up Sixth to West Ninth Street to see (on the left) Jefferson Market Courthouse ② and (on the right) Balducci's gourmet market.

Turn right at West 10th Street ③ to the Alexander Onassis Center for Hellenic Studies. A passageway at the front once led up to the Tile Club, a gathering place for the artists of the Tenth Street Studio, where Augustus Saint-Gaudens, John LaFarge and Winslow Homer lived. Mark Twain lived at 24 West 10th Street, and Edward Albee at 50 West 10th.

Back across Sixth Avenue is Milligan Place ④, a cluster of 19th-century houses, and Patchin Place ⑤, where the poets e e cummings and John Masefield both lived.

Farther on is the Ninth Circle bar ⑥ which, when it first opened in 1898, was known as "Regnaneschi's." It was the subject of John Sloan's painting *Regnaneschi's Saturday Night.* Playwright Edward Albee first saw the question "Who's afraid of Virginia Woolf?" scrawled on a mirror here.

Tips for Walkers

Starting point: *8th St/6th Ave.*
Length: *2 miles (3.2 km).*
Getting there: *Take subway train A, B, C, D, E or F to West Fourth Street-Washington Square station (Eighth Street exit). Fifth Avenue buses M2 and M3 stop at Eighth Street. From here, walk one block west to Sixth. The M5 bus loops around Washington Square back to Sixth Avenue and Eighth Street.*
Stopping-off points: *The Pink Tea Cup, 42 Grove Street, is good for lunch. The SoHo Kitchen & Bar, 103 Greene Street, is a typical soaring SoHo space, also known for its superb selection of wines.*

The doorway of Chumley's ⑩

Greenwich Village

Turn left at Waverly Place past the Three Lives Bookstore, a typical Village literary gathering spot, to Christopher Street and to the triangular Northern Dispensary ⑦.

Follow Grove Street along Christopher Park to Sheridan Square, the busy hub of the Village. Left is the Circle Repertory Theater ⑧, which premieres the plays of Pulitzer Prizewinner Lanford Wilson.

Facade in Washington Mews ⑬

Cross Seventh Avenue and bear left on to Grove Street. At the corner of Bedford Street, you can't miss "Twin Peaks" ⑨, a home for artists in the 1920s. Turn right to see Bedford: the unmarked door is Chumley's ⑩, a saloon not much changed since 1928 when it was a speakeasy *(see p28).* Writers Dylan Thomas, Simone de Beauvoir, Ernest Hemingway, William Faulkner, J.D. Salinger, Jack Kerouac and many others drank here. Covers of their books line the walls. 75 Bedford is the narrowest house in the Village, once the home of feminist poet Edna St. Vincent Millay.

Walk up Carmine to Sixth Avenue and turn right at Waverly Place. At 116 Waverly ⑪, Anne Charlotte Lynch, an English teacher, held weekly gatherings in her town house for such eminent friends as Herman Melville and Edgar Allan Poe, who gave his first reading of *The Raven* here.

A detour left of half a block will bring you to MacDougal Alley ⑫, a lane of carriage houses in which Gertrude Vanderbilt Whitney had her studio. She opened the first Whitney Museum here in 1932, just behind the studio.

Washington Square

Once back on MacDougal, turn left to Washington Square North, to see the finest Greek Revival houses in the United States. Writer Henry James set his *Washington Square* in No. 18, his grandmother's home.

Then pause at Fifth Avenue to look back at Washington Square Park for a perfect view

Washington Square Park and Arch

of the twin towers of the World Trade Center framed by the Washington Square Arch.

Go across to Two Fifth Avenue; opposite is Washington Mews ⑬, an elegant carriage house complex. John Dos Passos, Edward Hopper and Rockwell Kent lived in the studio at No. 14a at various times.

Go back up Washington Square North, past some elegant houses. Writer Edith Wharton lived at Seven Washington Square North. Walk beneath the arch and across Washington Square Park. On the left as you leave the park, is the fine Judson Memorial Church and Tower ⑭ by Stanford White and the NYU Loeb Student Center. The Center was once a boarding house, known as the "house of genius," and is where Theodore Dreiser wrote *An American Tragedy.*

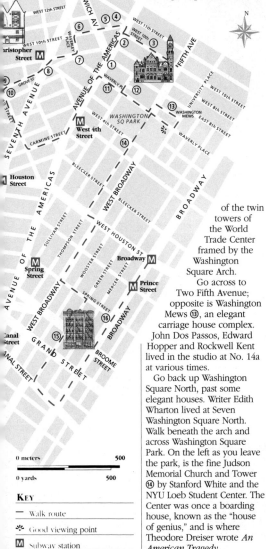

KEY

— Walk route

❊ Good viewing point

Ⓜ Subway station

SoHo

Walk south on Thompson, a typical Village street lined with clubs, cafés and shops. Turn left at Houston, SoHo's northern limit, and right on West Broadway, lined with some of the city's most famous galleries along with chic and arty boutiques.

Turn left at Spring Street for yet more tempting shops, then right at Greene Street ⑮, the heart of the Cast-Iron Historic District. Many of these fine buildings now house clusters of galleries. Turn left at the end of Greene Street to Canal Street, the end of SoHo, to see how quickly New York can change. This noisy street is full of hawkers and discount electronics stores. You can explore bargains for the next two blocks and then turn left up Broadway, soon finding yourself on the cutting edge of art, at the New Museum of Contemporary Art at 583 Broadway and the Guggenheim Museum SoHo ⑯ found at 575 Broadway *(see p105)*.

Cast-iron facade, Greene Street ⑮

A Two-Hour Walk in the Upper East Side

A PROMENADE ALONG upper Fifth Avenue and its environs will take you past the best remaining examples of New York's turn-of-the-century gilded age. A detour through the old German district of Yorkville leads to a riverside stroll to Gracie Mansion, official residence of the city's mayor, dating from 1799. For details on Upper East Side sights, see pages 180–201.

KEY

— Walk route

Good viewing point

[M] Subway station

From the Frick to the Met

Begin at the Frick mansion ①, built for coal magnate Henry Clay Frick in 1913–14. Allow some extra time to see Frick's art collection *(pp200–1)*. Many such mansions were built as New York's first families outdid each other with miniature Versailles, Loire-style châteaux and even Venetian palazzos. Most of the ones still standing have now become either institutions or museums. The apartment building opposite the Frick is typical of those where today's affluent New Yorkers live.

Church of the Holy Trinity ⑰

East on 70th are two of the city's top art galleries, the Knoedler Gallery and Hirsch & Adler ②. Walk up Madison to the corner of 72nd Street, to the big Polo-Ralph Lauren store ③, the 1898 French Renaissance home of Gertrude Rhinelander Waldo. Wander inside to see the elegant restored interior.

Walk back toward Fifth on the north side of 72nd, past two 1890s limestone beauties, now the Lycée Français de New York ④. Continue along Fifth Avenue to 73rd Street. Turn right to 11 East 73rd, Joseph Pulitzer's former home ⑤.

A few blocks on, between Lexington and Third, is a fine row of town houses ⑥. Back on Fifth, walk to 75th Street, to see 1 East 75th, the former residence of Edward S. Harkness, son of a founder of Standard Oil. It is now the Commonwealth Fund ⑦. At 1 East 78th, the tobacco millionaire James B. Duke's 18th-century French-style château has now become the New York University Institute of Fine Arts ⑧. At 79th Street and Fifth, the former home of financier Payne Whitney, is the French Embassy ⑨ and 2 East 79th is the Ukrainian Institute of America ⑩. On the southeast corner of 82nd is Duke-Semans House ⑪, one of the few grand Fifth Avenue residences still privately owned. Save another day for The Metropolitan Museum of Art ⑫ at 82nd.

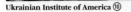

Ukrainian Institute of America ⑩

Carl Schurz Park Promenade

TIPS FOR WALKERS

Starting point: Frick Collection.
Length: 3 miles (4.8 km).
Getting there: Take subway train 6 to 68th Street and Lexington, then walk west (left) three blocks to Fifth Avenue. Or take the M1, M2, M3 or M4 bus up Madison Avenue to 70th Street and walk one block west.
Stopping-off points: The cafés at the Whitney and Guggenheim museums are pleasant. Or sample the German fare at Ideal, a restaurant at 238 E. 86th Street, or try the Heidelberg Café on Second Avenue off 86th Street. Madison Avenue between 92nd and 93rd has many places to eat, including Sarabeth's Kitchen, with its excellent weekend brunch.

Yorkville

Turn east on 86th Street for the vestiges of German Yorkville – Bremen House ⑬, Kleine Konditorei and Ideal, a restaurant that

serves large portions. Cross Second Avenue, then turn right to the Heidelberg Café and German deli, Schaller & Weber ⑭.

East River and Gracie Mansion

Henderson Place ⑮ at East End Avenue is a cluster of 24 red-brick Queen Anne town houses. Carl Schurz Park opposite was named after the city's most prominent German immigrant, editor of *Harper's Weekly* and the *New York Post*. The park promenade atop the east River Drive leads to a view of Hell Gate, where the Harlem River, Long Island Sound and New York harbor meet. From the walkway you can see the back of Gracie Mansion ⑯, the mayor's official residence. The path west along the fence leads to a better view. Walk west on 88th Street past the Church of the Holy Trinity ⑰ and at Lexington Avenue go to 92nd Street and west past two of the few wooden houses left in Manhattan ⑱.

The Cooper-Hewitt Museum ⑳

Carnegie Hill

Back on Fifth Avenue, turn downtown past the Felix Warburg Mansion of 1908, now the Jewish Museum ⑲, and continue to 91st Street and the huge Andrew Carnegie home, now the Cooper-Hewitt Museum ⑳. Built in 1902 in the style of an English country manor, it gave the area the unofficial name of Carnegie Hill. The James Burden House ㉑ at 7 East 91st Street, built for Vanderbilt heiress Adele Sloan in 1905, has a spiral staircase under a stained glass skylight that was known in society as "the stairway to heaven." At 9 East 91st, the financier Otto Kahn's Italian Renaissance-style residence was a show-place with a drive-through porch and interior courtyard. It is now the Convent of the Sacred Heart School.

Wooden houses on 92nd Street ⑱

A Three-Hour Walk in Brooklyn

A TRIP ACROSS New York's most famous crossing leads to Brooklyn Heights, the city's first suburb. This neighborhood has a 19th-century feel, mixed with a hint of Middle Eastern cultures. The riverfront promenade has unrivaled views of Manhattan. For more details on sights in Brooklyn, see pages 244–51.

Fire Station on Old Fulton Street

Fulton Ferry Landing

About 3,580 ft (1 km) long, the Brooklyn Bridge span yields thrilling views of the lower New York skyline and prize photo opportunities. Take a taxi, or, if feeling energetic, walk across to Brooklyn.

On the far side, follow the Tillary Street sign to the right, turn right at the bottom of the stairs, then take the first path through the park and walk down Cadman Plaza West ① under the Brooklyn-Queens Expressway; here Cadman becomes Old Fulton Street. You can see the bridge on the right as you head to the river at Water Street and the Fulton Ferry landing ②. During the Revolutionary War, George Washington's troops fled to Manhattan from here. In 1814, this was the depot for the ferry connecting Brooklyn and Manhattan Island. This transformed Brooklyn Heights from a predominantly farming area to a residential district. The area is still a favorite place to live. To the right are Bargemusic ③, a barge hosting chamber music concerts, and the River Café, whose fine cuisine and views make it one of New York's most exceptional dining spots.

Eagle Warehouse ④

Brooklyn Heights

From the landing, turn right to steep Everitt Street up Columbia Heights, past the former Eagle Warehouse ④ of 1893 to Middagh Street and along the streets of Brooklyn Heights. 24 Middagh ⑤ is one of the oldest, built in 1824.

Next turn right on Willow and left on Cranberry; here the town houses range from wooden clapboards to brick Federal-style to brownstones. Except for cars and a few modern buildings, you could be in the 19th century.

Many famous people have lived here. Truman Capote wrote *Breakfast at Tiffany's* and *In Cold Blood* in the basement of 70 Willow, and Arthur Miller once owned 155 Willow. Walt Whitman lived on Cranberry Street when he was editor of the *Brooklyn Eagle*. He set the type for his *Leaves of Grass* at a print shop near the corner of Cranberry and Fulton. The town houses now on the site are called Whitman Close.

Turn right along Hicks. The Hicks family, local farmers, inspired the name "hick" for a yokel. Turn left on Orange Street to the Plymouth Church ⑥, home of Henry Ward Beecher, an antislavery preacher. His sister, Harriet Beecher Stowe,

Entrance to the River Café

Truman Capote with feathered friend

wrote *Uncle Tom's Cabin*. At Clark Street are marquees of once-luxurious hotels, such as the Towers. Follow Clark Street to 142 Columbia Heights, where Norman Mailer lives ⑦. Invalid Washington Roebling lived at 110 – using a telescope, he directed the construction of Brooklyn Bridge from his room.

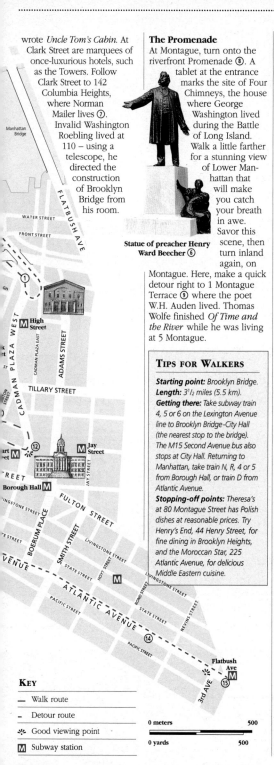

Statue of preacher Henry Ward Beecher ⑥

The Promenade
At Montague, turn onto the riverfront Promenade ⑧. A tablet at the entrance marks the site of Four Chimneys, the house where George Washington lived during the Battle of Long Island. Walk a little farther for a stunning view of Lower Manhattan that will make you catch your breath in awe. Savor this scene, then turn inland again, on Montague. Here, make a quick detour right to 1 Montague Terrace ⑨ where the poet W.H. Auden lived. Thomas Wolfe finished *Of Time and the River* while he was living at 5 Montague.

> #### TIPS FOR WALKERS
>
> **Starting point:** Brooklyn Bridge.
> **Length:** 3½ miles (5.5 km).
> **Getting there:** Take subway train 4, 5 or 6 on the Lexington Avenue line to Brooklyn Bridge-City Hall (the nearest stop to the bridge). The M15 Second Avenue bus also stops at City Hall. Returning to Manhattan, take train N, R, 4 or 5 from Borough Hall, or train D from Atlantic Avenue.
> **Stopping-off points:** Theresa's at 80 Montague Street has Polish dishes at reasonable prices. Try Henry's End, 44 Henry Street, for fine dining in Brooklyn Heights, and the Moroccan Star, 225 Atlantic Avenue, for delicious Middle Eastern cuisine.

The old Montague Street trolley, which led to the river and the ferry

Montague and Clinton Streets
Once back on Montague Street, walk to the heart of Brooklyn Heights, with all its cafés and boutiques. The baseball team, the Brooklyn Dodgers, got their name from dodging the trolley cars that once ran down the street. Walk to the intersection of Montague and Clinton to see the stained glass of the 1834 Church of St. Ann and the Holy Trinity ⑩. Walk a block left on Clinton to Pierrepont Street for the Brooklyn Historical Society ⑪. A block farther, at Court Street, is the 1849 Borough Hall ⑫, and the subway taking you back to Manhattan.

Brooklyn's Dodgers, who got their name from dodging trolley cars

Atlantic Avenue
Another option is to stay on Clinton and walk five short blocks to Atlantic Avenue. A left turn here leads to a whole string of Middle Eastern emporia ⑬, such as Sahadi Imports at 187 Atlantic Avenue, with a huge selection of foods. Rashid at 191 sells Arabic publications and records; and the Damascus Bakery at 195 makes the most delicious filo pastries. Two blocks on are numerous antique shops ⑭. At Flatbush Avenue, look left to the Brooklyn Academy of Music ⑮ and the grand front of the Williamsburg Savings Bank. Watch for signs to the subway back to Manhattan.

KEY
— Walk route
- - Detour route
≫ Good viewing point
Ⓜ Subway station

| 0 meters | 500 |
| 0 yards | 500 |

TRAVELERS' NEEDS

WHERE TO STAY

ITH OVER 70,000 hotel rooms available, New York offers something for everyone. The top hotels are not quite as expensive as those in Paris or London, but the best news for visitors is the increase in budget hotels. While many of these are basic rather than charming, they offer good value. Other budget options are furnished apartments and studios and bed and breakfast in private

Cole Porter's piano, in the Waldorf–Astoria bar *(see p281)*

homes, as well as youth hostels and YMCAs. From an inspection of over 200 hotels, we have selected 76 as the best of their kind. *Choosing a Hotel (pp274–45)* helps you make a choice based on your needs, but for more detailed descriptions, turn to the listings on pages 276–83. The map on page 272 highlights ten hotels, chosen as the best in their category.

Bathroom at the Paramount Hotel *(see p277)*

WHERE TO LOOK

THE EAST SIDE, roughly between 59th and 77th streets, is the traditional location for luxury hotels, but the renovation of certain landmark midtown properties, such as the St. Regis, and new hotels in famous chains from the Far East, such as the Peninsula Group, have increased competition in this price range.

Business travelers tend to favor midtown, especially the moderately priced hotels lining Lexington Avenue near Grand Central Terminal.

Those seeking relative quiet with access to midtown should look in the Murray Hill area, while theater lovers should note the revival of the Times Square area. Hotels within walking distance of theaters offer an advantage, since performances tend to end at the same time and cabs are hard to come by.

The Upper West Side hotels are less expensive. This popular residential area is convenient for Lincoln Center and offers easy access to public transportation.

The **New York Convention and Visitors Bureau** publishes a free, annually updated leaflet called "The New York Hotel Guide," listing current rates, toll-free numbers and fax numbers. Staff will offer advice about hotels but do not make reservations.

HOTEL PRICES

SOME HOTELS offer seasonal promotional rates and other off-peak reductions. For example, business travelers vacate hotels at the end of the working week, and you can take advantage of bargain weekend deals, even in luxury hotels, as prices drop *(see Special Breaks p270)*.

There is a growing number of all-suite hotels available in every price category. Suites offer about twice the amount of space as a normal hotel room – plus cooking facilities and a refrigerator – for the same price. Most suites can accommodate up to four people, a saving that makes them popular with families. Bear in mind that the location will be reflected in the cost.

Café Botanica at the Essex House Hotel *(see p278)*

HIDDEN EXTRAS

WHEN CALCULATING the cost of hotels in New York, note the price per room quoted by the hotel, then add the New York State sales tax (13.25%), the New York City hotel sales tax (6%) and a $2 occupancy tax per room per night on top of that. Room rates under $100 are not only easier on the wallet but lower the total tax rate to 14.25% (plus $2), accounting for an increase in rooms in the lower category.

Lobby phones, to reach a guest staying in the hotel

Suite at the Millenium *(see p276)*

Very few hotels include breakfast in the room price. In general, a standard hotel Continental breakfast before tax costs about $5 per person in the cheaper hotels, soaring to over $15 in some of the luxury hotels. To save money, head for the nearest deli or coffee shop and leave the hotel to business people having power breakfasts.

Hotel telephone charges are usually high; it may well be cheaper to use the pay phone in the lobby, particularly when calling overseas.

Tips are expected in the United States. Staff who take your luggage to the room are usually tipped a minimum of $1 per bag – more in a luxury hotel. The concierge need not be tipped for normal services such as arranging transportation or making dinner reservations, but should be rewarded for exceptional services.

When you order from room service, check the menu to see whether a service charge will also be included in the bill; if not, a 15% tip is customary.

Solo travelers will find that single room rates are usually at least 80% of the double rate and are sometimes the same as for two people.

FACILITIES

ALTHOUGH you'd expect hotel rooms in New York City to be noisy, most windows are double- or even triple-glazed to keep out the noise. Air-conditioning is almost a standard feature, so there is no need to open the windows in hot weather. Even so, some rooms are obviously quieter than others, if they are at the back of the hotel or overlooking a courtyard – check when reserving.

Television, radio and at least one telephone are usually provided in every room, even in modest lodgings, and most hotel bedrooms have in-suite bathrooms. Many mid-range hotels now offer fax outlets and machines in each room, a health club or exercise room and a full concierge service. Luxury facilities include minibars in the room, dual phones, private phone message systems and electronic checkout.

The hotels listed here are all within a few minutes' walk of a large number of shops and restaurants. Very few hotels have their own parking, but valets may park your car in areas reserved for guests' use in nearby public garages. A reduced (but still expensive) daily parking fee is normally offered. If there is no concierge at the hotel, front desk staff will be able to help with tourist information and to answer any queries.

The Art Deco lobby of the Edison Hotel *(see p277)*

HOW TO RESERVE

IT IS ADVISABLE to make hotel reservations at least one month in advance. While it's unlikely that the hotel will be fully booked, you may well find that the best rooms and suites have been taken, especially if a major convention is taking place. The busiest periods are at Easter, the New York Marathon week in late October or early November, Thanksgiving and Christmas.

Reserve directly with the hotel by telephone, letter or fax. Written confirmation of your telephone booking will be required, probably with a deposit as a guarantee of your arrival; any cancellation fees may be deducted from this. You can pay by credit card, international bank draft or money order, or dollar traveler's check. Advise the staff if you are going to arrive at the hotel after 6pm or you will lose your reservation, unless you have prepaid with a credit card.

You can also book a hotel through your travel agent or airline. Most hotels have a toll-free telephone number for use in the United States, but these numbers do not work from Europe and the UK. If the hotel is part of an international chain, an affiliated hotel in your country should be able to reserve a room for you.

SPECIAL RATES

HOTELS ARE BUSIEST during the week, when business travelers are in the city, so most of them offer cheap packages to encourage more weekend business. It's often possible to move from a standard to a luxury room for the weekend at the same rate.

A lower corporate rate is usually available to employees of large companies. But quite often, reservation clerks will grant corporate discounts on request without asking for a company affiliation.

Some reservation agencies offer discount rates. A good travel agent should be able to get the best current rates, but compare prices by contacting directly a discount reservation service such as The Room Exchange *(see p269)*. They offer discounts between 20% and 50% on last-minute bookings, depending on the time of year. You reserve by credit card and receive a voucher to present to the hotel.

Package tours can also provide savings on the usual price. These rates may not oblige you to stay with a tour group, only to use their air and hotel arrangements. These packages may also include airport transfers, an additional saving. Airlines frequently have their own special deals, particularly during slow travel seasons. Again, a knowledgeable travel agent should be able to tell you the current best deals, but newspapers often advertise special, limited offers that can be booked directly. At off-peak times you may net even bigger savings than with the package plans.

Lobby of the St. Regis Hotel *(see p282)*

Disabled Travelers

By law, new hotels must provide facilities for disabled visitors, and many older buildings have been renovated to comply, too. Guide dogs are allowed in most hotels, but it is advisable to check when reserving.

This guide's disabled access information is based upon each hotel's own assessment of its suitability. Let the hotel know of any specific needs when booking. The **Mayor's Office for People With Disabilities** also offers information about hotels.

Traveling with Children

American hotels generally have a very welcoming attitude toward children. Cots or cribs and lists of baby-sitters are normally widely available, and most hotel restaurants are happy to cater for young guests.

Traveling with children can be cheaper than anticipated. Many hotels do not charge for children if they stay in their parents' room, or make only a small charge for an extra bed. There is usually a limit of one or two children per room in these cases, and most hotels stipulate that the children must be under a certain age, often 12. Parents of older children are expected to pay the full price, although the age limit is occasionally extended to 18. Ask about family rates when reserving.

Bed-and-Breakfast

There is an increasing number of bed-and-breakfast accommodations to be had in private apartments. This varies from a room in an apartment with an owner-host in residence to an entire apartment to yourself, with its own kitchen and bathroom, yours while the owner is away.

Staying in a private apartment enables you to feel at home in a New York neighborhood and to visit local restaurants, usually far more reasonably priced than those in tourist areas.

Entrance to the Peninsula Hotel *(see p281)*

Bed-and-breakfast lodgings can be found through many free booking services. Some booking agencies have a two-night minimum. Rates for unhosted apartments vary from about $70 to $200, and for a double room range from $60 to $90 a night, depending on whether you have a private bathroom. There is a wide range of apartments, from spacious and luxurious to cramped and dowdy. Your costs will rise if the address is remote, requiring frequent cabs. Ask about location and amenities when you reserve.

Youth and Budget Accommodations

A youth hostel and many **YMCA** dormitories offer lodgings for those on a tight budget. For the longer-term visitor, the **92nd Street Y**, a nonsectarian hostel and lively cultural center situated in the Upper East Side, has good-value rooms from about $30 to $50 a night.

There are no campsites in Manhattan, and, sadly, youth hostels are not as prevalent in New York as they are in large European cities.

Sky-high swimming pool at the UN Plaza Hotel *(see p280)*

Using the Listings

Hotel listings are on pages 276–83. Each hotel is listed according to its area and price category. The symbols after each hotel's address summarize the facilities it offers.

all rooms with bath and/or shower unless otherwise indicated
1 single-rate rooms available
rooms for more than 2 people available, or an extra bed can be put in a double room
24 24-hour room service
TV television in all rooms
minibar in all rooms
nonsmoking rooms available
rooms with good view available
air-conditioning in all rooms
gym/fitness facilities available in hotel
swimming pool in hotel
business facilities: message-taking service, fax machine for guests, desk and telephone in each room, and meeting room within hotel
children's facilities: cribs/cots, baby-sitting service
wheelchair access
elevator
pets allowed in bedrooms (always check when reserving)
P valet parking available
garden/terrace open to guests
bar
restaurant
tourist information desk or personnel
Credit cards accepted:
AE American Express
DC Diners Club
MC MasterCard/Access
V VISA
JCB Japanese Credit Bureau

Price categories for a double room with bath per night, including tax and service:
$ under $120
$$ $120–$180
$$$ $180–$250
$$$$ $250–$320

New York's Best: Hotels

NEW YORK hotels range from the
ultimate in luxury to the
surprisingly cheap and cheerful. All
are within easy reach of shops,
restaurants and transportation. Some
are of historical or literary interest;
some are streamlined and high-tech;
others are old-fashioned and cozy.
From this wide variety, certain hotels
stand out, whether for character,
comfort or good value. The hotels
shown here have been selected from
the listings on pages 276–83 as the best
in their particular style or price range.

Plaza
*This land-
mark hotel has
been part of New
York life for over
100 years. Re-
furbishing has
restored its early
glamor.* (See
p281.)

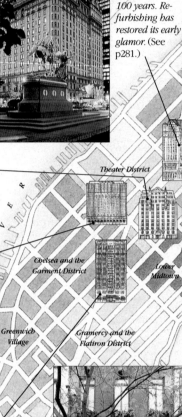

Wyndham
*Book well in
advance for a
winning com-
bination of
homey charm
and low prices.*
(See p278.)

Paramount
*Chic designer
Philippe Starck
set the style of
this ultra-smart,
yet sensibly-
priced,
hotel.*
(See
p277.)

Theater District

Upp
Midto

*Chelsea and the
Garment District*

*Lower
Midtown*

*Greenwich
Village*

*Gramercy and the
Flatiron District*

*SoHo
and
TriBeCa*

Algonquin
*Sip a cocktail
in the spot
where literary
wit Dorothy
Parker and
her circle
gathered in
the 1920s.*
(See p278
and p143.)

*Seaport
and the
Civic Center*

*Lower
East
Side*

*Lower
Manhattan*

Box Tree
*Two brownstones have been
converted into an intimate yet
sumptuous inn, complete with
superb restaurant.* (See p281.)

Carlyle
Old-world elegance, stunning views of Central Park and the mellow jazz notes of Bobby Short in the Café Carlyle combine to make this luxury hotel superb. (See p282.)

Mayfair Baglioni
A European air and an atmosphere of gracious sophistication attract an international clientele. The mirrored lounge is a favorite rendezvous for breakfast and tea. (See p282.)

Lowell
Luxurious suites offer all the comforts of a country house on the Upper East Side. (See p282.)

```
0 kilometers          2
0 miles            1
```

Pickwick Arms
Midtown's best bargain offers no-frills value for money in the heart of Manhattan. An unexpected bonus are the fine views of the encircling skyline from the simple, pleasant roof terrace. (See p280.)

UN Plaza
The soaring views from the bedrooms are outdone only by those from the glassed-in, 27th-floor pool. (See p280.)

Choosing a Hotel

THE 76 HOTELS listed in the following pages have all been individually inspected and assessed to help you make an informed decision. All the hotels are in Manhattan itself, within easy walking distance of museums, shops and restaurants. They are listed alphabetically in their price category.

		Number of Rooms	Large Rooms	Business Facilities	Children's Facilities	Recommended Restaurant	Concierge	Quiet Location	24-Hour Room Service
LOWER MANHATTAN (*See p276*)									
Millenium	$$$$	561		■	●		●		●
New York Marriott Financial Center	$$$$	504		■	●		●		
LOWER EAST SIDE (*See p276*)									
Holiday Inn Downtown	$$	227		■	●	■	●		
GREENWICH VILLAGE (*See p276*)									
Washington Square Hotel	$	180						■	
GRAMERCY AND THE FLATIRON DISTRICT (*See p276*)									
Carlton	$	210		■	●			■	
Gramercy Park	$	545		■				■	
Roger Williams	$	211	●					■	
CHELSEA AND THE GARMENT DISTRICT (*See p276*)									
Herald Square Hotel	$	120							
Stanford	$	130			●				
THEATER DISTRICT (*See p277–9*)									
Chatwal Inn on 45th Street	$	50		■			●		
Edison	$	900							
Iroquois	$	110		■					
Wellington	$	700		■					
Best Western President	$$	400		■			●		
Best Western Woodward	$$	200		■			●		
Days Hotel Midtown	$$	366		■					
Howard Johnson Plaza	$$	300		■	●				
Paramount	$$	610		■	●	■	●		●
Quality Inn Midtown	$$	200		■					
St. Moritz	$$	680							
Wyndham	$$	200	●						
Algonquin	$$$	165		■		■	●		
Embassy Suites	$$$	460	●	■	●		●		
Holiday Inn Crowne Plaza	$$$	770	●	■	●	■	●		●
Ramada Renaissance	$$$	305		■	●		●		
Salisbury	$$$	320	●	■					
Sheraton Manhattan	$$$	663		■	●		●		
Warwick	$$$	425		■					
Essex House	$$$$	593		■	●	■	●		●
Le Parker Meridien	$$$$	691		■			●		●
Macklowe	$$$$	629		■	●	■	●		
Michelangelo	$$$$	178	●	■			●		
Rihga Royal	$$$$	500	●	■	●		●		
Ritz–Carlton	$$$$	228		■	●	■	●		●
Royalton	$$$$	167		■	●	■	●		●
LOWER MIDTOWN (*See p279–80*)									
Journey's End	$$	189		■			●		
Roosevelt	$$	1070		■			●		
Doral Court	$$$	199	●	■		■	●	■	
Helmsley Middletowne	$$$	190						■	

Price categories for a double room per night, including tax and service:
$ under $120
$$ $120–$180
$$$ $180–$250
$$$$ $250–$320
$$$$$ over $320

CONCIERGE
Concierge available to advise, make reservations, etc.

BUSINESS FACILITIES
Message service; fax for guests; desk and telephone in each room; meeting room within the hotel.

CHILDREN'S FACILITIES
Family rooms; cots or cribs; baby-sitting service; children's portions; high chairs in dining area.

QUIET LOCATION
Quiet, residential neighborhood or quiet street in a busy area.

	Price	Number of Rooms	Large Rooms	Business Facilities	Children's Facilities	Recommended Restaurant	Concierge	Quiet Location	24-Hour Room Service
Jolly Madison Towers	$$$	246	●	■					
Roger Smith	$$$	130	●	■	●				
Doral Park Avenue	$$$$	188		■		■	●	■	
Doral Tuscany	$$$$	121		■		■	●	■	
Sheraton Park Avenue	$$$$	150	●	■		■	●	■	●
United Nations Plaza	$$$$	428		■	●	■	●		●
UPPER MIDTOWN (See p280–82)									
Pickwick Arms	$	400					●	■	
Beverly	$$	187	●	■	●		●		
Doral Inn	$$$	655		■			●		
Dorset	$$$	490	●	■			●		
Fitzpatrick Manhattan Hotel	$$$	92		■			●		
Plaza	$$$$	812	●	■	●	■	●		●
Waldorf–Astoria	$$$$	1410	●	■	●	■	●		●
Box Tree	$$$$$	13		■		■		■	
Peninsula	$$$$$	250	●	■	●	■	●		●
Pierre	$$$$$	206	●	■	●	■	●		●
St. Regis	$$$$$	322	●	■	●	■	●		●
Stanhope	$$$$$	141	●	■	●	■	●	■	●
UPPER EAST SIDE (See p282–3)									
Wales	$$	95		■			●		
Barbizon	$$$	344		■			●		
Mark	$$$$	180	●	■	●	■	●	■	
Carlyle	$$$$$	175	●	■	●	■	●	■	●
Lowell	$$$$$	61			●	■	●	■	
Mayfair Baglioni	$$$$$	201	●	■		■	●	■	●
Plaza Athénée	$$$$$	156		■		■	●	■	●
Regency	$$$$$	384	●	■	●	■	●		●
Westbury	$$$$$	231	●	■	●	■	●	■	●
UPPER WEST SIDE (See p283)									
Beacon	$	100					●	■	
Broadway American	$	200	●						
Excelsior	$	150	●						
Milburn	$	90	●	■	●		●	■	●
Radisson Empire	$$	375		■	●	■	●		●
Mayflower	$$$	377	●	■				■	

Lower Manhattan

Millenium

55 Church St, NY, NY 10007.
Map 1 B2. [C] 693-2001.
[FAX] 571-2317. **Rooms:** 561. 🛏 1
24 TV 🍴 ⛱ 🌊 🗄 🖥
🅿 🅃 🛗 🐾 P 🅃 🚹 🏋
AE, DC, MC, V. $$$$

At 58 stories high, the sleek
Millenium is designed to appeal to
the well-heeled who have business near Wall Street. Rooms are
not particularly large, but make
excellent use of space with furnishings that give the illusion of
being built-in. Bathrooms are in
dramatic black marble, lighting
fixtures are the very latest design,
and there are conveniences such
as two-line telephones with
speaker and conference capabilities, voice mail and a video
system that can be used to order
room service or settle your bill.
Most rooms face the World Trade
Center; lower floors overlook the
courtyard, while higher locations
provide river views. Some of the
most pleasant views are from the
side, where the fitness center and
large pool face the leafy churchyard of St. Paul's Chapel.

New York Marriott Financial Center

85 West St, NY, NY 10006. **Map** 1 B3.
[C] 385-4900. [FAX] 385-8136. **Rooms:**
504. 🛏 1 TV 🍴 ⛱ 🌊 🗄 🖥
🅿 🅃 🛗 🐾 P 🅃 🚹 🏋
🗄 *AE, DC, MC, V, JCB.* $$$$

A newcomer in the financial
district, the Marriott offers standard rooms and amenities. There
are, however, some welcome features, such as an indoor pool and
health club and outstanding
Hudson River views from higher
floors. Rates drop substantially on
weekends, making this a good base
for exploring Lower Manhattan.

Lower East Side

Holiday Inn Downtown

138 Lafayette St, NY, NY 10013.
Map 4 F5. [C] 966-8898.
[FAX] 966-3933. **Rooms:** 227. 🛏 1
🛗 TV ⛱ 🗄 🖥 🚹 🐾 P 🅃
🚹 🏋 🗄 *AE, DC, MC, V, JCB.* $$

This first hotel in Chinatown open-
ed in 1992. Its rooms are small and
undistinguished with Oriental
touches. Pacifica, its Hong Kong-
style gourmet restaurant, offers
excellent food but is unfortunately
more expensive than most
Chinatown restaurants. The hotel

is well located for anyone doing
business in the area, and for
tourists who want to take advan-
tage of its bargain weekend rates
and explore this fascinating
neighborhood, as well as adjacent
Little Italy and the Lower East Side,
popular for discount shopping.

Greenwich Village

Washington Square Hotel

103 Waverly Pl, NY, NY 10011.
Map 4 E2. [C] 777-9515.
[FAX] 979-8373. [TX] 126909. **Rooms:**
180. 🛏 170. 1 🛗 TV 🍴 🗄 🖥
🐾 🅃 🚹 🗄 *AE, MC, V, JCB.* $

This small hotel, just off the square
in the heart of Greenwich Village,
has tiny rooms but much to recom-
mend it nevertheless. Marble,
latticework and plants give an
old-world look to the lobby, while
the narrow hallways are accented
with Mexican tiles. The rooms are
decorated with cheerful fabrics,
bathrooms are new and there is a
coffee shop and a small fitness
center. Above all, it is the only
hotel in the heart of the Village.

Gramercy and the Flatiron District

Carlton

22 E 29th St, NY, NY 10016. **Map** 8 F3.
[C] 532-4100. [FAX] 889-8683. **Rooms:**
210. 🛏 1 🛗 TV 🗄 🖥 🚹
🐾 🅃 🚹 🏋 🗄 *AE, DC, MC, V.* $

Cheerful interior renovation of this
Beaux Arts building has provided
a reasonably priced haven on the
edge of Murray Hill. The lobby has
been spruced up, rooms are newly
decorated and bathrooms have
modern fixtures. There's a café off
the lobby and amenities such as
room service and valet service, not
often found in this price range.

Gramercy Park

2 Lexington Ave, NY, NY 10010.
Map 9 A4. [C] 475-4320.
[FAX] 505-0535. [TX] 668755. **Rooms:**
545. 🛏 🛗 TV 🖥 🗄 🚹 🐾 P
🅃 🚹 🗄 *AE DC, MC, V, JCB.* $

If the rooms matched the attractive
facade and the location on the
city's only private park, this would
be a wonderful place. As it is, the
paneled lobby is pleasant but the
decor is tired and rooms are
overdue for modernizing.
However, rates are reasonable, es-
pecially on weekends, and guests
can use the park, a feature that
attracts many European guests.

Roger Williams

28 E 31st St, NY, NY 10016.
Map 8 F3. [C] 684-7500.
[FAX] 576-4343. **Rooms:** 211. 🛏 1
 *AE, DC, MC, V.* $

Expect nothing fancy here – the
rooms could do with renovation,
and so could the plumbing. But
for relatively little money you get
a pleasant, convenient and safe
Murray Hill address with clean,
decent-sized rooms, an adequate
kitchenette, television and a
phone – all in all, a good deal.

Chelsea and the Garment District

Herald Square Hotel

19 W 31st St, NY, NY 10001.
Map 8 F3. [C] 279-4017.
[FAX] 643-9208. **Rooms:** 120. 🛏 108.
1 🛗 TV 🗄 🖥 🗄 *AE, MC, V,*
JCB. $. See p131.

This immaculate budget hideaway
has been renovated with taste and
charm. The gilded cherub over the
front door remains from the time
when this Beaux Arts building,
designed by Carrère & Hastings,
was the first home of *Life* maga-
zine. Vintage *Life* covers adorn the
hallways. The rooms are quite
small, but are brightened by this
pleasant pink decor. Bathrooms
are spanking new. The location is
convenient for visiting both
Macy's department store and the
Empire State Building. The neigh-
borhood, unfortunately, lacks a
wide range of restaurants, but
"Little Korea" is only a block away,
and has several interesting, cheap
eateries to choose from.

Stanford

43 W 32nd St, NY, NY 10001..
Map 8 F3. [C] 563-1480.
[FAX] 629-0043. [TX] 211283. **Rooms:**
130. 🛏 1 🛗 TV 🍴 🖥 🚹 🅃
🚹 🗄 *AE, DC, MC, V.* $

Popular with Asian visitors, this
clean, modern hotel on the "Little
Korea" block is a very good deal
for the price. In addition to the
standard amenities of a telephone,
television and radio, all rooms
have a refrigerator. Other features
not always found in a budget-
priced hotel include room service,
laundry and valet service. The
Stanford offers good Korean cuisine
in the Gamiok restaurant and an
American café in the lobby. The
location is also very convenient
for shopping at Herald Square as
well as visiting the Javits
Convention Center.

THEATER DISTRICT

Chatwal Inn on 45th Street

132 W 45th St, NY, NY 10036.
Map 12 E5. **(** 921-7600.
FAX 719-0171. **Rooms**: 50. 🛏 1
🏢 TV 🖥 🔒 🔖 🌀 🗡 🍴 🍺 AE, DC, MC, V, JCB. Ⓢ

The Chatwal Inn on 45th Street is a modest hotel in a convenient location for theatergoers. It is one of several small budget hotels owned by Indian restauranteur Sant Chatwal, all recently remodeled with new furnishings and bathrooms. A concierge and laundry service are among the amenities, and Continental breakfast is also included in the price.

Edison

228 W 47th St, NY, NY 10036.
Map 12 E5. **(** 840-5000.
FAX 719-9541. **Rooms**: 900. 🛏 1
🏢 TV 🖥 🌀 🗡 🍴 🍺 🍺
AE, DC, MC, V, JCB. Ⓢ

After its recent restoration, this old building has become one of the best values among hotels in the Theater District. The Art Deco lobby, brass doorways and period light fixtures of the original 1931 hotel have been beautifully restored. Rooms have also been refurbished, and now boast updated bathrooms and new attractive decor. The hotel has its own café, restaurant and bar.

Iroquois

49 W 44th St, NY, NY 10036.
Map 12 F5. **(** 840-3080.
FAX 398-1754. **Rooms**: 110. 🛏 1
🏢 TV 🖥 🌀 🗡 🍴 🍺 🍴 🍴
🍺 AE, DC, MC, V, JCB. Ⓢ

A budget choice on the same block as the Algonquin and Royalton, the Iroquois is unpretentious and comfortable. It has a friendly, multilingual staff to take care of the many foreign visitors who keep it booked. Several suites include kitchenettes. The location is handy for shopping and theaters.

Wellington

7th Ave at 55th St, NY, NY 10019.
Map 12 E4. **(** 247-3900.
FAX 581-1719. **TX** 66297. **Rooms**: 700. 🛏 1 🏢 TV 🖥 🌀 🗡 🍴
🍴 🍴 🍺 AE, DC, MC, V, JCB. Ⓢ

After a complete renovation, the Wellington lobby is resplendent with mirrors and elaborate light fixtures. Rooms have been updated with modern furnishings. The suites, and many of the bedrooms, have kitchenettes; family

rooms have two bathrooms. In a convenient midtown location and with a coffee shop, restaurant and bar on site, this reasonably priced, pleasant hotel is a good deal.

Best Western President

234 W 48th St, NY, NY 10036.
Map 12 E5. **(** 246-8800.
FAX 974-3922. **TX** 147057. **Rooms**: 400. 🛏 1 🏢 TV 🖥 🔒 🌀
🍴 🍴 🍴 🍴 🍺 AE, DC, MC, V, JCB. ⓈⓈ

The largest of the Chatwal properties, the President offers 500 small but adequate recently renovated rooms and suites in a convenient Theater District location. Continental breakfast is included in the rates.

Best Western Woodward

210 W 55th St, NY, NY 10019.
Map 12 E4. **(** 247-2000.
FAX 581-2248. **TX** 408363. **Rooms**: 200. 🛏 1 🏢 TV 🖥 🔒 🌀 🍴
🍴 🍴 🍴 🍺 AE, DC, MC, V, JCB. ⓈⓈ

A reasonably priced choice in a renovated Beaux Arts landmark building, the Woodward offers very few frills but does have all the necessary comforts, including good modernized bathrooms. It is situated within an easy walk of both shopping and theaters. Rates include Continental breakfast.

Days Hotel Midtown

790 8th Ave, NY 10019. **Map** 12 D5.
(581-7000. **FAX** 974-0291.
Rooms: 366. 🛏 1 🏢 TV 🖥 🔒
🍴 🍴 🍴 🍴 🍴 🍺 AE, DC, MC, V. ⓈⓈ

An outdoor rooftop swimming pool (open May–mid Sep) is the main attraction at this otherwise predictable Loews chain hotel in the Theater District. The entire hotel was recently renovated, including the lobby, which has some sleek banquettes and an attractive Art Deco chandelier. The rates are moderate, especially for families, as children under 18 can stay in their parents' room free. Definitely worth consideration.

Howard Johnson Plaza

851 8th Ave, NY, NY 10019.
Map 12 D4. **(** 581-4100.
FAX 974-7502. **Rooms**: 300. 🛏 1
🏢 TV 🖥 🔒 🌀 🍴 🍴 🍴
🍺 AE, DC, MC, V, JCB. ⓈⓈ

Although part of a chain of motels, this particular lodging may exceed your expectations. Comfortable rooms have recently been

refurbished. Many rooms have spacious areas for seating and lots of work space. There is an on-site restaurant and parking is available. Children under 18 can stay free with their parents. At the price, this is a reasonable choice.

Paramount

235 W 46th St, NY, NY 10036.
Map 12 E5. **(** 764-5500.
FAX 575-4892. **TX** 425918. **Rooms**: 610. 🛏 1 🏢 24 TV 🖥 🔒 🌀
🔒 🍴 🍴 🍴 🍴 🍺 AE, DC, MC, V, JCB. ⓈⓈ

Philippe Starck's spectacular floating stairway and lighting, inspired by the art of Joan Miró, are the first things you see in the Paramount. Ian Schrager designed it for the young and hip, and to prove that inexpensive hotels need not be boring. Playful design, such as prints of Vermeer's *Lacemaker* as headboards, make up for the small size of the tiny rooms. Public amenities include a children's playroom and a branch of Dean & DeLuca *(see p322)*, with take-out foods. There's a business center, and a video library that supplies the VCRs in every guest room. The bar, known as Whiskey, is one of the hottest spots in town.

Quality Inn Midtown

157 W 47th St, NY, NY 10036.
Map 12 D5. **(** 768-3700.
FAX 768-3403. **Rooms**: 200. 🛏 1
🏢 TV 🖥 🔒 🔖 🌀 🍴 🍴 🍴
🍺 AE, DC, MC, V, JCB. ⓈⓈ

The Quality Inn Midtown is yet another modest and modestly priced Chatwal property. A multilingual staff welcomes guests from all parts of the world. It is convenient for theatergoers, has small, recently renovated bedrooms with new bathroom fixtures. Complimentary Continental breakfast is included, making this no-frills hotel even more attractive.

St. Moritz

50 Central Park S, NY, NY 10019.
Map 12 E3. **(** 755-5800. **FAX** 319-9658. **Rooms**: 680. 🛏 1 🏢 TV
🌀 🔖 🍴 🍴 🍴 🍴 🍺
AE, DC, MC, V, JCB. ⓈⓈ

Standing in a superb location opposite Central Park, and with one of the best sidewalk cafés in the city, the St. Moritz has everything going for it – except youth. The hotel is old and looks it. At present, guests who don't mind the tired decor and plumbing can enjoy a budget stay in this posh neighborhood. Rumpelmayer's, the famous ice-cream parlor, is just off the lobby. Don't count the calories – just enjoy the experience.

For key to symbols *see p271*

Wyndham

42 W 58th St, NY, NY 10019.
Map 12 F3. ☎ *753-3500.*
FAX *754-5638.* ***Rooms****: 200.* [1] [TV] *AE, DC, MC, V.* $$

You will have to reserve well in advance if you hope to get a room in the hotel that many consider to be New York's best buy. The atmosphere is very homey and warm – the owners live there. The exceptionally large rooms are individually furnished and, although a little threadbare in places, are always personal and warm. This is a favorite place for actors, especially those seeking long-term lodgings during a Broadway run. The low prices mean that there is no room service, but there is a good restaurant in the hotel.

Algonquin

59 W 44th St, NY, NY 10036.
Map 12 F5. ☎ *840-6800.*
FAX *944-1419.* TX *66532.* ***Rooms****: 165.* [1] [TV] [i] *AE, DC, MC, V, JCB* $$$. *See p143.*

The Round Table of the 1920s may have gone, but the Algonquin still maintains its famous literary tradition. It is a favorite haunt of publishers, writers and theatrical types – even the friendly bartender is rumored to be finishing his second novel. Renovation has considerably freshened the decor and modernized most bathroom fixtures, but the old-fashioned feel of the rooms, which make up in coziness what they lack in size, has been very carefully preserved.

Embassy Suites

1568 Broadway, NY, NY 10036.
Map 12 E5. ☎ *719-1600.*
FAX *921-5212.* ***Rooms****: 460.* [1] [TV] [P] [i] *AE, DC, MC, V.* $$$

Embassy Suites Hotel is a Broadway hit for its spacious quarters and hospitality. A full breakfast and a two-hour daily cocktail reception are offered, all on the house. The hotel is dramatic, in keeping with its theatrical location, and has a sky-lit third-floor lobby, theatrical lighting and sleek Art Deco surroundings. The two-room suites offer three telephones, two remote control televisions, a fridge, microwave and coffeemaker, as well as a wet bar: a bar with a sink. Rooms have outlets for a fax and computer, with machines available on request, and guests have free use of a fitness center. Parents can leave children between ages three and 13 with attendants in the Cool Kat Kids Club.

Holiday Inn Crowne Plaza

1605 Broadway, NY, NY 10019.
Map 12 E4. ☎ *977-4000.*
FAX *333-7393.* ***Rooms****: 770.* [1] [24] [TV] [P] [i] *AE, DC, MC, V, JCB.* $$$

This is not a typical Holiday Inn, but the flagship of the chain's luxury Crowne Plaza division. For those who want a really big hotel right on Broadway, there is much to recommend this particular one, which one reviewer aptly called "brassy and classy." Public spaces are flashy and fun and, while their furnishings are predictable, the rooms are large and higher floors provide wonderful views of New York or the Hudson River. Guests can choose from three restaurants and have the use of a well-equipped business center, a health club and New York's largest indoor hotel swimming pool.

Ramada Renaissance

2 Times Sq, NY, NY 10036. **Map** 8 E1. ☎ *765-7676.* FAX *765-1962.*
Rooms*: 305.* [1] [TV] [P] [i] *AE, DC, MC, V.* $$$

This new high-rise modern hotel in the heart of Times Square is the American flagship of Ramada's upscale Renaissance properties. The hotel is determined to provide ultimate luxury. There are 21 butlers, one per floor, to oversee such services as packing and unpacking, drycleaning and room service. Rooms have custom-designed contemporary furnishings and a restful peach color scheme with black accents. Each has three phones, a minibar, a large-size television, a VCR, voice mail and outlets for a fax machine – the machine itself is available on request. The hotel also has a good health club and a business center.

Salisbury

123 W 57th St, NY, NY 10019.
Map 12 E3. ☎ *246-1300.*
FAX *977-7752.* TX *668366.* ***Rooms****: 320.* [1] [TV] [i] *AE, DC, MC, V, JCB.* $$$

Comfortably old-fashioned, the Salisbury is an exceptional buy in a wonderful location. It is right across from Carnegie Hall and an easy walk to the best Fifth Avenue shops. Rooms are undistinguished, but good size, and many of them have well-equipped kitchenettes, a bonus for families. The ambience is friendly and warm, and the neighborhood is convenient, safe and fun to be in.

Sheraton Manhattan

790 7th Ave, NY, NY 10019.
Map 12 E3. ☎ *581-3300.*
FAX *541-9219.* ***Rooms****: 663.* [1] [TV] [P] [i] *AE, DC, MC, V, JCB.* $$$

Across the street from the Sheraton New York Hotel and Towers, this smaller sister hotel has many features for its moderate price. These include a fitness center with saunas and a big, attractive, four-lane indoor pool with adjacent terrace – just the place to relax after a day of sightseeing. The modern rooms are predictable but comfortable, most in restful shades of rose, with a few extras such as a coffeemaker, and some rooms have sofa beds to accommodate families. A lobby receptionist greets and helps incoming guests, particularly those from outside the US, and a novel video checkout communicates in six languages. There's also a complete business center and a lobby bistro.

Warwick

65 W 54th St, NY, NY 10019.
Map 12 F4. ☎ *247-2700.*
FAX *489-3926.* ***Rooms****: 425.* [1] [TV] [P] [i] *AE, DC, MC, V.* $$$

A utilitarian hotel with a good location, the Warwick has revovated most, but not all of its rooms, with modernized bathrooms and such services as two-line telephones and voice mail. A beauty salon, barber, drugstore and valet service are all available, plus a restaurant and bar. A safe choice, but make sure you get a renovated room.

Essex House

160 Central Park S, NY, NY 10019.
Map 12 E3. ☎ *247-0300.*
FAX *315-1839.* ***Rooms****: 593.* [24] [TV] [P] [i] *AE.* $$$$

Fresh from a multimillion-dollar renovation by the Nikko hotel chain of Japan, the elegant Essex House is now dramatic Art Deco. There are stunning black marble columns standing tall in the lobby, coffered ceilings, etched brass elevator doors and newly enlarged windows, overlooking Central Park. Rooms are not overly large, but guests who have Park views may never notice. All rooms are decorated in tasteful, traditional English-style decor, and guests are treated to bathrobes, shoe shines, turndown service and 24-hour room service. The hotel offers a health spa and a business center.

Le Parker Meridien

118 W 57th St, NY, NY 10019.
Map 12 E3. **℡** 245-5000.
FAX 708-7477. **TX** 6801134. **Rooms:**
691. ⬛🚭 🔢 🛗 24 TV 📺 🛏
🍴 🏊 🛗 👵 🚬 🛋 P 🐕 🎾
🚻 🛗 AE, DC, MC, V.
$$$$$

The two main attractions at this hotel are the soaring public spaces and the exceptionally good fitness facilities. There is a rooftop pool, jogging track, squash courts and racquetball court, plus a well-equipped health club. The entrance, a two-story, block-long arcade, is quite impressive, and the lobby piano bar is a great place for a relaxing drink. Refurbishing is under way in all the rooms, which are perfectly adequate but surprisingly ordinary considering the rest of the hotel.

Macklowe

145 W 44th St, NY, NY 10036.
Map 12 E5. **℡** 768-4400.
FAX 768-0847. **Rooms:** 629. ⬛ 1
🔢 TV 📺 🍴 🛏 🛗 🚬 🛋
👵 🛋 P 🎾 🚻 🛗 AE, DC,
MC, V, JCB. $$$$

Sleek and streamlined, the high-tech Macklowe boasts a striking modernistic lobby and staff dressed all in robotlike gray. The hotel is justifiably proud of its electronic gadgetry, which includes voice mail in four languages, and the MackTel in-room system that allows guests to access airline schedules and restaurant menus, order tickets and make theatre reservations, review accounts and then check out of the hotel electronically. Though rooms are small for the price, they do have features such as 100% cotton bed linen and goose-down pillows. Guests also have the use of a state-of-the-art fitness center. The Macklowe is particularly recommended for business travelers, who are allowed use of the spacious, modern meeting room and conference facilities.

Michelangelo

152 W 51st St, NY, NY 10019.
Map 12 E4. **℡** 765-1900.
FAX 541-6604. **Rooms:** 178. ⬛ 🔢
24 TV 📺 🍴 🛏 🛗 🚬 👵
P 🎾 🚻 🛗 AE, DC, MC, V,
JCB. $$$$

The first luxury hotel to open near Broadway now has new owners, Star Hotels of Italy. They plan to maintain the hotel's first class reputation, and have already added such services as a fitness facility and complimentary Continental breakfast. Rooms here average 450 sq ft (42 sq m), have marble foyers and are furnished in various styles: Empire, Country French or Art Deco. Excellent dining choices include Bellini by Cipriani off the lobby and the excellent four-star Le Bernardin in the Equitable Center right across the street.

Rihga Royal

151 W 54th St, NY, NY 10019.
Map 12 E4. **℡** 307-5000.
FAX 765-6530. **TX** 2450170. **Rooms:**
500. 🔢 24 TV 📺 🍴 🛏 🛗 🍴
🚬 👵 🛋 P 🎾 🚻 🛗
AE, DC, MC, V, JCB. $$$$

In the lineup of the many luxury hotels near Broadway, the all-suite Rihga Royal stands out: – at 54 stories high, it is one of New York's tallest hotels. Rooms on the upper floors offer spectacular panoramic views. Each elegant suite has a living room with bay windows and one or two bedrooms, separated with mirrored French doors. Decor is classic and comfortable, and amenities in the rooms include dressing areas, mini-bars with icemakers, three tele-phones, two televisions, including cable and movie channels, a VCR and an electronic room safe. Guests can also enjoy a business and fitness center, free newspapers, shoe shines and transportation to Wall Street. Halcyon, the dining room off the lobby, was recently voted among the top four hotel restaurants in the city.

Ritz–Carlton

112 Central Park S, NY, NY 10019.
Map 12 E3. **℡** 757-1900. **FAX** 757-9620. **TX** 971534. **Rooms:** 228. ⬛
1 🔢 24 TV 📺 🍴 🛏 🛗 👵
🛋 P 🎾 🚻 🛗 AE, DC, MC,
V, JCB. $$$$

There's a private club feeling to the intimate Ritz–Carlton, and a definite English air, with its small, pine-paneled lobby, mahogany furnishings and traditional print fabrics. The leather and antique pine of the Jockey Club bar give it a masculine look, and the bar is a favorite gathering place at the end of the working day. Rooms are small, considering the rates, but the views of Central Park from the front windows are worth it. Rooms at the back are less expensive.

Royalton

44 W 44th St, NY, NY 10036.
Map 12 F5 **℡** 869-4400.
FAX 869-8965. **TX** 213875.
Rooms: 167. ⬛ 1 🔢 24 TV 📺
🍴 🛏 🛗 👵 🚬 🛋 🐕 🎾
🚻 🛗 AE, DC, MC, V.
$$$$

Ian Schrager and his late partner, Steve Rubell, who made their very distinctive mark with the trendy Studio 54 nightclub and then cemented their success with Morgans Hotel, really pulled out all the stops with the Royalton. Philippe Starck's design includes a space-age lobby, curving hallways and rooms rigged out like first-class cabins in a sleek ocean liner, with big built-in beds like bunks. Who likes this sort of thing? Well, the celebrity guest list includes directors David Lynch and Oliver Stone, actors Dudley Moore, Sean Penn and John Malkovich, the Manhattan Transfer singing group and other musical stars including Hammer and heavy-metal band Guns 'n' Roses. The 44 restaurant attracts trendy editorial types for lunch, and the small round bar, aptly called 44 Round, is equally popular.

LOWER MIDTOWN

Journey's End

3 E 40th St, NY, NY 10016. **Map** 8 F1.
℡ 447-1500. **FAX** 213-0972. **Rooms:**
189. ⬛ 1 🔢 TV 📺 🛏 🛗 👵
🛋 🚻 🛗 AE, DC, MC, V.
$$

A Canadian company that is best known for its motels has provided this clean, contemporary, no-frills midtown hotel with reasonable rates. The decor is, unsurprisingly, motel-like, but the rooms are furnished with functional work-tables and comfortable sitting areas, remote-control TV and clock radios, and guests receive complimentary morning newspapers and coffee. Many rooms have sofa beds for children, who can stay free in their parents' room. The location is within easy walking distance of theaters and shopping.

Roosevelt

Madison Ave at 45th St, NY, NY 10017.
Map 13 A5. **℡** 661-9600.
FAX 687-5064. **TX** 238944. **Rooms:**
1070. ⬛ TV 🍴 🛏 🛗 P 🎾 🚻
🛗 AE, DC, MC, V, JCB. $$

This business travelers' standby hotel near Grand Central Terminal is getting a sorely needed face-lift. The lobby is now finished and sports a new, smart gilt trim on the ceiling, freshly painted wrought-iron balconies and a magnificent, glistening chandelier. The room renovations are still in progress, and are scheduled to be completed by the end of March 1994. Redecorated rooms are more expensive than those still awaiting refurbishment. The central location is a plus point though.

For key to symbols *see p271*

Doral Court

130 E 39th St, NY, NY 10016.
Map 9 A1. **【** 685-1100.
FAX 889-0287. **TX** 679-0532.
Rooms: 199.
AE, DC, MC, V. $$$

This is the least assuming of three popular Doral properties in the residential Murray Hill area, The Doral Court is an appealing hotel. Among its many features are a small, warm, wood-paneled lobby and cheerful, light and airy rooms with entry foyers, walk-in closets, dressing areas and fluffy bathrobes. Other niceties include largescreen televisions, VCRs and guest privileges at the nearby Doral Fitness Center. The Courtyard Café is a popular dining spot. For skyline views, ask for one of the four terraced rooms on the 15th floor.

Helmsley Middletowne

148 E 48th St, NY, NY 10017.
Map 13 A5. **【** 755-3000.
FAX 832-0261. **Rooms**: 190.
AE, DC, MC, V, JCB. $$$

Of the city's several Helmsley hotels, the Middletowne Hotel is the least glitzy. It is a good bet for those who like the ambience of a smaller hotel but who also want a safe, convenient East Side location. The lobby is tiny and the rooms are small, but the bedrooms are pleasant, redecorated in bright colors and fresh fabrics. All have refrigerators, and many come with well-supplied kitchenettes.

Jolly Madison Towers

22 E 38th St, NY, NY 10016.
Map 9 A1. **【** 685-3700.
FAX 447-0747. **TX** 127692. **Rooms**: 246.
AE, DC, MC, V. $$$

A comfortable mid-range hotel, the Madison Towers is nothing fancy – but then neither are the rates. The rooms are reasonably large, but could do with redecorating, which the new owners, the Jolly chain from Italy, may undertake. The hotel offers a good health spa equipped with whirlpool and sauna. The pleasant Whaler Bar has a fireplace and murals with a nautical theme.

Roger Smith

501 Lexington Ave, NY, NY 10017.
Map 13 A1. **【** 755-1400.
FAX 319-9130. **Rooms**: 130.
AE, DC, MC, V. $$$

This used to be just yet another commonplace hotel, but its artistic new owners have done wonders. The lobby has been transformed with painting and sculpture and all the rooms have been refurbished; no two are alike and some have four-poster beds. Continental breakfast is offered on the balcony level, and Lily's Restaurant off the lobby serves good continental food. The arts-conscious owners also include tickets to the Museum of Modern Art in their weekend rates.

Doral Park Avenue

70 Park Ave, NY, NY 10016.
Map 9 A1. **【** 687-7050.
FAX 949-5924. **TX** 968872. **Rooms**: 188.
AE, DC, MC, V. $$$

A Murray Hill oasis that attracts sophisticated travelers who prefer smaller hotels, the Doral Park Avenue has distinctive Neoclassical decor accented with frescoes and ornate grillwork. Tranquil bedrooms in muted colors have such luxurious amenities as marble bathrooms, well-stocked minibars and free TV movies. Other guest privileges include the use of the Doral Fitness Center, shoe shines and a limousine service to Wall Street. The Saturnia restaurant serves healthy cuisine inspired by the Doral Saturnia spa in Florida.

Doral Tuscany

120 E 39th St, NY, NY 10016.
Map 9 A1. **【** 686-1600.
FAX 779-7822. **TX** 660243. **Rooms**: 121.
AE, DC, MC, V. $$$$

The most expensive of the Murray Hill Doral trio, the Tuscany attracts a loyal clientele who appreciate such details as fresh flowers, walk-in closets, television and telephone in the bathroom, and refrigerators well stocked with free soft drinks. Guests can use the Doral Fitness Center across the street, or request exercise bicycles in their own rooms. The aptly named Time and Again restaurant has been favorably reviewed.

Sheraton Park Avenue

45 Park Ave, NY, NY 10016.
Map 9 A2. **【** 685-7676.
FAX 889-3193. **Rooms**: 150.
JCB. $$$$

The Sheraton Park Avenue is decorated in English style, with wood-paneled walls, Chippendale furnishings and an entire library of leather-bound books. Bedrooms are comfortable, with long floral curtains, mantelpieces and prints of old New York on the walls. There's a good restaurant and a bar with jazz, and a multilingual concierge is always on duty. Understated, in a quiet location, it feels almost like a country inn.

United Nations Plaza

1 United Nations Plaza, NY, NY 10017. **Map** 13 C5. **【** 355-3400.
FAX 702-5051. **TX** 126803. **Rooms**: 428.
AE, DC, MC, V, JCB. $$$$.
See p156.

There is no more dramatic setting in New York than Kevin Roche's soaring skyscraper towering above the city, which is usually filled with an international clientele from the nearby United Nations. The sleek marble lobby has chrome accents and massive floral bouquets. Pastel-hued and very comfortable modern bedrooms begin on the 28th floor, and provide spectacular views. The 27th floor has a complete fitness center and a glass-enclosed swimming pool, and on the 38th floor is the only indoor hotel tennis court in Manhattan. The artwork throughout the hotel is unique, taken from the hotel's collection of antique tapestries and textiles gathered from every UN nation. The hotel also offers butler service, and provides complimentary transportation to Wall Street and other areas in the morning and to the Theater District during the evening.

UPPER MIDTOWN

Pickwick Arms

230 E 51st St, NY, NY 10022.
Map 13 B4. **【** 355-0300.
FAX 755-5029. **Rooms**: 400. 235.
AE, DC, MC, V. $

The Pickwick Arms is in a chic and safe location and is easily the best midtown choice in the budget range. Freshly redecorated, the hotel has an attractive lobby adorned with grand columns and a glistening chandelier. Plain but quite pleasant bedrooms offer television, AM/FM clock radios and room service. The single rooms that have a shared bathroom are very cheap. The studios offer extra space and a sofa bed for additional family members. On the hotel premises are a coffee shop and Torremolinos, a Spanish restaurant. This is a good affordable hotel with outstanding city views from the rooftop garden.

Beverly

125 E 50th St, NY, NY 10022.
Map 13 A4. ☎ *753-2700.*
FAX *753-2700.* TX *66579.* ***Rooms**: 187.* 🛁 [1] 👪 [TV] 🚭 ❄ 🖋 🧒 ⇅ [P] 🍸 🍴 [i] 💳 *AE, DC, MC, V, JCB.* $$

The Beverly is an unpretentious, friendly, family-owned hotel. It provides spacious suites, lovely, old-fashioned, comfortable furnishings, and attentive service at rates that are well below those of many of its neighbors on Lexington Avenue. It is, therefore, a good choice for business travelers on a budget as well as for families with young children. The hotel also has a reasonable restaurant and a charming coffee shop.

Doral Inn

541 Lexington Ave, NY, NY 10022.
Map 13 A5. ☎ *755-1200.*
FAX *319-8344.* TX *236641.* ***Rooms**: 655.* 🛁 [1] [TV] 🚭 ❄ 🏋 🖋 ♿ ⇅ 🍸 🍴 [i] 💳 *AE, DC, MC, V, JCB.* $$$

One of several modern Midtown hotels near Grand Central, the Doral Inn has well-decorated, moderately priced lodgings and offers extras such as a complimentary health club with a sauna and squash courts, a 24-hour café and a very convenient laundry room. The hotel is also popular with tour groups, which can cause delays at the desk.

Dorset

30 W 54th St, NY, NY 10019.
Map 12 F4. ☎ *247-7300.*
FAX *581-0153.* TX *4976429.* ***Rooms**: 490.* 🛁 [1] 👪 [TV] 🚭 ❄ 🖋 ⇅ 🐕 [P] 🍸 🍴 [i] 💳 *AE, DC, MC, V.* $$$

There is a gracious, old-fashioned feeling to the highly polished wood-paneled lobby and large rooms at the Dorset. Bedroom furnishings are in the style of Chippendale; rooms are light with attractive floral prints. If the bathrooms were a little more modern, the hotel would no doubt be far more expensive, but as it stands, this well-located and often-overlooked midtown oasis has many loyal admirers who come back time and time again. Also, about half the bedrooms are permanently leased. Service is good, and the bar-café is very popular with neighborhood residents. The hotel offers excellent weekend packages for guests, which often include the lavish "Prince of Wales" Sunday brunch buffet, a meal sure to leave you satisfied.

Fitzpatrick Manhattan Hotel

687 Lexington Ave, NY, NY 10022.
Map 13 A3. ☎ *355-0100.*
FAX *355-1371.* ***Rooms**: 92.* 🛁 [1] [TV] ❄ 🖋 ⇅ [P] 🍸 🍴 [i] 💳 *AE, DC, MC, V, JCB.* $$$

Emerald-green carpet, Waterford chandeliers and loads of Irish prints are unmistakable clues that this is a new American outpost for a Dublin-based hotelier. Other hints include a portrait of the Irish president and suites named after past presidents of the Irish Republic. This renovated former apartment hotel has 92 rooms, more than half of them suites, and a much better value than the small single rooms. Amenities offered include cable TV, voice mail, computer and fax outlets and whirlpool baths. Guests also have membership privileges at the Atrium Club, an excellent nearby fitness center. Fitzers, the in-house restaurant and bar, features delicious Dublin Bay prawns and oak-smoked salmon.

Plaza

768 5th Ave, NY, NY 10019.
Map 12 F3. ☎ *759-3000.*
FAX *759-3167.* TX *236938.* ***Rooms**: 812.* 🛁 👪 [24] [TV] 🥂 🚭 🌅 ❄ 🖋 🧒 ♿ ⇅ 🐕 [P] 🍸 🍴 [i] 💳 *AE, DC, MC, V, JCB.* $$$$
See p179.

There are smarter hotels and more elaborate rooms in New York, but for location, lobby and history, nothing compares with the Plaza. It is a national landmark, a local fixture and has been a favorite hotel for almost 100 years. The Plaza presides over Grand Army Plaza at the entrance to Central Park, and rooms facing the park have really fabulous green vistas. Among the Plaza's many amenities are a business center, theater ticket desk, meeting and banquet rooms, several shops and restaurants, a barber and a hair salon.

Waldorf–Astoria

301 Park Ave, NY, NY 10022.
Map 13 A5. ☎ *355-3000.*
FAX *759-9209.* TX *666747.* ***Rooms**: 1410.* 🛁 [1] 👪 [24] [TV] 🥂 🚭 ❄ 🏋 👔 🧒 ♿ ⇅ [P] 🍸 🍴 [i] 💳 *AE, DC, MC, V, JCB.* $$$$.
See p175.

There are really two Waldorfs: the big business-oriented hotel and the ultra-exclusive Towers, with its own private entrance and smart concierge and without doubt some of the most elaborate and beautifully furnished quarters in the city. The Towers is the frequent choice of presidents and visiting dignitaries. The main lobby is quite magnificent. It has been restored to its 1931 Art Deco glory, with bas-relief friezes and grillwork setting off the beautifully painted murals, deep mahogany paneling and elegant marble columns. The marvelous giant clock once stood in the legendary original hotel on 34th Street. Famous Peacock Alley is still a very popular place to go for drinks, and for those who like the services and choice of restaurants that a big hotel can offer, this is an excellent choice.

Box Tree

250 E 49th St, NY, NY 10017.
Map 13 B5. ☎ *758-8320.*
FAX *308-3899.* ***Rooms**: 13.* 🛁 [1] 👪 [24] [TV] ❄ 🖋 🐕 🍸 🍴 [i] 💳 *AE.* $$$$$

Only the red carpet on the front steps gives a clue that these two town houses in a row of look-alike brownstones actually comprise New York's most unusual lodging. The Box Tree is an opulent 13-room inn with restaurant, reflecting the extravagant tastes of Bulgarian-born owner Augustin Paege, who, having bought the brownstone next door, hopes to increase the number of rooms available. The rooms are small but sumptuous, with formal curtains, chandeliers, fur throws and working marble fireplaces. Each room has an individual theme, ranging from Chinese to English Gothic. Rates are high, but they do include a substantial restaurant credit per night. Children under the age of ten are not allowed in the hotel.

Peninsula

700 5th Ave, NY, NY 10019.
Map 12 F4. ☎ *247-2200.*
FAX *903-3949.* TX *4976154.* ***Rooms**: 250.* 🛁 👪 [24] [TV] 🥂 🚭 🌅 ❄ 🏋 🏊 🖋 🧒 ⇅ [P] 🌿 🍸 🍴 [i] 💳 *AE, DC, MC ,V, JCB.* $$$$$

Since the noted Peninsula group from Hong Kong took over at the hotel, things have been looking up at the 1905 Beaux Arts landmark, the former Gotham Hotel. A sweeping double stairway leads to the elegant lobby, resplendent with antiques and massive floral arrangements. The Art Nouveau bedrooms are gracious, and some of the baths come with 6 ft (2 m) whirlpool tubs. A highlight is the rooftop-level fitness center, health spa and pool. The Pen-Top bar opens on to a terrace and in summer is one of the pleasantest places in New York to go for a drink.

Pierre

2 E 61st St, NY, NY 10021.
Map 12 F3. ☎ *838-8000.*
[FAX] *940-8109.* [TX] *66376.* ***Rooms:*** *206.* 🛏 [1] ⊞ [24] [TV] 🍷 🚭 ❄ ▤ 🏋 🚸 ♿ ⇅ 🐕 [P] 🍸 🍴 [i] 💳 *AE, DC, MC, V, JCB.* $$$$$

Limousines stand outside the door, awaiting the presidents who are among the clientele of this ultra-luxurious hotel. The Pierre is a member of Canada's highly esteemed Four Seasons group. Half the rooms are leased on a permanent basis. Both lobby and bedrooms are full of antiques and Old-World elegance, and are lovelier than ever after recent refurbishing. Amenities and service are excellent, and the Café Pierre is one of New York's leading places for business breakfasts.

St. Regis

2 E 55th St, NY, NY 10022.
Map 12 F4. ☎ *753-4500.*
[FAX] *787-3447.* ***Rooms:*** *322.* 🛏 ⊞ [24] [TV] 🍷 🚭 ▤ 💼 🏋 🚸 ♿ ⇅ [P] 🍸 🍴 [i] 💳 *AE, DC, MC, V, JCB.* $$$$$

John Jacob Astor's Beaux Arts beauty, the toast of New York society back in 1904, has emerged from a $100 million, three-year restoration looking almost as good as new. Decorated in muted blues and greens, the high-ceilinged rooms contain silk wall coverings and Louis XV reproduction furniture. The St. Regis Roof is the scene of glittering social events, and Maxfield Parrish's mural of King Cole once more reigns behind the King Cole Bar. The price for all this magnificence and luxury is one of the highest room rates in the city.

Stanhope

995 5th Ave, NY, NY 10028.
Map 17 A4. ☎ *288-5800.*
[FAX] *517-0088.* ***Rooms:*** *141.* 🛏 ⊞ [24] [TV] 🍷 ▤ 🏋 🚸 ♿ ⇅ [P] 🌿 🍸 🍴 [i] 💳 *AE, DC, MC, V.* $$$$$

Small and opulent, the Stanhope stands in a superb spot right across the street from the Metropolitan Museum of Art. It has a Parisian-style terrace café that is one of the city's most popular. The public rooms are heavily adorned with French antiques. Each of the bedrooms is furnished with Louis XVI reproduction furniture and, besides the usual conveniences, comes equipped with CD and cassette players. Even if you can't afford to stay here, come for tea in Le Salon, a room with the feel of an indoor garden.

Upper East Side

Wales

1295 Madison Ave, NY, NY 10128.
Map 17 A3. ☎ *876-6000.*
[FAX] *860-7000.* ***Rooms:*** *95.* 🛏 [TV] ❄ ▤ 💼 [P] 🍸 🍴 [i] 💳 *AE, MC, V.* $$

A small, turn-of-the-century, almost European hotel, the Wales is one of a kind in New York. While far from luxurious, it has real genteel charm, thanks to renovation that has restored the fireplaces, marble stairs and oak paneling of the original 1901 hotel. The marble sinks and brass fixtures in the bathrooms are also original. Breakfast and tea are served in the Pied Piper Room, a Victorian drawing room on the second floor decorated with antique illustrations from children's books. The location is perfect for museum-hopping, and the neighborhood contains a wide choice of restaurants.

Barbizon

140 E 63rd St, NY, NY 10021.
Map 13 A2. ☎ *838-5700.*
[FAX] *753-0360.* ***Rooms:*** *344.* 🛏 [1] ⊞ [TV] ❄ ▤ 🏋 ⇅ [P] 🍸 🍴 [i] 💳 *AE, DC, MC, V.* $$$

Once a well-chaperoned residence for young ladies of good families, the Barbizon has been most handsomely renovated. The smart, modern, pastel-hued rooms are small but well priced for this popular East Side district. The tower suites have terraces with fine city views. More dramatic changes may be coming, because Ian Schrager, who transformed the Royalton and Paramount hotels so well, is now the new owner.

Mark

25 E 77th St, NY, NY 10021.
Map 16 F5. ☎ *744-4300.*
[FAX] *744-2749.* ***Rooms:*** *180.* 🛏 [24] [TV] 🍷 ▤ 🏋 🚸 ♿ ⇅ 🍸 🍴 [i] 💳 *AE, DC, MC, V, JCB.* $$$$

The Mark emerged from a recent lavish renovation as a leading contender among the posh palaces of the Upper East Side. The lobby mood is of discreet and yet contemporary elegance, with Biedermeier furniture, marble floors and 18th-century Piranesi prints on the walls. There is a 24-hour concierge service. The bedrooms have formal curtains matching the bedspreads, plants, antique prints and bathrooms in marble or Italian ceramic tile. Fine linen and down pillows are in all rooms, and most have pantries with minibars. There is a sumptuous bar with the atmosphere of a drawing room – a friendly setting for tea or drinks.

Carlyle

35 E 76th St, NY, NY 10021.
Map 16 F5. ☎ *744-1600.*
[FAX] *717-4682.* [TX] *620692.* ***Rooms:*** *175.* 🛏 [1] ⊞ [24] [TV] 🍷 ❄ ▤ 💼 🏋 🚸 ⇅ 🐕 [P] 🍸 🍴 [i] 💳 *AE, DC, MC, V.* $$$$$

A hushed, antique-filled lobby welcomes guests to what many consider New York's best hotel. An Upper East Side luxury outpost, the Carlyle has a reputation for exceptional personal service. The rooms are large and in understated good taste, decorated in traditional style and floral prints. Each has a kitchenette as well as a VCR, stereo, CD player, dedicated fax line and multiple-line hands-free phones. Several of the rooms have private terraces and dining rooms. A fitness center and sauna are available to all guests. Despite its subdued luxury, the Carlyle is very lively at night, a popular spot for drinks amid the amusing murals in Bemelmans' Bar, and songs by cabaret star Bobby Short in the Café Carlyle.

Lowell

28 E 63rd St, NY, NY 10021.
Map 13 A2. ☎ *838-1400.*
[FAX] *838-9194.* ***Rooms:*** *61.* 🛏 [1] [TV] 🍷 ▤ 🚸 ♿ ⇅ 🐕 [P] 🍸 🍴 [i] 💳 *AE, DC, MC, V, JCB.* $$$$$

This intimate, luxurious all-suite hotel is the only New York member of the select Relais et Châteaux group. Service is excellent, and the 61 suites offer such niceties as wood-burning fireplaces, libraries, real plants, fresh flowers, marble baths and full kitchens. Eclectic decor mixes French, Art Deco and Oriental pieces, always in the best of taste. The Pembroke Room on the second floor seats just 35 people and is a delightful place for tea or weekend brunch in a serene setting of lace curtains and discreet European charm. The Post House restaurant is also highly regarded.

Mayfair Baglioni

610 Park Ave, NY, NY 10021.
Map 13 A2. ☎ *288-0800.*
[FAX] *737-0538.* [TX] *236257.* ***Rooms:*** *201.* 🛏 [1] [24] [TV] ▤ 💼 🏋 ♿ ⇅ 🐕 [P] 🍸 🍴 [i] 💳 *AE, DC, MC, V, JCB.* $$$$$

Previously known as the Mayfair Regent, and for a long time near the very top of New York's hotel hierarchy, the Mayfair now has new Italian owners. Hopefully they will maintain the hotel's reputation for warmth and personal service that has made it a favorite stop for the well-heeled from Europe. The welcoming lobby offers wing chairs in front of a fireplace; and the mirrored lounge is a favorite New York rendezvous for breakfast and tea. Rooms are spacious, with every amenity expected of a luxury hotel plus a few extras, such as umbrellas in each closet. The fitness center has a five-hole golf putting green. Guests who can afford the bill will find the four-star Le Cirque restaurant just off the lobby an excellent choice (see p296).

Plaza Athénée

37 E 64th St, NY, NY 10021.
Map 12 F2. **C** 734-9100.
FAX 772-0958. **TX** 6972900. **Rooms**: 156. 🛏 1 🎛 24 TV 🍽 🛗 🔥 🖥 🛗 P Y 🛗 🔥 *AE, DC, MC, V, JCB.* $$$$$

The New York version of the Paris hotel is an elite enclave. It is very exclusive, albeit small, rooms and a host of amenities, including fresh flowers, shoe trees, safes, kitchenettes, bathrobes and room humidifiers. Decor is Louis XVI and every room has a replica of the gilt clock found in the famous Paris hotel. The hotel's restaurant, La Régence, receives good reviews for its food, served beneath a cloud-painted ceiling (see p297). The reader survey in *Institutional Investor* magazine has often named the hotel number one in Manhattan.

Regency

540 Park Ave, NY, NY 10021.
Map 13 A2. **C** 759-4100.
FAX 826-5674. **Rooms**: 384. 🛏 🎛 24 TV 🍽 🛗 🛗 🔥 🛗 🔥 P Y 🛗 🛗 *AE, DC, MC, V, JCB.* $$$$$

Hollywood moguls are likely to be among those alighting from the limousines in front of the Regency, many of them bound for magnificent suites. The name reflects the Regency decor that the rooms share, and the lobby is filled with mirrors and gilt. The Regency's 540 Restaurant is where New York's "power breakfast" was born; here, almost every morning, key players wheel and deal over muffins and croissants. The hotel provides first-class service to all guests and has every amenity, including 24-hour room service, a fitness center and business center.

Westbury

15 E 69th St, NY, NY 10021.
Map 12 F1. **C** 535-2000.
FAX 535-5058. **TX** 4976607. **Rooms**: 231. 🛏 1 🎛 24 TV Y 🍽 🛗 🛗 🔥 *AE, DC, MC, V, JCB.* $$$$$

Set amid the exclusive boutiques and galleries of Madison Avenue, the quiet Westbury exudes English charm. The rooms are pretty, and the lobby is an oasis of calm with its tapestries and huge bouquets of flowers. Indeed, the entire hotel seems wonderfully civilized. A health club has been added and the popular Polo restaurant has recently been refurbished.

UPPER WEST SIDE

Beacon

2130 Broadway, NY, NY 10023.
Map 15 C5. **C** 787-1100.
FAX 724-0839. **Rooms**: 100. 🛏 1 🎛 TV 🍽 🛗 🛗 🛗 🔥 *AE, DC, MC, V, JCB.* $

The smartest of the budget hotels sprouting on the Upper West Side, the Beacon is named after the famous theater next door. The recently refurbished lobby is stylish, with a floor of black and white tiles and an Oriental-style rug. Bedroom furnishings are unimaginative but adequately comfortable, and rooms are equipped with full kitchenettes.

Broadway American

2178 Broadway, NY, NY 10024.
Map 15 C5. **C** 362-1100.
FAX 787-9521. **Rooms**: 430. 🛏 40. 1 🎛 TV 🍽 🛗 🛗 🔥 🛗 *AE, DC, MC, V.* $

The Broadway American is a good find for budget-watchers. This recently renovated Upper West Side lodging is decorated in sparse Art Deco style, with bright, abstract modern art downstairs and some whimsical touches in the rooms. Room amenities include cable TV and refrigerators, and guests have use of kitchen facilities, a laundry, and vending machines on each floor. There is also a 24-hour café on the premises. Rooms sharing bathrooms are an excellent value.

Excelsior

45 W 81st St, NY, NY 10024.
Map 15 D4. **C** 362-9200.
FAX 721-2994. **TX** 205686. **Rooms**: 150. 🛏 1 TV 🍽 🛗 Y 🛗 🔥 *AE, MC, V.* $

An understated, reliable option on the Upper West Side, the Excelsior has a gracious, welcoming lobby and large, comfortable, old-fashioned rooms. Most of the rooms are suites, but even individual rooms come equipped with money-saving kitchens. For the best views, ask for a room right at the front, overlooking the Museum of Natural History.

Milburn

242 W 76th St, NY, NY 10023.
Map 16 D5. **C** 362-1006.
FAX 721-5476. **Rooms**: 90. 🛏 1 🎛 24 TV 🍽 🛗 🛗 🔥 🛗 🔥 *AE, DC, MC, V.* $

Newly refurbished and pleasantly decorated with art posters, this modest West Side hotel offers reasonably sized studios (the best buys) and a few two-room suites, all with fully equipped kitchens, including a microwave and a refrigerator. Bathrooms are new, and there is an in-house laundry for guests' use. The location is convenient to Lincoln Center, and to the many interesting shops and restaurants to be found on increasingly trendy Broadway and the rest of the Upper West Side.

Radisson Empire

44 W 63rd St, NY, NY 10023.
Map 12 D2. **C** 265-7400
FAX 765-4913. **TX** 428190. **Rooms**: 375. 🛏 1 🎛 24 TV 🍽 🛗 🛗 🔥 🛗 🔥 P Y 🛗 🛗 🔥 *AE, DC, MC, V.* $$

The old Empire has a totally new lease on life, thanks to a recent and stylish renovation. The high-ceilinged lobby now has the look of a Tudor castle, with its unusual wrought-iron candelabra and a beautiful carved mantelpiece. Rooms are pleasantly decorated in floral patterns. The hotel is almost close enough to Lincoln Center to hear the arias; music lovers will be pleased to note that each room comes equipped not only with television and VCR but with a stereo, tape deck and CD player. The onsite Empire Café is convenient for pre-concert dining.

Mayflower

15 Central Park West, NY, NY 10023.
Map 12 D2. **C** 265-0060.
FAX 265 2026. **Rooms**: 377. 🛏 1 TV 🍽 🛗 🛗 🔥 🛗 🔥 *AE, DC, MC, V, JCB.* $$$

Situated opposite Central Park and an easy walk from Lincoln Center, the Mayflower has a genteel Old World air. Although the rooms are well overdue for renovation, the hotel is nicely comfortable and unpretentious. Bedrooms have convenient small kitchenettes and refrigerators. The hotel is popular because of its location and the opportunities it presents for visitors to rub elbows with artists and Lincoln Center performers at the Conservatory Café. Park views from front rooms on the higher floors are glorious, and are well worth the extra expense.

For key to symbols see p271

RESTAURANTS AND BARS

NEW YORKERS love to eat well, and there are over 25,000 restaurants in the five boroughs catering to their wishes. City dwellers avidly read restaurant reviews in magazines such as *New York* to ensure that they are seen in the latest fashionable eatery. "In" places and cuisine change with great regularity, while some favorite places simply remain popular. The restaurants in our listings have been selected as the best that New York can offer. *Choosing a Restaurant* on pages 290 to 92 will help narrow down your choice, and the map on page 288 shows the highlights of the list. For lighter refreshment and casual meals, see *Light Meals and Snacks* on pages 304 to 305.

The classic Manhattan cocktail

RESTAURANT MENUS

MEALS IN MOST of the better restaurants consist of three courses: the appetizer (or starter), an entrée (the main course) and a dessert. Virtually all New York restaurants, except fast-food places, serve you rolls or bread and butter just after you're seated, at no extra charge – it's all part of the expected service. In some fine restaurants you may be offered a complimentary appetizer, such as a small

Street-corner hot dog stand

dollop of mousse or a tiny triangle of quiche. Appetizers at the better restaurants are often the chef's most creative dishes – many diners request two appetizers and no entrée. Italian menus offer a pasta dish as a second course before the main course, but in many places pasta is considered a main course. Coffee or tea and a dessert ordinarily conclude the meal in restaurants above the coffee-shop level. Your coffee cup may be refilled until you refuse any more.

The cheeseboard is a rarity in New York restaurants, although a few of the better French restaurants offer one.

PRICES

YOU WILL ALWAYS find a restaurant in New York to suit your budget. At inexpensive coffee shops, diners and fast food chains, $5 will buy you a filling meal. There are also hundreds of acceptable, even first-rate, restaurants where you can eat well at a moderate cost – around $20 per person for a filling and decent meal, not including drinks – in attractive surroundings. For dinner at a trendy New American venue with a star chef, the bill could be upward of $40 to $60 per person, excluding drinks. Many top restaurants do, however, offer fixed-price (or, as they are known in New York, prix-fixe) meals. These are normally much cheaper than items on the à la carte menu. Lunch is also less expensive than dinner in such places, and because of the profusion of business diners, lunch is also the busiest period of the day.

TAXES AND TIPPING

NEW YORK CITY sales tax of 8.25% will be added to your bill. Service is not usually included. Tipping can run from 10% at a coffee shop to 25% at the fanciest places, with 15% an average fair tip. Many New Yorkers just double the sales tax for a tip.

The bill is known as the "check" in New York, as all

A typical New York deli *(see p304)*

over the US. Commonly accepted credit cards are VISA, MasterCard and American Express. Traveler's checks are also taken in many restaurants. Luncheonettes and coffee shops accept cash only. In fast-food chains, you order at the counter and pay cash in advance.

DINING ON A BUDGET

DESPITE THE TALES of $200 business lunches, there are ways to stretch a meal budget in New York.

Order fewer courses than you would normally. American portions are huge, and an appetizer is often big enough for a light main course. You could share one with your companion or choose two appetizers and no entrée.

"Specials of the day" may be more expensive than items on the printed menu, so be sure to check prices.

Ask your waiter if there is a prix-fixe menu. Many expensive restaurants offer this at lunch and dinner – in the early evening it may often be called the pretheater menu. Or try a prix-fixe lunch buffet. These

Interior of Zen Palate *(see p300)* are popular in

Indian restaurants and other places and are very reasonably priced meals.

Go to bars featuring "happy hours." They often offer a variety of hors d'oeuvres, like Spanish *tapas*, which can make a meal in themselves. If you want to simply see inside the restaurants every visitor has heard about, just go to have a drink and soak up the atmosphere. Avoid breakfast in your hotel. Even its coffee shop is likely to be more expensive than an outside coffee shop or deli. Many restaurants post their menus or will let you see them before you are seated, good for checking prices in advance.

Waiting in style at the Café at Grand Central Terminal *(see p309)*

HOURS

BREAKFAST HOURS are usually from 7 to 10:30 or 11am. Sunday brunch is a popular meal, served at most better restaurants between about 11am and 3pm. Lunch runs from 11:30am or noon to 2:30pm at most places, but the busiest time of the day

Poolside at the Four Seasons *(see p293)*

is 1pm. Dinner is usually served from 5:30 to 6pm onward. The most popular time is around 7:30 to 8pm.

Some restaurants stop serving at 10pm during the week, or 11pm on Friday and Saturday. Certain informal restaurants, especially Chinese, are open from 11:30 am to 10pm. Coffee shops are open long hours, from 7am to midnight or even 24 hours.

DRESS CODES

FEW RESTAURANTS demand that male diners dress formally, though a jacket is required at classy restaurants, and jacket and tie at the very best. At most places, for both men and women, "casual but

smart" suffices. Women tend to dress up when dining at the expensive restaurants. If unsure, check the dress code when making a reservation.

RESERVATIONS

IT IS PRUDENT to make reservations at any restaurant above the luncheonette/fast food level. A few of the trendiest restaurants won't even accept reservations except for groups of six or more. It is essential to make reservations for lunch at a midtown restaurant. But you may still be seated at the bar, even if you have booked a table.

SMOKING

MOST RESTAURANTS in New York above the luncheonette level have smoking and non-smoking sections; many ask which you prefer when you call.

CHILDREN

WHEN EATING out with children, ask if there's a child's menu with half-portions. The prices are reduced, sometimes by half. Children are accepted in most New York restaurants, but if yours are unpredictable stick to casual spots, Chinatown Chinese or family-run Italian restaurants, burger bars, delis, cafés, fast food chains and luncheonettes. A few of the better restaurants have facilities for babies or toddlers; others may not be so well equipped. Dining out in the more formal New York restaurants is certainly not a family affair.

WHEELCHAIR ACCESS

WHILE MANY restaurants may be able to accommodate a wheelchair, it is always best to mention your requirements when making your reservation. Many smaller places cannot cater to disabled customers because of lack of space.

USING THE LISTINGS
Key to symbols in the listings on pp293–303.

[telephone number
≈ nonsmoking area
¶⊖ fixed-price menu available
V vegetarian or vegetarian specialties
☒ highchairs and/or children's portions
⊞ outdoor eating
& wheelchair access to all or part of restaurant
T jacket and tie required
♫ live music
♀ excellent wine list
★ highly recommended
⊘ credit cards accepted
AE American Express
DC Diners Club
MC MasterCard/Access
V VISA
JCB Japanese Credit Bureau

Price categories for a three-course meal for one, including a half-bottle of house wine and all unavoidable extra charges (sales tax and service):

$ Under $25
$$ $25–$35
$$$ $35–$50
$$$$ $50–$70
$$$$$ Over $70

What to Eat in New York

Hot dog

THE VARIETY OF FOOD found in New York is as varied as its cultural and ethnic makeup, and you can find virtually any food you want. For a hearty simple meal, such as marinated vegetables, pasta or salami and cheese, visit one of the Italian restaurants found in every neighborhood. For a more sophisticated meal try a Japanese restaurant for sushi and sashimi – as good in New York as anywhere in Japan. Or try such traditional Jewish foods as pastrami, blintzes and bagels, found in most delis and coffee shops. Spicy curries can be found in the many Indian restaurants around Manhattan. If you are really hungry, visit a steakhouse for juicy steaks, fresh seafood and some especially wicked desserts.

Bagel
This chewy Jewish bread roll is most popularly served with lox (smoked salmon) and cream cheese.

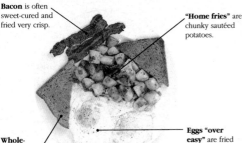

Pancakes
Thick, sweet pancakes are usually served with maple syrup as breakfast. Fresh or dried fruit may be mixed into the batter before cooking.

Bacon is often sweet-cured and fried very crisp.

"Home fries" are chunky sautéed potatoes.

Whole-wheat toast

Eggs "over easy" are fried on both sides.

French Toast
A breakfast dish of sliced bread dipped in egg then fried and often served with syrup.

Breakfast or Brunch
Breakfast (or brunch if eaten midmorning) can consist of anything from home fries, eggs, bacon and toast to sweet pancakes or croissants, often with unlimited coffee.

Egg Cream
This drink is made with milk, chocolate syrup and carbonated soda water.

Corned Beef on Rye
Cured beef is served on rye bread with mild mustard and a pickled dill gherkin.

Burger and Fries "To Go"
A hamburger and french fries may come with salad and onion rings.

Giant Pretzel
This savory bread twist is sold on many street corners.

Pork ribs are barbecued in a rich molasses-based sauce.

Corn bread muffins

Boiled, spiced collard greens

Black-eyed peas

Clam Chowder
The Manhattan version of this shellfish soup is made with tomatoes and garnished with crackers.

Soul Food
The cuisine of Harlem stems from America's Deep South. Simple foods are cooked with spices for a unique flavor.

Pizza
The street food of Italian festivals is available all over the city – this uptown version is topped with artichoke hearts.

Sushi
Japanese cuisine, like this ultrafresh raw fish and rice, is a New York favorite.

Dim Sum
Tiny steamed dumplings, stuffed with fish, meat or vegetables, are a speciality of Chinese cuisine.

Waldorf Salad
Created in the 1930s at the Waldorf Hotel, it's made out of apples, nuts and lettuce.

Cappuccino and Cookies
Frothy coffee sprinkled with chocolate is served with cookies in New York cafés.

Apple Pie à la Mode
This traditional American dessert is only "à la mode" when served with ice cream.

New York Cheesecake
This thick, baked Jewish dessert may be served plain or glazed with fruit.

Banana Split
Some New York ice cream concoctions will feed a family. No one will mind if you order extra spoons and share.

New York's Best: Restaurants, Cafés and Bars

RESTAURANTS CAN BE FOUND all over New York, catering to all tastes and budgets and open at all times of the day or night. New York's eating habits reflect the city's ethnic heritage, past and present, as new immigrant groups make New York their home. Witness the enduring popularity of Italian, Chinese and Japanese restaurants and the traditional Jewish deli. In the 37 pages of restaurant listings in the New York telephone directory, you can find virtually every imaginable cuisine, from Californian, New American, Cajun and southern barbecue to Thai, Vietnamese, Indian, Afghan, Burmese and Philippine. The restaurants here are just a few favorites, selected from the listings on pages 293 to 303 as the best in their particular field.

Carnegie Delicatessen
Try the giant "pastrami on rye" at this typical deli. (See p306.)

Zen Palate
The excellent vegetarian cuisine offered here is a clever blend of Oriental styles. (See p300.)

Chelsea and the Garment District

Union Square Café
This is the place to sample New American cuisine at its best. Seafood and desserts are both excellent. (See p295.)

Greenwich Village

Gramercy and the Flatiron District

Florent
This bistro is open around the clock for authentic food and atmosphere. (See p306.)

SoHo and TriBeCa

East Village

Lower Manhattan

Seaport and the Civic Center

Lower East Side

Caffè Vivaldi
Of many charming coffeehouses in New York, this is a favorite for its delicious sticky pastries. (See p306.)

Golden Unicorn
Chinatown's best Chinese food is served here. Their range of dim sum is not to be missed. (See p300.)

McSorley's Old Ale House
For atmosphere alone, try this bar. Sample the potent house beer with care. (See p309.)

N

Upper West Side

Central Park

Theater District

Upper East Side

Upper Midtown

Lower Midtown

E A S T   R I V E R

Café des Artistes
This New York classic is famed for both its saucy 1930s murals and its chocolate dessert tray. (See p296.)

Mezzaluna
It's just a short walk from Museum Mile to some of the best pizzas in town. (See p306.)

SERENDIPITY 3

Serendipity 3
Eccentric Victoriana amuses the adults, but kids vote this café a hit for its ice-cream sundaes. (See p306.)

The Four Seasons
Outstanding European and American food is served in two stunning rooms, one paneled in rosewood, the other centered around a pool. (See p293.)

Oyster Bar, Grand Central Terminal
The best seafood restaurant in Manhattan is this vaulted, golden room in the historic train station. The all-American wine list is excellent, too. (See p294.)

| 0 kilometers | | 2 |
| 0 miles | 1 | |

Hatsuhana
The freshest and most varied sushi available makes this Japanese restaurant stand out from the rest. Take a seat at the sushi bar and watch the skilled chefs at work. (See p301.)

Choosing a Restaurant

THE RESTAURANTS in this section have been selected for their good value or exceptional food. This chart highlights some factors that may influence your choice. For details see pages 293 to 303. Details of *Light Meals and Snacks* are on pages 304 to 306; for some of New York's best *Bars*, see pages 307 to 309.

	PAGE NUMBER	FIXED-PRICE MENU	LATE OPENING	CHILDREN'S FACILITIES	TABLES OUTSIDE	QUIET RESTAURANT	VEGETARIAN DISHES	SEAFOOD SPECIALTIES
LOWER MANHATTAN								
Hudson River Club *(American)* $$$$	294	●		●				
Cellar in the Sky *(American)* $$$$$	293	●						●
Windows on the World *(American)* ★ $$$$$	295	●				●		
SEAPORT AND THE CIVIC CENTER								
Bo Ky *(Chinese)* $	300	●		●				
Saigon *(Southeast Asian)* $$	301			●			■	●
LOWER EAST SIDE								
Canton *(Chinese)* $$	300			●				
Oriental Garden *(Chinese)* $$	300		■	●				●
Golden Unicorn *(Chinese)* $$$	300	●	■	●				
Sammy's Famous Roumanian *(Jewish/Romanian)* $$$$	303		■					
SOHO AND TRIBECA								
Savoy *(Mediterranean)* $$	303	●						●
Honmura An *(Japanese)* $$$	301	●				●	■	●
Provence *(French)* $$$	297	.	■	●	●			
Tommy Tang's *(Southeast Asian)* $$$	301			●			■	●
Alison on Dominick Street *(French)* $$$$	295					●		●
Chanterelle *(French)* ★ $$$$	296	●				●		
Montrachet *(French)* ★ $$$	297	●		●				
Raoul's *(French)* $$$$	297	●	■			■	■	
TriBeCa Grill *(American)* $$$$	295	●				■	■	
Zoë *(American)* $$$$	295			●			■	●
Bouley *(French)* ★ $$$$$	296	●						
GREENWICH VILLAGE								
Chez Jacqueline *(French)* $$$	296					■		
Cent' Anni *(Italian)* $$$	298						■	
Il Mulino *(Italian)* $$$	298		■	●			■	
La Métairie *(French)* $$$	297		■				■	
Gotham Bar & Grill *(American)* $$$$	294			●			■	
EAST VILLAGE								
Iso *(Japanese)* $$$	301	●	■					●
Siracusa *(Italian)* $$$	299							●
GRAMERCY AND THE FLATIRON DISTRICT								
An American Place *(American)* $$$	293			●			■	
Mesa Grill *(American)* $$$	294			●		●	■	●
Lola *(Caribbean)* $$$$	303		■	●				●
Periyali *(Greek)* $$$$	303					■		
Union Square Café *(American)* ★ $$$$	295			●			■	
The Water Club *(American)* $$$$$	295	●	■			■		
CHELSEA AND THE GARMENT DISTRICT								
Da Umberto *(Italian)* $$$$	298						■	●
Le Madri *(Italian)* ★ $$$$	298		■			■	■	
World Yacht Cruises *(American)* $$$$$	295	●		●				

Price categories include a three-course meal for one, half a bottle of house wine and all unavoidable extra charges, such as sales tax and service.
$ under $25
$$ $26–$35
$$$ $36–$50
$$$$ $51–$70
$$$$$ over $70

★ Means highly recommended.

FIXED-PRICE MENU
A fixed price for a set meal that is a lot cheaper than normal menu prices.
LATE OPENING
Last orders at or after 11:30pm excluding Sunday.
CHILDREN'S FACILITIES
Highchairs and/or child portions.
QUIET RESTAURANT
No piped music; peaceful atmosphere.
VEGETARIAN DISHES
Vegetarian restaurant or restaurant with good vegetarian selection.

	Price	Page Number	Fixed-Price Menu	Late Opening	Children's Facilities	Tables Outside	Quiet Restaurant	Vegetarian Dishes	Seafood Specialties
THEATER DISTRICT									
Afghan Kebab House *(Afghan)*	$	302	●					●	
Siam Inn Too *(Southeast Asian)*	$	301		●					
Jewel of India *(Indian)*	$$	302	●					●	
Zen Palate *(Chinese)*	$$	300						●	
B. Smith's *(American)*	$$$	293		●					
Cabana Carioca *(South American)*	$$$	303			●				
44 *(American)*	$$$	293		●					●
Orso *(Italian)*	$$$	299		●				●	
Mamma Leone's *(Italian)*	$$$$	298	●	●	●			●	
Remi *(Italian)*	$$$$	299		●		●			
Trattoria Dell'Arte *(Italian)*	$$$$	299		●			●	●	●
Le Bernardin *(French)*	$$$$$	296	●						●
Les Célébrités *(French)*	$$$$$	296	●		●		●		
Palio *(Italian)*	$$$$$	299	●					●	
The Rainbow Room *(French)* ★	$$$$$	297	●	●	●			●	●
Russian Tea Room *(Russian)*	$$$$$	303		●				●	●
San Domenico *(Italian)* ★	$$$$$	299		●			●		●
The Sea Grill *(Italian)*	$$$$$	294	●			●			●
LOWER MIDTOWN									
Ambassador Grill *(American)*	$$$	293	●		●		●	●	●
Grand Central Oyster Bar *(American)* ★	$$$	294			●				●
Tropica *(Caribbean)*	$$$$	303	●					●	●
Sparks Steakhouse *(American)*	$$$$$	294							●
UPPER MIDTOWN									
Hwa Yuan Szechuan Inn *(Chinese)*	$	300			●				
Akbar *(Indian)*	$$	302	●		●				
Contrapunto *(Italian)*	$$	298		●				●	
Zarela *(Mexican)*	$$	303							
Arizona 206 *(American)*	$$$	293	●	●	●			●	●
Chin Chin *(Chinese)*	$$$	300	●	●	●	●		●	●
Dawat *(Italian)*	$$$	302	●					●	
Hatsuhana *(Japanese)*	$$$	301	●						●
Il Nido *(Italian)*	$$$	299			●				
Sushisay *(Japanese)*	$$$	301							●
Bice *(Italian)*	$$$$	298				●		●	
La Caravelle *(French)*	$$$$	296	●				●		
Darbar *(Italian)*	$$$$	302					●	●	
Felidia *(Italian)*	$$$$	298						●	
Inagiku *(Japanese)*	$$$$	301							●
Lutèce *(French)* ★	$$$$	297	●						
Mitsukoshi *(Japanese)*	$$$$	301							●
Shun Lee Palace *(Chinese)*	$$$$	300							●
Smith & Wollensky *(American)*	$$$$	294		●					●
Aquavit *(Scandinavian)*	$$$$$	302	●					●	●
La Côte Basque *(French)*	$$$$$	296					●		
The Four Seasons *(American)* ★	$$$$$	293	●				●		●
Le Périgord *(French)*	$$$$$	297	●				●		
The '21' Club *(American)*	$$$$$	295	●	●			●	●	

Price categories include a three-course meal for one, half a bottle of house wine and all unavoidable extra charges, such as sales tax and service.
$ under $25
$$ $26–$35
$$$ $36–$50
$$$$ $51–$70
$$$$$ over $70

★ Means highly recommended.

FIXED-PRICE MENU
A fixed price for a set meal that is a lot cheaper than normal menu prices.
LATE OPENING
Last orders at or after 11:30pm excluding Sunday.
CHILDREN'S FACILITIES
Highchairs and/or child portions.
QUIET RESTAURANT
No piped music; peaceful atmosphere.
VEGETARIAN DISHES
Vegetarian restaurant or restaurant with good vegetarian selection.

	PAGE NUMBER	FIXED-PRICE MENU	LATE OPENING	CHILDREN'S FACILITIES	TABLES OUTSIDE	QUIET RESTAURANT	VEGETARIAN DISHES	SEAFOOD SPECIALTIES
UPPER EAST SIDE								
Bangkok House *(Thai)* $$	301	●	■	●	■		■	●
Pamir *(Afghan)* $$	302					■		
Pig Heaven *(Chinese)* $$$	300		■	●				
Arcadia *(American)* ★ $$$$	293	●		●	■			
Coco Pazzo *(Italian)* $$$$	298						■	
Elaine's *(Italian)* $$$$	298		■					
Jo Jo *(French)* $$$$	296	●	■			●		
Aureole *(French)* ★ $$$$$	295	●			■	●	■	
Le Cirque *(French)* ★ $$$$$	296	●						●
Le Régence *(French)* $$$$$	297	●						●
Sign of the Dove *(American)* $$$$$	294	●			■	●		
UPPER WEST SIDE								
Ollie's Noodle Shop & Grill *(Chinese)* $$	300		■	●				●
Café Luxembourg *(French)* $$$	296	●	■				■	
Carmine's *(Italian)* $$$	298			●				
Shun Lee West *(Chinese)* $$$	300		■				■	
Café des Artistes *(French)* ★ $$$$	296	●	■					●
MORNINGSIDE HEIGHTS AND HARLEM								
Sylvia's *(American)* $	294			●				
Rao's *(Italian)* $$$	299	●						●
The Terrace *(French)* $$$	297	●			■			●
BROOKLYN								
Moroccan Star *(Moroccan)* $	303	●		●				
Gage & Tollner *(American)* $$$	293	●		●				●
Peter Luger *(American)* $$$$	294	●		●				
The River Café *(American)* ★ $$$$$	294	●	■		■			
QUEENS								
The Water's Edge *(American)* $$$$$	295			●	■			●

AMERICAN

In New York restaurants, you are likely to find three types of American cuisine: American, New American and Regional American.

American cuisine, generally speaking, consists of grilled meats, deep-fried seafood, french fries and fresh tossed salads. Served in huge portions at reasonable prices, this food will be found in restaurants in almost every neighborhood.

New American cuisine is a spin-off from French nouvelle cuisine. Portions are generally small – and foods are chosen for interesting textures and color combinations. Adapting the old regional recipes and using fresh local ingredients with the infusion of Oriental items – such as ginger, soy, garlic, curry and fresh coriander – has become a touchstone of this cooking style. New American restaurants are easily among the very best and most expensive in New York.

Also to be found in the city is Regional American food. Cuisines in this category range from New England's seafood to the South's barbecued ribs and soul food, which is traditionally eaten by black Americans. Creole cuisine may include blackened fish, crayfish or gumbo (stew with poultry, rice, seafood and tomatoes); California cuisine uses mainly natural, fresh ingredients, often combining Asian food with nouvelle techniques. Restaurants serving regional food tend toward the middle of the price range.

Ambassador Grill

United Nations Plaza Hotel, 1 United Nations Plaza. **Map** 13 C5.
702-5014. **Open** 7–10:30am, noon–2pm & 6–10:30pm daily. AE, DC, MC, V.

American cuisine, with a particular French flourish, is served to a very mixed clientele of UN business-people and mature East Siders in this comfortable mirrored setting. Prices are reasonable, considering the quality of the food and the location, but by far the best buy is the all-you-can-eat Sunday lobster-and-champagne brunch buffet.

An American Place

2 Park Ave. **Map** 9 A2. 684-2122. **Open** 11:45am–3pm Mon–Fri, 5:30–10pm Mon–Sat. AE, DC, MC, V.

Chef-proprietor Larry Forgione has made a name for himself and his New American cooking style in this restaurant reminiscent of a hotel dining room of the 1930s. His inventive menu frequently changes and might include grilled boneless quail with cornbread stuffing, or crispy free-range duck with a minted wild-flower honey glaze. There are a few American boutique beers that go well with many of the robust dishes.

Arcadia

21 E 62nd St. **Map** 12 F2.
223-2900. **Open** noon–2:30pm Mon–Fri, 6–10:30pm Mon–Sat. **Closed** some hols. ★ AE, DC, MC, V.

For the practicing gourmet, a visit to this posh, beautifully decorated little uptown place is essential. The co-owner, Anne Rosenzweig, is one of the top young New American chefs. Virtually everything on the menu is appealing, and dining here can be a memorable experience. Unfortunately, its popularity means that it does get a little crowded, and the noise levels can then become intrusive.

Arizona 206

206 E 60th St. **Map** 13 B3.
838-0440. **Open** noon–3pm Mon–Sat, 5:30–11:30pm Fri, Sat, 5:30–10:30pm Sun. AE, DC, MC, V.

For a memorable meal, step into this whitewashed-walled, adobe-like interior, with its cozy wood fires, wood tables and knotty pine floors. An imaginative blend of the Southwest with New American flair produces dishes such as stuffed peppers, roasted quail with polenta and barbecued foie gras. Dinner is the best time to eat here, though it's noisy and extremely crowded. You can also sample a wide range of its superb appetizers at a fraction of the restaurant's cost in the attached Arizona 206 Café.

B. Smith's

771 Eighth Ave. **Map** 12 D5.
247-2222. **Open** noon–11pm Mon–Thu, noon–12:30pm Fri, Sat, noon–10:30pm Sun. AE, DC, V, MC.

Run by Barbara Smith, a former model, this high-ceilinged restaurant is a magnet for New York's elite, showbiz types. The well-priced and stylish New American food is good. Upstairs, in a vast glass-enclosed space, is B. Smith's Rooftop Café, where the audience is treated to nightly live music.

Cellar in the Sky

Windows on the World, 107th, 1 World Trade Center. **Map** 1 B2.
938-1111. **Open** 7:30pm Mon–Sat. AE, DC, MC, V, JCB.

Cellar in the Sky is on the 107th floor of the World Trade Center, a neighbor of Windows on the World, but without the incredible eye-popping city views. The emphasis is therefore on the food, which is terrific. There is only one seating, at 7:30pm. You will be served an excellent seven-course meal, continental style, with five superb wines to accompany it.

44

Royalton Hotel, 44 W 44th St. **Map** 12 F5. 944-8844. **Open** 7am–11pm Mon–Thu, 8am–midnight Fri, Sat. AE, DC, MC, V.

This hotel dining room is refreshingly stark in its all-gray decor, and it is a pleasant surprise to find the food as sophisticated as the location. It is convenient for the Theater District and has a good pretheater prix-fixe menu. The browned sea scallops in a creamy risotto is just one of many choices on the inventive menu.

The Four Seasons

99 E 52nd St. **Map** 1 3A.
754-9494. **Open** noon–2pm & 5–11:15pm Mon–Sat. **Closed** some hols. occasionally. ★ AE, DC, MC, V, JCB.

This restaurant, established in 1961, continues to attract power-lunch regulars to its magnificent, high-ceilinged Grill Room. More romantic, and a good place for a pretheater prix-fixe dinner, is the spacious Pool Room, with its marble pool. Wherever you sit, you'll enjoy consistently delicious New American and continental dishes. Don't miss the dessert cart. This will be an expensive treat but it will not disappoint. Reservations are required.

Gage & Tollner

372 Fulton St, Brooklyn.
(718) 875-5181. **Open** 11am–3pm, 5pm–10pm daily. AE, DC, MC, V.

It's worth making the journey to Brooklyn for some of the area's finest seafood, served in a restaurant that could pass as a set for the film *Gaslight*. Oysters and grilled clambellies are the best items here, as well as the chef's South Carolina specialties, like Charleston she-crab soup (crab meat and crab eggs mixed with cream, onion and sherry). The best time to come is at night, when there is an eclectic clientele, unless you want to listen to politics at lunch. At night take a taxi.

For key to symbols *see p285*

Gotham Bar & Grill

12 E 12th St. **Map** 4 E1.
☎ *620-4020.* ***Open*** *noon–2:30pm Mon–Fri, 5:30–10pm Mon–Thu, 5:30–11pm Fri, Sat, 5:30–9:30pm Sun.* 🚭 [V] 🧒 🍷 💳 *AE, DC, MC, V.* $$$$$

In a former warehouse, amid a Neoclassical setting of columns, high ceilings and a pink marble bar, you will find what is probably the best food in this part of town. Alfred Portale is a young and gifted French-trained chef whose most celebrated dish is his seafood salad, but all the seafood dishes are wonderful. Don't overlook his flair with game. This spot is pricey, but worth a visit for a memorable New American food experience.

Grand Central Oyster Bar

Grand Central Station, Lower Level. **Map** 9 A1. ☎ *490-6650.* ***Open*** *11:30am to last sitting at 9:30pm Mon–Fri.* ***Closed*** *some hols.* 🚭 🧒 ♿ 🍷 ★ 💳 *AE, DC, MC, V, JCB.* $$$

Some of the best seafood in New York is served in this cavernous, simply furnished space below the city's main railroad station. At lunch you can't hear yourself think, let alone talk, since sound bounces off the vaulted arches and ceilings. But the fish and shellfish are always fresh and simply prepared – and surprisingly well-priced. There's also a lengthy California wine list.

Hudson River Club

250 Vesey St. **Map** 1 A2.
☎ *786-1500.* ***Open*** *11:30am–3pm Mon–Fri, 5–10pm Mon–Sat, 11:30am–3:30pm Sun.* ***Closed*** *some hols.* 🚭 🍽 🧒 ♿ 👔 💳 *AE, DC, MC, V.* $$$$

This club is situated on the second floor in one of the World Financial Center towers, and the view of the harbor and the Statue of Liberty extends along the length of the dining room. The original menu highlights the foods and wines of the Hudson River Valley.

Mesa Grill

102 Fifth Ave. **Map** 8 F5.
☎ *807-7400.* ***Open*** *noon–2:15pm Mon–Fri, 11:30am–3pm Sat, Sun, 5:30–10:30pm Mon–Thu, 5:30–11pm Fri & Sat.* 🚭 ♿ 💳 *AE, DC, MC, V.* $$$

Spicy, inventive renderings of popular southwestern US dishes, mainly from Arizona and New Mexico, are served in this former clothing showroom. The restaurant is now a spacious and colorful evocation of the West as only a New York restaurateur would see it. It attracts the trend-setting crowd with its unusual combinations of grilled foods at reasonable prices.

Peter Luger

178 Broadway, Brooklyn.
☎ *(718) 387-7400.* ***Open*** *11:45am–10pm Mon–Thu, 11:45am–11pm Fri & Sat, 1–10pm Sun.* 🚭 🍽 🧒 ♿ $$$$

Carnivores insist that this is the best steakhouse in all of the five boroughs and well worth the taxi ride to indulge in an enormous well-charred porterhouse steak or double lamb chops. The main dining room has a German beer-hall look, with oak paneling and exposed wood beams, and the same kind of intimacy. The waiters, used to coping with many regulars and hordes of tourists, deal with their customers in a brusquely good-humored manner.

The River Café

1 Water St, Brooklyn. **Map** 12 F5.
☎ *(718) 522-5200.* ***Open*** *11:30am–11:30pm daily.* 🚭 🍽 ♿ 👔 ♫ ☂ 🍷 💳 *AE, DC, MC, V.* $$$$$

The River Café has some of the most spectacular skyline views of Manhattan, but it also has good creative New American cooking, notably prix-fixe and six-course "tasting" menus. Nighttime is the lovers' favorite, but views are great at lunch and brunch and it's much easier to reserve a table by the window.

The Sea Grill

Rockefeller Skating Rink, 18 W 49th St. **Map** 12 F5. ☎ *246-9201.* ***Open*** *noon–3pm Mon–Fri, 5–11pm Mon–Sat.* ***Closed*** *Memorial & Labor days.* 🚭 🍽 ♿ 👔 ☂ 💳 *AE, DC, JCB, MC, V.* $$$$$

Though this is something of a tourist trap, the fresh seafood here is excellent, if costly. In winter you can watch skaters at the outdoor rink while you eat, and in summer you can dine in the garden. The prix-fixe dinner is a good choice.

Sign of the Dove

1110 Third Ave. **Map** 13 B2.
☎ *861-8080.* ***Open*** *noon–2:30pm Tue–Fri, 11:30am–2:30pm Sat & Sun, 6–11pm Mon–Fri, 5:30–11:30pm Sat, 6–10pm Sun.* 🚭 🍽 ♫ ☂ 💳 *AE, DC, MC, V.* $$$$$

Couples gravitate to this charming hideaway of small rooms with well-separated tables, brick archways and mirrors. There is also a great conservatory with a sliding roof; it's wonderful dining here on starlit summer nights. Now one of the city's prime restaurants for its elegant American/French food, it serves such dishes as beef ravioli with morel mushrooms, *farfalle* (pasta) with braised rabbit and beef filet with foie gras.

Smith & Wollensky

201 E 49th St. **Map** 13 B5.
☎ *753-1530.* ***Open*** *11:45am–midnight Mon–Fri, 5pm–midnight Sat, Sun.* ***Closed*** *New Year's Day, Thanksgiving, Christmas.* 🚭 ♿ 🍷 💳 *AE, DC, MC, V.* $$$$

Brown leather banquettes, marble panels, and a dark, woody look create a men's club ambience at Smith & Wollensky. It is a long-time favorite venue for executive types, who throng here for the excellent steaks, chops, prime ribs and filet mignon (small cut of beef from the thin end of an undercut) for which the restaurant has become well known. There is also an extensive wine list of good American vintages.

Sparks Steakhouse

210 E 46th St. **Map** 13 B5.
☎ *687-4855.* ***Open*** *noon–3pm Mon–Fri, 5–11pm Mon–Thu, 5pm–11:30pm Fri & Sat.* 🚭 ♿ 🍷 💳 *AE, DC, MC, V.* $$$$$

The midtown location of this machismo place, which may just remind you of *The Godfather*, has made it into a business lunch favorite, so the decibel levels rise very quickly. Not surprisingly, steaks are the main item on the menu, though there are good lobsters, too, some of incredible size. The wine list is exceptional. Service is brusque – as usual for New York steakhouses.

Sylvia's

328 Lenox Ave. **Map** 21 B1.
☎ *996-0660.* ***Open*** *7:30am–10:30pm Mon–Sat, 1–7pm Sun.* ***Closed*** *Christmas.* 🚭 🧒 ♿ ♫ 💳 *AE.* $ *(See p228.)*

For a unique American cuisine experience, head for this soul food heaven in Harlem (taking a taxi is recommended). Barbecued ribs, fried chicken, black-eyed peas, collard greens and ham are a few things to try in this cozy outpost of South Carolina home cooking, where the waiters may call you "dear." Be sure not to miss the sweet potato pie. Breakfasts here are huge and very delicious.

TriBeCa Grill

375 Greenwich St. **Map** 4 D5.
📞 941-3900. **Open** noon–2:30pm
Mon–Fri, 5:30–10:45pm Sun–Thu,
5:30–11:15pm Fri & Sat, 11:30am–
3pm Sun. 🚭 🍴 📺 🚻 📶 ♿
🍷 AE, DC, MC, V. $$$$

You may see co-owner Robert De
Niro here, as well as many other
celebrities, especially at the large
round bar that is the centerpiece
of this brick-walled bistro. The bar
is therefore the place to sit if you
like to play spot-the-star, but the
inventive American food is
surprisingly good, despite the
frenetic nature of the place. Save
room for the many delicious
desserts, a house specialty.

The '21' Club

21 W 52nd St. **Map** 12 F4.
📞 582-7200. **Open** noon–midnight
Mon–Sat. **Closed** Sat in May–Aug.
🚭 🍴 📺 🚻 ♿ 🍷 AE, DC,
MC, V. $$$$$

Although the club's heyday is long
past, this former speakeasy, with
a black iron fence and jockey
statues outside, has developed a
younger coterie of fans in show
business and political circles who
enjoy the somewhat formal town-
house ambience. The American
food, however, is overpriced and
somewhat erratic in quality.

Union Square Cafe

21 E 16th. **Map** 8 F5. 📞 243-4020.
Open noon–2:30pm Mon–Sat,
6–10:30pm Mon–Thu, 6–11:30pm Fri
& Sat, 5:30–10pm Sun. 🚭 📺 🚻
♿ ★ 🍷 AE, DC, MC, V.
$$$$

This is one of New York's premier
restaurants and is well known for
its imaginative American, Italian and
French renderings. The Union
Square Cafe is surprisingly
moderately priced for all its fame.
Its very high ceilings and open-
plan setting attract the area's
publishing élite. Good acoustics
make it possible both to talk and
to listen. Seafood is treated well
here; try the fried *calamari*
(squid), grilled black sea bass or
grilled tuna. Desserts – lemon pie,
hot apple and pear tarts – are
superb, as is the friendly service.

The Water Club

500 E 30th St. **Map** 9 C3.
📞 683-3333. **Open** noon–11:30pm
daily. 🚭 🍴 ♿ 📶 🚻 🍷 AE,
DC, MC, V. $$$$

This restaurant is located in an
unusual glass-enclosed skylit pier
that connects two large barges. It
sets the stage perfectly for

sweeping river views and some
intriguing, and delicious, seafood
dishes, such as salmon steak with
pesto crust on steamed spinach.

The Water's Edge

44th Drive & East River, Long Island
City. 📞 (718) 482-0033. **Open**
noon–3pm & 6–11pm Mon–Sat. 🚭
🕴 ♿ 🍴 📶 🚻 ♿ AE, DC,
JCB, MC V. $$$$

From this large dining room's
windows, you'll have a view of
the MetLife and Chrysler buildings
and other midtown Manhattan
landmarks across the river. New
American food, prepared with a
certain amount of flair, as well as
singers, add to the often magical
experience created here. There's
also a free ferry service from East
34th Street to the restaurant dock.

Windows on
the World

1 World Trade Center, 107th fl, West
St. **Map** 1 B2. 📞 938-1111. **Open**
noon–3pm Mon–Fri, 5–10pm
Mon–Sat, 5–8:30pm Sun. 🚭 🍴
🕴 ♿ 🚻 ♿ ★ AE, DC, MC,
V. $$$$

Windows on the World is 107
stories above the harbor in the
World Trade Center. There are
stunning views in all directions,
though if the parapetlike windows
were wider, these would be even
better. This is the best place from
which to view all the events in the
harbor, such as the Tall Ships or
Fourth of July celebrations. The
food is expensive and not quite
up to the views, but a prix-fixe
menu helps considerably. It is a
membership club at lunch, but
nonmembers can still eat here, at
an extra charge.

World Yacht Cruises

Pier 81, W 41st St. **Map** 7 B4.
📞 630-8100. **Open** noon–2pm &
7–10pm Mon–Sat, 12:30–2:30pm
Sun. 🚭 🍴 🕴 ♿ 📶 🚻 ♿
AE, MC, V. $$$$

This is as close as you can get for
special events on the waterfront.
World Yacht Cruises is a fleet of
five boats, featuring year-round
lunch or dinner with dancing and
a wonderful movable feast of a
city view at a one-price cost. The
real surprise is that the American
and continental food is not bad.

Zoë

90 Prince St. **Map** 4 E3. 📞 966-6722.
Open noon–3pm, 6pm–
10:30pm Tue–Sun. 🚭 📺 🕴 ♿
🚻 🍷 AE, DC, MC, V. $$$$

This SoHo spot enjoys a good
reputation for its grilled meats
and fish, as well as its imaginative
New American cooking style. The
long dining room, with extremely
high ceilings, high columns and
open kitchen, appeals to the
many artists and young professionals who have been flocking
here since it opened in 1992.

FRENCH

Fine dining in New York usually
means French. The fashionable,
established French restaurants
tend to be expensive, serving
haute cuisine in settings profuse
with fresh floral arrangements. They
are usually located in midtown and
the Upper East Side. Some newer
places feature nouvelle cuisine
and can be very expensive. Many
of the places on the West Side and
in the Theater District are less
lavishly decorated and less pricey,
though still traditional in menu.

Bistros have become popular
recently, since they cater to the
trend for simple healthy fare,
informal settings and lower prices.

All three types, haute, nouvelle
and bistro, are at their very best in
New York. In most cases, the
chef-proprietor is French with
long restaurant experience.

Alison on Dominick
Street

38 Dominick St. **Map** 4 D4.
📞 727-1188. **Open** 5:30–10:30pm
Mon–Thu, 5:30–11pm Fri, Sat,
5:30pm–9:30pm Sun. 🍷 AE, DC,
MC, V. $$$$

You'll find a skillful mixture of
French, Mediterranean and New
American cuisines in this rather
off-the-track romantic place. The
setting is sleek and stylish. The
bar at the front is a scene in itself,
and the dining room is dark, cozy
and conducive to intimate dining.

Aureole

34 E 61st St. **Map** 13 A3.
📞 319-1660. **Open** noon–2: 30pm
& 5:30–10:30pm Mon–Thu,
noon–2:30pm & 5:30–11pm Fri &
Sat. 🚭 🍴 📺 🚻 📶 ♿ ★ 🍷
AE, DC, MC, V. $$$$$

In a well-restored brownstone, the
long, narrow rooms are cleverly
brightened by floral arrangements
and clever bas-relief decorations.
The garden is the place to dine in
warm weather. The transAtlantic
dishes are excellent and change
frequently. Order the wood-grilled
lamb chops when they're on the
menu. A prix-fixe menu helps
ease the pain of this rarefied
dining experience.

For key to symbols *see p285*

Le Bernardin

155 W 51st St. **Map** 10 E4. ☎ *489-1515.* ***Open*** *noon–2:30pm Mon–Fri, 6–10:30pm Mon–Thu, 5:30–11pm Fri & Sat.* ***Closed*** *some hols.* 🚭 🍽 ♿ 👔 🍷 💳 *AE, DC, MC, V, JCB.* [$][$][$][$][$]

To knowledgeable locals, seafood and Le Bernardin are synonymous. This is a large and beautiful place, with a teak ceiling, pale-blue walls and tapestry-covered chairs. The fish is served undercooked to let the freshness speak for itself, and very little sauce is used. It is very expensive but worth every penny. Desserts are special, too – try the sampler of caramel sweets.

Bouley

165 Duane St. **Map** 1 B1. ☎ *608-3852.* ***Open*** *noon–2:30pm Mon–Fri, 6–11pm Mon–Sat.* 🚭 🍽 👔 🍷 ★ 💳 *AE, DC, MC, V.* [$][$][$][$][$]

No detail is missed in this very comfortable dining room with its Romanesque-arched ceilings, well-spaced tables, fresh flowers and attentive service – even if you're not one of Bouley's usual celebrity guests. The modern French food, using only fresh ingredients, is exquisite, with many imaginative twists of chef David Bouley's own. The prix-fixe lunch and dinner menus are a steal for a place of this high caliber. There are no weaknesses here at all.

Café des Artistes

1 W 67th St. **Map** 12 D2. ☎ *877-3500.* ***Open*** *noon–3pm & 5:30pm–midnight Mon–Sat, 10am–3pm & 5:30–11pm Sun.* ***Closed*** *Christmas Day.* 🚭 🍽 👔 *after 5pm.* ★ 💳 *AE, DC, MC, V, JCB.* [$][$][$][$]

This crowded, jolly café is on everyone's list of favorites. The 1934 murals, by Howard Chandler Christy, of frolicking nymphs, set the light-hearted tone, and the excellent French food extends it. Desserts are a specialty here, especially the Hungarian *tortes* (small cakes), a plate of samples and the lavish chocolate creations that only the very strong-willed can resist. The mix of theater, television and publishing personalities who often drop by adds to the joie de vivre.

Café Luxembourg

200 W 70th St. **Map** 11 C1. ☎ *873-7411.* ***Open*** *noon–3pm Tue–Sat, 5:30pm–12:30am Mon–Sat, 11am–3pm & 6–11:30pm Sun.* 🍽 [V] 💳 *AE, DC, MC, V.* [$][$][$]

Café Luxembourg is a clean white-tile-walled, faux Art Deco favorite for just hanging out and people watching. The mix of French-American-Italian food is erratic, so stick to simple things on the menu, like soups. The cassoulet is an exception to this rule. Better yet, the location, very convenient for Lincoln Center, makes it a good drinking stop en route. The bar is the place to be seen.

La Caravelle

33 W 55th St. **Map** 12 F4. ☎ *586-4252.* ***Open*** *12:30–2:30pm Mon–Fri, 5:30–10:30pm Mon–Sat.* 🚭 🍽 ♿ 👔 🍷 💳 *AE, DC, JCB, MC, V.* [$][$][$][$]

For over thirty years this bastion of haute cuisine has been serving elegant French food in a really comfortable, softly lit room. The clientele of regulars is distinctly upscale. There have been some new flourishes in the kitchen of late, but the fresh foie gras and most seafood dishes are among the old favorites that are always good. Lunch, dinner and pre-theater prix-fixe menus are available.

Les Célébrités

Essex House Hotel, 160 Central Park South. **Map** 12 E3. ☎ *247-0300.* ***Open*** *6–10pm Tue–Sat.* 🚭 🍽 🧒 ♿ 👔 🍷 💳 *AE, DC, MC, V.* [$][$][$][$][$]

New, luxurious and theatrical, with huge gilded columns, thick carpeting and paintings by show-biz people, this French restaurant, with a mere 14 tables, is off the lobby of the Essex House Hotel. The food is remarkably good, with strong Oriental influences and light touches, the handiwork of the former chef at Maurice. The seafood is beautifully prepared, but so is everything on the menu.

Chanterelle

2 Harrison St (corner of Hudson). **Map** 4 D5. ☎ *966-6960.* ***Open*** *noon–2:30pm & 6–10:30pm Tue–Sat.* ***Closed*** *some hols.* 🚭 🍽 ♿ 👔 ★ 💳 *AE, DC, MC, V.* [$][$][$][$]

This small TriBeCa establishment seats 60 people and offers an excellent, albeit limited, prix-fixe menu. In a perfect, though rather minimalist, setting – with high ceilings, wood walls, columns and stunning flower arrangements – the French food tastes as good as its nouvelle arrangements look. Seafood is a treat, and the cheese tray is truly remarkable. For a lovely romantic splurge, this place is hard to beat.

Chez Jacqueline

72 MacDougal St. **Map** 4 D3. ☎ *505-0727.* ***Open*** *noon–3pm Mon–Fri, 6–11pm Sun–Thu, 6–11:30pm Fri & Sat.* ***Closed*** *Christmas, New Year's days.* 🏛 💳 *AE, DC, MC, V.* [$][$][$]

Pastel walls help make this tiny Village spot seem larger, and the familiar, if uneven, French bistro fare keeps regulars coming back, despite the overloud taped music. The crowd is mostly young, hip and international. Near to several Off-Broadway theaters and the Film Forum, this is a handy, moderately priced dinner stop.

Le Cirque

58 E 65th St. **Map** 13 A2. ☎ *794-9292.* ***Open*** *noon–2:30pm & 5:45–10:15pm Mon–Sat.* 🚭 🍽 ♿ 👔 🍷 ★ 💳 *AE, DC, MC, V.* [$][$][$][$][$]

Many of the locals consider this the city's finest restaurant, even though the tables and banquettes are crowded together and give the feeling of dining on stage. The rosy glow, flowers, Limoges china and murals are mere garnishes for an exquisitely prepared mix of French and Italian dishes. Try the risotto and leave room for a dessert, perhaps the famous crème brûlée. A much cheaper prix-fixe lunch menu is a strong incentive to eat among the many power-lunchers.

La Côte Basque

5 E 55th St. **Map** 12 F4. ☎ *688-6525.* ***Open*** *noon–2pm Mon–Sat, 6–10:30pm Mon–Fri, 6–11pm Sat.* ***Closed*** *some hols.* 🚭 🍽 ♿ 👔 🍷 💳 *AE, DC, JCB, MC, V.* [$][$][$][$][$]

In this outpost of traditional French cuisine, you will be professionally served classic dishes against a faux-rustic background of half-timbered walls. There is a beautiful mural of coastal France at the back. The upscale clientele appreciate one of the city's most extensive wine lists.

Jo Jo

160 E 64th St. **Map** 13 A2. ☎ *223-5656.* ***Open*** *noon–2:30pm, 6–11:30pm Mon–Sat.* 🚭 🍷 💳 *AE, MC, V.* [$][$][$][$]

Jo Jo is the creation of chef Jean-Georges Vongerichten, formerly of Restaurant Lafayette, and is set in a Parisian-style town house. If you like to eat in peace, ask to be seated upstairs in the vaguely Victorian parlor. The restaurant downstairs is much livelier and noisier. Fans of Vongerichten's modern cooking, with its inventive combinations at some surprisingly low prices, always fill the place up. There is a well-priced wine list and a prix-fixe lunch menu.

Lutèce

249 E 50th St. **Map** 13 B4.
【 752-2225. **Open** noon–2pm Tue–Fri, 6–10pm Mon–Sat. **Closed** Aug, some hols. 🖾 🍴 ♿ 🍷 🍺 ★ 🗩 AE, DC, JCB, MC. $$$$$

Trendy restaurants may come and go, but Lutèce is always popular. The clue to its continued success may be that its proprietor, André Soltner, and his staff treat first-timers with the same warmth as they show the well-heeled regulars. You can eat in the casual garden room, which has slate floors and latticework walls, or in the more formal upstairs dining room, with patterned walls and paintings. The wonderful food comprises many hearty, Alsatian-accented dishes. Don't miss the apple tart. The prix-fixe menu makes an occasional splurge possible.

La Métairie

189 W 10th St. **Map** 3 C2.
【 989-0343. **Open** noon–midnight daily. 🖾 ♿ 🍷 🍺 🗩 AE, DC, MC, V. $$$$

You may feel that this tiny rather crowded bistro, with room for only 20 customers, has tried too hard to be charming. It sports Dutch doors, white shutters and farm implements (a *métairie* is a small farm). However, the food is good, if not spectacular, robust French country fare, seasoned with plenty of garlic.

Montrachet

239 W Broadway. **Map** 4 E5.
【 219-2777. **Open** noon–2pm Fri, 6–10pm Mon–Thu, 6–11pm Fri, Sat. 🖾 🍴 🥗 ♿ 🍺 ★ 🗩 AE. $$$$

This restaurant is delightfully un-pretentious for one of New York's premier restaurants. Montrachet has a nondescript exterior that leads into three large high-ceilinged dining rooms (one for private parties) that are pleasant and spacious but hardly awe-inspiring. Once the food arrives, however, you'll find the decor of little consequence. Take your time choosing, for the menu offers a panoply of inventive, contemporary French dishes – game is especially good. Desserts must be sampled. A large French-cum-California wine list is as well-priced as the food for the quality. Lunch is served on Fridays only.

Le Périgord

405 E 52nd St. **Map** 13 C4.
【 755-6244. **Open** noon–3pm & 5:30–10:30pm Mon–Sat. **Closed** some hols. 🖾 🍴 🍷 🍺 🗩 AE, DC, MC, V. $$$$$

This established restaurant is a favorite of UN people who appreciate impeccably prepared dishes, such as pheasant breast on cabbage with juniper berries or snapper in lobster sauce. Rose-colored walls, fresh flowers, soft lighting and a low noise level allow for intimate dining.

Provence

38 MacDougal St. **Map** 4 D3.
【 475-7500. **Open** noon–3pm & 6–11:30pm daily. **Closed** some hols. 🖾 🥗 🍷 🍺 🗩 AE, MC, V. $$$

Provence is a well-priced bistro in a pleasant Greenwich Village spot. Pale-yellow walls, dried flowers and a garden for warm-weather dining all suggest Provence, France, an impression strongly enhanced by a menu of roasted eggplant tartlets, *bouillabaisse* (fish soup), roast lamb served with ratatouille and many other southern French favorites.

The Rainbow Room

GE Building, 65th floor, 30 Rockefeller Plaza. **Map** 12 F5.
【 632-5000. **Open** 5:30pm–1am Tue–Sat, 5:30–10:30pm Sun. 🖾 🍴 🥗 🥗 ♿ 🍷 🍺 ★ 🗩 AE. $$$$$

From this pinnacle, superb views cover the entire city. This is one of New York's most magical and luxurious places, where the food matches the atmosphere and you can dance to a live band – for a hefty price, of course.

Raoul's

180 Prince St. **Map** 4 D3.
【 966-3518. **Open** 6–11:30pm Sun–Thu, 6pm–2am Fri, Sat. **Closed** Thanksgiving, Christmas days. 🖾 🍴 🥗 🥗 🍺 🗩 AE, MC, V. $$$$

Raoul's is about as authentic a French bistro as you'll find in New York. Its pressed-tin ceiling, dark interior and chalkboard menu (which is changed daily) lend a cozy neighborhood feel. But what keeps artists and other habitués coming back is reliable, informal food, like the steak au poivre. It is pricier than a Parisienne counter-part might be. Raoul's on Varick Street (phone: 929-1630) is a bigger, brassier version with similar fare.

Le Régence

Hotel Plaza Athénée, 37 E 64th St. **Map** 13 A2. 【 606-4647. **Open** noon–2:30pm & 6–9:30pm daily. 🖾 🍴 ♿ 🍷 🗩 AE, DC, MC, V. $$$$$

The chandeliers and the cloud-painted ceiling are grandiose and a little misleading. The dishes are prepared with modern flair and inventiveness, making this one of the more memorable French restaurants. It is expensive, and there is a prix-fixe dinner menu.

The Terrace

400 W 119th St. **Map** 20 F3.
【 666-9490. **Open** noon–2:30pm & 6–10pm Tue–Sat. 🖾 🍴 🎵 🎵 🍺 🗩 AE, DC, MC, V. $$$$

Although this place is overpriced and over-praised, what redeems everything is the breathtaking view. Service can be erratic, but the setting invites lovers with its candlelit tables and ambitious French menu. Taxi back and forth, as the neighborhood is dubious.

ITALIAN

Italian restaurants vie with Chinese for being the most popular with New Yorkers, as well as the most prolific. Little Italy and Greenwich Village have long been strong-holds of southern Italian cooking, but northern Italian cuisine has recently become increasingly popular, and restaurants featuring it have blossomed in every part of the city. The main difference is that southern cuisine consists of hearty, more peasant-style food, while northern cuisine is more sophisticated. Another difference is price; southern Italian restaurants range from cheap to moderate, northern ones from moderate to expensive.

In southern Italian restaurants you may find Formica-topped tables and waiters on firstname terms with customers in a cheerful, noisy atmosphere. The food will usually feature soups, many shrimp and veal main courses, vegetable dishes such as *eggplant parmigiana* (eggplant, cheese and tomato sauce), ubiquitous *marinara* (tomato sauce), *fra diavolo* (red pepper), rich tomato-based sauces and deep-fried mozzarella.

Northern Italian restaurants are often more formal, elegant and pricy. They feature a variety of pastas in rich cream and cheese sauces, polenta, gnocchi, risotto, venison, game birds, truffles, many kinds of wild mushrooms, diverse herbs and such breads as foccacia and bruschetta.

For key to symbols *see p285*.

Bice

7 E 54th St. **Map** 12 F4.
(688-1999. **Open** noon–11pm,
daily. 🍴 🚻 ♿ 🌿 AE, DC, MC, V.
$$$$

A magnet for the rich and famous,
this offspring of Milan's Bice has
been packed since its sleek Art
Deco interior was opened in 1987.
The northern Italian food is light
with freshly made pastas, such as
lobster ravioli or pasta with quail
and arugula. The bill is usually as
heady as the ambience.

Carmine's

2450 Broadway. **Map** 15 C2.
(362-2200. **Open** 5–11pm
Mon–Thu, 5pm–midnight Fri & Sat,
2–10pm Sun. **Closed** Thanksgiving,
Christmas. 🍴 🧒 ♿ 🌿 AE.
$$$

Carmine's is the sort of southern
Italian restaurant that you would
expect to find in Little Italy, and it
has all the casualness of its Upper
West Side neighborhood. This
lively, cavernous Sicilian restaurant
is best enjoyed by groups; single
portions could feed armies of
people. It is very popular with
families who like plates piled high
with good food for relatively little
money – and who don't mind an
uneven culinary performance.

Cent' Anni

50 Carmine St. **Map** 4 D3.
(989-9494. **Open** noon–2:30pm,
5:30–11pm Mon–Thu, noon–2:30pm
& 5:30–11:30pm Fri, 5:30–11:30pm
Sat, 5–10:30pm Sun. **Closed** New
Year's Day, 10 days in July, Christmas.
🍴 V ♿ 🍷 🌿 AE. $$$$

This West Village favorite earns
good reviews for its robust
Florentine-style food and unusual
Tuscan vintages at pretty reasonable
prices – unfortunately, you'll also
find erratic service, crowds and
high noise levels. But for a classic
Village experience, it's fine.

Coco Pazzo

23 E 74th St. **Map** 16 F5.
(794-0205. **Open** noon–3pm &
6–11:30pm daily. **Closed** one wk
Aug. 🍴 V ♿ 🍷 🌿 AE, MC, V.
$$$$

This trendy hit with the "beautiful
people" is a contemporary ivory-
walled trattoria, part of the Le
Madri stable of stylish upscale
Italian restaurants. The tables are
close together, the resulting noise
level can often become distracting,
and service is sometimes slow, but
these points should not deter the
dedicated diner from the
remarkable risotto with seafood,

plus an assortment of robust,
delicious and mostly northern
specialties.

Contrapunto

200 E 60th St. **Map** 13 B3.
(751-8616. **Open** noon–
11:45pm Mon–Sat, 3–11pm Sun. 🍴
V AE, DC, MC, V. $$

Noisy, almost frenzied on weekends, this all-white pasta restaurant
is a favorite stop with shoppers
from Bloomingdale's, despite long
waits for tables in rush hours –
reservations are not taken here. A
wide selection of pasta offers
tasty choices at fair prices for the
neighborhood. The dishes,
especially the seafood, are almost
good enough to overlook the
often amateurish service.

Da Umberto

107 W 17th St. **Map** 8 E5.
(989-0303. **Open** noon–3pm
Mon–Fri, 5:30–11pm Mon–Sat.
Closed New Year's Day, Christmas.
🍴 🌿 AE. $$$$

In a tawny, softly lit front dining
room and an airier skylit one in
the rear, which is probably the
brighter lunch choice, hearty
Florentine fare, strong on game and
roasts, is served. You can watch
through windows as hefty
portions of baked pheasant with
herbs, veal chops and pork
studded with garlic are dished up
in the kitchen. The food is worth
the price.

Elaine's

1703 Second Ave. **Map** 17 B3.
(534-8103. **Open** 5:30pm–2am
daily. **Closed** New Year's Day,
Thanksgiving, Christmas. 🍴 🎹
piano Fri, Sat. 🌿 AE, MC, V.
$$$$

Only the star-struck will make the
trek to this celebrity hangout.
Otherwise, the routine Italian fare
could be considered much too
expensive to bother – but then,
nobody goes for the food. Try to
get a table as near to Elaine's as
possible to watch all the meeting
and greeting that goes on there.

Felidia

243 E 58th St. **Map** 13 B3.
(758-1479. **Open** noon–2:30pm
& 5–11pm Mon–Fri, 5pm–midnight
Sat. V 🍷 🍴 🌿 AE, DC, MC, V.
$$$$

Dinner in this much-acclaimed
restaurant is comfortably rustic,
with rows of brightly polished
copper pots, partial brick walls
and open wine racks. The Italian
regional food derives mostly from

Trieste, with such dishes as the
popular gnocchi all'Ortolana
(potato dumplings with fresh
herbs and vegetables), fresh pasta
with wild mushrooms and a
delicious mixed mushroom risotto.

Le Madri

168 W 18th St. **Map** 8 E5.
(727-8022. **Open** noon–3pm
daily, 6–12:30pm Mon–Sat,
5–10:30pm Sun. **Closed** one wk Sep.
🍴 V 🍷 🍴 ★ 🌿 AE, MC, V.
$$$$

Named after the female cooks,
"the mothers," who turn out some
of the most exquisite northern
Italian food in the entire city, this
is currently one of New York's
most fashionable restaurants. The
dining room is so understated it's
almost glum, saved only by
several witty food sculptures by
Gerd Verschoor, who also made
the unusual Leaning Tower of
Foccacia that is stacked in the bar.
Quail with red peppers and
sausage is just one of the many
culinary triumphs on the menu,
and the vegetarian dishes are
always highly recommended.

Mamma Leone's

261 W 44th St. **Map** 12 D5.
(586-5151. **Open** 7–10:30am &
11:30–10:45pm Mon–Sat, noon–3pm
& 4–10pm Sun. 🍴 🍱 V 🍴 ♿
🎵 🌿 AE, DC, MC, V. $$$$

Broadway's prime tourist trap is
still going strong, even though it
has moved to a new location. But
there are only two real reasons to
decide to have a meal here: the
extraordinary Neapolitan decor,
which has to be seen to be
believed, and the massive portions
of southern Italian food served at
moderate prices.

Il Mulino

86 W 3rd St. **Map** 4 D3.
(673-3783. **Open** noon–2:30pm
Mon–Fri, 5–11:30pm Mon–Sat.
Closed July, some hols.
🍴 V 🍴 🍷 🌿 AE. $$$$

Almost too dark at dinner, Il
Mulino's exposed brick walls, bent-
wood chairs and cramped quarters
seem more agreeable at lunch
since there are fewer customers
then. Aficionados, however, love
the lagniappe (small appetizer) of
delicious fried zucchini, served the
minute you sit down. Less
agreeable is the long wait at the
bar before you are seated, even if
you have reservations. Pasta
dishes are among the specialties
covering Italy's culinary map.
Many consider this the Village's
best Italian choice.

Il Nido

251 E 53rd St. **Map** 13 B4.
☎ *753-8450.* ***Open*** *noon-3pm & 5:30-11pm Mon-Sat.* ***Closed*** *July 4th, Thanksgiving, Christmas.* 🚭 [V] 🚸 [T] 💳 *AE, DC, MC, V.* $$$

One of the earliest northern Italian restaurants to set up in New York, Il Nido has been overshadowed recently by newer stars. Its charming Tuscan farmhouse interior prepares you for the many delicious dishes, like the risotto Nido and grilled scampi with anchovy caper sauce. For the upscale clientele, dining here is a fairly dressy affair.

Orso

322 W 46th St. **Map** 12 D5.
☎ *489-7212.* ***Open*** *noon–midnight Sun–Tue, Thu, Fri, 11:30am–midnight Wed, Sat.* ***Closed*** *Christmas Day.* 🚭 [V] 💳 *MC, V.* $$$

Orso is popular with journalists, theater people and their agents. It is convenient for Broadway; has a cheerful decor, with an open kitchen and a skylight; has large pizzas and other Italian standbys, plus a respectable Italian wine list. The menu is limited but has enough choices, especially pastas, at medium-range prices.

Palio

151 W 51st St. **Map** 12 E4.
☎ *245-4850.* ***Open*** *noon–2:30pm Mon–Fri, 5:30–11pm Mon–Sat.* ***Closed*** *some hols.* 🚭 🍴 [V] ♿ [T] 🍷 💳 *AE, DC, MC, V.* $$$$$

Palio is a favorite of elegant Broadwayites and workers in the Equitable Assurance Tower, in which the restaurant is located. The restaurant has a popular street-level bar with a vivid 124-foot-long, wraparound mural of Siena's famous Palio (horse-race festival) by Sandro Chia. Upstairs, the dining room is pretty, though the quality of the northern Italian food can be uneven – superb one evening, pedestrian the next. You can, however, always count on a pleasant quick lunch at the bar. A pretheater menu is available, too.

Rao's

455 E 114th St. **Map** 22 E3.
☎ *722-6709.* ***Open*** *7pm–9:30pm daily.* ***Closed*** *some hols, last wk Aug–1st wk Sep.* $$$$

To eat at Rao's, expect at least a two- to three-month wait on the reservations list. On the big evening, take a taxi, since finding the place can be difficult, though you will recognize it by the many Christmas tree lights that twinkle year-round as the main decoration on what seems from the outside just a corner bar in a shabby neighborhood. Once inside, you will find eight tables set against dark well-varnished wood walls behind a long bar. After all the waiting and effort to get to eat here, you'll find the southern Italian food both pleasant and unmemorable.

Remi

145 W 53rd St. **Map** 12 E4.
☎ *581-4242.* ***Open*** *11:45am–2:30pm & 5:30–11:30pm daily.* ***Closed*** *Thanksgiving, Christmas days.* 🚭 ♿ 🏨 🍷 💳 *AE, DC, MC, V.* $$$$

For dealmakers at lunch and the pre- and posttheater crowd at dinner, this lively, noisy restaurant is the place to be seen. There is a mural of Venice, reddish Brazilian maple floors with stripes of birch, comfortable chairs and banquettes, plus a glass wall facing a flowered arcade. The service is attentive and the northern Italian food first rate, prepared with panache. Desserts are stunning too, as is the lengthy Italian wine list, which includes more than four dozen types of grappa.

San Domenico

240 Central Park South. **Map** 12 E3.
☎ *459-9016.* ***Open*** *11:30am–2.30pm & 5:30–11:30pm daily.* 🚭 [V] ♿ [T] 🍷 ★ 💳 *AE, DC, MC, V.* $$$$$

Soft lighting, Florentine terra-cotta floors, well-spaced tables, supple leather chairs and impeccable service make this a luxurious and romantic setting for some of the best and most imaginative northern Italian food in town. San Domenico is arguably New York's best Italian restaurant. Grilled eel in vine leaves with balsamic vinegar is one of many superlative examples. A well-priced pretheater menu is available.

Siracusa

65 Fourth Ave. **Map** 4 F1.
☎ *254-1940.* ***Open*** *noon–11pm Mon–Sat.* 🚭 ♿ 💳 *AE.* $$$

A reliable choice, handy for the Public Theater and Cooper Union, therefore favored by theater types. This very well-established neighborhood Italian grocery has embellished its plain wood walls with Sicilian puppets and other Italian ornaments. The menu is short, with pastas featuring heavily, and the gelato is probably the best in the city. Prices aren't cheap.

Trattoria dell'Arte

900 Seventh Ave. **Map** 12 E3.
☎ *245-9800.* ***Open*** *noon–2:30pm daily, 5–11:30pm Mon–Sat, 5–10:30pm Sun.* ***Closed*** *Christmas Day.* 🚭 [V] 🏨 💳 *AE, MC, V.* $$$$

The two main advantages here, according to the Carnegie Hall – going clientele, are the bright, clever Milton Glaser interior designs and what is surely the biggest antipasto bar in the city. Share an amazingly well-priced platter of delicious antipasto items, enjoy the exuberant decor, then head across the street for the music. The rest of the menu, even the pizza, is uninspired.

CHINESE

Chinese restaurants are as numerous as Italian ones in New York. They range from take-out outlets and cheap hole-in-the-wall eateries – found in almost every neighborhood but extensively throughout Chinatown – to formal, very expensive restaurants, mostly located in midtown or on the Upper East Side. For a visitor on a tight budget, having a Chinese meal is probably the cheapest option.

Many of the Chinese restaurants in New York are of the chop-suey/chow-mein variety, Americanized for decades. The better Chinese restaurants are as good as any to be found outside Hong Kong and China. A large local Chinese population has created a much more demanding clientele. In general, by far the most authentic restaurants are in Chinatown; uptown restaurants tend to be more chic, serving, in some instances, nouvelle Chinese Westernized fare.

Szechuan and Hunan cooking swept New York in the early 1980s, creating a demand for the hot, sour and peppery cuisines of those regions of China. Of late, New Yorkers have become more interested in the delicacy and subtlety of Cantonese cooking. Most Chinese restaurants have large menus featuring a variety of regional dishes, so you can sample both spicy and mild. Desserts at a Chinese restaurant are limited, usually to ice cream, lychee nuts or pineapple.

Dim sum (which are small steamed or fried dumplings and other nibbles) are mainly served in Chinatown on weekend mornings and early afternoons and treated as a Chinese brunch. Diners choose their dishes from a trolley wheeled from table to table, generally drinking tea as an accompaniment.

For key to symbols *see p285.*

Bo Ky

80 Bayard St. **Map** 4 F5.
☎ *406-2292.* ***Open*** *8am–9:30pm daily.* ***Closed*** *two days Chinese New Year.* 🚭 🍴 👪 ♿ $

This Chinese restaurant is noisy and bustling; if there's a line, don't worry, it always moves quickly. Tables are shared, and the waiters speak only limited English. The many seafood noodle dishes and good soups are cheap, filling and delicious. The Vietnamese dishes are often the best items.

Canton

45 Division St. **Map** 5 A5.
☎ *226-4441.* ***Open*** *noon–10pm Wed–Thu, noon–11pm Fri & Sat, noon–9:30pm Sun.* ***Closed*** *4 weeks mid-July–mid-August.* 🚭 $$

The Canton offers better standards than usually found in Chinatown restaurants, in decor, service and food. Prices are higher, too, but its ardent uptown fans think it's worth paying the extra, especially for the seafood dishes. It has no alcohol license, but you can bring your own. No credit cards are accepted. Ask what the chef or waiting staff would recommend, since not all the dishes are written in English on the menu.

Chin Chin

216 E 49th St. **Map** 13 B5.
☎ *888-4555.* ***Open*** *11:30am–midnight daily.* 🚭 🍴 [V] 👪 ⛱ 🍷 💳 *AE, DC, MC, V.* $$$

Chin Chin is an upscale Chinese restaurant with understated Western decor, offering a very wide range of dishes from all over China. A number of offbeat items, such as snails with coriander and garlic broth as well as shredded roasted duck salad are usually on the menu. Or try the tea-smoked duck with spring onion pancake. Most of the dishes have a Western accent.

Golden Unicorn

18 E Broadway. **Map** 5 A5.
☎ *941-0911.* ***Open*** *8am–midnight daily.* 🚭 🍴 👪 💳 *AE, MC, V.* $$$

In this attractive, mirrored, two-story Hong Kong–style palace with a loyal clientele, you can get delicious dim sum and other authentic Cantonese food. Chinese families tend to form a majority of the diners, which is always a good sign. However, you also get noise, crowds and staff outfitted with walkie-talkies. You should try the delicious shark-fin dumpling in fragrant broth.

Hwa Yuan Szechuan Inn

236 E 53rd St. **Map** 13 B4.
☎ *355-5096.* ***Open*** *11:30am–11pm Mon–Thu, noon–11pm Fri–Sun.* 🚭 👪 💳 *AE, DC, MC, V.* $

Steer clear of the tourist menu here, as well as most of the Cantonese dishes and the many "chef specials," and choose only the Szechuan dishes. If, however, you want your food really hot, you'll have to be emphatic; as the menu markings for hot and spicy don't mean much. Prices are cheap to moderate.

Ollie's Noodle Shop & Grill

2315 Broadway. **Map** 15 C4.
☎ *362-3111.* ***Open*** *11:30am–midnight Sun–Thu, 11:30am–1am Fri, Sat.* ***Closed*** *Thanksgiving.* 🚭 👪 💳 *AE, MC, V.* $$

In this plain luncheonette-type noodle restaurant, the many different soups available, with wontons, vegetables, meats and/or seafood, are hearty, satisfying and budget-friendly.

Oriental Garden

14 Elizabeth St. **Map** 4 F5.
☎ *619-0085.* ***Open*** *8:30am–2am daily.* 🚭 👪 💳 *AE MC V.* $$

You will have to share Formica-topped tables with strangers in this packed restaurant and suffer the occasionally abusive waiter and the dreary surroundings, but don't let this put you off – the seafood is Chinatown's best. Cantonese dishes are good, too.

Pig Heaven

1540 Second Ave. **Map** 17 B4.
☎ *744-4333.* ***Open*** *11:30am–midnight daily.* 🚭 👪 ♿ 💳 *AE, DC, MC, V.* $$$

A firm favorite for its reliable and delicious Cantonese dishes, Pig Heaven specializes in pork, especially suckling pig. You can also eat duck, chicken or vegetable dishes here. The all-pink, all-pig decor is too cute for words.

Shun Lee Palace

155 E 55th St. **Map** 13 A4.
☎ *371-8844.* ***Open*** *noon–11pm daily.* ***Closed*** *Thanksgiving.* 🚭 ♿ 👔 💳 *AE, DC, MC, V.* $$$$

In the forefront of East Side Chinese chic for more than 20 years, this popular place has some devoted fans. It is spacious and elegant, with subtle, landscaped screens – there are no gilded dragons or other classic Chinese restaurant glitz here. The menu comprises slightly fancified Cantonese and Szechuan dishes; the wine list is long for a Chinese restaurant, and prices are very fair for the neighborhood.

Shun Lee West

43 W 65th St. **Map** 11 D2.
☎ *595-8895.* ***Open*** *noon–midnight daily.* ***Closed*** *Thanksgiving.* 🚭 [V] ♿ 💳 *AE DC, MC, V.* $$$

Handy for Lincoln Center, this West Side cousin of Shun Lee Palace has a devoted clientele, though both food and service can be uneven, especially at peak times. At their best, the Szechuan dishes have real sizzle and snap, with many regional winners, such as softshell crab in black-bean sauce, lobster in Szechuan sauce and a really delicious dish of shredded Szechuan beef.

Zen Palate

663 Ninth Ave. **Map** 12 D5.
☎ *582-1669.* ***Open*** *11:30am–10:45pm Sun–Thu & Sat, 11:30am–11pm Fri, Sat.* 🚭 [V] ♿ 💳 *AE, MC, V.* $$

A first for the Theater District: Zen Palate is a stylish vegetarian restaurant where original Chinese-accented vegetarian dishes are served with great elan. Travelers will also catch echoes of Japan and Indonesia in some of the tofu and other interesting dishes.

JAPANESE

Japanese restaurants are second in number to Chinese among Oriental restaurants in New York and serve perhaps the best Japanese food this side of Tokyo. Most are located in the midtown area and serve traditional dishes, such as sukiyaki (vegetables and meat stir-fried, then simmered), tempura (vegetables or seafood deep-fried in light batter) and teriyaki (meat or other foods marinaded several times in soy sauce, sweet rice wine and sugar, dried, then grilled). Many have sushi bars (see below) in the front or rear, where you can see the assortment of fresh uncooked seafood and choose accordingly. Sushi (cooked, vinegared rice wrapped around raw fish or lightly cooked shrimp) and sashimi (raw fish accompanied by a dip of soy, ginger and wasabi, Japanese horseradish) have become very popular and are always eaten with chopsticks. Some places offer traditional seating on tatami mats on the floor.

Hatsuhana

17 E 48th St. **Map** 12 F5. ☎ *355-3345.* ***Open*** *11:45am–2:45pm & 5:30–10pm Mon–Fri, 5–10pm Sat.* 🚭 🍽 💳 *AE, DC, MC, V.* $$$.

Just why this Japanese sushi and sashimi restaurant is so revered and so crowded may not seem apparent at first glance. However, connoisseurs have long since realized the sushi is some of the freshest and most varied in town. The best seats in the house are at the sushi bar, where you can watch the skilled chefs at work.

Honmura An

170 Mercer St. **Map** 4 E3. ☎ *334-5253.* ***Open*** *noon–2:30pm Wed–Sat, 6–10pm Tue–Thu & 6–10:30pm Fri, Sat, 6–9:30pm Sun.* ***Closed*** *1st week Jan, July 4 weekend, Labor Day weekend.* 🚭 🍽 [V] 💳 *AE, DC, MC, V.* $$$

Honmura An is new and elegant, and not just by noodle house standards. It sets a high level of stylishness, with service and food to match. House specialties are mostly *soba* (noodle) dishes.

Inagiku

Waldorf–Astoria Hotel, 301 Park Ave. **Map** 13 A5. ☎ *355-0440.* ***Open*** *noon–2:30pm Mon–Fri, 5:30–10pm daily.* ***Closed*** *some hols.* 🚭 ♿ 💳 *AE, DC, JCB, MC, V.* $$$$

With its tasteful, formal Japanese decor, Inagiku is possibly the most beautiful of its kind in town. Tempura, its specialty, is excellent, but if you're feeling rich order a Kaiseki ten-course classical dinner. This is a traditional and formal meal comprising set courses in the following order: clear soup, appetizer, a simmered dish, a grilled dish, a meat dish, vegetables, a large fried dish, boiled rice, an assortment of vinegared vegetables, miso soup and tea. The large selection of ingredients is seasonal.

Iso

175 Second Ave. **Map** 4 F1. ☎ *777-0361.* ***Open*** *5:30pm–midnight daily.* ***Closed*** *some hols, one week summer.* 🚭 🍽 💳 *AE, DC, MC, V.* $$$

Iso has contemporary art on the walls; the freshest, most inventive sushi and other seafood on the plates; and an East Village, warm ambience. Staff are friendly and prices not too high for the neighborhood. The teriyaki is also highly recommended.

Mitsukoshi

461 Park Ave. **Map** 13 A3. ☎ *935-6444.* ***Open*** *noon–2pm & 5:30–10pm Mon–Sat.* ***Closed*** *some hols.* 🚭 ♿ ♫ 💳 *AE, DC, MC, V.* $$$$

Elegant and very expensive, Mitsukoshi has several dining areas, including traditional tatami mat rooms – where you sit on a mat on the floor – and a highly popular sushi bar. It is located in the basement of a big Japanese department store and is decorated to give the restaurant a simple and traditional Japanese look. It also has some of the freshest, most varied and very best sushi/sashimi in town. Customers just keep on coming back for more, despite the high prices.

Sushisay

38 E 51st St. **Map** 13 A4. ☎ *755-1780.* ***Open*** *noon–2:15pm & 5:30–10:15pm Mon–Fri, 5–9pm Sat.* 🚭 💳 *AE, DC, MC, V.* $$$

This quietly understated and calm Japanese-style dining room is just below street level. Sushi and sashimi are the best choices here, especially at the always-crowded sushi bar, where you can sit and pick out your favorites from the display. Service is cheerful and friendly but can be slow, and the dishes on the regular menu are more humdrum.

Southeast Asian

Traditional Thai cuisine has become increasingly popular in America during the past five years, but by far the best Thai restaurants are actually found in other large cities in the US, such as Los Angeles. Thai restaurants in New York tend to be modest and tiny places where the dishes are authentically spicy and inexpensive. Thai cuisine is best known for its emphasis on the hot, sweet, sour and salty qualities of the varied dishes. The ingredients most commonly used are lemon grass, galanga (similar to ginger root), kafir lime leaves, tamarind, garlic, fresh coriander and hot chili oil. Thai curries are markedly different from the well-known Indian curries in that they are spicier and more delicate at the same time. One of the best accompaniments to this type of meal is to drink traditional Thai beer.

Vietnamese cuisine is slowly becoming more popular and combines a few elements of Thai with those of Chinese. It is delicate and spicy, but not as spicy as Thai.

Bangkok House

1485 First Ave. **Map** 17 C5. ☎ *249-5700.* ***Open*** *5–11pm Mon–Thu & Sun, 5–11:30pm Fri & Sat.* 🚭 💳 *AE, MC, V.* $$

You will find authentic spicy-hot Thai food in Bangkok House's pleasant and relaxed setting of spacious tables and comfortable chairs, enhanced by a helpful staff. Relatively inexpensive for the neighborhood, the prices are still on the high side.

Saigon

89-91 Mulberry St. **Map** 4 F5. ☎ *227-8825.* ***Open*** *11:30am–10:30pm Sun–Thu, 11:30am–11pm Fri & Sat.* 🚭 [V] 🚸 💳 *AE, DC, MC, V.* $$

There's nothing fancy in this simple, light, bright setting, but the authentic Vietnamese food has flair and authority, attracting legal eagles from courthouses in the neighborhood. The low prices reflect the restaurant's downtown location. Soups and seafood are the high points. There's a second branch, Saigon Seafood Restaurant II, at 89–91 Bayard Street (phone 732-8988), which serves similar dishes but places more emphasis on seafood.

Siam Inn Too

854 Eighth Ave. **Map** 12 D4. ☎ *489-5237.* ***Open*** *noon–3pm Mon–Fri, 5–11:30pm daily.* 🚭 [V] ♿ 💳 *AE, DC.* $

The decor is just a notch above the diner level in this tiny, crowded restaurant, but the authentic food compensates, and the prices are right. Hot, fresh, spicy Thai dishes are served in generous portions by friendly staff. *Pla lad prig* (deep-fried sea bass in chili-garlic sauce) is one of many very good dishes. The other branch is called Siam Inn Two on Eighth Avenue (phone 757-4006).

Tommy Tang's

323 Greenwich St. **Map** 1 B1. ☎ *334-9190.* ***Open*** *noon–2:30pm Mon–Fri, 6–10:30pm Mon–Thu, Sun, 6–11pm Fri, Sat.* 🚭 [V] 🚸 💳 *AE, DC, MC, V.* $$$

"Pop Thai" it's been called, but the Westernized Thai cuisine at Tommy Tang's appeals to both the trendy TriBeCa crowd and many tourists. The attractive decor is cool, blue and restful; the dining room is cavernous and noisy; the prices are upmarket. Try the Malaysian clams sautéed with roasted chili paste or the spicy mint noodles with beef.

For key to symbols *see p285.*

Indian and Afghan

Indian restaurants in New York have only recently become more adventurous, and they still have some way to go to match the standard of Indian restaurants in London, for example. Even so, they present some of the best dining-out values in the city. Most Indian menus feature curries and other dishes of lamb, chicken, shrimp and vegetables. Indeed, due to New York's scarcity of pure vegetarian restaurants, Indian restaurants make a terrific substitute. Some restaurants have tandoori ovens and specialize in chicken dishes and breads cooked in the oven's dry heat. While most Indian restaurants have alcohol licenses, the best drink with a meal is Indian beer. For non-drinkers, a yoghurt-based drink called lassi is a good substitute — mango lassi makes a refreshing alternative to traditional desserts, which are too sweet for Western palates.

There are only a few Afghan places in New York, also reasonably priced and informal. The food is similar to Indian, but less spicy and less diverse, though with some good variations on Indian cuisine.

Afghan Kebab House

764 Ninth Ave. **Map** 12 D4.
☎ *307-1612.* ***Open*** *noon–10pm daily.* 🍽 ♿ $

This is one of a chain of Afghan Kebab House restaurants offering remarkable value and zesty Afghan fare, especially their kebabs. The menu is slightly different at each site, but tiny space and minimal decor prevail at all. None of the three holds an alcohol license, but you can bring your own bottle. The other two restaurants are Afghan Kebab House II at 1345 Second Avenue (phone 517-2776); and Afghan Kebab House III at 155 West 46th Street (phone 768-3875).

Akbar

475 Park Ave. **Map** 13 A3.
☎ *838-1717.* ***Open*** *5–11pm daily.* 🚭 [V] 🍽 🧒 ♿ 💳 *AE, DC, MC, V.* $$

The all-white decor at Akbar makes a cool backdrop for reliably spicy Indian dishes and excellent breads. Well-seasoned tandoori-cooked and other properly spiced specialties make up for sometimes slow, neutral service. The prices are reasonable considering the location; the lunch buffets are a great value. Another branch is at 256 East 49th Street (phone 755-9100). The Park Avenue Akbar is consistently better.

Darbar

44 W 56th St. **Map** 12 F3.
☎ *265-1850.* ***Open*** *noon–3pm daily, 5:30–11pm Mon–Thu, 5:30–11:30pm Fri & Sat, 5:30–10:30pm Sun.* 🚭 [V] 🧒 ♿ 💳 *AE, DC, MC, V.* $$$$

At Darbar, consistently reliable, well-seasoned northern Indian food is served in surroundings congenial to privacy. The restaurant is multilevel and handsome. Try the generous lunchtime buffet and the fine vegetarian dishes.

Dawat

210 E 58th St. **Map** 13 B3.
☎ *355-7555.* ***Open*** *11:30am–3pm Mon–Sat, 5:30–11pm Sun–Thu, 5:30–11:30pm Fri & Sat.* 🚭 🍽 [V] ♿ 💳 *AE, DC, MC, V.* $$$

The imprimatur of famous Indian food writer Madhur Jaffrey, who acts as a consultant, is all over this Indian menu, which features hot food in a pale-apricot decor. Unusual and exquisitely seasoned dishes are the hallmark here. The surprise is the moderate cost for such originality, including a wide vegetarian choice that you won't see in most other Indian restaurants in New York.

Jewel of India

15 W 44th St. **Map** 12 F5.
☎ *869-5544.* ***Open*** *noon–3pm, 5:30–11pm daily.* 🍽 [V] ♿ 💳 *AE, DC, MC, V.* $ $

The location of this restaurant couldn't be handier for theater-goers or midtown shoppers: just west of Fifth Avenue. But step inside and you're far east of Suez... in north India to be exact. Service is as Indian as the decor, and the spicy, well-seasoned food is Indian to the core. While the tandoori and other à la carte dishes are well priced, the best deals here are the prix fixe dinner, lunch buffet and business lunch. There are also delicious free nibbles available during happy hour.

Pamir

1437 Second Ave. **Map** 17 B5.
☎ *734-3791. Open 5–11pm Tue–Sun.* 🚭 [V] ♿ 💳 *MC, V.* $$

Afghan food is still something of a novelty in New York, but this modest, well-priced place has built a following for its reliable lamb dishes, kebabs and yoghurt sauces. Service is friendly; the setting is cozy, but sometimes there are long waits for a table on the weekends. However, most customers feel that the food is worth the wait.

European and Middle Eastern

If you look hard enough, you might find any national cuisine in New York, but not necessarily in large numbers. The following are a few of the best in a range of European and Middle Eastern cuisines. Mediterranean cooking in general relies on fresh seafood, grilled meats, tomatoes, olives, peppers, garlic, olive oil and herbs. In most Greek restaurants, for example, you'll find peppers, salads with feta cheese, stuffed eggplants, *dolmadhakia* (stuffed vine leaves), roast lamb, seafood dishes, *spanakopitta* (spinach pie baked in filo pastry) and honeyed sweets like baklava. Moroccan cooks create such dishes as chicken or lamb roasted with prunes or figs and almonds, plus*couscous* (a semolina-like grain with a hearty meat-and-vegetable stew).

There are very few northern European restaurants in New York. Scandinavian restaurants specialize in seafood and tend to be formal and pricey. Russian and Jewish/Romanian restaurants are informal on the whole, though not inexpensive. (For Jewish kosher specialties, *see* Delis, *p304*.)

Aquavit

13 W 54th St. **Map** 12 F4.
☎ *307-7311.* ***Open*** *noon–3pm & 5:30–10:30pm Mon–Fri, 5:30–10:30pm Sat.* 🚭 🍽 [V] [T] 🍷 💳 *AE, DC, MC, V.* $$$$$

This was once Nelson Rockefeller's town house and now belongs to Unibank. It has become one of New York's most arresting restaurants specializing in Scandinavian cuisine. Ask to sit in the Atrium, the main dining room, which is an eight-story glass-topped atrium with a waterfall and decorative kites overhead facing the huge windows of the bar. A must is the smorgasbord plate appetizer (samples of the traditional five courses of pickled herring and potatoes; salmon, eels or sardines; hot beef, reindeer or liver paste; salad, fruit, cheese or vegetables). Seafood and game are always on the menu, with Arctic venison especially good. Lighter, cheaper fare is available upstairs at Café Aquavit, overlooking the Atrium.

Moroccan Star

205 Atlantic Ave, Brooklyn.
☎ *643-0800.* ***Open*** *12:30–11pm daily.* 🚭 🍽 🧒 💳 *MC, V.* $

The Moroccan Star twinkles on a street known for its modestly priced Middle Eastern restaurants. The chef has worked at the Four Seasons, so there are good continental dishes on the menu. Recommended Middle Eastern dishes are the chicken *tajine* (stew), *b'stilla* (chicken pie), lamb dishes and hummus. These are just a few of the many delights served in friendly, family-style, family-run, tidy simplicity, at unbelievably low prices.

Periyali

35 W 20th St. **Map** 8 F5.
☎ *463-7890.* ***Open*** *noon–3pm Mon–Fri, 5:30–11pm Mon–Sat.* ❄ 🪑 💳 *AE, DC, MC, V.* $$$$

The white stucco walls of Periyali, as well as its tiled floors and dark-beamed taverna decor, may transport you in spirit to a Greek island, though the billowy tent ceiling is more designer fantasy. The nouvelle Greek food, somewhat gentrified and more expensive than in any taverna, can be terrific. Try the spanakopitta and such seafood dishes as charcoal-grilled octopus and whole sea bass anointed with lemon, herbs and olive oil.

Russian Tea Room

150 W 57th St. **Map** 12 E3.
☎ *265-0947.* ***Open*** *11:30am–midnight Mon–Fri, 11am–midnight Sat, Sun.* ❄ 🍴 [V] 🎵 👔 *at dinner.* 💳 *AE, DC, MC, V.* $$$$$ *(See p147.)*

The most glamorous, most famous places like this expensive, long-established celebrity haunt may not have the best food in town, but that's not why you'll want to go here. Go, at lunch especially, for the blinis (small, savory pancakes), borscht (beetroot soup), chicken Kiev (chicken breast wrapped around butter and baked) and, of course, the caviar – then star-gaze to your heart's content in a setting as glitzy as many of the patrons. Try to avoid the very large upstairs dining room dubbed "Siberia," where noncelebs are often shunted. It's quieter but much less fun.

Sammy's Famous Roumanian

157 Chrystie St. **Map** 5 A4.
☎ *673-0330.* ***Open*** *3:30–10.30pm Sun–Thu, 3:30pm–midnight Fri–Sun.* ❄ 🎵 💳 *AE, MC.* $$$$

This is not kosher but Jewish-Romanian. This noisy, no-decor-to-speak-of place is where you'll catch the essence of the New York Jewish experience, famous for its stuffed cabbage, fried *kreplach* (small dumplings filled with cheese or meat, often served in soup), chicken soup and other passions. You don't have to be Jewish to enjoy the "let it all hang out" atmosphere of live music, loud talk and much laughing. On each table are ingredients to make the famous egg cream: milk, seltzer (carbonated mineral water) and chocolate syrup. The rib eye steak appetizers and stuffed *derma* (boiled and baked sausages), are terrific, but skip the desserts.

Savoy

70 Prince St. **Map** 4 F3.
☎ *219-8570.* ***Open*** *noon–3pm, 6pm–10.30pm, Mon–Thu, 6pm–11pm Fri, Sat.* ♿ [V] 🍴 $$

The cozy look of the Savoy is that of a SoHo-cum-country bistro. The Mediterranean fare is as inviting as the cheerful, friendly service. Grilled salmon in a Spanish almond and garlic sauce is the signature dish.

South American and Caribbean

Despite the influx of people from Latin America and the Caribbean into New York, there are only a few mainstream restaurants that feature their cuisines. Caribbean restaurants use such ingredients as coconut, banana, garlic, rice and beans. They also have lots of peppery dishes, such as conch stews and black bean soup.

Brazilian restaurants offer reasonable prices; a cheerful, casual ambience, and a number of authentic homey dishes. Look for the national dish, *feijoada,* a stew of black beans and various meats and vegetables.

Mexican restaurants in New York generally offer standard Tex-Mex food. Melted cheese poured over enchiladas (chicken or beef-stuffed corn tortillas), tamales (filled cornmeal parcels, wrapped and steamed in corn husks), fajitas (strips of grilled beef), refried beans and quesadillas (crisp pastry filled with cheese) are among the dishes to expect.

Cabana Carioca

123 W 45th St. **Map** 12 E5.
☎ *581-8088.* ***Open*** *noon–11pm Sun–Thu, noon–midnight Fri & Sat.* ❄ 👶 🎵 💳 *AE, DC, MC, V.* $$$

There aren't many Brazilian restaurants in town, but this very moderately priced place is without doubt one of the best. Arrive feeling hungry, since the portions are huge in this funky place with nonstop music, folk art frescoes on the walls and a high decibel level bouncing off them. *Feijoada* (a black bean and meat casserole) is served on Wednesday and Saturday, but you will always find hearty steak dishes, chicken and seafood. After a few gulps of *caipirinha*, the favorite Brazilian drink, you may find the noise less bothersome and may even join in.

Lola

30 W 22nd St. **Map** 8 F4.
☎ *675-6700.* ***Open*** *noon–3pm Mon–Sat, 6pm–midnight Mon–Thu, 6pm–1am Fri, Sat, 11:45am–2:30pm 6–10:30pm Sun.* ❄ 👶 ♿ 🎵 💳 *AE, MC, V.* $$$$

Lola's is a handsomely converted high-ceilinged loft mainly serving hot -and-sassy Caribbean dishes, though there's some American and Italian food, such as venison, pasta and seafood. The best of the many wonderful dishes is the fiery 100-spices Caribbean fried chicken. Lola has departed, but remaining are live blues, jazz and reggae nightly, plus a gospel music Sunday brunch that rocks the rafters. The fun surpasses the food.

Tropica

MetLife Bldg, 200 Park Ave. **Map** 13 A5. ☎ *867-6767.* ***Open*** *noon–3pm & 5–10pm Mon–Fri.* ***Closed*** *some hols.* ❄ 🍴 [V] 👶 ♿ 💳 *AE, DC, MC, V.* $$$$

This attractive restaurant evokes the tropics with its palms, airy upper levels, latticework and wicker chairs. Considering the location, the Caribbean food is more imaginative than its bustling business lunch crowd might demand. Seafood is good here; try the roasted cod with *saké* (Japanese rice wine) and black-bean sauce. It is pricey yet certainly worth the money for serious eaters who might be in the neighborhood.

Zarela

953 Second Ave. **Map** 13 B4.
☎ *644-6740.* ***Open*** *noon–3pm Mon–Fri, 5–11pm Mon–Thu, 5–11:30pm Fri & Sat, 5–10pm Sun.* ❄ 🎵 💳 *AE, DC.* $$

Light years from the standard Tex-Mex fare usually encountered north of the border, Zarela's is trendy in every way – menu, crowd (youthful) and especially price. You'll find delicious and authentic tamales and enchiladas as appetizers only. Fresh seafood is featured strongly here, prepared with the same subtle sophistication found in the dishes from Mexico's beautiful coastal region.

For key to symbols *see p285.*

Light Meals and Snacks

YOU CAN GET A SNACK almost anywhere, at any time, in Manhattan. New Yorkers seem to eat all the time – on street corners, at bars, in coffee shops or delis, before work and after, and long into the night.

Casual eating in New York might include soft pretzels from a corner stand; a Danish pastry and espresso; a slice of pizza from a local pizzeria; a huge take-out sandwich from a deli or sandwich shop; char-roasted chestnuts or a Greek gyro sandwich (lamb in pita bread) from a street vendor; a formal late-afternoon tea; a pretheater snack at a café; and a post-party binge at an all-night coffee shop, diner or bistro before heading home. While street fare and coffee shops are generally cheap, other light meals may cost considerably more.

DELIS

DELICATESSENS, a New York institution, are great sources for a hefty lunchtime sandwich. Try the wonderful corned beef and pastrami sandwiches from the famous **Carnegie Delicatessen**, considered by many to be New York's best deli.

Some delis, like **Katz's,** cater to older people who enjoy traditional, kosher food. Much deli business, though, is take-out, so delis are bustling places where you line up, quickly get your order and leave.

The huge sandwiches at most delis are still relatively cheap, but the counter staff is often impatient. Never take it personally, it's just the deli style. Rudeness is an essential part of visiting the **Stage Deli**, which is now more a tourist stop than the showbiz favorite it used to be.

For New York ethnic Jewish flavor, go to the **Second Avenue Delicatessen**, well-known for its homemade soups, pickles, corned beef sandwiches, chopped liver and other kosher goodies.

Ratner's Dairy Restaurant is another place for authentic New York kosher food. Dairy restaurants, as opposed to delis, serve milk-based kosher food, but Ratner's is worth a visit for its onion rolls, blintzes (pancakes with fillings of fruit or cheese usually eaten with sour cream) and poppy seed cake, even though the waiters are rather grumpy.

CAFÉS AND BISTROS

CAFÉS COME in various sizes, and range in style from country casual to chic casual. In general, cafés, like the newly popular bistros, serve lunch and dinner, but they also serve snack food and have separate menus for light meals in the off-peak hours.

One of the best is the **Chefs & Cuisiniers Café**, a casual spot where top chefs eat on their days off. The freshly made food is simple – lots of seafood, grilled chicken and softshell crabs in season. The best, and most crowded, time to come here is late evening.

Fans of Zabar's, the deli and gourmet food store, will happily cross town for Eli Zabar's **E.A.T.**, a Parisian-style café that sells Jewish favorites, like *challah* bread, as well as soups, salads and some really sinful desserts. Everything is top quality, and you pay accordingly.

A favorite of local artists, **Florent** offers delicious French bistro fare and huge breakfasts. **Elephant and Castle** has two minimally decorated but cozy cafés, named after the London tube stop. They are SoHo and Village favorites for soup-salad-omelette lunches and other light snacks. Their real forte is breakfast, served in ample portions at modest prices, though the lines can be long. The bar scene at both places is lively.

You'll find yourself "deep in the heart of Texas" at **Yellow Rose Café**, a cozy West Side hangout that offers huge portions for your money. Here you can sample typical Texas food, like barbecued meat, mashed potatoes, buttermilk biscuits and chili. Strictly speaking, **Sarabeth's Kitchen** defies categorization, but can probably be described as a bistro. The best time to visit is at breakfast and for weekend brunch, when families wolf down the wonderful waffles, omelets, French toast and pancakes.

Some bars double as cafés or have small cafés in the rear, where you can get standard American snacks.

PIZZERIAS

PIZZA IS AVAILABLE all over New York, from street vendors and fast-food places, which sell it by the slice for a few dollars, to traditional Neapolitan pizzerias.

But some pizzerias offer something more. **Arturo's Pizzeria** uses a coal oven for crisp, thin-crusted pizza pies and also offers live jazz. **Mezzogiorno** has a Tuscan menu and wonderful pizzas with unusual toppings, often called "designer" pizzas. The crowded **Mezzaluna** also specializes in brick-oven, thin-crusted pizzas. Restaurants like **Pizzeria Uno** specialize in Chicago-style pizza, which is made in a deep dish, then lavished with toppings.

Generally, pizza parlors are good places to go for a cheap, simple meal, especially with children. Most pizzerias won't take reservations, and popular ones, like **John's Pizzeria**, have long lines at mealtimes. Go early or late.

HAMBURGER PLACES

YOUR NOSE may lead you to some of the cheaper burger and hot dog stands on the street. However, there are many places in New York where you can buy a better-quality burger, even though prices for a top-grade, $1/4$-to-$1/2$ lb (125-to-250 g) all-beef burger can go up to $10.

Hamburger Harry's offers reasonably priced, large, juicy burgers, with a choice of over a dozen toppings and a huge fresh salad alongside. There are burgers at **Papaya King**, but their specialty is all-beef hot dogs. The food is cheap and satisfying. Bright and basic, the five outlets of **Jackson Hole** offer fat, juicy, meaty burgers that make kids feel at home on the range. Adults might prefer less glare and smarter decor, but they will like the price: cheap.

Children love **Mickey Mantle's,** which is covered with baseball memorabilia and TV screens. You can get great burgers and other snacks at the bar, while a more formal dining area in the rear is open at mealtimes.

Other popular places for hamburgers and snack food, but considerably more expensive, include **Planet Hollywood**, which is owned by film stars Bruce Willis, Arnold Schwarzenegger and Sylvester Stallone, and the perennial **Hard Rock Café**. Both feature loud rock music and are magnets for teenagers, despite the high prices for food. Portions are huge and you may enjoy the displays of showbiz memorabilia.

DINERS AND LUNCHEONETTES

Diners and luncheonettes, also called sandwich or coffee shops, can be found all over town. Food is usually indifferent but served in huge, cheap platefuls. A major advantage of such places is that they are usually open from breakfast until late evening, and you can drop in at almost any hour for coffee and something basic to eat.

A recent trend with diners has seen replicas of the old 1930s cheap-eats places. These new retrodiners often serve good, relatively inexpensive food.

One such is the Empire Diner (see p136). The **Broadway Diner**, a faithful recreation of a 1940s diner, offers a better-than-average breakfast, including thick-cut fries and tasty homemade

corned beef hash with eggs. **Bellevues** has a hip, young crowd who love its French dishes, sandwiches, croissants, and notch-above-diner decor.

Devotees swear by **Viand,** a luncheonette with cheap, ample American breakfast fare, also the best fresh turkey sandwiches in town.

You enter **Les Halles** through the meat market to find earthy French food. The **Kiev Restaurant** is well known for its Jewish European specialties, such as borscht.

Veselka is not the usual New York coffee shop: it offers Polish/Ukrainian food at rock-bottom prices.

The **Brasserie** has reliable food, fast lunches and is open for 24 hours a day. **Mangia** has some of the best take-out sandwiches, salads and pastries in the city. Mangia also delivers food.

TEAROOMS

About the only place you can be absolutely sure of getting a cup of real brewed tea is at a formal prix-fixe afternoon tea in a lounge at one of New York's pricier hotels, from 3 to 5pm.

Afternoon tea in the **Plaza Hotel's** Palm Court has cream cakes and hot buttered scones galore. For an extra-smart tea, served on Chippendale furniture, visit the **Carlyle Hotel**. The **Hotel Pierre** offers one of the better buys in hotel prix-fixe teas, served in the Rotunda room setting.

Tea at the **Waldorf–Astoria** comes with Devonshire cream, and the city's most expensive tea is in the Gold Room of the **New York Palace** (see p174). Less opulent than the hotels, but restful and cheap is **Le Train Bleu**, a copy of an Orient Express dining car in Bloomingdale's (see p179). The prix-fixe "Mayfair Tea" is a good choice.

Café Vienna at Bergdorf Goodman (see p311) offers one of the cheapest teas.

At the **Russian Tea Room** (see p147), you can choose between four prix-fixe afternoon tea menus, whose price depends on the caviar you choose. A cheaper tea is

served at **Book-Friends Café,** tucked away in a Chelsea bookstore. It also has tea-dancing every other Wednesday.

COFFEE AND CAKES

At most diners, luncheonettes and coffee shops, you can get a decent cup of coffee for as little as 75 cents with endless free refills. But there are also expensive coffeehouses. Some ice cream parlors and patisseries also serve good coffee, along with luscious pastries.

Some of the most charming coffeehouses are in Little Italy, such as **Caffè Biondo**, which serves cappuccino and sinful sweets. **Caffè Vivaldi**, in the West Village, serves coffees, teas and desserts on marble tables.

Caffè Ferrara, going strong since 1892, has moderately priced Italian pastries, good coffee and outdoor seating.

Caffè Dante is a favorite with New York University students who like to sit outside in warm weather.

On the Upper East Side at **Caffè Bianco,** desserts are fabulous, the coffee is good, and prices are cheap; **Les Délices Guy Pascal** has delicious French pastries.

Sant' Ambroeus Ltd. is a luxurious outpost of the Milanese *pasticceria*, with decadent desserts and a stand-up espresso bar in front.

Rumpelmayer's is New York's quintessential old-fashioned ice cream parlor and the place to have an egg cream (see p286) or an ice cream fantasia. A close runner-up is **Serendipity 3**, famous for its Victoriana, elaborate ice cream creations, coffee and mid-afternoon snacks. The **Coffee Shop** has basic decor and loud music, designed to attract the trendy set.

For a charming place in warm weather, head for the **Boathouse Café** in Central Park. The food is ordinary so just have coffee or a drink at the bar. **Zabar's Café** is nothing fancy – just stools and some of the best cappuccino in town.

DIRECTORY

LOWER EAST SIDE

Delis

Katz's Deli
205 E Houston St.
Map 5 A3.

Ratner's Dairy
Restaurant
138 Delancey St.
Map 5 B4.

Coffee and Cakes

Caffè Biondo
141 Mulberry St.
Map 4 F5.

Caffè Ferrara
195 Grand St.
Map 4 F4.

SOHO AND TRIBECA

Cafés and Bistros

Elephant and Castle
183 Prince St.
Map 4 D3.
One of two branches.

Pizzerias

Mezzogiorno
195 Spring St.
Map 4 D4.

GREENWICH VILLAGE

Pizzerias

Arturo's Pizzeria
106 W Houston St.
Map 4 E3.

Cafés and Bistros

Florent
69 Gansevoort St.
Map 3 B1.

Coffee and Cakes

Caffè Dante
79 MacDougal St.
Map 4 D3.

Caffè Vivaldi
32 Jones St.
Map 3 C2.

EAST VILLAGE

Diners and Luncheonettes

Kiev Restaurant
117 2nd Ave. **Map** 4 2F.

Veselka
144 2nd Ave.
Map 4 F1.

Delis

Second Avenue Deli
156 Second Ave. **Map** 4
F1.

GRAMERCY AND THE FLATIRON

Cafés and Bistros

Chefs & Cuisiniers Café
36 E 22nd St. **Map** 8 F4.

Diners and Luncheonettes

Les Halles
411 Park Ave. **Map** 9 A3.

Tearooms

Book-Friends Café
16 W 18th St. **Map** 8 F5.

Coffee and Cakes

Coffee Shop
29 Union Sq West.
Map 9 A5.

CHELSEA AND THE GARMENT DISTRICT

Diners and Luncheonettes

Bellevues
496 Ninth Ave. **Map** 8 D2.

Empire Diner
210 10th Ave. **Map** 7 C4.

THEATER DISTRICT

Delis

Carnegie Delicatessen
854 Seventh Ave. **Map** 12
E4.

Stage Deli
834 Seventh Ave. **Map** 12
E4.

Hamburger Places

Hamburger Harry's
145 W 45th St.
Map 12 E4.
One of several branches.

Hard Rock Café
221 W 57th St.
Map 12 E3.
One of several branches.

Planet Hollywood
140 W 57th St.
Map 12 E5.

Diners and Luncheonettes

Broadway Diner
1726 Broadway.
Map 12 E4.

Tearooms

Russian Tea Room
150 W 57th St.
Map 12 E3.

Coffee and Cakes

Rumpelmayer's
St. Moritz Hotel,
50 Central Park S.
Map 12 F3.

UPPER MIDTOWN

Hamburger Places

Mickey Mantle's
42 Central Park South.
Map 12 F3.

Diners and Luncheonettes

Mangia
54 W 56th St.
Map 12 F3.

The Brasserie
100 E 53rd St.
Map 13 A4.

Tearooms

Le Train Bleu
Bloomingdale's,
1000 Third Ave.
Map 13 A3.

New York Palace
455 Madison Ave.
Map 13 A4.

Plaza Hotel
Palm Court, 768 Fifth Ave.
Map 12 F3.

Waldorf–Astoria
301 Park Ave.
Map 13 A5.

UPPER EAST SIDE

Cafés and Bistros

E.A.T.
1064 Madison Ave.
Map 17 A4.

Pizzerias

John's Pizzeria
408 E 64th St.
Map 13 C2.

Mezzaluna
1295 Third Ave.
Map 17 B5.

Hamburger Places

Jackson Hole
232 E 64th St.
Map 13 B2.
One of several branches.

Papaya King
983 Third Ave.
Map 13 B3.

Diners and Luncheonettes

Viand
673 Madison Ave.
Map 13 A2.
One of several branches.

Tearooms

Café Vienna
Bergdorf Goodman,
754 Fifth Ave.
Map 12 F3.

Hotel Pierre
2 E 61st St.
Map 12 F3.

Carlyle Hotel
35 E 76th St.
Map 17 A5.

Coffee and Cakes

Caffè Bianco
1486 Second Ave.
Map 17 B5.

Les Délices
Guy Pascal
1231 Madison Ave.
Map 17 A3.

Sant' Ambroeus Ltd
1000 Madison Ave.
Map 17 A5.

Serendipity 3
225 E 60th St.
Map 13 B5.

CENTRAL PARK

Coffee and Cakes

Boathouse Café
Central Park, East Park
Drive & 72nd St.
Map 12 F1.

UPPER WEST SIDE

Pizzerias

Pizzeria Uno
432 Columbus Ave.
Map 16 Dl.
One of several branches.

Cafés and Bistros

Sarabeth's Kitchen
423 Amsterdam Ave.
Map 15 4C.

Yellow Rose Café
450 Amsterdam Ave.
Map 15 4C.

Coffee and Cakes

Zabar's Café
2245 Broadway.
Map 15 3C.

New York Bars

NEW YORK BARS are an institution; they play a huge part in the life and culture of the city. It is normal for New Yorkers to spend the evening in a succession of bars, because each usually offers something more than just alcohol. For example, there may be excellent food, dancing or live music. Another attraction may be the imported or American boutique beers. The bars are innumerable, spread all over the city, and there's one suited to every taste, budget and lifestyle.

RULES AND CONVENTIONS

BARS GENERALLY open at around 11am and close around midnight. Some stay open until 2 or 4am, when they have to close by law.

Many bars have a "happy hour" between 5 and 7pm, offering twofers (two drinks for the price of one) and a variety of free snack foods, such as small pizzas and quiches.

The legal minimum drinking age is 21; if the bartender suspects you are younger, you'll be "carded," or asked to show some identification that will prove your age. Children are not usually welcome in New York bars.

It is common to "run a tab" and pay your bill just before you leave. Tipping the bartender is expected – 10% of the bill or about 50 cents for a single drink. Shots are not premeasured, so if you want a bigger drink, it helps to "belly up" to the bar and tip the bartender accordingly for his or her generosity. If you sit at a table, you'll be served there and charged more.

A round of drinks can be expensive. You can save money by buying a quart or a half-gallon (two and a quarter liters) pitcher of beer.

Avoid the "free drinks for ladies" bars, which are often just pick-up joints. Some of New York's pubs did not admit women until forced to by law a few years ago. Even today, many women still feel uncomfortable drinking alone in certain pubs, taverns and sports bars. Safer bets for single women are hotel bars or singles bars, although it's still difficult to avoid being sexually harassed in these.

WHAT TO DRINK

YOU CAN GET almost any alcoholic drink you want in New York bars. The most popular drink is beer, served ice-cold. Mainstream bars serve standard beers from such big producers Budweiser, Coors and Miller, plus such high-profile imports as Bass ale, Becks and Heineken lagers, and occasionally Guinness. Some bars, especially the old publike ones, have a much wider variety of beer, which include boutique-type from the USA's small domestic breweries such as Samuel Adams, Sierra Nevada and Anchor Steam, and the local products, including such beers as Brooklyn Lager and New Amsterdam Amber.

Other popular drinks include cocktails during the happy hour; rum and coke; very dry martini; Scotch or bourbon, "straight up" (without ice) or "on the rocks" (with ice) and/or with club soda or water; vodka and tonic and gin and tonic. Wine, especially white, is also widely available at bars, though the "wine bar" concept has never really caught on in New York.

FOOD

MOST BARS SERVE some sort of food all day. It is usually such food as burgers, fries, salads, sandwiches and small snacks like spicy chicken wings (also called buffalo wings). Happy hour is an excellent time to fill up on delicious free snacks and appetizers in the smarter New York bars. Most bar kitchens stop serving just before midnight.

FASHIONABLE BARS

WITH ITS LONG, Art Deco interior and hip downtown location, the **Odeon** is a great place to catch the SoHo-TriBeCa art scene. Also downtown is **SoHo Kitchen and Bar**, a loft enlivened with colorful abstract paintings, tiered dining areas, a long brick bar, good pizzas, and probably one of New York's longest wine lists as well as a good range of beers.

On the Upper East Side, the bar at **Mortimer's** is a place to observe what passes these days for high society, without paying exorbitant prices for the restaurant's ordinary food.

After work, crowds go to **P.J. Clarke's**, the classic New York saloon with Irish bartenders and an incredibly bustling scene, or to one of the 11 branches of **Houlihan's**, a formulaic "standard bar," with friendly staff, a sizable beer selection, and American fare like burgers and sandwiches.

Another popular bar is **T.G.I. Friday's**, which has branches all over America. They are known for decent bar food, reasonable prices, good service and as favorite watering-holes for yuppies and singles after work.

BARS WITH VIEWS

FOR A HAWK'S EYE view of the harbor, **Hors d'Oeuvrerie** in the World Trade Center (see p73) is a great place to have a drink, nibble canapés and watch the city light up. There's live piano from 4:30pm and dancing from 7:30pm to 1am.

For drinks and views alone, pop into **City Lights** on the same floor to view the Statue of Liberty, and try Scotch from a collection of 130 varieties or gins from a choice of 75.

The **Tavern on the Green** has magical views of Central Park. It is very festive, with chandeliers, mirrored walls and 350,000 twinkle lights. It boasts an extensive selection of beers and wines to enjoy in the garden during the warmer weather. The food is also excellent.

HISTORIC AND LITERARY BARS

IF YOU SAMPLE only one New York bar, it should be **McSorley's Old Alehouse**, an old Irish saloon, often dubbed "McSurly's" because of the staff. It's been on the same site since 1854, making it one of New York's oldest bars. It's also known for its great beers, and ploughman's lunch.

The **Ear Inn** has a pedigree that goes back to 1812, when the first tavern opened on this site. Now the haunt of poets and writers, its cramped, dark interior and long wooden bar ooze no-nonsense authenticity.

Another oldie is **Pete's Tavern** dating to 1864. It is a Gramercy Park area hangout that is busy until 2am and known for its Victoriana, the house brew, called Pete's Ale, and the many beers on tap.

Old Town Bar, a typically Irish pub since 1892, has converted gas lamps, and is favored by advertising types.

A good, though rather touristy, place to go for a drink if you find yourself in the financial district is the **Fraunces Tavern** *(see p76)*.

Greenwich Village has some of the city's oldest bars, like **Chumley's**, which retains its character as a Prohibition era speakeasy and still has no sign outside. It is especially snug in winter when an open fire burns in the hearth.

The **Lion's Head** is another hangout for literary types, and has good snacks and burgers. Dylan Thomas's unpretentious old favorite, the **White Horse Tavern**, is still going strong, crowded with literary and collegiate types in the outside café in warm weather.

Peculier Pub is a beer-lover's paradise. There are over 360 varieties from all over the world to choose from, but you must be willing to tolerate the sometimes snappy and uninformed staff. The **Minetta Tavern** is one of the Village's oldest Italian bars and restaurants, with an original late-1930s mural.

Not the celebrity scene it once was, **Sardi's** is still a hangout for *New York Times* reporters, and is worth a stop

to inspect the "who's who" celebrity caricatures lining the walls, and for the generous drinks served in the second floor bar. Anyone leaving or arriving at Grand Central Station should drop into the **Café at Grand Central Station** overlooking the station's concourse *(see p285)* and renowned for its cheap snacks. Near Carnegie Hall is the unobtrusive and trendy **P.J. Carney's**, a watering hole for musicians and artists since 1927. It has a U-shaped bar, a few tables, Irish ales and a good shepherd's pie.

YOUNG AND TRENDY BARS

A FAVORITE AFTER-WORK spot is the **North Star Pub**, with its six English and Irish beers on tap and more than a dozen bottled varieties in this cozy English-style pub.

Not quite as far downtown is **Lucky Strike**, one of SoHo's most popular late-night scenes, inexpensive and always fun with a good mix of ages. **ZIP City Brewing Company** is New York's only brew pub, where you watch the brewing process at the big copper vats in the center of the room while drinking the fresh suds (beer).

Uptown at **Sam's Grill**, which is owned and run by actress Mariel Hemingway, the bar scene is one of the best for the young, single and stylish, and you can even get a good light meal. At **Brother Jimmy's BBQ**, college-age kids and many other twenty-somethings gather for beer and a good barbecue of the really old-fashioned southern, nothing-fancy type.

Brewsky's is "in" with the young microbrewery crowd. A microbrewery is a small, individually owned brewery, producing a limited amount of traditional beer. This is the place to sample some of America's boutique beers.

The unappetizingly named **Burp Castle** is next door to **Brewsky's** and is decked out inside like a monastery hall, complete with bartenders wearing monks' habits. Ignore the costumes, since this is the best source for some great

Belgian beers, and is utterly unique. **Manchester's** very name rings heavily with nostalgia. For homesick Brits, this is a cozy pub with a good range of British beers, which are not widely available in New York. Ten beers are on tap, including Watneys and Newcastle Brown Ale, and there are 27 bottled varieties. The shepherd's pie, fish and chips and other light meals aren't bad either.

SINGLES BARS

THE CHANCE to meet new people is offered in singles bars, which are extremely popular. These are mainly concentrated around midtown on the East Side. But check the prices before you order: a beer can cost more than $3.

Live Bait has a frenetic young singles scene frequented by skinny models. Despite the noise level, it's worth eating here since the Cajun food is quite good. At **Lucy's**, across town, young singles line up to get in. It's more popular for the socializing than the unexceptional Tex-Mex food.

GAY AND LESBIAN BARS

GAY BARS TEND to be found mainly in Greenwich Village, though there are some in SoHo, the East Village, Chelsea and Murray Hill. Lesbian bars are mainly found in Greenwich Village and the East Village. The *Native* newspaper has listings of bars, or call the Gay and Lesbian Switchboard *(see p343)*.

HOTEL BARS

IN A CENTRAL midtown location, the **Blue Bar** in the Algonquin Hotel *(see p143)* was a famous literary haunt in the 1920s and early 1930s and is now a good place for a quiet drink and conversation before dinner or the theater. Nearby, but much trendier, is the bar in the handsome lobby-lounge of the **Royalton Hotel**, a perfect place for a drink while watching the rich, fashionable and theatrical crowds drifting in and out all evening. Open 4pm to 4am, midtown's new fashionable bar, the **Whiskey** in the Paramount Hotel, has floor-to-ceiling windows and is frequented by fashion and theater people.

For comfort, try the **Sun Garden**, a glass-enclosed, tiered, elongated space above the lobby of the Grand Hyatt Hotel. It has separated private enclaves and is especially pleasant on winter afternoons, when the sun streams through the glass. The

Bull and Bear in the Waldorf–Astoria exudes comfort and a real sense of history (it dates back to the Prohibition era), with scores of exotic drinks and Bull and Bear ale on tap. At **Harry's New York Bar** in the Helmsley Palace, you can sit in velvet booths, sip costly drinks and enjoy piano music.

Uptown, the **Oak Room and Bar** at the Plaza Hotel is a very posh place to impress people – but for a high price. The newly refurbished **King**

Cole Room at the St. Regis Hotel is named after the mural by Maxfield Parrish behind the bar, in a stylish room of cherrywood-paneled walls.

Journeys in the Essex House Hotel provides an English club ambience, with hunting prints and mahogany paneling. Treat yourself at the **Warwick Bar** in the Warwick Hotel. During happy hour (5.30–7pm Mon–Fri), delicious free snacks are served.

SHOPPING

A VISITOR to New York will inevitably include shopping in his or her action plan. The city is the consumer capital of the world: a shopper's paradise that is a constant source of entertainment, with dazzling window displays and a staggering variety of goods for sale. Everything is available here, from high fashion to rare children's

Tiffany's clock

books, state-of-the-art electronics and a mouthwatering array of exotic food. Whether you are looking for a personal Hovercraft, read-in-the-dark eyeglass attachments, a designer bed for your pet gerbil or a Wurlitzer jukebox, this is the city of your dreams. Whether you have $50,000 or $5, New York is the place to spend it.

BEST BUYS

NEW YORK is a bargain hunter's dream, with huge discounts on anything from household goods to designer clothes. Some of the best shops are on Orchard Street and Grand Street on the Lower East Side, where designer goods are sold at

The 1920s-style Henri Bendel store (see p311)

20–50% below the retail price. You can find just about every imaginable item of clothing here, in addition to tableware, shoes, home furnishings and electronics. Shops in this area are closed on Saturday – the Jewish Sabbath – but are usually open all day Sunday.

. Another great area for fashion bargain hunters is the trendy Garment District, roughly between Sixth and Eighth avenues from 30th to 40th Street. The hub of it – Seventh Avenue – was renamed as Fashion Avenue in the early 1970s. Here, many different designers and manufacturers have showrooms, some of which are open to the public. They also have sales of many of their samples, announced on notices posted around the

area. Often the best time to go and visit these stores is just before one of the major gift-giving holidays.

SALES

ONE WORD you are likely to see all over the city, no matter what time of year you visit, is "Sale." So before you pay full price for anything, check the sale goods first. The best sales are during New York's sale seasons, which run from mid-June until the end of July and from December 26 until February. For information, look for ads in the local papers. A word of warning: along midtown Fifth Avenue there are signs announcing "Lost Our Lease" sales. But many of the shops have had these signs up for years and are best avoided.

HOW TO PAY

MOST SHOPS accept major credit cards, although there will often be a minimum purchase price. If you want to use your traveler's checks, identification is needed. Personal checks drawn in another currency will be refused. Some stores only take cash, especially during sales.

The Bulgari entrance at Hotel Pierre (see p282)

OPENING HOURS

MOST SHOPS in New York are normally open from 10am to 6pm, Monday to Saturday. Many department stores, though, are open all day Sunday and until 9pm at least two nights a week. The best time to avoid crowds is weekday mornings. The most crowded times are lunch hours (noon to 2:30pm), Saturday mornings, sales and holidays.

TAXES

THE NEW YORK city sales tax, 8.25%, is added to the price when you pay. But you may still be asked to pay duty on goods at customs if you exceed the allowance. If the goods are sent direct, you won't have to pay sales tax (see p352).

Designer dress at a New York sale

Shopping Tours

If you can't face the thought of braving the stores by yourself, why not go on one of the many shopping tours available in New York? Apart from visiting the main department stores, options include a visit to private designer showrooms, auction houses and fashion shows. Some operators will customize tours to suit your requirements.

Convention Tours Unlimited
545-1160.

Doorway to Design
221-1111.

Guide Service of New York
408-3332.

The Intrepid New Yorker
534-5071.

Window displays at Bloomingdale's *(see p179)*

Department Stores

Most of New York's large department stores are in midtown Manhattan. Allow plenty of time to explore, because all these stores tend to be enormous, with an amazing range of goods. Prices are often high, but you can get bargains during sales.

Stores such as Saks Fifth Avenue, Bloomingdale's and Macy's provide a diverse and extraordinary range of shopping services, including doing the shopping for you. But then you would miss out on what may be the shopping experience of a lifetime.

Abraham & Straus, more familiarly known as A&S, is a bustling store that carries reasonably priced ready-to-wear fashions for adults and

children. It is the centerpiece of an Art Deco–style mall, the largest in Manhattan.

Barney's New York is a favorite among young professional New Yorkers. It specializes in excellent, but expensive, designer clothes. A branch for men only is located in the glittering World Financial Center.

Bergdorf Goodman is luxurious, very elegant and understated. It carries high-quality contemporary fashions at high prices, specializing in European designers. The men's store is right across the street.

Almost every visitor to New York includes **Bloomingdale's** *(see p179)* on their sightseeing list. "Bloomies" is the Hollywood film star of the department stores, with many eye-catching displays and seductive goods. Its ambience is that of a luxurious exotic wonderland, filled with wealthy, immaculately dressed New Yorkers seeking out the newest, trendiest fashions. Bloomingdale's also has a high reputation for household goods and gourmet food – it has a shop devoted entirely to caviar. Extensive shopping services and amenities include a noted restaurant, Le Train Bleu *(see p306)*, and a theater ticket discount agency.

Everything found in **Henri Bendel's**, from the Art Deco jewels to beautiful handmade shoes, is displayed as though each were a priceless work of art. The store, which is laid out in a series of 1920s-style boutiques, is exclusive and sophisticated, and has a good selection of creative and innovative women's fashions.

Lord & Taylor is renowned for its classic and much more conservative fashions for men and women. The store places

A magnificent display offering household goods

an emphasis on US designers. You need comfy shoes and lots of spare time to wander.

Macy's, the self-proclaimed largest store in the world *(see p132–3)*, sprawls over an entire city block. It has ten floors and sells everything imaginable from can openers to massive antiques.

Saks Fifth Avenue is synonymous with style and elegance. It has long been considered one of the city's high-quality department stores, with service to match. It sells stunning designer clothes for men, women and children.

Addresses

Abraham & Strauss
33rd St at 6th Ave. **Map** 8 E2.
594-8500

Barney's New York
106 7th Ave. **Map** 8 E5.
929-9000.
Upper Level, 2 World Financial Center.
Map 1 A2.
945-1600.

Bergdorf Goodman
754 5th Ave. **Map** 12 F3.
753-7300.

Bloomingdale's
1000 3rd Ave. **Map** 13 B3.
355-5900.

Henri Bendel
712 5th Ave. **Map** 12 F4.
247-1100.

Lord & Taylor
424 5th Ave. **Map** 8 F1.
391-3344.

Macy's
151 W 34th St. **Map** 8 E2.
695-4400.

Saks Fifth Avenue
611 5th Ave. **Map** 12 F4.
753-4000.

New York's Best: Shopping

I N A CITY where you can literally shop 24 hours a day, the best plan is to shop the way New Yorkers do, by neighborhood.

Designer shoes from Madison Avenue

Each has its own character and specialties. Here are highlights of the best shopping districts – where they are and what you will find in each. If time is very tight, head for one of the huge department stores *(see p311)*, or if window shopping is your preference, stroll along Fifth Avenue, home to Manhattan's most glittering stores *(see opposite)*. For great bargains in a truly ethnic area, try the Lower East Side.

Greenwich and East Villages
Explore around Eighth Street and St. Mark's Place for shoes and avant-garde fashions, books, ethnic goods and flea markets. Move to lower Broadway for antiques (often "retro" 20th century). (See pp108–9 and pp116–17.)

SoHo
The area bordered by Sixth Avenue, Lafayette, Houston and Canal streets is bustling with contemporary art galleries, antiques, crafts, exclusive or unusual gifts and fashions. Weekend brunchtime gallery-hopping is very popular. (See pp102–3.)

Lower East Side
Sunday is the day when New Yorkers and visitors flock to Canal, Delancey, Orchard and Essex streets for great bargains in fashions, shoes, jewelry, electronics and household goods. (See pp94–95.)

South Street Seaport
This is a browser's paradise of crafts, gifts, toys, souvenirs, antiquarian and new books, and antiques with a seafaring connection. (See pp82–83.)

Chelse
and t
Garme
Distri

Greenwich
Village

SoHo and
TriBeCa

Ea
Villa

Seaport
and the
Civic
Center

Lower
Manhattan

Lower East Sid

HUDSON RIVER

N

Upper West Side

Central Park

Theater District

Upper East Side

See inset map

Upper Midtown

Lower Midtown

Gramercy and the Flatiron District

Columbus and Amsterdam Avenues
These are New York hot spots for exclusive but trendy designer clothes, quirky antiques, esoterica and upscale gift shops. (See pp210–11.)

Madison and Lexington Avenues
Shoppers come here for classics in art and antiques, designer clothes and shoes. The museum shops are also nearby. (See pp182–83.)

East 57th and 59th Streets
Exclusive antiques and high fashion are found on 57th Street – and be sure not to miss Bloomingdale's. (See p179.)

0 kilometers 2

0 miles 1

Herald Square and the Garment District
Here are two temples of retailing: A&S Plaza and, of course, Macy's. The surrounding area (especially Seventh Avenue) is the fashion wholesale center with major discounts during sales – but many stores accept only cash. (See pp130–31.)

FIFTH AVENUE

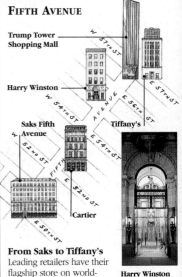

Trump Tower Shopping Mall

Harry Winston

Saks Fifth Avenue

Tiffany's

Cartier

From Saks to Tiffany's
Leading retailers have their flagship store on world-famous Fifth Avenue.

Harry Winston
(see p320)

New York Originals

NEW YORK IS A CITY where just about any kind of shop, no matter how esoteric, will always attract customers. Dozens of tiny shops scattered around the city specialize in unusual merchandise, from butterflies and bones to traditional Tibetan treasures and Shamrock sprigs from Ireland. Coming across these in some tucked-away corner is what makes shopping in New York such an entertaining experience.

SPECIALTY SHOPS

FOR BEAUTIFUL BRASS, onyx and pewter chess sets, and the opportunity to play a decent game, make a move to the **Village Chess Shop**. **Big City Kites Co.** has kites in different kinds of weird and wonderful shapes from fiery dragons to cuddly teddy bears, plus enough accessories to satisfy even the most dedicated kite flyer. For those with a bit more energy, **Blades** sells and rents out skates and also the trendiest skateboards plus all the safety equipment to go with them.

If you're looking for different or unusual buttons, a visit to **Tender Buttons**, which stocks millions, is a must. Whether you want enamel, wood or Navajo silver buttons – or perhaps want your own buttons made into cuff links or earrings – here you'll find just what you want – and more.

For the inveterate collector of sports cards, **Jeff's** has one of the largest selections. **Leo Kaplan Ltd.** specializes in paperweights and **Rita Ford's Music Boxes**, a 19th-century style shop, stocks an extensive range of music boxes. For unusual phones, the **Phone Booth** stocks every possible design including juicy puckered lips, Snoopy dogs and hamburgers.

The **New York Firefighter's Friend** sells an intriguing range of items related purely to fire-fighting, including toy fire engines, firemen's jackets, badges, scaled-down uniforms for children, stuffed toy dalmatians and a wide selection of T-shirts including a popular one with NYFD (New York Fire Department) on one side and "Keep back 200 feet" on the other.

For the true romantic who wants to impress, everything sold by **Only Hearts** is heart-shaped, including pillows, soap and jewelry. The **Magickal Childe** is an occult emporium full of potions, tarot cards and fragrant incense. Science fiction fans and comic collectors should head for **Forbidden Planet**. Then, step straight into the space age at **Star Magic** to buy celestial maps, holograms, prisms and scientific toys.

Cologne made especially for George Washington and the official soap of the White House during the Eisenhower era are just some of the many fascinating items for sale at **Caswell-Massey Ltd.**, the oldest pharmacy in the city.

Guitar gurus will want to visit **Rudy's**, Manny's or Sam Ash's guitar shop. You may bump into Eric Clapton or Lou Reed – both have their guitars made in this area – and you'll also find the best choice of instruments in the city.

Bibliophiles will find a range of gifts in both the **New York Public Library Shop** (see p144) (such as bookends of the lions guarding the main entrance) and the **Pierpont Morgan Library shop** (see pp162–3), including book-marks and writing paper.

University knickknacks and accessories are at **The Yale Club** gift shop and **The Princeton Club**.

The Shop at One East (Temple Emanu-El) sells Judaica and other household gifts for the Jewish home. **Hebrew Religious Articles** carries one of the largest selections of Jewish religious items in the city. **The Cathedral Shop** at the Cathedral of St. John the Divine is a large store selling books, artworks, herbs, jewelry and religious items.

MEMORABILIA

AT LINCOLN CENTER, the **Metropolitan Opera Shop** has records, cards, librettos, small binoculars and many other opera-related items. The **Performing Arts Shop** downstairs is a real treasure trove of theater, opera, ballet and music memorabilia. For ballet fans, everything from Nureyev T-shirts to dance records can be found at the **Ballet Shop**. For thousands of rare and classic film stills and posters visit **Jerry Ohlinger's Movie Material Store**.

If you're looking for an old Wurlitzer jukebox or a Coke machine, go to **Back Pages Antiques**. The **Carnegie Hall Shop** carries musically themed cards, T-shirts, games, posters, tote bags and much more. For something truly original and very American, be sure to visit **Lost City Arts** and **Urban Archaeology** in SoHo. Between these two shops, you'll unearth all sorts of relics from America's past, from Barbie Doll lunch boxes to furniture from traditional ice-cream parlors.

TOYS, GAMES AND GADGETS

FOR CHILDREN'S GIFTS, don't miss the legendary **F.A.O. Schwarz**. This is a massive store crammed from floor to ceiling with luxury toy cars, enormous stuffed animals and every kind of electronic toy imaginable. There are shoulder-to-shoulder crowds at Christmas, when you might have to line up to get in.

The Enchanted Forest (see p102) is a magical experience for children. Its handmade toys are artfully displayed among the trees of the delightful interior, built by a theatrical set designer.

The Last Wound-Up has a large selection of wind-up toys and music boxes in all possible shapes and sizes. **Penny Whistle Toys** sells a huge selection of quality toys, games and all kinds of different dolls.

For games for both children and adults, the **Game Show** has puzzles and games galore, from real classics like Monopoly to the latest yuppie favorite. **Red Caboose** and the **Train Shop** are for fans of model railways. **Toys 'R' Us** doesn't have Schwarz's style but it does stock over a million toys for all ages at reasonable prices.

If you're looking for a self-stirring saucepan or a pair of electric socks, then go to **Hammacher Schlemmer**. There are high-tech gadgets galore, some more fascinating than practical, but this was the first shop to sell the steam iron and pop-up toaster. Finally, if there's room in your life for a pencil you couldn't fit in your car or an aspirin even an elephant would find difficult to swallow, then these and other oversize versions of ordinary objects are for sale at **Think Big**.

MUSEUM SHOPS

SOME OF NEW YORK'S best souvenirs can be found in the city's many museum shops. In addition to the usual range of books, posters and cards, there are reproductions of the exhibits on display, including jewelry and sculpture. The **American Craft Museum** (see p169) has an excellent selection of American crafts. In addition to realistic model dinosaurs and rubber animals, the **American Museum of Natural History** (see pp214–15) has earth-awareness gifts, which include posters, bags and T-shirts, large selections of jewelry from throughout the world and Native American handicrafts. There is also a kids' shop with reasonably priced items such as shell sets, magnets and toys.

The **Asia Society Bookstore and Gift Shop** (see p185) has a striking selection of Oriental prints, posters, art books, toys and jewelry. Items related to interior design are offered at the **Cooper-Hewitt** (see p184). One of New York's largest collections of Jewish ceremonial objects, including menorahs and Kiddush cups, books and jewelry, is found in the small shop at the **Jewish Museum** (see p184).

For reproduction prints of famous paintings, and other exquisite gifts a visit to the **Metropolitan Museum of Art** (see pp188–95) gift shop is a must. The traditional **Museum of American Folk Art** (see p213) prides itself on its American country crafts, including wooden toys, quilts and weathervanes.

The **Museum of the City of New York** (see p197), specializes in pictures of old New York. The **Museum of Modern Art/MOMA Design Store** (see pp170–73) has a selection of innovative home furnishings, toys and kitchenware inspired by international designers such as Frank Lloyd Wright and Le Corbusier.

For a selection of nautical items, including charts, maps, model ships and scrimshaw, go to the **South Street Seaport Museum Shops** (see pp82–85). The **Whitney Museum's Store Next Door** (see pp198–9) stocks only American-made items, including jewelry, wooden toys and books and posters complementing current exhibitions. The **Hayden Planetarium** (see p216) has an interesting gift shop for budding astronomers, with books on all aspects of astronomy plus star-finders and charts, cards and prints.

THE BEST OF THE IMPORTS

NEW YORK is a massive melting pot of different nationalities, cultures and ethnic groups, all of which have made their mark on New York's diverse culture in one way or another. Many ethnic shops specialize in food or goods of a particular group. Some of the most interesting and unusual shops include the **Alaska Shop/Gallery of Eskimo Art**, which has a huge collection of Eskimo art, and the **Chinese Porcelain Company,** for exquisite Chinese decorative arts and furniture. **Back From Guatemala** has jewelry and decorative arts from Central and South America, and **Himalayan Crafts and Tours** stocks everything from paintings to Tibetan rugs. A wonderful collection of emerald green goods and items with a Celtic theme can be found in **Shamrock Imports**, which also sells hand-knitted Irish sweaters. **Things Japanese** has beautifully made crafts and unusual books. **Surma** is a Ukrainian general store that sells hand painted eggs and linens. **Common Ground** sells Native American baskets, weavings and jewelry, and **Tibet West** sells textiles and colorful jewelry.

ADDRESSES

Alaska Shop/Gallery of Eskimo Art
31 E 74th St. **Map** 16 F5.
[879-1782.

Back From Guatemala
306 E 6th St. **Map** 5 A2.
[260-7010.

Chinese Porcelain Company
822 Madison Ave. **Map** 13 A2.
[628-4101.

Common Ground
19 Greenwich Ave. **Map** 1 B1.
[989-4178.

Himalayan Crafts and Tours
1228 Lexington Ave. **Map** 17 A4.
[744-8892.

Shamrock Imports
Fifth level, A&S Plaza, 901 6th Ave.
Map 8 E2.
[564-7474.

Surma
11 E 7th St. **Map** 4 F2.
[477-0729.

Things Japanese
127 E 60th St.
Map 13 A3.
[371-4661.

Tibet West
19 Christopher St. **Map** 3 C2.
[255-3416.

DIRECTORY

SPECIALITY SHOPS

Big City Kites and Darts
1201 Lexington Ave.
Map 17 A4.
[472-2623.

Blades
105 W 72nd St.
Map 11 C1.
[787-3911.
One of several branches.

Caswell-Massey Ltd.
518 Lexington Ave.
Map 13 A5.
[755-2254.

The Cathedral Shop
Cathedral of St John the Divine, 1047 Amsterdam Ave. **Map** 20 E4.
[222-7200.

Hebrew Religious Articles
45 Essex St. **Map** 5 B4.
[674-1770.

Jeff's
150 2nd Ave. **Map** 4 F1.
[598-0180.

Leo Kaplan Ltd.
967 Madison Ave.
Map 17 A5.
[249-6766.

Magickal Childe
35 W 19th St. **Map** 8 F5.
[242-7182.

New York Firefighter's Friend
263 Lafayette St.
Map 4 F3.
[226-3142.

New York Public Library Shop
5th Ave at 42nd St.
Map 8 F1.
[930-0678.

Only Hearts
386 Columbus Ave.
Map 15 D5.
[724-5608.

Phone Booth
12 E 53rd St.
Map 12 F4.
[751-8310.

Pierpont Morgan Library Shop
Madison Ave at 36th St.
Map 9 A2.
[685-0610.

The Princeton Club
15 W 43rd St. **Map** 8 F1.
[840-6400.

Rita Ford's Music Boxes
19 E 65th St.
Map 12 F2.
[535-6717.

Rudy's
169 W 48th St
Map 12 E5.
[391-1699.

The Shop at One East
Temple Emanu-El,
1 E 65th St.
Map 12 F2.
[744-1400.

Star Magic
745 Broadway. **Map** 4 E2.
[228-7770.

Tender Buttons
143 E 62nd St. **Map** 13 A2.
[758-7004.

Village Chess Shop
230 Thompson St.
Map 4 D3.
[475-9580.

The Yale Club
50 Vanderbilt Ave.
Map 13 A5.
[661-2070.

MEMORABILIA

Back Pages Antiques
125 Greene St. **Map** 4 E4.
[460-5998.

Ballet Shop
1887 Broadway.
Map 12 D2.
[581-7990.

The Carnegie Hall Shop
881 7th Ave.
Map 12 E3.
[903-9610.

Jerry Ohlinger's Movie Material Store
242 W 14th St. **Map** 3 C1.
[989-0869.

Lost City Arts
275 Lafayette St.
Map 4 F3.
[941-8025.

Metropolitan Opera Shop
Metropolitan Opera House, Lincoln Center,

136 W 65th St.
Map 11 C2.
[580-4090.

Performing Arts Shop
Metropolitan Opera House, Lincoln Center,
136 W 65th St.
Map 11 C2.
[580-4356.

Urban Archaeology
285 Lafayette St.
Map 4 F3.
[431-6969.

TOYS, GAMES AND GADGETS

The Enchanted Forest
85 Mercer St. **Map** 4 E4.
[925-6677.

F.A.O. Schwarz
767 5th Ave.
Map 12 F3.
[644-9400.

Game Show
474 6th Ave. **Map** 12 E5.
[633-6328.

Hammacher Schlemmer
147 E 57th St.
Map 13 A3.
[421-9000.

The Last Wound-Up
1595 2nd Ave.
Map 17 B4.
[288-7585.

Penny Whistle Toys
448 Columbus Ave.
Map 16 D4.
[873-9090.
One of several branches.

Red Caboose
16 W 45th St, 4th Floor
Map 12 F5.
[575-0155.

Think Big
390 West Broadway.
Map 4 E4.
[925-7300.

Toys 'R' Us
Herald Center,
1293 Broadway.
Map 8 E2.
[594-8697.

Train Shop
Basement, 23 W 45th St.
Map 12 F5.
[730-0409.

MUSEUM SHOPS

American Craft Museum
40 W 53rd St. **Map** 12 F4.
[956-6047.

American Museum of Natural History
W 79th St at Central Park West. **Map** 16 D5.
[769-5100.

Asia Society Bookstore and Gift Shop
725 Park Ave.
Map 13 A1.
[288-6400.

Cooper-Hewitt
2 E 91st St.
Map 16 F2.
[860-6878.

Hayden Planetarium
Central Park West at W 81st St. **Map** 16 D4.
[769-5900.

Jewish Museum
1109 5th Ave.
Map 16 F2.
[423-3200.

Metropolitan Museum of Art
5th Ave at 82nd St.
Map 16 F4.
[535-7710.

Museum of American Folk Art
2 Lincoln Sq.
Map 12 D2.
[496-2966.

Museum of the City of New York
5th Ave at 103rd St.
Map 21 C5.
[534-1672.

Museum of Modern Art/MOMA Design Store
44 W 53rd St.
Map 12 F4.
[767-1050.

South St Seaport Museum Shops
207 Front St. **Map** 2 D2.
[480-4951.

The Whitney Museum's Store Next Door
943 Madison Ave.
Map 13 A1.
[606-0200.

Fashion

WHETHER YOU'RE LOOKING for a secondhand pair of 501s or the kind of ballgown Ivana Trump would wear, you'll find it in New York. The city is the fashion capital of America and an important center of clothing manufacture and design. Its clothing stores, like its restaurants, reflects the city's dramatically different styles and cultures. To save time it's probably best to visit one area at a time and wander from store to store. Alternatively, visit one of the major department stores for an excellent selection of fashion for everyone.

AMERICAN DESIGNERS

MANY AMERICAN designers sell their creations in boutiques within the large department stores, or have exclusive shops of their own. One of the most famous is Geoffrey Beene, known for sophisticated looks that are casual and comfortable.

Bill Blass is the king of American fashion whose clothes feature loads of different colors, wild patterns, innovative shapes and a lot of wit. Liz Claiborne's designs are always elegantly simple, casual and reasonably priced, including everything you could possibly need from tennis whites to casual professional wear for women.

The late Perry Ellis's style lives on with clothes designed by Marc Jacobs, known for his sportswear. James Galanos is an exclusive designer for the rich and famous, making one-of-a-kind *couture* clothes, and Betsey Johnson is popular with women able to wear figure-hugging fashions in fabulous fabrics.

Donna Karan's clothes include a range of outfits for the professional woman as well as cheaper sportswear. Anne Klein's much more traditional clothes, specializing in a more sophisticated look, have been continued by Louis dell'Olio, who took over after her death. Calvin Klein is renowned for comfortable, classic sportswear, including the sensuous and well-fitting underwear and jeans so familiar from his ads. Ralph Lauren is well known for his aristocratic and expensive clothes, a "look" favored by the exclusive and posh Ivy League, horsey set. Joan Vass specializes in moderately priced but exciting, colorful and innovative knitwear.

DISCOUNT DESIGNER CLOTHES

IF YOU'RE on the lookout for discount designer clothes, **Designer Resale**, **Encore** and **Michael's** sell a wide range. Oscar de la Renta, Ungaro and Armani are just some of the leading labels available. Clothes are either new or worn but near-perfect.

MEN'S CLOTHES

TWO OF THE city's most highly-regarded menswear stores are **Brooks Brothers** and **Paul Stuart**. Brooks Brothers is something of a New York institution, famous for its traditional, conservative clothing such as smart button-down shirts and Chinos. There's an ultra-conservative woman's line too. Paul Stuart prides itself on its very British look and offers a stylish array of superbly tailored fashions.

Go to the high-quality department store **Bergdorf Goodman Men** to find beautifully made Turnbull & Asser shirts and marvelous suits by Gianfranco Ferré or Hugo Boss.

Barney's New York has one of the most comprehensive men's departments in America, with a truly massive range of clothes and accessories. A smaller Barney's, at the World Financial Center, specializes in even smarter business clothes and suits for professionals.

The **Polo/Ralph Lauren** department store is packed from floor to ceiling with the so-called king of American Sportswear's simple and timeless fashions and his many stylish accessories.

Mano a Mano sells elegant clothes for the modern SoHo man; **Matsuda** sells very expensive, avant-garde Japanese chic for men and women. **Bijan Designer for Men** is so exclusive that clothes can be seen only by appointment.

The **Custom Shop Shirtmakers** specializes in custom-made suits and shirts in beautiful materials. Go to **F. R. Tripler & Co.** for superb traditional and formal wear, and to **Burberry Limited** for classic British trenchcoats.

J. Press sells classic, conservative yet elegant clothes. Uptown designer menswear boutiques include the renowned **Beau Brummel** with a selection of very stylish European clothes and for superb designer bargains, check out **Moe Ginsburg** for one of New York's largest selections of men's Italian clothing or **BFO** for discount Armani and Matsuda. Women, be advised: many of these stores also carry striking women's fashions.

CHILDREN'S CLOTHES

IN ADDITION to an excellent selection within the large department stores, there are several shops around the city that sell children's clothing exclusively. Take a look at **Bébé Thompson** for classic, designer outfits or **Bonpoint** for French-style charm.

Gapkids and BabyGap shops, often in the **Gap** shops, have comfortable, long-lasting cotton overalls, sweat pants, denim jackets, sweatshirts and leggings. The wonderfully named **Peanut Butter & Jane** sells trendy but particularly comfortable togs. **Space Kiddets** has everything from bibs and booties to cowboy and cowgirl clothes.

WOMEN'S CLOTHES

Women's fashion is subject to design trends, and New York stores keep pace with them all. Most of the city's most fashionable shops are found in the midtown area around Madison and Fifth avenues. These include some of the major department stores *(see p311)*, which stock a range of American designers, including Donna Karan, Anne Klein, Bill Blass and Claude Montana. Leading international names such as **Chanel**, **Fendi**, and **Valentino** also have shops here, as does one of the outstanding American designers, **Geoffrey Beene**. There is also a handful of popular ready-to-wear stores, including **Ann Taylor**, which is much favored by young, busy professionals looking for stylish, comfortable clothing.

Right at the heart of this area stands the pink-marbled Trump Tower, which houses a selection of exclusive shops, including **Galeries Lafayette**, the French department store.

Madison Avenue is packed with designers for the smart set, who have everything you could ever need, including **Givenchy** who sells show-stopping formal gowns at phenomenal prices, Valentino who has classic Italian clothes and **Emanuel Ungaro** who is relatively unintimidating and has something to suit most tastes from beautifully tailored jackets to more matronly full-figured and boldly patterned print dresses. **Missoni** is famous for richly textured sweaters in sumptuous wools and colorful patterns, **Sonia Rykiel** for knitwear and silk dresses. **Yves St Laurent Rive Gauche** has evening gowns, one-of-a-kind jackets, silks and extravagant blouses and beautifully cut pants suits. **Krizia** is full with eye-catching fashions by designer Mariucca Mandella. Sophisticated Italian looks are also available from Italian style kings **Giorgio Armani** and **Gianni Versace**. **Romeo Gigli's** Milanese clothing is so exclusive that his shop has no name on the door. **Gucci**, one of the oldest Italian shops in America, is for the wealthy and status-conscious.

The Upper West Side has many shops competing for attention with contemporary fashions, including **Betsey Johnson's** shop, with her whimsical, relatively inexpensive designs. **Charivari** is a fast-growing chain of stores that specialize in ultra-hip casual fashions. **French Connection** is known for its affordable separates, both casual and for the office.

The villages – the East Village in particular – are the best places to go for second-hand clothing and 1950s rock 'n' roll gear, with ever-changing interesting shops run by new and young designers and art school graduates. **B-Flat the Store** carries a huge selection of secondhand Levi's as well as hundreds of denim and leather jackets. **Dorothy's Closet** has classic dresses from the 1920s to the 1960s. **Panache** specializes in second-hand designer clothes in totally pristine condition. **Screaming Mimi's** is where you could unearth that pair of velvet bell-bottoms or go-go boots you've always dreamed of having. A more mainstream shop is **The Gap**, a chain store selling moderately priced, well-made casual and comfortable clothes for men, women and children.

Recently SoHo has come to rival Madison Avenue for designer boutiques specializing in expensive but interesting clothes – the fashions here are far more avant-garde. You'll find **Yohji Yamamoto**, among other exclusive stores. **Comme des Garçons** sells minimalist Japanese chic.

More mainstream is one of SoHo's most famous stores, the **Canal Jean Co.**, which has all the latest SoHo looks at affordable prices. Go to **Wearable Energy** for wall-to-wall spandex or **The Second Coming** for secondhand clothing and even furniture and household goods.

SIZE CHART

For Australian sizes follow the British and American conversions.

Children's clothing

American	2-3	4-5	6 6x	7-8	10	12	14	16	(size)
British	2-3	4-5	6-7	8-9	10-11	12	14	14+	(years)
Continental	2-3	4-5	6-7	8-9	10-11	12	14	14+	(years)

Children's shoes

American	7½	8½	9½	10½	11½	12½	13½	1½	2½
British	7	8	9	10	11	12	13	1	2
Continental	24	25½	27	28	29	30	32	33	34

Women's dresses, coats and skirts

American	4	6	8	10	12	14	16	18
British	6	8	10	12	14	16	18	20
Continental	38	40	42	44	46	48	50	52

Women's blouses and sweaters

American	6	8	10	12	14	16	18
British	30	32	34	36	38	40	42
Continental	40	42	44	46	48	50	52

Women's shoes

American	5	6	7	8	9	10	11
British	3	4	5	6	7	8	9
Continental	36	37	38	39	40	41	44

Men's suits

American	34	36	38	40	42	44	46	48
British	34	36	38	40	42	44	46	48
Continental	44	46	48	50	52	54	56	58

Men's shirts

American	14	15	15½	16	16½	17	17½	18
British	14	15	15½	16	16½	17	17½	18
Continental	36	38	39	41	42	43	44	45

Men's shoes

American	7	7½	8	8½	9½	10½	11	11½
British	6	7	7½	8	9	10	11	12
Continental	39	40	41	42	43	44	45	46

DIRECTORY

DISCOUNT DESIGNER CLOTHES

Designer Resale
324 E 81st St.
Map 17 B4.
(734-3639.

Encore
1132 Madison Ave.
Map 17 A4.
(879-2850.

Michael's
1041 Madison Ave.
Map 17 A5.
(737-7273.

MEN'S CLOTHES

Barney's New York
111 7th Ave. **Map** 8 E5.
(929-9000.
One of several branches.

Beau Brummel
1113 Madison Ave.
Map 17 A4.
(737-4200.
One of several branches.

Bergdorf Goodman Men
754 5th Ave. **Map** 12 F3.
(753-7300.

BFO
149 5th Ave. **Map** 8 F4.
(254-0059.

Bijan Designer for Men
699 5th Ave. **Map** 12 F4.
(758-7500.

Brooks Brothers
346 Madison Ave.
Map 9 A1.
(682-8800.

Burberry Limited
9 E 57th St. **Map** 12 F3.
(371-5010.

The Custom Shop Shirtmakers
618 5th Ave. **Map** 12 F4.
(245-2499.
One of several branches.

F. R. Tripler & Co.
366 Madison Ave.
Map 13 A5.
(922-1090.

J. Press
7 E 44th St. **Map** 12 F5.
(687-7642.

Mano a Mano
580 Broadway. **Map** 12 E5. **(** 219-9602.

Matsuda
156 5th Ave. **Map** 8 F4.
(645-5151.

Moe Ginsburg
162 5th Ave. **Map** 8 F4.
(242-3482.

Paul Stuart
Madison Ave at 45th St.
Map 13 A5.
(682-0320.

Polo/Ralph Lauren
Madison Ave at 72nd St.
Map 13 A1.
(606-2100.

CHILDREN'S CLOTHES

Bébé Thompson
98 Thompson St.
Map 4 D4.
(925-1122.

Bonpoint
1269 Madison Ave.
Map 17 A3.
(722-7720.

Gapkids
657 3rd Ave.
Map 18 B3.
(697-9007.
One of several branches.

Peanut Butter & Jane
617 Hudson St. **Map** 3 B1.
(620-7952.

Space Kiddets
46 E 21st St. **Map** 8 F4.
(420-9878.

WOMEN'S CLOTHES

Ann Taylor
3 E 57th St. **Map** 12 F3.
(832-2010.
One of several branches.

B-Flat the Store
125 E 4th St.
Map 4 F2.
(260-5220.

Betsey Johnson
248 Columbus Ave.
Map 16 D4.
(362-3364.
One of several branches.

Canal Jean Co.
504 Broadway. **Map** 4 E4.
(226-0737.

Chanel
5 E 57th St.
Map 12 F3.
(355-5050.

Charivari 57
18 W 57th St.
Map 12 F3.
(333-4040.

Charivari 72
257 Columbus Ave.
Map 12 D1.
(873-7242.

Workshop
441 Columbus Ave.
Map 12 D2.
(496-8700.

Sports
201 W 79th St.
Map 15 C5.
(799-8650.

Women
2315 Broadway.
Map 16 D3.
(873-1424.

Comme des Garçons
116 Wooster Street.
Map 4 E3.
(219-0660.

Dorothy's Closet
335 Bleecker St.
Map 3 C2.
(206-6414.

Emanuel Ungaro
803 Madison Ave.
Map 13 A2.
(249-4090.

Fendi
720 5th Ave. **Map** 12 F3.
(767-0100.

French Connection
304 Columbus Ave.
Map 12 D1.
(496-1470.
One of several branches.

Galeries Lafayette
4–10 E 57th St.
Map 12 F3.
(355-0022.

The Gap
354 6th Ave. **Map** 8 E1.
(777-2420.
One of several branches.

Geoffrey Beene
783 5th Ave. **Map** 12 F3.
(935-0470.

Gianni Versace
816 Madison Ave.
Map 13 A2.
(744-5572.

Giorgio Armani
815 Madison Ave.
Map 13 A2.
(988-9191.

Givenchy
954 Madison Ave.
Map 13 A1.
(772-1040.

Gucci
685 5th Ave. **Map** 12 F4.
(826-2600.

Krizia
805 Madison Ave.
Map 13 A2.
(628-8180.

Missoni
836 Madison Ave.
Map 13 A1.
(517-9339.

Panache
525 Hudson St.
Map 3 B1.
(242-5115.

Romeo Gigli
21 E 69th St.
Map 10 F1.
(744-9121.

Screaming Mimi's
22 E 4th St.
Map 4 E2.
(677-6464.

The Second Coming
72 Greene St.
Map 4 E4.
(431-4424.

Sonia Rykiel
792 Madison Ave.
Map 13 A2.
(744-0880.

Valentino
825 Madison Ave.
Map 13 A2.
(772-6969.

Wearable Energy
73 W Houston St.
Map 4 D3.
(475-0026.

Yohji Yamamoto
103 Grand St.
Map 4 E4.
(966-9066.

Yves St Laurent Rive Gauche
855 Madison Ave.
Map 13 A1.
(472-5299.

Accessories

IN ADDITION TO the following shops, all of the major Manhattan department stores have extensive accessory departments stocking a range of hats, gloves, bags, jewelry, watches, scarves, shoes and umbrellas.

JEWELRY

MIDTOWN FIFTH AVENUE is where to find the most dazzling jewelers, including the museum-like **Harry Winston**, which showcases its coveted jewels from around the world. **Buccellati** is well respected for its innovative Italian creations and excellent workmanship. **Bulgari** has an impressive collection that ranges in price from a mere couple of hundred to over a million dollars.

Housed in a Renaissance-style palazzo, **Cartier** is a jewel in itself and sells its beautiful baubles at unthinkable prices. **Fortunoff** has an enormous selection of elegant jewelry. **Tiffany & Co.** has ten floors of glittering crystal, diamonds and other jewels just waiting to be packed up for you and taken away in the store's signature sky blue boxes.

Diamond Row, a one-block area on 47th Street (between Fifth and Sixth avenues), is lined with shops displaying hundreds of thousands of dollars worth of diamonds, gold, pearls and other exotic jewels from around the world. Try not to miss the **Jewelry Exchange**, a new complex where 40 different crafts-people sell their unique creations direct to the public. Boisterous bargaining is very much alive here, so be prepared to play the game.

HATS

THE CITY'S OLDEST hat shop is **Worth & Worth**, which has the largest collection of hats in the city. You can get everything you could possibly want here, from original Australian bush hats to silk toppers and romantic con-coctions. Try **Lola Millinery** for unique whimsical hats. **Suzanne Millinery** is the hatmaker to the stars, popular with such celebrities as Whoopi Goldberg and Ivana Trump. **Don Marshall Millinery** has been worn everywhere by the rich and famous since 1946.

UMBRELLAS

THE MINUTE IT STARTS to rain in New York, hundreds of street vendors selling umbrellas seem to sprout like mush-rooms. Their umbrellas, at just a few dollars, are the cheapest in the city, but unlikely to last much longer than the downpour itself. For good-quality umbrellas, you'll find a fine selection of Briggs of London at **Worth & Worth**, a wide range of styles at **Uncle Sam**, and both trendy patterns and more traditional tartans and stripes at **Barney's New York**. World-famous **Gucci** has umbrellas to match its ties. There are expensive and telescopic ones found at **Hanae Mori**, and doorman-sized ones in solid black or the university's traditional colors of black and orange at **The Princeton Club**. **The Yale Club** has blue ones emblazoned with a white "Y".

HANDBAGS AND BRIEFCASES

TWICE A YEAR, during the January and August sales, a serpentine line of buyers wraps around the corner of 48th Street and Madison Avenue waiting to get into **Crouch & Fitzgerald**. An old New York institution, selling handbags, briefcases and luggage. All the well-known brands are sold here, including Judith Leiber, Ghurka, Dooney & Bourke and Louis Vuitton, as well as the firm's own line. Elsewhere in the city are such exclusive shops as **Bottega Veneta**, **Loewe** and **Prada**, where handbags are displayed like precious art, with prices to match. Younger and trendier places include **La Bagagerie**, crammed floor to ceiling with a wide range of contemporary bags, **Furla**, well-respected for its Italian designs, and the stylish **Il Bisonte**. **The Coach Store** is known for its simple, classic leather handbags.

For discount designer handbags go to the legendary **Fine & Klein**, and for bargain briefcases from slim envelopes to thick lawyer's bags, a visit to the **Altman Luggage Company** is a must.

SHOES AND BOOTS

MANHATTAN SHOE stores are well renowned for their extensive selections of shoes and boots, and if you shop around you are sure to to find what you want at a good price.

Most of the large depart-ment stores in New York also have shoe departments where you can find designer-label shoes in addition to other brands. **Bloomingdale's** *(see p179)* has a huge women's footwear department, and **Brooks Brothers** has one of the best selections of tradi-tional men's shoes in the city.

For both men's and women's shoes, the most exclusive shops are around the midtown area. **Susan Bennis/Warren Edwards** has fabulous shoes made from exotic and often unusual materials. **Maud Frizon** stocks the Parisiennes' favorite footwear, from cute little-girl round toes to more seductive high-heeled pumps. **Ferragamo** sells classic styles crafted in Florence. Go to **Botticelli** for whimsical shoe fashions and try **Charles Jourdan** for some very elegant designer creations.

For cowboy boots, head for **Billy Martin's**. There's an enormous selection of handmade boots, from basic, no-frills "ropers," which real American cowboys wear, to crocodile leather boots that sell for thousands of dollars. Billy Martin's also stocks all sorts of western garb and accessories, so you can clothe yourself in western gear from head to toe. For beautiful custom-made boots, try **St. Mark's Leather** or **Buffalo Chips Bootery**.

For the latest and best in children's shoes, **East Side Kids** stocks the trendiest fashions for kids. **Little Eric** has unusual, eye-catching footwear and **Shoofly** has imported shoes in all styles.

Both **Tru-Tred** and **Stride Rite** have everything a style-conscious child needs, from basketball sneakers to tap dancing shoes.

For discounted shoes, the greatest concentration of shops is around West 34th Street and West 8th Street between Fifth and Sixth avenues, and Orchard Street on the Lower East Side.

LINGERIE

EXPENSIVE and exquisite handmade silk lingerie can be found at the sensuous **La Lingerie** and **Montenapoleone**. More affordable is **Victoria's Secret**, which offers two floors of beautifully made lingerie in satin, silk and other fine fabrics.

DIRECTORY

JEWELRY

Buccellati
725 5th Ave. **Map** 12 F3.
(308-5533.

Bulgari
730 5th Ave. **Map** 12 F3.
(315-9000.

Cartier
653 5th Ave. **Map** 12 F4.
(753-0111.

Fortunoff
681 5th Ave. **Map** 12 F4.
(758-6660.

Harry Winston
718 5th Ave.
Map 12 F3.
(245-2000.

Jewelry Exchange
15 W 47th St.
Map 12 F5.

Tiffany & Co.
5th Ave at 57th St.
Map 12 F3.
(755-8000.

HATS

Don Marshall Millinery
120 E 56th St.
Map 13 A3.
(758-1686.

Lola Millinery
2 E 17th St.
Map 8 F5.
(366-5708.

Suzanne Millinery
700 Madison Ave.
Map 13 A3.
(593-3232.

Worth & Worth
331 Madison Ave.
Map 9 A1.
(867-6058.

UMBRELLAS

Barney's New York
See p311.

Gucci
685 5th Ave.
Map 12 F4.
(826-2600.

Hanae Mori
27 E 79th St.
Map 16 F5.
(472-2352.

The Princeton Club
15 W 43rd St.
Map 8 F1.
(840-6400.

Uncle Sam
161 W 57th St.
Map 12 E3.
(582-1976.

Worth & Worth
See Hats.

The Yale Club
50 Vanderbilt Ave.
Map 13 A5.
(661-2070.

HANDBAGS AND BRIEFCASES

Altman Luggage Company
135 Orchard St.
Map 5 A3.
(254-7275.

La Bagagerie
727 Madison Ave.
Map 13 A2.
(758-6570.

Il Bisonte
72 Thompson Street.
Map 4 D4.
(966-8773.

Bottega Veneta
635 Madison Ave.
Map 13 A3.
(371-5511.

The Coach Store
710 Madison Ave.
Map 13 A3.
(319-1772.

Crouch & Fitzgerald
400 Madison Ave.
Map 13 A5.
(755-5888.

Fine & Klein
119 Orchard St.
Map 5 A3.
(674-6720.

Furla
705 Madison Ave.
Map 13 A3.
(755-8986.
One of two branches.

Loewe
711 Madison Ave.
Map 13 A3.
(308-7700.

Prada
45 E 57th St. **Map** 12 F3.
(308-2332.

SHOES AND BOOTS

Billy Martin's
812 Madison Ave.
Map 13 A1.
(861-3100.

Botticelli
612 5th Ave. **Map** 12 F4.
(582-6313.

Bloomingdale's
See p311.

Brooks Brothers
See p319.

Buffalo Chips Bootery
116 Greene St. **Map** 4 E4.
(274-0651.

Charles Jourdan
Trump Tower, 725 5th Ave.
Map 12 F3.
(644-3830.

East Side Kids
1298 Madison Ave.
Map 17 A2.
(360-5000.

Ferragamo
717 5th Ave. **Map** 12 F3.
(759-3822.

Little Eric
1331 3rd Ave. **Map** 17 B5.
(288-8987.

Maud Frizon
19 E 69th St. **Map** 13 A1.
(249-5368.

St. Mark's Leather
7 St. Mark's Pl. **Map** 5 A2.
(982-3444.

Shoofly
465 Amsterdam Ave.
Map 15 C4.
(580-4390.

Stride Rite
730 Columbus Ave.
Map 16 D1.
(222-2219.

Susan Bennis/ Warren Edwards
22 W 57th St. **Map** 12 F3.
(755-4197.

Tru-Tred
1241 Lexington Ave.
Map 17 A4.
(249-0551.

LINGERIE

La Lingerie
792 Madison Ave.
Map 13 A2.
(772-9797.

Montenapoleone
789 Madison Ave.
Map 13 A2.
(535-2660.

Victoria's Secret
34 E 57th St.
Map 12 F3.
(758-5592.

Books and Music

As THE PUBLISHING CAPITAL of America, it's not surprising that New York has the country's best selection of bookstores. These range from vast general interest stores to hundreds of esoteric bookstores specializing in everything from sci-fi to suspense, selling new books and old. Music lovers will also find sounds for all tastes at reasonable prices, plus thousands of rare recordings.

GENERAL INTEREST BOOKSTORES

One OF THE MOST well-known of New York's bookstores is **Barnes & Noble** on Fifth Avenue, reputedly the world's largest bookstore. The store at 18th and Fifth is packed high with over three million books on every imaginable subject. The sales annex across the street has thousands of good buys.

Several blocks away is the main branch of New York's famous **Strand Book Store**. The Strand has an astonishing two million copies of new and secondhand books at some of the best prices in town. There is also a large rare book room for first editions. **Doubleday Book Shop** is very good for new titles, best-sellers and travel books. **B. Dalton's** flagship store on Fifth Avenue is stacked with the latest best-sellers, and **Coliseum Books** has a vast selection of paperbacks.

In the heart of midtown Manhattan you can find the excellent **Brentano's**. This is well stocked with all kinds of books and magazines. **Rizzoli** has an enormous selection of photography, foreign language, music and art books plus children's books and videos. **Gotham Book Mart**, a New York institution, is a tiny shop with hundreds of out-of-print books and limited editions.

Shakespeare & Co. offers a sensational selection of titles and is open late every night. **Endicott Booksellers** has a good range of hardcovers.

SPECIALTY BOOKSTORES

For THE BEST selection of art books in the city, visit **Hacker Art Books**. The **Burlington Book Shop** is crammed full with new and

secondhand books on art and literature. **Urban Center Books** has titles on urban planning and conservation.

Books and Co. is a magnet for literati, with an emphasis on poetry, art and philosophy. The city's largest selection of out-of-print books, especially for art and literature, can be found at **Academy Book Store**. Rare, out-of-print and old books about New York are the raison d'être of **New York Bound Bookshop**. The **Biography Bookshop** is the only midtown store specializing in diaries, letters, biographies and autobiographies. Theater buffs should try **Applause Theater & Cinema Books**.

For hundreds of titles on science, business, technology and computers visit **McGraw-Hill** and **Waldenbooks**. Both have general titles too.

Books on murder and suspense are the focus of three shops: **Murder Inc,** **Mysterious Bookshop** and **Foul Play**. Try **Forbidden Planet** for old and new science fiction books and comics. Sci-fi buffs will love the **Science Fiction Shop**, and the **Village Comics** has thousands of old and new comics.

Eeyore's Books for Children has the best selection of children's books. Try **Storyland** for lots of videos and tapes. **Books of Wonder** for hardcover and rare children's books.

The **Traveller's Bookstore** is run by three extremely knowledgeable bibliophiles who know every book they sell and every corner of the globe, too. **The Complete Traveller** stocks a wide selection of travel books and guides, as does the **The Civilized Traveller**. For an excellent range of maps visit the large **Rand McNally Map & Travel**

Store and the **Hagstrom Map & Travel Store**.

Cookbooks are on the menu at **Kitchen Arts & Letters**, with many out-of-print books and first editions.

Radicals should head for **Revolution Books** or **St. Mark's Bookstore,** which also has an excellent selection of literary and art titles. The **Oscar Wilde Memorial Bookshop** has a wide selection of gay and lesbian texts. Those into the occult will find plenty to interest them at **Samuel Weiser's**.

RECORDS, TAPES AND COMPACT DISCS

The BEST MANHATTAN record-store chain is **Tower Records**, whose many stores have everything from bebop to rap. **HMV** follow a close second. **J&R Music World** is a complete home entertainment store.

For out-of-print records, go to **Gryphon Records** and **G&A Rare Records Ltd.** Each is a treasure trove for collectors. The **Academy Book Store** has an excellent choice of classical, jazz and opera recordings. **Footlight Records** is for lovers of Broadway musicals and film soundtracks, and **Dayton's Records** has a large stock of out-of-print and rare records. **Bleecker Bob's Golden Oldies** Record Shop has everything from imports, rock and punk to rare jazz. Try **Midnight Records** for imports, reissues, American garage rock and psychedelia.

SHEET MUSIC

Just BEHIND Carnegie Hall is one of the best stores for classical sheet music, **Joseph Patelson Music House Ltd.** The **Frank Music Company** has a huge collection of classical music scores. For a wider variety of sheet music go to **The Music Exchange**. **Charles Colin Publications** specializes in jazz. For chart music and pop tunes try **Colony Record and Music Center** in the Brill Building.

DIRECTORY

GENERAL INTEREST BOOKSTORES

B. Dalton
666 5th Ave. **Map** 12 F4.
(247-1740.
One of several branches.

Barnes & Noble
105 5th Ave. **Map** 8 F5.
(807-0099.
One of several branches.

Brentano's
597 5th Ave. **Map** 12 F5.
(826-2450.

Coliseum Books
1771 Broadway.
Map 12 D3.
(757-8381.

Doubleday Book Shop
724 5th Ave. **Map** 12 F3.
(397-0550.
One of several branches.

Endicott Booksellers
450 Columbus Ave.
Map 16 D4.
(787-6300.

Gotham Book Mart
41 W 47th St. **Map** 12 F5.
(719-4448.

Rizzoli
31 W 57th St. **Map** 12 F3.
(759-2424.
One of several branches.

Shakespeare & Co.
2259 Broadway.
Map 15 C4.
(580-7800.

Strand Book Store
828 Broadway. **Map** 4 E1.
(473-1452.

SPECIALTY BOOKSTORES

Academy Book Store
10 W 18th St. **Map** 8 F5.
(242-4848.

Applause Theater & Cinema Books
211 W 71st St.
Map 11 C1. (496-7511.

Biography Bookshop
400 Bleecker St. **Map** 3 C2.
(807-8655.

Books and Co.
939 Madison Ave.
Map 17 A5.
(737-1450.

Books of Wonder
132 7th Ave.
Map 8 E5.
(989-3270.

Burlington Book Shop
1082 Madison Ave.
Map 17 A4.
(288-7420.

The Civilized Traveller
1072 3rd Ave.
Map 13 B2.
(758-8305.

The Complete Traveller
199 Madison Ave.
Map 9 A2.
(685-9007

Eeyore's Books for Children
2212 Broadway.
Map 15 C4.
(362-0634.
One of two branches.

Forbidden Planet
821 Broadway. **Map** 4 E1.
(473-1576.

Foul Play
13 8th Ave. **Map** 3 C1.
(675-5115.
One of several branches

Hacker Art Books
45 W 57th St. **Map** 12 F3.
(688-7600.

Hagstrom Map & Travel Store
57 W 43rd St. **Map** 8 F1.
(398-1222.

Kitchen Arts & Letters
1435 Lexington Ave.
Map 17 A2.
(876-5550.

McGraw-Hill Bookstore
1220 6th Ave. **Map** 12 E4.
(512-4100.

Murder Inc
2486 Broadway.
(362-8905.

Mysterious Bookshop
129 W 56th St.
Map 12 E3.
(765-0900.

New York Bound Bookshop
50 Rockefeller Plaza.
Map 12 F5.
(245-8503.

Oscar Wilde Memorial Bookshop
15 Christopher St.
Map 3 C2. (255-8097.

Rand McNally Map & Travel Store
150 E 52nd St. **Map** 13 A4.
(758-7488.

Revolution Books
13 E 16th St. **Map** 8 F5.
(691-3345.

St. Mark's Bookstore
12 St Mark's Pl. **Map** 5 A2.
(260-7853.

Samuel Weiser's
132 E 24th St. **Map** 9 A4.
(777-6363.

Science Fiction Shop
163 Bleecker St. **Map** 4 D3.
(473-3010.

Storyland
1369 3rd Ave. **Map** 17 B5.
(517-6951.

Traveller's Bookstore
Time Warner Building, 22
W 52nd St. **Map** 12 F4.
(664-0995.

Urban Center Books
457 Madison Ave.
Map 13 A4.
(935-3595.

Village Comics
163 Bleecker St.
Map 4 D3.
(777-2770.

Waldenbooks
57 Broadway. **Map** 1 C3.
(269-1139.
One of several branches.

RECORDS, TAPES, COMPACT DISCS

Academy Book Store
See Specialist Bookshops.

Bleecker Bob's Golden Oldies
118 W 3rd St.
Map 4 D2.
(475-9677.

Dayton's Records
4th Ave at 10th St.
Map 4 F1.
(254-5084.

Footlight Records
113 E 12th St.
Map 4 F1.
(533-1572.

G&A Rare Records Ltd.
2nd Floor, 139 W 72nd St.
Map 11 C1.
(877-5020.

Gryphon Records
251 W 72nd St.
Map 11 D1.
(874-1588.

HMV
2081 Broadway.
Map 15 C5.
(721-5900.
One of several branches.

J&R Music World
15, 23, 27 & 33 Park Row.
Map 1 C2.
(732-8600.

Midnight Records
263 W 23rd St.
Map 8 D4.
(675-2768.

Tower Records
692 Broadway. **Map** 4 E2.
(505-1500.
One of several branches.

SHEET MUSIC

Charles Colin Publications
315 W 53rd St.
Map 12 D4.
(581-1480.

Colony Record and Music Center
1619 Broadway.
Map 12 E4.
(265-2050.

Frank Music Company
250 W 54th St.
Map 12 D4.
(582-1999.

Joseph Patelson Music House Ltd.
160 W 56th St.
Map 12 E4.
(582-5840.

The Music Exchange
151 W 46th St. **Map** 12 E5.
(354-5858.

Art and Antiques

ANY ART-LOVING VISITOR to New York could easily spend several days gallery-hopping around the several hundred galleries found throughout New York. Antique lovers can find an exciting variety of goods, including Americana and many bargains, at the many flea markets; or they can browse through European and American fine antiques in one of the more exclusive antiques centers. To find out what's happening, pick up the free monthly *Art Now Gallery Guide*, available at most galleries, or check the local papers.

ART GALLERIES

ONE OF THE MOST well known galleries in SoHo is **Leo Castelli**, an important showcase for Pop Art during the early 1960s and now spotlighting new artists. **Mary Boone Gallery** features Neo-Expressionist artists such as Julian Schnabel. The **Pace Gallery** exhibits current stars, especially well-known painter-photographers, and the trendy gallery **Jay Gorney Modern Art** deals in contemporary art and sculpture. The **John Weber Gallery** features new talent but is famous for its many Minimalists and Conceptualists. **Metro Pictures** is known for experimental work.

Among the exclusive 57th Street galleries is the venerable **Sidney Janis Gallery**, which displays 20th-century masters. **Holly Solomon Gallery** has European and American contemporary painting, drawing and sculpture, while **Marian Goodman Gallery** features the European avant-garde.

Along the Upper East Side is **Knoedler & Company**, which exhibits contemporary paintings by modern masters. **Gagosian Gallery** has great works by Lichtenstein and Johns, and the **Hirschl & Adler Galleries** feature a good selection of European and American fine art.

AMERICAN FOLK ART

IF YOU'RE in the market for American folk art, go to **Susan Parrish Antiques** and to **Kelter-Malcé** for a selection of hooked rugs and other Americana. Similar goods are at **Cynthia Beneduce/Brian Windsor**.

American Hurrah Antiques has a good selection of quilts, Native American art and paintings, and **Hirschl & Adler Folk** is well stocked with American folk paintings, some beautiful quilts and needlework. **Laura Fisher** sells everything from decoys to hooked rugs.

ANTIQUES CENTERS

THE CITY HAS two major antiques centers, **The Manhattan Art & Antiques Center** and the **Place des Antiquaires**, each with dozens of dealers under one roof. The Manhattan Arts & Antiques Center has 104 galleries and a strong emphasis on fine jewelry. The Place des Antiquaires has over 60 shops, with expensive items ranging from rugs to toys.

AMERICAN FURNITURE

FOR FURNITURE from the 17th-, 18th- and 19th-centuries, try **Bernard & S. Dean Levy**, **Eagles Antiques**, **Leigh Keno American Furniture** or the highly regarded **Israel Sack**. **Judith James Milne** sells early American country furniture and a splendid collection of quilts. **Ruth Bigel Antiques** has American country furniture and folk art. Go to **Thomas K. Woodard American Antiques & Quilts** for a truly wonderful selection of Shaker pieces.

Collectors of Art Deco or Art Nouveau furniture should pay a visit to **Alan Moss** or **Alice's Antiques**. **Macklowe Gallery & Modernism** has a massive collection of fine Art Nouveau furniture. **Deco Deluxe** has everything from

perfume bottles to lacquered pianos, and **Minna Rosenblatt** and **Lillian Nassau** have Tiffany lamps and many Art Nouveau and Art Deco pieces.

Depression Modern and **Mood Indigo** have treasures from the 1930s and 1940s. **Fifty/50** is packed full with good examples of mid-20th-century American and European designs.

INTERNATIONAL ANTIQUES

IF YOU'RE LOOKING for English antiques, try **Arthur Ackermann & Son**, **Florian Papp** and **Kentshire Galleries**. For European pieces, visit **Betty Jane Bart Antiques**, **Kurt Gluckselig Antiques**, **The Little Antique Shop**, **Linda Horn Antiques**, and **Pierre Deux**. Oriental dealers include **Art Asia**, **Doris Leslie Blau**, **E. & J. Frankel** and **Flying Cranes Antiques**.

FLEA MARKETS

NEW YORK HAS a number of year-round weekend markets. The best time to go is at the crack of dawn.

Visit the **Annex Antiques Fair and Flea Market** for everything from secondhand clothing to antique furniture. The weekend **Canal Street Flea Market** has bric-a-brac; the **Columbus Avenue Flea Market** has new and second-hand clothing and furniture. For information on all street fairs and flea markets, check Friday's *New York Times*.

AUCTION HOUSES

MANHATTAN'S TWO most celebrated auction houses are **Christie's** and **Sotheby's**, selling collectibles ranging from coins, jewels and vintage wines to fine and decorative arts. Items for sale are usually previewed several days before the auctions. Admission is free, but the catalog cost about $20. For information on previews and auctions, check the Friday and Sunday editions of the *New York Times*.

DIRECTORY

ART GALLERIES

Gagosian Gallery
980 Madison Ave.
Map 17 A5.
(*744-2313.*

Hirschl & Adler Galleries
21 E 70th St. **Map** 12 F1.
(*535-8810.*
One of several branches.

Holly Solomon Gallery
172 Mercer St. **Map** 4 E3.
(*757-7777.*

Jay Gorney Modern Art
100 Greene St. **Map** 4 E4.
(*966-4480.*

John Weber Gallery
142 Greene St. **Map** 4 E4.
(*966-6115.*

Knoedler & Company
19 E 70th St. **Map** 13 A1.
(*794-0550.*

Leo Castelli
420 West Broadway.
Map 4 E4.
(*431-5160.*

Marian Goodman Gallery
24 W 57th St. **Map** 12 F3.
(*977-7160.*

Mary Boone Gallery
417 West Broadway.
Map 4 E4.
(*431-1818.*

Metro Pictures
150 Greene St. **Map** 4 E4.
(*925-8335.*

Pace Gallery
32 E 57th St. **Map** 12 F3.
(*421-3292.*

Sidney Janis Gallery
110 W 57th St. **Map** 12 E3.
(*586-0110.*

AMERICAN FOLK ART

American Hurrah Antiques
766 Madison Ave.
Map 13 A2.
(*535-1930.*

Cynthia Beneduce/ Brian Windsor
281 Lafayette St.
Map 4 F4.
(*274-0411.*

Hirschl & Adler Folk
851 Madison Ave.
Map 13 A1.
(*988-3655.*

Kelter-Malcé
361 Bleecker St. **Map** 3 C2.
(*989-6760.*

Laura Fisher
Manhattan Art & Antiques Center, 1050 2nd Ave.
Map 13 B4.
(*838-2596.*

Susan Parrish Antiques
390 Bleecker St. **Map** 3 C2.
(*645-5020.*

ANTIQUES CENTERS

The Manhattan Arts & Antiques Center
1050 2nd Ave. **Map** 13 A3.
(*355-4400.*

Place des Antiquaires
125 E 57th St. **Map** 13 B4.
(*758-2900.*

AMERICAN FURNITURE

Alan Moss
88 Wooster St. **Map** 4 E4.
(*219-1663.*

Alice's Antiques
505 Columbus Ave.
Map 16 D3.
(*874-3400.*

Bernard & S. Dean Levy
24 E 84th St. **Map** 16 F4.
(*628-7088.*

Deco Deluxe
Place des Antiquaires, 125 E 57th St. **Map** 13 A3.
(*751-3326.*

Depression Modern
150 Sullivan St. **Map** 4 D3.
(*982-5699.*

Eagles Antiques
1097 Madison Ave.
Map 17 A5.
(*772-3266.*

Fifty/50
793 Broadway. **Map** 12 F3.
(*777-3208.*

Israel Sack
15 E 57th St. **Map** 12 F3.
(*753-6562.*

Judith James Milne
506 E 74th St. **Map** 17 C5.
(*472-0107.*

Leigh Keno American Furniture
19 E 74th St. **Map** 16 F5.
(*734-2381.*

Lillian Nassau
220 E 57th St. **Map** 13 B3.
(*759-6062.*

Macklowe Gallery & Modernism
667 Madison Ave.
Map 13 A3.
(*644-6400.*

Minna Rosenblatt
844 Madison Ave.
Map 13 A1.
(*288-0257.*

Mood Indigo
181 Prince St. **Map** 4 E3.
(*254-1176.*

Ruth Bigel Antiques
743 Madison Ave.
Map 13 A2.
(*734-3262.*

Thomas K. Woodard American Antiques & Quilts
799 Madison Ave.
Map 13 A2.
(*988-2906.*

INTERNATIONAL ANTIQUES

Art Asia
1086 Madison Ave.
Map 17 A4.
(*249-7250.*

Arthur Ackermann & Son
50 E 57th St. **Map** 12 F3.
(*753-5292.*

Betty Jane Bart Antiques
1225 Madison Ave.
Map 17 A3.
(*410-2702.*

Doris Leslie Blau
15 E 57th St. **Map** 12 F3.
(*759-3715.*
By appointment only.

E. & J. Frankel
1040 Madison Ave.
Map 17 A5.
(*879-5733.*

Florian Papp
962 Madison Ave.
Map 17 A5.
(*288-6770.*

Flying Cranes Antiques
1050 2nd Ave. **Map** 13 B4.
(*223-4600.*

Kentshire Galleries
37 E 12th St. **Map** 4 E1.
(*673-6644.*

Kurt Gluckselig Antiques
1050 2nd Ave. **Map** 13 B4.
(*758-1805.*

Linda Horn Antiques
1015 Madison Ave.
Map 17 A5.
(*772-1122.*

The Little Antique Shop
44 E 11th St. **Map** 4 E1.
(*673-5173.*

Pierre Deux
367 Bleecker St. **Map** 3 C2.
(*243-7740.*
One of several branches.

FLEA MARKETS

Annex Antiques Fair and Flea Market
24th to 27th Sts at 6th Ave.
Map 8 E4.
(*243-5343.*
Open sat and sun.

Canal Street Flea Market
335 Canal St. **Map** 4 E5.

Columbus Avenue Flea Market
Columbus Ave, between 76th and 77th St.
Map 16 D5.
(*947-6302. Open sun.*

AUCTION HOUSES

Christie's
502 Park Ave. **Map** 13 A3.
(*546-1000.*

Sotheby's
1334 York Ave.
Map 13 C1.
(*606-7000.*

Food and Household Goods

Ｎew york's striking cultural and ethnic diversity is celebrated in its food – the city's food shops provide a truly international feast. There is also a dazzling array of household goods, electronics and photographic equipment available almost everywhere you turn.

Gourmet Groceries

Ｓcattered around town are several famous food emporiums that are tourist attractions in themselves. Remember, too, to visit the department stores, which often rival the specialty food stores.

Balducci's in Greenwich Village is a real Italian delight, with its own brands of cold meats, pastas, salami and fish. Food has been elevated to an art form at **Dean & DeLuca**, a chic delicatessen – don't miss the huge selection of take-out food. **Russ & Daughters** is one of the oldest gourmet shops, known as an "appetizing" store, full of ethnic food and famous for cream cheese, chocolates and bagels. **Zabar's** is arguably the finest food store in the world, with huge crowds jostling for the excellent smoked salmon, bagels, caviar and cheese.

Silver Palate Kitchens has revolutionized the picnic menu with its prepared dishes and desserts. For pâté de foie gras, Scottish smoked salmon, caviar and hand made chocolates, go to **Caviarteria**.

Specialty Food and Wine Shops

Ｆabulous bread and cake shops abound but one of the best is **Poseidon Greek Bakery**, renowned for its filo pastry. **H & H Bagels** bakes 60,000 of the best bagels in Manhattan every day. **Vesuvio** has Italian bread and some unusual pepper biscuits. Try **Fung Wong** for delicious Chinese pastries or purchase a traditional Sicilian loaf from **A. Zito & Son's Bakery**.

Cheese lovers should visit **Ben's Cheese Shop**, with its varieties of farmer's cheese. **Cheese of All Nations** has over 1,000 types on sale. Great confectionery shops include **Li-Lac** for handmade chocolates and **Mondel Chocolates** for chocolate animals. **Economy Candy** has a huge selection of dried fruit but for a real treat go to **Teuscher**, which has fresh champagne truffles flown in direct from Switzerland.

Myers of Keswick imports English food. For something more exotic, **Kam Man Food Products** is an Oriental grocery selling Chinese, Thai, and other oriental products. The **Italian Food Center** has great olive oils, dried pastas and sausages. Go to **Jefferson Market** for meat and fish, and **Citarella's** for its fine seafood. **Angelica's Traditional Herbs and Food** has 2,500 varieties of herbs and spices.

For fine burgundies, **Acker, Merrall & Condit** is a good choice. Go to **Garnet Liquors** for fine wines and champagnes at bargain prices. **SoHo Wines and Spirits** has an extensive selection of single-malt Scotch whisky. **Sherry-Lehmann** is New York's leading wine merchant. New York also has many fine coffee stores. Among the best are **Oren's**, **The Sensuous Bean**, **M Rohrs** and **Schapira Coffee**, each with a mouth-watering selection. For fruit and vegetables at reasonable prices, visit a farmers' market, but get there early. Among the most popular are **City Hall**, **Upper West Side**, **St. Mark's in-the-Bowery**, and **Union Square**. For information about the city's markets, phone: 788-7900.

Household Goods

Ｍost of the department stores offer a wide range of household goods. For a specialized shop, try **Broadway Panhandler**, a cook's heaven with outstanding baking and pastry-making equipment. **Bridge Kitchenware** is a household name among most restaurateurs. **Williams-Sonoma** has many cooking utensils and cookbooks. **Zabar's** has an excellent selection of cooking utensils.

Baccarat, **Daum**, **Lalique** and **Villeroy & Boch** are where you'll find the finest crystal, china and silverware. Other fashionable shops include **Orrefors Crystal** and **Tiffany & Co**. Go to **New Glass** for hand-blown glass, **Avventura** for crystal and china, and for classic American and European designs, visit **Contemporary Porcelain**. **Ceramica** which stocks lovely handmade Italian pottery, and or **La Terrine** and **Steuben Glass** for hand-painted ceramics.

Cheap linens can be found in most department stores. But for silk sheets and luxurious linens, visit **Descamps**, **D. Porthault & Co** and **Pratesi**. **ABC Carpet & Home** has an enviable reputation for home furnishings as does **Ad Hoc Softwares** for its bed linens and bathroom accessories.

Electronics and Photographic Equipment

Ｐerhaps the most competitive retailers in New York are the ones that sell electronics. Whatever you're buying, it pays to shop around. For the best buys of the week, check Tuesday's *New York Times*. If you're buying electrical goods to take to Europe, make sure they are compatible with the voltages and formats (many in other countries have different standards).

47th Street Photo sells equipment from cameras to fax machines. Another popular shop for electrical equipment is **Uncle Steve's**. **J&R Music World** sells very competitively priced equipment. **Nobody Beats the Wiz** is a large electronics chain that prides itself on never knowingly being undersold. For a wide variety of computers, videos and cameras try **Willoughby's**.

DIRECTORY

GOURMET GROCERIES

Balducci's
424 Ave of the Americas.
Map 12 E5.
(673-2600.

Caviarteria
29 E 60th St. **Map** 12 F3.
(759-7410.

Dean & DeLuca
560 Broadway. **Map** 4 E3.
(431-1691.

Russ & Daughters
179 E Houston St.
Map 5 A3.
(475-4880.

Silver Palate Kitchens
274 Columbus Ave.
Map 16 D5. (799-6340.

Zabar's
2245 Broadway.
Map 15 C4.
(787-2000.

SPECIALITY FOOD AND WINE SHOPS

A. Zito & Son's Bakery
259 Bleecker St. **Map** 3 C2.
(929-6139.

Acker, Merrall & Condit
160 W 72nd St.
Map 11 C1.
(787-1700.

Angelica's Traditional Herbs and Food
147 1st Ave. **Map** 5 A1.
(677-1549.

Ben's Cheese Shop
181 E Houston St.
Map 5 A3.
(254-8290.

Cheese of All Nations
53 Chambers St. **Map** 1 B1.
(732-0752.

Citarella's
2135 Broadway.
Map 15 C5.
(874-0383.

City Hall Green Market
Centre St and Chambers St.
Map 1 C1.

Economy Candy
108 Rivington St.
Map 5 A3. (254-1531.

Fung Wong
30 Mott St. **Map** 4 F3.
(267-4037.

Garnet Liquors
929 Lexington Ave.
Map 13 A1.
(772-3211.

H & H Bagels
2239 Broadway.
Map 15 C4. (595-8000.

Italian Food Center
186 Grand St. **Map** 15 C4.
(925-2954.

Jefferson Market
455 Ave of the Americas.
Map 12 E5. (675-2277.

Kam Man Food Products
200 Canal St. **Map** 4 F5.
(571-0330.

Li-Lac
120 Christopher St.
Map 3 C2. (242-7374.

M. Rohrs
1692 2nd Ave. **Map** 17 C3.
(427-8319.

Mondel Chocolates
2913 Broadway.
Map 20 E3.
(864-2111.

Myers of Keswick
634 Hudson St.
Map 3 C2.
(691-4194.

Oren's
1144 Lexington Ave.
Map 17 A4.
(472-6830.

Poseidon Greek Bakery
629 9th Ave. **Map** 12 D5.
(757-6173.

St. Mark's in-the-Bowery
E 10th St at 2nd Ave.
Map 4 F1.

Schapira Coffee
117 W 10th St. **Map** 4 D1.
(675-3733.

The Sensuous Bean
66 W 70th St. **Map** 12 D1.
(724-7725.

Sherry-Lehmann
679 Madison Ave.
Map 13 A3.
(838-7500.

SoHo Wines and Spirits
461 West Broadway.
Map 4 E4.
(777-4332.

Teuscher
25 E 61st St. **Map** 12 F3.
(751-8482.

Union Square
E 17th St and Broadway.
Map 8 F5.

Upper West Side
Columbus Ave at 77th St.
Map 16 D5.

Vesuvio
160 Prince St. **Map** 4 E3.
(925-8248.

HOUSEHOLD GOODS

ABC Carpet & Home
888 Broadway. **Map** 16 D5.
(254-7171.

Ad Hoc Softwares
410 W Broadway.
Map 4 E3.
(925-2652.

Avventura
463 Amsterdam Ave.
Map 15 C4.
(769-2510.

Baccarat
625 Madison Ave.
Map 13 A3.
(826-4100.

Bridge Kitchenware
214 E 52nd St. **Map** 13 B4.
(688-4220.

Broadway Panhandler
520 Broadway.
Map 4 E4.
(966-3434.

Ceramica
59 Thompson St.
Map 4 D4.
(941-1307.

Contemporary Porcelain
105 Sullivan St. **Map** 4 D3.
(219-2172.

D. Porthault & Co.
18 E 69th St. **Map** 12 F1.
(688-1660.

Daum
694 Madison Ave.
Map 13 A3.
(355-2060.

Descamps
723 Madison Ave.
Map 13 A2.
(355-2522.

Lalique
680 Madison Ave.
Map 13 A3.
(355-6550.

New Glass
345 West Broadway.
Map 4 E4. (431-0050.

Orrefors Crystal
58 E 57th St.
Map 13 A3.
(753-3442.

Pratesi
829 Madison Ave.
Map 13 A2.
(288-2315.

Steuben Glass
715 5th Ave. **Map** 12 F3.
(752-1441.

La Terrine
1024 Lexington Ave.
Map 13 A1.
(988-3366.

Tiffany & Co
See p321.

Villeroy & Boch
974 Madison Ave.
Map 17 A5.
(535-2500.

Williams-Sonoma
20 E 60th St. **Map** 12 F3.
(980-5155.
One of several branches.

Zabar's
See Gourmet Groceries.

ELECTRONICS AND PHOTOGRAPHIC EQUIPMENT

47th St Photo
67 W 47th St. **Map** 13 A5.
(921-1287.
One of several branches.

J&R Music World
See p322.

The Wiz
12 W 45th St. **Map** 11 B5.
(302-2000.
One of several branches.

Uncle Steve's
343 Canal St. **Map** 4 E5.
(226-4010.
One of several branches.

Willoughby's
110 W 32nd St. **Map** 8 E3.
(564-1600.

ENTERTAINMENT IN NEW YORK

NEW YORK CITY IS a non-stop entertainment extravaganza, every day, all year round. Whatever your taste, you can be sure the city will satisfy it on both a grand and an intimate scale. The challenge is to take advantage of as many of the entertainments as possible. If it's theater, you can enjoy a mainstream success on Broadway or take a chance on an experimental production in a loft. If it's music, there's the magnificence of opera at the Met or a jazz group blowing in a club in the Village. You can catch a spectacle of avant-garde dance in a café or try your own avant-garde dancing in one of the city's warehouse-sized clubs. Movie theaters abound. But perhaps best of all is wandering and watching the vast show that is New York.

Performance by the New York City Ballet

PRACTICAL INFORMATION

FIND OUT what you can choose from in the arts and leisure listings of the *New York Times* and the *Village Voice* newspapers and *New York* and *The New*

TKTS discount ticket booth

Yorker magazines. These briefly describe the entertainment and tell you which credit cards are accepted. At your hotel ask for *Where*, a free weekly magazine containing maps and information on the many different attractions.

Hotel staff may be able to answer some of your questions and should also carry a wide selection of brochures and leaflets. They may also be willing to reserve tickets for you. Some hotel TVs have a New York visitor information channel.

The efficient **New York Convention and Visitors Bureau** *(see p352)* is the city's official tourism data distribution point for literature, TV shows and schedules of events. They also have free and discount tickets such as "twofers" – which used to mean two for the

price of one but now just refers to a hefty discount. **TDF NYC/On Stage** is a telephone hotline for theater, dance and music; **Broadway Line** gives brief descriptions of current shows, schedules and the different prices; while **Movietime** gives recorded information on all the films.

BOOKING TICKETS

POPULAR SHOWS may well be sold out for weeks ahead, so purchase your seats well in advance. Theater box offices are open daily, except on Sundays, from 10am until one hour after the performance begins. Call in person or telephone the box office or a ticket agency and order your seats by credit card. The biggest agencies are **Hit-Tix, Telecharge**, **Ticketmaster** and **Ticket Central**. A small

handling fee of a few dollars will always be charged.

An independent ticket agent may also be able to find seats – good ones include **Prestige Entertainment** and **Union Tickets**; others are listed in the New York Yellow Pages. Fees will vary according to demand.

New York magazine has a free phone hotline with information on ticket availability. This is open from 10:30am to 4:40pm on Monday to Friday.

DISCOUNT TICKETS

DISCOUNT tickets for plays and musicals are sold on the day of performance by nonprofit **TKTS** booths. Discounts range from 25% to 50%, but the price will include a small handling fee and must be paid for in cash or by traveler's check.

There is a TKTS booth on Broadway, where matinée tickets are sold from 10am to 2pm every Wednesday and Saturday; evening tickets are sold from 3pm to 8pm, and Sunday tickets from noon until closing. The booth at the 2 World Trade Center mezzanine sells tickets from 11am to 5:30pm on Monday to Friday and 11am to 1pm on weekends. Saturday matinée tickets can be bought here on Fridays.

On the third floor of Bloomingdale's *(see p179)*, a **Ticketmaster** outlet sells a few day-of-performance tickets at discounts of 10% to 75% (with a small charge).

Bobby Short singing at the Café Carlyle *(p343)*

The Booth Theater on Broadway *(see p333)*

Day-of-performance half-price dance, concert, theater and opera tickets are sold at the nonprofit **Music and Dance Booth** in Bryant Park. A small handling fee will be charged on top of the ticket price. Credit cards are not accepted. It is also a Ticketmaster agency for advance purchase of full-price tickets. Opening hours are from noon to 2pm and 3 to 7pm on Tuesday to Friday (11am to noon on Wednesday and Saturday). Tickets for the Monday shows are sold on Sunday. Opening hours are from noon to 6pm on Sundays.

"SCALPERS" AND TOUTS

IF YOU BUY from a "scalper" (a ticket tout), tickets for the wrong day or wrong price, counterfeit tickets and outrageous prices are among the risks.

FREE TICKETS

FREE TICKETS to TV shows, concerts and special events are offered at the **New York Convention and Visitors Bureau,** which is open from 9am to 6pm on Monday to Friday and 10am to 6pm on weekends. "Cheap Thrills" in the *Village Voice* lists such events as poetry readings, recitals and experimental films. During the popular New York Shakespeare Festival, free tickets are given out on a

first-come, first-served basis and are restricted to one ticket per person. The line forms from noon on the day of the performance at the **Delacorte Theater**, in Central Park. Veteran playgoers take a picnic basket, blankets and cushions.

Royale Theater at night *(see p333)*

Free tickets for TV video-taping sessions are available by writing to the networks or from their on-street agents at **Rockefeller Center.**

HANDICAPPED ACCESS

BROADWAY THEATERS reserve a few spaces and cut-price tickets for the disabled. Call **Ticketmaster** or **Telecharge** well in advance for information about shows and also to reserve tickets. For Off-Broadway theaters, call their box offices.

USEFUL ADDRESSES

Broadway Line
[563-2929.

Delacorte Theater
Entrance via 81st St at Central Park W.
Map 16 E4.
[861-7277.

Hit-Tix
[564-8038.

Movietime
(see p337)
[777-FILM.

Music and Dance Booth
42nd St and Ave of the Americas.
Map 8 F1.
[382-2323.

New York Convention and Visitors Bureau
2 Columbus Circle.
Map 12 D3.
[397-8222.

New York Magazine
[880-0755.

Prestige Entertainment
[697-7788.

Network Tickets
ABC.
67th St and Columbus Ave.
[456-3537.

CBS.
524 W 57th St.
[975-2476

NBC.
30 Rockefeller Plaza.
[664-3055.

TDF NYC/On Stage
[768-1818.

Telecharge
[239-6200.

Ticket Central
[279-4200.

Ticketmaster
[307-7171.
Bloomingdale's Department Store.
Lexington Ave at 59th St.
Map 13 A3.
[705-2122.

TKTS
Broadway at W 47th St.
Map 12 E5.

2 World Trade Center.
Map 1 B2.

Union Tickets
[(800) 234-8497.

New York's Best: Entertainment

Greenwich Village jazz club

Nᴇᴡ ʏᴏʀᴋ is one of the great entertainment capitals of the world. Top names in every branch of the arts are drawn here to perform and often to live and work. Major sporting events are also constant, and as for nightlife, New York lives up to its reputation as "the city that never sleeps." From the huge choice offered, there are some venues and events that stand out as classics of their kind; this selection has been chosen from the listings on pages 332 to 347 as among those not to be missed. Even if you experience only one of them, you will have been part of something as essentially New York as the Empire State Building.

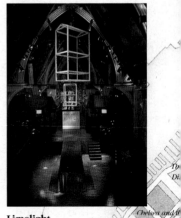

Limelight
Nightclubs come and go, but this converted church has become a firm favorite with New York's night owls. (See p342.)

Madison Square Garden
Top sporting action is found at "the Garden," including home games for basketball's New York Knicks and ice hockey's Rangers, plus the Golden Gloves boxing tournament. (See p340.)

Film Forum
At New York's most stylish arts movie theater you can see the latest foreign and American independent releases or catch up with a classic in a wide range of retrospectives. (See p336.)

Village Vanguard
The jazz clubs of Greenwich Village have played host to all the great names in jazz. Fans can catch the stars of today and tomorrow at the world-famous Village Vanguard and the Blue Note. (See p340.)

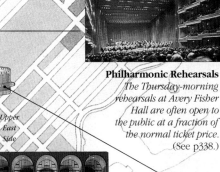

Philharmonic Rehearsals
The Thursday-morning rehearsals at Avery Fisher Hall are often open to the public at a fraction of the normal ticket price. (See p338.)

Metropolitan Opera House
Reserve well ahead and prepare to pay high prices to see the giants of the opera world. (See p338.)

Shakespeare in Central Park
If you are a summer visitor, set aside a day to get one of the rare free tickets for the Delacorte Theater's open-air Shakespeare featuring top Hollywood and Broadway names. (See p332.)

The Nutcracker
The Christmas event for children of every age is performed each year at Lincoln Center by the New York City Ballet. (See p334.)

The Fantasticks
The tiny Sullivan Street Playhouse has been home to America's longest-running play since May 1960. New Yorkers who saw it when they were young are now taking their own children to the show. (See p332.)

Carnegie Hall
Conveniently situated in the Theater District, Carnegie Hall is famous the world over as a showcase for the best in the musical arts. A backstage tour gives a fascinating insight into "the house that music built." (See p338.)

Upper West Side

Central Park

Upper East Side

Upper Midtown

mercy
d the
iron
strict

EAST RIVER

0 kilometers 2

0 miles 1

Theater and Dance

NEW YORK IS FAMOUS for its extravagant musicals and its ferocious critics. It is one of the world's greatest theater and dance centers, featuring every kind of production imaginable. Whether your preference is for the glitz and glamour of a Broadway blockbuster or something truly experimental, you'll find it here.

BROADWAY

BROADWAY HAS long been synonymous with New York's Theater District, but the majority of Broadway theaters are actually scattered between 41st and 53rd streets and from Sixth to Ninth avenues, with a few around the much-improved Times Square. Most were built between 1910 and 1930, during the heyday of vaudeville and the famous Ziegfeld Follies. The **Lyceum** (see p142) is the oldest theater still in operation (1903), and the **Majestic** is the newest (1986). Broadway theaters experienced a slump during the 1980s but are now enjoying a revival because of cutting costs, using big names to draw in the crowds and benefiting from urban renewal of the Broadway district.

This is where you will find the "power productions" – the big, highly publicized dramas, musicals and revivals starring many Hollywood luminaries (it is hoped) sure-fire money earners. Recent hits include such international imports as *Dancing at Lughnasa* and *Les Misérables; such* New York originals as *Falsettos* and *Jelly's Last Jam;* and great revivals like *Guys and Dolls* – Damon Runyon's nostalgic snapshot of Broadway and its denizens.

OFF-BROADWAY AND OFF-OFF-BROADWAY

THERE ARE about 20 Off-Broadway stages and 300 Off-Off-Broadway stages whose works will sometimes transfer to Broadway. Off-Broadway theaters have from 100 to 499 seats, and Off-Off-Broadway showplaces have fewer than 100. Both range from the well-appointed to the improvised, sited in lofts, churches and even garages.

Off-Broadway became very popular during the 1950s as a reaction to the commercialism of Broadway. It was also an ideal place for more cautious producers to try out works considered too avant-garde or unsuitable for Broadway at much lower operating costs. During the last two decades, Off-Off-Broadway theaters have become the venue for the more experimental pieces by these same producers.

Off-Broadway theaters are found all over Manhattan – from Greenwich Village's **Sullivan Street Playhouse** (where the longest-running show in New York, *The Fantasticks*, plays) to Central Park's open-air **Delacorte Theater**. Some are even in the traditional Broadway district. Farther afield can be found the **Brooklyn Academy of Music (BAM)** (see p246), the **Manhattan Theater Club** and the **92nd Street Y**. In these venues you will always find lively, unusual and experimental showcases for new talent as well as lots of uninhibited productions.

The Off-Broadway theatres mounted the first productions in New York of the works of playwrights Sean O'Casey, Tennessee Williams, Eugene O'Neill, Samuel Beckett, Jean Genet, Eugene Ionesco and David Mamet. They host new and very often irreverent treatments of the classics, and every imaginable theatrical presentation is floated.

Sometimes a more intimate, smaller Off-Broadway stage suits a production much better than a larger more established theater would, as proved by such long-running successes as *The Fantasticks* and the *Three-penny Opera*. Of course, there are flops occasionally – but that's show business.

PERFORMANCE THEATER

THIS EXTREMELY avant-garde art form can be found in several Off- and Off-Off-Broadway locations. Accurate descriptions and categorizations are almost impossible, but expect the bizarre and outlandish. The most likely venues to find this are **La MaMa**, **P.S. 122**, **CBGB's 313 Gallery**, **92nd Street Y**, **Symphony Space** and the Joseph Papp **Public Theater** (see p118). The latter is perhaps the most influential theater in New York. It was founded in the 1950s by the late director Joseph Papp, who introduced neighborhood tours to bring theater to people who had never seen it before.

The Public Theater created hits like *Hair* and *A Chorus Line;* it is most famous for its free summer performances of Shakespeare at the Delacorte Theater in Central Park (see p206). It usually has several productions running, and at 6pm on the day of performance, "Quiktix" tickets (limited to two per person) are sold in the Public Theater lobby.

THEATER SCHOOLS

NEW YORK is the best place in the country to see actors learning their trade. Foremost among the acting schools is **The Actors' Studio**. The late Lee Strasberg, the advocate of method acting – in which the actor aims for complete identification with the character being played – was its guru. His students included Dustin Hoffman, Al Pacino and Marilyn Monroe. "In progress" productions feature trainees and are usually open to the public. Sandy Meisner trained many actors, including the late Lee Remick, at the **Neighborhood Playhouse School of the Theater**. Its plays are also open to the public. The **New Dramatists** began in 1949 to develop new playwrights, helping the careers of the likes of William Inge. Play readings are open to the public and free.

Broadway Theaters

① **Ambassador**
215 W 49th St.
☎ *239-6200.*

② **Barrymore**
243 W 47th St.
☎ *239-6200.*

③ **Belasco**
111 W 44th St.
☎ *239-6200.*

④ **Booth**
222 W 45th St.
☎ *239-6200.*

⑤ **Broadhurst**
235 W 44th St.
☎ *239-6200.*

⑥ **Broadway**
1681 Broadway.
☎ *563-2266.*

⑦ **Brooks Atkinson**
256 W 47th St.
☎ *307-4100.*

⑧ **Circle in the Square – Uptown**
1633 Broadway.
☎ *239-6200.*

⑨ **Cort**
138 W 48th St.
☎ *239-6200.*

⑩ **Eugene O'Neill**
230 W 49th St.
☎ *239-6200.*

⑪ **Gershwin**
222 W 51st St.
☎ *307-4100.*

⑫ **John Golden**
252 W 45th St.
☎ *239-6200.*

⑬ **Helen Hayes**
240 W 44th St.
☎ *307-4100.*

⑭ **Imperial**
249 W 45th St.
☎ *239-6200.*

⑮ **Longacre**
220 W 48th St.
☎ *239-6200.*

⑯ **Lunt–Fontanne**
205 W 46th St.
☎ *307-4100.*

⑰ **Lyceum**
149 W 45th St.
☎ *239-6200.*

⑱ **Majestic**
245 W 44th St.
☎ *239-6200.*

⑲ **Marquis**
1535 Broadway.
☎ *382-0100.*

⑳ **Martin Beck**
302 W 45th St.
☎ *239-6200.*

㉑ **Minskoff**
Broadway at 45th St.
☎ *869-0550.*

㉒ **Music Box**
239 W 45th St.
☎ *239-6200.*

㉓ **Nederlander**
208 W 41st St.
☎ *307-4100.*

㉔ **Neil Simon**
250 W 52nd St.
☎ *307-4100.*

㉕ **Palace**
1564 Broadway.
☎ *307-4100.*

㉖ **Plymouth**
236 W 45th St.
☎ *239-6200.*

㉗ **Richard Rodgers**
226 W 46th St.
☎ *221-1211.*

㉘ **Roundabout**
1530 Broadway.
☎ *869-8400.*

㉙ **Royale**
242 W 45th St.
☎ *239-6200.*

㉚ **St. James**
246 W 44th St.
☎ *239-6200.*

㉛ **Shubert**
225 W 44th St.
☎ *239-6200.*

㉜ **Virginia**
245 W 52nd St.
☎ *239-6200.*

㉝ **Walter Kerr**
219 W 48th St.
☎ *239-6200.*

㉞ **Winter Garden**
1634 Broadway.
☎ *239-6200.*

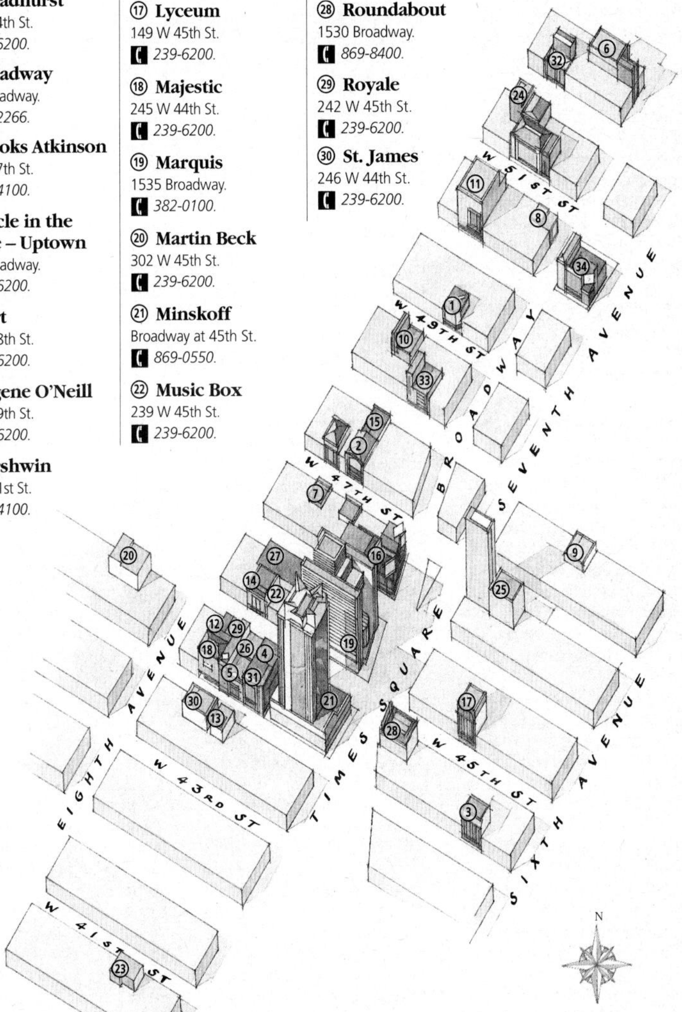

For other theaters *see p335.*

BALLET

AT THE HEART of the dance world is Lincoln Center (see p212), where the New York City Ballet performs pieces in the **New York State Theater**. This company was created by the legendary brilliant choreographer George Balanchine (see p46) and is probably still the best in the world. The current director, Peter Martins, was one of Balanchine's best dancers and continues the strict policy of ensemble dancing rather than "star turns." The season runs from November to February and late April to early June. The ballet school at the **Juilliard Dance Theater** also presents a spring workshop every year, and this is a good chance to see budding stars.

The American Ballet Theatre appears at the **Metropolitan Opera House**, which also hosts many visiting foreign companies, such as the Kirov, Bolshoi and Royal ballets. Its repertoire includes 19th-century classics, such as *Swan Lake*, and works by modern choreographers like Twyla Tharp and Paul Taylor.

CONTEMPORARY DANCE

NEW YORK is the center of many of the most important movements in modern dance. The **Dance Theater of Harlem** is world famous for its modern, traditional and ethnic productions. Other havens of experimental dance include the **92nd Street Y** and the **Merce Cunningham Studio** in Greenwich Village. The unusual **Dance Theater Workshop** has a packed program as well as an art gallery. **The Kitchen**, **La MaMa**, **Symphony Space** and **P.S. 122** are all multimedia venues with the latest in contemporary dance, performance art and avant-garde music. Choreographer Mark Morris's company performs at the **Manhattan Center**. **City Center** (see p146), a favorite venue for dance fans, used to house the New York City Ballet and the American Ballet Theater before Lincoln Center was built. As well as

featuring the Joffrey Ballet, City Center has held performances by all the great contemporary artists, including Alvin Ailey's blend of modern, jazz and blues and the companies of modern dance masters Merce Cunningham and Paul Taylor. Avoid the mezzanine as the view is restricted.

The city's single most active venue for dance is probably the **Joyce Theater,** where such well-established companies as the Feld Ballet, along with bold newcomers and visiting troupes, perform.

Each spring the Festival of Black Dance at the **Brooklyn Academy of Music (BAM)** (see p246) features everything from ethnic dance to hip-hop. During autumn the "Next Wave" festival of music and dance is held, celebrating international and American avant-garde dance and music. During winter the American Ballet Festival is held here.

During June, **New York University** (see p113) holds a Summer Residency Festival with lecture-demonstrations, rehearsals and performances, and **Dancing in the Streets** organizes summertime dance performances all over the city.

Throughout the month of August, **Lincoln Center Out of Doors** has a program of free dance events on the plaza, with such experimental groups as the American Tap Dance Orchestra.

The **World Financial Center** (see p69) has a free series at the Winter Garden, with such dance companies as the National Dance Institute.

At different times of the year, **Radio City Music Hall** holds several accomplished and spectacular shows, with different companies from all over the world. At Christmas and Easter, it features the Rockettes dance troupe.

Choreographers and dance companies frequently present works-in-progress and recitals to the public. Among the most interesting venue for these is **Alvin Ailey's Repertory Ensemble**. The **Hunter College Dance Company** performs new works by its student choreographers, and the **Isadora Duncan Inter-**

national Center for Dance re-creates her original dances. For contemporary choreographers the best place to go is **Juilliard Dance Theater**.

PRICES

THEATER is extremely expensive to produce, and ticket prices tend to reflect this. Even Off- and Off-Off-Broadway tickets are not cheap anymore. At one time, all tickets to previews of new plays sold at a much-reduced price, but not so today. Preview tickets are easier to get hold of, though, and it's fun to see a show before the reviews are in so you're able to make up your own mind.

For Broadway theater you can expect to pay $15 to $50; for musicals, up to $65; Off-Broadway, $15 to $40. For dance, $7 to $30 is the usual range, with up to $60 for the American Ballet Theatre. The **Music and Dance Booth** (see p329) in Bryant Park sells half-price day-of-performance tickets, worth the wait.

TIMES OF PERFORMANCE

THE GENERAL RULES for theater hours are: closed on Mondays (except for most musicals), with matinees on Wednesdays, Saturdays and sometimes Sundays. Matinees usually begin at 2pm, with evening performances at 8pm. Be sure to check the correct dates and times of the performance beforehand.

BACKSTAGE TOURS AND LECTURES

FOR THOSE INTERESTED in the mechanics of the theater and anecdotes on the stars, **Backstage on Broadway** conducts some fascinating backstage tours. The **92nd Street Y** organizes talks giving an insider's view of the theater, with famous directors, actors and choreographers taking part. Writers are often invited along to read or discuss their current works. **Radio City Music Hall** also hold tours.

DIRECTORY

OFF-BROADWAY

92nd Street Y
Lexington Ave.
Map 17 A2.
■ 415-5420.

Actors' Playhouse
100 Seventh Ave S.
Map 3 C1.
■ 307-7171.

American Place
111 W 46th St.
Map 12 E5.
■ 840-3074.

Brooklyn Academy of Music
30 Lafayette St., Brooklyn.
■ (718) 636-4100.

CBGB's 313 Gallery
313 Bowery. **Map** 4 F2.
■ 677-0455.

Circle in the Square – Downtown
159 Bleecker St.
Map 4 D3.
■ 254-6330.

Circle Repertory
99 Seventh Ave. **Map** 3 C2. ■ 924-7100.

Delacorte Theater
Central Park. (81st St.)
Map 16 E4.
■ 861-7277.

John Houseman
450 W 42nd St.
Map 7 C1.
■ 967-9077.

Lambs Theater
130 W 44th St.
Map 12 E5.
■ 997-1780.

Manhattan Theater Club
City Center, 131 W 55th St.
Map 12 E4.
■ 645-5848.

Provincetown Playhouse
133 MacDougal St.
Map 4 D2.
■ 777-2571.

Public Theater
425 Lafayette St.
Map 4 F2.
■ 598-7100.

Sullivan Street Playhouse
181 Sullivan St.
Map 4 D3.
■ 674-3838.

Symphony Space
2537 Broadway.
Map 15 C2.
■ 864-5400.

Vivian Beaumont
Lincoln Center.
Map 11 C2.
■ 362-7600.

OFF-OFF-BROADWAY

The Kitchen
512 W 19th St. **Map** 7 C5.
■ 255-5793.

Living Theater
■ 865-3957.
Touring group. Call for info.

Mabou Mines
■ 254-1109.
Touring group. Ring for info.

Performing Garage
33 Wooster St.
Map 4 E4.
■ 966-3651.

Theater at St. Peter's Church
Citicorp Center, 619 Lexington Ave.
Map 13 A4.
■ 246-8949.

PERFORMANCE THEATER

92nd Street Y
See Off-Broadway.

CBGB's 313 Gallery
See Off-Broadway.

La MaMa
74a E 4th St.
Map 4 F2.
■ 475-7710.

P.S. 122
150 First Ave. **Map** 5 A1.
■ 477-5288.

Public Theater
See Off-Broadway.

Symphony Space
See Off-Broadway.

THEATER SCHOOLS

The Actors' Studio
432 W 44th St.
Map 11 C5.
■ 757-0870.

Neighborhood Playhouse School of the Theater
340 E 54th St.
Map 13 B4.
■ 688-3770.

New Dramatists
424 W 44th. **Map** 11 C5.
■ 757-6960.

DANCE

92nd Street Y
See Off-Broadway.

Alvin Ailey American Dance Center
211 W 61st St. **Map** 11 3C.
■ 767-0940.

Brooklyn Academy of Music
See Off-Broadway.

City Center
131 W 55th St.
Map 12 E4.
■ 581-7907.

Dance Theater of Harlem
466 W 152nd St.
■ 967-3470.

Dance Theater Workshop
219 W 19th St. **Map** 8 E5.
■ 924-0077.

Dancing in the Streets
131 Varick St. **Map** 4 D4.
■ 989-6830.

Hunter College Dance Company
695 Park Ave.
Map 13 A1.
■ 772-5011.

Isadora Duncan International Center for Dance
91 Claremont Ave.
Map 20 D2.
■ 662-4591.

Joyce Theater
175 Eighth Ave at 19th St.
Map 8 D5.
■ 242-0800.

Juilliard Dance Theater
60 Lincoln Center Plaza, W 65th St.
Map 11 C2.
■ 769-7406.

The Kitchen
See Off-Off Broadway.

La MaMa
See Performance Theatre.

Lincoln Center Out of Doors
Lincoln Center, Broadway at 64th St. **Map** 11 C2.
■ 362-6000.

Manhattan Center
311 W 34th St.
Map 8 D2.
■ 307-4100.

Merce Cunningham Studio
55 Bethune St.
Map 3 B2.
■ 691-9751.

Metropolitan Opera House
Lincoln Center, Broadway at 65th St.
Map 11 C2.
■ 362-6000.

Music and Dance Booth
See page 329.

New York State Theater
Lincoln Center, Broadway at 65th St. **Map** 11 C2.
■ 870-5570.

New York University
Tisch Hall, 111 Second Ave.
Map 4 F1.
■ 998-1984.

P.S. 122
See Performance Theater.

Radio City Music Hall
50th St at Ave of the Americas. **Map** 12 F4.
■ 247-4777.

Symphony Space
See Off-Broadway.

World Financial Center
West St between Vesey and Liberty St. **Map** 1 B2.
■ 945-0505.

BACKSTAGE TOURS

92nd Street Y
See Off-Broadway.

Backstage on Broadway
■ 629-4282.

Radio City Music Hall
■ 632-4041.

Movies

NEW YORK is a film buff's paradise. Apart from new US releases, which show months in advance of London, many classic and foreign films are screened here.

The city has always been the testing ground for new developments in films, and it continues to be a hotbed of new and innovative talent. Many of the movies' most famous directors – like Spike Lee, Martin Scorsese and Woody Allen – were born and bred in New York, and the city's influence can be seen in many of their films. They, and others, can often be seen filming on the streets of the city – many of New York's landmarks have become famous after appearing in films.

Most of the TV networks based in New York offer free tickets to the taping of their shows. Watching the taping of a show, such as *The David Letterman Show* or *Donahue*, is popular with New Yorkers and visitors alike.

FIRST-RUN MOVIES

NEW YORK REVIEWS and box office returns are so vital to a film's success that most major American films have their premieres in Manhattan's major theaters. First-run films are shown mainly at the City Cinema chains, Loews, Guild and Cineplex Odeon, which are scattered widely around the city. Some theaters have recorded information giving the names and duration of the different films showing, with starting times and ticket prices.

Programs start at noon and are repeated every two to three hours until midnight. You should expect to line up for most evening and weekend performances of the more popular films. Making reservations using a credit card is possible at some theaters for an additional charge of about $1 per ticket. Matinées (usually before 4pm) are easier to get into. Senior citizens pay a reduced price for tickets: the required age may be over 60, 62 or 65 depending on the policy of the theater.

NEW YORK FILM FESTIVAL

A HIGH POINT of the year for film buffs is the New York Film Festival, now in its third decade. Organized by the **Film Society of Lincoln Center**, the festival starts in late September and continues for two weeks at the many Lincoln Center theaters. Outstanding new films from the United States and abroad are entered in a competition that has no prizes except for the huge prestige of winning an award. The successful films go on to have a limited release in New York's many art houses.

FOREIGN FILMS AND ART HOUSES

FOR THE LATEST foreign and independent films, go to the **Angelika Film Center**, which has six screens and an upscale coffee bar. Other good venues are the plush **Carnegie Hall Cinema** and the stylish **Film Forum** and **Lincoln Plaza Cinema**. The Plaza has many foreign and art films, as does the **68th St. Playhouse**. For Asian, Indian

FILM CERTIFICATES

Films in the United States are graded as follows:
G General audiences; all ages admitted.
PG Parental guidance suggested; some material unsuitable for children.
PG-13 Parents strongly cautioned; some material inappropriate for children under age 13.
R Restricted. Children under 17 need to be accompanied by a parent or an adult guardian.
NC-17 No children under 17 admitted.

ON LOCATION

Many New York locations have played starring roles in films. Here are a few:

The Brill Building (1141 Broadway) contained Burt Lancaster's penthouse in *Sweet Smell of Success*.
The Brooklyn Bridge was a great backdrop in Spike Lee's *Mo' Better Blues*.
Brooklyn Heights and the **Metropolitan Opera** appeared in *Moonstruck*.
Central Park has shown up in countless films, including *Love Story* and *Marathon Man*.
55 Central Park West will be remembered as Sigourney Weaver's home in *Ghostbusters*.
Chinatown played a major role in *Year of the Dragon*.
The Dakota was where Mia Farrow lived in the classic *Rosemary's Baby*.
The Empire State Building is still standing after *King Kong*'s last heroic battle.
Grand Central Station is famous for Robert Walker's meeting with Judy Garland in *Under the Clock* and the magical ballroom sequence in *The Fisher King*.
Harlem's tenements were the seedy settings for jazz musicians and dancers in *The Cotton Club*.
Katz's Deli was the setting for the café scene between Billy Crystal and Meg Ryan in *When Harry Met Sally...*
Little Italy appeared in *The Godfather I* and *II*.
Madison Square Garden was the setting for the dramatic climax of *The Manchurian Candidate*.
The Russian Tea Room was where Dustin Hoffman had lunch with his agent in *Tootsie*.
Tiffany & Co. was Audrey Hepburn's favorite shop in *Breakfast at Tiffany's*.
The United Nations Building featured in the thriller *North by Northwest*.
Washington Square Park was where Robert Redford and Jane Fonda walked *Barefoot in the Park*.

and Chinese films, you should visit the **Asia Society**. The **French Institute** screens many French films with English subtitles and plays host to the Asian American International Film Festival. The **Cinema 3** located in the Plaza Hotel shows new films in elegant surroundings. **Cinema Village** runs special film events, such as the Festival of Animation.

For late-night films, go to the **Eighth St. Playhouse**. This runs midnight performances of both old classics and more modern cult films. Classic late-night films are often screened at **Theatre 80**, with the more modern films being shown at the **Waverly** Cinema.

CLASSIC FILMS AND MUSEUMS

RETROSPECTIVES OF films by particular directors or featuring specific actors are shown at the **Film Society of Lincoln Center**, the **Public Theater** and the **Whitney Museum of American Art** (see pp198–9). The extensive **Museum of Modern Art** (see pp170-3) is one of the best places to see a wide range of classic and silent movies. The museum also screens films

on art and cultural subjects.

The **American Museum of the Moving Image** (see p244) screens old films and also has many exhibits of memorabilia from the film industry. The **Museum of Television & Radio** (see p169) has regular screenings of classic films; you can also see or hear specific television or radio programs. Students interested in classic, new and experimental movies will appreciate the really huge wealth of material at the **Anthology Film Archives**. "Naturemax," which is at the **American Museum of Natural History**, shows environmental films using the most up-to-date technology – like IMAX, 70-mm film that has incredible clarity of image – projected onto huge screens.

On Saturday mornings, take your young filmgoers to the **Film Society of Lincoln Center**, where special children's shows are held.

TELEVISION SHOWS

A NUMBER of TV programs originate in New York. By writing several months in advance, you may be able to see one or more of them as they are being taped for broadcast. These include the

highly popular Phil Donahue and David Letterman shows. To request free tickets for programs made by **ABC, CBS** and **NBC**, write to each company individually. Another good source of free tickets is the New York Convention and Visitors Bureau (see p352). On weekday mornings on Fifth Avenue around **Rockefeller Plaza**, free tickets for a number of TV programs are sometimes distributed by the program's production staff. There's absolutely no way that you can plan for this. It's simply a matter of good luck and being in the right place at the right time.

For those who want to get a glimpse behind the scenes of TV, NBC organizes studio tours, usually from 9am to 4pm on Monday to Saturday.

CHOOSING WHAT TO SEE

I F YOU FEEL bewildered by the huge range of films offered in New York, check the detailed listings in the art sections of *New York* magazine, the *New York Times*, the *Village Voice* and *The New Yorker*. "Movietime," a free telephone service, gives recorded information.

FILM VENUES

68th St. Playhouse
Third Ave.
Map 13 B1.
(734-0302.

ABC
See p329.

American Museum of the Moving Image
35th Ave and 36th St.
Astoria, Queens.
((718) 784-0077.

American Museum of Natural History
Central Park W at 79th St.
Map 16 D5.
(769-5650.

Angelika Film Center
18 W Houston St.
Map 4 E3.
(995-2000.

Anthology Film Archives
32 Second Ave at 2nd St.
Map 5 C2.
(505-5181.

Asia Society
725 Park Ave. **Map** 13 A1.
(517-2742.

Carnegie Hall Cinema
Seventh Ave at 56th St.
Map 12 E3. (265-2520.

CBS
See p329.

Cinema 3
2 W 59th St. **Map** 12 F3.
(752-5959.

Cinema Village
100 Third Ave. **Map** 9 B5.
(505-7320.

Eighth St. Playhouse
52 W 8th St. **Map** 4 D1.
(674-6515.

Film Forum
209 W Houston St.
Map 3 C3. (727-8110.

Film Society of Lincoln Center
Walter Reade Theater.
Map 11 C2. (875-5600.

French Institute
55 E 59th St. **Map** 12 F3.
(355-6160.

Lincoln Plaza
Broadway at 62–63rd St.
Map 12 D2. (757-2280.

Movietime
(777-FILM.

Museum of Modern Art
11 W 53rd St. **Map** 12 F4.
(708-9490.

Museum of Television & Radio
25 W 52nd St. **Map** 12 F4.
(621-6600.

NBC
See p329.

New York Film Festival
(875-5600.

Public Theater
425 Lafayette St.
Map 4 F4. (598-7171.

Rockefeller Plaza
47th–50th St. 5th Ave.
Map 12 F5.

Theatre 80
80 St. Mark's Pl.
Map 5 A2. (254-7400.

Waverly
323 Ave of the Americas.
Map 8 E1.
(929-8037.

Whitney Museum of American Art
954 Madison Ave.
Map 13 A1.
(570-0537.

Classical and Contemporary Music

NEW YORKERS HAVE A voracious appetite for music. Live concerts by the world's most celebrated musical performers may be enjoyed at famous halls throughout the year, and younger, newer artists and exotic imports always find receptive audiences.

TICKETS

FIND OUT WHAT you can choose from in New York by checking out the listings in the *New York Times* and the *Village Voice* and in *New York* and *The New Yorker* magazines. Day-of-performance half-price opera and concert tickets are sold at the **Music and Dance Booth** (*see p329*) in Bryant Park.

CLASSICAL MUSIC

THE ORCHESTRA in residence at **Avery Fisher Hall** in Lincoln Center (*see p213*) is the New York Philharmonic. It is also the annual site for the popular "Mostly Mozart" series and Young People's Concerts. The **Alice Tully Hall**, in Lincoln Center, is an acoustic gem and home to the Chamber Music Society.

One of the world's premier concert halls is the revamped **Carnegie Hall** (*see p146*). Upstairs in the Weill Recital Hall there are quality performances for reasonable prices. The **Brooklyn Academy of Music (BAM)** (*see p246*) is the home of the Brooklyn Philharmonic, which has recently gone into partnership with the Metropolitan Opera to produce lesser-known works.

The **Merkin Concert Hall** is host to some top chamber ensembles and soloists. For really excellent acoustics, go to the **Town Hall**. The **92nd Street Y's** Kaufmann Concert Hall also offers a lively menu of music and dance. Popular

museum venues include the **Museum of Modern Art's** sculpture garden for chamber and contemporary music. There's also the **Frick Collection** and **Symphony Space**, both of which offer a varied program ranging from gospel to Gershwin, classical to ethnic. The beautiful Gracè Rainey Rogers Auditorium in the **Metropolitan Museum of Art** is for chamber music and soloists, while **Bargemusic**, in Brooklyn, presents chamber music and soloists against the stunning backdrop of Manhattan's famous skyline.

The **Juilliard School of Music** and the **Mannes College of Music** are both considered excellent. Their students and faculties give many free recitals, and there are shows by many leading orchestras, chamber music groups and opera companies.

At 9:45am on the Thursdays of the New York Philharmonic concerts, the evening show is rehearsed at **Avery Fisher Hall** in Lincoln Center. Audiences are often admitted to listen, and rehearsal tickets are available at low prices. Phone beforehand to check.

OPERA

DOMINATING the city's operatic scene is **Lincoln Center** (*see p212*), home to the New York City Opera, and the **Metropolitan Opera House**, which has its own operatic company. The Met is the jewel in the crown, offering top international performers, but it is often criticized for being unadventurous. More accessible and dynamic is the New York City Opera. Its performances range from *Madame Butterfly* to *South Pacific*, with subtitles above the stage to help the audience understand the plot. Lower-priced quality perfor-

mances are staged by the up-and-coming singers at the **Village Light Opera Group**, the **Amato Opera Theater**, the **American Chamber Opera Co.** and the students at the **Juilliard Opera Center** in Lincoln Center.

CONTEMPORARY MUSIC

NEW YORK is one of the most important places in the world for contemporary music. Exotic, ethnic and experimental music is played in many first-rate venues. The **Brooklyn Academy of Music (BAM)** is the standard bearer of the avant-garde. Each autumn the Academy holds a festival of music and dance called "Next Wave"; this has helped launch the careers of many musicians, including Philip Glass.

An annual festival of serious modern music called "Bang on a Can" is performed at the **Ethical Culture Society Hall** and features composers like Pierre Boulez and John Cage. Experimentalists, such as Davie Weinstein with his "audio-visual acid test" music – a mix of CD players, amplified instruments, keyboards and sound effects – perform at the **Dance Theater Workshop**. Other venues include the **Asia Society** (*see p185*), with its jewel of a theater for many visiting Asian performers, and **St. Peter's Church**.

BACKSTAGE TOURS

BEHIND-THE-SCENES tours are offered by **Lincoln Center** and **Carnegie Hall**, which also holds a "Tour and Tea" package in the Russian Tea Room (*see p147*).

RELIGIOUS MUSIC

FEW EXPERIENCES are more moving than an Easter concert in the vast **Cathedral of St. John the Divine** (*see pp224–5*). Seasonal music is also offered at many of the city's museums and in almost every other available space – from Grand Central Station's main concourse (*see pp154–5*)

CLASSICAL RADIO

New York has four good FM radio stations that broadcast classical (and a selection of other) music: WQXR at 96.3, WKCR at 89.9, WNYC at 93.9 and WNCN at 104.3.

to bank and hotel lobbies.

For jazz vespers in a stunning modern building, visit **St. Peter's Church** (*see p173*). Most of these concerts are free for everyone, but you are encouraged to contribute.

AL FRESCO

FREE OUTDOOR concerts during the summer can be found in **Bryant Park**, **Washington Square** and **Lincoln Center's Damrosch Park**. The annual concerts on Central Park's Great Lawn and in Brooklyn's Prospect Park are performed by the New York Philharmonic and the Metropolitan Opera. In good weather, keep a look out for all the strolling musicians who perform at South Street Seaport, right on the steps of the **Metropolitan Museum of Art** (*see pp188–95*) and also around Washington Square.

MUSIC FOR FREE

THROUGHOUT the year free musical performances are given at the **Citicorp Atrium** (*see p173*), the fascinating **IBM Garden Plaza** (*see p169*), **The Cloisters** (*see pp234–7*) and the **Whitney Museum's** Philip Morris Building (*see p150*). Sunday-afternoon recitals are held at **The Dairy** in Central Park (*see p206*). You will also find music in the Winter Garden and Plaza of the **World Financial Center** (*see p69*) and **Federal Hall** (*see p68*). At **Lincoln Center**, free performances are held in the **Juilliard School of Music** and the **Library Museum of the Performing Arts**.

Other very popular venues include the **Mark Goodson Theater** (for chamber music) and the **Theodore Roosevelt Birthplace** (*see p125*).

Free concerts and talks in churches include **St. Paul's Chapel** and the **Trinity Church** (*see p68*).

MUSIC VENUES

92nd Street Y
1395 Lexington Ave.
Map 17 A2.
📞 996-1100.

Amato Opera Theater
319 Bowery at 2nd St.
Map 4 F2.
📞 228-8200.

American Chamber Opera Co.
6 E 87th St. **Map** 16 F3.
📞 781-0857.

Asia Society
70th St at Park Ave.
Map 13 A1.
📞 517-2742.

Backstage Tours
📞 903-9790.

Bargemusic
Fulton Ferry Landing,
Brooklyn. **Map** 2 F2.
📞 (718) 624-4061.

Brooklyn Academy of Music
30 Lafayette Ave, Brooklyn.
📞 (718) 636-4100.

Bryant Park
Map 8 F1.
📞 983-4143.

Carnegie Hall
881 Seventh Ave. **Map** 12 E3.
📞 247-7800.

Cathedral of St. John the Divine
Amsterdam Ave at 112th St. **Map** 20 E4.
📞 316-7400.

Citicorp Atrium
Lexington Ave at 53rd St.
Map 13 A4.
📞 559-9095.

The Cloisters
Fort Tryon Park.
📞 923-3700.

The Dairy
Central Park.
Map 12 F2.
📞 794-6564.

Dance Theater Workshop
See Dance p335.

Ethical Culture Society Hall
2 W 64th St.
Map 12 D2.
📞 874-5210.

Federal Hall
Broad St at Wall St.
Map 1 C3.
📞 866-2086.

Frick Collection
1 E 70th St. **Map** 12 F1.
📞 288-0700.

IBM Garden Plaza
590 Madison Ave.
Map 13 A3.
📞 745-3500.

Lincoln Center
155 W 65th St.
Map 11 C2.
📞 875-5400.

Alice Tully Hall
📞 875-5050.

Avery Fisher Hall
📞 875-5030.

Damrosch Park
📞 875-5400.

Juilliard Opera Center
📞 769-7406.

Juilliard School of Music
📞 799-5000.

Library Museum of the Performing Arts
📞 870-1630.

Metropolitan Opera House
📞 362-6000.

Mannes College of Music
150 W 85th St.
Map 15 D3.
📞 580-0210.

Mark Goodson Theater
2 Columbus Circle.
Map 12 D3.
📞 841-4253.

Merkin Concert Hall
129 W 67th St.
Map 11 D2.
📞 362-8719.

Metropolitan Museum of Art
Fifth Ave at 82nd St.
Map 16 F4.
📞 570-3949.

Museum of Modern Art
Sculpture garden
11 W 53rd St. **Map** 12 F4.
📞 708-9480.

Music and Dance Booth
42nd St at Ave of the Americas. **Map** 8 E1.
📞 382-2323.

St. Paul's Chapel
Broadway at Fulton St.
Map 1 C2.
📞 602-0747.

St. Peter's Church
54th St at Lexington Ave.
Map 13 A4.
📞 935-2200.

Symphony Space
2537 Broadway.
Map 15 C2.
📞 864-5400.

Theodore Roosevelt Birthplace
28 E 20th St.
Map 8 F5.
📞 866-2086.

Town Hall
123 W 44th St. **Map** 12 E5.
📞 840-2824.

Trinity Church
Broadway at Wall St.
Map 1 C3.
📞 602-0800.

Village Light Opera Group
227 W 27th St.
Map 8 E3.
📞 279-4200.

Washington Square
Map 4 D2.

Whitney Museum
(Philip Morris Building)
Park Ave at 42nd St.
Map 9 A1.
📞 878-2550.

World Financial Center
West St at Vesey St.
Map 1 A2.
📞 945-0505.

Rock, Jazz and World Music

THERE'S EVERY IMAGINABLE form of music in New York, from international stadium rock to the sounds of the 1960s, from Dixieland jazz or country blues to talented street musicians. The city's music scene changes at a dizzying pace, with many new arrivals (and departures) almost daily, so there's no way to predict what you may find when you arrive. Musical standards also vary.

PRICES AND PLACES

AT CLUBS, EXPECT a cover charge and possibly a one- or two-drink minimum (at $5 or more) requirement. The prices for concerts range from $8 to $40 for the major venues, with about $12 to $15 the norm. Many of the smaller concert venues are arranged for seating in certain areas and dancing in others – often with different prices for each.

The top international bands are usually to be found in the huge arenas at **Shea Stadium** in Flushing Meadows or at the **Meadowlands** and **Madison Square Garden** *(see p133)*. Here the likes of Elton John, Bruce Springsteen and David Bowie perform. Tickets for these events sell out very fast, so buy some as soon as you hear of a concert, unless you don't mind paying a lot for them through an agent or a scalper. During the summer, big outdoor concerts are held at Jones Beach *(see p253)* and **Central Park SummerStage**.

Medium-sized venues for mainstream bands include the Art Deco palace of **Radio City Music Hall** and the **Beacon Theater**, by far the most popular live-music venue in the Upper West Side area.

Many leading rock venues are basically bars with music. They will often book different bands every night, so check the listings in the *New York Times*, *Village Voice* or *New York* magazine or phone the place to find out what's happening and at what time during that particular week.

ROCK MUSIC

ROCK COMES IN many forms: gothic, industrial, techno, psychedelic, post-punk funk, indie and alternative music are among the latest crazes.

If you prefer to see more of a band than a giant video screen, the following venues have a much more intimate, friendly atmosphere. **CBGB**, New York's sleazy, dungeonlike cradle of new wave, launched such bands as Talking Heads and Blondie and is still a showcase for new indie bands.

The **Knitting Factory** has live jazz and new music. The **Limelight** has the latest sounds and the newest groups. **Marquee NY** presents the more avant-garde bands who perform just about everything from thrash metal to new music. **Tramps** is in a loft where relatively unknown rock groups play, as do the occasional famous country and blues musicians. Megastar Bruce Springsteen played his first recorded concert in the 1970s at the **Bottom Line**, and it still remains a record industry showcase for new and up-and-coming bands.

Bands appearing at the **Academy** range from indie stalwarts, such as Ride and the Soupdragons, to Ice-T's controversial *Body Count*. **Ritz** (the former Studio 54) is a very popular concert venue, with everything from voodoo groove and world music to hip-hop and such rappers as KRS One. There's balcony viewing as well as dancing at ground level. The **Palladium** is a vast old theater that has been really spectacularly revamped for dancing and rock concerts. **Roulette** has avant-garde sounds that are performed by appropriately named groups such as Woof, Quack and Miaow.

JAZZ

THE ORIGINAL Cotton Club and Connie's Inn, which were once crucibles of jazz, are long gone, as are the former speakeasies of West 52nd Street. But living legends such as Maynard Ferguson, Dave Brubeck and Les Paul still play, while others carry on the old traditions of Duke Ellington, Count Basie and other big bands.

In Greenwich Village, jazz temples from the 1930s survive and continue to foster great music. Foremost among them is the **Village Vanguard**, where some of the most highly revered jazz memories linger and newer ones are being fashioned by such groups as the McCoy Tyner and Branford Marsalis trios. **Blue Note** hosts big bands at high prices but has an excellent atmosphere.

The **Knitting Factory** and the **Bottom Line** tend to feature much more contemporary and avant-garde jazz, while **Bradley's** has small groups performing in a cozy, clublike restaurant. It's also a favorite watering-hole for many off-duty jazz musicians.

The **Birdland** features ex-Mingus alumni and musicians such as Bud Shank. Expect the great sounds of Dixieland jazz or small unknown groups in **Cajun**, a friendly New Orleans–style restaurant.

Fat Tuesday's is the place to go if you want to hear famous, small jazz groups perform their acts live. The club also has the occasional rock-and-roll performer.

Michael's Pub features jazz-pop singers and revues. Its really big draw is the New Orleans Funeral and Ragtime Orchestra, a Dixieland septet of uneven capabilities, which has been led by clarinetist-filmmaker Woody Allen on most Monday nights for the last 23 years.

One of the hottest tickets in town is the Sunday jazz brunch at **Sweet Basil**, which often features the trumpeter Doc Cheatham and his band. On Mondays, salsa meets jazz at that other great venerable institution in Manhattan, the **Village Gate**. **Time Café** presents the Mingus Big Band workshop every Wednesday. If you're in New York in June, don't miss the annual **JVC Jazz Festival**, where such famous jazz icons as Oscar Peterson, Nina Simone and B.B. King play at various clubs all around Manhattan. For information, phone ahead.

The end of July sees the annual Classical Jazz Series at Lincoln Center's **Alice Tully Hall**. The music ranges from Duke Ellington's New York sounds, under the direction of Wynton Marsalis, to Johnny Dodds' traditional New Orleans–style jazz.

FOLK AND COUNTRY MUSIC

FOLK, ROCK MUSIC and R&B (rhythm and blues) can be found at the famed but much-faded **Bitter End**, which once showcased James Taylor and Joni Mitchell but now specializes in new talent as does **Kenny's Castaways**.

For country-and-western music, with infusions of blues and rock, try the aptly named **Lone Star Roadhouse** – also doubling as a rock venue – or the equally evocative and excellent **Texas Café**.

BLUES, SOUL AND WORLD MUSIC

FOR BLUES, soul and world music, options include the **Apollo Theater** in Harlem (*see p228*). For nearly 60 years the near-legendary Wednesday Amateur Nights have "discovered" such stars as James Brown and Dionne Warwick. **China Club** is a soul music dance club that also hosts rock groups and impromptu jamming by visiting rock stars. This is currently one of the hottest places in town.

The **Cotton Club** is not the original, but it offers good blues, jazz and a Sunday real gospel brunch on Harlem's main street. **Manny's Car Wash** runs the gamut of blues, rock and soul with the likes of Bo Diddley, Jr., Tino Gonzales, and a free Sunday "Blues Jam." Don't miss "Mambo Mondays" with Nestor Torres at **SOB's** (Sounds of Brazil), a world music club specializing in the many Afro-Latin rhythms. Finally, there's **Wetlands**, for classic soul and 60's sounds.

DIRECTORY

MUSIC VENUES

Beacon Theater
2124 Broadway.
Map 15 C5.
☎ 496-7070.

Central Park SummerStage
Rumsey Playfield.
Map 12 F1.
☎ 360-2777.

Madison Square Garden
Seventh Ave at 33rd St.
Map 8 E2.
☎ 465-MSG1.

Meadowlands
50 Route 120,
East Rutherford, N J.
☎ (201) 935-3900.

Radio City Music Hall
See Dance p335.

Shea Stadium
126th St at Roosevelt Ave.
Flushing, Queens.
☎ (718) 507-TIXX.

ROCK MUSIC

Academy
234 W 43rd St. **Map** 8 E1.
☎ 249-8870.

Bottom Line
15 W 4th St. **Map** 4 D2.
☎ 228-6300.

CBGB
315 Bowery. **Map** 4 F2.
☎ 982-4052.

Knitting Factory
47 E Houston St. **Map** 4 F3.
☎ 219-3055.

Limelight
47 W 20th St. **Map** 8 F4.
☎ 807-7850.

Marquee NY
547 W 21st St. **Map** 7 C4.
☎ 249-8870.

Palladium
126 E 14th St. **Map** 4 F1.
☎ 473-7171.

Ritz
254 W 54th St. **Map** 12 E4.
☎ 541-8900.

Roulette
228 W Broadway. **Map** 4 E5.
☎ 219-8242.

Tramps
45 W 21st St. **Map** 8 F4.
☎ 727-7788.

JAZZ

Alice Tully Hall
See Classical Music p339.

Birdland
2745 Broadway. **Map** 22 E5.
☎ 749-2228.

Blue Note
131 W 3rd St. **Map** 4 D2.
☎ 475-8592.

Bottom Line
See Rock Music.

Bradley's
70 University Pl.
Map 4 E1.
☎ 228-6440.

Cajun
129 Eighth Ave. **Map** 8 D5.
☎ 691-6174.

Fat Tuesday's
190 Third Ave. **Map** 17 B5.
☎ 533-7902.

JVC Jazz Festival
☎ 787-2020.

Knitting Factory
See Rock Music.

Michael's Pub
211 E 55th St. **Map** 13 B4.
☎ 758-2272.

Sweet Basil
88 Seventh Ave S. **Map** 8 E5.
☎ 242-1785.

Time Café
380 Lafayette St. **Map** 4 F2.
☎ 533-7000.

Village Gate
160 Bleecker St. **Map** 3 C2.
☎ 475-5120.

Village Vanguard
178 7th Ave South.
Map 3 C1.
☎ 255-4037.

FOLK AND COUNTRY

Bitter End
147 Bleecker St. **Map** 4 E3.
☎ 673-7030.

Kenny's Castaways
157 Bleecker St. **Map** 4 E3.
☎ 473-9870.

Lone Star Roadhouse
240 W 52nd St.
Map 12 E4.
☎ 245-2950.

Texas Café
10 E 16th St.
Map 8 F5.
☎ 255-8880.

BLUES, SOUL AND WORLD MUSIC

Apollo Theatre
253 W 125 St. **Map** 19 A1.
☎ 749-5838.

China Club
2130 Broadway.
Map 15 C5.
☎ 877-1166.

Cotton Club
666 W 125th St.
Map 22 F2.
☎ 663-7980.

Manny's Car Wash
1558 Third Ave. **Map** 17 B3. ☎ 369-2583.

SOB's
204 Varick St.
Map 4 D3.
☎ 243-4940.

Wetlands
161 Hudson St.
Map 4 D5.
☎ 966-4225.

Clubs, Dance Halls and Piano Bars

Nᴇᴡ ʏᴏʀᴋ's ɴɪɢʜᴛʟɪғᴇ and club scene is legendary. Whatever your preference – be it for a noisy disco, stand-up comedy or the soothing melodies of a Harry Connick, Jr. soundalike in a piano bar – you'll be really amazed at the choice. There was a rash of big discos in the 1980s, few of which have survived the recent trend toward the comfort and style of supper clubs.

Wʜᴇɴ ᴀɴᴅ Wʜᴇʀᴇ

Tʜᴇ ʙᴇꜱᴛ and hippest time for clubbing is during the week – it's also a lot cheaper. Take a fair amount of money and some ID to prove you're old enough to drink (which is over 21) – but beware, all the drinks are very expensive.

The trendiest clubs roll on until 4am or later. Fashions and club nights change all the time, so go to Tower Records on Broadway for all the latest leaflets, check club details in the listings magazines (see p328) and read the Village Voice. The most interesting places nowadays are often popularized by word of mouth. Your best bet is to go somewhere like the **Limelight** and hope someone will tell you where to go on to – often invitations to other clubs are given out there as well.

Dᴀɴᴄɪɴɢ

Nᴇᴡ ʏᴏʀᴋᴇʀꜱ thrive on music and dancing. The dance floors available all around the city range from the handkerchief-sized **Hors d'Oeuvrerie** – for jazz, dancing, a 107th-floor view and hors d'oeuvres – to a few huge basketball-court-sized places, such as **Roseland**. This has ballroom dancing every Thursday and Sunday and is New York's classic Broadway ballroom, revealing a tantalizing glimpse of older Broadway culture. It also has a good megasize, (700-seater), restaurant-cum-bar.

For mainstream danceable music, the **Rainbow Room** is reliable. For rock and roll, there's the fun **China Club**, and if you want something really different, try **Barbetta**, where Boris and Yvgeny play a combination of gypsy music and Viennese waltzes.

The **Copacabana**, which once starred the likes of Dean Martin and Frank Sinatra, is now a disco alternating with live bands. It also stages wild parties on the last Thursday of every month, with go-go boys, drag queens and disco divas. **El Morocco**, the upscale, famous nightspot with its original 1940s decor, is currently a disco alternating with Latin bands.

The **Limelight**, which started as an enormous 1980s disco, has been transformed into a mixed venue that has ground-floor dancing as well as spectator seats up in the balconies. It always advertises upcoming events. To reserve tickets ahead, telephone Ticketmaster (see p329).

Some of the most popular clubs for disco dancing, which also feature the latest music groups, are the Ritz, the Academy, Marquee, CBGB, Tramps, Manny's Carwash and the Knitting Factory (see p340–41). Few of these have strict membership policies. Be sure to get there early and be prepared to line up for entry.

Nɪɢʜᴛᴄʟᴜʙꜱ

Nɪɢʜᴛᴄʟᴜʙꜱ are the places to see a show. New York shows are less flashy than in the 1940s and 1950s but still have a variety of acts. Expect to pay a cover charge; many of the clubs also require that you have at least two drinks.

The Ballroom is a simple, breezy room that adjoins a Spanish restaurant and often has vocalists singing hits from Broadway musicals. **Maxim's** usually has one room open that features revues, plus another with singers. For some spectacular views, an elegant room, revues plus singers, go to the **Rainbow & Stars**. **Steve McGraw's** is a

theater supper club. The smart **Supper Club** surrounds you with gold lamé draperies and features big band music downstairs. Cabaret singers perform upstairs in their intimate Blue Room. **Tatou** is very expensive to eat in, and acts range from jazz to disco. Central Park's venerable indoors/outdoors **Tavern on the Green** now offers jazz in its Chestnut Room.

Gᴀʏ ᴀɴᴅ Lᴇꜱʙɪᴀɴ Vᴇɴᴜᴇꜱ

Tʜᴇ ᴘᴀꜱᴛ ᴛᴡᴏ decades have seen the arrival of clubs and restaurants specifically geared to gay and lesbian clientele. Although the entertainment is varied, transvestite revues predominate. Though all the clubs are open to heterosexuals and often to the opposite sex, too, some can make "interlopers" feel extremely uncomfortable. The current popular gay cabarets include the **Duplex**, which has a mix of stand-up comics, comedy sketches and singers. The very fashionable nightclubs and bars for men include the trendy uptown **Town House**, a piano bar with restaurant, and **Julius**, known as Greenwich Village's top neighborhood bar. **Don't Tell Mama** is a long-established gay bar, that presents good musical revues and spoofs.

Henrietta Hudson and **Crazy Nanny's** cater solely to women, as does **Grolier**. **Marie's Crisis** piano bar is a mixed venue and **Splash** is open daily with a happy hour between 5pm and 9pm..

The Village Voice has good listings of what's happening in the gay communities, and the Gay Yellow Pages covers the gay scene. For more information, phone the **Gay and Lesbian Switchboard**.

Cᴏᴍᴇᴅʏ Sʜᴏᴡᴄᴀꜱᴇꜱ

Mᴀɴʏ ᴏғ New York's best current comedy clubs or showcases have evolved from earlier "improvisational" comedy. Leading the pack are the aptly named **Catch a Rising Star**, **Improvisation** and **Caroline's**. Also good for a visit are the **Comic Strip**, **Stand-Up New York**, **Mostly Magic**, **55 Grove St.**, **Dangerfield's**, and **Comedy Cellar**. Each club presents a nightly batch of comics.

PIANO BARS AND HOTEL "ROOMS"

CABARETS HAVE become a New York institution. Such cozy, just-for-listening places are often called "rooms" and

are located in hotels. Most operate from Tuesday to Saturday (usually with a cover charge or drink minimum) and most take credit cards.

The **Algonquin's** Oak Room has had song stylists such as Michael Feinstein. For a classic piano lounge with a panoramic Manhattan view, visit the **Beekman Tower**. The "long-distance hummer" award goes to the suave and sophisticated Bobby Short, who has played his piano for over a quarter of a century at the atmospheric Café Carlyle

in the **Carlyle Hotel**. In the same hotel is Bemelman's Bar, with whimsical murals and attracting a relaxed crowd who enjoy first-class crooners. Hear tinkling keys and fine songs in the lounge of the **Drake Swissôtel**. Performers such as Barbara Cook play the **Hilton Hotel's** Club 53, and Café Pierre's singer-pianist Kathleen Landis holds court at the **Pierre Hotel**. Piano music is heard at the Ambassador Lounge in the **UN Plaza Park Hyatt Hotel**.

DIRECTORY

DANCING

Barbetta
321 W 46th St.
Map 12 D5.
[246-9171.

China Club
See p341.

Copacabana
10 E 60th St.
Map 12 F3.
[755-6010.

El Morocco
307 E 54th St.
Map 13 B4.
[750-1500.

Hors d'Oeuvrerie
1 World Trade Center.
Map 1 B2.
[938-1111.

Limelight
See p341.

Rainbow Room
30 Rockefeller Plaza.
Map 12 F4.
[632-5100.

Roseland
239 W 52nd St.
Map 12 E4.
[247-0200.

NIGHTCLUBS

The Ballroom
253 W 28th St.
Map 8 E3.
[244-3005.

Maxim's
680 Madison Ave.
Map 13 A3.
[751-5111.

Rainbow & Stars
30 Rockefeller Plaza.
Map 12 F4.
[632-5000.

Steve McGraw's
158 W 72nd St.
Map 12 D1.
[595-7400.

Supper Club
240 W 47th St.
Map 12 D5.
[595-7400.

Tatou
151 E 50th St. **Map** 13 A4.
[753-1144.

Tavern on the Green
Central Park west side at 67th St.
Map 12 D2.
[921-1940

GAY AND LESBIAN VENUES

Crazy Nanny's
21 Seventh Ave South.
Map 3 C1.
[366-6312.

Don't Tell Mama
343 W 46th St.
Map 12 D5.
[757-0788.

Duplex
61 Christopher St.
Map 3 C2.
[255-5438.

Five Oaks
49 Grove St.
Map 3 C2.
[243-8885.

Gay and Lesbian Switchboard
[777-1800.

Henrietta Hudson
438 Hudson St.
Map 3 C3.
[243-9079.

Julius
159 W 10th St.
Map 4 D1.
[929-9672.

Marie's Crisis Café
59 Grove St.
Map 3 C2.
[243-9323.

Town House
236 E 58th St.
Map 13 B4.
[754-4649.

COMEDY SHOWCASES

55 Grove St.
Map 3 C2.
[366-5438.

Caroline's
1626 Broadway.
Map 12 E5.
[757-4100.

Catch a Rising Star
1487 First Ave.
Map 17 B5.
[794-1906.

Comedy Cellar
117 MacDougal St.
Map 4 D2.
[254-3630.

Comic Strip
1568 Second Ave.
Map 17 B4.
[861-9386.

Dangerfield's
1118 First Ave.
Map 13 C3.
[593-1650.

Improvisation
358 W 44th St.
Map 12 D5.
[765-8268.

Mostly Magic
55 Carmine St. **Map** 4 D3.
[924-1472.

Stand-Up New York
236 W 78th St.
Map 15 C5.
[595-0850.

PIANO BARS AND HOTEL "ROOMS"

Algonquin Hotel
Oak Room, 59 W 44th St.
Map 12 F5.
[840-6800.

Beekman Tower
3 Mitchell Pl.
Map 13 C5.
[355-7300.

Carlyle Hotel
35 E 76th St.
Map 17 A5.
[744-1600.

Drake Swissôtel
440 Park Ave.
Map 13 A3.
[421-0900.

Hilton Hotel
Club 53, 53 Ave of the Americas. **Map** 12 E4.
[586-7000.

Pierre Hotel
Café Pierre, 2 E 61st St.
Map 12 F3.
[586-7000.

UN Plaza Park Hyatt Hotel
1 UN Plaza at 44th St.
Map 13 C5.
[355-3400.

Sports and Fitness

NEW YORKERS ARE SPORTS MAD, and there are activities to suit every taste. If you're a doer not a viewer, you can choose from health clubs and horseback riding to pumping iron and swimming, playing tennis or jogging. Spectator sports are provided by two professional baseball teams, two hockey teams, a basketball team and two football teams, while for tennis fans there are the US Open and Virginia Slims tournaments.

TICKETS

THE EASIEST WAY to get hold of your tickets is through Ticketron or Ticketmaster (*see p329*). For the big games, you may need a ticket agent.

FOOTBALL

THE CITY'S two professional football teams are the New York Giants and the New York Jets. They both play their home games across the river at **Giants Stadium** in New Jersey. Tickets for the Giants are almost impossible to obtain, but they may be available for the Jets.

BASEBALL

TO CAPTURE the essence of this American institution, first time spectators should go to **Yankee Stadium**, home of the New York Yankees. **Shea Stadium**, the Mets' base, is also convenient. The season runs from April to September.

BASKETBALL

THE NEW YORK KNICKS play their home games from October to April at **Madison Square Garden**; you may also catch the ever-popular Harlem Globetrotters there.

BICYCLING

THE BEST PLACE to cycle is in Central Park during the weekend, when it is closed to cars. Bikes may be rented from **AAA Bicycle Rentals**.

BOXING

PROFESSIONAL boxing matches are more often seen on Paramount's wide TV screen than in the flesh at **Madison Square Garden**.

FITNESS CENTERS, GYMS AND HEALTH CLUBS

FACILITIES INCLUDING jogging tracks, Nautilus machines and swimming pools are now found in such hotels as the UN Plaza and Peninsula (*see pp280–81*). Many of the commercial gyms and health clubs are open only to those with an annual membership, but it is possible to use the facilities at a **YMCA** if you are a member or buy a day pass.

GOLF

PRACTICE YOUR swing at the **Midtown Indoor Golf Club** or play mini-golf at the **Wollman Memorial Rink**. The city owns several courses in the boroughs, such as **Pelham Bay Park** in the Bronx and **Silver Lake** on Staten Island. For information, call 360-8204; or to make a reservation, phone 225-GOLF.

HORSE RIDING AND RACING

THE ONLY riding stable in Manhattan is **Claremont Riding Academy**. You can ride in its indoor arena or go trotting in Central Park.

Harness racing, in which horses pull sulkies (small carts), takes place year-round at **Yonkers Raceway**. Flat races are held daily, except Tuesday, October to May at the **Aqueduct Race Track**, and May to October at the **Belmont Park Race Track**.

ICE HOCKEY

THE ICE FLIES, as do the players' fists, when the New York Rangers meet their competition at **Madison Square Garden**. The season runs from October to April.

ICE-SKATING

THE OUTDOOR Rockefeller **Plaza Rink** is glamorous. **Lasker Skating (City) Rink** is an outdoor pool in summer. The **Wollman Memorial Rink** has ice-skating in winter, roller-skating and mini-golf in summer. Indoor sites include **Rivergate Ice Rink** and the **Ice Studio**.

INDOOR SPORTS AND RACQUET GAMES

A LARGE SPORTS complex called **Hackers, Hitters & Hoops** has batting cages, mini-golf, Ping-Pong, racquetball (similar to squash) and other activities. There's also the **Printing House Fitness & Racquet Center**.

JOGGING

SOME PARKS are safe for joggers, others are not, so be guided by your concierge. None is safe after dark, at dusk or before dawn. The most popular route is around the reservoir in Central Park (*see p206*). The **International Running Center** has weekly running clinics and races.

MARATHON

TO BE ONE of the 25,000 who enter the New York Marathon, you have to sign up six months in advance. The race is held on the first Sunday in November. Phone 860-4455 for information.

SPORTS BARS

TOP BARS include **The Sporting Club**, which has a huge electronic scoreboard with right-up-to-the-second information, plus nine life-sized TV screens. At **Mickey Mantle's** you can watch the fixtures on ten elephantine video screens.

SWIMMING

MANY MANHATTAN hotels have pools with free access during your stay. If yours does not, look for the public pools listed in the Yellow Pages "Government Offices" section. There are also various outdoor pools.

Try the spectacular Jones Beach State Park (see p253) along Long Island's shoreline.

TENNIS

THE TOP TENNIS tournament in New York is the US Open, played each August at the **National Tennis Center**. Also good is the women's Virginia Slims Championships in November at **Madison Square Garden** (see p133).

If you want to play tennis rather than watch it, look in the telephone directory under "Tennis Courts: Public and Private." For private courts, you can expect to pay up to about $50 an hour. For public courts, you will need a $50 permit, available from the **NY City Parks & Recreation Department**. You will also need an identity card before you are allowed to play. Courts must be reserved at least a week in advance. **The Tennis Center** and the **Manhattan Plaza Tennis Center** are two possibilities.

TRACK AND FIELD

THE MILLROSE GAMES are normally held in early February, and the Amateur Athletic Union (AAU) championships, where most of the top athletes usually appear, are held in late February at **Madison Square Garden**.

OTHER ACTIVITIES

IN CENTRAL PARK, options include renting rowboats from **Loeb Boathouse** or playing chess – pick up the pieces from The Dairy (see p206). Bowling is available at the **Leisure Time Recreation Center**. Pool can be played in bars and pool halls such as the **Julian Billiard Academy** and **Chelsea Billiards**. Farther afield are fishing trips from **Sheepshead Bay**.

SPORTS ADDRESSES

AAA Bicycle Rentals
The Boathouse, Central Park. **Map** 16 F5.
(861-4137.

Aqueduct Race Track
Ozone Park, Queens.
((718) 641-4700.

Belmont Park Race Track
Hempstead Turnpike, Long Island.
((718) 641-4700.

Chelsea Billiards
54 W 21st St. **Map** 8 E4.
(989-0096.

Claremont Riding Academy
175 W 89th St.
Map 15 C3.
(724-5100.

Giants Stadium
Meadowlands
East Rutherford, NJ.
((201) 935-8222.
New York Giants.
((201) 935-8500.
New York Jets.

Hackers, Hitters & Hoops
123 W 18th St. **Map** 8 E5.
(929-7482.

Ice Studio
1034 Lexington Ave.
Map 17 A5.
(535-0304.

New York Road Runners' Club
9 E 89th St. **Map** 17 A3.
(860-4455.

Julian Billiard Academy
138 E 14th St. **Map** 4 F1.
(475-9338.

Lasker Skating (City) Rink
110th St at Lenox Ave.
Map 21 B4.
(722-9781.

Leisure Time Recreation Center
625 Eighth Ave. **Map** 8 D1.
(268-6909.

Loeb Boathouse
Central Park. **Map** 16 F5.
(517-4723.

Madison Square Garden
Seventh Ave at 33rd St.
Map 8 E2.
(465-MSG1.

Manhattan Plaza Tennis Center
450 W 43rdSt.
Map 7 C1.
(594-0554.

Mickey Mantle's
42 Central Park South.
Map 12 E3.
(688-7777.

Midtown Indoor Golf Club
7 W 45th St.
Map 12 F5.
(869-3636.

National Tennis Center
Flushing Meadows Park, Queens.
((718) 271-5100.

NY City Parks & Recreation Department
Arsenal Building
64th St and Fifth Ave.
Map 12 F2.
(408-0100.

Pelham Bay Park
Bronx.
((212) 885-1258 or (718) 225-4653.

Plaza Rink
Rockefeller Center.
1 Rockefeller Plaza, Fifth Ave.
Map 12 F5.
(757-5731.

Printing House Fitness & Racquet Center
422 Hudson St.
Map 3 C3.
(243-7777.

Rivergate Ice Rink
401 E 34th St.
Map 9 C2.
(689-0035.

Shea Stadium
126th St at Roosevelt Ave,
Flushing, Queens.
((718) 507-TIXX or (718) 507-8499.

Sheepshead Bay
(For information on fishing trips call Mike's Tackle & Bait Shop.)
((718) 646-9261.

Silver Lake
915 Victory Blvd,
Staten Island.
((718) 447-5686 or (718) 225-4653.

The Sporting Club
99 Hudson St.
Map 4 D5.
(219-0900.

The Tennis Center
331 E 38th St.
Map 4 D5.
(685-5135.

Wollman Memorial Rink
Central Park. Fifth Ave at 59th St. **Map** 12 F2.
(517-4800.

Yankee Stadium
River Ave at 161st St
The Bronx.
(293-6000.

47th St YMCA
224 E 47th St.
Map 13 B5.
(755-2410.

92nd St YMCA
1395 Lexington Ave.
Map 17 A2.
(427-6000.

West Side YMCA
5 W 63rd St.
Map 12 D2.
(787-4400.

Yonkers Raceway
Yonkers
Westchester County.
((914) 968-4200.

Late-Night New York

N EW YORK IS INDEED a city that never sleeps. If you wake up in the middle of the night – with a craving for fresh bread, a need to be entertained or an urge to watch the sun rise over the Manhattan skyline – there are always plenty of options to choose from.

BARS AND CLUBS

T HE BEST and friendliest bars are often the Irish ones. Sing-alongs happen at **Katie O'Toole's** on Thursdays, and daily (except Mondays) at **Tommy Makem's**. Have a late-night dry martini at the **Temple Bar**. The best piano bars are in the hotels: try the Café Carlyle in the **Carlyle Hotel** or the Oak Room in the **Algonquin Hotel**.

For hot American jazz until 4am, go to **Sweet Basil** or the **Blue Note**. Traditional jazz and swing entertain the diners and dancers at the **Rainbow Room** and the **Red Blazer Too. Cornelia Street Café** is a snug and lively nook for prose, poetry and theater readings. Poetry, theater and Latin music can be found at the **Nuyorican Poets Café**.

MIDNIGHT MOVIES

S PECIAL MIDNIGHT showings and a youthful crowd can be found at Eighth Street Playhouse. Late movies are also screened at the Angelika Film Center and the Film Forum *(see pp336–7)*.

SHOPS

O N FIFTH AVENUE, the huge Doubleday Book Shop is open to 10pm; the St. Mark's Bookshop and Shakespeare & Company Booksellers are also open late. The Upper West Side HMV record store is open till midnight, East Side HMV until 10pm. Both Tower Records close at midnight, as does Gryphon Records. Bleecker Bob's Golden Oldies Record Shop stays open until 3am on weekends *(see Shopping pp322-3).*

Late-night video stores include the enormous **Palmer Video Store** on Hudson and **Video Access**.

Among the many Village clothing stores that stay open late on weekends are the **Antique Boutique** (open until midnight) and **Trash and Vaudeville** (open till 8pm on Fridays and Saturdays). For aspirin and other health essentials, **Kaufman Pharmacy** is open 24 hours a day and **Plaza Pharmacy** until 11pm every night.

TAKE-OUT FOOD AND GROCERIES

A FEW TAKE-OUT food stores are open 24 hours a day, including the **Delmonico Gourmet Food Market** and the **West Side Supermarket**. Many Korean greengrocers also stay open all night. The **Food Emporium** is a supermarket chain open until midnight (around the clock at the York Avenue branch). On Saturdays, **Zabar's** stays open until midnight. Liquor stores are usually open until 10pm and many deliver.

For the best in bagels, go to **H & H Bagels East**, **Bagels On The Square** and **Jumbo Bagels and Bialys.** There are many pizzerias and Chinese restaurants that stay open late, and most deliver. Many ice cream parlors are also open late.

DINING

C LUBBERS AND the trendy set often frequent **La Jumelle**, **Florent** and **Les Halles** for good French dishes. Twentysomethings will seek out the **Coffee Shop** for late-night beer and Brazilian food. You'll find delicious and legendary sandwiches at the **Carnegie Deli**. **Caffè Reggio** in Greenwich Village has been a favorite for late-night coffee and desserts since 1927. It is also possible to find good food in dinner clubs. **Le Bar**

Bat is popular for its bat cave décor and Vietnamese cuisine. **Tatou's** offers jazz and real old-fashioned Creole food, and at the 1930s **Rainbow Room**, the continental dishes add to the magic of this special place.

SPORTS

T HERE IS round-the-clock play at **Chelsea Billiards** or until 5am at the **Billiard Club** on weekends. Have late-night beers and burgers with the New York University crowd at **Bowlmore Lanes** bowling alley.

SERVICES

M IDNIGHT EXPRESS CLEANERS, of Long Island City, picks up garments in Manhattan until midnight and has them ready the next day. It also delivers until midnight. **Rialto** can arrange a bouquet until midnight any day of the week. On Thursdays hairdresser **George Michael of Madison Avenue/Madora Inc** is open until 10pm and will also make house calls.

TOURS AND VIEWS

O NE OF NEW YORK'S most enjoyable walks is along the Hudson River at the World Financial Center's **Battery Park City**, open (and safe) at all hours. Piers 16 and 17 at South Street Seaport attract strollers and revelers all night long and the **Harbor Lights** restaurant on Pier 17 is open until 4am for a middle of the night pick-me-up. Or enjoy the city lights by taking a **Circle Line** two-hour tour of the nighttime harbor.

Try the Riverview Terrace at Sutton Place: the benches offer a peaceful and quiet place to watch the sun rise over the East River, Roosevelt Island and Queens. Two of the most sensational views with the Manhattan backdrop are (looking west) from the **River Café** and (looking east) from **Arthur's Landing** restaurant.

Take a trip on the **Staten Island Ferry** *(see p76)* to see the Statue of Liberty and the Manhattan skyline in the dawn light, or a take a taxi across Brooklyn Bridge *(see pp86–9)* to watch the sun rise over New York harbor. Go to the **Beekman Tower Hotel's** Top of the Tower for some panoramas of the city's East Side up to 1am. Perhaps the ultimate view is from the **Empire State Building**: its Observation Deck *(see pp134–5)* stays open until midnight. Have breakfast 107 floors up, at the World Trade Center's **Windows on the World** restaurant, overlooking the city, river and harbor.

Château Stables has rides in horse-drawn carriages and **Island Helicopter** runs spectacular flights over the glittering city at night. If you want to experience something a little bit different, try one of **Elite 'Wild-Side' Tours'** escorted evening barhopping walks, or see the night lights with **Happy Apple Tours**. And if you still can't sleep, visit the bustling downtown **Fulton Fish Market** at 6am.

DIRECTORY

BARS AND CLUBS

Algonquin Hotel
See Piano Bars p343.

Blue Note
See Jazz p341.

Carlyle Hotel
See Piano Bars p343.

Cornelia Street Café
29 Cornelia St. **Map** 4 D2.
(989-9318.

Katie O'Toole's
134 Reade St. **Map** 1 B1.
(226-8928.

Nuyorican Poets Café
236 E 3rd St. **Map** 5 A2.
(505-8183.

Rainbow Room
See Dancing p343.

Red Blazer Too
349 W 46th St.
Map 12 D5.
(262-3112.

Sweet Basil
See Jazz p341.

Temple Bar
332 Lafayette St.
Map 4 F4.
(925-4242.

Tommy Makem's
130 E 57th St. **Map** 12 E3.
(759-9040.

SHOPS

Antique Boutique
712–714 Broadway.
Map 4 E2.
(460-8830.

Kaufman Pharmacy
See Survival Guide p355.

Palmer Video Store
470 Hudson St. **Map** 3 C3.
(463-9377.

Plaza Pharmacy
251 E 86th St. **Map** 17 B3.
(427-6940.

Trash and Vaudeville
4 St. Mark's Pl. **Map** 5 A2.
(982-3590.

Video Access
2617 Broadway.
Map 15 C1.
(316-6666.

TAKE-OUT FOOD AND GROCERIES

Bagels On The Square
7 Carmine St. **Map** 4 D3.
(691-3041.

Delmonico Gourmet Food Market
55 E 59th St. **Map** 12 F3.
(751-5559.

Food Emporium
1498 York Ave.
Map 17 C4.
(879-9555.

H & H Bagels East
1550 2nd Ave.
Map 17 B4.
(734-7441.

Jumbo Bagels and Bialys
1070 2nd Ave. **Map** 13 B3.
(355-6185.

West Side Supermarket
2171 Broadway. **Map** 15 C5.
(595-2536.

Zabar's
2245 Broadway. **Map** 15 3C.
(787-2000.

DINING

Caffè Reggio
119 MacDougal St.
Map 4 D2.
(475-9557.

Carnegie Deli
Restaurants and Bars p306.

Coffee Shop
Restaurants and Bars p306.

Florent
Restaurants and Bars p306.

La Jumelle
55 Grand St. **Map** 4 E4.
(941-9651.

Le Bar Bat
311 West 57th St.
Map 12 D3.
(307-7228.

Les Halles
Restaurants and Bars p306.

Rainbow Room
Restaurants and Bars p306.

Tatou
151 East 50th St.
Map 13 A4.
(753-1144.

SPORTS

Billiard Club
220 W 19th St.
Map 8 E5.
(206-POOL.

Bowlmore Lanes
110 University Pl.
Map 4 E1.
(255-8188.

Chelsea Billiards
See Sport p345.

SERVICES

George Michael of MadisonAvenue/ Madora Inc
420 Madison Ave.
Map 13 A5.
(752-1177.

Midnight Express Cleaners
25–15 41 Ave,
Long Island City.
(921-0111.

Rialto
707 Lexington Ave.
Map 13 A4.
(688-3234.

TOURS AND VIEWS

Arthur's Landing
Port Imperial Marina,
Pershing Circle,
Weehawken, NJ.
((201) 867-0777.

Battery Park City
West St. **Map** 1 A3.

Beekman Tower Hotel
1st Ave 49th St.
Map 13 C5.
(355-7300.

Château Stables
608 W 48th St.
Map 15 B3.
(246-0520.

Circle Line
W 42nd St. **Map** 15 B3
(563-3204 .

Elite 'Wild-Side' Tours
((800) 275-3548.

Empire State Building
See pp134–5.

Fulton Fish Market Tours
(669-9400.

Happy Apple Tours
((800) 421-4518.

Harbor Lights
89 Fulton St.
Map 2 D2.
(227-2800.

Island Helicopter
(683-4575.

River Café
See Restaurants and Bars p306.

Staten Island Ferry
See Getting Around New York p369.

Windows on the World
See Restaurants and Bars p295.

CHILDREN'S NEW YORK

YOUNG VISITORS soon catch the contagious excitement in the air in New York. Attractions for all ages abound, and plenty are designed especially for children. More than a dozen theater companies, two zoos and three imaginative museums are for just the young, backed up with special events at many museums and parks. The chance to visit a TV studio is a treat, and New York's own Big Apple Circus is a perennial delight. With more to do than can ever be squeezed into a single visit, you'll never hear the cry "I'm bored!" Best of all, there's no need to spend a fortune to have fun.

A young visitor making New York his very own playground

PRACTICAL ADVICE

NEW YORK is family-friendly. Many of its hotels allow children in parents' rooms free, and will supply cots or cribs if needed. Most museums charge half price or less for children, while others are free. Children under 44 in (112 cm) also ride free on subways and buses when accompanied by an adult. Travel between 9am and 4pm to avoid rush hours.

Supplies such as diapers and medicines are readily available, and the Kaufman Pharmacy *(see p357)* is open 24 hours a day. Finding changing tables in public toilets is less easy, but no one objects if a counter is used. Best bets are the facilities in libraries, hotels and department stores. Most hotels will arrange babysitters; another reliable source is the **Baby Sitters' Guild**.

To find out more about the range of current activities for children, get a copy of the free quarterly calendar of events, available from the New York Convention and Visitors Bureau *(see p352)*. Weekly listings can be found in *New York* magazine.

NEW YORK ADVENTURES

THE CITY can seem like a giant amusement park for youngsters. Elevators whisk you sky-high for bird's-eye views from atop the world's highest buildings. Or you can set sail on the classic **Circle Line** tour around Manhattan; the sailboat **Petrel**; a choice of tall ship or paddlewheeler from South Street Seaport *(see p84)*; or the bargain roundtrip on the Staten Island Ferry *(see p76)*. The Roosevelt Island Tram *(see p179)* is a Swiss cable car offering an airborne ride over the East River. Central Park *(see pp202–7)* is a source of rides of every kind – from the old-fashioned charm of the carousel to real horseback and ponycart rides. Children who prefer a faster pace can join the rollerblade skaters who cruise around the park, away from the traffic, every weekend.

Cooling off in a playground in Central Park

MUSEUMS

WHILE MANY of New York's museums appeal to all ages, some are designed just for the young. High on the list is the imaginative Children's Museum of Manhattan *(see p217)*, a multimedia world in which children can produce their own videos and newscasts. Farther afield are the **Staten Island Children's Museum**, where a huge climb-through anthill is one of the favorite items, and the Brooklyn Children's Museum *(see p245)*. The *Intrepid* Sea-Air-Space Museum *(see p147)* is a real aircraft carrier, with exhibits including the fastest spy plane in the world. Finally, be sure to see the dinosaur displays at the American Museum of Natural History *(see pp214–15)*.

OUTDOOR FUN

IN SUMMER, all of New York comes out to play. Central Park is a child's wonderland, from skating rinks to

Skating with Santa at Rockefeller Center

boating lakes, bicycle paths to miniature golf. The park has free entertainment galore—such as guided walks by park rangers on Saturdays, toy sailboat races and summer storytelling. The zoo is relatively small in scale, which makes it just right for children.

All children will be fascinated by the International Wildlife Conservation Park *(see pp242–3)* where there are also plenty of friendly animals to be petted.

Orchard and **Rockaway** beaches and Coney Island *(see p247)* are just a subway ride away. Winter brings the chance to skate at Rockefeller Center *(see p142)* or in Central Park on a rink fringed with views of skyscrapers.

INDOOR FUN

NEW YORK children's theater is of a quality and variety matching that for adults. Some favorite companies are the **Paper Bag Players** and **Theaterworks USA**, whose shows sell out fast; get schedules and reserve seats early.

The New York City Ballet's annual Christmas production of *The Nutcracker* at Lincoln Center *(see p212)* opens at about the same time that the **Big Apple Circus** sets up its tent nearby. Ringling Brothers and Barnum & Bailey Circus is in action at Madison Square Garden *(see p133)* for several weeks each spring.

Opportunities for youngsters to work off energy in winter are many, from indoor skating rinks to bowling alleys.

SHOPPING

THERE WILL be no complaints about shopping trips if they include **F.A.O. Schwarz**,

Centerpiece clock at toy store F.A.O. Schwarz

one of the world's biggest and best toy stores. Other children's favorites are **Enchanted Forest** and **The Last Wound-Up** (the latter packed with mechanical toys), and youngsters are welcomed for storytelling sessions at children's bookstores, such as **Books of Wonder**.

EATING OUT

HAMBURGER-and-pasta chain **Ottomanelli's Cafés** is very popular with children, and even adults find it hard to finish their huge burgers. The lively **Hard Rock Café** is another hit, and most children enjoy the foods sold around Chinatown and Little Italy. For a quick hot snack, pizza-by-the-slice is worth a try, or stave off hunger pangs with pretzels and hot dogs from street vendors. Sure to sweeten young dispositions are the legendary ice-cream parlors, **Rumplemayer's** *(see p305)* and **Peppermint Park**. If all else fails, there are scores of fast food places, including McDonalds, with more than 40 branches.

Storytelling session at South Street Seaport

SURVIVAL GUIDE

PRACTICAL INFORMATION

Visitors to New York are treated very much the same as anyone else. While you may not be given special treatment, as long as you follow a few guidelines on personal security *(see pp356–7)* you'll be able to explore the city as freely as any native New Yorker. Buses and subway trains *(pp372–5)*

Visitors resting on the steps of the Metropolitan Museum of Art

are reliable and cheap; there are lots of cash machines *(pp358–9)*, and money can be easily exchanged at banks, hotels and foreign money brokers. The wide range of prices offered by all the many hotels *(pp274–5)*, restaurants *(pp290–92)* and entertainment venues *(pp328–47)* means your New York trip can be both fun and affordable.

SIGHTSEEING TIPS

New York's rush hours extend from 8 to 10am, 11:30am to 1:30pm and 4:30 to 6:30pm, Monday to Friday. During these times, every form of public transportation will be crowded, and the streets will be much harder to navigate on foot. Plan your day accordingly.

It's worth trying to visit a cluster of sights in the same area – see the *Street-by-Street* plans of each area – instead of exhausting yourself rushing from one distant attraction to another. Buses are a comfortable and reliable way to get around, and you'll see the city as you travel.

It's best to avoid passing through certain areas of the city, especially at particular times *(pp356–7)*. Public toilets in train stations, bus stations and subways should always be avoided. They attract many drug users and the homeless, even when there's an attendant.

If you need help with street directions or, for whatever reason, feel a need to get off the street, try and find a hotel doorman. There is one on duty at the entrance to most hotels 24 hours a day.

Hotel doorman

OPENING HOURS

Business hours are generally from 9am to 5pm with no lunchtime closing. Only banks close earlier, at 3pm, although some do have longer hours

(8am–6pm) and are open on Saturday mornings. Many museums close on Mondays and major holidays. Some open on Tuesday or Thursday evenings during certain seasons (phone for details).

MUSEUMS

In New York, *museums* is used as a blanket term to include institutions that offer diverse holdings. The city's museums are described on pages 34 to 37. Museums in the city either charge admission, starting at around $2, or require a "donation." There are usually discounts for senior citizens, students and children. The leading museums schedule free guided tours and lectures. Museum Mile *(see pp166–7)*, on or near Fifth Avenue, groups a number of major museums close together. Of these, the Frick Collection and the Cooper-Hewitt are small enough to see in one or two hours, but the larger Guggenheim and Whitney museums may take far longer than this.

ETIQUETTE

It is illegal to smoke on buses and trains; in taxis; or in office lobbies, shops and enclosed public places. Restaurants, theaters and cinemas have smoking areas but ban pipes and cigars.

Business travelers need not bring a gift for their hosts. Such tokens are not expected

and may even be considered improper. If you do bring something, it should be something cheap and preferably representative of where you live.

Tipping is an integral part of New York life: for taxi drivers leave 10 to 15%; waiters 15 to 20%, cocktail waiters 15%, hotel room service 10% (when not added to the bill); coat check $1; hotel maids $1 or $2 per day after the first day; hotel bellhops about $1 per bag; hair stylists 15 to 20% and barbers 10 to 20%.

TOURIST INFORMATION

Advice on any aspect of life in New York is available from the **New York Convention and Visitors Bureau**. Its literature racks and information desk attendants provide information on current events and exhibitions at museums and art galleries.

Useful information

New York Convention and Visitors Bureau, 2 Columbus Circle. **Map** 12 D3. 397-8222. **Open** 9am–6pm Mon–Fri, 10am–6pm Sat, Sun.

Information racks at the New York Convention and Visitors Bureau

ENTERTAINMENT LISTINGS

A NUMBER of cheaply priced or even free publications listing current exhibitions and leisure activities are available at newsstands, hotels or galleries throughout New York.

Among the more popular ones are *New York* magazine and *The New Yorker's* "Goings On About Town" roster. Both magazines list offerings at the city's many museums, clubs, theaters, galleries, restaurants, cinemas, colleges and libraries, plus impending auctions.

The *Village Voice* focuses on events in SoHo, TriBeCa and Greenwich Village, plus other major cultural activity in the city. The *New York Times* Friday and Sunday editions list current visual and performing arts events in their respective "Weekend" and "Arts and Leisure" sections. *Art News* is a monthly magazine that lists major art events and auctions and reviews exhibits.

There are also various free magazines. The weekly *Where* is distributed through hotel concierges and lists major museums, their opening hours, locations and any exhibitions they have on. *Art Now/New York Gallery Guide* is released in art galleries each month. It lists current exhibitions and has many very useful maps showing where they are located.

***New York* magazine has weekly comprehensive entertainment listings for all of New York**

GUIDED TOURS

However you want to see New York – with the help of a pre-recorded walk or by an exciting trip in a helicopter, boat or horse-drawn carriage – organized sightseeing trips, planned by someone else, can save a lot of time, effort and often money.

Boat Tours

Circle Line
Sightseeing Yachts
Pier 83, W 42nd St.
Map 7 A1. 563-3200.
A three-hour trip circumnavigating Manhattan.

Circle Line Statue of
Liberty Ferry
South Ferry, Battery Park.
Map 1 C4. 363-3200.

Seaport Line
Pier 16 at South Street
Seaport. **Map** 2 E3.
233-4800. *Paddlewheeler and steamboat
harbor cruises.*
669-9417. *A two-hour
sail on the Pioneer.*

Spirit of New York
99 Wall St. **Map** 2 D3.
742-PARTY. *Cruises
include lunch or dinner.*

Staten Island Ferry
South Ferry. **Map** 2 D4.
806-6940.
Manhattan–Staten Island.

World Yacht, Inc
Pier 81 W 41st St.
Map 2 D5. 929-7090.
*Cruises include lunch,
dinner and entertainment.*

Helicopter tour

Carriage Tours

59th St at Fifth Ave and
along Central Park S.
*Horse-drawn carriages
gather outside the Plaza
Hotel (**Map** 12 F3),
days and evenings. The
usual itinerary takes in
Central Park.*

Coach Tours

Allied Tours
165 W 46th St.
Map 12 E5.
869-5100.

Gray Line of New York
254 W 54th St.
Map 12 E4.
397-2600.

Short Line Tours/American
Sightseeing NY
166 W 46th St.
Map 12 F5.
354-5122.

Helicopter Tours

Island Helicopter
Sightseeing
One Penn Plaza. **Map** 8 E2.
683-4575.

Liberty Helicopter Tours
Heliport at W 30th St and
Twelfth Ave. **Map** 7 B3.
629-5370.

Walking Tours

Backstage on Broadway
228 W 47th St.
Map 12 E5.
575-8065.
*Behind-the-scenes tours of
Broadway shows.*

CityWalks
410 W 20th St. **Map** 7 C5.
989-2456.
Historic neighborhoods.

Harlem Spirituals, Inc.
1697 Broadway.
Map 12 E4.
757-0425.
*A tour soaking up Harlem's
history and culture.*

Museum of the City of
New York
103rd St and Fifth Ave.
Map 21 C5.
534-1672.
Architecture and history.

NBC Studio Tour
30 Rockefeller Plaza,
49th St at Sixth Ave.
Map 12 F5.
664-3055.

92nd Street YMCA
1395 Lexington Ave.
Map 17 B5.
427-6000.
Culture and history.

Talk-a-Walk
30 Waterside Plaza.
Map 9 C4.
686-0356.
Recorded itineraries.

Talking Tours
25 E 21st St.
Map 8 F4.
737-5137.
Recorded itineraries.

Carriage ride in Central Park

DISABLED TRAVELERS

DISABLED PEOPLE will find New York more accessible than most cities. Many of the city's buses have ramps that can be lowered to help people in wheelchairs board. The buses also "kneel" to help those with restricted mobility.

Hotels, large stores and office buildings are also often well equipped for wheelchair access, and some museums offer tours for the deaf, blind and disabled. Several city theaters have systems to aid hearing-impaired patrons as do a growing number of telephones. *Access Guide to New York City*, free from the **Junior League of the City of New York**, lists buildings accessible to the disabled.

Useful information Junior League of the City of New York, 130 E 80th St. **Map** 17 A4. **C** 288-6220. The Mayor's Office for People with Disabilities. **C** 788-2830.

A New York city bus "kneeling" to help the elderly board

CUSTOMS AND IMMIGRATION

AT PRESENT ALL British and Canadian passport holders, whether they are on vacation, business travelers or students, do not need visas if staying in the US for 90 days or less. Australians and New Zealanders require passports, visas and onward passage tickets. Some nationals also must show proof they have $500 or more. Check with a travel agent if in any doubt.

Customs allowances per person when you enter the US are 200 cigarettes, 50 cigars or 4.4 pounds (2 kilograms) of tobacco; no more than 2 pints (1 liter) of alcohol; gifts which are worth no more than $100; no meat or meat products (even in cans), seeds, growing plants or fresh fruit.

Upon arrival at one of New York's airports, you should follow signs stating "other than American passports" to immigration counters where your passport will then be inspected and stamped. Once you have reclaimed your baggage from the appropriate area (again, follow the signs), you will be approached by a Customs officer. He or she will examine the Customs declaration you should have received and filled in on your flight and direct you either toward the exit or to a Customs inspector who will then search your luggage.

According to American Customs officials, only 5% of all travelers will have to have their luggage searched. There are no red or green Customs channels – you're cleared and free to go once the Customs officer has seen your fully completed declaration.

STUDENT TRAVELERS

MANY MUSEUMS and theaters allow students a discount on admission. To receive this, however, you will need to carry proof of your student status at all times.

An International Student ID Card can be purchased quite cheaply, provided you have the right credentials, from the **New York Student Center** or the **Council on International Educational Exchange**. At the same time, ask for a copy of the *ISIC Student Handbook*. This invaluable booklet identifies places and services throughout the US that offer a range of discounts to card holders. Included are accommodations, various museums, theaters, tours and attractions, nightclubs, restaurants and even Carey transportation (buses from Manhattan to New York's airports, *see p363*).

Normally, it is extremely difficult to obtain permission to work in the US; students are an exception. Any branch of the Student Travel Association in the UK, Australia or New Zealand will be able to help you with details of working holidays in New York. In London, contact the **University of London Union** for advice.

STUDENT INFORMATION

International Educational Exchange
205 E 42nd St. **Map** 9 B1.
C 661-1414.

New York Student Center
895 Amsterdam Ave.
Map 20 E5.
C 666-4177.

University of London Union
Malet St, London WC1E 7BY.
C 071-580 9551.

CONVERSION CHART

Bear in mind that 1 US pint (0.5 liter) is a smaller measure than 1 UK pint (0.6 liter).

Imperial system:
1 inch = 2.5 centimeters
1 foot = 30 centimeters
1 mile = 1.6 kilometers
1 ounce = 28 grams
1 pound = 454 grams
1 US pint = 0.5 liter
1 US gallon = 3.8 liters

Metric system:
1 millimeter = 0.04 inch
1 centimeter = 0.4 inch
1 meter = 3 feet 3 inches
1 kilometer = 0.6 mile
1 gram = 0.04 ounce

International Student ID Card

New York daily newspapers

A newspaper-dispensing machine

NEWSPAPERS, TELEVISION AND RADIO

Y OU CAN BUY foreign newspapers, usually the previous day's issue, at **Hotalings**. Vendors are also at airports, hotels and newsstands near international business areas like the World Trade Center and Wall Street.

Comprehensive schedules of TV programs can be found in the weekly *TV Guide* magazine and the television section of Sunday's *New York Times*.

The choice of TV stations available in New York is vast. CBS operates on channel 2, NBC on channel 4, ABC on channel 7 and WNYW (Fox) on channel 5. PBS offers cultural and educational fare, including some vintage BBC programs, on channel 13. Cable TV offers everything from the Arts and Entertainment Network (channel 14) to public access programs.

AM radio stations include WCBS News (880Hz) and WFAN Sports (660Hz). Among the many FM stations are WNEW rock (102.7M), WBGO jazz (88.3M) and WNCN classical (104.3M).
Useful information Hotalings,142 W 42nd St. **Map** 8 E1. 📞 *840-1868.*

ELECTRICAL APPLIANCES

A LL AMERICAN electric current flows at a standardized 115 to 120 volts AC (alternating

current). You will need to bring an adapter plug and a voltage convertor that fits standard US electrical outlets. US plugs have two flat prongs.

Most modern New York hotels provide wall-mounted electric hair dryers in bathrooms. In addition, some hotels have wall plugs capable of powering both 110- and 220-volt electric shavers, but little else – not even radios. It can, in fact, be dangerous to connect anything more powerful. If you bring along sophisticated electrical appliances with you, be certain to take a battery pack as well. You will also need an adapter to recharge your spare batteries.

Few New York hotel rooms provide irons or coffee- or tea-makers. However, room service should be able to provide you with an iron upon request.

Standard plug

EMBASSIES AND CONSULATES

Australian Consulate General
636 Fifth Ave. **Map** 12 F5.
📞 *245-4000.*

British Consulate General
845 Third Ave. **Map** 13 B4.
📞 *752-8400.*

Canadian Consulate General
1251 Sixth Ave and 50th St.
Map 12 E4. 📞 *768-2400.*

Consulate General of Ireland
515 Madison Ave. **Map** 17 A5.
📞 *319-2555.*

New Zealand Embassy
37 Observatory Circle, NW, Washington, DC 20008.
📞 *(202) 328-4880.*

RELIGIOUS SERVICES

T HERE ARE SOME 4,000 places of worship in New York, catering to almost any faith. Most hotels have lists of local organizations and service times. Among the leading churches and temples are:

Catholic
St. Patrick's Cathedral
Fifth Ave at 50th St.
Map 12 F4.
📞 *753-2261.*

Episcopalian
St. Bartholomew's
109 E 50th St. **Map** 13 A4.
📞 *751-1616.*

Jewish
Reform
Temple Emanu-El
Fifth Ave at 65th St.
Map 12 F2.
📞 *744-1400.*

Orthodox
Fifth Avenue Synagogue
5 E 62nd St. **Map** 12 F2.
📞 *838-2122.*

Lutheran
St. Peter's
619 Lexington Ave. **Map** 17 A4.
📞 *935-2200.*

Methodist
Christ Church United Methodist
520 Park Ave. **Map** 13 A3.
📞 *838-3036.*

Nondenominational
Riverside Church
122nd St at Riverside Dr.
Map 20 D2.
📞 *222-5900.*

Riverside Church

Personal Security and Health

Police badge

IN 1990, NEW YORK was a distant 30th on the Federal Bureau of Investigation's total crime index of American cities. This ranks it below such towns as Boston and Columbus, Ohio, neither of which has New York's international reputation for violent crime. The city's police force concentrates on foot patrols in tourist areas, and security is being beefed up in midtown, in the transit system and at airports. While there are places where any traveler would be foolish to tread after dark – and sometimes in daylight – if you keep your wits about you and stick to the following guidelines, you should enjoy a trouble-free visit.

Curtis Sliwa, founder of the Guardian Angels

LAW ENFORCEMENT

THE NEW YORK police department has around-the-clock foot, horse and car patrols. These are concentrated in specific areas at critical times – for instance, the theater district during show times. There are also platoons of parking violations officers and a small army of transit police who patrol the subway stations and trains.

You will probably also see youths wearing red berets. As their T-shirts proclaim, they are Guardian Angels. Always unarmed, these safety patrols "police" the subways and midtown streets. Although tolerated by the police and often a welcome sight, they have no official powers.

GUIDELINES ON SAFETY

BE ALERT and walk as if you know where you're going. Avoid making eye contact and confrontations with down-and-outs.

If someone asks you for money, be careful; do not be drawn into conversation.

Never use deserted streets. At night, if you can't afford a taxi, try to travel with a group and avoid such areas as the Lower East Side, Chinatown, midtown west of Broadway (except the Lincoln Center plaza) and, uptown, generally north of 82nd Street. Even the side streets around Times Square and the Broadway theaters can be unsafe. The Financial District (except for the World Financial Center) is deserted after business hours, and some TriBeCa and SoHo streets can be risky after dark if you are alone.

Parks are often used for drug dealing. They are safest when there is a crowd for a rally, concert or other event. If you want to go for a jog, ask your hotel concierge for a map of safe routes and follow his or her advice. Keep your wallet in an inconspicuous place and have enough change handy for phone calls and bus fares. It's best not to have to dig into your purse or wallet while standing in line. Never stop to count your money on the street. Defeat purse snatchers by carrying your bag with the clasp facing toward you and the shoulder strap right across your body.

Leave valuable jewelry at home or stored at your hotel. If you wear it casually, it will only mark you as a target for robbery or worse.

Do not allow anyone except hotel and airport personnel to carry your luggage or parcels.

Stow your valuables and camera in a locked suitcase or dresser or closet safe when you do leave your hotel room.

Mounted police officers

LOST AND FOUND

THE CHANCES are poor of recovering anything lost in New York City. There is no citywide lost and found.

Two armed New York City police officers

Cap and badge worn by city police

If you do happen to misplace something, ask your hotel concierge where you should start looking for it.

USEFUL INFORMATION

Lost and Found Offices
Bus and subway services
 (718) 625-6200.

Taxis
(840-4734.

Missing Credit Cards
American Express
((800) 528-4800 (freephone).

Diners Club
((800) 525-9135 (freephone).

JCB
((800) 736-8333 (freephone).

MasterCard
((800) 627-8372 (freephone).

VISA
((800) 336-8472 (freephone).

TRAVEL INSURANCE

TRAVEL INSURANCE is highly recommended, mainly because of the high cost of medical care. There are many types of coverage, with prices dependent on the length of your trip and the number of people covered on the policy.

Among the most important features are: accidental death, dismemberment, emergency medical and dental care, trip cancellation, and baggage and travel document loss. There are many policies that include all these items. Your travel agent or insurance company should recommend a suitable policy.

MEDICAL TREATMENT

BE PREPARED to undergo an expensive experience: some of the city's practitioners and facilities are among the

best around, and medical fees in the US are unregulated. Be sure to protect yourself well with insurance. A few physicians and dentists may accept credit cards, but they are much more likely to want payment in cash or traveler's checks. Hospitals accept most credit cards (see p358).

Kaufman's Pharmacy, open all night

EMERGENCIES

IN THE EVENT of your being involved in a medical emergency, proceed at once to a **Hospital Emergency Room**. Should you need an ambulance, telephone 911 and one will be sent. If your medical insurance is properly in order, you won't have to worry about costs.

Unless you are particularly impoverished, it is better to avoid the overworked and regularly overcrowded city-owned hospitals listed in the telephone book blue pages. Instead, choose one of the many private hospitals listed in the yellow pages in the telephone directory. Dial 411 and ask the operator to give you the number of the nearest public or private hospital to you. Other options include asking your hotel to call a doctor or dentist to visit you in your room, or finding one yourself through the **Doctors Emergency Service** or **Dental Emergency Service**. For more general advice and information ring **Travelers' Aid**, a national organization geared to helping travelers.

New York ambulance

Banking and Currency

NEW YORK IS THE NATION'S banking center. It has a wealth of local, regional and major national banks, plus some retail branches of the leading foreign banks. NatWest and Barclays are well represented in New York; the banks of Australia, Canada, Ireland, Montreal, Nova Scotia and Scotland all have offices or branches.

Foreign currency exchange counter at Chequepoint USA

BANKING

NEW YORK banks are generally open weekdays from 9am to 3pm. There are, however, a number of banks that open earlier or close late evening to suit commuters' needs. Tellers are behind a counter. At most banks, all the tellers will cash traveler's checks and exchange your foreign currency.

Automated teller machine (ATM)

AUTOMATED TELLER MACHINES

A CONVENIENT development in banking has been the introduction of the automated teller machine (ATM). These are found in nearly all bank lobbies and enable you to obtain American currency 24 hours a day by electronically tapping into your own bank account. ATMs usually issue American banknotes in $20 denominations.

Before you leave for New York, check with your bank about which New York City banks and ATM systems will accept your bank card and what fees and commissions will be charged on each transaction. Most ATM machines are in either the

Cirrus or Plus network. They accept various US bank cards, MasterCard and VISA cards and certain others. Among the many advantages of ATMs is the swift, secure exchange of your money at the wholesale rate used between the banks when they make their million-dollar deals.

On a more cautionary note, robberies of customers using ATMs have recently increased in New York. It is therefore prudent to use them only in daylight hours or when the streets are crowded.

CREDIT CARDS

MASTERCARD, American Express, VISA, JCB and Diners Card are widely accepted throughout the United States, regardless of which company or bank issues them. These cards can also be used to obtain cash advances from various ATM machines. They may also be upgraded to confer higher spending limits. In the US you can use a credit card to pay for nearly everything imaginable, from groceries to restaurant and hotel bills, and telephone orders for movie and theater tickets. Major expenses such as tours, travel packages and expensive rentals are all best paid for by credit card. Try to avoid carrying huge sums of money around with you.

CASHING CHECKS

DOLLAR TRAVELER'S checks issued by American Express and Thomas Cook are widely accepted without a fee by most of New York's department stores, shops, hotels and restaurants. Traveler's checks in other currencies, including sterling, are not universally accepted. They can usually be

exchanged by your hotel cashier, but may require a visit to a bank. Exchange rates are printed daily in the *New York Times* and *Wall Street Journal*, and may be posted in the windows of banks that invite currency-exchange business. American Express checks are always exchanged without a fee at American Express offices. Major hotels have cashiers equipped to exchange your traveler's checks.

Foreign exchange brokers are few. Among the most solidly established are **Thomas Cook Currency Services Inc.** and **MTB**. The ones listed on the opposite page have late hours. Others are listed in the city's telephone yellow pages under *Foreign Money Brokers*. Expect to pay a fee, which will vary widely from one place to the next, plus a commission.

There are scores of hole-in-the-wall check-cashing shops in Manhattan. They are listed in the yellow pages classified section. They may not be willing to cash your traveler's checks though, and they are very unlikely to accept or cash foreign checks.

EXCHANGE ADDRESSES

Thomas Cook Currency Services
Rockefeller Center, 630 Fifth Ave.
Map 12 F5. █ 757-6915.
One of several other branches.

MTB Banking Corporation
151, No.1 World Trade Center.
Map 1 B2. █ 775-1440.

Coins

American coins (actual size shown) come in 25-, 10-, 5- and 1-cent pieces. 50-cent and $1 coins are also minted but are rarely used. Each value of coin has a more popular name: 25-cent pieces are called quarters, 10-cent pieces are called dimes, 5-cent pieces are called nickels and 1-cent pieces are known as pennies.

**25-cent coin
(a quarter)**

**10-cent coin
(a dime)**

**5-cent coin
(a nickel)**

**1-cent coin
(a penny)**

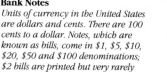

Bank Notes

Units of currency in the United States are dollars and cents. There are 100 cents to a dollar. Notes, which are known as bills, come in $1, $5, $10, $20, $50 and $100 denominations; $2 bills are printed but very rarely circulated. A "buck" is the popular slang for a dollar.

**An American Eagle
on a $1 bill**

1-dollar bill ($1)

5-dollar bill ($5)

20-dollar bill ($20)

50-dollar bill ($50)

100-dollar bill ($100)

AFTER-HOURS FOREIGN CURRENCY EXCHANGE

American Express

Bloomingdale's, 59th St and Lexington Ave. **Map** 13 A3. 🄲 *705-3171.* **Open** *10am–6pm Mon–Wed and Fri, Sat, 10am– 8pm Thu. One of several branches.*

Chequepoint USA

551 Madison Ave and 55th St. **Map** 13 A4. 🄲 *980-6443.* **Open** *8am–8pm Mon–Fri, 10am–8pm Sat, 10am–6pm Sun.*

Freeport Currencies

132 W-45th St. **Map** 12 E5. 🄲 *730-8339.* **Open** *9am–6pm Mon–Fri, 10am–5pm Sat & Sun.*

Harold Reuter & Co

Grand Central Station. **Map** 13 A5. No telephone. **Open** *7am–7pm Mon–Fri, 8am–3pm Sat & Sun.*

Thomas Cook

1 Herald Square, 33rd St and Sixth Ave. **Map** 8 E2. 🄲 *736-9790.* **Open** *9:30am–5:30pm Mon–Fri, 10am–3pm Sat. Also at 41 E 42nd St.* 🄲 *883-0400.* **Open** *9am–5pm Mon–Fri, 10am–3pm Sat.*

Using New York's Phones

Sign for public payphones

Public payphones can be found at many street corners, in hotel and office lobbies, restaurants, bars, theaters and department stores. Very few use credit cards, and none use prepaid phone cards. Most are coin-operated and take 5-, 10- and 25-cent coins. Hotels are free to set their own rates, and so calls made from your room can be more expensive than using a public payphone. Avoid this by making calls from a public phone in the lobby.

New York Time

New York is on Eastern Standard Time. When making international calls, calculate the time in the country you are calling. For the UK add 5 hours; for Australia add 15 hours; and for New Zealand add 17 hours.

Public Telephones

The standard payphone has a hand receiver and 12-button key pad and is pillar- or wall-mounted. In some locations the payphone may belong to an independent company. These phones often look similar to those of New York Tel but usually work differently. The independents are usually more expensive and definitely less reliable.

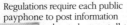

Independently operated payphone

Regulations require each public payphone to post information about charges, toll-free numbers and how to make calls using other carriers. Look for the New York Telephone Company name or logo on the box to be sure the phone will reach all numbers at the standard rates. To complain about service, call the **Public Service Commission**. **Useful information** Public Service Commission [(800) 342-3355 (tollfree number).

Payphone Charges

Within the New York boroughs, the standard charge, around 25 cents, buys five minutes' talking time. If your call lasts more than five minutes, the operator will request additional payment.

Domestic long-distance rates for direct-dial calls decrease by 35% from day rates after 5pm and by 60% after 11pm on weekdays. On weekends the 60% discount also applies, except for Sundays from 5 to 11pm when the 35% rate resumes. These discounts also apply to calls to Canada, but they take effect an hour later.

Using a Coin-Operated Phone

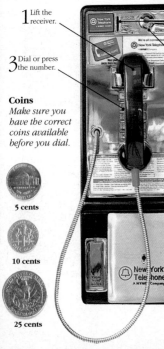

1 Lift the receiver.

2 Insert the necessary coin or coins. The coin drops as soon as you insert it.

3 Dial or press the number.

Coins
Make sure you have the correct coins available before you dial.

4 If you do not want to complete your call or it does not get through, retrieve the coin(s) by pressing the coin return.

5 If the call is answered and you talk longer than the allotted five minutes, the operator will interrupt and ask you to deposit more coins. Payphones do not give change.

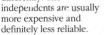

5 cents

10 cents

25 cents

A New York Telephone Company phone stand

International long-distance rates for calls dialed direct vary from country to country. For calls to the UK, the discount rate starts at 1pm, then drops to an economy rate from 6pm until 7am the next day.

USEFUL NUMBERS

Local Directory Inquiries
🄲 411.

Main Post Office
🄲 967-8585.

Operator Assistance
🄲 0.

Speaking Clock
🄲 976-1616.

International Directory Inquiries
🄲 00.

REACHING THE RIGHT NUMBER

• Two prefixes (area codes) are used in New York: 212 for Manhattan and 718 for Brooklyn, the Bronx, Queens and Richmond (Staten Island). An 800 prefix means the call will be free.
• To call a number outside your own area, first dial 1. For example, to dial Queens from Manhattan dial 1 (718) (number).
• To call long distance from a payphone: dial 0 followed by the area code and then the number. The operator will answer and tell you how much money you need to deposit.
• To make an international direct call: dial 011 followed by the country code (New Zealand; 64, Australia: 61; UK: 44), then the city or area code (minus the first 0) and the local number.
• To make an international call via the operator: dial 01 followed by the country code, the city code (minus the first 0) and then the local number.
• International Directory Inquiries are on 00. If you have problems, call international operator assistance on 01.
• **In an emergency, dial 911.**

Sending A Letter

APART FROM post offices, letters can be mailed at your hotel concierge desk (which usually also sells stamps); in letter slots in office building lobbies; in air, rail and bus terminals; and in the occasional street mailbox. These are always painted blue, or red, white and blue. Mail in most mailboxes is not picked up on weekends. Post offices are shown on the *Street Finder* maps *(see pp378–9)*.

US state mail logo

POSTAL SERVICES

THE CITY'S main **General Post Office** is open 24 hours a day. Stamps can be bought here or from branch offices (a handy one is in the Empire State Building) or from coin-operated machines in pharmacies, department stores and bus and train stations. There is a 25% charge on stamps bought anywhere other than a post office. All letters go first class.

The federal post office offers two special delivery services. The **Express Mail** service is for next-day delivery, and the **Priority Mail** service is for two-day delivery. Priority Mail will also pick up letters on weekdays for an extra charge. Private express

Colorful US stamps

mail can be arranged through hotel concierges or with one of the delivery services listed in the telephone book. Two international companies are **DHL** and **Federal Express**.

Useful information General Post Office, 421 Eighth Ave. **Map** 8 D2. 🄲 967-8585. Priority Mail and Express Mail 🄲 (800) 222-1811. Federal Express 🄲 (800) 238-5355. DHL 🄲 (800) 225-5345.

HELD MAIL

LETTERS AND parcels will be held for you for 30 days at the General Post Office's General Delivery window. Mail can be sent to other post offices by giving the zip code or name. Address mail with: Name, General Delivery, US Post Office, New York, NY10001.

Express Mail   **Priority Mail**

Mailboxes
Mailboxes can be few and far between on New York streets, and it may be easier to find a post office (see Street Finder pp378–9). *Instructions on how to use each mailbox are written on the box. If you use Express or Priority services, weigh your letters at a post office to figure out the postage needed.*

Standard mailbox

GETTING TO NEW YORK

MANY INTERNATIONAL airlines have direct flights to New York. It is also very well served by charter and domestic services. Price wars between airlines have reduced fares, and domestic flights now prove a viable alternative to bus and train tickets; group tour package prices are often

Aerial view of Manhattan

unbeatable. The *QE2* is one of several cruise ships that dock in the city. Long-distance trains serving New York are clean and comfortable. Interstate and long distance buses are comfortable, with air-conditioning and on-board toilets. For information on arriving in New York see the map on pages 366–7.

AIR TRAVEL

NEW YORK CAN be reached by air direct from most major cities. The flight from London takes about eight hours. However, there are no direct flights from Australia or New Zealand. Instead, the airlines fly to the west coast, which takes around 14 hours, land, refuel and then continue on to New York.

Among the main carriers to New York are **Air Canada**, **Delta**, **Canadian Air**, **Continental**, **British Airways**, **American Airlines**, **Virgin Atlantic** and **United Airlines**. All international flights arrive at Newark or JFK airports *(see pp364–5)*.

APEX (Advance Purchase Excursion) tickets for the scheduled airlines are usually the cheapest return fares apart from package tours. But they must be bought in advance and are valid for a stay of 7 to 30 days. Some airlines offer cheaper fares if you limit your stay to specified periods. Senior citizens may also receive discounts.

AIRLINE NUMBERS

Major Carriers

Air Canada
[(800) 776-3000 (tollfree).

American Airlines
[(800) 433-7300 (tollfree).

British Airways
[(800) 247-9297 (tollfree).

Canadian Air
[(800) 426-7000 (tollfree).

Continental
[(800) 231-0856 (tollfree).

Delta
[(800) 241-4141 (tollfree).

United Airlines
[(800) 241-6522 (tollfree).

Virgin Atlantic
[(800) 862-8621 (tollfree).

SEA TRAVEL

NEW YORK IS a regular port of call for the *QE2* which docks there, via Southampton, 25 times a year. It also makes

Long-distance Greyhound coach

voyages to Australia and New Zealand. Sea travel offers an expensive, but relaxing, way of traveling to New York. Ships dock at the Hudson River piers in mid-town Manhattan.

COACH TRAVEL

ALL LONG-DISTANCE buses such as **Greyhound Coaches** arrive in the city at the **Port Authority Bus Terminal**. Buses from here also connect with the three airports. With over 6,000 coaches arriving and leaving daily and carrying some 172,000 passengers, the atmosphere is chaotic. Many hotels are also accessible directly from the terminal.
Useful information Greyhound Coaches [971-6363 *(24 hrs)*. Port Authority Bus Terminal. W 40th St and Eighth Ave. **Map** 8 D1. [564-8484 *(24 hrs)*.

TRAIN TRAVEL

AMTRAK TRAINS from Canada, upstate, southern, northeastern and western states all stop at Penn Station *(see p376)*. Metro North lines from upstate and Connecticut arrive at Grand Central Terminal.

Ocean liner approaching Manhattan

New York Airports

Transatlantic jet

THE THREE MAIN airports (Newark, JFK and La Guardia) are all well connected to central Manhattan. Look for uniformed "skycaps" – scarlet-capped porters wearing distinctive badges, who will help you with your luggage. Never trust anyone else to help carry your bags – you may never see them again. Taxi dispatchers will help you into a licensed taxi at the taxi area.

GETTING INTO MANHATTAN

THE GROUND Transportation center at each airport will give you information on the ways you can continue your trip. The most useful services, operating from La Guardia and JFK, are the **Carey Airport Express** and **Gray Line Air Shuttle**. The small shuttle vans will drop you anywhere in Manhattan between 23rd and 63rd streets. They are more expensive than buses, but the door-to-door service saves a taxi fare. New Jersey Transit buses and **Olympia Airport Express** also go to Manhattan.

Shared vehicle rides are offered at JFK and La Guardia by **Classic Airport Share Ride** and **Westchester Express**. You can share a taxi and toll charges with up to three other people. Many car rental firms

Signs for connections to Manhattan at La Guardia

have courtesy telephones at the baggage-claim areas. Telephone numbers for advance reservations are listed on page 371.

BUS COMPANIES

Carey Airport Express
[*(718) 632-0500/0509.*

Classic Airport Share Ride [*(516) 567-5100.*

Gray Line Air Shuttle
[*315-3006.*

Olympia Airport Express
[*964-6233.*

Westchester Express
Taxi dispatcher [*(718) 624-6900.*

LA GUARDIA (LGA)

PRINCIPALLY SERVING business travelers, La Guardia lies 8 miles (13 km) east of Manhattan on the north side of Long Island in Queens.

Upon arrival, you can rent luggage trolleys cheaply from the baggage-claim area next to the luggage carousels. Skycaps are on hand to assist you. Baggage can also be left in the Tele-Trip business center on the departure level. Bureaux de change are located around the Central Terminal.

Uniformed taxi dispatchers at the airport are on duty at peak hours; or ask one of the Port Authority Police for help. Only use yellow taxis licensed by the city. The cost of tolls, plus a small surcharge after 8pm and all day Sunday, will be added to the fare shown on the meter (about $25–30 to central Manhattan). **Useful information** Airport Information Service [*(718) 533-3400.*

Check-in desk at La Guardia

PLAN OF LA GUARDIA AIRPORT

A frequent free bus service runs between each of the terminals and parking areas. Buses and taxis into the city and its suburbs depart from the first floor of the Central Terminal building.

Central Terminal building

Marine Air Terminal

Delta Shuttle Terminal

US Air Shuttle Terminal

Trump Shuttle Terminal

Delta Terminal

Grand Central Parkway to New York

KEY

P Parking

🚌 Bus service between terminals

JFK Airport

NEW YORK'S main inter-
national airport, JFK, lies
15 miles (24 km) southeast of
Manhattan, in the borough of
Queens. American Airlines,
British Airways, Delta, TWA,
and United have their own
arrivals buildings, complete
with customs and immigration
facilities. Other airlines use the
International Arrivals Building.

Luggage trolleys can be
hired from the baggage-claim
area. Your bags can also be
left at the check-in counter

Airport information signs at JFK

**Main Hall at the International
Arrivals Building, JFK**

of the International Arrivals
Building. Bureaux de change
are in all terminals.

The Ground Transportation
services desk is on the ground
level near the baggage-claim
area. Transportation into
Manhattan can be arranged
here 24 hours a day.

The quickest way to reach
Manhattan is by helicopter. But
the price for a 15-minute flight
is double or more the cost of
a taxi fare. Courtesy phones
are provided by the car rental
companies. Most have shuttle

service to their rental offices.
Taxis wait at stands outside
the terminals. A trip to the city
center normally takes up to an
hour and costs around $30.

Buses can take up to an hour
and a half to the city center,
but the Carey Airport Express
bus service is very reliable,
relatively cheap and safe, and
operates 24 hours a day.

For early morning flights
there are hotels very near the
airport. City center hotels can
be booked at the Meegan
Services reservation desk.

Useful Addresses

**Airport Information
Service**
☎ *(718) 656-4520.*

Hilton JFK Airport
138–10 135th Ave, Queens.
☎ *(718) 322-8700.*

Holiday Inn JFK
144–02 135th Ave, Queens.
☎ *(718) 659-0200.*

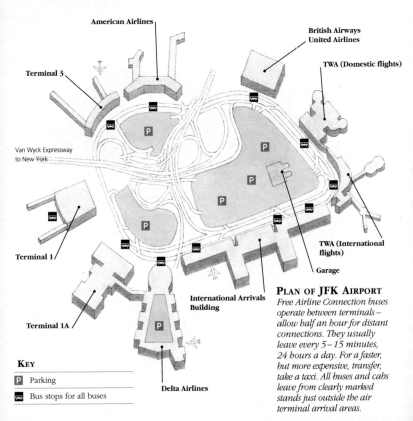

American Airlines

British Airways
United Airlines

TWA (Domestic flights)

Terminal 3

Van Wyck Expressway
to New York

TWA (International
flights)

Garage

Terminal 1

International Arrivals
Building

Terminal 1A

Delta Airlines

Key

P Parking

▦ Bus stops for all buses

Plan of JFK Airport

*Free Airline Connection buses
operate between terminals –
allow half an hour for distant
connections. They usually
leave every 5–15 minutes,
24 hours a day. For a faster,
but more expensive, transfer,
take a taxi. All buses and cabs
leave from clearly marked
stands just outside the air
terminal arrival areas.*

NEWARK AIRPORT

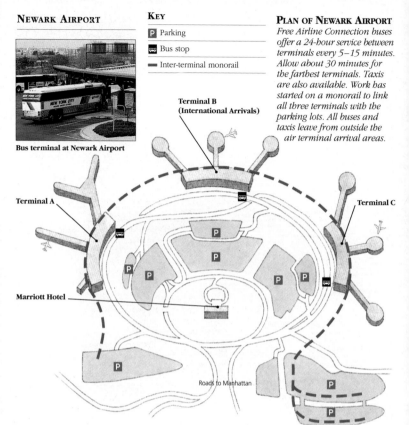

Bus terminal at Newark Airport

KEY

P Parking

🚌 Bus stop

— Inter-terminal monorail

**Terminal B
(International Arrivals)**

Terminal A

Terminal C

Marriott Hotel

Roads to Manhattan

PLAN OF NEWARK AIRPORT

*Free Airline Connection buses
offer a 24-hour service between
terminals every 5–15 minutes.
Allow about 30 minutes for
the farthest terminals. Taxis
are also available. Work has
started on a monorail to link
all three terminals with the
parking lots. All buses and
taxis leave from outside the
air terminal arrival areas.*

Newark, NEW YORK'S second largest international airport, is located about 16 miles (26 km) southwest of Manhattan, in New Jersey.

All international flights arrive at Terminal "B". Baggage trolleys can be rented near the luggage carousels in the baggage-claim area on the ground level. There is, however, no left luggage office. Bureaux de change are available in each terminal.

The Ground Transportation services desk, open 24 hours a day, is next to the baggage-claim area. Courtesy phones are provided by limousine and car rental firms. Many of these have a free shuttle service to their rental offices.

If you want a taxi, line up at one of the many taxi stands located outside most arrival areas. Uniformed taxi dispatchers will also help you hail a cab. Never accept a ride into town from anyone

who approaches you in the terminal: they will probably have no insurance and could charge an outrageous fare. The journey into Manhattan takes about 40-60 minutes and will cost you up to $30.

Buses and coaches can take anywhere from 40 minutes to over an hour to reach Manhattan, but cost about $10. Electronic boards around the terminal list departure times of all these services.

For early morning flights, there are hotels located in and around the airport grounds. City hotels can be booked on arrival through the courtesy

phones that are linked directly to various Manhattan hotels. At Newark, these are located in all three terminals.

USEFUL ADDRESSES

**Airport Information
Service**
📞 (201) 961-2000.

**Holiday Inn
International**
1000 Spring St, Elizabeth, N J.
📞 (800) 465-4329.

Marriott Hotel
Newark Airport grounds.
📞 (800) 228-9290.

Monitors for ground transportation information, Newark Airport

Arriving in New York

THIS MAP SHOWS the links between New York's three airports and the center of Manhattan. It also illustrates rail connections linking New York to the rest of the United States and Canada. Travel information, including journey times for subway, bus, rail and helicopter services, is listed in each information box. The passenger ship terminal, once New York's key point of arrival for the flood of post-war immigrants, is located a short distance from the center of Manhattan. Port Authority Bus Terminal, on the west side provides services across the city.

Ships at the passenger terminal

PASSENGER SHIP TERMINAL
Piers 88–92 for QE2 and other cruise ship arrivals and departures.

KEY

✈ Airport *see pp363–5*	
⛴ Seaport *see p362*	
🚆 Rail link *see p362*	
🚌 Bus station/link *see p362*	
Ⓜ Subway link *see pp374–5*	
⛴ Water shuttle	
🚁 Helicopter link *see p364*	
— Carey Airport Express and Gray Line Air Shuttle *see p363*	
— Water shuttle	
— Helicopter *see p364*	
— Long Island Rail Road *see pp376–7*	
— New Jersey Transit buses *see p363*	
— Olympia Airport Express *see p363*	
— Shuttle bus *see p364*	
— Subway line, A train *see p374*	

PORT AUTHORITY BUS TERMINAL
All long-distance buses arrive and depart here; links to all city airports.

Passenger Ship Terminal

Port Authority Bus Terminal

🚆 PENN STATION
*Long-distance trains from **Canada** and other US states arrive and depart here; daily commuter train services to **Long Island** and **New Jersey**.*
🚆 *Amtrak, Long Island Rail Road and New Jersey Transit services.*
Ⓜ *A, C, E, 1, 2, 3, 9.*

Penn Station

Chelsea and the Garment District

Greenwich Village

Gray Line Air Shuttle buses take passengers to any point between 23rd and 63rd streets.

SoHo and TriBeCa

East Village

Seaport and the Civic Center

Lower East Side

World Trade Center
🚆 *Metro-North.*
Ⓜ *A, C, E, 2, 3.*

Lower Manhattan

Pier 11

✈ NEWARK
Bus service to central Manhattan every 20–30 mins.
🚌 *Olympia Airport Express every 20–30 mins to the **World Trade Center, Penn Station** and **Grand Central Terminal.***
🚌 *New Jersey Transit buses every 15–20 mins to the **Port Authority Bus Terminal.***

Delta Water Shuttle from La Guardia

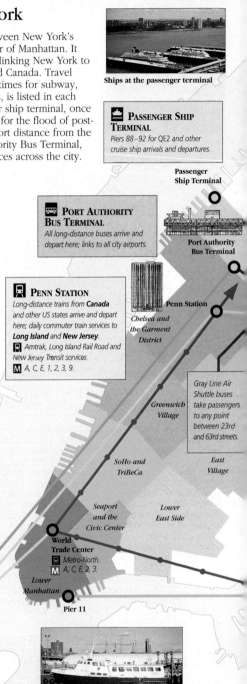

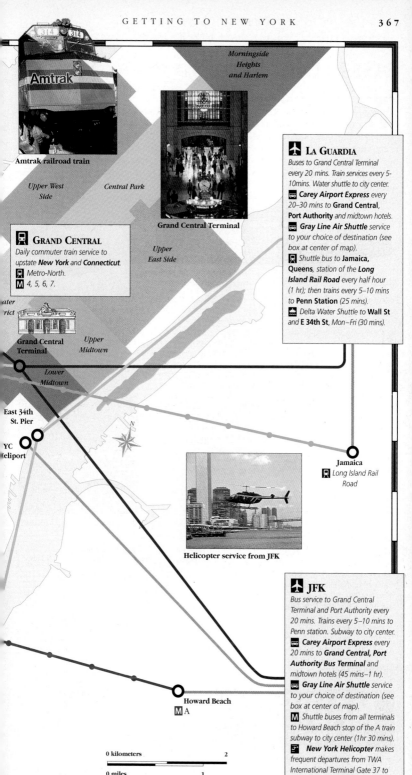

Amtrak railroad train

Morningside Heights and Harlem

Upper West Side

Central Park

Grand Central Terminal

🚁 LA GUARDIA
Buses to Grand Central Terminal every 20 mins. Train services every 5-10mins. Water shuttle to city center.
🚌 *Carey Airport Express every 20–30 mins to* **Grand Central, Port Authority** *and midtown hotels.*
🚌 *Gray Line Air Shuttle service to your choice of destination (see box at center of map).*
🚊 *Shuttle bus to* **Jamaica, Queens,** *station of the* **Long Island Rail Road** *every half hour (1 hr); then trains every 5–10 mins to* **Penn Station** *(25 mins).*
⛴ *Delta Water Shuttle to* **Wall St** *and* **E 34th St,** *Mon–Fri (30 mins).*

Upper East Side

🚊 GRAND CENTRAL
Daily commuter train service to upstate **New York** *and* **Connecticut**.
🚊 *Metro-North.*
Ⓜ *4, 5, 6, 7.*

ater rict

Grand Central Terminal

Upper Midtown

Lower Midtown

East 34th St. Pier

YC eliport

Jamaica
🚊 *Long Island Rail Road*

Helicopter service from JFK

🚁 JFK
Bus service to Grand Central Terminal and Port Authority every 20 mins. Trains every 5–10 mins to Penn station. Subway to city center.
🚌 *Carey Airport Express every 20 mins to* **Grand Central, Port Authority Bus Terminal** *and midtown hotels (45 mins–1 hr).*
🚌 *Gray Line Air Shuttle service to your choice of destination (see box at center of map).*
Ⓜ *Shuttle buses from all terminals to Howard Beach stop of the A train subway to city center (1hr 30 mins).*
🚁 *New York Helicopter makes frequent departures from TWA International Terminal Gate 37 to* **34th Street Heliport**.

Howard Beach
Ⓜ A

| 0 kilometers | 2 |
| 0 miles | 1 |

GETTING AROUND NEW YORK

WITH OVER SIX thousand miles of streets, walking around New York could prove difficult. But the city is a network of districts and many of the major sites can be visited area by area. Taxis are best for door-to-door transit but can be held up in traffic jams, especially during rush hours. The city's bus service is reliable and cheap but often slow. Subways are quick, reliable and cheap, and make stops throughout central Manhattan. There are no weekly or day passes valid for all public transportation, but buses and trains have their own forms of travel passes.

Stretch limousine, the preferred travel for New York's glitterati

NEGOTIATING THE AVENUES AND STREETS

MANHATTAN'S avenues run approximately north to south; its streets (except in the older areas) run east to west. Fifth Avenue is used as an arbitrary center line for the measurement of East and West addresses; Five West 40th Street is, for example, a few doors west of Fifth Avenue on 40th Street, and Five East 40th is a few doors to the east.

Most streets in midtown are one-way. In general, traffic is eastbound on even-numbered streets and westbound on odd-numbered streets. Avenues also tend to be one-way, alternating northbound or southbound.

First, Third (above 23rd Street), Madison, Eighth, Avenue of the Americas (6th Ave) and Tenth avenues, are all northbound, while Second, Lexington, Fifth, Seventh,and Ninth avenues and Broadway below 59th Street are southbound. There is two-way traffic on York, Park, Eleventh and Twelfth avenues and Broadway above 60th Street.

Although most city blocks north of Houston Street are rectangular, they are not very uniform: east–west blocks are three or even four times longer than north–south blocks.

When asking directions from a New Yorker, you may get confused over certain streets. For instance, Avenue of the Americas is also Sixth Avenue, and Seventh Avenue is often called Fashion Avenue. Many intersections and plazas have titles commemorating famous people and events.

Rush-hour gridlock in Manhattan

FINDING AN ADDRESS

A useful formula has been devised to help pinpoint any **Avenue Address**. By dropping the last digit of the address, dividing the remainder by 2, then adding or subtracting the **Key Number** given here, you will discover the nearest cross street. For example: To find No. 826 Lexington Avenue, first you have to drop the 6; divide 82 by 2, which is 41; then add **22** (the key number). Therefore, the nearest cross street is 63rd Street.

A road sign for Madison Avenue positioned at an intersection with a street

Avenue Address	Key Number	Avenue Address	Key Number
1st Ave	+3	9th Ave	+13
2nd Ave	+3	10th Ave	+14
3rd Ave	+10	Amsterdam Ave	+60
4th Ave	+8	Audubon Ave	+165
5th Ave, up to 200	+13	Broadway above	
5th Ave, up to 400	+16	23rd St	-30
5th Ave, up to 600	+18	Central Park W, divide	
5th Ave, up to 775	+20	full number by 10	+60
5th Ave 775–1286,		Columbus Ave	+60
do not divide by 2	-18	Convent Ave	+127
5th Ave, up to 1500	+45	Lenox Ave	+110
5th Ave, up to 2000	+24	Lexington Ave	+22
(6th) Ave of the		Madison Ave	+26
Americas	-12	Park Ave	+35
7th Ave below		Park Ave South	+08
110th St	+12	Riverside Drive, divide	
7th Ave above		full number by 10	+72
110th St	+20	St Nicholas Ave	+110
8th Ave	+10	West End Ave	+60

However, the maps in this guide use the place names that most New Yorkers know and regularly use.

PLANNING YOUR JOURNEY

THE STREETS and sidewalks are busiest during the rush hours – 8 to 10am, 11:30am to 1:30pm and 4:30 to 6:30pm, Monday to Friday. Throughout these periods it is better to face the crowds on foot than attempt any journey by bus, taxi or subway. At other times of day and during certain holiday periods *(see p53)*, the traffic is often much lighter and you should reach your destination quickly.

There are, of course, a few exceptions. Fifth Avenue should always be avoided on parade days (St. Patrick's Day and Thanksgiving Day are the worst). Celebrity visits or one of the regular demonstrations at City Hall *(see p90)* can cause major disruption to the traffic. The area around Seventh Avenue, south of 42nd Street, is likely to be busy during the day with the truck and handcart traffic of New York's garment industry.

WALKING

MOST INTERSECTIONS between avenues and streets have lampposts with name-markers and electric traffic signals. The traffic lights show red (stop) and green (go) for vehicles and "Walk–Don't Walk" for pedestrians. You

Pedestrian crossing

Do not cross the road

You may cross the road

will quickly come to realize, however, that most New York pedestrians rely on their eyes and judgment rather than on the numerous "Walk" signs.

Remember that vehicles keep to the right. There are no cautionary "Look Left" signs to alert you to the direction of oncoming traffic. There are, however, numerous one-way streets, so it's best to look both ways before you cross. Beware, too, of cars, trucks and taxis turning the corner behind you as you start to cross the road.

There are pedestrian crossings at some intersections. These are officially designated pedestrian crossing points, although they are more often than not ignored by both pedestrians and motorists alike. Do not rely on them. The city has few underground walkways for pedestrians.

Staten Island Ferry leaving Battery Park

Circle Line tour boat

FERRIES

There are two ferries of interest to visitors *(see also p353)*: the Circle Line runs a ferry to the Statue of Liberty and Ellis Island several times each day from Battery Park at the southern tip of Manhattan. The 24-hour Staten Island ferry service from Battery Park travels the channel, offering splendid sea views of Manhattan, the Statue of Liberty, the bridges and Governors Island for only 50 cents. You can also stay on board and return to Manhattan without having to pay any extra charge.

CYCLING

FOR VISITORS who want to cycle around New York it is probably safer to stick to park pathways (in Central Park and along the East and Hudson rivers) and to use them only during daylight hours. You can rent bikes at AAA Bicycle Rentals in Central Park.
Useful information AAA Bicycle Rentals. [861-4137.

Cyclist in Central Park

Driving in New York

H EAVY TRAFFIC AND EXPENSIVE rental cars make driving in New York a frustrating experience. You must wear a seat belt. The speed limit is 35 mph (56 km/h) – which is difficult to exceed because of Manhattan's pot-holes and traffic. Most streets are one-way, and there are traffic lights at every corner. Driving is on the right.

Traffic on Sixth Avenue

RENTING A CAR

T O RENT A CAR you must be able to prove that you are at least 25 years old. You will need a valid driver's license (for foreign visitors an Inter-national Driver's License is useful) and a credit card or you will have to pay a large deposit.

Unless you are adequately covered by your own insu-rance policy, you should also take out damage and liability protection, as vandalism and theft are common. Refill with gas before you return the car or you'll pay double the normal price for fuel. It is cheaper to rent a car in the city than at the airports.

TRAFFIC SIGNS
Black-and-white zebra-striped markings on many street crossings mean that pedestrians have right of way. At intersections, they indicate that traffic should keep out when the traffic light is red. Unlike the rest of New York State, you can never turn right on a red light.

Traffic flows in a single direction

PARKING

P ARKING IN Manhattan is difficult and costly. Parking areas and parking garages post their rates at the entrance. Some hotels include parking charges in their room rates.

In some areas there are meters at the curb for short-term (20–60 minutes) parking. Don't be tempted to park at out-of-order meters – you may receive a parking ticket. Yellow street and curb markings mean no parking.

"Alternate-side" parking applies on most of the city's side streets. Cars may usually be left all day and night but must be moved to the other side of the street before 8am the next day. For specific information call the **Trans-portation Department.**

PENALTIES

I F YOU RECEIVE a parking ticket, you have seven days to pay the required fine or to appeal against it. If you have any queries about your ticket call the **Parking Violations Bureau** between 8:30am and 7pm on any weekday.

New York's tow-away brigades are extremely active, and one-third of cars towed suffer damage. If you cannot

find your car at its parking place, first of all call the traffic department's tow-away office. The pound is open 24 hours a day, Monday to Sat-urday. You can redeem your car for a hefty fine of $150, plus $5 per day storage fee. Traveler's checks, certified checks, money orders and cash are all accepted. There is an ATM machine *(see p358)* on the premises. If you have rented the car, the rental contract must be produced, and only the authorized driver (you'll need your license) may collect the car. If your car is not there, report its loss to the police.

Useful information Police 【 *911;* Parking Violations Bureau 【 *477-4430;* Traffic Dept, Tow Pound, Pier 76, W 38th St and Twelfth Ave. **Map** 7 1B. 【 *788-7800;* Transportation Dept 【 *566-2525.*

Police Department traffic officer

CAR RENTAL AGENCIES

I F YOU NEED TO rent a car while in New York, agencies are listed in the telephone directory under *Automobile Renting.* The major rental companies include:

Avis
【 *(800) 331-1212.*

Budget
【 *(800) 527-0800.*

Dollar
【 *(800) 800-4000.*

Hertz
【 *(800) 654-3131.*

National
【 *(800) 227-7368.*

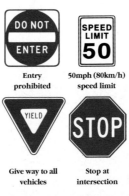

DO NOT ENTER

Entry prohibited

SPEED LIMIT 50

50mph (80km/h) speed limit

YIELD

Give way to all vehicles

STOP

Stop at intersection

New York's Taxis

New York taxi cab

Aᴸᴸ ʟɪᴄᴇɴꜱᴇᴅ ᴛᴀxɪ cabs are yellow. If their roof numbers are lit up, they are available for hire and can be flagged down. Occupied cabs have their top lights switched off. Taxis that are not on duty have their "Off-Duty" sign lit. Only licensed cabs are authorized to pick up people who hail them from the street; accepting a ride from anyone else can be dangerous and expensive.

Tᴀᴋɪɴɢ ᴀ Cᴀʙ

Eᴠᴇʀʏ ʏᴇʟʟᴏᴡ ᴄᴀʙ has a meter and many can issue printed receipts. A taxi can carry up to four passengers with a single fare covering everyone on board.

Taxi stands are scarce; hotels, Penn Station and Grand Central Terminal are by far the best places to seek cabs.

Licensed taxis undergo periodic inspections and are insured against accidents and losses. Non-licensed or "gypsy" cabs are unlikely to have these safeguards.

Once the cab driver accepts a passenger the meter starts ticking at around $1.50. The fare increases about 25 cents after each additional 292 yards (320 meters). Surcharges will then be added for waiting time and journeys between 8pm and 6am. A few drivers now accept credit cards but most will want to be payed in cash. Tip the driver no more than 15%.

Cab driving is a traditional occupation of newly arrived immigrants and, as such, communication can be a problem. Although owners of licensed cabs must pass exams in English comprehension and the layout of the city they will not necessarily understand either. Make sure your driver understands exactly

```
I ♥ NEW YORK
TRIP#    004653
09:11AM 11-15-92
MEDALLION# 6N64
DIST       2.30
FARE $     6.00
TLC:212-221-TAXI
```

A printed receipt available from most taxi cabs

where you want to go before you start your journey.

By law, a driver must take you anywhere in the city unless the off-duty sign is lit and the roof light is off. The driver should not ask you your destination until after you've sat down, and must follow your requests not to smoke, to open or close a window, and to pick up or drop off passengers as you direct. If he or she doesn't comply you can then report them to the **Taxi & Limousine Commission**.

Each yellow cab displays the driver's photograph and registered number next to the meter. Drivers can be sullen, or try to overcharge or not cooperate with some of your requests. Make a note of the driver's number or the license or·receipt number (if you have requested one), and report it to a policeman.

Heavy one-way traffic on one of the city's avenues

Tᴀxɪ Nᴜᴍʙᴇʀꜱ

Taxi & Limousine Commission
℃ 840-4577.

Yellow Cab Information
℃ 840-4572.

Lost and Found
℃ 840-4737.

If you would prefer to use a radio-dispatched taxi, call:

Bell Radio Taxi
℃ 691-9191
or (800) 344-3974 (tollfree).

Big Apple Car
℃ 517-7010
or (800) 251-5001 (tollfree).

Chris Limousines
℃ (718) 356-3232.

A meter will display your fare as it mounts up. Additional costs are then shown separately.

The roof-light illuminates the cab's number as well as the driver's "Off-Duty" sign.

Charge rates are listed clearly on the outside of the front passenger door.

I.N.Y.C. TAXI 7B72

Traveling by Bus

THE CITY'S 3,700 BLUE-AND-WHITE buses cover more than 200 routes in the five boroughs. Many run 24 hours a day, every day. The buses are modern, clean and air-conditioned. Traveling by bus is a good way to take in many of New York's sights. Buses are also considered very safe and tend not to get too crowded. Smoking is forbidden on all public buses, and animals (except guide dogs) are not allowed.

The fare box is just inside the entrance doors, next to the driver.

TICKETS

FARES MUST BE paid using a subway token, bought from a station or an "out-of-system" site like McDonald's *(see p374)*, or with the correct change (only nickels, dimes and quarters are accepted – no bills). The fare is a flat one, and you won't get any change if you overpay. Have your fare ready.

Subway token

If you need to change buses to reach your destination, you can request a free paper transfer when you pay your fare. This is valid for an hour and allows you to travel on any connecting bus.

There are discount fares for senior citizens and the disabled. Most buses can "kneel," which helps elderly people board *(see p354)* and are also accessible to wheel-chairs via a platform at the rear.

Bus transfer

RIDING THE BUS

BUSES WILL STOP only at the designated bus stops. They follow north–south routes on the major avenues, stopping every two or three blocks. Crosstown buses, running east–west, stop at every block *(see p368)*. Many routes run a 24-hour daily service, which becomes a lot less frequent during the evening and at night; other bus services operate only during the peak hours of 7am to 10pm.

Bus stops are marked by red, white and blue signs and yellow paint along the curb. Most also have bus shelters. A route map and schedule is posted at each stop. When you have identified your bus, enter at the front door and deposit your coins or a subway token in the fare box. Request a transfer if you will be changing to another bus.

Bus stops often have three-sided, glass-walled shelters.

This bus map shows the route and main stopping-off points for route M15.

The majority of New York's bus drivers are very friendly and will call out your stop if you ask them to.

To request a stop when traveling on the bus, press the vertical call strip between the windows. A "Stop Requested" sign, above the driver's head, will light up.

Leave through the double door located toward the rear of the bus. The driver will activate the door release as soon as the bus has stopped, but you then have to push the door to open it. If you do not keep a firm grip on the door handle it is liable to swing back and hit you, so take care.

RECOGNIZING YOUR BUS

Each bus stop serves more than one route, so look for the route number posted on the front of the bus and on the side, near the front door. Ask the driver if he or she will be stopping at your destination or close to it.

Exit the bus through the double doors toward the rear.

Route numbers appear on the front and side of the bus.

Enter the bus through the doors at the front.

LONG-DISTANCE & COMMUTER BUSES

Buses to the rest of the US and Canada leave from the **Port Authority Bus Terminal**. Another terminal, at the Manhattan end of the George Washington Bridge, is for local buses to northern New Jersey and New York's Rockland County.

Bus tickets at Port Authority are on sale in the main concourse. The long-distance bus company, Greyhound Bus Lines, and the commuter line, Short Line, each has its own ticket counter. There are no reservations on Greyhound, but Short Line does take reservations.

There are bathrooms open from 6am to 10pm, but caution is advised. The homeless congregate in Port Authority.

A Greyhound bus arriving in New York en route to Port Authority

BUS INFORMATION

Route Maps
Available from MTA, 370 Jay St, Brooklyn, NY 11201.

Travel Information
☎ *(718) 330-1234 (24 hrs).*

Port Authority Bus Terminal
West 40th St and Eighth Ave.
Map 8 D1.
☎ *564-8484.*

George Washington Bridge Terminal
178th St. and Broadway.
☎ *564-1114.*

Lost Property
☎ *(718) 625-6200.*

SIGHTSEEING BY BUS

For a pleasant and cheap alternative to a tour bus, hop on a city bus and see New York with the New Yorkers. Bus route M1 goes from 59th Street, along Fifth Avenue and onward to the Battery, returning north via the Wall Street area and Madison Avenue. Route M5 gives fine views of the Hudson River as buses travel north on Riverside Drive to the George Washington Bridge at 178th Street. Route M104 travels from the United Nations at First Avenue across 42nd Street, through Times Square, then follows Broadway north by Lincoln Center to Columbia University at 125th Street.

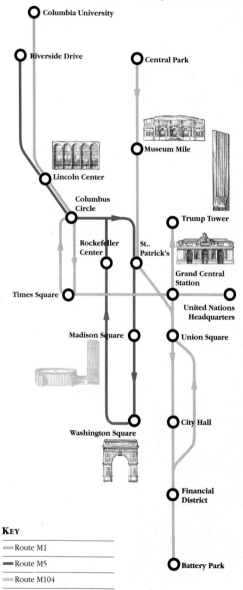

KEY

— Route M1
— Route M5
— Route M104

Using the Subway

New York subway logo

T HE SUBWAY is the quickest and most reliable way to travel in the city. The vast system extends over 714 miles (1142 kilometers) and has 469 stations. Most routes operate 24 hours a day, throughout the year. Night services are less frequent, and fewer trains run on weekends. In the last few years the subway system has been completely upgraded and the trains are now air-conditioned, well lit and much more comfortable.

NEW YORK SUBWAY

M ANY SUBWAY entrances are marked by illuminated spheres: green where the token booth is manned around the clock, red where there is restricted entry. Others are marked by a sign bearing the name of the station and the numbers or letters of the routes passing through it.

The subway system runs 24 hours a day, but some routes do have restricted operating times. The basic service is between 6am and midnight.

Always bear in mind that there are two types of train. Local trains stop at all stations and express trains are faster and stop at fewer stations. Both types of stop are distinguished on every subway map.

Safety on the subway has improved tremendously. If you travel between the rush hours of 8am to 6pm anywhere south of Central Park you should be safe. However, women should not travel alone after the evening rush hour and no one

should travel to the outer boroughs, Bronx and Harlem, unless with a large group of people. Your hotel concierge will tell you the stations to avoid. Stand in well-lit spots, use the central cars and avoid eye contact with unsavory characters. In an emergency, contact the guard.

Subway information New York City Transit Authority █ *(718) 330-1234.*

SUBWAY TOKENS

T HE FARE is the same no matter how far you travel on the subway. There are no discount passes. Purchase a token from an attendant in a booth or from a token machine. You can also buy tokens from several out-of-system locations including major tourist attractions and over 100 McDonald's. Tokens are valid at all times, can be used anywhere in the subway system, and can be used on buses and as tips.

Subway token

READING THE SUBWAY MAP

Each route is identified on the subway map (*see inside back cover*) by color, by the names of the stations at each end of the line, and by a letter or number. For instance, the green (6) route links Woodlawn and Utica avenues, and is served by number 4 trains. Local and express stops and interchange points are identified. The letters and numbers

below the station names indicate which routes serve that particular station. A letter or number in heavy type indicates that trains on that route stop there between 6am and midnight; letters in lighter type mean that the route is served by a part-time service only; a boxed letter or number shows the last stop on the line. The maps posted in all the subway stations have a comprehensive guide that explains the trains and timetable of each route.

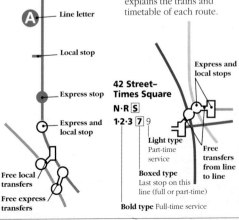

A — Line letter

— Local stop

— Express stop

— Express and local stop

Free local transfers

Free express transfers

42 Street– Times Square

N·R S

1·2·3 7 9

Express and local stops

Light type — Part-time service

Free transfers from line to line

Boxed type — Last stop on this line (full or part-time)

Bold type Full-time service

This station's green sphere shows that it is staffed continuously

MAKING A JOURNEY BY SUBWAY

1 There is a map of the subway system on the back inside cover of this book. Large-scale maps are also positioned in prominent areas in every station, usually very near the token booth.

Subway map

Booth with agent

2 Buy a token from an agent in a booth or from a token machine.

Token machine

3 Deposit the token in the turnstile to pass through to the platform.

Token deposit slot

4 Follow the directions for the train you want. For safety, stay in sight of the token booth as you wait for your train; at night, stay in one of the yellow off-hours waiting areas.

→ Uptown Local ① ⑨

Off-hours waiting area

5 Each train displays its route number or letter in the appropriate color, plus the names of the terminal stations.

9 242 St–Van Cortlandt Park Bronx
South Ferry Manhattan

Route indicator

① ⑨ Broadway Skip-Stop Express

6 Once aboard, you will find a system map next to the door on each side of the car. Use it to follow your progress. Stops are announced on the public address system, and you will also see the station names at each platform. The doors are operated by the driver. For safety, be sure to enter a well-populated car or one where the guard can be found.

7 After leaving the train, look for signs giving directions to the exit. If you need to change trains, then follow the signs to the connecting platforms.

→ Exit 33 St 7 Av — Penn Station, Madison Square Garden, Amtrack LIRR NJ Transit

Traveling by Train

Nᴇᴡ ʏᴏʀᴋ ʜᴀs ᴛᴡᴏ main train stations. Grand Central Terminal is served by commuter trains from New York's suburbs and Connecticut, while Pennsylvania (Penn) Station is the terminal for long-distance services from the rest of the US and also Canada. Most commuter trains have no buffet cars on board, so it's best to buy any food and drink you want before boarding the train. Seat reservations are only available on the long-distance intercity services.

An Amtrak train

Gʀᴀɴᴅ Cᴇɴᴛʀᴀʟ Tᴇʀᴍɪɴᴀʟ

Gʀᴀɴᴅ ᴄᴇɴᴛʀᴀʟ Terminal *(see pp154–5)* on Park Avenue between 41st and 42nd streets is the main terminal for **Metro-North** commuter trains (Hudson, New Haven and Harlem lines), which run north and east of New York and serve Connecticut and Westchester County. From Grand Central you might travel by train to such destinations as the International Wildlife Conservation Park – formerly the Bronx

Long Island Rail Road logo

Zoo – *(see pp242–3)* and President Franklin D. Roosevelt's Hyde Park estate.

The 4, 5 and 6 trains on the green (Lexington) line and number 7 on the purple (Flushing) line serve Grand Central subway station, below the main terminal. A shuttle service links Grand Central to Times Square. Many bus lines stop at Grand Central.

Pᴇɴɴ Sᴛᴀᴛɪᴏɴ

Pᴇɴɴ sᴛᴀᴛɪᴏɴ, between Seventh and Eighth avenues and from 31st to 33rd streets, is a modern terminal that was rebuilt in 1963 underneath the Madison Square Garden complex *(see p133)*. Commuter trains, New Jersey Transit trains and **Amtrak** trains from Canada and other parts of the US terminate at this station. There are no luggage trolleys, but redcap porters will help.

You will find taxis at street level. Buses run downtown on Seventh Avenue and uptown on Eighth Avenue. The blue (8th Avenue) subway lines, A, C, and E run on the Eighth Avenue side of the station; the red (Broadway) lines, 1, 2, 3 and 4 run on the Seventh Avenue side of the station. The ticket counters and waiting rooms are one level below; the trains leave from an even lower level.

From Penn Station, you could head for New Jersey and Long Island or farther on Amtrak trains to such destina-

Grand Central Terminal

tions as Canada, Philadelphia or Washington. Also in Penn Station are ticket offices and departure points of the **Long Island Rail Road (LIRR)**, mainly a commuter line, but with trains to such Long Island resorts, as the Hamptons and Montauk Point.

Pᴀᴛʜ Tʀᴀɪɴs

Pᴀᴛʜ ᴛʀᴀɪɴs operate round the clock between New Jersey stations (Harrison, Hoboken, Jersey City and Newark) and Penn Station in Manhattan. They also stop at Christopher Street, the World Trade Center, 9th, 14th, 23rd and 33rd streets and Avenue of the Americas (6th Avenue).

LIRR train at Penn Station

Aᴍᴛʀᴀᴋ

Aᴍᴛʀᴀᴋ ɪs ᴛʜᴇ ᴜs national railroad passenger service linking New York with other US cities and Canada. Some Amtrak trains have carriages with reclining seats; others have dining facilities and lounge cars. Sleeper cars are available on all long-distance routes. Some fast trains operate on certain Amtrak routes, such as the **Metroliner** between Boston and Washington via New York.

Tickets can be bought at Penn Station, as well as from Amtrak Travel Centers. Buy your ticket before getting on the train as there is a penalty for buying tickets on board. Senior citizens receive a 15% discount; the conductor will ask for proof of age. There are no student discounts. Seat reservations made by phone with a credit card need to be made at least 10 days in advance of travel if you want the tickets mailed to you.

Amtrak also offers a Great American Vacations package and various promotional fares during the year. Ask for information when you book.

Information board at Penn Station

TICKETS AND TRAVEL

TICKETING AREAS at all train stations are well lit and generally crowded at all times of the day. Ticket offices will accept most credit cards, as well as cash. There are a variety of ticket types, most based on a one-way fare; a return fare is twice the single fare. If you are planning a number of trips, Metro-North and LIRR offer weekly passes that will save you money.

Train times, destination and gate numbers are continually updated on numerous large information boards. Watch for signs indicating the major interim stops and transfer points, listed next to the gate for departing trains. Wait for the opening of the gate posted for your train. Metro-North and LIRR carriages are all one class, and have no reserved seating, Amtrak trains offer both. The conductor will ask to see your ticket after the train has left the station.

Penn Station and Grand Central Terminal have minimal facilities, but both have bathrooms plus shops and restaurants.

TRAIN INFORMATION

Amtrak Travel Centers
12 West 51st St. **Map** *12 F4.*
1 East 59th St. **Map** *12 F3.*
1 World Trade Center. **Map** *1 B2.*
📞 *(800) USA-RAIL (Information).*
📞 *(800) 321-8684 (Reservations).*

Long Island Rail Road (LIRR)
📞 *(718) 217-LIRR (Information).*
📞 *(718) 990-8384 (Lost property).*

Metroliner
📞 *(800) 523-8720.*

Metro-North
📞 *532-4900 (Information).*
📞 *340-2555 (Lost property).*

PATH Trains
📞 *(800) 234-7284.*

DAY TRIPS BY TRAIN

There are some beautiful places outside New York city, which, if your time allows, are well worth a visit. Below is a list of some recommended sights within 125 miles (200 km) of New York city center. For further details, call the New York Convention and Visitors Bureau *(see p352).*

A scenic view of Tarrytown

Stony Brook
Peaceful north shore village. Entrance to the Three Villages historic district.
🚆 *58 miles (93 km) east. Long Island Rail Road from Penn Station. 2 hrs.*

The Hamptons
Chic bars and boutiques in a weathered, historic setting. The Beverly Hills of Long Island.
🚆 *100 miles (161 km) east. Long Island Rail Road from Penn Station. 2 hrs, 50 min.*

Montauk Point
State park on the eastern-most tip of Long Island; windswept ocean views.
🚆 *120 miles (193 km). LIRR from Penn Station. 3 hrs.*

Westbury House, Old Westbury
John Phipps's 1906 re-creation of a Charles II mansion with exquisite English formal gardens.
🚆 *24 miles (39 km) east. Long Island Rail Road from Penn Station. 40 min.*

Tarrytown
Washington Irving's home "Sunnyside" and Jay Gould's mansion.
🚆 *25 miles (40 km) north. Metro-North from Grand Central, then taxi. 40–50 min.*

Hyde Park
Springwood estate of Franklin D. Roosevelt and the Vanderbilt mansion.
🚆 *74 miles (119 km) north. Metro-North from Grand Central to Poughkeepsie, then taxi. 2 hrs.*

New Haven, Connecticut
Home of Yale University.
🚆 *74 miles (119 km). Metro-North from Grand Central Terminal. 1 hr, 46 min.*

Hartford, Connecticut
Mark Twain's riverboat-style house, Atheneum Museum and Old State House.
🚆 *112 miles (180 km) north. Amtrak from Penn Station. 2 hrs, 45 min.*

Winterthur, Delaware
Henry du Pont's collection of Early American art, museum and gardens.
🚆 *116 miles (187 km) north. Amtrak from Penn Station to Wilmington, then bus to Winterthur. 2 hrs.*

Yale University in New Haven, Connecticut

STREET FINDER

THE MAP REFERENCES given with all sights, hotels, restaurants, bars, shops and entertainment venues described in this book refer to the maps in this section (*see* How Map References Work *opposite*). These maps cover the whole of Manhattan. A complete index of street names and all the places of interest marked on the maps can be found on the following pages.

The key map *(below)* shows the areas covered by the *Street Finder*, within the various districts. The maps include all of Manhattan's sight-seeing areas (which are color-coded), with all the districts important for hotels, restaurants, bars, shops, theaters and entertainment.

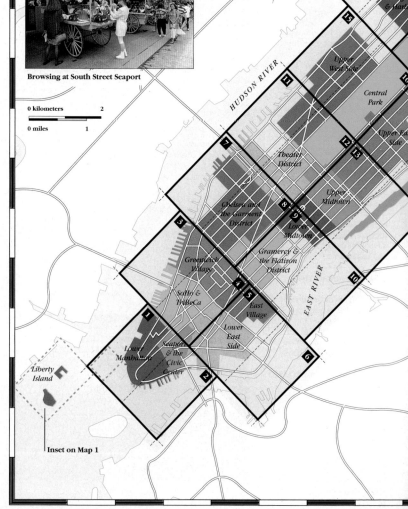

Browsing at South Street Seaport

0 kilometers 2

0 miles 1

Liberty Island

Inset on Map 1

HUDSON RIVER

EAST RIVER

Morning Heights & Harlem

Upper West Side

Central Park

Upper East Side

Theater District

Upper Midtown

Chelsea and the Garment District

Lower Midtown

Greenwich Village

Gramercy & the Flatiron District

SoHo & TriBeCa

East Village

Lower East Side

Lower Manhattan

Seaport & the Civic Center

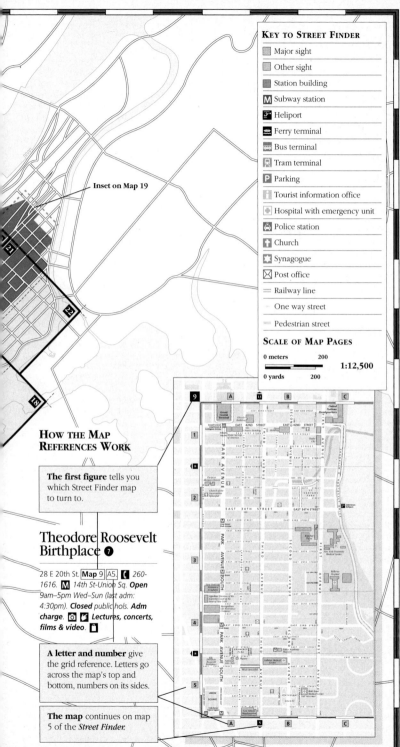

KEY TO STREET FINDER

- ▢ Major sight
- ▢ Other sight
- ▢ Station building
- **M** Subway station
- **🚁** Heliport
- **⛴** Ferry terminal
- **🚌** Bus terminal
- **🚊** Tram terminal
- **P** Parking
- **i** Tourist information office
- **✚** Hospital with emergency unit
- **⌂** Police station
- **✝** Church
- **✡** Synagogue
- **✉** Post office
- ═ Railway line
- One way street
- Pedestrian street

SCALE OF MAP PAGES

0 meters	200	
0 yards	200	**1:12,500**

Inset on Map 19

HOW THE MAP REFERENCES WORK

The first figure tells you which Street Finder map to turn to.

Theodore Roosevelt Birthplace ❼

28 E 20th St. **Map 9** **A5.** 【 260-1616. **M** 14th St–Union Sq. **Open** 9am–5pm Wed–Sun (last adm: 4:30pm). **Closed** public hols. **Adm charge.** 📷 🎦 **Lectures, concerts, films & video.** █

A letter and number give the grid reference. Letters go across the map's top and bottom, numbers on its sides.

The map continues on map 5 of the *Street Finder.*

Street Finder Index

Each place name is followed by its borough (unless in Manhattan) and then by its Street Finder reference

Each place name is followed by its borough (unless in Manhattan) and then by its Street Finder reference

Each place name is followed by its borough (unless in Manhattan) and then by its Street Finder reference

Each place name is followed by its borough (unless in Manhattan) and then by its Street Finder reference

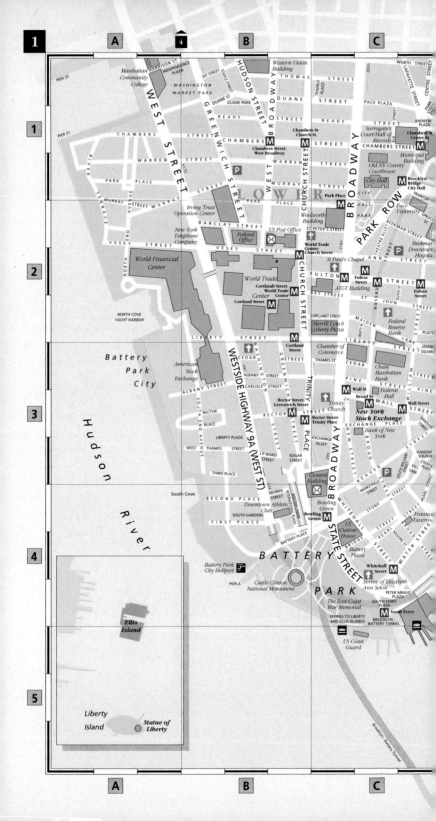

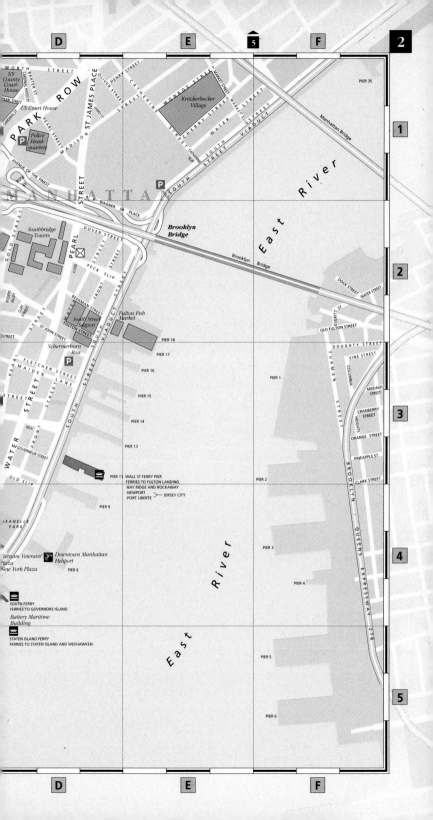

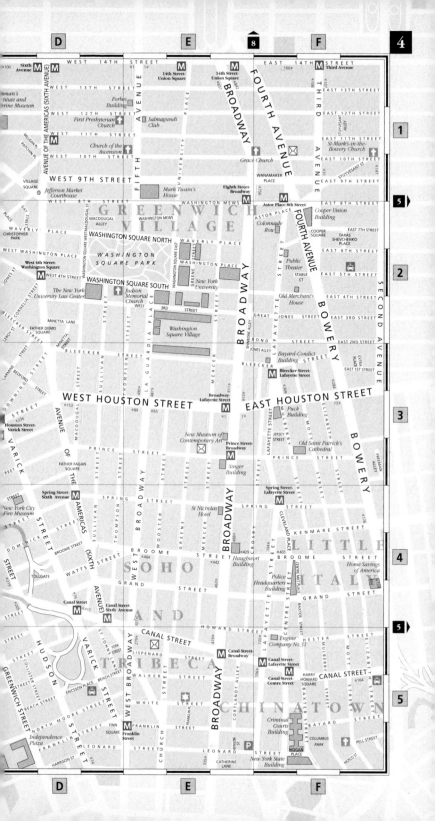

NORTH 9TH STREET

NORTH 8TH STREET

NORTH 7TH STREET

NORTHUE 6TH AVENUE STREET

NORTH 5TH STREET

NORTH 4TH STREET

NORTH 3RD STREET

METROPOLITAN AVENUE

NORTH 1ST STREET

GRAND STREET

SOUTH 1ST STREET

SOUTH 2ND STREET

SOUTH 3RD STREET

SOUTH 4TH STREET

SOUTH 5TH STREET

Williamsburg Bridge

SOUTH 6TH STREET

DUNHAM PLACE

BROADWAY

SOUTH 8TH STREET

SOUTH 9TH ST

SOUTH 11TH ST

DIVISION AVENUE

WYTHE AVENUE

BERRY STREET

KENT AVENUE

RIVER STREET

EAST

Athletic Field

RIVER

PARK

MANGIN STREET

BARUCH PLACE

FRANKLIN D ROOSEVELT DRIVE

STREET

SOUTH

EAST

Fireboat Station

RIVER

SAMUEL A SPIEGEL SQUARE

STREET

PARK

CHERRY STREET

CORLEARS HOOK PARK

VIADUCT

Corlears Hook

PIER 44

Wallabout Channel

US Naval Reserve Center

Wallabout Bay

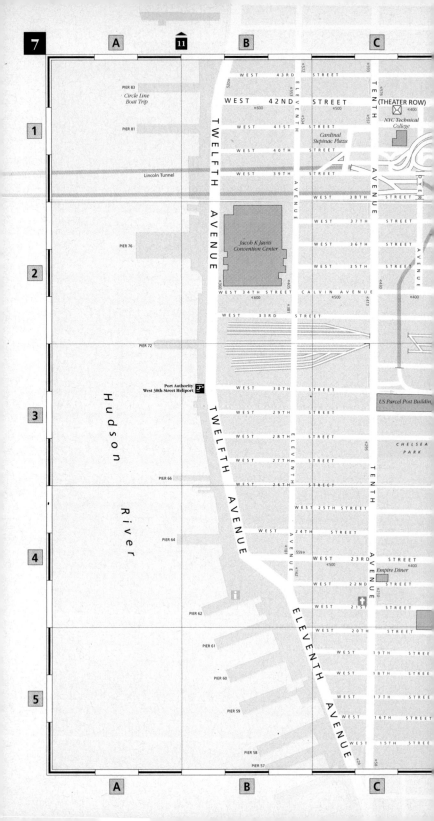

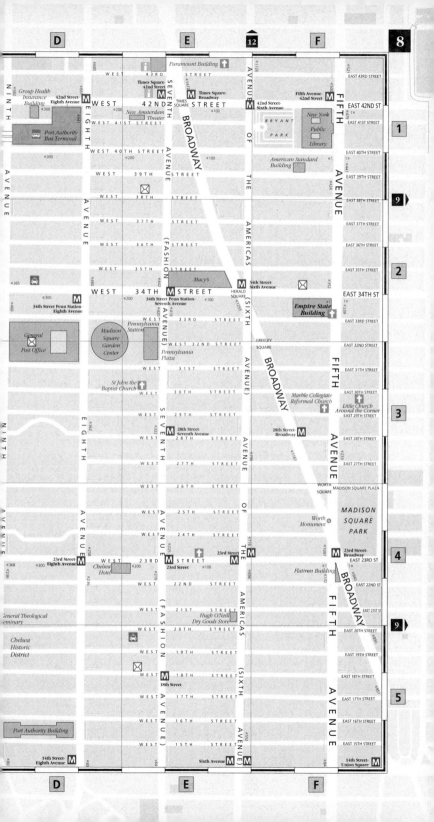

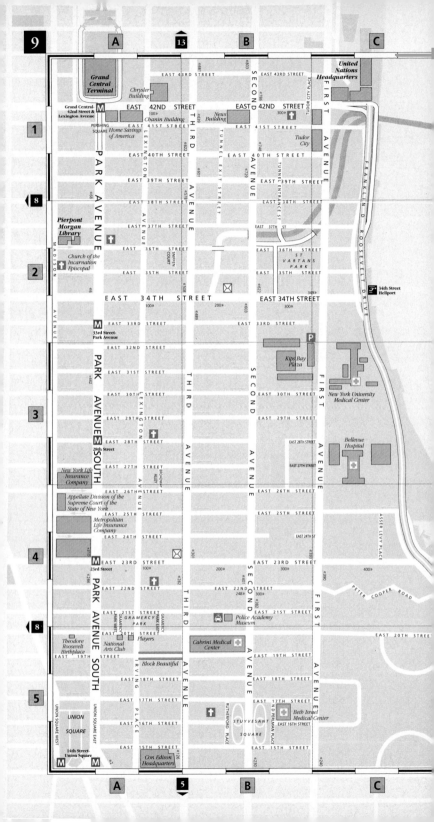

East River

Belmont Island

Queens - Midtown Tunnel 495

50TH AVENUE
51ST AVENUE
BORDEN AVENUE

M Vernon Jackson Boulevard

Long Island City Station

54TH (FLUSHING) AVENUE

55TH AVENUE

56TH AVENUE

Newton Creek

Pulaski Bridge

VERNON BOULEVARD
JACKSON AVENUE
2ND (10TH) STREET
5TH STREET

MANHATTAN AVENUE
255TH STREET
BOX STREET
COMMERCIAL STREET
CLAY STREET
DUPONT STREET
FRANKLIN STREET
EAGLE STREET
WEST STREET
FREEMAN STREET
GREEN STREET
HURON STREET
OAK STREET
INDIA STREET
JAVA STREET
KENT STREET
GREENPOINT AVENUE

Manhattan Marina

East River

PIER 70

PIER 69

PIER 68

PIER 67

FRANKLIN D ROOSEVELT DRIVE (EAST RIVER DRIVE)

AVENUE C

AVENUE C

EAST 16TH STREET

EAST 15TH STREET

1
2
3
4
5

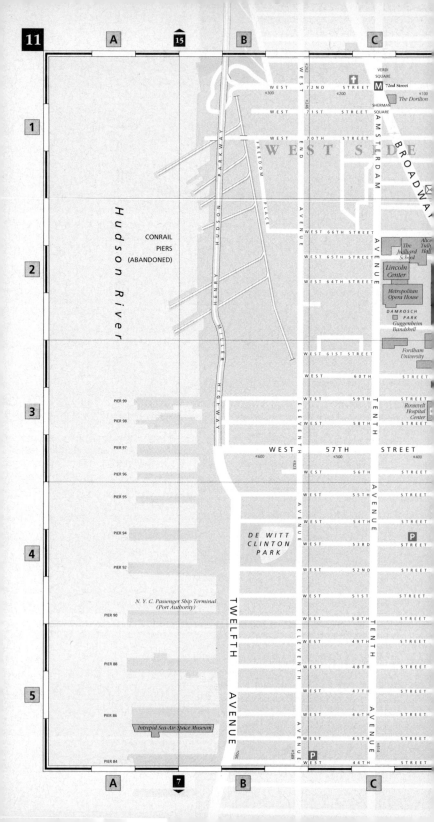

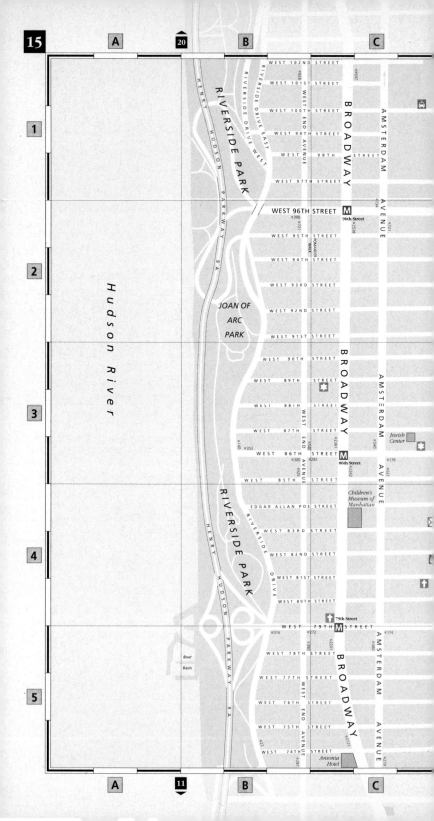

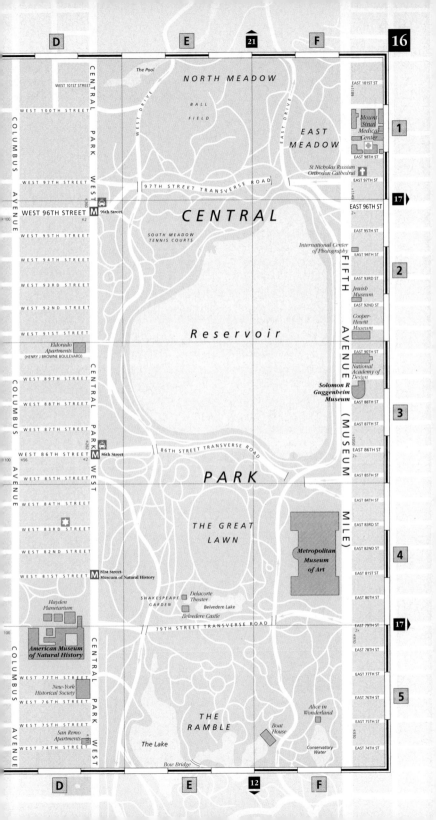

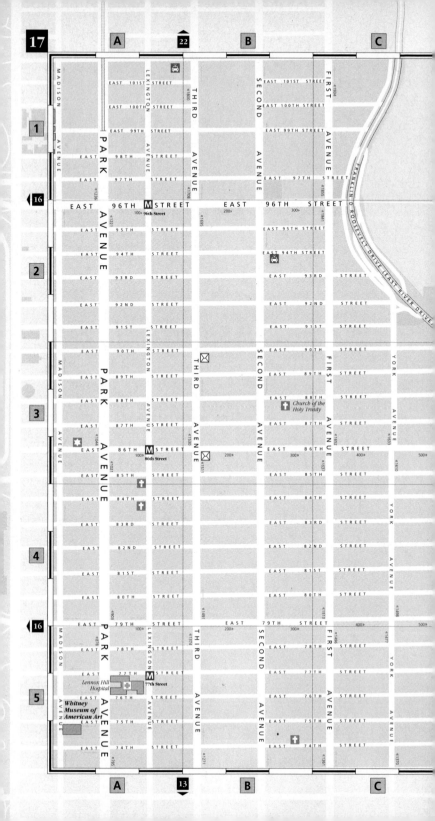

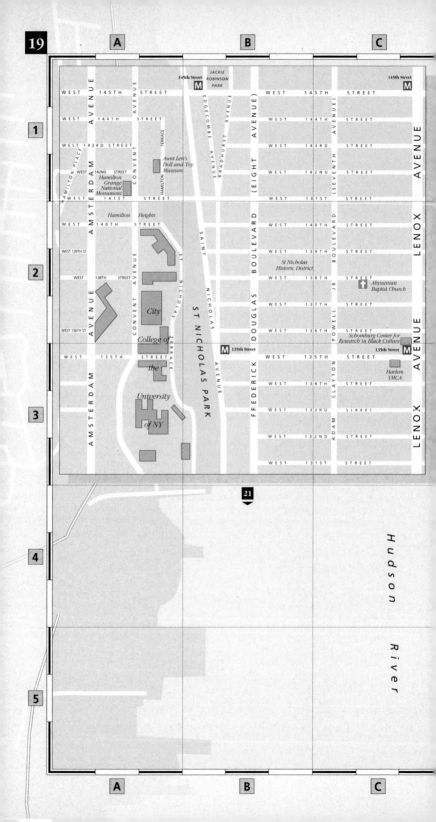

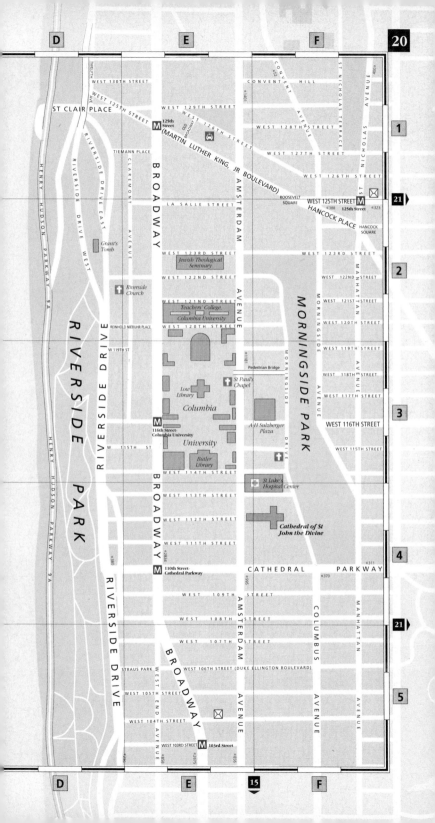

H a r l e m   R i v e r

Willis Avenue Bridge

EAST 127TH STREET

EAST 126TH STREET

THIRD AVENUE

SECOND AVENUE

25th Street
(MARTIN LUTHER KING, JR BOULEVARD)

LOUIS
GUVILLIER
PARK

Triborough   Bridge

RANDALL'S

ISLAND

PARK

FRANKLIN D ROOSEVELT DRIVE (EAST RIVER DRIVE)

PALADINO AVENUE

RONALD E MCNAIR PLACE

SYLVAN PL

FIRST AVENUE

EAST 120TH STREET

EAST 119TH STREET

EAST 118TH STREET

EAST 117TH STREET

PLEASANT AVENUE

16th Street
(LUIS MUÑOZ MARIN BOULEVARD)

THIRD AVENUE

SECOND AVENUE

EAST 115TH STREET

EAST 114TH STREET

EAST 113TH STREET

JEFFERSON

PARK

EAST 112TH STREET

EAST 111TH STREET

110th Street

EAST 110TH STREET

EAST 109TH STREET

EAST 108TH STREET

Benjamin
Franklin
Plaza

EAST 107TH STREET

FIRST AVENUE

SECOND AVENUE

THIRD AVENUE

FRANKLIN D ROOSEVELT DRIVE (EAST RIVER DRIVE)

RECREATION
PIER

H a r l e m

R i v e r

EAST 106TH STREET

EAST 105TH STREET

EAST 104TH STREET

EAST 103RD STREET

103rd Street

Foot Bridge

General Index

Acknowledgments

DORLING KINDERSLEY would like to thank the many people whose help and assistance contributed to the preparation of this book.

MAIN CONTRIBUTOR
Eleanor Berman is a widely published travel writer living in New York. Her *Away for the Weekend: New York* guide has been a best-seller since 1982. Other titles include *Cape Cod and the Islands; Away for the Weekend: New England; Away for the Weekend: Mid-Atlantic;* and *Reflections of Washington, DC.* She was also a contributor to the *Penguin Guide to New York.*

MUSEUM CONTRIBUTORS
Michelle Menendez, Lucy O'Brien, Heidi Rosenau, Elyse Topalian, Sally Williams.

DORLING KINDERSLEY wishes to thank the following editors and researchers at Websters International Publishers: Sandy Carr, Matthew Barrell, Sara Harper, Miriam Lloyd, Ava-Lee Tanner, Celia Woolfrey.

ADDITIONAL PHOTOGRAPHY
Edward Hueber, Eliot Kaufman, Karen Kent, Norman McGrath, Howard Millard, Paul Solomon, Chuck Spang, Chris Stevens.

ADDITIONAL ILLUSTRATIONS
Steve Gyapay, Kevin Jones, Dinwiddie MacLaren, Janos Marffy, Chris D. Orr, Nick Shewring, John Woodcock.

CARTOGRAPHY
Advanced Illustration (Cheshire), Contour Publishing (Derby), Europmap Ltd (Berkshire). Street Finder maps: ERA-Maptec Ltd (Dublin) adapted with permission from original survey and mapping by Shobunsha (Japan).

CARTOGRAPHIC RESEARCH
Roger Bullen, Tony Chambers, Ruth Duxbury, Ailsa Heritage, Jayne Parsons, Laura Porter, Donna Rispoli, Joan Russell, Jill Tinsley, Andrew Thompson.

DESIGN AND EDITORIAL ASSISTANCE
Keith Addison, Ron Boudreau, Linda Cabasin, Michelle Clark, Carey Combe, Diana Craig, Maggie Crowley, Guy Dimond, Tom Fraser, Alex Gray, Marcus Hardy, Sasha Heseltine, Pippa Hurst, Kim Inglis, Jane Middleton, Helen Partington, Leigh Priest, Nicki Rawson, Marisa Renzullo, Ellen Root, Liz Rowe, Anaïs Scott, Anna Streiffert, Clare Sullivan, Andrew Szudek.

SPECIAL ASSISTANCE
Beyer Blinder Belle, John Beatty at the Cotton Club, Peter Casey at the New York Public Library, Nicky Clifford, Linda Corcoran at the International Wildlife Conservation Park, Susan Ely at the Morgan Library, Jane Fischer, Deborah Gaines at the New York Convention and Visitors Bureau, Dawn Geigerich at the Queens Museum of Art, Peggy Harrington at St. John the Divine, Pamela Herrick at the Van Cortlandt House, Marguerite Lavin at the Museum of the City of New York, Robert Makla at the Friends of Central Park, Gary Miller at the New York Stock Exchange, Laura Mogil at the American Museum of Natural History, Fred Olsson at the Shubert Organization, Dominique Palermo at the Police Academy Museum, Royal Canadian Pancake House, Lydia Ruth and Laura I. Fries at the Empire State Building, David Schwartz at the American Museum of the Moving Image, Joy Sienkiewicz at the South Street Seaport Museum, Pam Snook at the New York City Transit Authority, the staff at the Lower East Side Tenement Museum, Msgr. Anthony Dalla Valla at St. Patrick's Cathedral.

RESEARCH ASSISTANCE
Christa Griffin, Steve McClure, Sabra Moore, Jeff Mulligan, Marc Svensson, Vicky Weiner, Steven Weinstein.

PHOTOGRAPHIC REFERENCE
Duncan Petersen Publishers Ltd.

PHOTOGRAPHY PERMISSIONS
DORLING KINDERSLEY would like to thank the following for their kind permission to photograph at their establishments: American Craft Museum, American Museum of Natural History, Aunt Len's Doll and Toy Museum, Balducci's, Home Savings of America, Brooklyn Children's Museum, The Cloisters, Columbia University, Eldridge Street Project, Federal Hall, Rockefeller Group, Trump Tower.

PICTURE CREDITS
t = top; tc = top center; tr = top right; cla = center left above; ca = center above; cra = center right above; cl = center left; c = center; cr = center right; clb = center left below; cb = center below; crb = center right below; bl = bottom left; bc = bottom center; br = bottom right.

Every effort has been made to trace the copyright holders, and we apologize in advance for any unintentional omissions. We would be pleased to insert the appropriate acknowledgments in any subsequent edition of this publication.

Works of art have been reproduced with the permission of the following copyright holders: © ADAGP, Paris and DACS, London 1993: 67cl (*Four Trees,* April 1971-July 1972, by Jean Dubuffet), 170bl, 186tl, 187crb, 199crb; *Alice In Wonderland,* 1959 © Jose de Creeft/DACS, London/VAGA, New York 1993: 53cl, 205cl; © DACS 1993: 34tr, 113tc, 160tr (donated by the Norwegian Government, 1952), 171cb, 172cr, 186bl, 187cra, 187bl, 188cla; © Estate of STUART DAVIS/DACS, London/VAGA, New York

1993: 199cr; © DEMART PRO ARTE BV/DACS 1993: 172cl; *The American Merchant Mariners Memorial*, 1991, © MARISOL ESCOBAR/DACS, London/VAGA, New York 1993: 55bc; © JASPER JOHNS/DACS, London/VAGA, New York 1993: 199ca; © ROY LICHTENSTEIN/DACS 1993: 140tr (commissioned by The Equitable Life Assurance Society of the United States), 173tl, 198clb; © Estate of DAVID SMITH/DACS, London/VAGA, New York 1993: 199bl.

© 1993 THE GEORGIA O'KEEFFE FOUNDATION/ARS, New York: 198c; © 1993 FRANK STELLA/ARS, New York: 190tr.

By permission of ELLSWORTH KELLY: 35cr.

By permission of E. JAN NADELMAN: 199br.

Printed by permission of the NORMAN ROCKWELL FAMILY TRUST © 1961 the Norman Rockwell Family Trust: 161br.

© 1993 THE ANDY WARHOL FOUNDATION FOR THE VISUAL ARTS, INC: 198cla.

© THE WHITNEY MUSEUM OF AMERICAN ART, NY: 35br (*The Brooklyn Bridge: Variation On An Old Theme*, 1939, by Joseph Stella), 198bl.

The Publishers are grateful to the following museums, companies, and picture libraries for permission to reproduce their photographs:

ALGONQUIN HOTEL, N.Y: 272bl; AQUARIUS, UK: 169c; AMERICAN MUSEUM-HAYDEN PLANET-ARIUM, NY: 216tl; AMERICAN MUSEUM OF THE MOVING IMAGE: Carson Collection © Bruce Polin, 246tl; AMERICAN MUSEUM OF NATURAL HISTORY, NY: 37bl, 214ca; ASHMOLEAN MUSEUM, Oxford: 15tc, 16c; THE ASIA SOCIETY, NY: 185cl; AVERY ARCHITECTURAL AND FINE ART LIBRARY, Columbia University in the City of New York: 135cl; AVERY FISHER HALL: © N. McGrath 1976 331tr.

© THE GEORGE BALANCHINE TRUST: *Apollo*, choreography by George Balanchine, photo by P. Kolnik 5tc; *Stravinsky Violin Concerto*, choreography by George Balanchine, photo by P. Kolnik 328tc; George Balanchine's *The Nutcracker*, SM, photo by P. Kolnik 331cb; THE BETTMANN ARCHIVE, NY: 4br, 16bcl, 17cla, 17cr, 17bl, 18cl, 20cbr, 20bl, 20-21, 23br, 25cra, 26cla, 26cra, 26crb, 26br, 30cla, 31tl, 40tl, 43cbl, 47cr, 47bc, 49c, 54bc, 71tl, 74cl, 79cr, 79br, 109bl, 175cla, 183br, 207t, 210cla, 223cr, 229t, 239tr, 265tr; BETTMANN NEWS-PHOTOS/REUTERS: 31tr; BETTMANN/UPI: 27cra, 27bc, 28bcr, 29br, 30cra, 30bl, 30br, 31ca, 31br, 44cl, 47cra, 48cl, 49bl, 72c, 72ca, 78cl, 151cl, 161cl, 264br, 265cr; BLOOMINGDALE'S: 27cbr; BFI: courtesy of Paramount Pictures 46b; © Roy Export Company Establishment 173tr; THE BRITISH LIBRARY, London: 14;

BROOKLYN HISTORICAL SOCIETY: (detail) 89tl; THE BROOKLYN MUSEUM: 34crb (*Climbing Into The Promised Land*, 1908, photo by Lewis Wick Hine), 36cl, 37c, 248cra, 248bl, 249t, 249cra, 249c, 249bl, 250t, 250br, 251cr, 251bl; The Cantor Collection 251cl; photo by J. Kerr 248c, 250bl; photo by P. Warchol: 249cr; BROWN BROTHERS: 67br, 71bl, 82cra, 90t, 104br.

CAMERA PRESS: 28cbr, 28bl, 31cb, 125cr; R. Open 48tr; T. Spencer 30cb; THE CARLYLE HOTEL, NY: 273tr, 328bc; CARNEGIE HALL: © H. Grossman 331br; J. ALLAN CASH: 31bl, 362cr; CBS ENTERTAINMENT/DESILU TOO: "Vacation from Marriage" 169br; COLORIFIC!: A. Clifton 373cl; Colorific/ Black Star 47tl, 79cra; T. Cowell 221cr; R. Fraser 74t; H. Matsumoto 368cr, 371tr; D. Moore 29bl; T. Spiegel 13cr, 349tl; CULVER PICTURES, INC: (inset) 9 , 17crb, 18cbl, 19bl, 21tl, 21br, 24tl, 24cl, 27cb, 27bl, 46tr, 47cb, 48br, 49tr, 74bl, 75cra, 75cb, 76tl, 78crb, 83c, 83crb, 119bl, 122tc, 125bl, 135cr, 145c, 147cl, 227t, 227bc, 227cr, 257bl, 259crb.

DAILY EAGLE: (detail) 89cl; DAILY NEWS: 354tl, 354tr.

ESSEX HOUSE, NY: 268cr; COLLECTION THE EQUITABLE LIFE ASSURANCE SOCIETY: Photo by G. Gorgoni 140tr; ESTO: P. Aaron 330bl; MARY EVANS PICTURE LIBRARY: 22br, 46clb, 47br, 87br, 104bl.

CHRIS FAIRCLOUGH COLOUR LIBRARY: 369bcl; THE *Forbes Magazine* COLLECTION, NY: 112tl; FRAUNCES TAVERN MUSEUM, NY: 20cla; Copyright THE FRICK COLLECTION, NY: 35bl (*St. Francis In The Desert* by Giovanni Bellini), 200ca, 200cl, 200clb, 200b, 201tl, 201ca, 201cr, 201bc, 201br.

GARRARD THE CROWN JEWELLERS: 143c; THE SOLOMON R. GUGGENHEIM MUSEUM, NY: *Blue, Green, Yellow, Orange, Red*, 1966, by Ellsworth Kelly, photo by D. Aronowitz 35cr; photo by D. Heald 186tl, 186bl, 186bc, 186br, 187t, 187cra, 187crb, 187bl.

ROBERT HARDING PICTURE LIBRARY: 362tc, 362bl; HARPERS NEW MONTHLY MAGAZINE: 87tl; HARPERS WEEKLY: 351c; MILTON HEBALD: *Prospero and Miranda* 203t, *Romeo and Juliet* 331cr; THE HOTEL MILLENIUM, NY: 269tl.

THE IMAGE BANK: 89br; M. Hilaire 75t; P. McConville 377c; M. Melford 10t, 377br; P. Miller 367tr; A. Satterwhite 75br.

THE JEWISH MUSEUM, NY: 182tr, 184c.

Copyright © 1993 K-III MAGAZINE CORPORATION: All rights reserved. Reprinted with the permission of *New York* Magazine 352tr; T. KHAPA: 252bc; THE KOBAL COLLECTION: 211tc.

FRANK LESLIE'S ILLUSTRATED NEWSPAPER: 86br, 87tr, 267c; LIBRARY OF CONGRESS: 18bc, 21cla, 25bl, 25br; LIFE MAGAZINE © Time Warner Inc/Katz/A. Feininger: 8–9; GEORG JOHN LOBER: *Hans Christian Anderson*, 1956, 204br; THE LOWELL HOTEL, NY: 273cl; MARY ANN LYNCH: 310bc, 356cl.

MADISON SQUARE GARDEN: 132r, 330cr; MAGNUM PHOTOS: © H. Cartier-Bresson 173c; Erwitt 33cr; G. Peres 12br, 92; THE MAYFAIR HOTEL, NY: 273cr; METRO-NORTH COMMUTER RAILROAD: F. English 154tr, 154cla; THE METRO-POLITAN MUSEUM OF ART, NY: 33bl (*Young Woman With A Waterjug* by Johannes Vermeer), 35crb (*Figure of a Hippopotamus*, faience, Egypt, 12th Dynasty), 180tc, 188cla, 188clb, 188bc, 188br, 189tl, 189tr, 189cr, 189bl, (photo Al Mozell) 189br, 190tr, 190c, 190bl, 190br, 191tl, 191tr, 191c, 191bl, 192tl, 192tr, 192c, 192b, (detail) 193tl, 193tr, 193b, 194t, 194cl, 194cr, 194b, 195tl, 195cr, 195bl, 234tr, 234cl, 234cr, 234b, 235ca, 235cr, 235bl, 235br, 236tl, 236tr, 237tr, 237c, 237b; MORRIS-JUMEL MANSION, INC NY: 17tl; A. Rosario 21crb; THE MUSEUM OF THE CITY OF NEW YORK: 15b, 16cra, 16–17, 17tr, 18ca, 19crb (photo J. Parnell), 20tl, 20cbl, 22tl (attributed to Samuel Lovett Waldo), 22cla, 22clb, 23cr, 23crb, 23bc, 24cb, 25tl, 25crb, 25cb, 26bl, 27tr, 28tl, 28cr, 29tc, 29c, 30tr, 35tr (silver porringer), 87cr (Talfour); THE MUSEUM OF MODERN ART, NY: 33ca (*The Starry Night* by Vincent Van Gogh, 1889), 34t (*The Goat* by Pablo Picasso, 1950), 6bl (Cisitalia "202" GT car), 165tc, 170c, 170bl, 171tc, 171cra, 171crb, 171cb, 171bl, 172cl, 172cr, 172bc, 173tl, 173b.

NATIONAL BASEBALL LIBRARY, Cooperstown, NY: 4tr, 23bl, 28cl; NATIONAL PARK SERVICE: Ellis Island Immigration Museum 78ca, 78br; Statue of Liberty National Monument 75bl; THE NEW MUSEUM OF CONTEMPORARY ART, NY: 105cl; NEW YORK CITY TRANSIT AUTHORITY: 374bc; Collection of THE NEW YORK HISTORICAL SOCIETY: 47tr; Neustaadt Collection 216tr; THE NEW YORKER MAGAZINE INC: Cover drawing by Rea Irvin, © 1925, 1953, All rights reserved, 28bcl; THE NEW YORK PALACE, NY: 25tr; NEW YORK POST: 354tl; NEW YORK PUBLIC LIBRARY: Special Collection Office, Schomburg Center for Research in Black Culture 28ca, 29cla; Stokes Collection 21tr; NEW YORK STATE DEPARTMENT OF MOTOR VEHICLES: 370b; THE NEW YORK TIMES: 354tl; NPA: © CNES 1993 10b; THE PENINSULA, NY: 271bc; PERFORMING ARTS LIBRARY: Clive Barda: 210bl; Collection of THE PIERPONT MORGAN LIBRARY, NY: 34cr (*Blanche of Castille and King Louis IX of France, author dictating to a scribe*, moralized Bible, c1230), 162bc, 162clb, 162br, 163tl, 163c, 163bl, 163br; POPPERFOTO: 29cra, 29cr, 71crb, 260cla; PLAZA HOTEL, NY: 272tr.

COLLECTION OF THE QUEENS MUSEUM OF ART: purchased with funds from the George and

Mollie Wolfe World's Fair Fund 29cbr; Official souvenir, purchase 30cbr.

RENSSELAER POLYTECHNIC INSTITUTE: 86-87, 87bl; REX FEATURES LTD: 376tl; Sipa-Press 52tr, 52br; Courtesy of the ROCKEFELLER CENTER © The Rockefeller Group, Inc: 29cbl.

LUIS SANGUINO: *The Immigrants*, 1973, 256b; THE ST. REGIS, NY: 270c; SCIENTIFIC AMERICAN: May 18 1878 edition 86tr; November 9 1878 edition 88bl; THE SOCIETY OF ILLUSTRATORS: 196tl; SPECTRUM COLOUR LIBRARY: 376bl; FRANK SPOONER PICTURES: Gamma 158cl; Gamma/ B. Gysenbergh 367tl; Liaison/Gamma/ Anderson front endpaper clb, 158tl, 159cla; Liaison/Levy/Halebian: 42tr, 45c; Sygma/ A. Tannenbaum 47ca.

TURNER ENTERTAINMENT COMPANY: 135br, 183br.

UNITED AIRLINES: Goldstag 363tl; UNITED NATIONS, NY: 159cra, 160tr, 160bc, 161tc, 161cla, 161br; © US POSTAL SERVICE: 361t, © THE US POSTAL SERVICE 1981: 361ca, © US POSTAL SERVICE 1991: 361c. Used with permission; UN PLAZA HYATT HOTEL, NY: 273bl.

© JACK VARTOOGIAN, NY: 61bc, 156t.

JUDITH WELLER: *The Garment Worker* 128t; LUCIA WILSON CONSULTANCY: Ivar Mjell 2-3, 13br, 164; Collection of THE WHITNEY MUSEUM OF AMERICAN ART, NY: 198cla, 198c, 198clb, 199t, 199ca, 199cr, 199crb (purchase with funds from a public fundraising campaign in May 1982. One half of the funds were contributed by the Robert Wood Johnson Jr. Charitable Trust. Additional major donations were given by The Lauder Foundation; the Robert Lehman Foundation, Inc.; the Howard and Jean Lipman Found-ation, Inc; an anonymous donor; The TM Evans Foundation, Inc.; MacAndrews & Forbes Group Incorporated; the DeWitt Wallace Fund, Inc; Martin & Agnes Gruss; Anne Phillips; Mr. and Mrs. Laurance S. Rockefeller; the Simon Foundation, Inc.; Marylou Whitney; Bankers Trust Company; Mr. and Mrs. Kenneth N. Dayton; Joel and Anne Ehrenkranz; Irvin and Kenneth Feld; Flora Whitney Miller. More than 500 individuals from 26 states and abroad also contributed to the campaign), 199bl, 199br (purchase with funds from the Mr and Mrs Arthur G. Altschul Purchase Fund, the Joan and Lester Avnet Purchase Fund, the Edgar William and Bernice Chrysler Garbisch Purchase Fund, the Mrs. Robert C. Graham Purchase Fund in honor of John I.H. Baur, the Mrs. Percy Uris Purchase Fund and the Henry Schnakenberg Purchase Fund in honor of Juliana Force); WHEELER PICTURES: 78t.

YU YU YANG: *Untitled*, 1973, 57br.